MOON

ARIZONA
& THE GRAND CANYON

TIM HULL

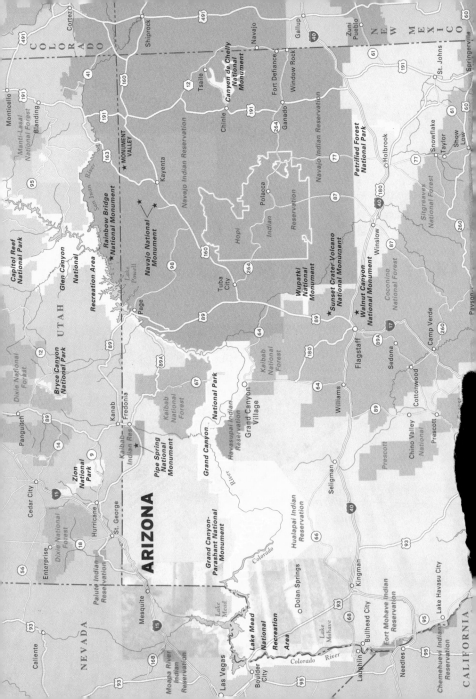

Contents

DISCOVER

Arizona & the
Grand Canyon

Arizona is authentic. It's too hot to fake it, too rugged to tell tall tales, too beautiful to commit to the hard sell. All of its institutions, its attractions, and even its mythologies were forged through hard experience, trial, and error.

This is even true of the land, built by the movement and explosion of the earth—canyons ripped open and mountains kicked up over millennia of shaking and oozing. This roiling has provided a wonderland of diversity, building—all at once—hot and verdant desert scrublands, cool evergreen mountain forests, dry sweeping grasslands, and red-rock, river-carved, fairy-tale canyons, all of which merge with a horizon lit most evenings with postcard-ready sunsets. It remains one of the most exotic destinations in North America, with endless variety, iconic scenery, and a dark history of which the world has never tired.

You will be surprised and changed by Arizona. Here you can easily happen upon an old pioneer graveyard, forgotten and ignored, on a strip of undeveloped desert right next to a gathering of just-built dream homes. This may be the perfect image for the dichotomies of this landscape. Everything here is either ancient or five minutes old.

There's a reason all those road movies feature scenes in the Grand Canyon State. There's no better way to see all the state has to offer than to pile in a car and hit the open road. Less than a day's drive from anywhere, you can discover something unexpected, whether it be the calm and sunny ease of life along the lower Colorado River, where houseboats and water-skiers pass by great monuments to engineering, or a chance meeting with a rare tropical bird hiding out in the riparian mist of a sky island.

In many a traveler's imagination, this place is the home to rattlesnakes, tumbleweeds, and vast tracts of arid wilderness. Luckily, Arizona still has all of these; there are still trackless spaces to explore. But the face Arizona shows to most of the world belies the leaps this once isolated territory has made. The youngest state in the lower 48 is one of the fastest-growing regions in the nation, and while nearly constant growth makes for sometimes rancorous debates about land use and natural resources, it serves to create in Arizona a dynamism—a flux that perpetuates itself. It is never boring here, and it is always beautiful and unknowable. There is always something, or someone, being created anew … changing … blooming.

Planning Your Trip

Where to Go

Phoenix, Scottsdale, and the Valley of the Sun

Arizona's largest metro area holds 10 cities linked together to create a sprawling megalopolis of glass high-rises and labyrinthine, stacked freeways spreading out over a hot Sonoran Desert valley. Visitors and residents alike tend to refer to the whole area as the Valley of the Sun, or simply Phoenix, after the valley's largest city. There are pockets of urbanity out in the sprawl, like Scottsdale with its art galleries, high-style eateries, and resorts and golf courses, and Tempe with its college-town nightlife, shopping, and museums. This area has the state's best resorts and restaurants, nightlife, museums, and Arizona's largest airport. The city's rural desert outskirts are home to old mining towns, river canyons, and saguaro forests.

Tucson and Southern Arizona

Tucson, the state's second-largest city and the one with the most character and history, anchors this region of saguaro forests, sweeping grasslands, and quirky desert outposts. Towering sky island mountain ranges shoot up from the long desert seas, and the nearby Mexican border looms equally large in this region's culture and history. Even better, they say a few of those myths and legends of the Old West actually happened here.

Flagstaff and North-Central Arizona

Arizona's sap-scented high country begins around mile-high Prescott and rises to a great ponderosa pine forest stretching east and north. Even higher is snowy Flagstaff and the bald-rock tip of the San Francisco Peaks, their slopes variegated by white-and-yellow aspens among the evergreens. Below the Mogollon Rim, the green edge of a great plateau, posh Sedona offers fine dining, self-healing, red-rock buttes, and shady streambeds.

Navajo and Hopi Country

The high desert grasslands in Arizona's northeastern plateau country are dotted with a few old cattle and railroad towns, trading posts, and an empty pastel-painted desert strewn with broken swirling-stone trees. The vast Navajo Nation is cut deep with red-sandstone canyons in which abandoned cliff-face cities and the tracks of dinosaurs create a timeless atmosphere that can be entrancing. On the edge of Black Mesa, the Hopi live atop high cold cliffs occupied for more than a thousand years.

The White Mountains and the Gila Valley

Rising in northeastern Arizona near the New Mexico border, the White Mountains region has small towns, rental cabins, trout steams, cold-water lakes, hiking trails, and wolves.

IF YOU HAVE . . .

- **ONE WEEK:** Visit Tucson, Southern Arizona, and the Grand Canyon.

- **TWO WEEKS:** Add North-Central Arizona, Phoenix, Scottsdale, and the Valley of the Sun.

- **THREE WEEKS:** Add the Navajo Nation, Hopi, the High Desert, the White Mountains, and the Gila Valley.

- **FOUR WEEKS:** Add the Lower Colorado River region.

Tombstone, in Southern Arizona

Much of the evergreen, mountainous wilderness is home to the Western Apache, and their ancient culture pervades the region, as does that of the Mormon pioneers and cattle ranchers who settled here in the Territorial era and never left. Below the highlands, the Gila Valley, where deserts collide and hot springs burst from the hot ground, spreads out along the last flowing remains of the once mighty desert river.

The Grand Canyon and the Arizona Strip

The Kaibab Plateau rises in northwestern Arizona; river-cut more than a mile deep into the plateau is Arizona's signature attraction and one of the world's most sought-after landscapes—the only canyon on earth deserving of the grand title. Between the canyon's forested rims is the lonely Arizona Strip, empty save for high barren red cliffs, sagebrush plains, and the water-and-red-rock mazes of Lake Powell.

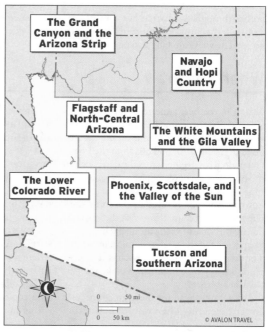

wildflowers in spring

aspen trees in winter

The Lower Colorado River

The Colorado River flows the length of far western Arizona to Mexico, creating a river-border through this barren hot zone of jagged rock mountains populated by bighorn sheep. The views are long and empty save for the toughest cactus, scrub, and wildflower. The river is a blue-and-green band of rustling, splashing life, and all living things here are drawn to it, whether they be rare birds or water-skiers.

When to Go

Spring is the best time to be on Arizona's lowland deserts. From late February through May, the weather is gorgeous on the deserts, often in the high 70s and 80s from the Lower Colorado River region across the desert belt to the New Mexico border. Spring is also bloom-time on the desert, when all the dormant wildflowers come to life, and all the spiny cacti burst with vivid color. If you visit the lowlands during this time of year, you are likely to come away with a vastly altered opinion of aridity. The desert-country tourist season is at its high point during these months, so make reservations in advance.

In summer, head for the high country. It is warm, tending often toward hot during the day, and cool, clear, and star-filled at night. In late summer the rains come, late-afternoon downpours that clean the air and get the creeks rising. Summer is the busy tourist season in this region that includes the Grand Canyon, North-Central Arizona, and Indian Country. You are bound to encounter crowds at most of the major attractions, and you'll need to make reservations.

It typically stays triple-digit hot on Arizona's deserts deep into October, so fall isn't really a recognized season in Phoenix and Tucson. By November the weather will have cooled off to mimic what is considered spring in other places; and then, seemingly overnight, it starts to get cold. In most years, from December through about February it is winter in the desert. During this time of year, from about October until about May, the snowbirds flock to Arizona from the Midwest, the Northeast, and Canada, crowding the roads, stores, and restaurants of Tucson and the Valley of the Sun.

Of course, things are different in the high country. From October through December, fall blesses the highlands with cool, pleasant days, crisp nights, turning and falling leaves, and chimney smoke. This is an ideal time to visit North-Central Arizona and the Grand Canyon, but don't forget your jacket. Above 7,000 feet or so, the cold and the snow have been known to arrive as early as November or December, but ski season doesn't usually get going in the White Mountains and Flagstaff until January. In winter, especially in a wet year (of which there have been very few lately), expect to find the mountain country somewhat crowded on the weekends with skiers and snowboarders.

Before You Go

A trip to Arizona requires a certain amount of advance planning, especially if you're going to be hiking the Grand Canyon, riding the Colorado's rapids, or renting a houseboat. A permit to spend even one night inside the canyon requires a reservation at least six months in advance, more if you want to stay in the gorge's only lodge, Phantom Ranch. If you're hoping to float down the Colorado, start planning at least a year in advance. Bring your passport along if you're planning to cross the U.S.-Mexico border.

You need to be prepared for a lot of car time. The towns, sights, and attractions are scattered throughout the state, and most of them are far from the two main urban centers of Phoenix and Tucson. You must have a car, and you can't really avoid spending a good deal of time in it.

What to Take

Your Arizona-bound knapsack should include a few essential items no matter what the season. These include, first and foremost, a good pair of hiking or walking shoes. Don't get a big, bulky, arctic-expedition pair, but day-hikers or at least a pair of tough running shoes or trainers are a necessity. At nearly every national park or national monument that you'll visit, there's some kind of short hike you have to take in order to *really* appreciate what you're seeing. A water bottle is always nice to have around, and you'll probably want to include a small pack for carrying snacks and water on day hikes or sightseeing excursions. Sunscreen is a necessity in any season; if you're not in a hot harsh-sun desert, you're in mountain country, where the sun shines hard and dangerous. A hat is a must, and one with a brim wide enough to cast a shadow on your neck is recommended. Think about bringing along a pair of binoculars; they are always handy when spotting bighorn sheep, petroglyphs, and rare birds.

Even if you're going to be in the desert in the summer, bring along a light jacket. In some of the outer regions away from the city the air cools a bit, and if you rise in elevation, which is easy to do, the nights will be much cooler. In the high country, layers will serve you best. It is often warm in the day and cold at night, even in summer.

As for style, think casual and utilitarian—everybody else does. If you're going to be staying or dining at any of the top resorts, a few fancy outfits might be in order. Otherwise, jeans and T-shirts, shorts and tank tops, flip-flops, rock sandals, and general outdoor style are the norm.

The Best of Arizona

The best way to see Arizona is from behind the wheel of your own car. A road trip through the heart of the American Southwest provides a unique opportunity to see this exotic region from the ground up.

Day 1

Arrive at Sky Harbor Airport in Phoenix, head to a hotel in downtown Phoenix, Scottsdale, or Tempe. Introduce yourself to the desert by taking a scenic drive along Highway 51 about 30 miles or 45 minutes out to Cave Creek and Carefree. Have dinner at El Encanto in Cave Creek.

Day 2

Get an early start and spend the morning touring Taliesin West, the Heard Museum, or the Phoenix Art Museum. Leave the city via I-17 to Prescott, about 100 miles north, a drive of about 1.5 hours. Stop for a late lunch and a slice of pie midway at the Rock Springs Café, 45 minutes north of Phoenix along I-17. Spend the night at one of downtown Prescott's historic hotels or bed-and-breakfasts. Have dinner at The Palace and hit up a few Whiskey Row watering holes.

Day 3

Get up early and eat breakfast at the Dinner Bell. Walk around downtown Prescott and tour the museums, shops, and galleries. Be sure to visit the Sharlot Hall Museum. Head north on scenic Highway 89A to Jerome, a 35-mile drive that takes about an hour. Stay at the Jerome Grand Hotel and have dinner at The Asylum.

Day 4

Have breakfast at the Mile High Grill and take a walk around Jerome. Head down Highway 89A to Sedona, a 28-mile drive that takes about 40 minutes. Check into your hotel, and then head out to explore the red rocks, galleries, and shops of Sedona. Eat dinner at Oaxaca Restaurant in Uptown.

Day 5

Spend the day shopping, hiking, sightseeing, and exploring Sedona and the Verde Valley.

the Heard Museum in Phoenix

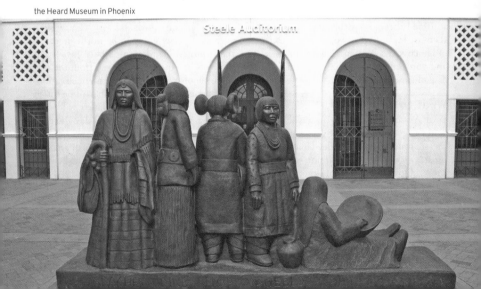

Feel the Heat: A Hot Summer Weekend

When the mercury rises above 100°F in the Sonoran Desert (usually around late May), the resorts in Phoenix and Scottsdale lower their prices to levels most of us can actually afford. Not only does this offer a chance to have a romantic getaway on a budget, it gives the neophyte an opportunity to experience the heat of the desert in all its glory.

You haven't truly experienced the Arizona desert until you've "felt the heat," and a romantic weekend at one of the valley's resorts offers a comfortable way of doing so. Example: The historic, Frank Lloyd Wright-inspired **Arizona Biltmore Resort and Spa,** still the state's most romantic and stylish resort, offers inclusive "romance" packages with spa treatments, chocolate-covered strawberries, a gourmet dinner, and more, which are discounted by about $300 per night late May-mid-September. Individually, the same room that goes for $685 in April costs about $189 in July.

Other sumptuous resorts that lower their prices or offer affordable getaway packages in the summer include the magnificent **Boulders Resort** in Scottsdale, with summer prices starting at $129 per night, and the **Fairmont Scottsdale Princess,** with rooms starting at $189 per night. In March, when the weather in the valley is usually perfect, similar accommodations will cost you at least $450 per night.

When you're not lolling poolside in a shady cabana or getting a pedicure, consider spending part of one day touring the (air-conditioned) **Phoenix Art Museum** or the **Heard Museum,** or even **Taliesin West**–though this option won't be as comfortable as the others. Since you're saving all that money at the resort, summer is a perfect time to do some shopping at one of the high-end (and climate-controlled) shopping centers in Scottsdale and Phoenix, like **Scottsdale Fashion Square** and **Biltmore Fashion Park.** The golf prices go down considerably during the summer as well, and you might just be able to survive a round or two if you start early in the morning. But you won't want to spend too much time out on the course. First of all, it's dangerous–literally. Plus, this is a couple's getaway, and there's no place cooler (or hotter for that matter) than your affordable room at one of the world's top resorts.

Check out Montezuma Castle, hike into red-rock country, or take a jeep tour through the redlands.

Day 6

Eat breakfast at the Coffee Pot in Sedona, then head north on Highway 89A through Oak Creek Canyon. Stop for a hike or to splash around in the water at Slide Rock State Park. Continue north to Flagstaff, about an hour drive from Sedona. Check into one of the historic hotels downtown. Stroll and shop downtown, then have dinner and beers at Beaver Street Brewery.

Day 7

Wake up and head out to visit the Museum of Northern Arizona in Flagstaff, about 3 miles north of downtown on Highway 180, then go north and east for a tour of Wupatki, Sunset Crater, and Walnut Canyon, all within a half hour of Flagstaff. In the late afternoon, drive east for about an hour on I-40 to Winslow and check into La Posada. Have dinner in the Turquoise Room. Order a box lunch from the restaurant for the next day.

Day 8

Spend the morning touring the Painted

The Ruins of Lost Cultures

the red sandstone ruins at Wupatki National Monument

Arizona and the Southwest are home to many native cultures that are no longer around to tell their stories and legends. Luckily, the ruins of the Hohokam, Anasazi, Salado, Sinagua, and others are protected throughout the state by federal law. You could make a whole trip out of visiting these mysterious structures, discovering the lost cultures that once scraped much more than subsistence out of the uncaring land.

HOHOKAM AND SALADO TRIBES

Use Phoenix and the Valley of the Sun as your base as you discover ruins left behind by the Hohokam and Salado tribes.

- **Pueblo Grande Museum and Archaeological Park:** Discover how the Hohokam coaxed an empire out of the Salt River Valley here at the ruin and museum in the middle of the city, near the ruins of the canals the Hohokam built to irrigate the desert.

- **Tonto National Monument:** Take the back-country route called the **Apache Trail** past Roosevelt Dam, east of the city, and witness a well-preserved cliff dwelling once inhabited by the Salado tribe that rises above slopes crowded with saguaros.

- **Casa Grande Ruins National Monument:** Located between Phoenix and Tucson, this monument is the largest example of Hohokam architecture left, the huge molded-dirt apartment building called Casa Grande.

SINAGUA TRIBE

Use Sedona or Flagstaff as your base for visiting the awesome ruins of North-Central Arizona's vanished Sinagua tribe.

- **Montezuma Castle National Monument:** This Verde Valley cliff dwelling is one of the best preserved in the Southwest.

- **Walnut Canyon National Monument:** East of Flagstaff is this lost world where a long-gone culture once built a busy village on the rim and along the walls of a hidden canyon.

- **Wupatki National Monument:** Just north of Flagstaff, this monument preserves the ruins of several awesome red-sandstone great houses.

ANASAZI TRIBE

- **Navajo Nation:** The abandoned cliff cities of the Anasazi are on display here in northeastern Arizona.

- **Navajo National Monument:** While visiting Tsegi Canyon, you can spot the ruin called **Betatakin** from the rim, nestled in a rock alcove above a bottomland forest.

- **Keet Seel:** Sign up for a 16-mile round-trip hike below the rim of Tsegi Canyon to spend the night near the spectacularly preserved ruin hidden deep in the canyon.

- **Canyon de Chelly National Monument:** Also on Navajoland, don't miss this area where you can hike down a slickrock trail and stand in awe before the **White House Ruin.**

Canyon de Chelly

Desert and the Petrified Forest near Holbrook, 52 miles or about an hour from Winslow on I-40. Then take I-40 to Highway 191 north to Chinle on the Navajo Reservation, a distance of 123 miles, about 2.5 hours. Stay at the Thunderbird Lodge near Canyon de Chelly or at one of the chains in Chinle.

Day 9

Spend the morning hiking into Canyon de Chelly to the White House Ruins and driving the scenic rim roads, or hire a Navajo guide and go deeper into the canyon. After lunch head north on Highway 191, west on Highway 160, then north on Highway 163 to Kayenta, a distance of 73 miles, about 1.5 hours. Get a hotel room in Kayenta and drive through Monument Valley late in the afternoon and watch the sun set. Monument Valley is 50 miles from Kayenta, a drive that takes about an hour.

Day 10

Eat breakfast in Kayenta at The Blue Coffee Pot and then head west on Highway 160 past Tuba City to U.S. Highway 89 then south to Cameron, about 100 miles or 1.5 hours. Take Highway 64 west 30 miles to Grand Canyon National Park and make your way to the east entrance. Check out the Desert View sights, then drive on into Grand Canyon Village and have lunch at El Tovar. Spend the night at El Tovar or the Bright Angel Lodge. Get up early and hike down one of the South Rim trails for as far as you feel like going. If you're not a hiker, take a mule ride to the river and back. Spend the remainder of the day looking around the rim and staring into the gorge.

Day 11

This day will be spent mostly in the car driving from the high country down to Tucson and Southern Arizona, a drive of about 340 miles or five hours. Leave the Grand Canyon early through the south entrance and take I-40 east to I-17 south. In Phoenix, follow the signs to I-10 south to Tucson. You'll probably arrive in the late afternoon. Check into the Hotel Congress, the Arizona Inn, or one of the area's bed-and-breakfasts, and then head to Mi Nidito for a Mexican-food dinner.

Top Five Hikes

The wrinkled land of Arizona is a hiker's paradise. The Grand Canyon State's varied landscapes, not to mention the great canyon itself, are crisscrossed with hundreds of well-maintained and well-used trails of various lengths and difficulties. Whether you're looking for an easy walk in the desert or a multiday expedition deep into the canyon's depths, the five hikes listed below are among the best of the best.

- **White House Ruin Trail** (Canyon de Chelly National Monument; 2.5 miles round-trip, 2-3 hours, elevation gain 550 feet, moderate): High sandstone walls tower above as you descend into the Navajo Nation's Canyon de Chelly, where the otherworldly White House Ruin awaits, carved into the cliffs.

- **Brown Mountain Trail** (Tucson Mountain Park; 4.8 miles round-trip, 2-3 hours, elevation gain 260 feet, moderate): This trail winds through the saguaro forests on Tucson's wild western edge, rising to traverse a ridgeline with spectacular views of the surprisingly verdant Sonoran Desert.

- **West Fork of Oak Creek Trail** (north of Sedona; 6.5 miles round-trip, 3-4 hours, elevation gain 200 feet, easy): A rare example of a high desert streamside forest environment, dark green evergreens mingle with red rocks and trickling water here to create an exotic Southwestern Eden.

- **Humphreys Peak Trail** (Snow Bowl Ski Area, Flagstaff; 9 miles round-trip, 5-6 hours, elevation gain 3,833 feet, difficult): This hike isn't easy, but the effort is richly rewarded when you're looking out over Arizona from its highest point, more than 12,000 above sea level.

- **Bright Angel Trail to Phantom Ranch** (Grand Canyon Village; 9.6 miles one way, overnight, elevation gain 4,380 feet, moderate to difficult): Obtain a permit and head down the ancient Bright Angel Trail to the mighty Colorado River and the peaceful confines of Phantom Ranch in the mystical depths of the Grand Canyon. It takes a bit of planning, but this is truly the hike of a lifetime.

Bright Angel Trail at sunset

Chiricahua National Monument

Day 12

Get up early and spend the morning walking around Saguaro National Park (west) and visiting the nearby Arizona-Sonora Desert Museum. Have lunch at the museum's café, or at The Coyote Pause Café about five miles south. Then continue south see San Xavier del Bac. After visiting the church, keep heading south to Tubac and Tumacacori. Stroll through the shops and galleries at Tubac or check out Mission San Jose de Tumacacori. Have dinner at Wisdom's Café in Tumacacori or continue south on I-19 and walk across the U.S.-Mexico border at Nogales, about 25 miles south on I-19, and eat at one of the restaurants in the tourist district. Drive back to your hotel in Tucson, about an hour's drive depending on where you're staying, and relax.

Day 13

This day is a kind of Southern Arizona grab bag. Drive through the San Pedro Valley or the Mountain Empire. Do some wine-tasting in Elgin, shop in Bisbee, or drive the dirt roads into the Huachuca Mountains and up to the Coronado National Memorial. Visit Chiricahua National Monument, Cochise Stronghold, Patagonia, Madera Canyon, Kartchner Caverns, or Tombstone. A full, busy day will allow you to make, say, three or four major stops, depending on your personal interests and the amount of time you spend at any one place. You'll likely arrive back at your hotel in Tucson late.

Day 14

Wake up early and take a stroll through one of Tucson's downtown neighborhoods or 4th Avenue and the University District. On your way north on I-10 to the airport in Phoenix, a distance of 116 miles, 1.5 hours, stop off at Picacho Peak State Park for a last hike, or detour to Casa Grande Ruins National Monument for a last look at native Arizona.

Bright Angel Creek

A Grand Canyon Family Adventure

The Grand Canyon, while a backcountry-lover's paradise, is also a fun place for families—just ask TV's Brady Bunch. This itinerary includes one night below the rim and so requires you to secure reservations and permits far in advance. The best time to go is spring or October.

Day 1

Take an early morning flight into Phoenix's Sky Harbor Airport, rent a car, and drive north to Williams (170 miles). Park your car and catch the Grand Canyon Railway to Grand Canyon National Park's South Rim. Check into your family-sized cabin at Bright Angel Lodge, and then explore and go sightseeing around Grand Canyon Village, getting acclimated to the huge gorge in front of you. Eat dinner at El Tovar.

Day 2

Tour the South Rim, visiting all the historic buildings and the lookouts. If your kids are around the ages of 4-12, before you start your sightseeing, take them to the Visitor Center at Canyon View Information Plaza and get them in the Junior Rangers program. The ranger will give them age-appropriate booklets, and throughout the day they'll earn a Junior Ranger badge and patch by fulfilling the fun and educational requirements, which include attending one of the ranger-led programs offered throughout the day. Have dinner at one of the casual eateries on the South Rim and get a good night's sleep—you'll need it.

Day 3

If you are hiking, get a very early start down either the Bright Angel Trail or the South Kaibab Trail. Don't carry your own bags.

riding into the Grand Canyon

Spend a few extra bills to have the mules do it, so you and the family can enjoy the hike and really see the scenery. If you're riding with a mule-train to the bottom, show up at the appointed time and place and saddle up. You'll arrive at Phantom Ranch near the Colorado River late in the day. (You have to reserve a cabin and meals at the cantina up to a year beforehand. A mule trip will be all-inclusive, but if you're hiking you'll need to make separate reservations.) Take a shower, explore Phantom Ranch, dip your feet in Bright Angel Creek, walk to the river, and relax in the inner gorge. Eat a hearty meal at the cantina and attend a ranger-led program before collapsing into bed.

Day 4

Get up early, eat breakfast at the cantina, and spend the day exploring the inner gorge, the river, and Phantom Ranch. The rangers can tell you the best day hikes and sights in the inner canyon and suggest all kinds of fun activities for the kids.

Day 5

Wake up early, eat breakfast, and head out, either on a mule or on foot. It'll take you most of the day to get out of the canyon. If you're hiking and you came down the Bright Angel Trail, head up the South Kaibab for a different view. If you came down the South Kaibab, hike out using the Bright Angel so you can see lush Indian Gardens. When and if you make it out of the canyon, treat yourselves to a nice dinner and relax and recover for the rest of the day.

Day 6

Spend the morning seeing the canyon for the last time and shopping for souvenirs. Catch the train back to Williams and check into the Grand Canyon Hotel. Have dinner at Rod's Steakhouse in Williams, then head back to the hotel to swim or soak in the hot tub.

Day 7

Head south to Phoenix after breakfast at the Pine Country Restaurant in Williams. Make the long drive south to Phoenix, stopping for a late lunch just outside of the city at Rock Springs Café. Catch your flight at Sky Harbor, and head home.

in the San Francisco Peaks

near the Grand Canyon's North Rim

A Week in the Forest

Most people who don't live in Arizona would say that it's primarily a desert state of cactus, tumbleweeds, and rattlesnakes. Of course, that's only a part of the story. More than one third of the Grand Canyon State—including the South and North Rims of the Grand Canyon—is covered in evergreen forests. This travel strategy, which starts in Flagstaff, the capital of the state's forested northland, will take you through these forests along cool, secluded, tree-lined highways, and to the top of the tallest mountains in the state. The best time to go is in the summer, when the deserts are too hot for comfort.

Day 1

Arrive in Flagstaff the night before and stay at one of the historic hotels downtown (the Weatherford or the Monte Vista). Wake up early in the morning and have breakfast at the Morning Glory Café, and head out to the San Francisco Peaks. Hike through the pine-and-aspen forest on the Humphreys Peak Trail

to the top of Arizona, at 12,600 feet. If you're not into hiking, ride the ski lift Skyride up to the top of a lesser peak at about 11,500 feet. After a day in the forest, relax at one of the restaurants or bars in downtown Flagstaff.

Day 2

Get up early and drive to Williams, where you'll park your car and hop on the Grand Canyon Railway. The historic train will drop you at the forested South Rim of the Grand Canyon, where you can spend the day looking into the gorge and exploring the charming buildings in Grand Canyon Village, and walking along the Rim Trail or taking a bike ride to Hermit's Rest. Catch the train back to Williams and stay the night at the Grand Canyon Hotel and have dinner at Rod's Steak House.

Day 3

Rise early once again and take Highway 89A through Oak Creek Canyon to Sedona,

Back to the Old West

Bisbee, in Southern Arizona

The conquistadores, miners, cowboys, outlaws, and mythmakers of the Old West all left an imprint on Arizona, and their descendants do what they can to keep those imprints from fading back into the deserts and the canyons. Listed below are some of the fascinating historical sights you can visit in Arizona.

SOUTHERN ARIZONA

Southern Arizona represents the northern extreme of the Spanish crown's American empire, while southwestern Arizona is full of the legends and kitsch of the Old West. Here you will find the following:

- **Tubac State Historic Park:** Visit this historic park, which preserves the memories and artifacts of Spain's American empire.

- **Coronado National Monument:** Tour the remote monument in the Huachuca Mountains that marks the trail used by Coronado as he trudged north toward the Seven Cities of Cibola.

- **Bisbee:** Visit an example of an Old West mining town rich with antique stores and artisan boutiques.

- **Tombstone:** Examine several forensic exhibits on that world-famous seconds-long gunfight that took place in the town's still-dusty streets.

- **Yuma Prison State Historic Park:** See what awaited those outlaws and bandits who ran afoul of territorial law.

NORTH-CENTRAL ARIZONA

- **Zane Grey Cabin:** Pay your respects to one of the Old West's greatest mythmakers. Here you can see an exact replica of Grey's hunting cabin (the real one burned down in 1990), complete with period decorations and furniture, and learn all about the prolific author's passion for Arizona's Mogollon Rim region.

- **Jerome:** See the history of hard-rock mining in this preserved mountainside town.

- **Riordan Ranch State Park:** Peek into the private lives of two 19th-century Flagstaff lumber barons featured at this state park.

- **Pipe Spring National Monument:** Discover what it was like to live on a lonely fortified ranch in the late 1800s at this Arizona Strip sight.

Scenic Byways

along Historic Route 66

Gas up the car, grab some road food and sodas, make that perfect highway mix for the stereo (pick songs that go well with long, empty views), and hit the road on one of these scenic drives around Arizona.

THE DESERT

Open spaces and strange scenery abound on these routes through the hot, rocky deserts of western Arizona.

- **Joshua Tree Forest Parkway:** Take Highway 60 northwest from Phoenix through Wickenburg and keep going when it turns to Highway 93, known for its stands of Joshua trees.

- **Highway 95 from Yuma to Bullhead City:** Head through the empty, jagged desert north of Yuma, keeping an eye out for bighorn sheep; from Parker on, drive against the Colorado River as it flows down the western border of Arizona, passing through small towns along the blue river and stopping every now and again to dip your feet in.

- **Historic Route 66:** Drive the remains of the Mother Road on the dry northwestern plains, where you can jump back to a slower time, passing through Kingman, stopping at the **Historic Route 66 Museum,** and spending some time in Seligman, the center of a Route 66 cultural rebirth.

THE FOREST

You'll be driving uphill on these scenic drives; watch as the vegetation changes from desert to a transitional bushy scrub to highland evergreen forests, all while you sit comfortably behind the wheel.

- **Highway 60 from Globe to Show Low:** The forest comes on pretty quick as you leave the central scrublands around Globe and rise along a twisty highway into the White Mountains. Make sure to stop for a photo-op at majestic **Salt River Canyon.**

- **Highway 89A from Prescott to Jerome:** Take Highway 89A up over forested **Mingus Mountain,** stopping to enjoy a sweeping view of the Verde River Valley

along Highway 95 near Yuma

- **Swift Trail Parkway:** Negotiate a twisting forest road from the desert Gila Valley to the top of **Mount Graham** at over 10,000 feet, the highest of Southern Arizona's sky islands–it's the equivalent of driving from Mexico to Canada in about an hour.

THE PLATEAU

The vast, sparsely populated Colorado Plateau has many lonely, scenic roads. On some of them, the traffic is so thin that you could take a nap on the center stripe.

- **The Vermilion Cliffs Highway:** Perhaps the loneliest of Arizona's lonely routes, this scenic road snakes across the **Arizona Strip** in northwestern Arizona, just below the border with Utah, and passes towering red-rock cliffs and vast bunchgrass plains.
- **Kayenta-Monument Valley Scenic Road:** The short drive from Kayenta to **Monument Valley Navajo Tribal Park** on the Navajo Reservation is almost as scenic as the famous Valley itself, with strangely eroded sandstone monuments rising from the sweeping red-dirt plains.

below when you reach the pass at the top of the hill. A little farther on and you're in the old copper mining town of **Jerome,** now home to boutiques and restaurants.

Oak Creek flows past red rocks in Sedona.

stopping along the way to admire the babbling, forested creek. Stay at the Matterhorn Inn in Sedona and have dinner at René at Tlaquepaque.

Day 4

Have breakfast in Sedona, and hit Highway 179 south from Sedona to I-17, then pick up Highway 260 east to the Mogollon Rim region. Drive through the forest along Highway 87, stopping in the small forest communities of Pine, Strawberry, and Payson to shop, hike, and eat. Check out the Zane Grey Cabin in Payson and consider stopping at the gorgeous Tonto Natural Bridge State Park. Stay at the Majestic Mountain Inn in Payson and have dinner at Gerardo's.

Day 5

Get an early start for a drive across the Mogollon Rim to the White Mountains region. Drive slowly across the rim along Forest Road 300 for 51 miles to the Mogollon Rim Visitor Center, where there's a paved trail and some breathtaking views, stopping often to

explore and enjoy the forest along the escarpment. Stay the night in Show Low or Pinetop-Lakeside in the White Mountains region.

Day 6

Rise early and lace up your hiking boots for a trek either to the top of Mount Baldy, the second highest peak in the state, or Escudilla Mountain, the third highest peak. Escudilla is the easier hike, and along the way you'll see some of the most beautiful old-growth forests in the state. Have dinner at the Rusty Cactus Restaurant in Alpine or at Bistro Escudilla in Nutrioso, and rest up for your last forest drive of the trip.

Day 7

Gas up the car and head south along The Coronado Trail, a 120-mile twisting, forested two-lane from the mountains down to the desert. Stop often to admire the wildflowers growing along the road, and keep a vigilant watch for wildlife. If you feel up to it, there are many trails along the route that lead into the forest.

PHOENIX, SCOTTSDALE, AND THE VALLEY OF THE SUN

If you spend enough time in the desert basin known locally as the Valley of the Sun (often just "the Valley"), there will undoubtedly come a time when you will ask yourself, "Why would they build a megalopolis *here*?"

This question will likely come up during the month of July or thereabouts, when it's 110°F in the shade and you're slogging

HIGHLIGHTS

LOOK FOR 【 TO FIND RECOMMENDED SIGHTS, ACTIVITIES, DINING, AND LODGING.

【 Heard Museum: Discover the histories and ways of life of Arizona's many Native American communities at this renowned institution, filled with artistic, ceremonial, and daily-life artifacts from both ancient history and more modern times (page 34).

【 Phoenix Art Museum: Spend hours browsing through one of the Southwest's top cultural depositories, where you'll see a spectacular array of the art of the American West and of the Western world (page 36).

【 Taliesin West: Tour architect Frank Lloyd Wright's desert masterpiece, a rare example of how humans can settle on the wild desert without marring or destroying it in the process (page 84).

【 The Apache Trail: Take a daylong backroad adventure on the city's rugged desert edges, passing by three glassy blue lakes ringed by saguaro, and through a few sleepy and forgotten mining towns (page 100).

【 Casa Grande Ruins National Monument: Explore the mysterious remains of a crumbling Hohokam great house (page 105).

to your car through a heat-storing parking lot somewhere. Don't lose heart, though. There is much in this mostly urbanized valley to do and see, eat and watch, find and buy.

A loose affiliation of cities and suburbs anchored by Phoenix and spreading to the wild northern Sonoran Desert that waits along its edges, the Valley of the Sun is one of the largest metro areas in the nation and as such can boast world-class hotels, restaurants, museums, theaters, sports, and shopping.

It's the logical place to begin an Arizona adventure; it's the transportation, government, and cultural hub of the state. Here you will see the hubris and shortsightedness that oftentimes have typified the settling of the urban West. But here also you will see novel attempts to live with the desert and its strange beauty, like Frank Lloyd Wright's Taliesin West and the ruins of the ancient canal-building Hohokam.

And if you're here during one of the two or three "springs" that soothe the long summer's violent tendencies, and you're playing golf in December, or hiking around the rugged

Superstition Mountains in January in shorts, you might end up forgetting that you ever questioned the wisdom of the valley's founders and instead ask yourself, "Why don't I live here?"

HISTORY

Phoenix wasn't really discovered so much as it was rediscovered, as its name suggests. The Salt River Valley, once home to prehistoric canal-crossed, mud-mound cities and thousands of Hohokam, was largely depopulated and ignored from about 1500 until the 1860s, when a few farmers moved in to supply hay and sundries to the troops at Fort McDowell, a nearby U.S. Army outpost. Soon a group of moneymen from Wickenburg, a mining community just to the northwest, looked out over the arid valley, still crisscrossed by the husks of the well-built ancient canals, and envisioned an agricultural empire. An educated British speculator among them got drunk and proclaimed the valley would henceforth be called Phoenix, as it would rise, like the mythical bird, from the Hohokam ashes to become a great American city. Or so the story goes.

The first lots went on sale in 1870, and many of them sold to residents of Prescott, the territorial capital 100 miles to the north. By the 1880s the railroad had arrived and farmers had rebuilt the Hohokam canals, tapping the wild Salt River, a major tributary of the Gila, to great effect. Victorian homes soon replaced adobe shacks, and the Anglos went about turning the desert into a pretty typical, if a bit stifling, American city—and a steadily growing one at that. From its very beginnings Phoenix has been a largely Anglo town, and it has less of the historic Latino cultural influence one sees in Tucson.

Before long the territorial capital was moved from Prescott to Phoenix, which would become the center of power and influence in the new state as well. Energetic community boosters would brand the Salt River Valley—for the sake of gathering tourism and health-seeker money to the desert—the Valley of the Sun. But the Salt, like many arid-land rivers, was fickle and wild, flooding one day and trickling the next,

making large-scale agriculture a risky endeavor. Valley farmers wanted it controlled, and the federal government, under the auspices of the Reclamation Act of 1902, put up the money to build Roosevelt Dam, then the largest of its kind in the world, to hold back and mediate the river. The dam transformed the valley and led to an agriculture boom concentrated largely on cotton and citrus. The two world wars increased demand for the valley's agriculture products and brought in military installations and military industry to spur an already steady growth rate. After World War II, and especially after 1951, when air-conditioning became affordable, growth became torrential, and it hasn't really let up yet. The city keeps sprawling, and now relies on its own growth as its primary economic engine. Where once there were cotton fields and citrus groves, now single-family tract housing and chain-store strip malls predominate. Phoenix is today the largest city in the Southwest and the fifth largest city in the nation. Forecasters have been saying for years that, one day not long in the future, the sprawl will reach unbroken all the way through Tucson and on to the Mexican border, and to the west and north in similar proportions.

PLANNING YOUR TIME

The Valley of the Sun comprises 10 incorporated cities and some 2,000 square miles, but most of the uniform sprawl deserves only pinpointed attention from the visitor. To see the highlights deeply and to taste the desert-city thrills, you'll need a week at least, but a long weekend suffices for a memorable once-over. An extra day could be spent touring the outer desert rings. If you're planning on spending time in other parts of Arizona during your trip, don't spend more than two or three days in Phoenix, depending on how much time you have. It is best used as a transportation hub and jumping-off station—the best place to begin but not the main focus of an Arizona journey.

That being said, going deep into the valley's offerings has its rewards. You could spend a week touring the area's museums, especially the Phoenix Art Museum, the Heard Museum,

PHOENIX

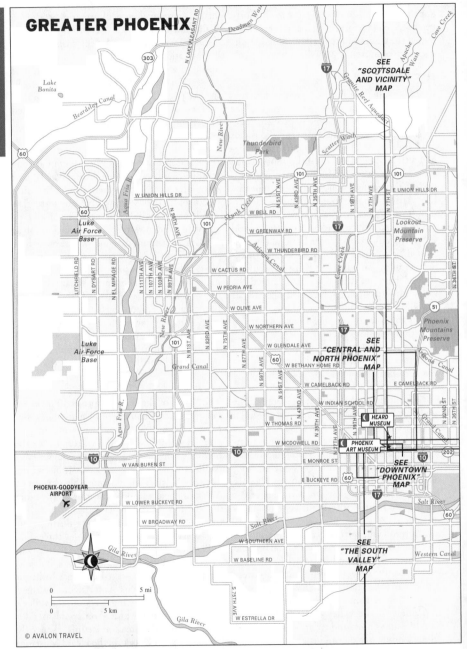

GREATER PHOENIX

SEE "SCOTTSDALE AND VICINITY" MAP

SEE "CENTRAL AND NORTH PHOENIX" MAP

SEE "DOWNTOWN PHOENIX" MAP

SEE "THE SOUTH VALLEY" MAP

HEARD MUSEUM

PHOENIX ART MUSEUM

Lake Bonita

Luke Air Force Base

Luke Air Force Base

PHOENIX-GOODYEAR AIRPORT

Thunderbird Park

Lookout Mountain Preserve

Phoenix Mountains Preserve

N LAKE PLEASANT RD
Deadman Wash
Cave Creek
Apache Wash
New River
Skunk Creek
Arizona Canal
Cave Creek
Scatter Wash
Granite Reef Aqueduct
Agua Fria R.
New River
Grand Canal
Beardsley Canal
Agua Fria R.
Gila River
Salt River
Salt River
Western Canal
Gila River
Grand Canal
Arizona Canal

303
17
60
60
101
101
17
51
101
60
10
10
202
17
60

W UNION HILLS DR
E UNION HILLS DR
W BELL RD
W GREENWAY RD
W THUNDERBIRD RD
W CACTUS RD
W PEORIA AVE
W OLIVE AVE
W NORTHERN AVE
W GLENDALE AVE
W BETHANY HOME RD
W CAMELBACK RD
E CAMELBACK RD
W INDIAN SCHOOL RD
W THOMAS RD
W MCDOWELL RD
W VAN BUREN ST
E MONROE ST
E BUCKEYE RD
W LOWER BUCKEYE RD
W BROADWAY RD
W SOUTHERN AVE
W BASELINE RD
W ESTRELLA DR

N 51ST AVE
N 43RD AVE
N 35TH AVE
N 19TH AVE
N 7TH AVE
N 7TH ST
N 36TH ST
N 92ND ST
N 32ND ST
N 111TH AVE
N 107TH AVE
N 103RD AVE
N 99TH AVE
N 91ST AVE
N 83RD AVE
N 75TH AVE
N 67TH AVE
N 59TH AVE
N 51ST AVE
N 43RD AVE
N 35TH AVE
N 27TH AVE
LITCHFIELD RD
N DYSART RD
N EL MIRAGE RD
S 75TH AVE

0   5 mi
0   5 km

© AVALON TRAVEL

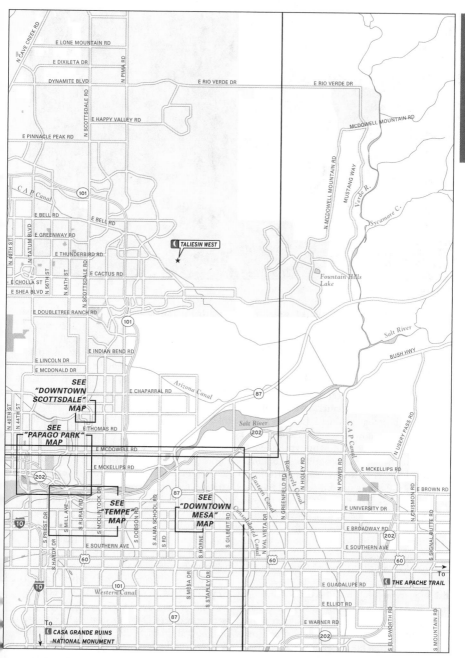

© TIM HULL

downtown Phoenix

the Arizona Museum of Natural History, the contemporary art museums in Mesa and Scottsdale, and the art and natural history museums at Arizona State University. You could spend a full day or two checking out the excellent Phoenix Zoo, the Phoenix Botanical Garden, the Mormon Temple in Mesa, the Deer Valley Rock Art Center, and the Pueblo Grande archaeological site. A full day could be given over to downtown Scottsdale, shopping and eating, or to downtown Phoenix, looking at the historic buildings, shopping, and lunching. An afternoon spent strolling, shopping, and eating on Tempe's Mill Avenue or in Glendale's historic downtown is never a waste of time. Another full day or more could be spent driving the rugged Apache Trail and exploring the dusty old mining towns on the valley's outer edges.

From May until the end of October, a full half of the year, a visit to Phoenix includes the risk of extreme heat. Risk becomes ridiculous folly June through September, when temperatures can and do reach 110°F and higher, as the heat-island effect created by all that concrete and asphalt turns the valley into a monstrous

oven that doesn't really cool down even when the moon replaces the angry sun. It is, yes, a dry heat—but does someone cooked alive in an oven scream less than one boiled alive in a pot? Seriously though, it does make a difference—90°F with high humidity is much worse than 110 with none at all. Still, experiencing Phoenix in the summer is likely to be a bit uncomfortable, though these days it's possible to feel the heat only on rare occasions; say, walking from your car through a parking lot and into a store—a brief burn of reality between air-conditioned sanctuaries. It is best to avoid daytime outdoor activities during the worst days of summer, but summer is also a good time to find a deal. If you can take the heat, you'll find prices at the high-class resorts in town drastically reduced, offering a chance for those of us who aren't movie stars and millionaires to experience a little pampering and stylish lounging. The best days to be in the valley are from October through November and March through May. These are the "spring" months, when all is right and perfect in the desert. December through February isn't too bad either, though expect to be wearing sweaters and light jackets, especially at night.

ORIENTATION

Phoenix proper sits at the center of a large basin surrounded by rugged ranges: the McDowell Mountains to the northeast; the White Tank Mountains to the west; the Sierra Estrella to the southwest; the Superstition Mountains to the east; and the South Mountains to the south. In the northeasterly portion of the metro area the Phoenix Mountains provide a convenient landmark in an otherwise rather flat and repetitive urban landscape. The mountains surrounding the Salt River Valley are rocky and dry, topped by cactus and creosote, much shorter and hotter than the 9,000-foot and higher sky islands of the southern Sonoran region. The Salt River used to run through the whole basin, but the Roosevelt Dam and other factors long ago dried up the riverbed scar.

Although there are many incorporated towns across the basin, for the purposes of the traveler and tourist, the valley can be conveniently sliced into a few general regions that make the megalopolis easier to digest. These include **Downtown and Central Phoenix,** wherein you'll find many of the valley's sights and stops, bounded, roughly, by 7th Street on the east and 7th Avenue on the west, and by I-17 on the south and Camelback Road on the north; the **east valley,** which includes **Tempe, Arizona State University,** and **Mesa; Scottsdale and**

the North Valley, which includes Scottsdale, just to the northeast of central Phoenix, and the small resort towns of Carefree and Cave Creek; and the **west valley,** which includes Glendale. Even longtime residents rarely distinguish between the towns when they're deciding which restaurant or shopping center to patronize, though it is true that if you live in Tempe or Scottsdale, you're not often found in Glendale. Unless you're paying close attention, you won't notice right away that you've left one city and entered another. The area's many freeways make getting around somewhat easy, though you should expect traffic jams everywhere during the rush hours, roughly 6am-10am and 4pm-7pm on weekdays.

I-10 runs east-west through the center of the valley and then turns south along the eastern flank of central Phoenix, skirting Sky Harbor Airport and heading southeast to Tucson and beyond. I-17 runs east-west from its interchange with I-10 near 7th Street on the east, and then, around 7th Avenue on the west, it moves north through the northwest valley all the way to Flagstaff. The Loop 202 freeway runs mostly east-west through the east valley, continuing east from where the I-10 turns south; and the Loop 101 runs north-south and east-west in a loop around the northern, western, and eastern outer edges of the city.

Sights

DOWNTOWN AND CENTRAL

Over the last several decades, downtown Phoenix has been going through a kind of renaissance, an effort that has dubbed it **Copper Square.** The area roughly bounded by 7th Street on the east, 7th Avenue on the west, Fillmore Street on the north, and Jackson Street on the south is the historic heart of the city and should be visited to get an idea of where the metropolis has been and where it hopes to go. The **Downtown Phoenix Partnership** (101 N. 1st Ave., Ste. 1450, 602/254-8696, www. coppersquare.com) watches over the 90-block

area, where you'll find museums, restaurants, theaters, sports arenas, shops, hotels, and parks. The partnership's orange-shirted ambassadors (hotline: 602/495-1500) can help you with any questions or concerns you have while in the area.

The whole downtown area comes alive from 6pm to 10pm (or later) on the first Friday of every month during the **First Friday Art Walks.** This is the time to see downtown at its most vibrant and creative, as more than 70 galleries and art spaces throw open their doors and put on shows and special performances, and thousands of Phoenicians mingle in the streets of downtown's up-and-coming neighborhoods. Along Roosevelt there's always a block party, with street performers and live bands and vendors selling all manner of handmade and one-of-a-kind items. The art walk is self-guided and begins at the **Phoenix Art Museum** (1625 N. Central Ave., 602/257-1222), where you can park and pick up a map and talk to a volunteer about what to do, and hop on a free shuttle (or walk or ride a bike). For more information contact the good folks at **Artlink** (602/256-7539, www.artlinkphoenix.com), who put on this popular event.

Heritage Square

Phoenix was founded by Anglo Americans, most of whom were Victorians through and through, despite their isolation out here in adobeland. With the coming of the railroad in the 1880s, building materials other than mud and rocks became available, and the homes in the valley began to reflect this; suddenly the adobe huts of the early years were replaced by red-brick and lumber homes, some of them as big and ornate as anything in the East. The remains of Phoenix's Victorian past can be seen at this downtown collection of museums and restaurants known as **Heritage Square** (115 N. 6th St., 602/262-5071, www.phoenix.gov/parks/parks/heritagepk.html), especially through a tour of the **Rosson House** (602/262-5029, www.rossonhousemuseum.org, 10am-4pm Tues.-Sat., noon-4pm Sun., $7.50 adults, $4 children under 12), a refurbished Victorian showcase built in 1895 at a cost of about $8,000. The tour takes about 45 minutes and will likely disabuse you of any lingering notions that what passed for the good life in late 19th-century America didn't find its way out to the frontier. Nearby, **Nobuo at the Teeter House** (602/254-0600, www. Nobuofukuda.com, 11am-4pm, 5:30pm-close Tues.-Sun.), a little Midwestern bungalow built in 1899, is now a Japanese tearoom during the day and an *izakaya*, or Japanese-style bar, when the sun goes down. The **Stevens House**, a red-brick Midwestern bungalow built in 1901,

now houses the **Arizona Doll and Toy Museum** (602/253-9337, 10am-4pm Tues.-Sat., noon-4pm Sun., closed Aug., $5 adults, $2 children) of interest to kids and other toy enthusiasts. They are closed during the month of August.

Arizona Science Center

Kids and adults alike will enjoy the popular, futuristic-looking silver-winged **Arizona Science Center** (602/716-2000, www.azscience.org, 10am-5pm daily, $14.95 adults, $11 children under 17, IMAX Planetarium extra) in Heritage Square, where you can move a ball with your brain, lie on a bed of nails, and ride a bike across a line rope like a trapeze artist (with a net below, of course). The climbing wall will challenge your inner ape, right after you watch an IMAX film about our closest primate cousins (there's also a spectacular movie about sea life). Even teenagers will like this excellent museum, which has a permanent collection of more than 300 hands-on exhibits and a planetarium. There are displays on water and how we use it, and on all the parts and technologies that go into the typical single-family home. There are also really good exhibits on the human body and the brain, and hands-on displays about gravity and other natural forces, geology, and other earth sciences.

There's a unique and eye-opening exhibit on various kinds of networks and an interactive display about music and how it works. A few exhibits are somewhat Arizona-specific, but most of the museum is general and geared toward kids. On a weekday during school hours you're liable to run into a rowdy school tour group. There's also an on-site café that's a bit pricey but offers sandwiches and snacks without a lot of grease and junk food. Several of the more exciting attractions cost extra.

◖ Heard Museum

It is possible for the observant visitor to the **Heard Museum** (2301 N. Central Ave., 602/252-8848, www.heard.org, 9:30am-5pm Mon.-Sat., 11am-5pm Sun., $18 adults, $7.50 children 6-12) to come away with a rather deep knowledge of the cultures, religions,

PHOENIX

© AVALON TRAVEL

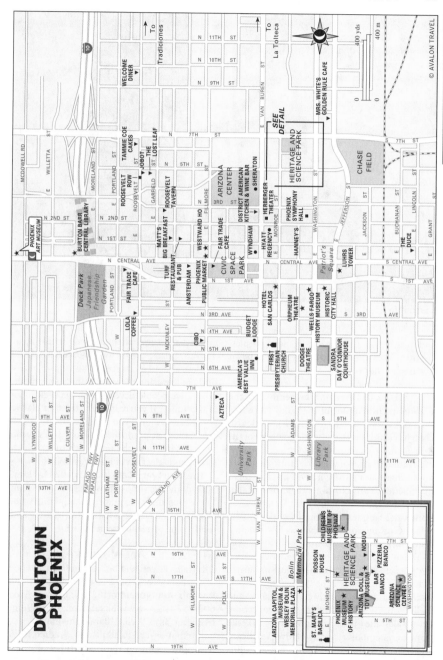

DOWNTOWN PHOENIX

To Tradiciones

To La Tolteca

WELCOME DINER

SEE DETAIL

MRS. WHITE'S GOLDEN RULE CAFE

CHASE FIELD

PHOENIX ART MUSEUM

BURTON BARR CENTRAL LIBRARY

TAMMIE COE CAKES

JOBOT

THE LOST LEAF

ROOSEVELT ROW

ROOSEVELT TAVERN

ARIZONA CENTER

SHERATON

DISTRICT AMERICAN KITCHEN & WINE BAR

HERBERGER THEATER

PHOENIX SYMPHONY HALL

HERITAGE AND SCIENCE PARK

Deck Park

Japanese Friendship Garden

FAIR TRADE CAFE

MATT'S BIG BREAKFAST

WESTWARD HO

FAIR TRADE CAFE

CIVIC SPACE PARK

WYNDHAM

HYATT REGENCY

HANNEY'S

Patriot's Square

LUHRS TOWER

THE DUCE

LOLA COFFEE

TURF RESTAURANT & PUB

AMSTERDAM

PHOENIX PUBLIC MARKET

HOTEL SAN CARLOS

ORPHEUM THEATRE

WELLS FARGO HISTORY MUSEUM

HISTORIC CITY HALL

CIBO

BUDGET LODGE

FIRST PRESBYTERIAN CHURCH

DODGE THEATRE

SANDRA DAY O'CONNOR COURTHOUSE

AMERICA'S BEST VALUE INN

AZTECA

University Park

Library Park

Papago Fwy

W GRAND AVE

Bolin Memorial Park

CHILDREN'S MUSEUM OF PHOENIX

ROSSON HOUSE

HERITAGE AND SCIENCE PARK

NOBUO

PHOENIX MUSEUM OF HISTORY

ARIZONA DOLL & TOY MUSEUM

BAR BIANCO

PIZZERIA BIANCO

ARIZONA SCIENCE CENTER

ARIZONA CAPITOL MUSEUM & WESLEY BOLIN MEMORIAL PLAZA

ST. MARY'S BASILICA

0 400 yds

0 400 m

Rosson House in Heritage Square

and histories of the state's indigenous peoples. If you're planning on spending any time in Arizona's other regions, a stop here first will enhance your trip.

This essential Arizona museum was the 1929 brainchild of one of the valley's most influential couples, Dwight and Maie Heard. Dwight Heard was the onetime publisher of the *Arizona Republican,* now the *Arizona Republic,* the state's largest newspaper both then and now. There was hardly a civic improvement in Phoenix's early 20th-century history that didn't have Dwight's hand in it, including the Roosevelt Dam. It was primarily Maie who developed the museum, however, as Dwight died just before its official opening.

Today the museum has 10 galleries featuring the art, artifacts, and historical narratives of each of the state's tribes. The large display on the Hopi is particularly comprehensive and includes Barry Goldwater's kachina collection. It's not all static history though; several galleries feature contemporary art by Native Americans and others. Sculptures dot the grounds while artists demonstrate their methods to onlookers. There are also galleries for kids, with hands-on displays about Native American culture, many of them featuring the various ingenious methods native people developed to live well in an arid country. If you're in the market for Native American art (or if you just like looking at it), especially that produced by Hopi and Navajo artists, don't miss the museum's store, which has a good selection of books as well.

The Courtyard Café (602/251-0204, 11am-3pm daily) serves Southwestern-tinged food in the museum's enchanting, shady courtyard, offering appetizing salads, sandwiches, and soups, plus coffee, beer, and wine.

Phoenix Art Museum

The state's largest and best art museum and one of the better collections in the Southwest, the **Phoenix Art Museum** (1625 N. Central Ave., 602/257-1222, www.phxart.org, 10am-9pm, free after 3pm Wed., 10am-5pm Thurs.-Sat., noon-5pm Sun., $15 adults, $6 children 6-17, free 6pm-10pm on the first Friday of every

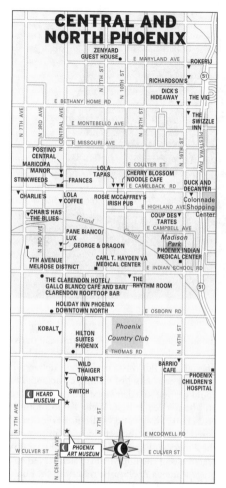

CENTRAL AND NORTH PHOENIX

Remington, and other well-known Western artists. One particular highlight is an otherworldly Arizona landscape by the fantasist illustrator Maxfield Parrish, who manages to capture that strange, fantastical vibe the desert sometimes gives off. There's also a worthy collection of Latin American art, featuring paintings by Frida Kahlo, Rufino Tamayo, and others, along with Spanish-era art and religious items. The eclectic modern and contemporary galleries manage to be challenging without becoming ridiculous, and there are interesting displays on fashion and Asian art. The miniatures gallery should not be overlooked, with its little model-room displays on interior design through the ages. Plan on spending several hours or even half a day here.

After you've spent time in the galleries, you can grab a bite or a drink at the museum's restaurant, **Palette** (11am-8pm Wed., 11am-3:30pm Thurs.-Sat., 11am-3:30pm Sunday brunch, $10.50-16), which serves sandwiches, salads, and desserts made with local organically grown ingredients, as well as a fine selection of Arizona-made beer and wine. The gift shop sells a wide selection of prints, books, and the usual museum store fare. Art lovers would do well to check the museum's website before traveling, as several large special exhibitions are put on every year.

Arizona Capitol Museum and Wesley Bolin Memorial Plaza

A neoclassical copper-domed monument to power on the western edge of downtown, the Arizona Capitol, built in 1901, is no longer the center of day-to-day legislative work here at the bustling state capitol complex. It's now the **Arizona Capitol Museum** (1700 W. Washington St., 602/926-3620, 9am-4pm Mon.-Fri., free), with displays on the state's political history, its flora and fauna, and its symbols and industries. Definitely worth seeing are the large paintings with heroic and mythical depictions of Arizona's past painted by famous local artist Lon Megargee in 1913-1914 to celebrate statehood and a few exhibits of historic furniture and other items from the

month) is the high-water mark of the valley's sometimes rather shallow cultural stream. Here you will find exactly what you'd expect from an art museum in the West as well as much that will likely surprise you.

What you'd expect is an excellent collection of Western-American art; the museum has that very definitely and is home to the Cowboy Artists of America annual show and sale. There are important and representative works by Eanger Irving Couse—whose arresting *The Captive* should not be missed—Fredric

© TIM HULL

Phoenix Art Museum

territorial days. Just east of the Capitol is a large plaza crowded with monuments to various heroes of Arizona and American history, including a large equestrian statue of Padre Kino and a black-wall memorial to the state's Vietnam veterans. This is a good place for a springtime walk, but it isn't worth visiting in the summer unless you have a particular interest in Arizona history. If you do, neither of these sights should be missed.

Wells Fargo Museum
The small **Wells Fargo Museum** (145 W. Adams St., 602/378-1852, www.wellsfargo.com/about/history/museums/phoenix, 9am-5pm Mon.-Fri., free) features an intact stage coach similar to those used by the trail-blazing banking and delivery company during the Gold Rush and subsequent settling of the West. There's also a shiny replica of the stage coach that the kids can climb, along with dozens of black-and-white photographs and artifacts from the frontier era, and even an old telegraph machine that you can tap on. Here you'll learn

the story of the early days of commercial transportation in the sparsely populated and bandit-stalked Old West, back when delivering the mail or a passel of mining-camp supplies could get you killed at worst, and mighty sore and bone tired at best. Wells Fargo's founders, Henry Wells and William Fargo, partnered with John Butterfield in 1850 to form the American Express Company and later operated along the famed Butterfield Overland Stage Route, a 2,795-mile trail from St. Louis to San Francisco that passed through Arizona along the way. (It went from Yuma in the far west of the state to Tucson, and from Tucson to New Mexico.) The story of Wells Fargo in Arizona is proof—as if it were still needed—that those who got rich and powerful during the Gold Rush were not miners. But even if you have no interest in transportation history, you should consider stopping here, if only to peruse the gallery full of N. C. Wyeth paintings and illustrations. Known for his detailed and iconic illustrations from Robert Louis Stevenson's *Treasure Island* and other classics, N. C. Wyeth

© TIM HULL

Arizona Capitol Museum

was a superior interpreter of the Old West in paintings and magazine and book illustration, and this little museum displays more of his Western-themed work than any other.

Hall of Flame Fire Museum

It makes a kind of poetic sense that the **Hall of Flame Fire Museum** (6101 E. Van Buren St., 602/275-3473, www.hallofflame.org, 9am-5pm Mon.-Sat., noon-5pm Sun., $6 adults, $4 children 6-17, $1.50 children 3-5), with its engaging collection of relics from the history of firefighting, has its home in a city named after a fiery bird. Firefighting on the southwestern frontier was largely a volunteer enterprise, as it still is in many of Arizona's rural communities. Most of the settlements from the territorial period, including Phoenix, burned to the ground a few times before surviving in their most current forms. After a series of fires that destroyed most of Washington Street in 1886, the city borrowed money to acquire equipment for a volunteer force—this about 15 years after the town was established. The Hall of Flame

displays nearly 100 different firefighting machines from the United States, Europe, and Japan, spanning more than two centuries (1725-1969). There's also a collection of firefighter helmets from around the world and throughout history. The almost one-acre museum near Papago Park includes the **National Firefighting Hall of Heroes,** a tribute to firefighters killed in the line of duty, and a display on the history of wildland firefighting, a particularly important occupation in the flame-prone pine forests of northern Arizona and southern Arizona's arboreal sky islands.

Burton Barr Library

Take a quick ride up through the "Crystal Canyon," the five-story glass atrium that divides this star of Phoenix's underrated architecture scene, to the 5th floor's **Great Reading Room** for an expansive view of the Valley of the Sun that nearly beats any vista you'd gain by hiking into the desert mountains. Along the way, make sure to check out the art on the walls—it's an amazing collection, with

© TIM HULL

Burton Barr Library

paintings by some of the Southwest's best artists.

Architect Will Bruder designed Phoenix's main library branch, the **Burton Barr Library** (1221 N. Central Ave., 602/262-4636, www. phxlib.org, 9am-5pm Mon., 1pm-5pm Tues.-Thurs., 9am-9pm Fri.-Sat., free), to suggest one of the great sandstone buttes of Monument Valley on the Navajo Reservation. Step in around noon on June 21, also known as the summer solstice, when round skylights with special lenses project illusory flames; people usually gather to watch the event. The 43,000-square-foot Great Reading Room is one the nation's largest, and it offers workstations where you can glom onto the wireless network. Throughout this beloved local landmark the sleek, modern, modular furnishings and exposed wires and cables create a futuristic-utilitarian atmosphere that clashes evocatively with those bookshelves full of ancient stories—all of it washed in filtered desert light. A 2nd-floor room holds the library's **Arizona Collection,** a place to get lost in the fascinating history of the

Grand Canyon State. The ground floor holds the **Central Gallery,** a space featuring exhibits by mostly local artists, and nearby there's a small store selling used and discarded books at very fair prices.

Civic Space Park

This expanse of stylish green space downtown, hovered over by the unique net-sculpture *Her Secret Is Patience,* by artist Janet Echelman, is hopefully an example of the direction urban design in the desert is headed. Opened in 2009, the **Civic Space Park** (424 N. Central Ave., 602/262-4734, http://phoenix.gov/parks/civicprk.html, 5am-11pm daily), which is right next to the light rail station on Central Avenue, has sustainable features such as solar panels, still-developing shade trees, and pervious concrete that captures rain runoff. The valley's rainstorms are often short and violent, especially during the summer "monsoon" rainy season. With all the paved surfaces that have replaced the thirsty desert floor, not much of the rushing rainwater from such storms soaks into the ground; instead it runs off quickly into the gutters and is wasted. The pavers and pervious concrete here allow more water to seep in, making the field of cool and inviting green grass seem like a gift for outdoor loungers rather than a waste of precious resources. Solar panels on the roofs of several shade structures provide the electricity for ghostly blue lights that illuminate Echelman's sculpture—which, inspired by the life-giving clouds that so infrequently visit the valley's wide skies, is suspended by cables 38 feet above the ground. A kid-entrancing **Splash Pad** (5pm-9pm Wed.-Sun.) also lights up, though with purplish hues, after the sun goes down, making nighttime an ideal time for a visit. The renovated red-brick **A. E. England Building** within the park has a notable gallery featuring local and national work, and hosts the **Fair Trade Café** (7am-3pm Mon.-Fri.).

St. Mary's Basilica

St. Mary's Basilica (231 N. 3rd St., 602/354-2100, www.saintmarysbasilica.org, 9am-4pm Mon.-Fri.), the white-stone and red-tile Spanish

© TIM HULL

St. Mary's Basilica

Revival church downtown whose tall, cross-topped towers have been points on the valley's skyline for nearly a century, is one of several vital sights in Arizona for the religious soul, though at just under 100 years old, it's also one of the youngest (considering that San Xavier del Bac and Mission Tumacacori in southern Arizona were founded in the 1600s). The current building, which replaced an older church on the same spot, held its first masses in 1915. The soaring interior, lined and lit by dozens of stained-glass windows (the largest collection in the state, in fact), should be seen by anyone interested in religious architecture. Before visiting Arizona in 1987, Pope John Paul II, who drew thousands of Catholics from the state's rural hinterlands and across the valley to a huge mass at Sun Devil Stadium, made St. Mary's a "minor basilica" (an important church with special ceremonial rights), and it is still today Arizona's only one. On the east side of the building the **Via Assisi Gift Shop** (10am-3pm Thurs.-Fri., 10am-6:30pm Sat., 9am-1pm Sun.) sells Catholic gifts.

Children's Museum of Phoenix

Arizona's children's museums have a knack for reusing grand old buildings that have been tossed aside and forgotten by the renewal-mad developers of the urban Southwest. Tucson's small museum for kids took over a stately old Carnegie library, while the larger **Children's Museum of Phoenix** (215 N. 7th St., 602/253-0501, www.childrensmuseumofphoenix.org, 9am-4pm Tues.-Sun., $11 adults and children over 1, children under 1 free) is housed in the **Historic Monroe School Building,** designed in 1913 by noted California architect Norman Marsh. Half the fun of taking the kids to these hands-on play centers is experiencing the soul of a beautiful old space. Of course, that's not what the kids will say. They'll enjoy scrambling up and all over the 37-foot-high pile of steel, tubes, planks, and passageways called **The Climber,** or serving plastic food in the make-believe restaurant, or pretending to be a firefighter in turnouts and helmet, or getting lost in a forest of foam noodles hanging from the ceiling, or doing a shift in the nursery, with lifelike dolls to feed and change, or creating some artistic masterpiece in the craft center, or throwing paint in imitation of Abstract Expressionist master and Monroe Elementary School alum Jackson Pollock, or . . . Don't expect to make a quick visit. The hands-on, interactive, and deceptively educational activities here will appeal to kids under 10.

Japanese Friendship Garden

A perfect slice of green Japan in the middle of downtown Phoenix, the **Japanese Friendship Garden** (1125 N. 3rd Ave., 602/256-3204, www.japanesefriendshipgarden.org, 10am-4pm Tues.-Fri., 10am-4pm Sat.-Sun., closed June-Sept., $5 adults, $4 children), a sculpted and manicured "strolling garden" with a trickling creek, rushing waterfall, and crowded koi pond, celebrates the valley's relationship with Himeji, Japan, Phoenix's sister city. Called *Ro Ho En* in Japanese, the 3.5-acre refuge holds four different vegetation zones (and more than 50 different kinds of plants) that gradually rise into a "mountain zone" above a large pond topped with water lily beds. A creek trickles down from the mountains and spills into the pond over a 12-foot waterfall. It's an enchanting place for a stroll on a warm, breezy fall day in the desert (the garden closes for the torrid summer months). Easy paved paths snake around the deceptively secluded property, past sculpted trees, hanging lanterns, and bamboo fences, over stone footbridges to the pond, swarming with fat, multicolored koi. The garden also has a traditional Japanese tea garden and an elegant tea house, where on the second Sunday of every month you can vie for a seat at a traditional **Japanese Tea Ceremony** ($22 per person). It's essential to call ahead for a reservation: The garden hosts just five ceremonies each time, with only eight to nine guests per ceremony.

Pueblo Grande Museum and Archaeological Park

The valley's ubiquitous construction cranes can usually be seen bending and rising at work from the smooth-dirt mound tops of the ancient Hohokam ruin at **Pueblo Grande Museum and Archaeological Park** (4619 E. Washington St., 602/495-0900, www.pueblogrande.org, 9am-4:45pm Mon.-Sat., 1pm-4:45pm Sun., closed Sun.-Mon. May-Sept., $6 adults, $3 children under 17), a canal-side city that reached the peak of its power and population just before it was abandoned around 1450. Here you'll also see the remains of one of the hundreds of canals the Hohokam dug through the valley to harness the Salt River—canals that formed the basis for modern agricultural pursuits as well. A short trail takes you to various points around the main ruin, which looks like a well-worked mound of dirt. Particularly interesting is the collection of Hohokam model homes along the trail, built according to what archaeologists think domestic structures may have looked like in the valley's ancient past. The contrast with today's tract homes and McMansions is striking to say the least. Though not as large as the spectacular Casa Grande to the east, Pueblo Grande, a rare city-center ruin, is recommended to anyone interested in the Hohokam and to those who want to learn how past cultures have tried to live with the desert rather than against it. A small, informative museum has displays on the Hohokam—who they were, how they developed, and where they went.

Encanto Park

A lush duck-pond park east of the city center, **Encanto Park** (2605 N. 15th Ave., 602/261-8991, 5:30am-11pm daily) was once the place to go on a hot Phoenix afternoon, and it's still a really peaceful, green, trickling-water oasis within the heat-island sprawlscape. It borders one of the valley's most tourable residential neighborhoods, the **Encanto-Palmcroft Historic District.** This district, with its winding, manicured streets, each home more elegant and each lawn better landscaped than the next, was Phoenix's first and best garden-style suburb, planned and built in the 1920s by Dwight Heard. It's fun to drive slowly through the neighborhood and see the style

The Hohokam

The Sonoran Desert is not a wasteland of shifting dunes, nor a place to make it through at all costs but never to stop and settle. While such may be the popular conception of a desert, first-time visitors to central and southern Arizona are often surprised to see so much vegetation, so much diversity, and so much evidence of eons of human habitation.

That's not to say it has always been easy to live here; prior to the damming of the Southwest's rivers, a drought or a flood could wipe out a lifetime's worth of progress, and you never really knew with any confidence if the annual rains would come too heavy or too light or not at all. There are usually two rainy seasons in the Sonoran Desert: In midsummer the Mexican Monsoon sends moisture north every late afternoon, and in winter the rains come again, hopefully. The twice-a-year rains, though scant compared to nearly every other place (the whole 100,000-square-mile desert gets less than 15 inches per year), allow for myriad dryland-adapted plants and animals to thrive here.

People too have thrived here for thousands of years, taking advantage of the once-perennial desert rivers like the Gila, the Salt, the Santa Cruz, and the San Pedro. Because of damming, overuse, and other factors, none of these rivers is much of a river anymore, but each of them long ago provided a healthy, if unpredictable, lifeline for the complex culture of the Hohokam, desert farmers who lived in the Sonoran river valleys from the beginning of the common era (AD 1) to about 1450. They disappeared from the valleys about 100 years before the Spanish arrived, leaving behind great mud ruins and more than 1,000 miles of irrigation canals built with stone and wooden tools.

The Hohokam culture went through several stages before reaching its golden age from around 1150 to 1450, also called the classic period. During this time, the tribe's irrigation farming of the Salt River Valley produced a surplus of maize, beans, squash, and cotton, and the culture grew more complex, the buildings bigger, and the population denser. Ball courts like those found in Mesoamerica were built in Hohokam villages, and pottery became more beautiful and less strictly utilitarian. At the culture's high point, there were as many as 40,000 Hohokam living in the valley, irrigating some 100,000 acres of farmland using canals that were still intact and usable when Anglo Americans arrived in the 19th century. Evidence of this golden age can be seen at ruins like Pueblo Grande in Phoenix and Casa Grande between Phoenix and Tucson.

Then, around 1450, it all fell apart. This is roughly the same time when the Anasazi cultures of the Four Corners region were also coming to an abrupt end, and the theories behind both collapses are similar, though by no means universally accepted. The culprits include soil salinization, disease, warfare, flood, drought, climate change, internal unrest, overpopulation, and various combinations thereof. The O'odham cultures, formerly called the Pima and Papago Indians, tell stories about how their ancestors overthrew the Hohokam cities along the Salt River because they had grown arrogant. Many archaeologists believe that the Hohokam were the ancient forebears of today's Sonoran Desert tribes, and oral tradition among the Hopi of northeastern Arizona links that culture to the Hohokam as well.

and grace that upper-middle-class merchants and city leaders once brought to valley living. The Spanish Colonial Revival and Monterrey Revival homes and the tall palms lining many of the streets—nonnative to Arizona except in a small pocket canyon near Yuma—give the whole neighborhood a dreamy pre-World War II California feel. Over at the park, kids will enjoy the old-school county fair-style rides at **Enchanted Island Amusement Park** (602/254-1200, www.enchantedisland.com, $1.15 for single ride, $14.25 all-day pass for kids under 54 inches tall); check the website for hours, as they change often.

Wrigley Mansion

A mere "winter cottage" to William Wrigley Jr., of the chewing gum Wrigleys, the shining-white, 16,000-square-foot **Wrigley Mansion** (2501 E. Telawa Tr., 602/955-4079, www.wrigleymansionclub.com, one-hour tours at 10am and 3pm Tues.-Sat., please arrive 15 minutes early, reservations required, summer hours may vary, $15;they also offer a lunch-tour package), perched on a hill overlooking central Phoenix, is still one of the valley's most beloved reminders of the pre-World War II cityscape. Wrigley, who also owned the Arizona Biltmore Resort just down the hill, built the home in 1931 in a kind of California-Spanish Colonial style with a lot of art deco flourishes. Another scion of American industry, composer and founder of L.A.'s legendary Village Recording Studio, George "Geordie" Hormel, bought the 24-room palace in the 1990s, and after a costly re-furbishing opened a bar and restaurant inside. The place is a "club" that offers memberships for $10 per year, following the letter if not the spirit of the zoning laws. But you can have a drink in the lounge, which has an impressive view of the valley, or attend the popular Sunday brunch ($45 per person) without becoming a member. It's essential to call ahead for brunch reservations. The most interesting part of a visit to this landmark hilltop, which bicyclists like to climb on weekend mornings, is the tour of the home, which reveals all the details and flourishes that you couldn't otherwise see.

Tovrea Castle and Carraro Cactus Garden

Perched on a cactus-covered hilltop just west of the I-10 freeway nearing the east valley, and resembling a many-tiered cake made of stone, the newly restored Phoenix landmark **Tovrea Castle** (5025 E. Van Buren St., 602/256-3221, www.tovreacastletours.com, $15 adults, $10 children 12 and under) is mostly seen these days from the seat of a car as you fly by at 75 miles per hour. It was built in 1928 by San Francisco businessman Alessio Carraro in a typical fit of passion for the desert, but sold soon after to Della Tovrea. The unique home

was Tovrea's winter getaway while she lived in Prescott with her second husband, a newspaper publisher, and she used it as her full-time residence after he died until her own death in 1969. The City of Phoenix purchased the large cactus garden, the home, and some adjacent property in the 1990s, and has since led a mul-timillion-dollar effort to renovate the property. Guides lead tours 7:30am-11am Friday-Sunday, though the exact times vary slightly by season. Call ahead to make a reservation for a specific time.

Phoenix Zoo

The excellent **Phoenix Zoo** (455 N. Galvin Pkwy., 602/273-1341, www.phoenixzoo.org, 7am-2pm daily June-Aug., 9am-5pm daily Sept.-Nov., 9am-4pm daily Nov. 6-Jan. 12, 9am-5pm daily Jan. 13-May 31, $20 adults, $10 children under 12) in Papago Park was called the "Maytag Zoo" when it first opened in 1962 in honor of its main booster, Robert Maytag, a scion of the appliance family. Today it's the nation's largest privately owned, non-profit zoo, hosting more visitors every year than any other valley attraction. You'll see all the usual suspects here, from the mountain lions and bighorn sheep that stalk Arizona's wild-lands to the rare Arabian oryx, which the zoo is credited with saving from near extinction. Along the way, as you walk along three paved trails through the zoo's clean, lush grounds, you'll commune with lions, elephants, camels, giraffes, and too many birds to name. You can catch a ride on a camel, walk through the fre-netic Monkey Village, and stare for as long as you want to at the invariably sleepy big cats. A newer exhibit lets you get up close and personal (sort of) with stingrays and even sharks. Don't miss Baboon Kingdom, where you can watch those exceedingly humanlike creatures inter-act (often hilariously), and be sure to walk the Arizona Trail, where you'll witness what you're missing out there in the desert. Plan on spend-ing at least half of the day here, and happily so.

Desert Botanical Garden

A 50-acre garden in Papago Park, the **Desert**

Botanical Garden (1201 N. Galvin Pkwy., 480/941-1225, www.dbg.org, 7am-8pm daily, $18 adults, $10 children 13-18, $8 children under 13) is the very best place to go to learn about the desert's unique flora, other than the wild desert itself, of course. Actually, the garden might be even better than the raw desert—you aren't risking your life by coming here in the summer, and there are signs everywhere explaining what each stickery bush and thorn-heavy succulent is called and why. There are several special exhibitions each year, including art installations by visiting artists. You can eat here at the small, delicious Patio Café and purchase a strange alien cactus for yourself. If you have any interest in the desert Southwest's unique and always-threatened plant life, consider spending a few hours strolling the garden's easy pathways. In the summer it can be trying, but it's not completely out of the question, as all that plantlife growing close together gives off a cooling vibe and a shady feeling, even when the sun is beating incessantly.

TEMPE AND THE EAST VALLEY

Tempe, a self-contained college town along the banks of the once-mighty Salt River, is home to Arizona State University, the state's largest university and one of the largest public land-grant schools in the Southwest. The east valley includes Mesa, a crowded, seemingly unending band of sprawl east of Tempe, that is the third-largest city in Arizona and the part-time home to thousands of snowbirds and RV parks. Mesa was founded in the late 19th century by Mormon pioneers from Utah and is still a largely Mormon-dominated town with the state's biggest Latter-day Saints temple. Chandler and Gilbert are also nearby, both of them former agricultural burgs that have grown and spread mightily during the housing booms of the last few decades.

Arizona Sealife Aquarium

The colorful, family-oriented **Arizona Sealife Aquarium** (5000 Arizona Mills Cir., Tempe, 480/478-7600, www.visitsealife.com/arizona, 10am-7:30pm Mon.-Sat., 10am-6pm Sun., $20 adults, $15 children under 12) at Tempe's Arizona Mills mall is not cheap; indeed, it's a bit pricey for what it is. If you don't have kids with you, it's not worth the price of admission. That being said, kids up to about 12 years old or so will likely enjoy this innovative, educational, and eye-catching attraction. The 26,000-square-foot space features a series of galleries with aquariums in all different shapes and sizes, holding more than 5,000 creatures of the sea, including eerie, flat black rays, sharp-toothed sharks, and goofy seahorses. There's a tidal pool display that allows kids to touch a few creatures, and several super fun observation bubbles get them up close and surrounded on all sides by sea life. At the end of the trail, after you've passed through each gallery and peaked into all 30 tanks, there's a big indoor climbing-and-sliding apparatus that will likely keep you on-site for another hour or so.

Arizona Historical Society Museum at Papago Park

So much of what tourists and historical re-enactors find most interesting about Arizona history—cowboys and Indians, placer miners and improbable gunfights in the streets—happened before the dawning of the 20th century. For many people the state's history stops at the O.K. Corral. But many of the more peculiar events that have occurred in the last state among the lower 48 happened in the 1900s, not the 1800s. The **Arizona Historical Society Museum at Papago Park** (1300 N. College Ave., 480/929-9499, www.arizonahistoricalsociety.org, 10am-4pm Tues.-Sat., noon-4pm Sun., two-for-one admission first Tues. of each month, $5 adults, $4 children 12-18, children 11 and under free) concentrates on the state's urban, 20th-century history, explaining how the Valley of the Sun became one of the largest cities in the country and illuminating the city's and the state's essential role during World War II. There are also a few displays on the state's popular culture, including the memorable local cartoon show hosts Wallace and Ladmo, which will have longtime Arizonans chuckling with

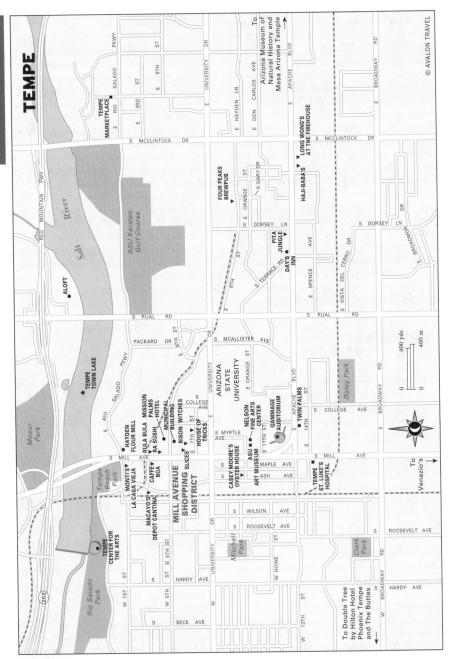

TEMPE

© AVALON TRAVEL

recognition. Don't miss the exhibit on the mass escape of German prisoners of war from the nearby Camp Papago Park. In December 1944, after digging a 176-foot-long tunnel in the hard desert soil, 25 German POWs got away, but the cruel desert expanses proved to be too much for most of them.

Tempe Town Lake

Tempe Town Lake (620 N. Mill Ave., 480/350-8625, www.tempe.gov/lake, free), a large, city-center waterway just off Tempe's main street, represents an ambitious, long-term attempt to bring back a bit of the Salt River, at least for the sake of pedal-boating and waterside jogging, to the Salt River Valley. It's a pleasant place to stroll, jog, and bike, or you can even lounge around on the grass at **Tempe Beach Park** (www.tempe.gov/lake), where there's always something going on. You can rent a pedal boat or a kayak, or take an electric-boat cruise on the lake. Kids will love to put on their swimsuits and dash around the cool water features at **Cox Splash Playground** (10am-7pm daily, free), where they'll also learn about water and why it's so important here in the desert. At the western edge of the park, near the inflatable dam that holds the lake together, check out the gleaming new **Tempe Center for the Arts** (700 W. Rio Salado Pkwy., 480/350-2822, www.tempe.gov), which hosts Broadway-style shows, local theater, music, and dance performances; it also has a small gallery.

Arizona State University (ASU)

If you walk around the sprawling, palm tree-lined campus of **Arizona State University** (University Dr. and Mill Ave., 480/965-9011, www.asu.edu) at any time during the spring or early fall months, you might wonder whether school is actually in session. You'll probably see students lounging around the grass and several Frisbee and football games going on. It's not that ASU students aren't serious—most of them are, and the university is among the top state schools in the nation in several categories—but it's truly difficult to take life too seriously when the weather is

so perfect, and it usually is while school is in session.

Along with prime people-watching, there are two museums that may entice the visitor to campus. The **ASU Art Museum** (480/965-2787, www.asuartmuseum.asu.edu, 11am-8pm Tues., 11am-5pm Wed.-Sat., free) has some excellent contemporary art pieces, and the Americas Gallery has an extremely varied display of paintings and drawings from across the Western Hemisphere, arranged in a kind of living room wall-style that is very effective. Don't miss Luis Jimenez's lithograph, *Southwest Pieta*—an indigenous take on the classic Christian art pose. The **ASU Museum of Anthropology** (480/965-6224, 11am-3pm Mon.-Fri. during school year, closed in summer, free) puts on several interesting exhibits throughout the year relating to human cultures in the Southwest and around the world. Every year from November through January, a Día de los Muertos (Day of the Dead) exhibition interprets and celebrates this most mysterious and fascinating of New World traditions.

an entrance to the Arizona State University campus

© TIM HULL

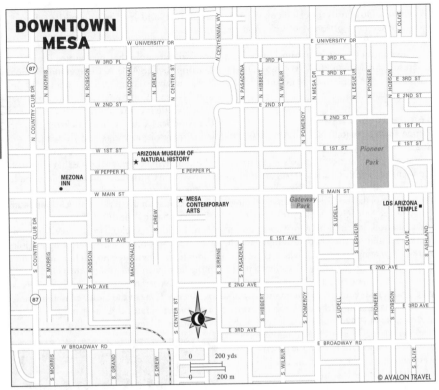

Mesa Contemporary Arts

One wouldn't expect to find this excellent contemporary art museum in staid Main Street, Mesa, but here it is. **Mesa Contemporary Arts** (1 E. Main St., 480/644-6500, www.mesaartscenter.com, 10am-5pm Tues., Wed., Fri., Sat., 10am-8pm Thurs., noon-5pm Sun., free) is highly recommended to anyone who wants to witness the most current moment in painting, sculpture, and other media. Three galleries in this cool, spare space inside the **Mesa Arts Center** show revolving exhibitions featuring primarily artists from the Southwest, California, and Mexico, but not necessarily—in fact rarely—what most would think of as Southwestern-style art. The shows are typically provocative and singular—a recent exhibition featured works by Latino artists from the collection of Cheech Marin, of Cheech and Chong fame. This museum, along with a similar contemporary space in nearby Scottsdale, is must-see proof that the valley isn't exactly the cultural graveyard it can sometimes appear to be.

Arizona Museum of Natural History

The valley's only natural history museum, the **Arizona Museum of Natural History** (53 N. MacDonald, 480/644-2230, www.azmnh.org, 10am-5pm Tues.-Fri., 11am-5pm Sat., 1pm-5pm Sun., $10 adults, $6 children under 12, $8 students over age 13 with I.D.) has quite a few hulking dinosaur skeletons in its Dinosaur Hall, and its three-story Dinosaur Mountain is definitely something to see, but the most interesting exhibits here are related to the history of the Southwest, including models of a

Spanish-era mission and a territorial jail. The exhibition about Arizona in the movies is fascinating, and the newer exhibit on the Hohokam is one of the best around. This is a great place to stop prior to traveling to other parts of the state, a kind of one-stop lesson on the nature and people of Arizona and the Southwest through the ages—especially recommended to parents who are hoping to sneak a little education into a Southwestern vacation.

Arizona Temple Visitor's Center

Non-Mormons can't go inside the beautiful **Arizona Temple** (525 E. Main St., Mesa, 480/964-7164, www.lds.org/placestovisit, 9am-9pm daily, free), on 20 green acres near the original Mesa townsite, but those interested in the mysterious and fascinating world of the Latter-day Saints church can stop by and see the outside (which some say resembles the biblical Temple of Herod). Construction on the LDS temple, the first built in Arizona—a state that has welcomed Mormon settlers for generations—began in 1922, and the building was dedicated in 1927. The grounds include a cactus garden and reflecting pools, and the visitors center has some displays and a film about the LDS church.

THE SOUTH VALLEY
Mystery Castle

From the early 19th century through the mid-20th, American doctors had a simple, if life-altering, prescription for patients suffering from tuberculosis and other chest ailments: seek dry air. As a result, the mountains and deserts of the interior West, especially the arid Southwest, became a popular place for the dying to live out their final days. Phoenix's early boosters did much to attract these "health seekers" to the Valley of the Sun, and thus shouldered Arizona and the desertlands early on with a reputation as a wide-open infirmary for the diseased and aged—a reputation the state still can't shake entirely thanks to its many retirement communities. And so the American West is littered with the failed and half-realized dream projects of those living

in a kind of surrealistic gulf between this and the afterworld, and this 18-room, stacked-stone **Mystery Castle** (800 E. Mineral Rd., 602/268-1581, mymysterycastle.com, 11am-4pm Thurs.-Sun. Oct.-May, $10 adults, $5 children 5-15) near South Mountain is one of the more fantastical among them. Something of a masterpiece of folk architecture, the odd, fascinating home's tubercular builder, Boyce Luther Gulley, came to the valley in 1930 from Seattle, Washington, leaving his wife and daughter behind. He spent the remaining years of his life cobbling together the sprawling, fairy-tale house out of stones found around the property and salvaged materials like telephone poles and railroad ties, believing he was constructing a walk-in sand castle for his daughter. His methods, and the resulting structure, were not that different from the mesa-top stone homes built for centuries by the Hopi of northeastern Arizona, whose methods and aesthetic were copied by Mary Colter, one of the Southwest's finest designers and architects, when she built the famous stone structures that line the South Rim of the Grand Canyon. Gulley's project was unfinished when he died in 1945, but his wife and beloved daughter, Mary Lou Gulley, moved in anyway, and Mary Lou and the home were famously featured in a 1948 article in *Life* magazine.

The home is open for tours from October to May, a truly one-of-a-kind attraction that should be seen by anyone interested in architecture, design, art, or an inspiring and illuminating story of one man's obsession. (Call ahead to make sure that tours are being offered.)

Rawhide Western Town at Wild Horse Pass

Pan for gold, ride a mechanical bull, and put the kids on the strong back of a cute burro for a ride around the dusty streets of **Rawhide Western Town** (5700 W. North Loop Rd., Chandler, 480/502-5600, www.rawhide.com, hours vary by season, summer hours: town and steak house 6pm-9:30pm Tues.-Sun., saloon 6pm-11pm Sat.), a "replica 1880s" frontier

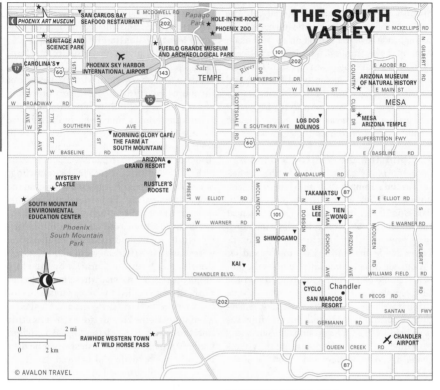

town theme park—though it replicates an average Western movie set more than it does a real Arizona town in the territorial era. But that's certainly not the point here, where you can spend an hour playing in the theme park with the kids and shopping for unique Old West souvenirs and cowboy kitsch, and then have a thick steak and some cowboy beans at the steak house. Every night a group of actors has a shoot-out, complete with stunt falls and other high action. It's free to walk around the town, but you have to shell out $3-10 to do anything fun. It costs $3 per person to watch the gunfights, which go down nightly at 7pm and 8pm. Rawhide is part of the Wild Horse Pass casino, resort, and golf course complex just off I-10 on the Gila River Indian Community Reservation. You'll find it about 20 miles southeast of downtown on the south side of I-10, Exit 162.

NORTH VALLEY
Musical Instrument Museum

Musicians and music-lovers will want to check out the **Musical Instrument Museum** (4725 E. Mayo Blvd., 480/478-6000, www.mim.org, 9am-5pm Mon.-Sat., first Friday of the month open until 9pm, 10am-5pm Sun., $18 adults, $14 children 13-19, $10 children 4-12), a gorgeous museum and concert hall about 20 miles north of downtown via Route 51. This elegant state-of-the-art museum showcases musical instruments from around the world and throughout history, offering a free audio tour with admission (bring your own headphones if you want to). A stroll through the museum's galleries reveals the astonishing beauty and variety of musical instruments throughout the world, and brings one into close personal contact with the totems of rock-and-roll. Some of the displays are permanent, others come and go. In recent times the museum has shown a Rickenbacker guitar purchased in 1963 by George Harrison, next to the very piano on which John wrote *Imagine*. If that's not worthy of a pilgrimage, nothing is. Plan to spend at least two hours here.

THE WEST VALLEY
Deer Valley Rock Art Center
The **Deer Valley Rock Art Center** (3711 W. Deer Valley Rd., 623/582-8007, http://dvrac.asu.edu, 9am-5pm Tues.-Sat. Oct.-Apr., 8am-2pm Tues.-Sat. May-Sept., $7 adults, $3 children under 12) in the far northwest valley is protected by ASU, and scholars are involved in ongoing research here into the forms and meanings of the petroglyphs that cover the Southwest. The more than 1,500 works of rock art on this 46-acre preserve were scraped and scratched by the Hohokam and other tribes that once inhabited the valley, and are believed to date from about AD 900-1100. There's a museum and visitors center before a quarter-mile trail that you can walk along to view some of the state's finest examples of the ancient medium. Consider bringing along binoculars (or you can rent them at the center), as some of the best work is off the trail. The center is about 20 miles northwest of downtown among the volcanic rock piles called the Hedgepeth Hills. The easy trail winds around the black basalt boulders, which seem to have made the perfect canvas for the largely inscrutable but no less fascinating figures and shapes. The center's 7,000-square-foot "boomerang-shaped" building, made of weathered steel and precast concrete and tucked in low among the creosote and cactus, is an attraction itself. It's the work of Will Bruder, the groundbreaking architect who also designed the masterful Burton Barr Library downtown.

Wildlife World Zoo & Aquarium
It's a long, 30-mile drive from downtown to reach the privately owned **Wildlife World Zoo & Aquarium** (16501 W. Northern Ave., 623/935-9453, www.wildlifeworld.com, zoo 9am-6pm daily, aquarium 9am-9pm daily, $29 adults, $14.25 children 3-12) in the far northwest valley. It is best visited combined with some other west valley pursuit, perhaps a visit to grandparents in nearby Sun City. The zoo doesn't match the more conveniently located Phoenix Zoo, but if you're already in the area it makes a fun, if a bit pricey, outing with the kids. Set among the valley's remaining agriculture lands and shaded by big, mature eucalyptus trees, the zoo keeps dozens of different exotic animals—giraffes that gladly accept offerings of food pellets, freaky albino alligators, and lions, tigers, and other big cats that lounge around haughtily, bored with it all. The newish aquarium is probably the best attraction here, and there's a water ride on which you pass through a glass tunnel swarming with sea life.

Entertainment and Events

NIGHTLIFE
There are a lot of young people in Phoenix—it's in many ways a very young city. There are also a lot of retirees, and even a few people in between somewhere. They all manage to come together when the sun goes down. Like so many desert creatures, they love the nightlife. There's upscale and dive-scale, there are sports bars and ultracool lounges, rock bars, honky-tonks, and hookahs. Hidden somewhere out in that hot sprawl there's a place that offers what you want. The best place to identify both the new and the classic is the *Phoenix New Times,* an alternative weekly you'll find free everywhere.

Downtown and Central
BARS AND PUBS
The sports and rock-and-roll memorabilia on the walls and the classic rock cover-bands on the stage make Phoenix native Alice Cooper's

combo "rock-'n'-jock" restaurant and bar **Alice Cooperstown** (101 E. Jackson St., 602/253-7337, www.alicecooperstown.com, 11am-9pm Mon.-Thurs., 11am-10pm Fri.-Sat., bar open later after sports events, $5-22) a fun place to spend an evening in downtown Phoenix, especially after a D-Backs or Suns game, when the place is usually packed. Ready-made Irish and English "pubs" are starting to pop up all over the country these days, but central Phoenix's **George & Dragon Pub** (4240 N. Central Ave., 602/241-0018, www.georgeanddragonpub.net, 11am-2am daily, $8-12) is the real deal, and it has been around forever. A fabulous selection of beers on tap—heavy on the delicious brews of the British Isles—a well-stocked jukebox, billiards, and good eats (the bangers and mash are particularly good) make this authentic pub a perfect place to spend an hour or ten. **The Vig** (4041 N. 40th St., 602/553-7227, www.thevig. us, 11am-close daily, $9-16), with its refined interior of red-brick walls, pale wood tables, and chocolate-brown booths, and its cool, shady, and laid-back patio, is one of the best hangouts in the valley. Try one of their $9 "vignature cocktails," perhaps the "Cougar Juice": infused vanilla vodka, Chambord, amaretto and champagne. Spend the afternoon or evening drinking on the patio, playing bocce ball, and sampling the hummus, guacamole, and spicy edamame. In downtown's Heritage Square adjacent to Pizza Bianca, the British pub atmosphere of **The Rose and Crown** (628 E. Adams St., 602/256-0223, 11am-2am Mon.-Sat, 10am-2am Sun.) is all you need most nights. There's a pool table and a dart board, a convivial atmosphere of fellow beer drinkers downing pints of Guinness, Tetley's, Smithwick's, and the like, The Clash on the stereo and on the wall, and a menu of tasty, rib-sticking pub eats to soak up the booze. The **Ice House Tavern** (3855 E. Thomas Ave., 602/244-1179, www. icehousetavernphx.com, 1:30pm-2am Mon.-Thurs., 11am-2am Fri.-Sun., sometimes open earlier for college football games) is a fun dive-style hangout, where you can grab a beer and watch the game, then stick around and dance to a local garage band. The bar has an ice-hockey theme, and you can watch through a big window as skaters attempt to stay up at the Arcadia Ice Arena.

LOUNGES AND WINE BARS

Housed in an old department store downtown that was hailed as a local masterpiece of the International Style when it opened in 1947, the retro-modernist lounge and restaurant **Hanny's** (40 N. 1st St., 602/252-2285, www. hannys.net, 11am-1:30am Mon.-Fri., 5pm-1:30am Sat.-Sun., $8-25) is an essential bar-hopping stop for anyone who appreciates urban renewal done the right way. This sophisticated lounge serves food—gourmet pizzas, appetizers, and sandwiches—until 1am, and a large menu of creative, expertly mixed (though expensive) cocktails, wine, and beer until 1:30am. It's the perfect place for a nightcap: the Petite Midnight Martini (just $2.50) is billed as the "last chance for romance." For a top-notch glass of wine, a plate of cheese and olives and bruschetta, and a quiet, laid-back but elegant atmosphere, head to **Postino** (3939 E. Campbell 602/852-3939, www.postinowinecafe.com, 11am-11pm Mon.-Thurs., 11am-midnight Fri., 9am-midnight Sat., 11am-10pm Sun., $8.50-14), where they'll squeeze an orange and mix you one of the best mimosas you've ever had. The wine program changes frequently, and they offer a decent selection of beers, most of them in bottles. Just across Camelback Road from the Biltmore Fashion Park, the upscale **MercBar** (2525 E. Camelback Rd., 602/508-9449, 5pm-2am Mon.-Fri., 7pm-2am Sat.-Sun., $6-17) claims to be "just a bar," but it is far beyond that: It is a civilized and darkly inviting lounge that you might not want to leave once you sit down at a small round table in a deep leather chair and taste one of the signature concoctions the expert bartenders mix up here. It's pricey, and you should wear your slickest duds, but it is worth it for the atmosphere and the tasty mixes. This is an ideal place to stop for a before- or after-dinner cocktail if you are on a hot date and want to impress. With its rustic exposed brick and wood floors contrasting with a Mid-Century Modern meets urban hip decor, the **SideBar** (1514 N. 7th Ave., 602/254-1646, www.sidebarphoenix.com, 4pm-2am Mon.-Fri., 5:30pm-2am Sat.-Sun., $2-10), at the southwest corner of 7th Avenue and McDowell, has atmosphere to spare. They also take their mixing seriously, with fresh-squeezed juices, perfectly balanced simple syrups, and a range of top-shelf booze both familiar and exotic. Stop in at **Carly's Bistro** (128 E. Roosevelt St., 602/262-2759, www.carlysbistro.com, 10am-2am Mon.-Wed., 11am-2am Thurs.-Fri., 10am-2am Sat., 10am-midnight Sun., $6-10) for a glass of real absinthe, a perfectly made White Russian with soy milk, or a carafe of sangria for the table. This bistro and hangout has a good selection of beers and a warm atmosphere that will keep you sampling from their exciting cocktail menu. Don't forget about **Durant's** (2611 N. Central Ave., 602/264-5967, www.durantsaz.com, lunch 11am-4pm Mon.-Fri., dinner 4pm-10pm Mon.-Thurs., 4pm-11pm Fri., 5pm-11pm Sat., 4:30pm-10pm Sun., $10-50), where they have more than excellent steaks and prime rib; they also serve one of the best martinis in town, with an old-school upscale mood to start a night on the town. The **Clarendon Rooftop Bar** (401 W. Clarendon Ave., 602/252-7363, www.theclarendon.net, 8am-10pm Sun.-Thurs., 8am-11pm Fri.-Sat., $5-15), on the roof of the Clarendon Hotel downtown, offers amazing views of the valley in an ultraposh atmosphere, but it's not always easy to get up there. They enforce a strict numbers limit, but it's worth a try for the peace you'll feel looking out over the desert city as the sun dips away, cocktail in hand and coursing through your veins.

GAY AND LESBIAN

The **Amsterdam** (718 N. Central Ave., 602/258-6122, www.amsterdambar.com, 4pm-2am daily) is the hottest club this side of Scottsdale, with a fun, mixed crowd of the young and not-so-young, and a large offering of creative martinis. This place is packed most weekends, and most other nights too, with revelers dancing to bumping hip-hop and Top 40 remixes on a big dance floor, lounging on the patio couches, and hanging in the upstairs bar. This should be the first stop for visitors looking to party. The vibe at **Charlie's** (727 W. Camelback Rd., 602/265-0224, www.charliesphoenix.com, noon-4am Mon.-Thurs., 2pm-4am Fri., noon-4am Sat., noon-2am Sun.) is a little more down-home. The home of the Arizona Gay Rodeo Association is all about shuffling your cowboy boots across the floor and getting in on a good line dance, and the DJs often (but not always) spin country hits rather than Lady Gaga. They also have drag shows, proms, and tons of other special events. In Park Central Mall, **Kobalt** (3110 N. Central Ave., Ste. 125, 602/264-5307, www.kobaltbarphoenix.com, 11am-2am Mon.-Fri., 10am-2am Sat.-Sun.) claims to have the best selection of karaoke music in town. This is a fun, trendy, and popular place; it has a kind of a local watering-hole vibe and hosts all kinds of fun games and drink specials, and has a comfortable, open patio. The **Cash Inn Country** (2140 E. McDowell Rd., 602/244-9943, www.cashinncountry.net, 2pm-1am Tues.-Thurs, 2pm-2am Fri., noon-2am Sat., noon-1am Sun.) is a friendly, countrified lesbian bar with a welcoming atmosphere. There's a lot of line dancing and two-stepping going on here, and if you don't know how, they offer lessons. If you're not a dancer, they've got pool tables, dart boards, poker, karaoke, and a big patio for hanging out and drinking cheap beer, which they offer in several different brands.

LIVE MUSIC

The **Crescent Ballroom** (308 N. 2nd St., 602/716-2222, www.crescentphx.com, 11am-1am or 2am Mon.-Fri., 5pm-1am or 2am Sat.-Sun.) downtown brings the best artists to the valley, from classic rockers, beloved alternative cult-leaders, and contemporary singer-songwriters. It's an intimate little place just a block west of the Van Buren Light Rail Station. There are no bad seats here; if you're not standing in front of the stage watching spit fly out of the singer's mouth, you're perched middle-center on a small set of bleachers, gulping a martini. The Ballroom's restaurant, **Cocina 10**

(11am-midnight Mon.-Thurs., 11am-1am Fri., 5pm-1am Sat., 6pm-midnight Sun.) serves excellent overstuffed burritos with variety of fillings to choose from. Parking is $5 at a lot next to the Ballroom; bring exact change, or better yet just take the light rail.

A hip, wood-and-brick lounge in a converted home, **The Lost Leaf** (914 N. 5th St., 602/258-0014, www.thelostleaf.org, 5pm-2am daily), at 5th Street and Roosevelt, offers more than 100 beers, meads, ciders, sakis, and wines (one of the smartest selections of beers in the valley), and hosts the best bands and musicians you've never heard nearly every night. All the shows are free, and it also costs nothing to look at the typically astounding, confusing, and haunting art on the walls. **The Blooze Bar** (12014 N. 32nd St., 602/788-4574, www.thebloozebar.com) has rockabilly and alternative rock bands on a regular basis and a young crowd. The **Rhythm Room** (1019 E. Indian School Rd., 602/265-4842, www.rhythmroom.com) is an excellent venue to catch local and national touring acts playing blues, rock, and country, and on any given night of the week there's likely to be some roots-heavy band that you'll be happy you stumbled onto tearing up the stage. For blues, jazz, and funk music that you can dance to by some of the tightest groups in the region, check out **Char's House of Blues** (4631 N. 7th Ave., 602/230-0205, www.charshastheblues.com), where you can also watch all the valley's sports teams on big TVs.

Right next to StandUpLive in downtown's CityScape development, **Copper Blues** (50 W. Jefferson St., 480/719-5005, www.copperblueslive.com, 11am-10pm Mon.-Tues., 11am-11pm Wed., 11am-midnight Thurs., 11am-2am Friday, 4pm-2am Sat., 4pm-10pm Sun., happy hour 3pm-6pm Mon.-Fri., 4pm-6pm Sat.-Sun., $5-15) has more than 60 beers on tap, which you can sample while live local and regional bands rock your socks off. Most of the shows are free, and so are three hours of parking with validation. Copper Blues also serves excellent stone-oven pizzas with all kinds of creative toppings, plus sandwiches, burgers, salads, and much more. This fun, laid-back place is located

right next to the light rail stops at Jefferson and 1st Avenue Station and Washington and Central Avenue Station, and has a comfortable patio for enjoying those perfect Valley of the Sun nights.

COMEDY

Located in the thick of all the downtown action in the bustling CityScape development, **StandUpLive** (50. W. Jefferson St., 480/719-6100, www.standuplive.com, hours vary according to show schedule, $10-30) brings A-list comedians to the valley and serves frosty drinks for you to blow out your nose while laughing. Check the club's online calendar for upcoming shows. A ticket to a show comes with a three-hour parking validation, but it's also easy to take the light rail to either the Jefferson and 1st Avenue Station or the Washington and Central Avenue Station.

Tempe and the East Valley

Head over to **Mill Avenue** in Tempe to party with the ASU crowd; there are several clubs and bars along Mill, and there's bound to be a fashionable and beautiful crowd anywhere you stop.

BARS AND PUBS

Casey Moore's (850 S. Ash Ave., 480/968-9935, www.caseymoores.com, 11am-2:30am daily) is a favorite among ASU students, faculty, and still-partying alumni, with a mist-cooled patio, a large selection of beers, and huge plates of oysters. For one of the best handcrafted beers in the valley, try the **Four Peaks Brewing Company** (1340 E. 8th St., 480/303-9967, www.fourpeaks.com, 11am-2am Mon.-Sat., 10am-2am Sun.) near campus, but you can also find Four Peaks beers at most of the better bars and restaurants in the valley. At **Dos Gringos Tempe Trailer Park** (3000 S. Priest, 480/753-4577, 11am-2am daily) you'll think you've died and landed in some beachside town on permanent spring break; a continual college bacchanalian vibe rules here, especially during happy hour and college sports games. The food isn't bad either, and they serve their hot, filling Mexican grub until 2am. The crowd at

Robbie Fox's Public House (640 S. Mill Ave., 480/642-6442, www.robbiefoxs.com, 11am-2am daily, $8-16) on Mill Avenue is a bit more refined, in that they scream at the soccer game rather than the football game. This is one of the most authentic Irish pubs in the valley, and if you don't believe it, just listen to the BBC One playing on the stereo and the thick accent of the proprietor when he stops by your table with a welcome. There's also a lot of interesting Irish pop-culture memorabilia and JFK items on the walls to keep you busy while you're waiting for your perfect pint. The best place in Tempe to get a big basket of wings and a cold lager and watch the Cardinals game is **Doc & Eddy's** (909 E. Minton Dr., 480/831-0635, www. docandeddystempe.com, 11am-2am daily), a real sports bar with cheap drink specials, tasty eats, and friendly people who love sports as much as you do. If you're more into hustling pool than watching it on television, head east to Main Street in Mesa to **Main Street Billiards** (1749 W. Main St., 480/969-7898, www.mesa-billiards.com, noon-2am Sun.-Thurs., noon-3am Fri.-Sat.). It's the largest poolroom in the valley, with 42 tables, and there's a small menu of bar food.

LIVE MUSIC
The **Yucca Tap Room** (29 W. Southern, 480/967-4777, http://yuccatap.com, 6am-2am daily) is a legendary ASU-area bar that hosts local and touring rock bands and musicians in a dive-bar setting near campus. A leader in the renowned Tempe music scene of the 1990s, the Yucca Tap Room is still one of the best places in the valley to see live music. **The Sail Inn** (26 S. Farmer Ave., 480/966-9565, www.the-sailinn.com, 2pm-2am Mon.-Fri., 11am-2am Sat.-Sun.) has two stages, one indoor and one outdoor, on which local and touring rock bands play several nights a week (including both Phish and Grateful Dead tribute bands), and on the other nights they offer karaoke, so you can pretend you're up on stage.

The **Tempe Tavern** (1810 E. Apache Blvd., 480/794-1706, http://tempetavern.com, 10am-2am daily) just south of ASU on Apache Boulevard puts on local and regional bands most nights, from rock to punk to hip-hop, for a largely college-age crowd. The restaurant here serves pretty good burgers, wings, onion rings, salads and sandwiches until midnight.

PERFORMING ARTS
The excellent **Phoenix Symphony** (602/495-1999, www.phoenixsymphony.org) puts on dozens of pops and classics concerts throughout the year at downtown's beautiful **Symphony Hall** (75 N. 2nd St.). The hall is also home to the **Arizona Opera Company** (602/266-7464, www.azopera.org), which presents mostly classic, well-known operas with creative set designs and top-notch performers. A few blocks away, the spectacular **Comerica Theatre** (400 W. Washington, 602/379-2800, www.comericatheatre.com) welcomes a constant stream of headlining national acts, including an impressive array of big-name comedians and rock bands. But perhaps the best seat in the valley is at the intimate **Celebrity Theatre** (440 N. 32nd St.,

© TIM HULL

Comerica Theatre

602/267-1600, www.celebritytheatre.com). The theater's round stage makes every seat in the house a perfect one, and a wide variety of performers appear every year—jazz bands, crooners, rappers, classic rock, and nearly everything else. The acts here aren't usually as big as the ones that play at the Comerica or at the huge outdoor **Ak-Chin Pavilion** (2121 N. 83rd Ave., 602/254-7200, www.cricket-pavilion.com), but you'll want to check the website; if any band or performer you like is playing at Celebrity Theatre, you should definitely think about going. The valley's premier live theater venue is the **Herberger Theater Center** (222 E. Monroe St., 602/254-7399, www.herberger-theater.org) downtown—you'll know you've found it when you see the fascinating dancing nude sculptures out front. Here you can see original productions by the **Arizona Theatre Company** (502 W. Roosevelt, 602/256-6995, www.aztheatre.org), one of the nation's finest regional theater companies, and one that is never daunted by difficult, unique work. The smaller **Actor's Theatre of Phoenix** (5110 N. 44th St., 602/253-6701, www.actorstheatrephx.org) also puts on plays at the Herberger, offering theatergoers a chance to catch some cutting-edge productions as well as entertaining favorites. Even if you don't have tickets to see one of the many theater, music, and live performances put on at the classic **Orpheum Theatre** (203 W. Adams St., 602/262-6225, http://orpheum-theater.com), you might want to step into the gorgeous old venue for a look around. The theater, one of the valley's oldest, recently went through a multimillion-dollar reformation and has been restored to its 1927 glory. If style and beauty and design are the ultimate criteria, this is probably the best venue in the valley.

CINEMA

For art-house and independent films, Tempe's **Harkin's Valley Art** (509 S. Mill Ave., 480/446-7272, harkinstheatres.com) is the best venue in the valley, showing the films you won't see at the multiplex in a cool, if a bit rickety, old building on Mill Avenue.

© TIM HULL

The Phoenix Symphony and Arizona Opera Company perform at the Symphony Hall.

COMEDY

The **Tempe Improv Comedy Theater** (930 E. University, 480/921-9877, www.tempeimprov.com) is where *Saturday Night Live* alum and Tempe favorite son David Spade cut his stand-up teeth. The Improv hosts mostly mid-level stand-ups, though often a big name like Dana Carvey or Richard Lewis will take the stage. The kitchen serves pretty good dinners—hamburgers, chicken dishes, and even prime rib ($10-18). The comedy here is usually very funny, and a night spent before the stage gives you an opportunity to see some rising stars and to laugh until your drink comes out your nose.

CASINOS

For Vegas-style gaming and entertainment in the valley, you can't do much better than **Wild Horse Pass Resort and Casino** (5040 W. Wild Horse Pass, 800/946-4452, www.wildhorsepass.com), the biggest American Indian casino in the region. The 100,000-square-foot casino, hotel, and resort on the Gila River Indian Community Reservation, just off I-10 in the southeast valley, has 875 slot machines willing to take your money, plus poker (both live and video) and blackjack tables. Wild Horse Pass also has a buffet for when you need to refuel, and live entertainment for when you lose all your money and need a little cheering up.

FESTIVALS AND EVENTS

At the end of December and into the first days of January, the valley celebrates college football with the Fiesta Bowl Parade, Fiesta Bowl Block Party, and, of course, the **Fiesta Bowl** (www.fiestabowl.org) at University of Phoenix Stadium in Glendale. In February the popular **VNSA Book Sale** (602/265-6805, www.vnsabooksale.org) has more than 600,000 used books for sale at the fairgrounds.

In March the **Heard Museum Guild Indian Fair & Market** (602/253-8848, www.heardguild.org) includes more than 600 artists, and Spring Training and **Cactus League** (www.cactusleague.com) brings MLB teams to the valley for a game every day of the month. In April **NASCAR Subway Fresh Fit 500** (www.nascar.com) roars into town, bringing the popular sport's top drivers with it.

In October the **Arizona State Fair** and the **Heard Museum Spanish Market** keep locals and visitors busy, and in November the cars return for the **NASCAR Checker Auto Parts 500.** In December, don't miss the popular **Pueblo Grande Museum Indian Market** (602/495-0901, www.pueblogrande.com).

Shopping

DOWNTOWN AND CENTRAL
Shopping Districts

Even if you don't feel like shopping, take a walk around the gardens and ponds at downtown's **Arizona Center** (400 E. Van Buren St., 602/271-4000, www.arizonacenter.com), a big open-air mall with an eclectic assortment of shops, boutiques, restaurants, and a movie theater. This is a great place to shop for Arizona-style gifts, especially if what you're looking for is a bit on the kitschy side. If you can't find anything to buy, you won't regret the stroll through one of the valley's greenest attractions. The upscale **Biltmore Fashion Park** (24th St. and Camelback Rd., 602/955-8400, www.shopbiltmore.com) along Camelback Road is the valley's finest shopping mall, with Saks Fifth Avenue, Ralph Lauren, and dozens of other high-end shops. You'll want to spend the whole day here if you're a shopping enthusiast with money to burn, and there are several restaurants to choose from for a memorable lunch or dinner. On 7th Avenue between Camelback and Indian School Roads, in the **Melrose District,** you'll find a host of retro boutiques, thrift stores, and hip home-decor shops. The increasingly busy and stroll-worthy **Roosevelt Row** (Roosevelt St. between Grand Ave. and

16th St.) has a host of funky locally owned boutiques, cafés, bars, artist studios, and galleries and a pedestrian-friendly vibe that sets it apart from the valley's strip-mall wastelands. The district hosts the **Second Saturday Sidewalk Sale** (10am-8pm, every second Saturday of every month), with lots of street vendors and live music and people-watching; and during the popular downtown event known as **First Fridays** (6pm-10pm), this section of downtown gets busy and vibrant with revelers, shoppers, and art lovers. For more information about these events and Roosevelt Row, contact **Roosevelt Row Community Development Corporation** at the **MADE art boutique** (1202 N. 3rd St., 602/772-0083, www.rooseveltrow.org)—a perfect example of the kind of unique businesses that are opening in this section of downtown—or check out their website. The **Chinese Cultural Center** (668 N. 44th St., 602/273-7268, www.phxchinatown.com), a gathering of Chinese-style buildings housing restaurants, stores, and gardens near Sky Harbor Airport, is the closest thing to Chinatown this side of California. There are several good restaurants here, serving seafood, Szechuan, Cantonese, and Shanghai-style cuisine in sleek Asian-modern interiors. There are also stores selling authentic Chinese gifts, furniture, household items, clothing, and herbs. The beautiful Chinese gardens recreate the architecture and landmarks of ancient Chinese cities. This is a great place to go for lunch and a stroll around the gardens and the shops, where you may find something unique that you had no idea you'd see in Phoenix.

Farmers Market

The most popular farmers market in the valley is the **Downtown Phoenix Public Market** (721 N. Central Ave., 602/253-2700, www.foodconnect.org), which gathers hundreds of vendors together downtown to sell locally grown fruits and vegetables, locally prepared foods, arts and crafts, and other items that you can't get anywhere else. There's also usually live music and a lot of interesting people to meet. The **Open-Air Market** (14 E. Pierce/721 N. Central—the northeast corner of Central Ave. and Pierce St.), every Wednesday (5pm-8pm) and Saturday (8am-noon May-Sept., and 8am-1pm Oct.-April) happens all year, even in the summer and the rainy season.

TEMPE AND THE EAST VALLEY

If the clothes at the Biltmore's Saks are too expensive, drive over to Tempe and the **Arizona Mills** (5000 Arizona Mills Cir., 480/491-7300, www.arizonamills.com, 10am-9pm Mon.-Sat., 11am-6pm Sun.), an outlet mall that has a Saks outlet (called Off 5th) and dozens of other outlet shops, including Ann Taylor, Kenneth Cole, and many more. This mall is huge and clean and has a fun gaming center for the kids and several restaurants. Also in Tempe, take a stroll along Mill Avenue, where you'll find all kinds of hip shops and boutiques; while Mill used to be quite a bit funkier than it is today, the bigger corporate stores that overtook it about a decade ago still have a lot of good shopping to offer.

WEST VALLEY
Shopping Districts

Historic Downtown Glendale (59th Ave. and Glendale Ave.) and the nearby **Catlin Court Historic District** (bounded by Gardenia Ave., 59th Ave., Palmarie Ave., and 58th Ave.) in the northwest valley offer the valley's quaintest shopping; the streets of downtown Glendale are lined with gas lamps and crowded antique stores, while Catlin Court is a historic residential neighborhood whose white picket fence-fronted bungalows have been turned into boutiques and restaurants. This area is a must-visit for those who enjoy walking in picturesque small-town settings and finding unique and unknown items to take home.

Bookstores

The valley isn't exactly a book-hunter's paradise, but there are a few stores worth checking out. The best bookstore in town is the legendary **Changing Hands Bookstore** (6428 S. McClintock Dr., 480/730-0205, www.changinghands.com, 10am-9pm Mon.-Fri.,

9am-9pm Sat., 10am-6pm Sun.) in Tempe, which sells an excellent mixture of new and used books. The statewide chain **Bookmans,** selling all manner of used media, including books, CDs, DVDs, games, and much more, has two well-stocked locations in the valley, one in the north valley (8034 N. 19th Ave., 602/433-0255, www.bookmans.com, 9am-10pm daily) and one in Mesa, in the east valley (1056 S. Country Club Dr., 480/835-0505, www.bookmans.com, 9am-10pm daily). All Bookmans locations offer free wireless Internet.

Music

If you prefer browsing in the real world for your CDs, and you still enjoy the warm sounds and cover art of vinyl records, there are a few places in the valley that you should not miss. At the Arizona and Nevada chain **Zia Records** (1940 W. Indian School Rd., 602/241-0313, www.zianation.com, 10am-midnight daily; and 105 W. University, Tempe, 480/829-1967, www.zianation.com, 10am-11pm Mon.-Sat., 10am-10pm Sun.), you'll find stacks of new and used CDs in all genres, plus movies, books, and magazines, and a relatively large selection of used vinyl. **Stinkweeds** (12 W. Camelback, 602/248-9461, www.stinkweeds.com, 11am-9pm Mon.-Sat., noon-6pm Sun.), at the northwest corner of Central and Camelback, has been a valley favorite since 1987, back when we had little choice other than bricks-and-mortar stores to buy our music, and the biggest worry of the independent record store was the coming of the superchains. This stubborn little store, which specializes in independent record labels and hard-to-find music, offers hours of browsing potential for new and used CDs and vinyl.

Sports and Recreation

Phoenicians love to get outdoors—with more than 300 sunny days a year, they really don't have a choice in the matter. They keep their parks and recreation areas immaculate. There are well-trod desert hiking trails a short drive from just about anywhere in town. But Phoenix's official sport is golf, and there are many courses to choose from and play on year-round.

HIKING AND BIKING

The valley's hiking trails sometimes seem more like running tracks with all the Lycra and MP3 players strapped to tan sweaty arms one is apt to see in any of the urban-area desert preserves, so close to the bustle and yet almost secluded if it weren't for all those people. Still, if you're staying in Phoenix for more than a few days, any one of these easily accessible desert parks makes for a pleasant outing. If you want a real desert hike, though, save your energy for a trek into the Superstition Mountains on the valley's eastern edge.

Phoenix Mountains

Here you will find the valley's favorite hiking trail, the **Piestewa Peak Summit Trail** (2701 E. Squaw Peak Ln., www.phoenix.gov/parks/trails/location/piestewapeak, 5am-11pm daily), a 1.2-mile one-way hunched-over climb up to what was, prior to the Iraq War, one of the more politically incorrect landmarks in the state—Squaw Peak. The term *squaw* has long had negative connotations for Native Americans, so in 2003 the peak was renamed Piestewa Peak, after Lori Piestewa, a Navajo soldier who was killed in Iraq. You are sure to run into a crowd on the trail on any given day, but if any of those days are clear, you can see all of the valley and beyond spread out before you. The Piestewa Peak Summit Trail is a really easy, if vertical, hike, and kids won't have a problem with it.

A little bit tougher is the hike up **Camelback Mountain** (www.phoenix.gov/parks/trails/locations/camelback), just a touch higher than its nearby sister at 2,704 feet. Within the **Echo Canyon Recreation Area** (5959 Echo Canyon Dr., 602/256-3220, sunrise to sunset), the mile-long one-way **Summit Trail** is a popular hike, and you may have to wait for a parking spot on weekends. You gain more than 1,000 feet on the way up, so it's not to be taken lightly. There are parts of the trail that are hewn out of slickrock, with handrails alongside for help. From the top you can see everything, whether you want to or not.

South Mountain Park and Preserve

Forming the valley's southern border, the obviously named South Mountains can't be missed—they are the ones with all the communication towers and antennae shooting up from their peaks like pins in a hard-rock cushion. The 16,000-acre **South Mountain Park and Preserve** (10919 S. Central Ave., www.phoenix.gov/parks/trails/locations/south, 5am-7pm, trails open until 11pm, daily) is popular with valley residents as an exercise field; bicyclists in particular enjoy climbing the high, twisting paved road to the lookout peak and then shooting rocketlike back down to the desert floor. One feels a little bad cruising slowly behind them on the curvy way up to Dobbins Point, the park's highest accessible point at 2,300 feet, which is a favorite pastime of less active Phoenicians and their visitors. There are several dry, rocky trails through the rugged cactus-and-creosote desert, most of them accessed off the main road up to the top and most of them up-and-down routes that aren't too difficult. Right after the main entrance, there's a trail-map station across from the Civilian Conservation Corps-built rock house, in which you'll find public bathrooms. The trails, nearly 58 miles of them, are open to hikers, mountain bikers, and horses. Mountain bikers will find some fun, moderately tough single-track here. For an easy and representative loop hike or bike ride, try a 3.5-mile round-trip jaunt on the **National Trail** to Hidden Valley. The trail is rough and rocky, and slick from wear in some places, but the views are spectacular and the saguaros plentiful. You pick up the trail at the top of the Summit Road at the Buena Vista

Lookout. The National Trail crosses the entire park, if you're really feeling ambitious.

Papago Park

A twisting red-rock desert park just east of central Phoenix, **Papago Park** (625 Galvin Pkwy., 602/495-5458, www.phoenix.gov/parks/trails/locations/papago) is a fun place to tear around on a mountain bike for a while or scramble up to **Hole-in-the-Rock,** a big hole in a jutting-rock hill through which the valley opens up beautifully. It's an easy climb up a very short trail, and then you can sit in the little smooth notch—which, the archaeologists will tell you, lines up perfectly with a building at Pueblo Grande a few miles to the southwest—and look out over the land. Facing west, this is a particularly good spot for sunset viewing. Walking trails crisscross the park, and there are dozens of picnic tables and even a lagoon for fishing.

GOLF

Seen from the air, the Valley of the Sun appears to be stamped illogically with wide swaths of short green grass, all dotted with man-made duck ponds and sandy beach interruptions. The 300-plus days of sunshine enjoyed here allow for year-round golf—the waking dream of your average Rust Belt duffer. As such, an inordinate amount of desert has been rolled over with grass, creating a golfer's paradise and a fairly questionable use of resources. The golf lover will likely disagree, however, especially during a bright morning round in November, the raw desert mountains beautifully framing the impossibly green fairways. There are dozens of courses throughout the valley, many of them linked to famous resorts. The valley also has some of the most popular municipal courses in the nation, each of them a bargain compared to the fancier places and competing just fine when it comes to lushness and creative design. Many of the municipal courses host more than 100,000 rounds of golf per year, so it's a good idea to make tee times in advance. You might want to book a tee time at a course before traveling—the city's golf course web pages

the view from Hole-in-the-Rock in Papago Park

© TIM HULL

allow for easy online reservations up to eight days in advance.

Perhaps the valley's most environmentally thoughtful course is the municipal **Cave Creek Golf Course** (15202 N. 19th Ave., 602/866-8076, www.phoenix.gov/recreation/rec/facilities/golf, $12-31 for residents, $12-43 nonresidents), a par 72 built on a reclaimed landfill; but you won't notice—it's green and tree-lined and is the valley's most popular public course. One of the oldest courses in the state, built in 1935 near Encanto Park, the city center's lush and attractive oasis, **Encanto Golf Course** (2755 N. 15th Ave., 602/253-3963, www.phoenix.gov/recreation/rec/facilities/golf, $12-31 for residents, $12-43 for nonresidents) is a par 70 municipal course lined, like its titular park, with tall shaggy palm trees. At Papago Park in the east valley, the green of the links at **Papago Golf Course** (5595 E. Moreland St., 602/275-8428, www.papagogolfcourse.net, $10-39 residents, $20-44 nonresidents, including cart) contrasts perfectly with red-rock hills all around. The par 72 municipal

course is very popular and hosts the Phoenix Open qualifying rounds. Just south in Tempe, the **ASU Karsten Golf Course** (1125 E. Rio Salado Pkwy., 480/921-8070, www.asukarsten.com, $25-108) stretches out near the bed of the Salt River, catching the shadow of Sun Devil Stadium—a rolling and twisting course that is particularly difficult.

HORSEBACK RIDING

There's nothing like a slow horseback ride among the saguaro forests to make you feel like a real cowboy or cowgirl, and there's no better way to meet a real cowboy or cowgirl than to hire one to guide you on a trail ride. The desert preserves around the valley are filled with trails perfect for horseback riding, and there are myriad companies offering one-hour to all-day rides through the unforgettable desert scenery. You can book an early morning ride to see the desert come alive, or a sunset ride to watch it settle down, colorfully as always. There's usually a weight limit of 225-250 pounds, and kids generally need to be eight years old or older.

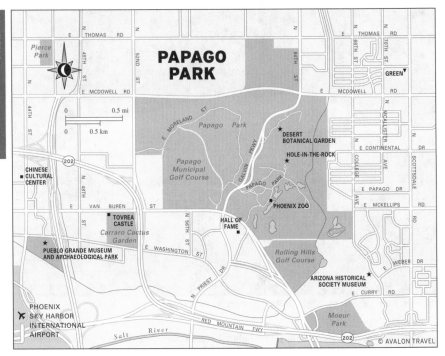

Most of the companies offer full-day rides with lunch, or evening rides with dinner around a campfire. It's a good idea to call ahead and make a reservation. Horseback riding in the valley is not recommended during the summer months, and it's not fun either. Most places are closed for summer anyway.

The best stables, and the ones closest to downtown, are the **Ponderosa Stables** (10215 S. Central Ave., 602/268-1261, www.ponderosastablesaz.com) in South Mountain Park, just before the park's main entrance. They offer trail rides from one to eight hours ($33-135) along the park's many trials, among the saguaro and the creosote and the petroglyphs. They are open year-round, but they suspend rides when the temperatures reach 100 degrees or above, which generally means they are closed during the day for a good part of the summer and open in the early evening for sunset rides. The guides

here are friendly and knowledgeable, and if you don't like to hike or tear around on a mountain bike, this is the best way to see South Mountain. While you're on your tour of the Apache Trail and the Salt River region in the far east valley, on the edge of the Tonto National Forest, consider a stop at **Saguaro Lake Trail Rides** (13020 Bush Hwy., 480/984-0335, www.saguarolaketrailrides.com). The friendly guides here will take you on 1.5- to 4-hour rides ($55-130) through the wild desert that the sprawl has yet to kill; on many rides you'll ford the Salt River on your steady mount and ride near the gemlike lakes made by the Roosevelt Dam. In the western desert the **White Tanks Riding Stables** (20300 W. Olive Ave., 623/935-7455, www.whitetanksriding.com) offer one- and two-hour rides (one-hour rides 9am, 1:30pm, 3pm, two-hour rides 10:30am Nov.-April, $37-60) through the saguaro-dotted **White**

Tank Regional Park with guides who are knowledgeable about the desert and its lore.

SALT RIVER TUBING

A leisurely, convivial float down the Salt is a desert-living tradition, especially during the unrelenting shine of summer. **Salt River Tubing and Recreation** (480/984-3305, www.saltrivertubing.com, 9am-6:30pm daily May-Sept., last tube rented at 3pm, $15 cash only per person, per tube, includes shuttle to launch) rents out tubes all summer, shuttling seekers of cool water to a launch on the Salt River just below Saguaro Lake, east of the city in the Tonto National Forest. You can rent an extra inner tube to hold your ice chest, and stock it with cans of beer and soda (no glass allowed) and sandwiches—and make sure to include some water, too. The party can get a bit drunken and adult on some days, especially the weekends. Kids must be at least eight years old and four feet tall to go along. There are some fun rapids and a quick current in places, depending on the water release schedule at the lake, but mostly it's a slow and sunny float along a thin band of shallow, cool, green-blue water, flanked by rock- and saguaro-lined canyon walls and thick riparian greenbelts. There are several beach landings along the way where floaters stop and picnic. Don't expect to be alone, and don't count on quiet or the sounds of nature all the time; a few waterborne revelers along the way will typically blast music and hoot and yell, depending on how much beer is left. You can choose from two-, three-, and five-hour trips weekdays, and a six-hour trip is offered on weekends. To get to the rental office, head north for 15 miles from U.S. Highway 60 on the Power Road in Mesa. Always call before going out there, though; the trips are subject to weather and water flow.

SPECTATOR SPORTS

Everybody in the valley is from somewhere else, or so the conventional wisdom says. The metropolis is indeed a transient city in a transient state; people are always moving in and out, and the new replaces the barely old at a whirlwind clip. This reality is both good and bad for the city's several major league sports clubs. There's always a built-in crowd of local devotees, and casual fans will usually turn out in droves when one of the big Midwestern or Eastern teams is in town. When the Chicago Cubs come to visit every summer, it's sometimes difficult to see the Diamondbacks fans among all those blue shirts. That being said, most of the local teams have been able to ingratiate themselves with the natives, the longtime residents, and the new arrivals alike simply by doing what a sports team is supposed to do: win.

The Arizona Diamondbacks

One of the more successful of Arizona's teams in recent times has been Major League Baseball's **Arizona Diamondbacks** (602/462-6500, http://arizona.diamondbacks.mlb.com), franchised in 1998 and with a World Series trophy in the clubhouse by 2001. With one of the best scouting programs in the game, lately the D-Backs have skewed younger, introducing future superstars to big-time playoff baseball and beginning a new tradition of smart, fast, and fundamental National League ball that has locals filling the seats at **Chase Field** (401 E. Jefferson St., 602/462-6799 or 800/821-7160, tours offered 9:30am, 11am, and 12:30pm Mon.-Sat. year-round, $7 adults, $5 children under 12) downtown, one of the few ballparks in the world with a retractable roof. The roof is closed during most of the season with the air conditioners blasting—the only way baseball can be played in the desert without killing players. Individual game tickets range in price from $5 for nosebleed seats to $215 for a clubhouse box. A decent seat will cost you between $15-40. Though the team is very popular in the valley, most of the time tickets can be purchased the day of the game at the ballpark. If one of the big Midwestern or Eastern teams is in town, like the Chicago Cubs or, during interleague play, the Detroit Tigers, you will need to plan far ahead.

PHOENIX

© TIM HULL

Chase Field, home of the Arizona Diamondbacks

The Phoenix Suns

The quick play of the **Phoenix Suns** (602/379-7900, www.nba.com/suns) has made the NBA team a beloved institution in Arizona. The Suns also have a long and storied history, with the likes of Charles Barkley, Dan Majerle (who still has a restaurant in town and now coaches Grand Canyon University's basketball team), Danny Ainge, and Dennis Johnson, and of course Shaquille O'Neal, once wearing the purple and orange. The Suns often battle the L.A. Lakers for supremacy in the Western Conference's Pacific League, and the stands at the huge **U.S. Airways Center** (201 E. Jefferson St.) downtown are always packed with fans.

The Arizona Cardinals

The most consistently disappointing of Phoenix's sports teams, the **Arizona Cardinals** (602/379-0102, www.azcardinals.com) hadn't had much in the way of wins since they moved to the Valley of the Sun from St. Louis in 1987 until they reached the

Super Bowl in 2009. There are a few good reasons for future hope, however. In 2006 the team opened **University of Phoenix Stadium** (1 Cardinals Dr., Glendale), a gleaming new headquarters that has fans more excited about the team than they have been in years.

ASU Sports

The various teams that play under the name **ASU Sun Devils** (480/965-2381, www.thesundevils.cstv.com, box office open beginning Aug. 16 and throughout school year, 9am-5pm Mon.-Fri., 9am-noon Sat.) are typically pretty good, and often, especially in baseball and football, very good. The students and the many ASU alumni who stuck around the valley really get into it, and tickets for the bigger games aren't easy to come by. Barry Bonds played his college baseball here, as did many other big leaguers. Jake "The Snake" Plummer, former quarterback for the Arizona Cardinals and then the Denver Broncos, was a college star on the Sun Devil football field.

Cactus League Baseball

In many parts of the country, March is a month for scraping ice off windshields, digging out of snow drifts, and hoping that global warming hurries up just a bit with all that melting. Spring may be just around the corner, but that corner seems way up ahead.

In the Valley of the Sun, however, March is perfect: a little brisk in the morning, warm in the afternoon, and light-jacket cool at night. Oh, and every single day of the month there are several Major League Baseball games played at intimate ballparks all over town.

Fifteen big league teams play in the Valley of Sun's Cactus League from late February to late March. The **Arizona Diamondbacks** and the **Colorado Rockies** play at **Salt River Fields** (7555 N. Pima Rd., Talking Stick Resort, 480/270-5000). The **Chicago Cubs** are based at **Hohokam Stadium** (1235 Center St., Mesa, 480/964/4467). The **Los Angeles Dodgers** and the **Chicago White Sox** share the huge, 13,500-seat **Camelback Ranch Stadium** (10710 W. Camelback Rd., Glendale, 623/302-5000). The **Cleveland Indians** and the **Cincinnati Reds** share the **Goodyear Ball Park** (1933 S. Ball Park Way, Goodyear, 623/882-3120). The **Kansas City Royals** and the **Texas Rangers** are based at **Surprise Stadium** (15850 N. Bullard Ave., Surprise, 623/222-2222). The **Milwaukee Brewers** play at **Maryvale Baseball Park** (3600 N. 51st Ave., Phoenix, 623/245-5555); the **Oakland Athletics** play at **Phoenix Municipal Stadium** near Papago Park (5999 E. Van Buren St., Phoenix, 620/392-0074). The **San Diego Padres** and the **Seattle Mariners** are based at **Peoria Sports Complex** (16101 N. 83rd Ave., Peoria, 623/773-5700). The **Los Angeles Angels of Anaheim** are based at **Tempe Diablo Stadium** (2200 W. Alameda Dr., Tempe, 480/350-5205), and the **San Francisco Giants** play at **Scottsdale Stadium** (7408 E. Osborn Rd., Scottsdale, 480/312-2580).

Ticket prices range $7-22 for most games. A great place to start planning your Spring Training vacation is at www.cactusleague.com, which has all the information and schedules; or you can call the individual stadiums for ticket information.

Accommodations

The accommodations scene in the valley is ruled by the big chains and resorts. If you're hoping to find something a bit more distinctive and independent, expect to pay for it accordingly. The best time to find bargains is in summer, when nearly every big hotel and resort slashes its prices to attract business to the infernal desert. Year-round deals can be found in Tempe, in the east valley, where there are a few independent hotels that offer a nice room for a fair price.

DOWNTOWN AND CENTRAL
$50-100

The best deal in town is the **Hosteling International Phoenix** (1026 N. 9th St., 602/254-9803, www.phxhostel.org, $20-23 dorm room, $32-45 private room), but you really have to be a hostel kind of person to enjoy it. You can stay in a dorm room or pay extra for a private room, but you share the bathrooms and kitchen area. There's a shady courtyard, coin-operated laundry, and a common area with a piano; the staff is friendly and laid-back, and the house is centrally located downtown.

The **⟨ ZenYard Guest House** (830 E. Maryland Ave., 602/845-0830, www.zenyard. com, $60-90) is a magical little place with four sumptuous rooms, individually decorated and offering free wireless Internet, wood floors, entrances onto the pool area and patio, and a complimentary continental breakfast. This beautiful home near downtown has a koi pond, two hot tubs and a solar-heated saltwater pool, and a lush patio that is a favorite haunt for hummingbirds where you can lounge poolside in a covered cabana. Three of the rooms have private bathrooms while one has a semiprivate bath.

The **Budget Lodge Motel** (402 W. Van Buren, 602/254-7247, $45-89) is inexpensive and basic, though the neighborhood is a bit on the dodgy side.

$100-250

Downtown's big, beautiful **Hyatt Regency Phoenix** (122 N. 2nd St., 602/252-1234, www. phoenixhyatt.com, $139-289) is right in the beating heart of the city center, right in the thick of it all. The towering hotel has three restaurants, an outdoor wading pool and hot tub, and comfortable, high-style rooms. The most distinctive accommodation in the valley is the historic (**Hotel San Carlos** (202 N. Central Ave., 602/253-4121, www.hotelsancarlos.com,

Hyatt Regency Phoenix

© TIM HULL

$98-240), located right downtown with a facade that brings back the golden age of big-city hotels. As it was with other historic Arizona hotels, the San Carlos, opened in 1928, was a favorite stop of Hollywood stars during the first half of the 20th century, and was one of the first high-rise hotels in the Southwest with full air-conditioning and electric elevators. The hotel now celebrates its glory days with themed rooms and memorabilia. The rooms are comfortable and chic, and the whole place has a kind of overstuffed retro-cool ambience that you'll get nowhere else.

The **Clarendon Hotel** (401 W. Clarendon Ave., 602/252-7363, www.theclarendon.net, $115-275) is a popular hangout owing to its amazing rooftop deck that overlooks the city and the desert. It also has gorgeous, spacious rooms with cool and comfortable beds, and a pool area to beat any in the valley. This is one of the hippest places you can stay in the valley, and it's a favorite of visiting pop stars and other luminaries. The charming Mission Style (**Maricopa Manor** (15 W. Pasadena Ave., 602/264-9200, www.maricopamanor.com, $190-240) offers the best in bed-and-breakfast-style accommodations in the valley. Located in north-central Phoenix just minutes from everything, this historic hideaway has lush, grassy grounds and a beautifully tiled pool area with a waterfall, spa, and several shady ramadas for lounging. The inn offers six rooms, each with a private bath and free wireless, and many of them open on to the pool area and patio. In the morning, don't worry about getting dressed to face the other guests around a communal table; here they deliver your breakfast to your doorstep in a basket. The **Hotel Highland at Biltmore Ave.** (2310 E. Highland Ave., 602/956-5221, www.hotelhighlandatbiltmore. com, $150-200) is a stylish boutique hotel with elegantly decorated rooms, plush bedding, free wireless, and a relaxing pool and spa. You can spend the evening at the patio lounge talking around the romantic fire pit. They also offer a free continental breakfast come morning.

Families should consider the **Embassy**

© TIM HULL

Hotel San Carlos

Suites Phoenix-Biltmore (2630 E. Camelback Rd., 602/955-3992, www.embassysuites.com, $89-199), conveniently located along the central Camelback Corridor and offering affordable suites with refrigerators, TVs, and a lot of space; amenities include a pool and hot tub, free made-to-order breakfast, and a complimentary cocktail hour every night. The kids will love the **Pointe Hilton at Squaw Peak** (7677 N. 16th St., 602/997-2626, www.pointehilton.com, $160-200) for its **Hole-in-the-Wall River Ranch,** a four-acre watery playground of linked pools, water slides, spas, cabanas, and all sorts of other watery fun. This is a very nice place that is also relatively affordable, especially during summer, when they offer cut-rate deals that no family in need of a vacation should pass up. Also a great place for families is the **Pointe Hilton Tapatio Cliffs Resort** (11111 N. 7th St., 602/866-7500, www.pointehilton.com, $160-190), which has a gorgeous series of pools and cabanas called the **Falls Water Village,** with several waterfalls, whirlpools, a water slide, and hidden, romantic spots to soak up the sun. There's also a golf course, spa, and several restaurants.

Over $250

The **Arizona Biltmore** (2400 E. Missouri Ave., 602/955-6600, www.arizonabiltmore. com, $205-675), covering 39 acres at the base of the Phoenix Mountains, is the valley's most famous, and still in most ways its best, resort. Other places may come and go, but this Frank Lloyd Wright-inspired (and, many contend, designed—Wright received a consulting fee on the project) "Jewel of the Desert" just keeps getting better with age. There are 738 guest rooms, including one- and two-bedroom villas, eight swimming pools, seven tennis courts, two 18-hole golf courses at the country club next door, a spa, an enormous outdoor chess set, and four restaurants. The Arizona Biltmore History Package ($238-437) is a great way to discover the resort; it includes a tour of the grounds, dinner, a night in one of the historic rooms, plus two tickets to Wright's Taliesin West.

© TIM HULL

the Arizona Biltmore

The **Renaissance Phoenix Downtown** (50 E. Adams St., 602/333-0000, www.mariott. com, $280-449) is downtown's biggest and nicest high-rise, right in the middle of everything and offering spacious, tasteful rooms—style, elegance, and haute comfort galore. The **Ritz-Carlton** (2401 E. Camelback Rd., 602/468-0700, www.ritzcarlton.com, $349-429), along the Camelback Corridor, is a gorgeous hotel with large, comfortable rooms and great views of the mountains and valley. It has all the amenities one would expect for the price, including a truly spectacular pool area. Though it's not exactly centrally located, the **Sheraton Wild Horse Pass Resort and Spa** (5594 W. Wild Horse Pass Blvd., 602/225-0100, www.wildhorsepass-resort.com, $275-350), on the Gila River Indian Community Reservation southeast of downtown, has some of the most amazing accommodations in the valley. The whole resort, which includes two golf courses, a spa, several restaurants, and a Wild West theme park, is decorated in a stylish contemporary Native American theme that melds the past and the present into something quite wonderful and unique. Plus, there's gambling, of course. Located near South Mountain Park, the **Arizona Grand Resort** (8000 S. Arizona Grand Pkwy., 602/438-9000, www.arizonagrandresort.com, $375-500) has well-appointed, comfortable rooms, a golf course for the adults, a water park for the kids, a health club, a spa, six pools, and seven restaurants. This is a great place to take the family for an unforgettable getaway. The **Royal Palms** (5200 E. Camelback Rd., 602/840-3610, www.royalpalmshotel.com, $400-600), right by the Phoenician at the base of Camelback Mountain, is a lush hideout with all the amenities and then some. The rooms are all decorated with antiques and other stylish touches; the grounds resemble some king's well-kept gardens, with Camelback Mountain shining in the background. This wonderful resort offers comfortable rooms, private casitas, and sprawling villas, plus the usual pool, spa, fitness center, and excellent gourmet dining.

TEMPE AND THE EAST VALLEY
$50-100

The **Twin Palms** (225 E. Apache Blvd., Tempe, 480/967-9431, www.twinpalmshotel.com, $79-159), right near Arizona State University, is a good bargain; it has a pool, free high-speed Internet, complimentary breakfast, and access to ASU's huge fitness and recreation center. It's close to everything in Tempe and the east valley and isn't too far from central Phoenix. The rooms are basic and comfortable, and each one has a refrigerator and a microwave. Another good bargain is the **Mezona Inn** (250 W. Main St., Mesa, 480/834-9233, www.mezonainn. com, $69-169), located in downtown Mesa, with a pool and clean, basic rooms.

$150-250

Formerly known as the Fiesta Inn, the newly remodeled **❰ DoubleTree by Hilton Hotel Phoenix Tempe** (2100 S. Priest Dr., Tempe, 480/967-1441, http://doubletree3.hilton.com, $149-189) remains a favorite among visiting ASU parents. It isn't the only valley hotel to call itself Frank Lloyd Wright inspired, but it is certainly the most affordable. This high-end but not-too-pricey resort has tasteful Old Southwest-style rooms and common areas, acres of saltillo tile, and sharp, rustic-looking decor all around. It has a big glistening blue pool, heated in the winter, a great restaurant and lounge with complimentary finger foods at happy hour, and service that rivals much pricier places.

Over $250

The **Tempe Mission Palms** (60 E. 5th St., Tempe, 480/894-1400, www.missionpalms. com, $259) in downtown Tempe is a beautiful property, with a huge pool and tennis courts on the roof overlooking the entire valley. It has its own cozy bar and restaurant, and is within walking distance to the shops and restaurants

on Mill Avenue. The rooms have a Southwest style, and the courtyards are lush and watered. This is one of the most luxurious places to stay in Tempe, and a bit less pricey than similarly appointed places in Phoenix and Scottsdale. Near Tempe Town Lake, **Aloft** (951 E. Playa Del Norte Dr., 480/621-3300, www.aloft-tempe.com, $325-375) is a contemporary, chic destination with complimentary spa products in your room and a plug-and-play station to charge your gadgets. The hotel offers free wireless, superbly comfortable beds, a hip bar, oversized shower heads in sleek walk-in showers, and so much style that you'll want to take photos of your room and the lobby.

As its name suggests, **The Buttes** (2000 Westcourt Way, 602/225-9900, www.marriott.com/phxtm, $250-275) overlooks the east valley from atop a 25-acre promontory in Tempe. This gorgeous resort offers free wireless Internet, sumptuously comfortable rooms, two large swimming pools and a water slide, a full-service spa, and all manner of other fun and relaxing amenities.

WEST VALLEY

In historic downtown Glendale, the **Glendale Gaslight Inn** (5747 W. Glendale Ave., 623/934-5466, www.gaslightinnaz.com, $99-349) is a charming, upscale place right in the middle of the west valley shopping and dining district, offering several individually decorated rooms of various sizes, including some with kitchens. The inn offers wireless Internet throughout and serves pastries and coffee in your room every morning. There's a well-stocked and romantic wine bar on the premises with live jazz on the weekends.

At Glendale's **Westgate** complex just a few miles west of historic downtown on Glendale Avenue, you'll find several big chain hotels right next to the stadiums—homes of the NFL's Arizona Cardinals and the NHL's Phoenix Coyotes. The Westgate center also has a host of midrange and upscale shopping and eating options, all conveniently located right next to the stadiums.

The historic **Wigwam Hotel** (300 E. Wigwam Blvd., Litchfield Park, 623/935-3811, www.wigwamresort.com, $280-350), which opened in 1929 and still has some of its original adobe casitas, offers a bit of classic Arizona in the west valley. The citrus trees that used to crowd the valley before the population boom still live on at this retro resort, and the whole place smells like oranges and lemons. It's far from the action, but worth the drive for the classic touches and historic feel. The resort has the **Red Door Spa,** a golf course, and all the other amenities you'd expect from a legendary desert hideaway.

Food

In many ways, Phoenix and the Valley of the Sun began as clean slates, uncluttered by too much history and tradition, available for residents and visitors to scrawl on at will, creating amalgams and collages by cross-pollinating everything they'd seen or heard or tasted before arriving in the desert. The new always finds a foothold here, right up until it is replaced by something else. This is especially true of the area's dining life. But while the details may be changing all the time, the lifestyle remains constant: creative and eclectic, with a particular dedication, like the valley's residents now and throughout history, to fusion.

If none of the recommendations below appeal, the daily *Arizona Republic* keeps an excellent, up-to-the-second guide to the valley's constantly changing dining scene on its website, www.azcentral.com/ent/dining; and the alternative weekly *Phoenix New Times* (www.phoenixnewtimes.com) publishes entertaining and knowledgeable reviews and listings on valley eateries.

It's always a good idea to call ahead and attempt to make a reservation, even though for most places you probably won't need one; this is especially smart in the valley, where you may have to drive a ways through busy traffic to get anywhere. At most of the area's fancier places, reservations are recommended, if not required. Only the highest-end restaurants are going to have anything approaching a dress code, and that is usually business casual for the most part, but with a jacket. The vast majority of valley hosts and hostesses won't bat an eye at your jeans or even your flip-flops, especially during summer.

DOWNTOWN AND CENTRAL
American
Even if the New American creations at **Wright's at the Biltmore** (2400 E. Missouri Ave., 602/381-7632, www.wrightsbiltmore.com, 5pm-10pm Tues.-Sat., 10am-2pm Sun. brunch buffet, $34-40, $25 for brunch), the famous resort's signature restaurant, weren't consistently memorable, the interior, stamped with the etched-concrete block soul of Frank Lloyd Wright, would still require a visit from restaurant connoisseurs. The three-course tasting menu provides the best opportunity to dig deep into the restaurant's charms. The best main courses are usually fresh river fish with some sort of fabulous, native materials-built sauce. Reservations are a good idea. Wright's also has a great bar that's open daily 2:30pm-1am.

Tucked in a Safeway strip mall along Camelback, **NOCA** (3118 E. Camelback Rd., 602/956-6622, www.restaurantnoca.com, 5:30pm-10pm Tues.-Sat., 5:30pm-9pm Sun., open Mondays Dec.-March, $18-33) serves creative New American food in an elegant, professional atmosphere. The friendly waitstaff starts you out with some kind of bafflingly appetizing *amuse-bouche,* and by the time you're done with that it will be difficult to turn down one of the inspired starters, such as the wildly delicious hot buttered lobster roll or the grilled octopus; then it's on to the relatively large menu of handmade pasta, fish, lamb, and beef dishes, all with unique touches. If you're in the mood for a feast, try the chef's four-course tasting menu ($50), which is the best value if you want to get at the true heart of this remarkable restaurant. Reservations are recommended. A bit more whimsical but no less deserving of a slice of your take-home pay, **Fez** (3815 N. Central, 602/287-8700, www.fezoncentral.com, 11am-midnight Mon.-Thurs., 11am-1am Fri., 10am-1am Sat., 10am-midnight Sun.. $9.95-21.95) serves a unique blend of classic American food with the spices and techniques of Morocco and the Mediterranean. A representative example of their approach is the "Tangier Burger": an Angus patty slathered with hummus and herb pesto, held together with ciabatta. The menu has a lot of appealing salads and other burgers, but the most interesting and memorable dishes are the *Kisras,* herb-infused flat bread with lamb, chicken, or shrimp, and all sorts of enticing spreads and cheeses and vegetables. With its retro-chic lime green, orange, and brown interiors, large patio and urban-cool atmosphere, Fez is a fun place for a few drinks and an appetizer even if you're not staying for dinner. The same holds for the **Tuck Shop** (2245 N. 12th St., 602/354-2980, www.tuckinphx.com, 5pm-10pm Tues.-Sat., $9-22), a fun nightlife spot that's also a very serious foodie haven. They bill their inventive, filling single-plate, tapas-style dishes as "neighborhood comfort food"—and that is it. Try the "Savory Cupcakes": beet, onion, or cornbread cakes topped with cream cheese, smoked salmon, or horseradish whip cream. The herbed potato fries topped with gruyere cheese and mushroom gravy are a wonderful variation on another classic American comfort food. The reformed Desert Modern bungalow in which the restaurant serves is something to see in itself.

Since the valley stopped being a farming center, the seasons have very little to do with the average resident's life. In summer you stay inside, the rest of the year you go outside as much as you can. That's about it. Not so at ◖**Quiessence** (6106 S. 32nd St., 602/276-0601, www.quiessencerestaurant. com, 5pm-close Tues.-Sat., $9-32), an enchanting restaurant in a converted farmhouse, set among the gardens and organic crops at **The Farm at South Mountain.** The restaurant, with its green-grass patio, serves "handcrafted American cuisine" based on what is seasonally available from local farms, gardens, ranches, and streams. They also serve a program of unique and delicious cocktails. The menus, changed daily, usually include fish, beef, and vegetable dishes, all made with locally or regionally produced ingredients. This is an ideal place to spend an adventurous, fun, and, yes, educational night with friends, sampling the many foods (feta cheese from Snowflake, Arizona? Who knew?) that are grown, raised, and made right here in the Grand Canyon State. It's as if the railroad never connected this far-flung territory to the rest of the world, and the food is definitely better for it. The **Half Moon Sports Grill** (2121 E. Highland Ave., 602/977-2700, www.halfmoonsportsgrill. com, 11am-2am daily, $7.49-12.49) has top-notch, award-winning wings (please try them if you are a wings lover) and Angus burgers, plus a wildly diverse selection of tasty entrées in a high-energy sports bar atmosphere.

Be prepared to wait a bit for a table at tiny ◖**Lo-Lo's Chicken & Waffles** (1220 S. Central Ave., 602/340-1304, www.loloschickenand-waffles.com, 9am-7pm Mon.-Sat., 9am-4pm Sun., $5-13), a classic and very popular soul-food joint on Central. Lo-Lo's serves crispy Southern-fried chicken and big waffles (a combination whose inventor was surely a culinary genius), macaroni and cheese, greens, and many other Southern favorites. But you may find yourself liking the huge "jar of drank" the best: a fruit jar filled with red Kool-Aid, the finest drink on the planet. They also recently opened a Scottsdale location (2765 N. Scottsdale Rd., 480/945-1920, www.loloschickenandwaffles. com, 9am-7pm Mon.-Thurs., 9am-midnight Fri., 9am-9pm Sat., 9am-4pm Sun., $5-13).

Breakfast and Lunch

The tasteful diner **Matt's Big Breakfast** (825 S. 1st St., 602/254-1074, www.mattsbigbreak-fast.com, 6:30am-2:30pm Tues.-Sun., $5.95-7.50) always seems to have a line outside,

© TIM HULL

Two Hippies Magic Mushroom Burgers

especially on the weekends. That's because they serve some of the best breakfast food in the valley. The well-prepared, deceptively simple classic breakfasts here will keep you full for most of the day. From classic American breakfast to the classic American lunch: **Two Hippies Magic Mushroom Burgers** (802 E. Indian School Rd., 602/265-3525, www.twohippiesburgers.com, 11am-8pm Mon.-Sat., $5-7) is your lunchtime go-to for the titular magical meat, plus a host of other succulent burgers, sliders, chicken sandwiches, salads, and dogs, all in a hippie-slum atmosphere—just look for the hole-in-the-wall with the corrugated tin roof with a giant plastic hot dog.

For something a tad more refined, head over to **Pane Bianco** (4404 N. Central Ave., 602/234-2100, 11am-9pm Mon.-Thurs., 4pm-10pm Fri.-Sun., $2-8), Chris Bianco's (of the famous Pizzeria Bianco) casual sandwich hut, which has a very small menu of gourmet sandwiches—tuna, house-made mozzarella, or Italian salami, plus a revolving "market sandwich," and a few salad choices.

French

For inspired French fusion try James Beard Award-winning chef Christopher Gross's **Christopher's** and the **Crush Lounge** (2502 E. Camelback Rd., 602/522-2344, www.christophersaz.com, 11am-9pm Mon.-Tues., 11am-10pm Wed.-Sat., noon-8pm Sun., plus happy hour and food in the kitchen bar, lunch $6.95-13, dinner $16-45), at Biltmore Fashion Park along the Camelback Corridor. The truffle-infused filet mignon makes one weak at the knees, and the wood-oven pizzas are legendary. You can sit at the casual **Kitchen Bar** and order small plates and watch the chefs at work, or sit in the stylish dining room, and then retire for a cocktail to the patio and the lounge.

Steaks and Chops

Durant's Fine Foods (2611 N. Central Ave., 602/264-5967, www.durantsaz.com, 11am-10pm Mon.-Thurs., 11am-11pm Fri., 5pm-11pm Sat., 4:30pm-10pm Sun., lunch $8.95-29.95, dinner $18.95-51.50) downtown is the archetypal retro-haute steak house and lounge, where you can get a juicy slice of prime rib, a perfectly cooked steak, and an expert martini served by the professional, tuxedoed waitstaff. Durant's has been serving the same food in the same location for more than 50 years and has a loyal following, so you'll probably want to get reservations.

Mexican

Aunt Chilada's Squaw Peak (7330 N. Dreamy Draw Dr., 602/944-1286, www.auntchiladas.com, 11am-2am Mon.-Fri., 10am-2am Sat.-Sun., $6.75-15.95) serves delicious Mexican food in a historic building in the shadow of the Phoenix Mountains. **Los Dos Molinos** (1044 E. Camelback, 602/528-3535, http://losdosmolinosphoenix.com, Tues.-Sat. 11am-9pm) downtown has a fun, cluttered atmosphere and basic northern Mexico favorites.

The **Barrio Café** (2814 N. 16th St., 602/636-0240, www.barriocafe.com, 11am-10pm Tues.-Thurs., 11am-10:30pm Fri., 5pm-10:30pm Sat., 11am-9pm Sun., brunch 11am-3pm, $10-26, brunch $17-26) gets quite a bit more creative, serving a rare (for Arizona) modern Mexican cuisine from many different regions. This is not the place for chimichangas and chicken enchiladas. Try the slow-roasted pork, and somebody at the table should order Oaxacan black mole, one of Mexico's famous sauces created by nun-chefs in the 19th century. The bar has over 200 different varieties of tequila.

Irish Pub

Downtown's **Seamus McCaffrey's** (18 W. Monroe, 602/253-6081, www.seamusmccaffreys.com, 10am-2am daily, $6-9.50), right below the San Carlos Hotel, has excellent fish and chips and pours a perfect pint of Guinness. This is a friendly, laid-back place for lunch, dinner, or drinking.

Italian and Pizza

Another valley winner of the prestigious James Beard Award, Chris Bianco operates **Pizzeria Bianco** (623 E. Adams St. at Heritage Square, 602/258-8300, www.pizzeriabianco.com, 11am-9pm Mon., 11am-10pm Tues.-Sat., $9-16) out of a historic brick building at downtown's Heritage Square. The pizza is the best in the valley, and, according to many critics, the best in the nation as well. This is a small, romantic, and very hip place, and it takes a while to get a table and an equal while to get your pizza. It is all without a doubt worth it. Go here if you love pizza; you'll be sorry to miss it. Next door **Bar Bianco** (602/528-3699, 11am-9pm Mon., 11am-10pm Tues.-Sat.) has a wide selection of wine and a warm atmosphere, with picnic tables on a grassy, candlelit patio. Though more on the casual slice-of-pie side of the pizza scene, **Mamma Mia** (3937 E. Indian School Rd., 602/508-0444, www.phoenixbestpizza.com, 11am-10pm daily, $6.29-15.99) moved to the valley from New Jersey in 1980 and has been serving some the best and most authentic East Coast-style pies in town ever since. They also have wonderful calzones and subs.

Asian

Sing High Chop Suey House (27 W. Madison

© TIM HULL

Pizzeria Bianco, in historic Heritage Square

St., 602/253-7848, www.singhighphx.com, 11am-9pm Sun.-Thurs., 11am-10pm Fri.-Sat., $8-13), holding on to its romantic Old West name, is the oldest Chinese place in the valley, operated by the same family since 1928 in what used to be Phoenix's Chinatown long ago. The dishes here are consistently good, all the basics and some surprises, too.

Vegetarian

 Loving Hut (3239 E. Indian School Rd., 602/264-3480, www.lovinghut.us, 11am-2:30pm and 5pm-9pm Tues.-Sat., 4pm-8pm Sun., closed last Sunday of every month, $5.50-10) is 100 percent vegan, but you wouldn't know it unless they told you so. The delicious and spicy Asian-style dishes are prepared with all kinds of faux-meat protein that adds depth and zest to the dishes. Vegetarians, especially vegans, will be in ecstasy here.

Greek

Voted the valley's favorite Greek restaurant for more than 20 years in a row, **Greekfest** (1940 E. Camelback Rd., 602/265-2990, www.thegreekfest.com, lunch 11am-2:30pm, dinner 5pm-10pm Mon.-Sat., lunch $6.50-14, dinner $14-28) serves authentic and well-prepared Greek dishes with lamb, seafood, chicken, and beef, in charming white-walled dining rooms with archways and exposed vigas. It is simply the best Greek restaurant in Arizona.

Jamaican

For something delightfully different, try the authentic Jamaican food at **The Breadfruit** (108 E. Pierce St., 602/267-1266, www.the-breadfruit.com, lunch 11am-2pm Mon.-Fri., dinner 5pm-9pm Mon.-Thurs., 5pm-10pm Fri., noon-10pm Sat., $10-25), a stylish grill downtown with big windows and a warm interior. Anything "jerked"—a favorite spice style of Jamaican cuisine—is worth trying, as are the roasted plantains and the brown stew chicken. They also serve a selection of fine sipping rums, and sometimes have live music.

TEMPE AND THE EAST VALLEY
American

The strange New Native American cuisine at **Kai** (5594 West Wild Horse Pass Blvd., reservations accepted noon-5pm Tues.-Sat. at 602/385-5726, outside these times 602/225-0100, www.wildhorsepassresort.com, 5:30pm-9pm Tues.-Thurs., 5:30pm-9:30pm Fri.-Sat., closed July 28-Sept. 5, $14-54), one of the most unusual five-star restaurants in the West, seems at first completely foreign, but you soon realize that most of the foreign-sounding ingredients are actually as native as can be. Indeed, the chefs at Kai, which means "seed" in the local O'odham language, are so dedicated to the local-food revolution that they serve baby lettuce hand-picked by children from the Gila River Indian Reservation. The menu is fascinating, and the decor is proof that Native American motifs can be made new and surprising again. Business casual dress: no T-shirts, shorts, hats, or open-toed sandals for gentlemen, and denim is not preferred.

The enchanting atmosphere at the **House of Tricks** (114 E. 7th St., 480/968-1114, www.houseoftricks.com, lunch 11am-4pm, dinner 4pm-10pm, Mon.-Sat. lunch $9.50-14, dinner $23-36), housed in a 1920s-era cottage and adjacent 1903 adobe house just off Mill Avenue, with a patio shaded by old trees and a warm, homey vibe, is nearly as attractive as the New American cuisine cooked up in its kitchen. Almost. The seasonally inspired menus, which change often, feature the freshest meats, fish, and produce all mixed up into eclectic and creative dishes you won't find anywhere else.

Breakfast and Lunch

You'll likely see a few hungover ASU students trying to quell their head-fire in bacon grease at **Harlow's Café** (1021 W. University Dr., 480/829-9444, 7am-2pm daily, $5-8), a favorite and filling greasy spoon in Tempe. Head here for no-frills, short-order comfort food for breakfast or lunch. Special fans of the genre should definitely visit.

Burgers and Steaks

Monti's La Casa Vieja (100 South Mill Ave., 480/967-7594, www.montis.com, 11am-10pm Sun.-Thurs., 11am-11pm Fri.-Sat., $8-40) occupies the oldest standing building in Tempe, across from the now-closed flower mill and ferry stop that gave the riverside suburb its life in the early days. Monti's has atmosphere to spare; good steaks, burgers, and prime rib; and a crowded, fun cantina. Another valley favorite is **Rustler's Rooste** (8383 S. 48th St., 602/431-6474, www.rustlersrooste.com, 5pm-10pm daily, $14.95-29.95), a cowboy-style steak house that seeks to re-create a rough-hewn ranch mess hall near South Mountain. Here you'll get pots of cowboy beans and steaming ears of corn, thick steaks, as well as an always-celebratory atmosphere and expansive views of the desert and city. This place is great for families and has a relatively inexpensive kids' menu offering small steaks and ribs. If you're just visiting Arizona, this may be your one chance to try fried rattlesnake.

You won't find many handcrafted microbrews better than the varieties served at **Four Peaks Brewing Company** (1340 E. 8th St., 480/303-9967, www.fourpeaks.com, 11am-2am Mon.-Sat, 10am-2am Sun.), happy hour 2pm-6pm daily, $6.50-17), near campus in Tempe, and the pub eats and entrées—burgers, sandwiches, pizzas, and some really excellent starters—are equally good.

Irish Pub

Stop into **Rúla Búla** (401 S. Mill Ave., 480/929-9500, www.rulabula.com, 11am-2am daily) on Mill for your fix of fish and chips, a pint of Guinness, bangers and mash, and a fun, friendly atmosphere.

Middle Eastern

■ **Haji-Baba Middle Eastern Food** (1513 E. Apache Blvd., 480/894-1905, 10am-8pm Mon.-Sat., noon-4:30pm Sun., $4-14), a storefront in a strip mall just south of the ASU campus in Tempe, serves without a doubt the best Middle Eastern food in Arizona. The baba ghanoush is amazing, as are the hummus, gyros, kabobs, and falafel. The place is laid-back and casual, with a bustling grocery store operating behind a thin partition; it's often packed, and the service can be a bit lackadaisical, but the food is perfect and cheap.

Italian

Caffe Boa (398 S. Mill Ave., 480/968-9112, www.cafeboa.com, 11am-10pm Mon.-Wed., 11am-11pm Thurs.-Sat., brunch 10am-3pm and dinner 4pm-10pm Sun., $9-37) serves the east valley's best Italian and Mediterranean food in an intimate setting in the busy Mill Avenue District. The panini here are particularly good for lunch, and there's a new dinner menu every month, always featuring delectable and creative pasta dishes grounded in tradition.

Mesa's **Organ Stop Pizza** (1149 E. Southern Ave., 480/813-5700, www.organstoppizza.com, 4pm-9pm Mon.-Thurs., 5pm-10pm Fri.-Sat., 3pm-9pm Sun. Thanksgiving-mid-April, 5pm-9pm Sun.-Thurs., 5pm-10pm Fri.-Sat. mid-April-Thanksgiving) is one of the most unique pizza joints in the valley. Here you can see the restaurant's famous **Mighty Wurlitzer,** a 1927 organ that was once used to spice up silent movies, on which world-class organists perform as you chomp up your delectable pizza, pasta, or sub.

Indian

Perhaps the best Indian food in the state is served out of the **Delhi Palace** (933 E. University Dr. #103, 480/921-2200, 5pm-10pm daily, 11am-2:30pm lunch buffet Mon.-Fri., 11am-3pm Sat.-Sun., $8.95-15) near ASU, offering the well-known dishes prepared well; the service can be patchy, but you will never leave unsatisfied, especially after partaking in the buffet.

The **Udupi Café** (1636 N. Scottsdale Rd., 480/994-8787, www.udupiaz.com, 11am-3pm and 5pm-9:30pm Sun.-Thurs., 11am-3pm and 5pm-10pm Fri.-Sat., $8-12) serves rather different Indian fare, dishes that may be unfamiliar to haunters of American-style Indian joints exclusively. If you're feeling a bit experimental, though, this is the place to go. Some 80 percent of the food here is vegan, so those brave souls will want to go crazy.

The foods and flavors of Punjab are served at **The Dhaba** (1874 Apache Blvd. E., 480/557-8800, www.the-dhaba.com, 11am-2:30pm and 5pm-10pm Mon.-Fri., noon-10pm Sat.-Sun., $8-20), a spectacular Indian restaurant named for the casual, road-food joints that line the highways of India and Pakistan. Enjoy meats cooked in the restaurant's authentic tandoors (clay ovens) as well as many appetizing rice dishes and vegetarian options.

Vegetarian

The folks at **Green** (2240 N. Scottsdale Rd., 480/941-9003, www.greenvegetarian.com, 11am-9pm Mon.-Sat., $6-9), a "New American Vegetarian" restaurant, use mock meats and fresh vegetables and sauces to create 100 percent vegan meals. This is a place that even avid meat eaters will enjoy. They've got the best vegan chili fries and vegan chicken wings in town, and the "no harm chicken parm sandwich" is so tasty that it's difficult to believe *no harm* was done in its creation.

Mexican

The food at **Casa Reynoso** (3138 S. Mill Ave., 480/966-0776, www.casareynoso.com, 11am-8:30pm Tues.-Thurs., 11am-9:30pm Fri.-Sat., 11am-8pm Sun., $7-15) is prepared from old family recipes passed down from an older place in the Central Arizona mining region of Globe-Miami. The Mexican food here is a bit more authentic than your average chimichanga hut, and the hacienda-style building gives the place an Old Mexico aura that makes for a fun night out just slightly north of the border.

WEST VALLEY

If you're in the northwest valley around breakfast time, don't miss **Kiss the Cook Restaurant** (4915 W. Glendale Ave., 623/939-4663, www.kissthecookrestaurant.com, 6am-2:30pm Mon.-Fri., 7am-3pm Sat., 7am-1pm Sun., $5-9), which serves the old American favorites in an antique-shop interior.

Try the authentic and tasty German food (and don't miss the beer garden) at valley favorite **Haus Murphys** (5739 W. Glendale Ave., 623/939-2480, www.hausmurphys.com, 11am-2:30pm Tues.-Fri., noon-2:30pm Sat., noon-8pm Sun., $5-20).

Information and Services

TOURIST INFORMATION

The Downtown Phoenix Visitor Center (125 2nd St., 877/225-5749, www.visitphoenix.com, 8am-5pm Mon.-Fri.) has stacks of information and literature, and the helpful staff will answer all your questions.

MEDIA

The two best newspapers in the valley, and in the state for that matter, are the daily *Arizona Republic* (www.azcentral.com), the largest newspaper in Arizona, and the weekly *Phoenix New Times* (www.newtimes.com), which is the best source for investigative reporting, off-center opinions, and cultural coverage.

HOSPITALS AND EMERGENCY SERVICES

If you get hurt in the valley or have any kind of emergency medical situation, the simplest thing to do is call 911. There are several top-notch hospitals around the valley, and many of them have satellite centers in every major subregion around the basin. **St. Joseph's Hospital and Medical Center** (350 W. Thomas Rd., 602/406-3000) is a Catholic hospital started by the Sisters of Mercy in the late 19th century and is consistently ranked one of the top hospitals in Arizona. It operates a Level 1 Trauma Center, one of just a few in Arizona.

St. Luke's Medical Center (1800 E. Van Buren, 602/251-8100, www.stlukesmedcenter.

com) is located near downtown Phoenix and has an updated and state-of-the-art emergency room that includes an innovative Chest Pain Emergency Center dedicated to preventing heart attacks. **Maricopa Medical Center**

(2601 E. Roosevelt St., 602/344-5011, www. mihs.org) is one the nation's top hospitals, offering a full range of services including a Level 1 Trauma Center and an infant ICU.

Getting There and Around

All the information below applies to the entire Valley of the Sun, not just Phoenix proper. If you spend time in the sprawling valley, you'll soon realize that it is easier viewed as one big city rather than many midsized cities. Though the cities around the valley each have something unique to offer, in terms of getting there and around, the differences are negligible. If you're going to be in the valley more than a day, you are going to need a car. The bus system is reliable and comfortable, but it is not realistic to employ it for sightseeing tours. The light rail system moves past most of the downtown and central sights, restaurants, and accommodations.

AIR
Phoenix Sky Harbor International Airport
Phoenix Sky Harbor International Airport (3400 E. Sky Harbor Blvd., 602/273-3300, www.phxskyharbor.com) is one of the Southwest's largest, with three terminals served by 16 domestic and international airlines, offering flights to about 80 domestic and 20 international destinations, most of them in Mexico and Canada. If you're traveling to Arizona by air, you will likely land at Sky Harbor.

Transportation
Sky Harbor is just five miles or so east of downtown Phoenix. If you're leaving the airport in a rental car, head east on Sky Harbor Boulevard to Route 143 South. Go south on Route 143 and after about two mile take exit 1B and get on I-10 going west. It should take about 10 minutes, or up to 20 in

traffic, to get downtown from the airport. If you're headed to Tempe and Arizona State University, take Sky Harbor Boulevard east to North Priest Drive. Turn right onto North Priest and then turn left on West University Drive. The airport is about five miles from campus, which could take up to 15 minutes in traffic.

METRO LIGHT RAIL AND SKY TRAIN
The Metro Light Rail goes to the airport ($2 per ride)—take the light rail to the 44th Street and Washington Valley Metro Station to get to terminals 1-3. From the Metro station, you can catch the free "Sky Train" to get to terminal 4 and the economy parking lots. The "Sky Train" runs all day and night and there's never a wait of more than five minutes or so. There's also a free shuttle that travels from the economy parking lots to the terminals.

SHUTTLES
SuperShuttle (602/244/9000, www.supershuttle.com) offers rides to the airport from destinations all over the valley. Sky Harbor contracts with the shuttle giant to provide the service, and the ride is typically reliable and not unpleasant. You have to make a reservation. Shuttles run every 15 minutes 9am-9pm daily. Expect to pay from $12-38 for the first person in your party, depending on how far you are from the airport, and $7 for each additional passenger regardless of where you are. Catch the shuttle from Terminal 2 on the north curb; from Terminal 3, wait at the north or south curbs; and from Terminal 4, head down to the first floor and wait at the north or south curb.

TAXIS

Three taxicab companies contract with Sky Harbor to provide transportation at a set rate ($5 first mile, $2.30 each additional mile, $23 per hour traffic delay, $15 minimum fare, $1 per trip surcharge): **Apache Taxi** (480/557-7000), **AAA/Yellow Cab** (480/888-8888), and **Mayflower Cab** (602/955-1355).

You can meet a taxi on the north curb outside Terminal 2's door No. 8, on the north curb of Terminal 3, outside door No. 8, or on the first floor of Terminal 4 on the north curb, outside door No. 7.

You can get a taxi to take you anywhere in the valley; however, considering the long distances involved, they can get expensive pretty quickly. On the weekends you'll find taxis waiting outside of popular drinking and partying areas like downtown Phoenix, Scottsdale, and Tempe, but most of the time you're going to have to call a company and arrange for a pickup. Ultimately, taxis are not really an efficient way of getting around the valley.

CAR

The easiest way to get to, from, and around Phoenix and Arizona is by car. Phoenix's charms are a mere preamble to the wonderland that is Arizona, and the best way to see that wonderland is in your own car, preferably with your roadtrip mix on the stereo.

I-10 passes through the valley's heart and lungs on its way to and from the California coast. Phoenix is 372 miles east of Los Angeles, a straight five-hour shot on I-10. Continuing east on I-10 another 100 miles or so and you're in Tucson, Arizona's second city. The valley is connected to the I-40 east-west corridor by I-17, which runs north 150 miles from central Phoenix to Flagstaff, an I-40 town and one of the gateways to the Grand Canyon. The trip north from the desert of Phoenix to the cool pines of Flagstaff takes just over two hours.

Car Rental

It is easy to rent a car at the airport, but the exorbitant airport taxes and fees make doing so

a bad idea; you'll get price shock that will ruin your trip in advance. That said, Sky Harbor provides a free **Rental Car Shuttle** from the baggage claim at each terminal to the **Rental Car Center** (1805 E. Sky Harbor Circle South, 602/683-3741), just west of the airport. All the major rental companies are represented at the center, including **Hertz** (602/267-8822 or 800/654-3131, www.hertz.com) and **Budget** (800/527-7000, www.budget.com).

It's better to head outside the airport to rent a car. Try the locally owned **Phoenix Car Rental** (2934 E. McDowell Rd., 602/269-9310 and 3625 W. Indian School Rd., 602/269-9310, www.rentacarphoenix.com). The McDowell Road site is about seven miles from the airport. Take Sky Harbor Boulevard east to Priest, then get on the 202 Loop to exit 1C or 32nd Street, then turn left on McDowell. You can also arrange for them to pick you up.

LONG-DISTANCE BUS

Phoenix's **Greyhound Bus Station** (2115 E. Buckeye Rd., 602/389-4200) is located right near Sky Harbor International Airport. **Arizona Shuttle** (800/888-2749, www.arizonashuttle.com, $45 per person, one way) offers several daily trips between Flagstaff's Amtrak station and Sky Harbor Airport.

TRAIN

Amtrak's (800/872-7245, www.amtrak.com) Sunset Limited train, which runs along the southern route through humid south and dry desert southwest three times a week from New Orleans, stops in Maricopa, Arizona, about 30 miles east of Phoenix. However, as of this writing, transportation options from Maricopa to Phoenix are tough to come by and expensive.

PUBLIC TRANSPORTATION
Buses

Valley Metro (602/253-5000, www.valley-metro.org), the valley's public transportation authority, runs bus service ($2 per ride) everywhere, including Glendale, Scottsdale, Tempe, and Mesa.

Metro Light Rail

The best thing to happen to the valley since affordable air-conditioning, the sleek **Metro Light Rail** (602/253-5000, www.valleymetro. org), which opened for riders in late 2008, is beginning to transform the city's one-person, one-car culture into something more sustainable. The current system is 20 miles long, beginning in the northwest at Montebello and 19th Avenue, where there's a large parking lot, and traversing the valley all the way to Mesa in the east. Along the way the futuristic people mover stops at or near most of the valley's top sights, including downtown's Heard and Phoenix Museums, and Tempe's Mill Avenue and Town Lake. It's a great way to get around and to see the sights without having to get in and out of a car every 20 minutes, let alone finding parking (though this strategy is recommended only in spring and winter). Fares start at $2 per ride, and the last trip begins at 11pm Sunday-Thursday and 2am Saturday and Sunday. For a complete map and fare schedule, go to www.valleymetro.org.

Scottsdale

Scottsdale suffers somewhat from its reputation as being high-toned, high-dollar, and maybe even a little pretentious. This isn't the case, however, in most corners of the city, which has won numerous national awards for being generally livable, clean, and attractive. It's true that you see more Hummers and Beemers within Scottsdale's city limits than in other parts of the valley (save Paradise Valley, a mostly residential community that is one of the richest in the nation), but a day's visit here will likely reveal that there is much more to Scottsdale than beautiful rich people and their high-walled resorts.

SIGHTS
Downtown

Visitors to Scottsdale, a citrus-growing suburb turned international resort destination and art center, primarily come to stroll, shop, and eat in the city's bustling downtown area (www.downtownscottsdale.com), which includes Old Town, Fifth Avenue, and the Arts District, among others. There are dozens of Native American and Western art galleries and trading posts, boutiques selling Southwestern-style items both authentic and touristy, contemporary art galleries with a flair for the most current styles, restaurants from hamburger huts to highbrow gourmet, and lots of coffeehouses and cool watering holes.

Downtown Scottsdale is roughly defined by Chaparral Road on the north, Osborn Road on the south, Miller Road to the east, and 68th Street on the west. Within these general boundaries there are several distinct districts, though they all kind of meld into one another. The attractions here are art-searching, shopping and window-peering, eating and drinking, and general strolling and people-watching. In the Arts District, between Goldwater Boulevard and Scottsdale Road, you'll find a collection of art galleries to rival any other artsy block in the Southwest, home to a popular Art Walk every Thursday night. On Fifth Avenue you'll find more than 80 boutiques and shops selling mostly Southwestern and Native American items. Here you'll also find **Bob Parks's Horse Fountain,** a collection of wild, galloping stone horses jumping out of a large fountain. There are several kiosks scattered around downtown that are stuffed with pamphlets, free magazines, and handouts about visiting Scottsdale.

HISTORIC OLD TOWN SCOTTSDALE

The stretch of downtown where Scottsdale's founder, Eastern banker Albert G. Utley, first staked out a townsite (roughly bounded by Scottsdale Rd., Brown Ave., Indian School, and 2nd St.) has a collection of shops and eateries, some of them with Old West-style facades and hitching posts out front. The main shopping, sauntering, and people-watching area is

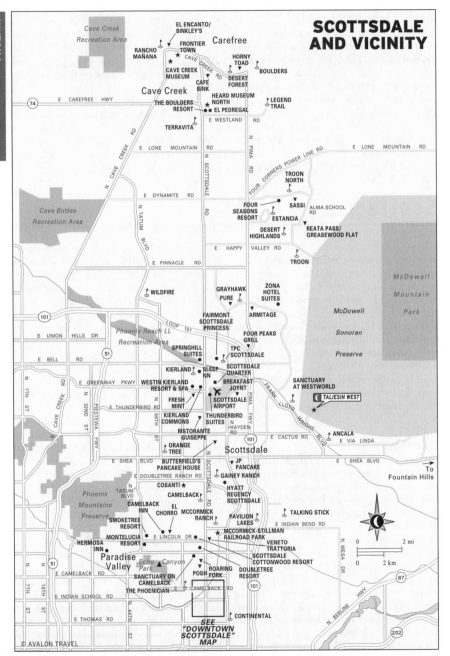

SCOTTSDALE AND VICINITY

Cave Creek Recreation Area

EL ENCANTO/BINKLEY'S

Carefree

RANCHO MAÑANA

FRONTIER TOWN

HORNY TOAD

CAVE CREEK MUSEUM

DESERT FOREST

BOULDERS

CAFÉ BINK

Cave Creek

74   E CAREFREE HWY

THE BOULDERS RESORT

HEARD MUSEUM NORTH

EL PEDREGAL

LEGEND TRAIL

TERRAVITA

E WESTLAND   RD

E LONE   MOUNTAIN   RD

E LONE   MOUNTAIN   RD

N CAVE CREEK RD

N SCOTTSDALE RD

N PIMA RD

FOUR CORNERS POWER LINE RD

Cave Buttes Recreation Area

E DYNAMITE   RD

TROON NORTH

N TATUM   BLVD

FOUR SEASONS RESORT

SASSI

ALMA SCHOOL RD

ESTANCIA

DESERT HIGHLANDS

REATA PASS/GREASEWOOD FLAT

E PINNACLE   RD

E HAPPY   VALLEY RD

TROON

McDowell

Mountain

Park

WILDFIRE

GRAYHAWK

ZONA HOTEL SUITES

PURE

McDowell

101

E UNION   HILLS   DR

LOOP 101

FAIRMONT SCOTTSDALE PRINCESS

ARMITAGE

Sonoran

Phoenix Reach LL Recreation Area

51

E BELL   RD

FOUR PEAKS GRILL

Preserve

SPRINGHILL SUITES

TPC SCOTTSDALE

N 7TH   ST

E GREENWAY PKWY

KIERLAND

SLEEP INN

SCOTTSDALE QUARTER

N 32ND   ST

WESTIN KIERLAND RESORT & SPA

BREAKFAST JOYNT

SANCTUARY AT WESTWORLD

E THUNDERBIRD RD

FRESH MINT

SCOTTSDALE AIRPORT

TALIESIN WEST

PIESTEWA FWY

N 56TH   ST

KIERLAND COMMONS

THUNDERBIRD SUITES

FRANK LLOYD WRIGHT BLVD

RISTORANTE GUISEPPE

N HAYDEN RD

101

E CACTUS RD

ANCALA

ORANGE TREE

Scottsdale

E VIA LINDA

E SHEA   BLVD

BUTTERFIELD'S PANCAKE HOUSE

JP PANCAKE

E SHEA BLVD

DOUBLETREE RANCH RD

GAINEY RANCH

To Fountain Hills

N TATUM BLVD

COSANTI

N SCOTTSDALE RD

Phoenix Mountains Preserve

CAMELBACK

HYATT REGENCY SCOTTSDALE

CAMELBACK INN

EL CHORRO

MCCORMICK RANCH

TALKING STICK

N MESA DR

0   2 mi

SMOKETREE RESORT

PAVILION LAKES

E INDIAN BEND RD

0   2 km

MONTELUCIA RESORT

E LINCOLN DR

MCCORMICK-STILLMAN RAILROAD PARK

HERMOSA INN

VENETO TRATTORIA

51

Paradise Valley

Echo Canyon Park

SCOTTSDALE COTTONWOOD RESORT

N 16TH ST

E CAMELBACK   RD

SANCTUARY ON CAMELBACK

ROARING FORK

DOUBLETREE RESORT

87

POSH

101

N 7TH ST

E INDIAN SCHOOL   RD

THE PHOENICIAN

E   CAMELBACK   RD

N 44TH ST

E THOMAS   RD

CONTINENTAL

SEE "DOWNTOWN SCOTTSDALE" MAP

N BEELINE HWY

202

© AVALON TRAVEL

sculptor Bob Parks's Horse Fountain in downtown Scottsdale

along Main Street just before Brown Avenue. In the old days Main Street here was lined with homes, but in the 1940s Scottsdale began selling itself as "The West's Most Western Town," and the homes were turned into businesses with faux frontier-era facades. Main Street ends at the 21-acre **Scottsdale Civic Center Mall,** prime strolling grounds with lots of grass and shade-giving trees and public art both silly and thought provoking. Just as you reach the mall off Main Street, look for the **Little Red Schoolhouse,** also known as the **Scottsdale Historical Museum** (7333 E. Scottsdale Mall, 480/945-4499, www.scottsdalemuseum.org, 10am-2pm Wed.-Sun., Sept.-June, 10am-5pm Wed.-Sun., Oct.-May). Inside this charming brick structure, built in 1909 and used as the town's school, city hall, courthouse, and library at various times over the years, there are several exhibits on Scottsdale's history. Every Tuesday at 10am January-March, a docent leads a one-hour **Downtown Historic Walking Tour** that begins at the schoolhouse. All around Old Town and in the other touristy districts of

downtown, you'll see quite a few horses doing draught duty in front of some restored carriage or wagon, loaded down with couples and kids. **KC's Classic Carriage Co.** (480/855-3180, www.horsencarriage.com, $20-100), which operates from the entrance to the Scottsdale Civic Center Mall at Brown Avenue and Main Street, will take you on a carriage ride through Old Town, or even through all of downtown if you so desire.

SCOTTSDALE MUSEUM OF CONTEMPORARY ART

It's fitting that the only art museum in Arizona dedicated strictly to the new and the now is in Scottsdale, one of the magnetic centers of art in the Southwest. You won't find any howling coyotes or Kokopelli here; the works are edgy, sometimes confusingly avant-garde, and always interesting. **SMoCA** (7374 E. 2nd St., 480/874-4666, www.smoca.org, noon-5pm Tues., Wed., Sun., noon-9pm Thurs., noon-5pm Fri.-Sat., $7 adults, $5 students, children under 15 free, admission free noon-9pm Thurs.) is located just

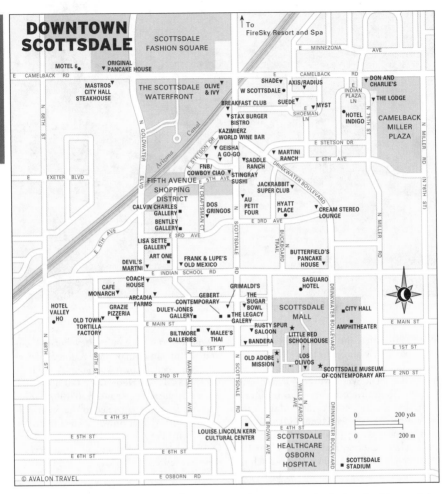

across the street from the Center for the Arts and has five galleries in a spare, modern space that used to be a movie theater. Special shows and exhibitions rotate often, and there's always at least one gallery showing work from the museum's permanent collection.

OLD ADOBE MISSION

The **Old Adobe Mission** (7655 E. Main St., 480/947-4331, www.olphaz.com), a small chapel in the heart of the Old Town district, was built in 1933 by a group of Mexican and Yaqui

Indian families. If it looks a bit like a miniature San Xavier del Bac, that's because it's supposed to: They say architect Robert Evans had Tucson's famous "White Dove of the Desert" in mind when he designed this little mission-style gem. It was built by volunteer labor out of some 14,000 adobe bricks made from a mixture of dirt, straw, and horse manure. Local tinsmith Barnebe Herrera made—and signed—the church's stained-glass windows. The chapel is undergoing a $450,000 renovation, and there's often a volunteer on-site to talk about

Scottsdale's Old Adobe Mission

the building, its history, and the important effort to save it.

Central Scottsdale and Paradise Valley
COSANTI

Known for his visionary, utopian architecture, the late Paolo Soleri, founder of the living architecture research facility in central Arizona called Arcosanti, was a powerful figure in the valley, if only because he represented what could be when it comes to humans living in resource-sparse environments. His round, organic, fairy-world structures, which seem to have been waiting there in the desert for some mad genius to tell them to rise up, are part Frank Lloyd Wright (who brought Soleri to the valley to study at Taliesin West), part Native American, and part artistic fantasy. His Paradise Valley desert complex, established in 1956, has a gallery, studio, living spaces, and a foundry, where students make the famous **Soleri Windbells,** which are sold throughout the world to fund the ongoing urban design experiments at Arcosanti. You

can watch the bells being made most weekday mornings. An ideal way to visit **Cosanti** (6433 E. Doubletree Ranch Rd., 480/948-6145, www.cosanti.com, 9am-5pm Mon.-Sat., 11am-5pm Sun., free) is to combine it with a tour of Taliesin West, which is located only about eight miles to the northeast.

McCORMICK-STILLMAN RAILROAD PARK

The kids and train enthusiasts will love **McCormick-Stillman Railroad Park** (7301 E. Indian Bend Rd., 480/312-2312, www.therailroadpark.com, most days 10am-6pm, call first as hours vary slightly by season, free), dedicated to the old iron horse. Tickets for rides are $1 each (carousel costs one ticket, train costs two tickets). A replica of a Colorado narrow-gauge railroad called **The Paradise and Pacific Railroad** makes you feel like a giant as it moves around a one-mile track running through the green park. There are also several old trains in the park that are worth a look, as well as a museum featuring exhibits on the history of the railroad and how it changed the valley—housed in a 1914 Santa Fe Railroad baggage car. Another highlight is a presidential Pullman car used by Eisenhower and FDR. Don't skip a ride on the restored old carousel—pure, forgetful joy.

North Scottsdale
HEARD MUSEUM NORTH

A small, two-gallery tentacle of Arizona's best Native American museum, the **Heard North** (32633 N. Scottsdale Rd., 480/488-9817, www.heard.org/north/index.html, 10am-5pm Mon.-Sat., 11am-5pm Sun., $5 adults, $2 children under 12) has a permanent exhibition showing pieces from the main museum's unmatched collection of pottery, jewelry, and other items made by Arizona's American Indian tribes. They also host a few changing exhibitions every year on Native American subjects, and there's a sculpture garden and café. It's not necessary to visit this outlet of the main downtown museum, which is a vital attraction that should not be missed by anyone; but if you want to make the drive to north Scottsdale, you surely won't regret it.

HUHUGAM KI MUSEUM

In an adobe building on the **Salt River Pima-Maricopa Indian Community,** two of the state's river-bred tribes preserve their history and cultural customs. Huhugam Ki means "House of the Ancestors," and the ancestors they are talking about are the mysterious Hohokam, who irrigated and grew corps in the Salt River Valley hundreds of years ago. The **Huhugam Ki Museum** (10005 E. Osborn Rd., 480/362-7400, www.srpmic-nsn.gov/history_culture/museum.asp, 9:30am-4:30pm Mon.-Fri., free) tells the stories and histories of the Pima Indians, now commonly referred to in their own language as the Akimel O'odham (River People)—cousins to southern Arizona's Tohono O'odham (Desert People)—and the Maricopa, or Xalychidom Piipaash, a tribe that migrated to the valley from the banks of the Gila and Colorado Rivers, through exhibits, old photographs, pottery, and other artifacts. The

Akimel O'odham are known for their basket making, and a highlight of a visit to this small museum is the live demonstrations of the intricate art by tribal members.

TALIESIN WEST

Architect Frank Lloyd Wright spent the money he made from his masterpiece Falling Water on a large swath of desert northeast of Scottsdale, and from about 1937 onward he spent a portion of each year living in the desert with his apprentices and building what would become **Taliesin West** (12621 Frank Lloyd Wright Blvd., 480/860-2700, recorded tour info 480/860-8810, www.franklloydwright.org, 9am-4pm daily). If every house built in the desert used the natural landscape in the same way as this wondrous complex does, the valley would be a very different, better place today. Familiar Wright motifs, like his ubiquitous compression-and-release entranceways, Oriental touches, and native-rock-and-mortar aesthetic, are on display at this truly unique and important attraction.

You can see Taliesin only by tour, but the guides are knowledgeable and very enthusiastic about Wright's work and legacy. Since the complex is still used and lived in today by fellows of Taliesin Associated Architects, a group carrying on the spirit of Wright's work, some buildings may be off limits during a tour. There are several tours to choose from, including an in-depth, three-hour, behind-the-scenes look around ($75). The most popular tour is the 90-minute **Insights Tour** (9am-4pm daily, every half hour Nov.-April, every hour May-Oct., $36 adults, $17 children 12 and under), which includes a look at the beautiful Garden Room and the living quarters as well as all of the sights included in the one-hour **Panorama Tour** (10:15am and 2:15pm daily, $28 adults, $10 children 12 and under). They change the tour schedules sometimes, so it's a good idea to call before you go. Arrive a little early so you can check out the excellent bookstore and gift shop, which sells Frank Lloyd Wright-inspired knickknacks and just about every book ever published by or on the master.

Frank Lloyd Wright in the Valley of the Sun

In 1940 Frank Lloyd Wright published an essay in *Arizona Highways* in which he eloquently pleaded for a different kind of architecture for the desert, one not based on previous models but on the unique colors and contours of the desert itself: "The ever advancing human threat to the integral beauty of Arizona might be avoided if the architect would only go to school in the desert…," he wrote, "and humbly learn harmonious contrasts or sympathetic treatments that would, thus, quietly, belong."

Certainly the best of the very few real-world examples of what Wright had in mind is his own **Taliesin West,** Wright's most famous desert-land building. He designed a few other distinctive structures in the valley, and some of them are accessible to fans of the nation's greatest architect. In addition to a church and an auditorium, Wright built nine private homes in the valley, eight of which still exist. One of the finest of his private homes is a small bungalow Wright designed for his friend Raymond Carlson, then the editor of *Arizona Highways.*

Many critics and scholars include the 1928 **Arizona Biltmore** (2400 E. Missouri St., Phoenix), then as now the state's most stylish resort, on the short list of public structures Wright designed in the valley. Though the architect of record is his former apprentice, Albert Chase McArthur, Wright was paid a consulting fee on the project and left his mark on the design, as anyone with even a passing knowledge of Wright's quirks and obsessions will see during a stroll around the magnificent "Jewel of the Desert."

Wright created the design for the north valley's **First Christian Church** (6750 N. 7th Ave., 602/246-9206, www.fccphx.com) in 1950 as part of the Classical University commission that never got off the ground. In 1972, church leaders obtained the unused plans and started construction on the sanctuary, considered by many the best example of Wright's church architecture. You can stop in for a look around, or attend one of the services held Sundays at 9am and 10:30am.

Wright originally designed Arizona State University's **Grady Gammage Memorial Auditorium** (1200 S. Forest Ave., Tempe, 480/965-5062) as an opera house for Baghdad, Iraq. In 1957, when Wright was 90 years old, the king of Iraq commissioned him to design several public buildings in Baghdad. Unfortunately, the king was killed the next year, so the project fell apart. Later, the design for the Baghdad opera house was changed a bit to become Gammage Auditorium. It is not one of the critics' favorites—a bit puffy and sappy for some tastes—but the acoustics, as in all of Wright's performance spaces, are absolutely perfect.

Journalist Lawrence Cheek wrote a slim but comprehensive book about Wright's desert work, *Frank Lloyd Wright in Arizona* (Rio Nuevo, 2006), that should be read by anybody interested in Wright's westerly masterpieces.

CAREFREE AND CAVE CREEK

Drive north on Scottsdale Road (about 15 miles from Phoenix) through a beautiful, if disappearing, stretch of desert to these tiny resort-style towns full of galleries, antique stores, restaurants, and artisan shops—a perfect daylong escapade to the valley's northeastern outer reaches. Along the way, watch for the large signs on the side of the road pointing out various representative Sonoran Desert flora. In late February, the **Carefree Fine Art & Wine Festival** attracts artists, artisans, and wine lovers from across the nation. This drive is very popular with motorcycle groups, and on any given weekend (though not so much in the summer) the area is likely to be somewhat crowded.

ENTERTAINMENT AND EVENTS
Nightlife

Scottsdale is somewhat known as a playground for the beautiful and the rich, and it is that in some quarters—a meat market with a premium on the tanned and tightened, dancing to repetitious beats, and peeking into debauched VIP rooms to catch some minor celebrity. But there are a lot of down-to-earth watering holes and scenes here too. Last call is usually 2am, per the state legislature, but many bars and clubs stay open for hours afterward, offering late-night menus and after-hours fun. Dress is generally casual, unless you're going to the highest of the high-end places. Most of the restaurants listed under the Food section double as nightspots as well.

Downtown's **Entertainment District** (roughly bounded by Camelback Rd., Scottsdale Rd., Miller Rd., and 6th Ave.) is as good a place as any to start your night on the town in Scottsdale, and you'll likely find enough clubs, bars, and lounges to keep you busy for quite a while.

BARS AND PUBS

The **Living Room at the W Scottsdale** (7277 E. Camelback Rd., 480/970-2100, 4pm-midnight Sun.-Thurs., 4pm-2am Fri.-Sat.) provides a perfect introduction to the high-end Scottsdale nightlife scene, with its moneyed and tanned patrons, high-priced, handcrafted cocktails, and swanky Modernist-fusion interiors. You might even see a few celebrities staying at the hotel.

American Junkie (4363 N. 75th St., 480/990-3000, http://americanjunkieaz.com, noon-2am Mon.-Fri., 10am-2am Sat.-Sun.) is a cozy, posh urban-style bar with little candle-lit tables and comfortable lounge seating, and a patio for smoking and enjoying the night air.

If you're looking for something a bit more rowdy, try the cowboy-dive **Rusty Spur Saloon** (7245 E. Main St., 480/425-7787, www.rustyspursaloon.com, 10am-1am Mon.-Thurs., 10am-2am Fri.-Sat.), a historic Scottsdale saloon housed in a building that opened first in 1921 as a bank. The vault is still here, but they keep booze in it now, and there's all kinds of cool old Western memorabilia on the walls and relaxed, neighborhood-joint atmosphere here, and they serve heaping plates of rib-sticking bar food and offer live bands as well.

5th and Wine restaurant and wine bar

Right across from the famous Horse Fountain in downtown Scottsdale, **5th and Wine** (7051 E 5th Ave., 480/699-8001, www.5thandwine.com, 11am-9pm Sun.-Mon., 11am-10pm Tues.-Thurs., 11am-11pm Fri.-Sat., $10-30) is an elegant but casual place to sit back with a glass of wine and a plate of bruschetta or a sampling of pears, figs, and brie with a side of fried pickles. The atmosphere here is the very definition of Scottsdale chic—upscale and laid-back all at the same time. Don't worry if you're not a wine drinker; they also have a full menu of beers and expertly made cocktails to sample, as well as an eclectic food selection that includes panini, pasta dishes, salads, and burgers made with, of course, wine.

DANCING AND LIVE MUSIC

The downtown mainstay **Martini Ranch** (7295 E. Stetson Dr., 480/970-0500, www.martiniranchaz.net) attracts a mid- to upscale crowd, and features live, mostly local music on its stage, and lots of scantily dressed young women dancing with cologne-scented young men in

The **Shaker Room,** a nightclub with DJs and risqué theme nights.

The **Firehouse Scottsdale** (4312 N. Brown Ave., 480/265-6989, www.ilovefirehouse.com, 10:30am-2am daily, $9-13) in Old Town has a huge patio, a young and beautiful clientele and a restaurant that serves breakfast, lunch, and dinner (burgers, pizzas, pitas, sandwiches, and breakfast burritos, etc.). Most nights there's some kind of party going on here, often featuring a DJ, dance music and all sorts of scantily clad 20-somethings sliding around drinks in their hands.

CASINOS

The **Salt River Pima-Maricopa Indian Community** operates two casinos in Scottsdale, though both require a bit of a drive from downtown. **Casino Arizona at Salt River** (524 N. 92nd St., 480/850-7777, www.casinoarizona.com), east of the Loop 101 at McKellips, has 900 slots, 34 gaming tables, keno, and a showroom that hosts touring acts and a review featuring look-and-sound-alikes of the superstars of American music. At the new **Casino Arizona at Talking Stick** (9700 E. Indian Bend Rd., 480/850-7777, www.talkingstickresort.com), about a mile east of the Loop 101 on Indian Bend Road, there are 700 slots and 50 gaming tables.

Performing Arts

The **Scottsdale Center for the Performing Arts** (7380 E. 2nd St., 480/499-8587, www.scottsdaleperformingarts.org) is a huge complex of theaters, classrooms, and grassy knolls right downtown. Inside, the **Virginia G. Piper Theater** and a few smaller spaces nearby host a wide range of theater, dance, comedy, and music—mostly classical and jazz. Acts like Laurie Anderson and Arlo Guthrie have performed here, as have jazz legend Dave Brubeck and many others.

Festivals and Events

More than 100 artists, many of them internationally known in art circles, participate in the popular **Arizona Fine Art Expo** (Scottsdale Rd. and Jomax Rd., www.arizonafineartexpo.com) from January through March, during which you can stroll in and out of galleries and cabanas set up streetside and watch the artists at work. Also in January, the famous **Barrett-Jackson Antique Auto Auction** (7400 E. Monte Cristo Ave., 480/421-6694, www.barrett-jackson.com) gets under way, selling auction-style the most expensive and spectacular automobiles in existence. Hundreds of white tents go up at Scottsdale Road and the Loop 101 from January through March for the **Celebration of Fine Art** (www.celebrateart.com), while inside, juried artists create their works before your eyes and sell them directly.

The **Scottsdale Arabian Horse Show** (Westworld, 16601 N. Pima, www.scottsdaleshow.com) brings equestrian enthusiasts from all over the world to town in February, and in March the **Scottsdale Arts Festival** (75th St. and Main St., www.scottsdaleperformingarts.org) attracts about 10,000 visitors to the Scottsdale Center for the Performing Arts for three days of art sales, demonstrations, and performances. In April, just before it starts to get hot, the shining stars of the eating scene gather for the **Scottsdale Culinary Festival** (www.scottsdaleculinaryfestival.org).

SHOPPING
Shopping Centers and Districts
If you're a serious shopper with serious money, don't miss the upscale centers for which this part of the valley is famous. Even if you don't have sacks of money, it's fun to walk around these always well-landscaped and fashionable shopping centers, bustling with beautiful people and stocked with luxury items from all over the globe, to get an idea of how the other one percent lives. Scottsdale's busy downtown areas provide the best shopping in town, and nearby **Scottsdale Fashion Square** (7014 E. Camelback Rd., 480/945-5495, www.fashionsquare.com, 10am-9pm Mon.-Sat., 11am-6pm Sun.) is the largest enclosed mall in the Southwest, featuring high-end department stores, boutiques, and restaurants.

Kierland Commons (6166 N. Scottsdale Rd.

© TIM HULL

Gilbert Ortega Gallery & Museum

and Greenway Pkwy., 480/348-1577, www.kierlandcommons.com, 10am-5pm Mon.-Sat., noon-6pm Sun.) has about 70 upmarket shops and eateries, including Anthropologie, Restoration Hardware, and Crate & Barrel.

The Shops at Gainey Village (Scottsdale Rd. and Doubletree Ranch Rd., www.theshopsgaineyvillage.com, 10am-6pm Mon.-Sat., noon-6pm Sun.) is perhaps the most stylish of them all, featuring unique boutiques (including a shop for the ultrapampered dog in your family), interior design shops, furniture stores with custom-made items you won't find anywhere else but you'll have to pay dearly for, contemporary art galleries, and even, because this is Scottsdale, a shop selling "baby couture."

Downtown
CLOTHING
It might be hard to swallow Scottsdale's claim as "The West's Most Western Town" when you are, say, sipping a cocktail in some urban-chic lounge; but when you visit **Saba's Western Wear** (3965 N. Brown Ave., 480/947-7664,

www.sabas.com), a fixture in Old Town since back when it was merely Town, you might start to sympathize a bit. Members of the Saba family, longtime valley merchants with nine stores (including one just across the street), still sell the finest, most authentic working-cowpoke Western wear you can find—plus an unparalleled selection for the equally authentic urban cowboy and cowgirl.

NATIVE AMERICAN ARTS
Scottsdale has long been known as one of the three or four top places to see and buy Native American arts in the Southwest. There are several galleries and shops along Main Street downtown, and the **Gilbert Ortega Gallery & Museum** (3925 N. Scottsdale Rd., 480/990-1808, 10am-6pm Sun.-Tues., 10am-9pm Wed.-Sat.) is worth a perusal.

For Hopi kachina dolls, Hopi and Zuni pottery, and Zuni fetishes, don't miss the **River Trading Post & Traditional Pueblo Arts** (7033 E. Main St., Ste. 102, 480/444-0001, www.rivertradingpost.com, 11am-5pm Tues.-Sat., noon-4pm Sun.). This museumlike shop has a superior collection of Navajo rugs, and sculptures and frontier-era furniture. The **Old Territorial Indian Arts** (7077 E. Main St., #7, 480/945-5432, www.oldterritorialshop.com, 10am-4pm Mon.-Sat.) is the oldest among Scottsdale's many Native American Arts dealers; they've been selling and showing wonderful antique Navajo rugs, Hopi pottery and kachina dolls, Native American jewelry, folk art, and baskets for more than 40 years.

FARMERS MARKET

Every Saturday the **Old Town Farmers' Market** (www.azcommunitymarkets.com, 8:30am-11am Sat., Oct. 23-May 29), in the city parking facility at the corner of Brown Avenue and 1st Street, features local farmers and artists, food artisans, and food lovers selling and promoting their unique wares.

GALLERIES

Scottsdale is second only to Santa Fe as a center for the Southwestern art scene. The **Scottsdale Arts District** (west of Scottsdale Rd. to 70th St., north along Marshall Way to 5th Ave.) has more than 100 galleries, many of them featuring the work of classic Southwestern artists and contemporary masters. But it's not all about regional expectations; be prepared to see a lot that defies preconceived notions about what Southwestern art is and should be. It's not all about Southwestern art, either. There are several galleries that have little to do with it at all, displaying instead a general contemporary style that is always intriguing. One of the best ways to see all that the downtown Scottsdale art scene has to offer is to embark on the famed **Scottsdale Artwalk** (480/377-9366, 7pm-9pm Thurs.). Every Thursday for two hours (and sometimes longer), the galleries along Main Street, Marshall Way, Stetson, and 6th Avenue throw open their doors to hundreds of art lovers, and you can walk along the lit-up streets, stop in for a drink at one of the area's many watering holes, and dip in and out of dozens of galleries. The weekly event has been going on since 1976 and is one of the nation's

© TIM HULL

Shops on Scottsdale's 5th Avenue sell mostly Southwestern and Native American items.

oldest art-walk events. For more information, and for a complete list of galleries, check out the **Scottsdale Gallery Association** website (www.scottsdalegalleries.com).

The **Wilde Meyer Gallery** (4142 N. Marshall Way, 480/945-2323, www.wildemeyer.com, 10am-5:30pm Mon.-Fri., 10am-6pm Sat.) shows an eclectic mix of paintings by mostly contemporary artists, many of whom have infused the Southwestern landscape with a surreal sensibility. The work here is some of the most exciting and baffling in the Arts District. At the **Trailside Galleries** (7330 Scottsdale Mall, 480/945-7751, www.trailsidegalleries.com, 10am-5:30pm Mon.-Sat.) on Scottsdale Mall, which has been around since 1963, you'll find mostly realistic Western art in the form of bucking-bronc bronzes, noble Indian chiefs, and tired old cowboys lounging on their saddles. They also have a fine collection of landscape paintings. **Scottsdale Fine Art** (7116 E. Main St., 480/990-3100, www.scottsdalefineart.com, 10:30am-6pm Mon.-Sat. and 7pm-9pm Thurs. Oct. 2-May 31; 10am-5pm Tues.-Sat. June 1-Oct. 1) has a wonderful collection of landscape art by contemporary masters of light and shadow and unique forms of the Southwest, and at **Bonner David Galleries** (7040 E. Main St., 480/941-8500, www.bonnerdavid.com, 10am-5:30pm Mon.-Sat., open until 9pm Thurs.) you'll find a thrilling mix of abstracts, landscapes, and realistic sculpture. If you're a film fan, and especially if you love old movies, don't miss the **Femmes Fatales & Fantasies Art Museum & Gallery** (7013 E. Main St., 480/429-6800, www.fffmovieposters.com, www.sherrygoldbergart.com, 10am-6pm, Tues., Wed., Fri., Sat., 1pm-9pm Thurs.), where they have a spectacular collection of framed, original movie posters from *The Big Sleep* to *Back to the Future* and pretty much everything in between.

SPORTS AND RECREATION

Scottsdale is a bit greener than many desert cities, and there are quite a few parks and open spaces within the relatively small area of the town. One of the best of these is the long multi-use trail that winds through the center of the mostly residential neighborhoods along Hayden Road from Indian Bend Road south to Tempe—about 13 miles of greenspace for bikers, joggers, walkers, and skaters called the **Indian Bend Wash Greenbelt** (Scottsdale Parks and Recreation, 7340 Scottsdale Mall, 480/312-7957, www.scottsdaleaz.gov). Along this unique flood-control system, which channels intermittent desertland floods—mostly in the late summer monsoon season—into Indian Bend Wash while at the same time creating a fine exercise and recreation belt through the length of the town, you'll see a steady stream of bikers, in-line skaters, and joggers, especially in the mornings. The path passes through several city parks and golf courses as it makes its way south all the way to Tempe Town Lake. There's not really a set-aside, signed starting block for the greenbelt, but a good place to pick it up is at **Chaparral Park** (5401 N. Hayden Rd., 480/312-2353).

Hiking and Biking

If you'd like to get out of the city a bit and into the desert, head out to **McDowell Mountain Regional Park** (16300 McDowell Mountain Park Dr., 480/471-0173, www.maricopa.gov/parks/mcdowell), a 21,000-acre desert preserve northeast of Scottsdale proper with miles of desert hiking, biking, and equestrian trails. This is an excellent setting for getting to know the Sonoran Desert. To get to the park from Scottsdale, take Shea Boulevard east to Fountain Hills Boulevard, which heads north and turns into McDowell Mountain Road leading into the park. If you've got some extra time, think about stopping in the retirement haven of Fountain Hills and seeing the world's biggest fountain; continue on Shea past Fountain Hills Boulevard, and then turn north on Saguaro Boulevard, which will take you right past **Fountain Park** and **The Fountain,** and then meets with Fountain Hills Boulevard, which leads to the preserve.

Inside the park, there are various trails for hiking and biking and horseback riding; one of the more popular short hikes is the 3-mile

North Trail. The 15-mile Pemberton Trail is the toughest and longest hike in the park.

McDowell Sonoran Reserve

McDowell Sonoran Reserve (various trailheads around Scottsdale, 480/312-7013, www.scottsdaleaz.gov/preserve, sunrise-sunset daily, free) in Scottsdale holds back the sprawling cityscape from some 27,000 acres of beautiful desert around the McDowell Mountains. The area is northeast of the city center and has dozens of varied trails for hiking, all of them roughly near each other. The largest and most developed trailhead is the **Gateway Access Area** (18333 N. Thompson Peak Pkwy.), about 15 miles north of downtown Scottsdale via the Route 101 Loop. Other access areas with trails include **Lost Dog Wash** (12601 N. 124th St.), 14 miles north of downtown via the 101 Loop; **Quartz** (10215 E. McDowell Mt. Ranch Rd.), also 14 miles north on the 101; **Ringtail** (12300 block of N. 128th St.), 14.5 miles north on the 101; **Sunrise** (12101 N. 145th Way), 16 miles north of downtown via the 101, and **WestWorld** (15939 N. 98th St.), 13 miles from downtown on the 101.

Golf

There are about 200 golf courses in the Valley of the Sun, and about 50 of them are in Scottsdale, a town as famous for its golf as for its galleries and resorts. You'll likely find the golf courses in Scottsdale to be a bit more challenging and considerably more beautiful and dramatic than those in surrounding communities, but they are also considerably more expensive. But for a true golf lover, this is where you'll want to splurge.

Kierland Golf Club (15636 N. Clubgate Dr., 480/922-9283, www.kierlandgolf.com) is a gorgeous 27-hole, par 36 desert course along Scottsdale Road just south of Frank Lloyd Wright Boulevard. It's part of the Weston Kierland Resort and Spa but is open to the public. The greens are shocking against the hard desert scenery, which has been left to itself along the edges of the greenery, making for a uniquely Arizona golfing experience. It's not cheap. It'll cost you about $109-189 per person in the high season, and about $49-69 per person during the hottest days of the summer. The course offers some twilight hour prices that are significantly cheaper, however. You can book a tee time online, and it's recommended that you do so before traveling if you want to play any of Scottsdale's courses.

The fabulous **Troon North Golf Club** (10320 E. Dynamite Blvd., 480/585-5300, www.troonnorthgolf.com) in the far northeast valley is a much-sought-after golfing experience for duffers the world over. It's probably the most beautiful public course in the valley, though one could say that about many fairways here. There are two courses at the club, both lined with desert boulders and saguaro; the Monument Course, the better of the two, is so named because of the 14-foot boulder rising off the fairway. Expect to pay more than $200 per person in the high season.

Starfire at Scottsdale Country Club (11500 N. Hayden Rd., 480/948-6000, www.starfiregolfclub.com) is a more centrally located course—head north on Hayden Road and you'll find it—and more reasonably priced than some of the fancier desert courses north of the city. The 27-hole course, lined with eucalyptus and palm trees, was designed by Arnold Palmer and is moderately challenging. Expect to pay about $40-50 per person during the high season.

TPC of Scottsdale (17020 N. Hayden Rd., 480/585-4334, http://tpc.com/scottsdale) is where the PGA pros play one of the most popular tournaments of the year in late January; the **Waste Management Open** (www.phoenixopen.com), formerly the Phoenix Open, is one of the oldest tournaments on the pro tour and draws some of the biggest crowds of any tournament. In the off-season you're likely to see one of the local PGA tour members practicing here. You'll find two exquisite, famous courses—one of them, the Champion's Course, was completely remodeled in 2007. The Scottsdale Princess Resort is linked with the course, and to stay and play here is to engage in the height of luxury and challenging golf, but it's going to cost you. Greens fees will run you about $287 per person in the high season, and about $77 in the deep summer, with discounts for evening play.

Spas

Scottsdale is known far and wide as a place to pamper your body and soul. There are dozens of spas in this upscale desert burg, and many of them are associated with the city's many world-famous resorts. A half day or a full day at one of these spas may be just what you need to get your life back on track, or to celebrate how on-track your life already is. Regardless, it's going to cost you. Check the individual websites for current pricing, but don't expect to do anything, or have anything done to you, for much under $100, and that's just to get started. During the summer months, however, most of the spas, like their parent resorts, cut prices somewhat to attract business to the hot valley. It's a good idea to call ahead for a reservation in any season.

With a name like **The Centre for Well-Being at the Phoenician** (6000 E. Camelback Rd., 480/843-2392, www.thephoenician.com, 7am-7pm daily) you'd expect this place to take your health and comfort very seriously, and you'd be right. They offer 75 different treatments at this 22,000-square-foot spa that will put you through a vigorous workout, give you a facial, massage, and a makeover and then send you on your way after you've stopped at the "waters bar" and found your center in the meditation room. **The Spa at Camelback Inn** (5402 E. Lincoln Dr., 800/922-2635, www.camelback-spa.com, 6:15am-7:30pm daily) has a gorgeous spa, with plunge pools, Turkish baths and saunas, and a beautiful pool area where you can rent a spa cabana for a day of relaxation. They offer all manner of body wraps and facial treatments, massages, and other body work in a truly stunning setting. They also have exercise classes, personal training and consultations, and a spa restaurant serving healthy and wholesome foods. At **The Sanctuary Spa at Sanctuary Resort** (5700 E. McDonald Dr., Paradise Valley, 480/607-2326, www.sanctuaryoncamelback.com, 6am-8:30pm daily) you

can get a variety of Asian treatments, such as the medicinal herb massage called "luk pra kope," as well as acupuncture, reiki, shiatsu, and Thai reflexology. This refined, tranquil space on the grounds of the Sanctuary Resort also offers a host of other treatments, including Swedish massage, facials, makeovers, and personal training. The **Willow Stream—The Spa at Fairmont Scottsdale Princess** (7575 E. Princess Dr., 480/585-4848, www.willowstream.com/scottsdale, 6am-10pm daily) was inspired by Havasupai (also called Supai), a small village in the western Grand Canyon where blue-green waterfalls tumble into deep pools and the walls of the canyon shine red. This gorgeous resort spa has re-created one of the famous canyon waterfalls, and has a rooftop pool area where you can rent a cabana and relax with some spectacular views. Then it's time to check out the large menu of body and facial treatments, including a Havasupai Body Oasis Experience, a two-hour pampering that features a eucalyptus footbath, scalp acupressure, aromatherapy wraps, and all sorts of exfoliations and massages.

If you're in downtown Scottsdale and find yourself in need of a massage, facial, and sauna, stop into the relaxing **Spa Du Soleil** (7040 E. 3rd Ave., 480/944-5400, www.spadusoleil.com, 10:30am-7pm Mon.-Fri., 9am-7pm Sat.). Their leafy, outdoor "rainforest room" is a perfect setting for a massage, and they offer an array of different water rooms and bath treatments. **The Lamar Everyday Spa** (5115 N. Scottsdale Rd., 480/945-7066, www.thelamar.com, 10am-7pm Sun.-Thurs., 9am-7pm Fri.-Sat.) offers massages, facials, pools and saunas, and all the other soothing treatments in a friendly, coed atmosphere that was voted one of the valley's best places for a romantic date. The prices here are generally a bit lower than those of the resort spas.

ACCOMMODATIONS

In Scottsdale, world-class accommodations and pampering are available to a great degree, but only to those who have the resources to buy them; those who don't, however, can still find a middle ground here, and there are even a few places for the budget-minded traveler. If you don't mind braving the heat, summer prices at the top resorts and getaways dip down into the real world.

$50-100

The **Motel 6 Scottsdale** (6848 E. Camelback Rd., 480/946-2280, www.motel6.com, $62-70) is located right downtown and close to everything; it features a pool ringed by palm trees and a breakfast place where it's hard to get a table on the weekends. The **Comfort Suites** (3275 Drinkwater Blvd., 480/946-1111, www. comfortinn.com, $64-70) is also centrally located and one of the few options here for the budget-minded traveler looking for something clean, basic, and comfortable.

$100-250

The **3 Palms** (7707 E. McDowell Rd., 800/450-6071, www.scottsdale-resort-hotels. com, $82-170) is one of the middle-brow resort-style accommodations in Scottsdale, offering most of the comforts and style of the more expensive places with just a slightly less ritzy sheen. This boutique hotel has cool contemporary interior design in all the rooms, and a large pool area perfect for lounging in the hot sun while sipping drinks. Another relatively affordable place is the **Chaparral Suites Resort** (5001 N. Scottsdale Rd., 480/949-1414, www. chaparralsuites.com, $99-199), which has comfortable rooms and a lush central courtyard and pool area. The **Hotel Indigo** (4415 N. Civic Center Plaza, 480/941-9400, www.scott-sdalehiphotel.com, $125-200) is an upscale boutique hotel with tasteful rooms featuring big comfortable beds and retro-chic couches. The pool area and the outdoor lounge is a perfect place to gather for drinks around the fire. Built up over many decades from the Paradise Valley studio of famed valley artist Alonzo "Lon" Megargee, the **Hermosa Inn** (5532 N. Palo Cristi, 602/955-8614, www.hermosainn. com, $170-707) is one of the most enchanting places to stay in Arizona. With its 34 detailed, high-rustic hacienda-style rooms, its gorgeous pool and myriad hidden outdoor spaces, and surrounding desert scenery, it's truly a desert original. The 1930s-era Arizona details, reflecting Megargee's time, add to the romance and enchantment that pervade here.

Over $250

The **FireSky Resort & Spa** (4925 N. Scottsdale Rd., 480/945-7666, www.fireskyresort.com, $275-330) is a sumptuous, gardenlike place downtown with all kinds of secluded and secret spots—lagoons and hot tubs and cozy cabanas—leather chairs and flat-screen TVs in the rooms, and a full-service spa. The **Fairmont Scottsdale Princess** (7575 E. Princess Dr., 480/585-4848, www.fairmont.com/scotts-dale, $450-3,500) is a five-diamond resort in downtown Scottsdale with unbelievably comfortable and richly decorated rooms, suites, and casitas, as well as golf courses, three restaurants, and one of the top spas in the nation. **The Boulders Resort and Golden Door Spa** (34631 N. Tom Darlington Dr., Carefree, 480/488-9009, www.theboulders.com, $150-400), out in the wild desert of Carefree, has been named America's top spa more than a dozen times. This unique desert property offers gorgeous suites, casitas, villas, and haciendas in a secluded setting outside of the city. It provides far and above the norm in comfort, style, and recreation. The spectacular **◖ Sanctuary Camelback Mountain Resort and Spa** (5700 E. McDonald Dr., Paradise Valley, 480/607-2326, www.sanctuaryoncamelback.com) is on 53 acres of preserved and manicured desert in Paradise Valley, with elegant, private casitas tucked among the rocks, all watched over by the jagged dry mountain and with the valley spread out below. Inside the casitas, with their wood and limestone interiors, you'll find huge beds and deep tubs, and the spa and exercise regime will have you rejuvenated in no time, if lounging by the pool in your own private cabana doesn't do the trick. Voted by Condé Nast readers as the best resort in the nation, the Sanctuary is a prime and triumphant example of all a desert resort can be. The **◖ Hotel Valley Ho** (6850 E. Main St., 480/248-2000, www.hotelvalleyho.com, $199-736) recalls the days of the mid-20th-century high-end hipster style, with a Trader Vic's on-site and rooms decorated like Frank Sinatra's pad in *The Tender Trap*. **Hotel Theodore** (7353 E. Indian School Rd., 480/648-2513, www.hoteltheodore.com, $295-495) is a playpen for the rich and famous, or just the rich and glamorous, with rooms like art installations and courtyards behind its high city walls that hold manicured jungles and oasis hideaways; service, food, and spa treatments here match the world's top destinations. You definitely get what you pay for. **The Phoenician** (6000 E. Camelback Rd., 480/941-8200, www.thephoenician.com, $365-775), along the Camelback Corridor, has an excellent golf course, high-end style, and a Center for Well-Being. The **Camelback Inn** (5402 E. Lincoln Dr., 480/596-7040, $375-425) has well-appointed guestrooms with French doors that open onto a private patio. The long pool, with luxurious lounging areas, looks out over unspoiled desert scenery, and the spa offers relaxation and balance in a secluded, peaceful setting. The **Four Seasons Resort Scottsdale at Troon North** (10600 E. Crescent Moon Dr., 480/515-5700, www.fourseasons.com/scottsdale, $425-500), just below jagged Pinnacle Peak, is a stunning resort that takes full advantage of its desert setting, with casitas set among the creosote and saguaros. The whole place has a white-washed hacienda look, with exposed vigas, iron-work touches, and fireplaces. Many of the rooms have balconies that look out over the desert, and the pool area is spectacular and watched over by the landmark peak. **The Westin Kierland Resort & Spa** (902 E. Greenway Pkwy., 480/624-1000, www.kierlandresort.com, $430-470) makes a great choice for families looking for different resort experiences: golf, spa treatments, and a super-fun water slide, the holy trinity of modern family happiness.

Cave Creek

Not surprisingly, this mid- to high-end burg has not a few bed-and-breakfasts. The **Spur Cross Bed & Breakfast** (38555 N. School House Rd., Cave Creek, 480/473-1038, www.spurcrossbnb.com, $139-400) rents four nice rooms with outside entrances and has a hot tub and wireless Internet.

FOOD

Scottsdale has many of the valley's poshest restaurants, and the scene is always changing and evolving. You'll find enough variety here to make your head and your palate spin. It's not all high-toned and intimidating, though; most of the best restaurants here are serious about food and design and service, but they don't take themselves too seriously. Many of Scottsdale's restaurants serve late-night menus and have busy bars as well as packed dining rooms. Reservations are always a good idea.

Brunch

The Hangover (4312 N. Brown Ave., 480/425-0111, www.mickeyshangover.com, 4pm-2am Mon.-Wed., 4pm-3am Thurs., 4pm-4am Fri., 10am-4am Sat., 10am-3pm brunch Sat.-Sun., $5-13) is a thrift store-chic clubhouse downtown where you'll always hear Bob Marley on the stereo and where you can order a jug of Mad Dog 20/20 ($10) and put your feet up on the coffee table. If you're not a happy and healthy dissipater (and especially if you are), try the brunch on weekends. It serves tasty and creative entrées based on the classic brunch dishes and concocts some of the valley's best mimosas and Bloody Marys.

American

Cowboy Ciao (7133 E. Stetson Dr., 480/946-3111, www.cowboyciao.com, 11:30am-2:30pm daily, 5pm-10pm Sun.-Thurs., 5pm-11pm Fri.-Sat., $10-32), a standout among Scottsdale's posh eateries, relishes fusions, mixing Italian motifs with cowboy-camp and Old West wood and metal, and serving strange, enticing dishes like elk strip loin and mushroom pan fry. Its take on the grilled cheese, adding brie and pickled tomatoes, is worth the trip itself. The salads and soups here are also particularly good.

AZ 88 (7353 Scottsdale Mall, 480/994-5576, www.az88.com, 11:30am-12:30am

Mon.-Fri., 5pm-12:30am Sat.-Sun., $7.50-16.50) is an ultracool lounge and restaurant with delicious, simple dishes like hamburgers and chicken sandwiches, DJs spinning many nights, and consistently interesting art on the walls, changed out regularly. Free Wi-Fi daily. **Rancho Pinot** (6300 N. Scottsdale Rd. #101, 480/367-8030, www.ranchopinot.com, 5:30pm-9:30pm Mon.-Sat. in winter, 5:30pm-9pm Mon.-Sat. in summer, lunch starting in Oct. 11:30am-2pm Mon.-Fri.) is a leading light of the slow food movement in the valley, serving a seasonally based, always today-fresh menu of truly feel-good food. The "salad-y" plates include locally and regionally grown vegetables and fruits and some seafood, while the "Savory Plates" are topped with lamb ribs, grilled quail, and stuffed squash blossoms—Arizona-bred eating at its best. They also have a top-notch wine and cheese selection. The talented, brave chefs at **Posh** (7167 E. Rancho Vista Dr., 480/663-7674, www.poshscottsdale.com, 5pm-close Tues.-Sat., $15-30), a sleek urban space downtown, practice "improvisational cuisine," and they do so without a net. This place is for the most adventurous and daring foodies out there. The dishes are seasonally based, and are typically intricate and wonderful. They offer a four- to seven-course tasting menu ($45-110) if you want to truly find out what they do here. ❰**Lon's at the Hermosa** (5532 N. Palo Cristi Rd., 602/955-7878, www.lons.com, breakfast 7am-10am, lunch 11:30am-2pm, dinner 5:30pm-10pm daily, brunch 10am-2pm Sat.-Sun.) has "comfort cuisine" carefully prepared with regional flair and ingredients, including many grown in the organic gardens on the grounds of this boutique resort, which was built out of the original desert studio of renowned valley artist Lon Megargee. The desert hideaway atmosphere enhances the spectacular New American cuisine. The tortilla soup is a classic, and you really must try the "truffle-scented" macaroni and cheese.

Tucked into the Civic Center Plaza, **The Orange Table** (7373 E. Scottsdale Mall, 480/424-6819, www.scottsdalebreakfast.com, 7am-3pm daily, $6-14) offers outstanding variations on American café food, offering a large menu for breakfast, lunch, and dinner, and their own take on burgers, sandwiches, salads, and pancakes. The **Sugar Bowl** (4005 N. Scottsdale Rd., 480/946-0051, www.sugarbowlscottsdale.com, 11am-10pm Sun.-Thurs., 11am-midnight Fri.-Sat., $5.25-10.50) has been a Scottsdale institution since it opened in 1958, serving delicious and filling sandwiches, soups, chili, burgers and dogs, and decadent ice cream treats in a family atmosphere. Bil Keane, who lived in nearby Paradise Valley, featured the Sugar Bowl several times in his famous "Family Circus" cartoon.

Lo-Lo's Chicken & Waffles (2765 N. Scottsdale Rd., 480/945-1920, www.loloschickenandwaffles.com, 9am-7pm Mon.-Thurs., 9am-midnight Fri., 9am-9pm Sat., 9am-4pm Sun., $5-13), with its original location in central Phoenix, is a soul-food joint that serves up crispy Southern-fried chicken and big waffles, macaroni and cheese, greens, and other Southern favorites.

Italian

Marcellino Ristorante (7114 E. Stetson Dr., 480/990-9500, www.marcellinoristorante.com, lunch 11:30am-3:30pm daily, dinner 5pm-10pm Mon.-Thurs., 5pm-11pm Fri.-Sat., 5pm-9pm Sun., bar 11:30am-close daily, $19.95-38.95) offers the very best in upscale, authentic Italian food, with the wine list to match. The large selection of handmade pasta creations and the romantic Old World elegance here make this one of the best Italian restaurants in the valley.

Steaks and Chops

Reata Pass Steakhouse (27500 N. Alma School Pkwy., 480/585-7277, www.reatapass.com, 11am-9pm Tues.-Thurs., 11am-11pm Fri.-Sat., noon-9pm Sun., $6.95-23.95) is another of Arizona's cowboy-style steak houses, with rustic Old West interiors and picnic tables holding beans, corn, ribs, and steaks; these places are always fun, especially for kids. On the site of what used to be a stagecoach stop in the McDowell Mountains, Reata Pass bills itself as the most authentic of the bunch. A more elegant but still comfortably casual protein-rich meal can be had at valley favorite **Don & Charlie's** (7501 E. Camelback Rd., 480/990-0900, www.azeats.com/DonAndCharlies/default.htm, 5pm-9:30pm Tues.-Sat., 5pm-9pm Sun., $10.95-44.95), a Chicago-style, old-school steak house with great prime rib and even better ribs. Pâté and crackers are served when you sit down, and you'll be mesmerized away from the menu by all the unmatched sports memorabilia covering the walls.

Southwestern and Mexican

Downtown's **Old Town Tortilla Factory** (6910 E. Main St., 480/945-4567, www.old-towntortillafactory.com, 5pm-9pm Sun.-Thurs., 5pm-10pm Fri.-Sat., $13.99-32.99) has an enchanting patio and serves gourmet Southwestern-style creations with pork, fish, chicken, shrimp, and beef. The tortillas are made on-site, come in several different flavors, and are served hot and fresh. The **Tequilaria** inside has shelves of tequila and makes great margaritas. For Southwestern food with a New Mexican flair, try **Carlsbad Tavern and Restaurant** (3313 N. Hayden Rd., 480/970-8164, www.carlsbadtavern.com, 11am-2am daily, $9.60-23.50), where green chilies take over the menu and bats take over the decor. Carlsbad serves hamburgers and sandwiches as well as New Mexican-style dishes. The Mexican food at **Dos Gringos** (4209 N. Craftsman Ct., 480/423-3800, www.dosgringosaz.com, 11am-2am daily, $3-11) downtown is delicious and filling, but it's the patio-party atmosphere that draws daytime drinkers here. The sunny rooftop patio, the chips and salsa and burritos, the buckets of Corona on the tables—how can you resist?

Don't leave Cave Creek without stopping for lunch or dinner at ◖ **El Encanto** (6248 E. Cave Creek Rd., 480/488-1752, www.elencantorestaurant.com, 11am-10pm daily, $7-17), serving what is perhaps the valley's best Mexican food from comfortable booths that look out on a Spanish-style enclosed courtyard with a pond, atop which elegant swans float

Dos Gringos

© TIM HULL

lazily. Try the prickly-pear margarita—sweet and delicious with a perfect kick.

Seafood

The **Salt Cellar** (550 N. Hayden Rd., 480/947-1963, www.saltcellarrestaurant.com, 5pm-11pm Mon.-Thurs., 5pm-midnight Fri.-Sat., $22.95-43.95), which actually feels like it's in a cellar, though a very nice one, serves the freshest, best-prepared, top-shelf but not pretentious seafood in the valley. You can even get three pounds of live Maine lobster ($70) if you so desire. The **Wildfish Seafood Grille** (7135 E. Camelback Rd., 480/994-4040, www.wildfishseafoodgrille.com, 4pm-close daily, $13-40) is a sophisticated urban seafood-and-steak restaurant that serves inventive entrées and has a fun Scottsdale-chic bar. Spend some time at the fresh oyster bar, or have a gulf shrimp cocktail with your other cocktail.

Japanese

With its smooth pale-wood surfaces and contemporary, upscale setting, **Roka Akor** (7299

N. Scottsdale Rd., 480/306-8800, www.rokaa-kor.com, lunch 11:30am-2:30pm Mon.-Fri., dinner 5pm-10pm Sun.-Thurs., 5pm-11pm Fri.-Sat., lunch $6-13.50, dinner $5-25) is the top destination for valley sushi lovers. They serve delectable skewers and meats grilled on roba-tayaki, authentic Japanese charcoal grills, and a full menu of sushi, sashimi and rolls, tempura, and specialty cocktails. **Sushi on Shea** (7000 E. Shea Blvd. #1510, 480/483-7799, www.sushionshea.com, 11am-10pm Mon.-Sat., 3pm-9pm Sun., $8-35) serves excellent sushi at affordable prices and has hypnotizing fish tanks throughout.

INFORMATION

While you're downtown, stop by the **Scottsdale Convention & Visitors Bureau** (4343 N. Scottsdale Rd., Ste. #170, 800/782-1117, www.scottsdalecvb.com) at the Galleria Corporate Center on the corner of Drinkwater Boulevard and Stetson Drive for all the Scottsdale-related information and literature you'll ever want. Parking is available either on the street or in the parking structure east of the entrance.

GETTING THERE AND AROUND

The best way to get from Phoenix to Scottsdale is to take one of the surface streets east from downtown; that way you'll get to see more of the ground-level city instead of breezing past everything on the freeways. If you take Camelback Road east from downtown Phoenix, you'll run right into downtown Scottsdale. If you're heading from Scottsdale to Tempe, take Scottsdale Road south, and you'll run right into the college town.

Valley Metro (602/253-5000, www.valleymetro.org), the valley's public transportation authority, provides bus service ($2 per ride) throughout the area, including Glendale, Scottsdale, Tempe, and Mesa.

Each downtown district in Scottsdale runs into the next and is easy to walk to, and there's a **free trolley** (11am-6pm daily, Thurs. evenings until 9pm, runs every 15 minutes) that will take you all around the downtown area if you don't like to walk.

© TIM HULL

Scottsdale's free trolley provides transportation all over the downtown area.

Around the Valley of the Sun

On the far eastern edge of the spreading cityscape, the desert holds a strong line in the Tonto National Forest. In this cactus, creosote, and mesquite wilderness, dashed with fallen slabs and boulders covered in faded-green dry lichen, you will experience the real Central Arizona outback, a rugged and storied stretch of the upper Sonoran Desert. If you have an SUV or a similarly high vehicle (or even, most of the time, a regular car), don't hesitate to drive the Apache Trail (State Route 88), a mostly dirt route that takes you deep into the desert, past several man-made lakes to one of the state's huge reclamation-era dams. You can then loop around to U.S. Highway 60, where you'll cruise through several old mining towns and past the jagged Pinal Mountains before heading back into the city. Or detour north for about 40 miles on U.S. Highway 60 from Globe to get a jaw-dropping look at Salt River Canyon. All along the way there are pull-offs and stops, trailheads, and historic markers. You can tour these eastern and northeastern reaches of the valley in one long day, unless you want to hike, then you'll need to mount a separate expedition.

If you're headed to Southern Arizona from the valley along I-10, veer off the main route for a few hours and visit the mysterious Casa Grande, the largest remaining Hohokam ruin. Or stop at Picacho Peak State Park just off the interstate to hike along a ragged rock spine towering over the desert.

About 60 miles northwest of the city on U.S. Highway 60 you'll find the old mining town of Wickenburg, which still has a bit of Old West charm. Continue north on U.S. Highway 89 for a twisting and scenic mostly two-lane drive through the chaparral and scrub midlands, through a lush ranching region, and on up to the pine forests of Prescott. And if you're taking the quick route to the northland along I-17,

consider stopping at Arcosanti, an ongoing experiment in architecture and living.

THE SUPERSTITION MOUNTAINS

These rugged desert mountains rise to about 5,000 feet off the desert floor and are the main component of the 160,000-acre **Superstition Wilderness Area** in the Tonto National Forest. The Superstitions pale in comparison to other Arizona mountains both in elevation and diversity, but they are an ideal place to get an introduction to the Sonoran Desert and spend some time in a wilderness close to the city. The trails are rocky, and some are quite worn in places; the landscape is rough, gray-green desert, rugged and hot and crowded with mobs of saguaro reaching into the always clear blue and huge sky, and carpeted with creosote, brittlebush, prickly pear, and all the other desert familiars. In February and March, especially after a winter of plentiful rainfall, and from April through June, large patches of the desert pop open with purple, red, yellow, and blue—everything that was waiting dormant explodes into bloom. This is the best time to be in the Superstitions. Don't go in the deep summer.

It is possible to get very far away from the city and everything else by going far into the wilderness area. Most, however, stick to the well-trod but still impressive sights along the popular **Peralta Trail,** a moderately difficult, approximately 6-mile round-trip hike that leads to a saddle with a fine view of Weavers Needle, a fantastically eroded butte. From Phoenix take U.S. Highway 60 east through Gold Canyon, then turn east on Peralta Road and drive about 8 miles to the trailhead for the Peralta and the **Dutchman's Trail,** on which you can take an 18-mile journey through the wilderness area. Expect to pay a $6 per vehicle user fee in the Tonto. For more on hiking in the Superstitions, check out the Tonto National Forest's trail

© ANTON FOLTIN/123RF.COM

Superstition Wilderness Area

guide at www.fs.fed.us/r3/tonto. The folks at **Superstition Search and Rescue** (480/620-0299, www.superstition-sar.org) keep an excellent website with trail descriptions, maps, and information on desert hiking safety.

Lost Dutchman State Park

A stop at small **Lost Dutchman State Park** (6109 N. Apache Trail, 480/982-4485, www.azstateparks.com/Parks/lodu/index.html, sunrise-10pm daily, $7 per vehicle) at the base of the Superstitions is a good way for families and day hikers to see the range and to spend some time walking around the desert on relatively easy trails. The park has 70 campsites ($15, no hookups) with showers, as well as tables and grills perfect for picnics. The **Treasure Loop Trail** is an easy way to see the park and get an idea of what the desert is like at about 2,000 feet. It's 2.4 miles round-trip, moderate and well marked, starting and beginning at either picnic area. Using the **Siphon Draw Trail,** you can climb up to

about 5,000 feet, first to a high overlook spot called the Flatiron and then on to the top of Superstition Peak, a hard 5-mile round-trip hike that rewards the tough with some striking desert views.

Superstition Mountain Museum

The small **Superstition Mountain Museum** (4087 N. Apache Trail, 480/983-4888, www.superstitionmountainmuseum.org, 9am-4pm daily, $5), at the beginning of the Apache Trail just outside of Apache Junction, makes for an interesting stop if you have an extra half hour to an hour. The displays on local mining legends, especially the infamous whopper about the **Lost Dutchman Mine** (which people still hunt for today, believing that 1890s prospector and "Dutchman" Jacob Waltz died before revealing the route to the world's richest gold mine somewhere deep in the Superstitions), and other Old West history lessons will enhance and contextualize the backcountry drive you're about to take.

Goldfield

Heading out of Apache Junction, the Apache Trail passes the Old West-show tourist trap **Goldfield** (4650 N. Mammoth Mine Rd., 480/983-0333, www.goldfieldghosttown.com, 10am-5pm daily), a rebuilt 1890s town on the site of what used to be a mining camp with about 5,000 people, settled after gold was discovered in the Superstitions and depopulated soon after the mining stopped. It's a kind of a mining-camp theme park now, with a working narrow-gauge railroad, theme shops along a boardwalk main street, a couple of cowboy-style restaurants, a saloon, a mine tour, gold panning, staged gunfights, and Jeep tours into the Superstitions. Kids will likely enjoy this attraction; everybody else should move on down the trail.

◖ THE APACHE TRAIL AND VICINITY

A tour of the Apache Trail (Route 88) and the Old West Highway (U.S. 60), a 120-mile round-trip loop along the wild edges of the sprawl-choked valley, begins just outside Apache Junction and eventually winds around the Superstition Mountains to Roosevelt Dam, then on through the Pinal Mountains and a few old mining towns.

The route follows in places the course of the Salt River, the damming of which first made all that sprawl possible. But it also created several desert lakes, each improbably beautiful and surrounded by an arid army of saguaros peering down from jagged-rock cliffs into the miragelike waters, wondering what all the fuss is about. The Apache Trail itself came about as a result of the dam, built as it was to cart materials and workers to and from the great construction site, though the route had been regularly traversed by native inhabitants long before the reclamation project began.

The best place to eat and get gas is at Globe, at the trail's end. However, if you find yourself in a bind, there's a good, fun restaurant at Tortilla Flat, plus restaurants and gas at each of the marinas along the route. Make sure you bring water with you and check your tires and fluids before you go.

Apache Junction, a sprawling suburb east of Phoenix at the base of the Superstition Mountains, marks the beginning of the Apache Trail from the west, and it ends at Tonto National Monument, 49 miles from Apache Junction and just outside of Globe. To reach Apache Junction from downtown Phoenix, go 40 miles east on U.S. Highway 60, a drive of about an hour. The Apache Trail, which is well marked, is Route 88, which is right off of U.S. 60.

Needle Vista to Tortilla Flat

The wild portion of the Apache Trail really gets started about 8 miles outside of Apache Junction at **Needle Vista,** which provides a sweeping view of the rough country and good look at Weaver's Needle, a distinctive rock formation. There are bathrooms here. Continuing east on the paved road, you next come to **Canyon Lake,** about 12 miles from Apache Junction. The smallest of the Salt River Project lakes, and the first you come to along the trail

© TIM HULL

along the Apache Trail

from Phoenix, Canyon Lake has 950 surface acres and 28 miles of shoreline. The headquarters here is the **Canyon Lake Marina and Campground** (16802 NE Hwy. 88, 480/288-9233, www.canyonlakemarina.com), which has a restaurant and campground with sites for tents and RVs with hookups, tables, grills, fire rings, and showers ($30 for waterfront campsite, 2 tents per site, 6 people, 1 vehicle; $45 for pull-through RV site with hookups; $20 each for additional vehicles). In normal times you're allowed to ride personal watercraft and water ski on Canyon Lake, and there's even an excursion steamboat and dinner cruise.

About five more miles east and you're at the old **Superstition Restaurant and Saloon** (20909 E. Apache Trail, 480/984-1776, 11am-9pm Mon.-Fri., 9am-5pm Sat.-Sun. June-Sept., 9am-6pm daily Oct.-May, $5-15) at **Tortilla Flat**, which was once a stage stop and is now a . . . well, a stage stop—only now its burgers, homemade chili, Mexican food, and beers and saddle-topped barstools are popular with Harley riders, who haunt the trail in large numbers on

the weekends. This strange, charming little place, restored from the original but still romantically rustic, is named after a butte nearby that looks a bit like stacked tortillas.

Apache Lake

Continuing on the trail another five miles east, a saguaro and scrub forest spreads out on either side, boulders strewn about and rising from the earth, the Superstitions looming like the petrified rock remains of giant jagged teeth; then the route descends precipitously just before it turns to dirt and washboards near spectacular Fish Creek Canyon, where you'll probably want to stop and take a few photos. Then it's on to the next of the desert lakes, Apache Lake, where the **Apache Lake Marina and Resort** (Rte. 88, 928/467-2511, www.apachelake.com) rents clean and basic lakeside rooms at the **Apache Lake Motel** ($90-105), including suites with kitchenettes. The 17-mile-long lake is popular with Phoenicians who enjoy water skiing, riding personal watercraft, and fishing for small- and largemouth bass.

© TIM HULL

Tortilla Flat

PHOENIX

© TIM HULL

Roosevelt Dam

Roosevelt Dam and Roosevelt Lake

After Apache Lake, the dirt trail follows a narrow band of river below the dam, then climbs up a bit and that sheer rock wall holding back the river comes into sight, about five miles from the last lake. You can stop here and read some plaques about the dam and look at it from a promontory. Then the road passes a large bridge over the dam and the highway heading north to Payson and the Rim Country. The largest of the Salt River Lakes with a peak fill of 22,000 surface acres, Roosevelt Lake can be accessed through the **Roosevelt Lake Marina** (Rte. 88, 928/467-2245, www.rlmaz.com/rlmaz.html, $6 day use, $4 boat fee, $10 camping, first-come, first-served). There are four motels near the lake and an RV park. You can rent a boat here, skid around on personal watercraft, or explore hidden coves and fishing spots.

Tonto National Monument

Pass Roosevelt Lake and turn at the sign to get to **Tonto National Monument** (8am-5pm daily, $3), a picturesque cliffside ruin once inhabited by the Salado people from about 1150 to 1450. It's so well preserved it appears as if—from far away, at least—people could still live here in the cool shade of a natural rock alcove high above the saguaro and cholla. The paved **Lower Ruin** trail is about a mile round trip, most of it straight up, and is open to the public. The visitors center below the ruin has some interesting artifacts of the Salado, and a good bit of information on this often-overlooked tribe. Tonto is about 49 miles from Apache Junction and marks the end of the Apache Trail from the west and its beginning from the east.

Globe and Superior

Follow Route 88 through several old Central Arizona mining towns, and then head back west on a scenic stretch of U.S. Highway 60 called the Old West Highway. Both Globe and Superior, in the shadow of the rocky Pinal Mountains, have quaint old downtowns that have yet to be discovered by hippies and

© TIM HULL

the ruins of a Salado cliffhouse at Tonto National Monument

artists and shop owners and shoppers—sort of like Bisbee before the craft boom. They are mostly boarded up now but seem ripe for discovery, especially Superior, which has a few really cool but disused buildings (long ago fancy hotels and shops) that could be expensively hipped up for the ever-growing retro-loving crowd.

In Globe, the kids will have fun climbing around the largely rebuilt Hohokam and Salado ruins at **Besh-Ba-Gowah Archaeological Park** (1324 Jess Hayes Rd., 928/425-0320, 9am-5pm daily, $3 adults, children under 11 free). Unlike most ruins in Arizona, these modest reconstructed pit houses and courtyards are open for scrambling and exploring, and there's a small but interesting museum with exhibits on the lifestyles of those long-lost tribes.

If you're feeling hungry, try the Mexican food at **Guayo's on the Trail** (14249 S. Hwy. 188, Globe, 928/425-9969, 10:30am-9pm Mon. and Wed.-Sat., 10:30am-8:30pm Sun., $6-9), which serves up outstanding traditional Mexican food based on old family recipes. This casual place has been around since 1938, and it's very popular with Apache Trail travelers, especially the motorcycle crowd.

Salt River Canyon

Take a detour north on Route 77 (which doubles as U.S. 60 for this stretch) from Globe along the edge of the Apache Mountains for about 40 miles to spectacular **Salt River Canyon,** one of the more impressive roadside natural wonders in a state chock-full of them. Once used as a hideout by the Apache during the Indian wars, this 2,000-foot-deep jagged desert gorge is where the Salt River runs free and wild. There's a parking area before the bridge where you can learn about the canyon and take pictures, and easy paved trails lead down to the flowing river. If you've got a four-wheel drive, you can head off on a riverside Jeep trail and explore the canyon in more depth. The traffic along Route 77 near the canyon bridge can get heavy and frustrating, especially on the weekends.

© TIM HULL

downtown Globe, ready to be rediscovered

Boyce Thompson Arboretum State Park

A stroll around the unique **Boyce Thompson Arboretum** (37615 U.S. Hwy. 60, 520/689-2811, www.ag.arizona.edu/bta/location.html, 8am-5pm daily Sept.-Apr., 6am-3pm daily May-Aug., $7.50 adults, $3 children 5-12) is the perfect capstone to an Apache Trail tour. Just three miles west of Superior along U.S. Highway 60, the arboretum was developed in the early 20th century by wealthy do-gooder and mining magnate Col. William Boyce Thompson. He built his own dreamland here, a kind of desert-country Hearst Castle, and endeavored to grow several different ecosystems on his property. Here you can walk on well-trod and easy paths leading through otherworldly cactus gardens, across a cottonwood-covered stream, along the shores of a desert lake, and even through an Australian eucalyptus forest, all surrounded by the huge, telltale boulder-mountains of the Central Arizona outback. This is not recommended in summer.

West to Phoenix

Phoenix sits about 60 miles west of the arboretum via U.S. 60, a scenic stretch that passes the edge of the Superstition Mountains and passes through Florence Junction and Gold Canyon. There's not much to look at along the route back to Phoenix save for awesome desert scenery. U.S. 60 becomes the Superstition Freeway once you're back in the city.

FROM PHOENIX TO TUCSON

The small towns southeast of the metro area are a snapshot of rural America in a state of flux, adapting to the city's spread and trying to hold on to some kind of identity as commuters move in and take over. The southeast, known to most Arizonans as the area you have to drive through to get from Phoenix to Tucson, was once dedicated to agriculture, though these days many of those fields are covered not with cotton but with stuccoed homes and RV parks. The area is prone to blowing dust storms, especially during the summer rainy season.

◖ Casa Grande Ruins National Monument

An ancient and fragile molded-mud apartment building just outside of the old farming town of Coolidge, **Casa Grande Ruins National Monument** (1100 W. Ruins Dr., 520/723-3172, www.nps.gov/cagr, 9am-5pm daily, $5 adults, children under 15 free) is all that remains of one of the largest prehistoric structures ever built in North America. It's an easy 10- to 15-minute detour off I-10 (Exit 211 halfway between Phoenix and Tucson—watch for signs).

There are still a lot of unanswered questions about how and why Casa Grande grew to dominate the Salt River Valley and beyond at its peak in about 1350, and even more questions about what caused its catastrophic decline around 1450. It's an amazing sight to see nonetheless—almost like a huge, human-sized sand castle covered by a towering metal roof to keep out the elements. The monument's excellent museum interprets and explains what we do know about the Hohokam, those ancient arid-land agriculturists who inspired the valley's modern-day settlers to attempt to turn the desert into an Eden.

Picacho Peak State Park

Small **Picacho Peak State Park** (just off I-10, Exit 219, 520/466-3183, www.azstateparks. com/parks/pipe/index.html, 5am-10pm daily, trails close at sunset), about 40 miles north of Tucson and 60 miles south of Phoenix, sits in the shadow of a dramatic 1,500-foot rock upcropping in the middle of an otherwise mostly flat desert plain. **Picacho Peak** has always been a natural landmark in this part of the state, and nearby, in 1862, soldiers fought Arizona's only Civil War battle, an event reenacted at the park every year. There are several good trails that lead up and along the rough spine of the peak; the area is particularly popular in spring, when the bajada stretching out from the cliffsides is often carpeted with multicolored wildflowers. Try the two-mile round-trip **Hunter Trail,** a rather difficult and steep route to the top that

© TIM HULL

Casa Grande Ruins National Monument

begins on the north side and requires negotiation of steel cables anchored into the rock in some places. The three-mile round-trip **Sunset Vista Trail** is a bit easier but longer, starting on the south side and heading to the top. Either way, the views from the top are amazing and well worth the climb.

WICKENBURG

This old mining town northwest of the valley on U.S. Highway 60 still has a bit of Old West charm and makes for a fun day trip from Phoenix or a couple of hours' detour during a drive north. If you're headed to Prescott from Phoenix, consider taking the back way along U.S. 60 through Wickenburg, then on to Route 89 north, cruising along a twisting rural two-lane through a sleepy but scenic mining and ranching region that most visitors miss.

Sights

Fans of Western art will want to spend an hour or so at the **Desert Caballeros Western Museum** (1 N. Frontier St., 928/684-2272, www.westernmuseum.org. 10am-5pm Mon.-Sat., noon-4pm Sun., closed Mon. June-Aug., $7.50), a very decent regional art museum that has some unique exhibits on life in the Old West.

Hikers and birders shouldn't miss the beautiful riparian area at the **Hassayampa River Preserve** (7am-11am Fri.-Sun. in summer, 8am-5pm Wed.-Sun. in winter, $5), run by the Nature Conservancy, where you can walk along the creek beneath cottonwoods and willows and watch for all manner of water-loving birds darting among the bushes.

Food

A good place to stop for lunch in Wickenburg is **Anita's Cocina** (57 N. Valentine Dr., 928/684-5777, www.azod.com/webs/anita, 8am-9pm Mon.-Fri., 7am-9pm Sat.-Sun., $4-9), a popular place with locals where they serve delicious and inexpensive Mexican favorites in a casual atmosphere.

NORTH ON I-17

If you've got a little time to spare during a drive north to Prescott, Sedona, or Flagstaff along I-17, stop by C **Rock Springs Café** (35769 S. Old Black Canyon Hwy., I-17 Exit 242, 623/374-5794, www.rockspringscafe.com, 7am-9pm Sun.-Thurs., 7am-10pm, Fri.-Sat.), an old cowboy-style saloon, historic general store, soda fountain, and café that serves locally famous hamburgers, steaks, barbecue, and homemade pies that you'll want to send home in a refrigerated crate. The whole place has a kind of dark, wood-and-stone air of historic authenticity, and it's been the site of one dusty travelers' wayside or another since the late 19th century. On the first Saturday of the month October-June Rock Springs Café puts on a **Hogs 'n Heat Barbecue and Nut Fry,** featuring "mountain oysters" from local cattle, live country music, and plenty of draft beer.

A bit farther north on I-17, the **Agua Fria National Monument** (623/580-5500, www.blm.gov/az/st/en/prog/blm_special_areas/natmon/afria.html, free), offers a relatively easy hike through a lush riparian area, which includes access to a petroglyph site. The trailhead is about 40 miles north of downtown Phoenix via I-17. Get off the interstate at Exit 256, Badger Springs, and follow the dirt road for about a mile east to the parking area at the trailhead. The trail runs through Badger Springs Wash, which you may find to be filled with a bit of water outside of deep summer, and follows the wash for about two miles one way.

A little farther north, as the ever-reaching imprint of the valley's insatiable growth begins to disappear and the midland desert scrublands open up wide, veer off at the Cordes Junction exit (Exit 262) and follow the signs to take a tour of the fascinating "urban laboratory" being built by architect and artist Paolo Soleri and his followers at **Arcosanti** (928/632-7135, www.arcosanti.

org, 10am-4pm daily, $10). It looks a bit like the buildings on Luke Skywalker's home planet of Tatooine, and the sweeping high-desert locale adds to its evocative otherworldliness. The approximately one-hour tour takes you through the settlement, as a guide explains the history and philosophy of the project. There's a small café and a gift shop where you can buy one of the world-famous handmade bells that support this ongoing experiment in "Arcology"—an architectural theory that seeks to lessen our imprint on the earth by bringing together architecture and ecology.

TUCSON AND SOUTHERN ARIZONA

The Sonoran Desert is a deceptive landscape. The soft greens and yellows can appear monotonous, yet stop and look closely and they reveal staggering variety. It rains here only rarely, yet there is a season, popularly called the monsoon season but more accurately termed the summer rainy season, when this so-called arid land is positively lush. Once a year, in the spring,

© TIM HULL

HIGHLIGHTS

LOOK FOR ◖ TO FIND RECOMMENDED SIGHTS, ACTIVITIES, DINING, AND LODGING.

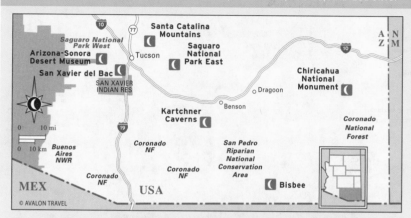

© AVALON TRAVEL

◖ **Arizona-Sonora Desert Museum:** See the region's wonders up close—mountain lions, wolves, bighorn sheep, and other rare Sonoran natives (page 123).

◖ **Saguaro National Park East:** Drive, walk, or ride a bike through the Sonoran Desert's unique saguaro forests in the eastern section of the famed national park, the older and larger of the park's two sections (page 127).

◖ **Santa Catalina Mountains:** Drive to the top of a sky-island peak and cool off in the high green forests (page 130).

◖ **San Xavier del Bac:** See Arizona's answer

to the Sistine Chapel, a white jewel of a mission on the desert plain (page 134).

◖ **Kartchner Caverns:** Enter an otherworldly cave still being formed by slowly dripping water (page 189).

◖ **Bisbee:** Explore an old mining boomtown, now an enclave for artists and antique shops (page 192).

◖ **Chiricahua National Monument:** Marvel at the "Land of Standing Up Rocks," a forest of hoodoos and twisted rock high in the evergreen mountains (page 197).

the land bursts with otherwise dormant wildflowers, like a one-night-only command performance. The region is dominated by desert, a flat land stretching out like a vast forgotten sea, yet increase your elevation into one of the region's sky islands and you will be hunting for tropical birds in a misty creek bed, or, if you go high enough, clamping on a pair of skis.

So it is with the culture in Tucson and Southern Arizona. If ever there was a melting pot in America it bubbles here, its heat

source being the triple-digit days come July. Traveling the region it is difficult to escape constant reminders that not too long ago this land was considered not the southern end of the United States but rather the northern end of Mexico. The Anglo and Hispanic settlers have since come to terms with each other for the most part, and their mixing has created a unique culture that can only be described as Southwestern. While this true Southwestern experience can be experienced and studied in

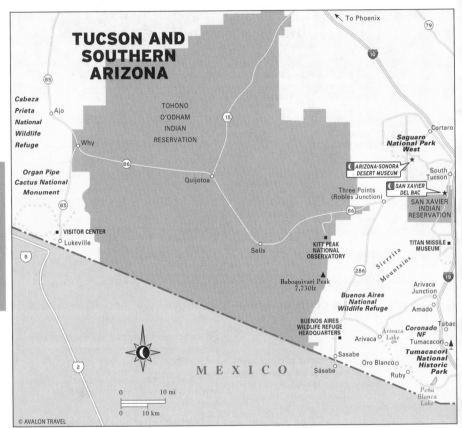

a few other places, nowhere is it more authentic and at the same time more dynamic than in Southern Arizona. There is proof of this in the region's art, music, and writing, all of which thrive on the arid climate and cultural complexity.

A short drive south, you'll experience the dynamic border region with all its bustling, and sometimes tragic, color. Go east and you'll find the remains of the Old West at its most iconic. Look a little closer and you'll find the new as well, in the artists and artisans who find Southern Arizona's quaint towns like Tubac and Bisbee so inviting. This is a fascinating, exotic region, and one you might find yourself happily lost in.

PLANNING YOUR TIME

You can do Tucson and Southern Arizona in one busy week; to sample some of the sky island trails and hideaways, take two weeks. The best times to visit are March through May and September through November. It is very hot on the desert in summer and perfect in the mountains, and in July and August count on near-daily late afternoon thunderstorms. Though hot and humid during the day, the months of the monsoon are a wonderful time to be alive in the Sonoran Desert. It's best to use Tucson as a base and explore the outlying areas by car unless you have more than a week or two to explore. All of the major sights in this region are within a few hours of the city.

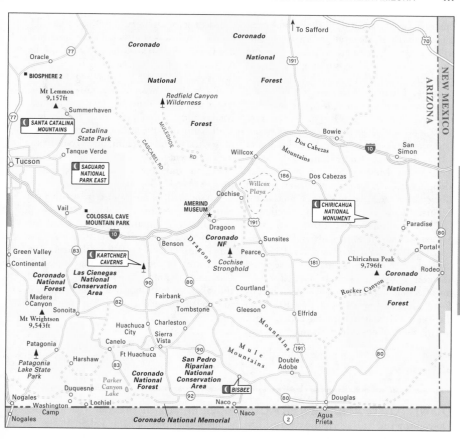

Tucson's charms deserve at least three days of concentration. Spend a full day visiting the West Side's Saguaro National Park, Tucson Mountain Park, the Arizona-Sonora Desert Museum, and San Xavier del Bac, and another day hanging around Downtown and Fourth Avenue, sampling the desert's urban side. Then head up the Sky Island Highway to Mount Lemmon to see a completely different view of Southern Arizona from the forested mountain heights. You can visit the Santa Cruz Valley and the Border Region, and even take a stroll into Mexico at Nogales, in a long day-trip from Tucson. You can also visit Bisbee, Tombstone, the Amerind Foundation, and even Chiricahua National Monument in a long, rather exhausting day trip. However, these and the other fascinating sites along the Cochise Trail, especially wondrous Kartchner Caverns, are best explored slowly and carefully, and Bisbee, which is relatively close to all the sites, is a romantic and memorable place to spend a night or two.

ORIENTATION

As it is with most Southwestern cities of a certain size, the Tucson metropolitan area encompasses several small towns as well as the City of Tucson proper. In this section of the guide, sights, accommodations, and restaurants are listed according to their proximity to downtown, which remains at least the sentimental heart of the city and will likely become even more than that in the future as long-term plans to reenergize the area are realized under the city's ambitious and long-suffering Rio Nuevo project.

Native Tucsonans have tried to hold onto a semblance of the small, funky city character that once dominated the Old Pueblo, and there are still no real freeways in the city as a result. I-10 provides the only quick throughway, and I-19 is the primary route south to the Santa Cruz Valley. Most of the time, plan to slog along busy surface streets. Traffic is moved along with some speed, however, thanks to the left arrow lights at most major intersections.

The main commercial corridors run west to east—22nd Street, Broadway Boulevard, Speedway Boulevard, and Grant Road. Dozens of hotels, motels, and restaurants can be found along any of these main roads in the city's midtown section, bordered roughly on the east by Swan Road and on the west by I-10. South Tucson is a separate incorporated city, a mile square, south of downtown Tucson.

North of the city, on Oracle Road/Route 77, are the small towns of Oro Valley, Catalina, and Oracle all nestled in the backside foothills of the Santa Catalina Mountains. To the southeast is the old mining and ranching district of Vail and the Rincon Valley, now peppered with suburban housing developments, and beyond that the communities along the Cochise Trail. South on I-19 are the big open-pit copper mines, the bedroom community of Sahuarita, the retirement haven of Green Valley, the artist's colony and shops of Tubac, and then on to the U.S.-Mexico Border.

Tucson itself is surrounded by mountains, with the mighty Santa Catalinas to the north, the Rincon Mountains to the east and the Tucson Mountains to the west. Far south in the Santa Cruz Valley along I-19 are the Santa Rita Mountains. If you remember that the Santa Catalinas, the most imposing range around the valley, are to the north, it isn't too difficult to navigate Tucson.

Sights

DOWNTOWN AND CENTRAL

Downtown Tucson is where the city first rose from the desert. The general area can be expanded to include 4th Avenue and the historic neighborhoods of El Presidio, Armory Park, Barrio Historico, and those around the University of Arizona, all of which are pedestrian friendly—something rare in the Southwestern cityscape.

Tucson Museum of Art and Historic Block

The permanent collection at the **Tucson Museum of Art** (140 N. Main Ave., 520/624-2333, www.tucsonmuseumofart.org, 10am-5pm Wed. and Fri.-Sat., 10am-8pm Thurs., noon-8pm Sun., $10 general admission, $8 seniors, $5 students) features the mysterious artifacts of the Americas prior to Columbus's

arrival, the art of the American West, and contemporary art with a Latin and Southwestern flavor. This is a good place to introduce yourself to that tricultural mixing that makes Southern Arizona unique. The museum puts on several special exhibitions every year; recent years have seen a heavily attended Warhol retrospective and the largest showing of the Arizona paintings of Maynard Dixon anywhere. Five historic homes built in the last half of the 19th century survive next to the museum. Just beyond the museum's wide Main Avenue entrance is the oldest of the Historic Block's buildings (and probably the oldest building in Tucson), La Casa Cordova, its two west rooms built several years before the Gadsden Purchase made Tucson part of the United States in 1854. The home is a perfect example of the style of Mexican townhouse that once lined the city's

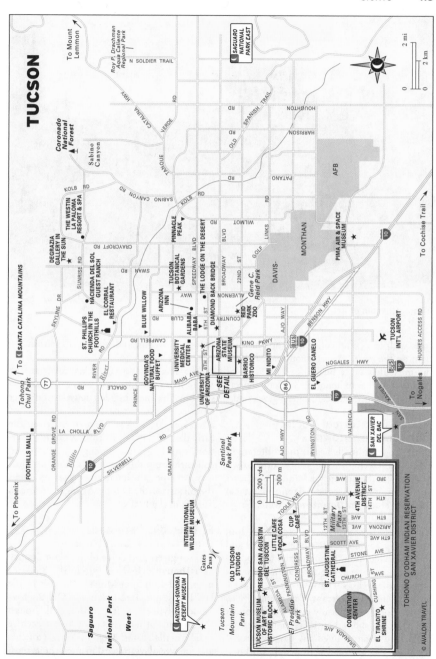

TUCSON

TUCSON

To Mount Lemmon

Coronado National Forest

Santa Catalina Mountains

To Phoenix

Saguaro National Park West

SAGUARO NATIONAL PARK EAST

Roy P. Drachman Aqua Caliente Regional Park

N SOLDIER TRAIL

AFB

DAVIS-MONTHAN

PIMA AIR & SPACE MUSEUM

To Cochise Trail

THE WESTIN LA PALOMA RESORT & SPA

DEGRAZIA GALLERY IN THE SUN

PINNACLE PEAK

TUCSON BOTANICAL GARDENS

THE LODGE ON THE DESERT

ARIZONA INN

DIAMOND BACK BRIDGE

Gene C. Reid Park

REID PARK ZOO

ST. PHILLIPS CHURCH IN THE FOOTHILLS

HACIENDA DEL SOL GUEST RANCH

EL CORRAL RESTAURANT

BLUE WILLOW

ALIBABA

ARIZONA STATE MUSEUM

BARRIO HISTORICO

MI NIDITO

EL GUERO CANELO

TUCSON INT'L AIRPORT

GOVINDA'S NATURAL FOOD BUFFET

UNIVERSITY MEDICAL CENTER

UNIVERSITY OF ARIZONA

SEE DETAIL

Sabino Canyon

Sentinel Peak Park

Tohono Chul Park

FOOTHILLS MALL

INTERNATIONAL WILDLIFE MUSEUM

Gates Pass

OLD TUCSON STUDIOS

ARIZONA-SONORA DESERT MUSEUM

Tucson Mountain Park

San Xavier District

To Nogales

SAN XAVIER DEL BAC

TOHONO O'ODHAM INDIAN RESERVATION SAN XAVIER DISTRICT

4TH AVENUE DISTRICT

Military Plaza

TUCSON MUSEUM OF ART & HISTORIC BLOCK

PRESIDIO SAN AGUSTIN DEL TUCSON

LITTLE CAFE POCA COSA

CUP CAFE

El Presidio Park

ST. AUGUSTINE CATHEDRAL

CONVENTION CENTER

EL TIRADITO SHRINE

© AVALON TRAVEL

2 mi

2 km

0 200 yds
0 200 m

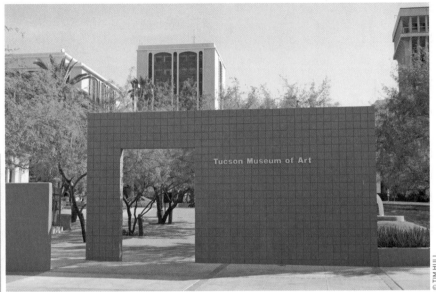

© TIM HULL

Tucson Museum of Art

core, with its central courtyard and entrance right on the street. A shady courtyard behind the museum's main building, The Plaza of Pioneers, has a wall honoring Tucson pioneers from the Spanish, Mexican, and Anglo periods.

Arizona Historical Society Museum Downtown

Until shopping malls began to proliferate in midtown starting in the 1960s, downtown Tucson was the commercial and social heart of the city, a fact that the **Arizona Historical Society Museum Downtown** (Wells Fargo Building, 140 N. Stone Ave., 520/770-1473, www.arizonahistoricalsociety.org, 10am-4pm Tues.-Fri., $3 adults, $2 students 12-18 and seniors) celebrates. Though there are ongoing attempts to revitalize downtown through a project called Rio Nuevo, it's unlikely the once bustling, mixed-use area will ever return to its former glory, when locally owned department stores, barber shops, boutiques, hotels, restaurants, and theaters lined the narrow streets, the sidewalks crowded with people working,

shopping, living, and playing all within the same few blocks.

The small museum, tucked away in the Wells Fargo building on Stone Avenue—a still-busy, business-minded downtown district crowded on the weekdays but largely deserted after 5pm Friday—shows artifacts from the early days of downtown through to its desertion, with large, rare photographs and saved ephemera from different eras of the city's history. An especially interesting installation tells the history of the Dillinger gang's capture in Tucson in the 1930s.

El Presidio Park and Pima County Courthouse

The sea-green tiled dome of the **Pima County Courthouse** (115 N. Church St., 8:30am-noon and 1pm-5pm Mon.-Fri.), built in the late 1920s, is a landmark of the Old Pueblo's modest skyline, and it's worth a walk around the grounds of the city's government beehive to take in the Spanish Colonial revival touches and, on weekdays, to see downtown at its most

El Presidio Historic District

El Presidio Historic District is where Tucson began as a place of human habitation, a mixture of adobe row houses and Victorian mansions that is several chapters in the city's history writ in architecture. The district is bounded roughly by Granada on the west, 6th Street on the north, Church Street on the east, and Alameda Street on the south.

Though turned back to desert now, the Royal Presidio de San Agustin del Tucson once stood here, the farthest north the Spanish crown dared to go. The presidio, or fort, had 12-foot-high adobe walls and covered 11 acres, housing a small contingent of soldiers and their families, a population that spent a good deal of its time fearing and fighting Apaches. Much later, archaeologists discovered that the fort had been built close to a Hohokam site that flourished from about 700-900, proving humans had made their lives on the banks of the Santa Cruz River for as long as nearly anywhere else in the union. A self-guided tour pamphlet of this district and other downtown-area historic sites is available at the Tucson Visitors Center at La Placita.

When the Americans took over in 1856, the fort was dismantled, its walls used to build homes and businesses for new arrivals. As more Anglos settled in, the district became a mixture of adobe row houses and eastern-style mansions for early-20th-century Tucson's rich and powerful. Many of these old mansions and adobes have been restored and now serve as offices and private residences.

industrious. On the weekends, especially in the summer, you'll likely find the area mostly deserted but still inviting. Walk across the front courtyard through a few arches and you'll be in **El Presidio Park,** with its fountains and memorial to the Mormon Battalion, which occupied the presidio briefly in late 1846. There are also memorials and statues in this large urban government-center park honoring WWII veterans, John F. Kennedy, and various pioneers of the Old West. There's usually a hot-dog cart on the plaza on weekdays, and plenty of opportunities for people-watching and shade.

Presidio San Agustín del Tucson

Experts on the history, lifeways, and architecture of the early Spanish settlers have recreated a portion of the old **Presidio San Agustín del Tucson** (at the downtown corner of Washington and Church Sts., 520/884-4214, www.tucsonpresidiotrust.org, 10am-4pm daily Oct.-May, 10am-3pm Thurs.-Sun. June-Sept., free). Within the newly raised adobe walls there's a large, realistic mural depicting daily life in and around the fort. There are a few dark, cool adobe rooms set up in period style to show visitors what life was like on the far, lonely northern edge of the Spanish Empire in 1775, when an Irishman working for the Crown rode north to Tucson from Tubac to establish a fort in an effort to outrun Apache predations. During the week parking is available in a nearby parking garage on Alameda Street; metered parking is available on nearby streets. On weekends, street parking is free.

Barrio Historico

The photogenic Sonoran-style row houses in the **Barrio Historico District** (bordered by Stone Ave., I-10, Cushing St., and 18th St.) on the southwest edge of downtown are well adapted to the desert environment. Their front entrances hug the property line (unlike their Anglo counterparts with large front and back yards) to make space for central courtyards hidden from the street, which provide a shaded outdoor living space within the home. Many of the adobes here have been lovingly and colorfully restored and now serve as offices, working galleries, and private residences. Sometimes called Barrio Viejo (the Old Neighborhood), the barrio has been on the National Register of

TUCSON

© TIM HULL

El Presidio Park, with the Pima County Courthouse dome visible

Historic Places since the 1970s. It dates from the mid-1850s and, as its dominant architecture suggests, has traditionally been a Mexican enclave. Once, several neighborhoods sprawled out here to create a large quarter referred to as Barrio Libre (Free Neighborhood), due either to the anything-goes atmosphere in some corners or because the Mexican population was mostly left alone to follow its own rules and culture. Much of the quarter was razed in the late 1960s to make way for the "urban renewal" program that built the Tucson Convention Center. The best examples of the adobe rowhouses can be found along Myer, Main, and Cushing. Along Myer look for the old Teatro Carmen, a Spanish-language theater that opened in 1915. Now empty, the old adobe building, which over the years served as a movie house, a boxing arena, and an Elks Lodge, still retains the charm and historic interest that once pervaded this district.

El Tiradito Shrine

Roadside shrines are common in Southern Arizona even in the most out-of-the-way places, but only one is dedicated to a folk-saint who was, by the church's standards, an unredeemed sinner. El Tiradito (The Castaway) dates to the 1870s, when Juan Oliveras, a young shepherd, fell in love with his mother-in-law and the two gave in to an illicit passion. They were discovered by her ax-wielding husband, who killed Oliveras and tossed his dead body away on the land that now holds the shrine (such is the tradition, anyway). The church wouldn't allow the doomed lover to be buried on consecrated land, so the people of the barrio interred him where he was "cast away" and erected a shrine. Some say that if you make a wish at the shrine by night and leave a lit candle, and you find it still burning in the morning, your wish will come true—this is why **El Tiradito** (221 S. Main Ave.) is sometimes called the "Wishing Shrine." Next door to the shrine is **La Pilita,** an old adobe house that has a small museum and store selling handmade items by local schoolchildren, with a few exhibits on local history created by neighborhood kids. There's an

© TIM HULL

El Tiradito, the "Wishing Shrine"

excellent mural on the south wall that tells the story of Tucson's Hispanic community.

St. Augustine Cathedral

Facing Stone Avenue on the eastern edge of the Barrio Historico, **St. Augustine Cathedral** (192 S. Stone Ave., 520/623-6351, www.augustinecathedral.org, mass at 7am and noon Mon.-Fri., church open all day Sat.-Sun.), dedicated to Tucson's patron saint, was built in 1896 and remodeled several times over the years. The facade has stone-carved yucca, saguaro, and horned-toad flourishes, and there are statues of the Virgin Mary and the titular saint near the big, heavy-wood entrance. Catholics or anyone interested in regional variations on the Mass should attend the lively mariachi mass, held at 8am every Sunday. Inside, one of the bells formerly used in the original Spanish-era cathedral is preserved in the vestibule.

The Diamondback Bridge

Artist Simon Donovan completed this rather literal work of public art (spanning Broadway near Euclid) in 2002 to be a kind of memorable entrance to a downtown that has been undergoing a slow revitalization for at least the past 20 years. **The Diamondback Bridge,** spanning Broadway Boulevard just as the busy street dips into the central city, has since become a popular local landmark. In 2003 it won the prestigious American Public Works Project of the Year award. The bridge, which looks like a monster-sized rattlesnake taking it easy, albeit with its jaw perpetually stretched open, is 300 feet long and cost about $2.7 million to build. There's a small, pleasant park on either end of the snake. The easiest way to see it is to pull over at Euclid and Broadway, park, and walk across. Just after the snake bridge, as you enter downtown, you'll see huge black-and-white photographs on both sides of the underpass. These are photographs from the 1940s and 1950s of Tucsonans walking, shopping, and generally bustling about downtown,

TUCSON

Downtown Walking Tours

For walking tours of downtown, try Alan Kruse of **KruseArizona Tours** (4517 E. Patricia Pl., 520/881-1638, www.KruseArizona.com, $15 per person); he dresses in period costume for a two-hour walk around downtown and serves pastry and coffee. Similarly, Julia Benites Arriola of the **Arizona Historical Society** (949 E. 2nd St., 520/622-0956, $10 per person) serves Mexican pastries and hot beverages on her colorful two-hour tour. The **Tucson Museum of Art and Historic Block** (520/624-2333, ext. 104, mhayes@tucsonarts. com, 10am-4pm Mon.-Sat., noon-4pm Sun.) offers a 2.5-hour tour for $10, by reservation.

TUCSON

© TIM HULL

St. Augustine Cathedral

back when it used to be a place where people did such things.

4th Avenue District
Lined with chic thrift stores, exotic clothing boutiques, smoke shops, ethnic food restaurants, and cocktail lounges, this is an ideal place to people watch, and there are some really good places to eat and treasures to be found in the quirky shops. Twice a year, in fall and spring, the area closes to vehicle traffic for a street fair featuring artisan booths, concerts, and greasy food galore. Located between downtown and the University District, 4th Avenue is just a short walk from campus, and on Friday and Saturday nights expect hordes of college kids out looking for inebriation. It's best to avoid driving in this area on weekend nights altogether.

UNIVERSITY OF ARIZONA (UA)
Since it was founded in 1885 as the first institution of higher learning in the Arizona Territory, the fate of the University of Arizona and that of its host pueblo have been inextricably linked. It's difficult to imagine what Tucson would be without the shady central campus. A land-grant school that has educated countless Arizona leaders and citizens, UA has nearly 37,000 students (more than the number of residents of most Arizona towns) and is active in the U.S. space program, specifically in Mars exploration. Not surprisingly, the school is world-renowned for its arid-land research, and has a center for integrative medicine founded by best-selling healer-doctor Andrew Weil. It's also the place where anthropology, archaeology, and many other disciplines were revolutionized through the discovery of tree-ring dating.

The university is also becoming known for contributing to space exploration in a big way. Check out the displays on the HiRISE Mars Camera, the Phoenix Mars Lander, and Cassini mission to Saturn at the **Sonett Visitor Center** (northwest corner of University Blvd. and Cherry St., 520/626-7432, 9am-5pm Mon.-Fri., free).

On campus you'll find a number of museums and galleries, and the entire campus itself is an arboretum. Indeed, the green central campus claims to be the "oldest continually maintained green space in Arizona." Flora enthusiasts can stroll around the campus and take in a cactus garden, a collection of rare tropical trees, and various arid land species that have been brought to UA from all over the world. If you want to learn more about the campus's natural wonders, go by the **Campus Arboretum** at Herring Hall (520/621-7074, http://arboretum.arizona.edu, 9am-5pm Mon.-Fri., free). Don't miss the **Joseph Wood Krutch Cactus Garden** in the center of the campus's long, grassy mall.

Kids will enjoy the hands-on exhibits, laser shows and sky-watching at **Flandrau: The UA Science Center** (1601 E. University Blvd., 520/621-7827, www.flandrau.org, 10am-3pm Mon.-Fri., 6pm-9pm Fri., 10am-9pm Sat., 1pm-4pm Sun., $7 adults, $5 children 5-15). Downstairs at Flandrau, you'll find the **UA Mineral Museum** (520/621-4227, www.UAMineralMuseum.org, 9am-3pm Thurs.-Fri., 6pm-9pm Fri., noon-9pm Sat., noon-4pm Sun., free), which has on display a wondrous collection of rocks from Arizona and beyond.

There are also numerous public art installations on campus. One that should not be missed is the hulking border commentary called **Border Dynamics,** created by artists Alberto Morackis and Guadalupe Serrano. It's not always easy to find parking on campus, and it's impossible during sporting events. Visitors can pay to park at the Park Avenue Garage at the corner of Park and Helen Street, and at the Main Gate Parking Garage at Euclid Avenue and East 2nd Street.

Arizona Historical Society Museum

Just south of the main gate wall along North Campus Drive is the **Arizona Historical Society Museum** (949 E. 2nd St., 520/628-5774, www.arizonahistoricalsociety.org, 10am-4pm Mon.-Sat., $5 adults, $4 students 12-18 and seniors), the largest of the Arizona Historical Society's three Tucson museums.

Exhibits include a full-scale reproduction of the cramped canvas-tent home early miners lived in, and a walk through a dark underground mine. There's also an old Studebaker on display; this make of car was once so popular with Arizona's sheriffs that the car company sent an author to the young state to write a public relations pamphlet that included exciting stories of frontier law enforcement. This is an interesting stop for Arizona history buffs, and there are several hands-on exhibits for the kids.

Arizona State Museum

Established in 1893, the **Arizona State Museum** (1013 E. University Blvd., 520/621-6302, www.statemuseum.arizona.edu, 10am-5pm Mon.-Sat., $5) is the oldest anthropology museum in the Southwest. Here you'll find several rooms of fascinating displays on the state's various Native American tribes and the world's largest collection of Southwest Indian pottery, including many contemporary pieces that prove pottery making is certainly not a lost art. Every year in February the museum's grassy grounds play host to the Southwest Indian Art Fair, one of the more important and well attended of such events in the Southwest. A permanent exhibition inside the stately old building explains the origins and histories of 10 of Arizona's Native American groups, including the Hohokam, the O'odham, and the Apache, all of whom ruled Southern Arizona at one time or another.

University of Arizona Museum of Art

The permanent collection of the **University of Arizona Museum of Art** (UA campus near Park Ave. and Speedway Blvd., 520/621-7567, http://artmuseum.arizona.edu, 9am-5pm Tues.-Fri., noon-4pm Sat.-Sun., closed Mon. and UA holidays, $5) has mostly minor works (but still worth seeing) by Tintoretto, Piazzetta, Goya, Brueghel, Rodin, Picasso, Hopper, Pollock, Rothko, O'Keeffe, and many more. Asian and Latin American traditions are also well represented. Special shows often feature the work of well-known local artists and artists from Mexico. The museum has an impressive collection of Spanish medieval art, the signature piece of which is the 26-panel **Retablo of Ciudad Rodrigo,** an altarpiece depicting the sweep of biblical events from Genesis through the life of Jesus Christ to the Last Judgment.

Center for Creative Photography

UA's **Center for Creative Photography** (1030 N. Olive Rd., 520/621-7968, www.creativephotography.org, 9am-5pm Mon.-Fri., 1pm-4pm Sat.-Sun., free) has one of the largest photography collections in the world; it holds the archives of Ansel Adams, Edward Weston, and dozens more major artists. The center mounts a few exhibitions a year, so it's a good idea to check the website before traveling to see what's on display. You can even make an appointment to personally view a few of the 80,000 prints accessible to the public (520/621-7968).

Southern Arizona Transportation Museum

When the railroad reached the isolated town of Tucson in the 1880s, it transformed the city and the region. The small **Southern Arizona Transportation Museum** (414 N. Tooele Ave., 520/623-2223, www.tucsonhistoricdepot.org, 11am-3pm Tues.-Thurs. and Sun., 10am-4pm Fri.-Sat., free) at the refurbished 1940s rail depot downtown explains all the myriad ways the railroad, and later the car and the Interstate system, changed Tucson and the Southwest, opening it up to visitors and settlers and linking it more with the United States rather than Mexico, as it had been before the train's arrival. There's a lifelike statue of Wyatt Earp and Doc Holiday nearby, and a plaque that tells the story of a bit of revenge and/or murder that went down right here back in the old violent days of the territory.

Tucson Children's Museum

Housed downtown in Tucson's original Carnegie Library, the **Tucson Children's Museum** (200 S. 6th Ave., 520/792-9985, www.tucsonchildrensmuseum.org, 9am-5pm Tues.-Fri., 10am-5pm Sat.-Sun., $8 adults, $6 seniors and children 2-18), a nonprofit, interactive learning center, is a local family favorite. Parents will appreciate the creativity and attention to detail. There are 12 permanent exhibits here, all of them hands-on and featuring some kid-mesmerizing subjects like dinosaurs, electricity, ocean life, and trains. There's also an "enchanted rainforest" for preschoolers. It's not always easy to find parking because the museum has no lot of its own; there are metered spaces around the museum, and $1 in change will get you about two hours during the week; on weekends parking is free.

Reid Park Zoo

Take Broadway Boulevard east to Randolph Way at Reid Park to Tucson's small but prestigious zoo. **Reid Park Zoo** (1100 S. Randolph Way, 520/791-4022, www.tucsonzoo.org, 9am-4pm daily, $9 adults, $7 seniors, $5 children 2-14) specializes in anteater research, and there are several of these strange beasts to look at here. There's also a polar bear, Boris, who seems to be very happy living in what you'd think would be the absolute opposite circumstances in which a polar bear would want to find himself. Not so, zookeepers say. The arctic, a cold desert, is actually drier than Tucson, so as long as they keep the air-conditioning pumping and his water hole cold he'll be staying for years.

Make sure to take the kids to the giraffe habitat, where for $1 they can buy some treats to feed the long-necked residents, who stick out their long, purple tongues, dripping with saliva, to capture the treat—much to the squealing delight of the feeders. A gift shop sells all kinds of zoo-related stuffed animals, shirts, and books, and a fast-food style eatery serves hamburgers, corn dogs, and the like.

If you get there early enough, you might catch a glimpse of the elegant black jaguars, sisters born at a wildlife park outside of Phoenix, lounging in the cool of the morning. The zoo is small enough that little kids aren't likely to get too tired out. Plan about three hours, less if you don't have kids.

Howard Hughes in Tucson

Everybody's heard about those weird few years that Howard Hughes spent hiding out on the top floor of a Las Vegas hotel, going mad.

Well, there are hints that the Old Pueblo could have been the site of Hughes's infamous hideout instead of Vegas. Bob Maheu, Hughes's right-hand man and official public face during the Vegas years, told Geoff Schumacher, author of the 2008 book *Howard Hughes: Power, Paranoia, and Palace Intrigue*, that in the mid-1960s before moving to Vegas Hughes first considered moving to Tucson, where he'd already set up a manufacturing plant in 1951.

Hughes loved the desert, considering it free of the germs that stalked him. There's a great scene in *The Aviator* in which the young Hughes, played by Leonardo DiCaprio, sees a stand of saguaros in a film he's watching and whispers something like, "so clean..." Ultimately, though, Hughes soured on the desert around Las Vegas due to his inability to stop nuclear testing at the Nevada Test Site, fallout from which he obsessively feared.

Though he never moved to Tucson, Hughes did of course have a presence here. Hughes Aircraft built the Falcon, the world's first air-to-air guided missile, and many other missiles and weapons here, employing thousands of workers. Hughes Missile Systems was eventually bought by Raytheon, which is today Southern Arizona's largest private employer.

Tucson Botanical Gardens

Gardeners and anybody who appreciates beauty should stop at the **Tucson Botanical Gardens** (2150 N. Alvernon Way, 520/326-9686, www.tucsonbotanical.org, 8:30am-4:30pm daily, $13 adults, $7.50 children 4-12), a midtown oasis, for a few hours. Flat walking trails wind around the nearly six-acre property, which feels secluded and hidden away even though it's right in the path of busy midtown. There are benches throughout on which to sit and contemplate the various gardens—16 in all, each one showcasing a different gardening tradition. Especially lovely is the Mexican-influenced garden, Nuestro Jardín (Our Garden), with its shrine of the Virgin of Guadalupe and found items. A cactus and succulent garden has examples of cacti not just from the nearby deserts but also from around the world, and the xeriscape garden demonstrates how you can grow desert-adapted plants without using a lot of water.

If you go between October and March, you'll get to see **Butterfly Magic,** a live tropical butterfly exhibit. Call ahead for times and availability. For the price of admission you can take advantage of one of several tours of the gardens. Different tours are offered throughout the month, and not every tour is offered every day, so it's best to call ahead or check the website. The **Garden Gallery** has rotating art shows that can be viewed 8:30am-4:30pm daily.

Mini Time Machine Museum of Miniatures

Built by passionate collectors of all things miniature, the charming **Mini Time Machine Museum of Miniatures** (4455 E. Camp Lowell Drive, 520/881-0606, www.theminitimemachine.org, 9am-4pm Tues.-Sat., noon-4pm Sun., $9 adults, $6 children) in midtown is a great place to take kids, who generally find all the tiny objects and detailed dioramas endlessly fascinating. They'll also like the Enchanted Tree, with its big face and fairytale trunk-life. The museum has a permanent collection of nearly 300 miniatures, both contemporary and antique, and presents special exhibits from time to time that explore a particular theme or style in depth and, of course, in miniature.

WEST OF DOWNTOWN

Take Speedway Boulevard west under I-10. The road becomes Gates Pass Road and then runs into Kinney Road. Follow the signs to each of the following sights, some of Tucson's most representative attractions. You can do it in one long day, though the Desert Museum and Saguaro National Park stand up to a full day each. To get to the Desert Museum, take Speedway Boulevard west for about 12 miles through the desert and then turn right onto Kinney Road. The International Wildlife Museum is along the way, and Old Tucson is nearby as well.

Sentinel Peak and Tumamoc Hill

Also called "A" Mountain for the large white—or, since 9/11, red, white, and blue—"A" re-painted on its face every year by University of Arizona students (a tradition that began in 1915), **Sentinel Peak** (1000 S. Sentinel Peak Rd., 8am-8pm Mon.-Sat., 8am-6pm Sun.) served the early populations of the Tucson valley with spring water and black basalt. When Father Kino first rode into the valley in the 1690s, he found the native population living in the small peak's shadow, and it was surely an important landmark in the basin for eons before that. During the presidio days it earned its name as a promontory from which soldiers would scan the desert for Apaches. Now there's a park on the peak, reached by a paved, winding road to the top. Take Congress Street west under I-10 and follow the signs. There are a few short trails around the park, a little rock shelter to sit under, charcoal barbecues, and some great views of the valley. The hill just to the north of Sentinel Peak, called **Tumamoc Hill** (Tumamoc Hill Rd.), is the home to a living desert laboratory founded in 1903. For thousands of years indigenous residents of the Tucson valley farmed on and around Tumamoc Hill, as evidenced by numerous archaeological sites found there. Among the legends of the Tohono O'odham is the story of a giant horned lizard that threatened to devour the tribe had not the god I'itoi, in response to prayers, turned the great reptile into a hill, hence the name Tumamoc (horned lizard) Hill.

International Wildlife Museum

As you drive west toward Gates Pass and the Tucson Mountains, off on the north side of the road, partly obscured by the thick desert, a large, castle-esque building holds the impressive taxidermy collection of the **International Wildlife Museum** (4800 W. Gates Pass Rd., 520/629-0100, www.thewildlifemuseum. org, 9am-5pm Mon.-Fri., 9am-6pm Sat.-Sun., $8 adults, $3 children 4-12), a private, nonprofit natural history museum. There are more than 400 stuffed and preserved mammals, birds, insects, and spiders here, including "Big Terror," a stuffed tiger who still looks a bit hungry. The mighty beast was killed in 1969 in India, after he'd reportedly devoured between 8 and 12 people. This is a fun and educational place to bring kids, but if you have limited time, I'd recommend skipping it in favor of the Arizona-Sonora Desert Museum a few miles up the road, where the mountain lions, rattlesnakes, beavers, and scorpions are all indigenous, and alive.

Tucson Mountain Park and Gates Pass Scenic Overlook

Robert Gates was a typical Southwestern frontier entrepreneur: He did a little mining, a little ranching, a bit of saloon keeping, some homesteading. In 1883, in order to connect his Avra Valley mine with his other interests in Tucson, he set about building a precipitous route over the Tucson Mountains, and in the process set the stage for local officials, about 50 years later, to establish one of the largest public parks of its kind in the nation. Thus we have the 37-square-mile Sonoran Desert preserve called **Tucson Mountain Park** (Speedway west from downtown over Gates Pass to Kinney Rd., 7am-10pm daily, free). The 20,000 acres of wild desert features one of the largest saguaro forests in the world, and has something like 62 miles of trails for hiking and mountain biking. The park has a rifle and pistol range, three large picnic areas with grills and ramadas and picnic tables, and within its boundaries is the world-renowned Arizona-Sonora Desert Museum. If all these activities seem a bit sweaty and active for your taste, at least make it to the top of the road named for the man who conquered the comparatively short Tucson Mountains at **Gates Pass.** You can drive to the pass and park at a large lot with bathrooms and a ramada and two little stacked-rock huts decorated inside with eons of graffiti. There are short trails out to a promontory from which you can see the whole sweeping expanse of the desert below. It's one of the best views in Arizona—a state that has no shortage of sweeping views. If you want to stay the night at the park, the **Gilbert Ray Campground** (8451 W. McCain Loop, off Kinney Rd., 520/883-4200, $10-20) has sites with RV hookups, picnic tables, restrooms, and a dumping station.

◖ Arizona-Sonora Desert Museum

A big part of the fun of a visit to the **Arizona-Sonora Desert Museum** (2021 North Kinney Rd., 520/883-2702, www.desertmuseum.org, 7:30am-5pm daily Mar.-Sept. daily (until 10pm Sat. June-Aug.), 7:30am-5pm daily Oct.-Feb., $14.50 adults, $5 children 6-12) is getting there. Driving west out of Tucson

over dramatic Gates Pass, you'll see thousands of sentinel-like saguaros standing tall on the hot, rocky ground below, surrounded by pipe-cleaner-like ocotillo and fuzzy cholla, creosote, and prickly pear.

But the saguaro forests of Tucson Mountain Park and Saguaro National Park West, both of which surround the Desert Museum, are only one of several distinctive desert life zones you'll see and learn about at this world-famous museum and zoo, where native mammals, birds, reptiles, amphibians, fish, and arthropods live in displays mimicking their open-desert habitats.

This is the best place to learn about both the general structure and the minute details of the surrounding desert, and probably your only realistic chance to see all of the unique creatures that call it home.

Easy trails wind through the beautiful 21-acre preserve, passing exhibits on semidesert grasslands and mountain woodlands similar to those surrounding and growing on the Sonoran Desert's high mountain ranges. The Desert

TUCSON

© FLORENCE MCGINN/123RF.COM

a bobcat at the Arizona-Sonora Desert Museum

Loop Trail leads through a lowland scrub and cacti landscape with javelina and coyote. In Cat Canyon, a bespeckled ocelot sleeps in the shade and a bobcat lounges on the rocks. A mountain lion can be seen close up through a viewing window, and a black bear strolls along a man-made stream and sleeps on a rock promontory. There are also rare Mexican wolves, white-tailed deer, bighorn sheep, and adorable prairie dogs with which to commune.

A riparian habitat has beavers and otters, water lovers that are once abundant in the Southwest. There's a desert garden exhibit, a cactus and succulent garden, and a butterfly and wildflower display. There are also displays on desert fish, dunes, and a walk-in aviary that holds dozens of native birds. Docents are scattered throughout the complex to help with questions and give presentations on special topics. All this, plus a restaurant, snack bars, and a gift shop that sells excellent Pueblo Indian crafts make the Desert Museum Tucson's very best attraction. If you're planning on doing any exploring in the desert, do so after a trip to the Desert Museum, where you'll get a comprehensive mini-course in desert ecology.

Old Tucson Studios

Since 1939 **Old Tucson** (201 S. Kinney Rd., 520/883-0100, www.oldtucson.com, 10am-5pm daily Oct.-May, $16.95 adults, $10.95 children 4-11) has been the setting for more than 400 film productions, the majority of them Westerns. It was originally constructed to make the film *Arizona,* starring Jean Arthur and William Holden, which tells the story of Tucson's territorial days.

In the 1950s, impresario Bob Shelton bought the disused property and rebuilt its circa-1860s town, again drawing productions west from Hollywood, several starring Shelton's friend John Wayne. It remained popular as a movie set as long as Westerns were popular at the box office, and so went through boom and bust periods along with the genre. Shelton added gunfight shows and other family-oriented tourist attractions to ride out the lean times. Today a rebuilt Old Tucson (the town burned to the

ground in the 1990s) concentrates on re-creating a movie-house version of the Old West for tourists.

Make sure to check out the collection of vintage posters from the films produced at the studio. Tours talk about the history of the studio and the stars who walked its dusty streets, and musical acts and vaudeville-style revues go on all day. There are several restaurants on-site, including **Big Jake's,** which serves up good barbecue and beans, and **El Vaquero,** offering Southwestern-style entrées and a wide variety of specialty drinks. Unless you're a Western-film buff, Old Tucson is a little stale. If you're into the genre, you'll find the film-related aspects worth a look. Kids might enjoy it, but the entry price is rather expensive for what you get.

Saguaro National Park West

This is where the icon of arid America holds court. The split **Saguaro National Park** (www. nps.gov/sagu, 7am-sunset daily, visitors center 9am-5pm daily, $10 per car, receipt valid for seven days, good at both sections) has a western section at the base of the Tucson Mountains and a larger eastern section at the base of the Rincon Mountains. Both are worth visiting, but if you have time only for one, go to the eastern section, which is older and larger. (Then again, there are a few other sights around the western portion, while the eastern is a bit on its own, save for nearby Colossal Cave.) Together they protect about 91,300 acres of magnificent Sonoran Desert landscape, including large and crowded saguaro forests surrounded by a thick underbrush of ocotillo, prickly pear, cholla, mesquite, and paloverde. If you want to see an accessible and wondrous example of the Sonoran Desert at its best, there are few better places to go.

The saguaro (pronounced sa-WAH-ro) is much more than a strange-looking plant to the native inhabitants of the Sonoran Desert, be they cactus wrens, coyotes, screech owls, or Tohono O'odham tribespeople. It is so supremely adapted to the arid environment, in which moisture from the sky comes but twice a year, that it anchors an entire busy community

© TIM HULL

There are many ancient petroglyphs in Saguaro National Park West.

of living things, providing food and shelter to all sorts of desert creatures.

The great cactus-tree grows slowly, and only during the summer rainy season. After living, shaded and protected by a mesquite tree, for 15 years, a saguaro is still only about a foot tall. But, then again, these green, ribbed giants can live to be 150 years old or more, so there's really no hurry. Not until it reaches 75 years old does a saguaro even begin to sprout its identifying arms; so when you see a tall and fat one with many arms—and there are many in both sections of the park—know that it is a venerable old plant, deserving of respect and awe.

The place to start your tour of the western park is the **Red Hills Visitor Center** (2700 N. Kinney Rd., 520/733-5158), where you can learn about the ancient symbiotic friendship between the Tohono O'odham and the saguaro. Here you'll find a guide to the park's 40 miles of trails, and you can also book a tour with a naturalist and peruse the bookstore stocked with titles on local history and nature.

A good way to see the park, especially in the

heat of summer, is to drive the six-mile **Bajada Loop** through a thick saguaro forest. The route is graded dirt and it can get dusty, but you can also walk or bike the loop. Or you can drive the loop and stop at the **Valley View Overlook Trail,** an easy one-mile round-trip trail off the loop road that rises to an expansive view of the Avra Valley and the saguaro-lined desert and the skulking rock mountains. A half-mile round-trip walk to the **Signal Hill Picnic Area** offers a look at ancient petroglyphs. Both trails can be accessed off the Bajada Loop drive and are well marked. There are also a few very short, paved walks around the visitors center featuring interpretive signs about the saguaro and other desert fauna.

Ironwood Forest National Monument

The long-lived tree that gives **Ironwood Forest National Monument** (520/258-7200, www. blm.gov), a 129,000-acre Sonoran Desert preserve about an hour's drive northwest of Tucson, its name is likely to appear a bit

TUCSON

© TIM HULL

a prickly pear cactus, covered with sweet red fruit

underwhelming to the uninitiated. The gray-green monotony of the surface-level desert tends to blur the vision, and one bushy little tree tends to look a lot like another. As it usually is, however, the truth is in the details. The ironwood, which can live as long as 800 years or more, is an anchor for a deceptively busy desert ecosystem, providing shade and succor for a whole host of flora and fauna unique to the region. Like most of Arizona's BLM-monitored national monuments, Ironwood Forest is a vast and empty place, inviting to hikers and hunters and campers and other outdoor types. There's no visitors center, no campgrounds or rangers. It is a perfect place for a long daytime drive through the desert on its dirt roads, which are mostly smooth and accepting of regular cars, although an SUV is best. More so than even Saguaro National Park, Ironwood is a place where the wild desert is there for you to discover—unvarnished, uncultivated, and unforgiving. It's not a good idea to venture out here in the summer. If you want to head out to this wilderness, the easiest way to see it is to drive slowly along the dirt roads that traverse part of the monument, stopping here and there to look into the details. The best way to do this is to take I-10 north to Avra Valley Road, then follow the road until it turns to dirt around the waste-pile remainders of the Silverbell Mine. Just follow the road through the monument, passing the mine, the Silverbell Mountains, Ragged Top Mountain, and Wolcott Peak. Take Silverbell Road out of the monument and back to the interstate. The whole trip could take all day if you stop enough to look around. Archaeologists have said that people have been living out here for about 5,000 years, though these days there are usually only campers and hunters hanging around this glorious desert outback.

EAST AND NORTH OF DOWNTOWN

The north end of Tucson, on the bajada and the foothills of the Santa Catalinas, is known for its mission-revival and Spanish Colonial homes, many of them designed by famed architect

Josias Joesler, and its high-end accommodations. The mighty mountains, reaching 10,000 feet and hosting an entirely different world from the desert below, rise northeast of downtown and are easily reached by taking Grant east from midtown to Tanque Verde (Catalina Highway), then the Mount Lemmon Highway north into the range. To the east you'll find caves, mountains, and saguaros as far as the eye can see.

◖ Saguaro National Park East

The eastern portion of **Saguaro National Park** (3693 S. Old Spanish Trail, 520/733-5153, 7am-sunset daily, visitors center open 9am-5pm daily, $10 per car, receipt valid for seven days, good at both sections) is backed by the 8,600-foot Rincon Mountains. The visitors center has a bookstore and exhibits about the desert. The easiest way to see this section is to stroll, bike, or drive very slowly along the paved Cactus Forest Drive, an eight-mile one-way that begins at the visitors center and winds up and across the bajada. The desert here is gorgeous, especially after a rainstorm or early in the morning during the bloom months. There are more than 100 miles of trails here, including one that goes to Rincon Peak above 8,000 feet. The park's newspaper guide has a full description of the major trails.

Vista del Rio Cultural Resource Park

Before the Spanish arrived in Southern Arizona, before the Mexicans, before the Americans, even before the Tohono O'odham and the Apache ruled this desert, it was home to the Hohokam people, arid-land farmers who lived in the Sonoran Desert's river valleys, building a highly complex culture that survived for centuries. Though the Tucson valley doesn't have any spectacular Hohokam ruins on the order of Casa Grande just off I-10 halfway between Tucson and Phoenix, **Vista del Rio Cultural Resource Park** (7575 E. Desert Arbor St., dawn-dusk), a four-acre archaeological park on the east side, preserves the humbler ruins of a village occupied by the Hohokam from about AD 1000 to 1150. Even if you're less than fascinated by the dirt-mound ruins, this is a quiet and peaceful park with walking paths and sitting areas, perfect for relaxation and contemplation among the ghosts of a long-lost nation.

Colossal Cave Mountain Park

Sure it's a "dead cave," and certainly it has become in recent years but a poor country cousin to the living underground wonderland that is Kartchner Caverns State Park just a few dozen miles to the southeast, but **Colossal Cave Mountain Park** (16721 E. Old Spanish Trail, 520/647-7275, www.colossalcave.com, 8am-5pm daily Mar. 16-Sept. 15, 9am-5pm daily Sept. 16-Mar. 15, park entry $5 per car with up to five people, cave tours $13 adults, $6.50 children 6-12) near Vail, about a half-hour drive through the desert east of Tucson proper, has many charms nonetheless. The cave has been used as a shelter, an altar, a hideout, and a tourist attraction by various bands of natives and colonists for the last 1,000 years or so, according to prehistoric artifacts and historic local newspaper accounts. In the 1930s the Civilian Conservation Corps built a few structures near the cave's entrance in that inimitable stacked native stone style, and installed lights and railings through about a half mile of the sprawling grotto. The typical tour follows this route, while the guide narrates a general natural history of the cave with a bit of human history (including a tale of outlaws) peppered in. It's all very basic, but interesting and really fun, especially with kids. Those looking for a more adventurous route should check out the Saturday night "Ladder Tour" (5:15pm-9pm, $35 with dinner, must be at least 12 years old and fit, reservations required), on which you'll shimmy and squeeze through passageways far off the tourist path in a helmet and headlamp. After the cave tour, there's a gift shop and a café and long views of the desert. A few miles down the road but still within the park, the mid-1870s **La Posta Quemada Ranch** offers more activities, particularly for children. In addition to trail rides and a gift shop, the ranch features a large sundial, displays on the cave and the

TUCSON

CCC's work in the park, and a habitat for two old desert tortoises, Henry and Big Nasty. It's unlikely you'll see either tort unless you arrive in the morning, especially during the hotter months. There are plenty of shady and peaceful places to picnic here, and you can even camp if you make a reservation.

Trail Dust Town

The best way to visit **Trail Dust Town** (6541 E. Tanque Verde Rd., 520/296-5442, www.traildusttown.com, 5pm-8pm daily, $2-3 for each attraction), an Old West-themed family attraction on the east side, is to wrap it up with a cowboy steak-and-beans dinner at Pinnacle Peak Steak House. If you don't have kids, rethink the entire venture. I'm not saying that there's nothing for the adult at Trail Dust Town; anyone interested in the more popularized notions of Old West culture might get a kick or two here—there's some movie-set style buildings, a miniature train that circles the property, a few on-cue gunfights in the dusty streets, and various shops and displays featuring touristy gifts and frontier artifacts; there's a gold-panning game, a shootout gallery, and a lot of other commotion. If you have young or even youngish children, though, you and the spouse can sit in the saloon and wait for your table while the kids explore the attractions.

St. Philips Church in the Foothills

St. Philips Church in the Foothills (4440 N. Campbell Ave., 520/299-6421, www.stphilipstucson.org) was originally designed in 1936 by Josias Joesler, a Swiss-born architect who designed the majority of the Foothills structures and is responsible for the amalgam of native and revival architecture sometimes known as the Tucson Style. Joesler's structures can be counted on to mimic Mexican, Spanish, and Moorish styles with upscale flourishes, many of them stylish desertland haciendas on the bajada of the Catalinas, an area long reserved for the region's wealthy. A longtime Tucson architect said that Tucson, at least when it came to architecture, divorced itself from Mexico (and thereby Spain and its Moorish traditions) too

quickly; these styles, with their courtyards and native materials and passive solar heating, are ideal for living in the hot, dry Sonoran Desert, certainly much better than the cheaply built tract homes that proliferate in the valley these days. Very few Tucsonans build homes in the Joesler style anymore (to do so, or to live in one that's already built, is out of the financial question for most of us), and that's too bad, because Joesler, like the originals he was inspired by, had it right. St. Philip's is along the busy River Road corridor and yet retains a peaceful atmosphere with gardens and fountains behind thick, silent walls. The building and grounds have been added to and changed over the years, but always with respect to the original vision. Church officials welcome visitors and students of architecture and anybody else who wants to look around. It's best not to go on a Sunday if you're just looking, and it's best to go before 4pm weekdays if you want to talk to someone about the church and its history.

Tohono Chul Park

Tohono Chul Park (7366 N. Paseo del Norte, 520/742-6455, www.tohonochulpark.org, 8am-5pm daily, $8 adults, $6 seniors, $4 students, $2 children 5-12), a 49-acre desert preserve, is worth the short drive north on Oracle Road out into Tucson's sprawl. Turn left on Ina Road, then right on Paseo del Norte, and you'll find native-plant gardens with easy trails punctuated by interpretive signs. The **Ethnobotanical Garden,** with rows of maize and other crops once planted by the O'odham and the Spanish settlers, demonstrates the different methods used by each group to coax subsistence out of the dry ground.

Kids will love the miniature stream, in which they can float little boats shaped like fish in the **Garden for Children,** where they can also see some old desert tortoises lolling about. If you stay quiet and sit by one of the many fountains or other water features on the grounds, you might get a glimpse of the many bobcats or javelina that call the preserve home. One night a year, in June or July, the garden's **Night-Blooming Cereus** comes to life, an event

© TIM HULL

Tohono Chul Park features a variety of succulents and cacti.

so rare and spectacular that there's a hotline (520/575-8468) for visitors to keep up-to-date on the expected bloom.

There are gift shops and galleries on the property, and exhibits generally feature Native American and Hispanic folk and fine arts. Don't miss the locally famous scones at the **Tohono Chul Park Tea Room** (520/797-1222, 8am-5pm daily, $2.95-12), a perfect place to lounge after exploring the grounds.

Roy P. Drachman
Agua Caliente Regional Park

Approaching the shock of wet greenery among the otherwise gray-green of the foothills, it's easy to see why this spring-fed oasis has been a popular spot for humans for the last 5,000 years or more. Now **Roy P. Drachman Agua Caliente Regional Park** (12325 E. Roger Rd., 520/749-3718, 7am-sunset daily; visitors center and art gallery 1pm-4pm Wed.-Fri., 8am-4pm Sat.-Sun. Nov.-Apr.), a 100-acre public park with a visitors center, gallery, nature shop, and wildlife-attracting spring-water ponds, the

site has over the millennia been a stopover for hunter-gatherers and the farming Hohokam culture, as well as a ranch and a resort built to exploit the supposedly curative powers of the springs. Much of the vegetation here, as well as the fish and the log-lounging turtles you'll see everywhere, are decidedly nonnative. The shaggy palms, encircling the ponds like some spice road camp, were planted long ago, but the 200-year-old mesquite tree next to the former ranch house, a tree that hosts a whole ecosystem of its own, is native to the area and one of the oldest mesquites in the valley. This is a contemplative, peaceful spot, a good place for a walk or a picnic or a long talk by the 87-degree ponds, with lazy turtles listening in.

DeGrazia Gallery in the Sun

A lot of art lovers turn up their noses at Ettore "Ted" DeGrazia. His little sad-eyed native children are ubiquitous here, on mugs and Christmas ornaments and whatever else, and all the work can look the same and seems to offer little in the way of depth. A visit to

© TIM HULL

Ettore DeGrazia built this chapel near his studio and dedicated it to the Virgin of Guadalupe.

the **DeGrazia Gallery in the Sun** (6300 N. Swan Rd., 520/299-9191, http://degrazia.org, 10am-4pm daily, free), the amazing foothills home and gallery that he largely built himself, changes opinions of the artist. When you see the home he built and get a close-up look at the more serious paintings that hang throughout the gallery—epic cycles about the Mexican Revolution, the "founding" of the Southwest by Cabeza de Vaca and his doomed companions, and the lives and traditions of the Tohono O'odham, to name just a few—you may conclude, as I did, that, far from being a hack, DeGrazia actually created some of the most enduring impressionistic visions in the Southwest. A native of Southern Arizona, DeGrazia attended the UA and published his first work in *Arizona Highways* magazine. He went on to study in Mexico with muralists Diego Rivera and Jose Clemente Orozco. He died in 1982 at the age of 73, but the DeGrazia Foundation carries on his memory at the Gallery in the Sun, DeGrazia's first studio and gallery in Tucson, built in honor of Padre Kino and dedicated

to Our Lady of Guadalupe. A mission on the grounds features DeGrazia murals, with a roof open to the sky. The gallery has a gift shop stocked with DeGrazia reproductions for sale. Even if you can't muster an appreciation of this admittedly overexposed artist's work, go for the native architecture and design to be found at his Gallery in the Sun, which may, after all, be DeGrazia's greatest work of art.

◖ Santa Catalina Mountains

In the arid basin and range territory, most living goes on in the basins, while most of the longing targets the cool, arboreal heights of the ranges. A range's relative accessibility usually determines the long-term happiness of the population sweating away on lower ground, so it stands to reason that Tucson's residents, living as they do in the shadow of the Santa Catalina Mountains, are quite content.

About 30 miles, an hour or so up a twisty, paved two-lane from the desert floor northeast of midtown, and you're at nearly 10,000 feet—the trip, it is often said, is like traveling from

TUCSON

© ANTON FOLTIN/123RF.COM

saguaros in the Santa Catalina Mountains

Mexico to Canada in one short scenic drive. It wasn't until the 1930s that Tucsonans could reach the cool heights in great numbers. It was then that former U.S. Post Master General Frank Hitchcock called in some federal favors and secured money and convict labor to begin building a road into the mountains. The indomitable Civilian Conservation Corps eventually finished the job, and in the 1940s real estate agents began selling lots in what is now **Summerhaven,** a little cabin village at 7,840 feet with a few gift shops and cafés. Just up a bit from the village are the 22 runs of **Ski Valley** (10300 Ski Run Rd., 520/576-1321, snow report 520/576-1400, 9am-4pm daily, $11-32), the nation's southernmost ski hill. The season runs, roughly, from mid-December to early April in a good year. The chairlift operates year-round, and it's fun to ride it to the green and cool mountaintop in the summer while the rest of the world sweats below.

There are dozens of trails on the range, and there are several public bathrooms, campgrounds, and lookout points. It's a good idea to

stop at the **Palisade Visitor Center** (520/749-8700, 8:30am-4:40pm daily) at 7,200 feet, which has trail maps, a bookstore, and displays about the mountain's ecology. There's a $5 per car user fee to go up the mountain, paid at a fee station along the road, or you can buy an annual pass for $20, which will allow you to access the Catalinas, the Santa Rita Mountains in the Santa Cruz Valley, and Sabino Canyon as many times as you like for one year.

Expect not to be alone when you're exploring the Catalinas; this is an extremely popular area among locals for picnicking and hiking, especially in the spring and summer. That being said, while the weekends are sometimes bumper-to-bumper, on weekdays, even in the summer, it's possible to avoid large crowds.

Sabino Canyon

Though in the range's foothills, Sabino Canyon is inextricably linked to the Santa Catalinas because without the mountains there would be very little water to fill up Sabino Creek, and without Sabino Creek this Edenic desert canyon would be just another rugged notch dominated by saguaro.

As it is, though, Sabino Creek starts as springs high up in the mountains, gathering snowmelt and runoff as it descends into the foothills, where it rushes through Sabino Canyon with sometimes-deadly vigor, creating a riparian oasis of cottonwoods, willow, walnut, sycamore, and ash, while saguaro, barrel cactus, prickly pear, and cholla dominate the rocky canyon slopes away from the creek's influence. It is a truly spectacular place that should not be missed.

Sabino Canyon Recreation Area, about 13 miles northeast of downtown Tucson, is easily accessible, user-friendly in the extreme, and heavily used—best estimates say 1.25 million people visit every year. Many locals use the canyon's trail system for daily exercise, and hikers, picnickers, and sightseers usually pack the canyon on any given day in any given season.

A paved road rises nearly four miles up into the canyon, crossing the nearly always running creek in several places. During Southern Arizona's summer and winter rainy seasons, it is nearly impossible to cross the small overflowing bridges without getting your feet wet. The Forest Service closed the road to cars in 1978. It's a relatively easy walk along the road to the top of the canyon and access to trails that go far into the Santa Catalinas. If you don't feel like walking, the **Sabino Canyon Shuttle** (520/749-2861, www.sabinocanyon.com, $8 adults, $4 children 3-12, children under 2 free) runs 45-minute, narrated trips into the canyon all day, pausing at nine stops along the way to take on or let off hikers at various trailheads. From July through mid-December the shuttle runs 9am-4pm weekdays and 9am-4:30pm on weekends and holidays. From mid-December to June it runs 9am-4:30pm daily.

From the last tram stop 3.8 miles up in the canyon, hikers can get off and take an easy stroll down the road, crossing the creek at nearly every turn, or try the **Phoneline Trail** winding along the canyon slopes and overlooking the riparian beauty below. Perhaps the most popular trail in the entire Tucson Valley is the

hike through nearby **Bear Canyon** to **Seven Falls,** a wonderful series of waterfalls and collecting pools. You can access the **Bear Canyon Trail** from just outside the visitors center, or take the shuttle to a trailhead 1.5 miles on. To the falls it's a total of 3.8 miles one way, and worth every step. The Bear Canyon shuttle leaves the visitors center every hour on the hour, 9am-4pm daily ($3 for adults, $1 children 3-12).

The **Sabino Canyon Visitors Center and Bookstore** (520/749-8700, www.fs.fed.us/r3/coronado, 8am-4:30pm Mon.-Fri., 8:30am-4:30pm Sat.-Sun.) has trail guides and sells gifts and books. There are bathrooms, drinking fountains, and dozens of tucked-away picnic areas throughout the canyon, and many of the trails link up with one another, so it is easy to cobble together a loop hike that will take you through all of the various life zones. The canyon is open from sunup to sundown every day, and bikes are allowed in the canyon only before 9am and after 5pm, never on Wednesday or Saturday, and never on trails that lead into the **Pusch Ridge Wilderness Area.**

To get to the canyon from midtown take Speedway Boulevard east until it turns into Tanque Verde Road, then turn north on Sabino Canyon Road to the recreation area, just north of Sunrise Road. There's $5-per-car fee for one day, or $10 for a week. An annual pass can be had for $20.

Catalina State Park

Catalina State Park (State Hwy. 77, mile marker 81, 520/628-5798, www.azstateparks.com, 5am-10pm daily, $7 per car), a popular desert reserve just north of Tucson in the saguaro-dotted foothills of the Santa Catalinas, is heavily used, especially on weekends. Hikers shouldn't be surprised to pass large families carrying coolers and bags of chips up the trail.

The 5,500-acre park has eight trails—most of them easy to moderate—picnic areas, charcoal grills, and a small gift shop. It's an easily accessible place to see the desert, lush here thanks to the runoff and snowmelt that barrels down from the mountains through boulder-strewn washes. In the early spring and late summer there are many natural pools that fill up with runoff, some of them deep enough to be called swimming holes.

The seven-mile **Romero Canyon Trail** will take you to an array of natural pools—and you don't have to hike the whole trail to get there. If you want to get off the beaten track a little, veer right about a mile into the trail near a bench and pick your way down into the wash, then head up the wash following a footpath that leads to some out-of-the-way less-used pools. For an easy walk, take the 0.5-mile round-trip **Romero Ruin Interpretive Trail** to an ancient Hohokam site. The ranger station/gift shop has a guide to all the park's trails, some of which link up to other trails all the way up into the mountains.

Biosphere 2

In the early 1990s eight scientists took up residence in **Biosphere 2** (32540 S. Biosphere Rd., 520/838-6200, www.b2science.org, 9am-4pm daily, $20 adults, $13 children 6-12), a 3.14-acre simulation of the earth (which would, of course, be Biosphere 1), in hopes of lasting two years and gaining important knowledge about how humans will survive in the future. They weren't able to remain self-contained, owing to problems with the food supply, but two members of the team fell in love at least. The unique laboratory may yet save the world, however, as the UA is now running experiments under the dome and researching ways to combat climate change.

While the science is fascinating—there are actually small savannas, rainforests, deserts, and even an ocean under the glass—many who take the tour seem more fascinated by the doomed experiments in togetherness. Indeed, the tour takes you into the "Biospherians'" apartments and kitchen, and through their garden, and guides field more questions on this part of the tour than all the others. The tour lasts about 45 minutes and is not wheelchair accessible. The Biosphere is in a beautiful 35-acre desert setting about 30 minutes north of Tucson near the small town of Oracle.

TUCSON

© TIM HULL

the world-famous Biosphere 2

Oracle

This small historic town about 30 miles north of Tucson on the northeastern slopes of the Santa Catalina range has a few historic buildings and a proliferation of high-desert-dwelling artists. The **Acadia Ranch Museum** (825 Mount Lemmon Rd., 1pm-5pm Fri.-Sat., free) tells the colorful history of the ranch—once a sheep ranch and later a sanatorium for sufferers of TB and other ailments—and of the town, which today has about 3,500 people, many of them artists and other desert runaways. The **Oracle Union Church** (695 E. American Ave.) is on the National Register of Historical Places and is worth a look, as is a nearby state park. There are several restaurants, including a historic steak house, and even a few little B&Bs, if you'd rather stay out here in the relative cool of 4,000 feet.

SOUTH OF DOWNTOWN

Head south from downtown and you reach South Tucson, a largely Latino community incorporated as a separate city. The airport is farther south, and to the southeast is the Pima Air and Space Museum, on the southwest edge of Davis Monthan Air Force Base. To the southwest, reached via I-19, is San Xavier del Bac.

Jardin de Cesar Chavez

A tiny park on the edge of South Tucson, dedicated to the Mexican American labor organizer and human rights activist (a native of Yuma, Arizona), **Jardin de Cesar Chavez** (Stone Ave. and Sixth St.) is worth seeing for its brilliant mural depicting ancient Aztec gods lounging around and seemingly passing stern judgment on all who pass. Artist Melchor Ramirez, known for painting the heroes and legends of the Aztec and Maya, painted the mural in vibrant yet earthy colors, and the names and dates of well-known human rights advocates—Tolstoy, Gandhi, etc.—are scrawled alongside the oversized figures. There's not a parking lot or anything, and you'll likely miss the sight unless you're looking for it. As you drive south on Stone Avenue, look to your right as you approach Sixth Street. There are several benches perfect for sitting and contemplating the fascinating paintings as the traffic zips by.

Pima Air and Space Museum

One of the largest museums of its kind in the West, the **Pima Air and Space Museum** (6000 E. Valencia Rd., 520/574-0462, www.pimaair. org, 9am-5pm daily, $15.50 adults, $12.75 seniors/military, $9 children 7-12) has interesting exhibits and an impressive number of decommissioned aircraft that tell the story of our fascination with defying gravity. Nearly 300 rare airplanes, many of them military, rest on the grounds and in six different hangars.

The Air and Space Museum is operated by the same group that operates the Titan Missile Museum near Green Valley, and for one price you can see both attractions. War plane enthusiasts will want to take the hour-long bus tour to the **Aerospace Maintenance and Regeneration Center (AMARC)** to see the hundreds of dust-gathering planes ending their days in this "boneyard."

◖ San Xavier del Bac

Founded in 1692 by Father Eusebio Francisco Kino and then built slowly over decades by other priests, missionaries, and natives, the mission **San Xavier del Bac** (1950 W. San Xavier Rd., 520/294-2624, www.sanxaviermission. org, 7am-5pm daily, free, donations encouraged) sits pure white against the perpetually blue sky about nine miles south of Tucson on the Tohono O'odham's San Xavier Indian Reservation. It is considered by many to be the foremost example of mission architecture remaining in the United States, blending elements of Moorish, Byzantine, and late Mexican Renaissance architecture.

Few Arizona landmarks have received as much worldwide attention as the "White Dove of the Desert," which has been called America's answer to the Sistine Chapel. Mass is still celebrated daily in the church (check website for times), but non-Catholic visitors are encouraged and welcomed.

Most days there are tables and booths set up in the mission's plaza selling burritos, fry bread,

© TIM HULL

San Xavier del Bac

and other delicious eats, and across from the mission to the south is a small shopping area called **San Xavier Plaza,** with a snack bar and several shops selling Native American crafts.

Statues and paintings of St. Francis Xavier and the Virgin of Guadalupe decorate the cool, dark interior of the domed church. A continuous videotape about the mission runs throughout the day as a self-guided tour, and there's a gift shop on-site that sells religious items and books about the history of the mission and the region. A small museum presents the history of the area's native inhabitants and the construction and ongoing rehabilitation of the mission. The mission is continually being worked on, but the seemingly ever-present scaffolding doesn't detract too much from its grandeur.

Entertainment and Events

NIGHTLIFE

Tucson's most vibrant nightlife takes place on three blocks within easy walking, or stumbling, distance of each other: Congress Street downtown, 4th Avenue, and Main Gate Square near the UA. There are always plenty of cabs waiting around outside the bars in these neighborhoods, especially on the weekends. When school's in session these areas are fairly packed with scantily clad young women and boys in flip-flops and baseball caps (a large contingent of the UA's student body is from California). But Tucson's nightlife and entertainment scene is fairly casual and mixed, drawing drunken college kids, postcollege slackers and go-getters, thirty-something urban workers, hip parents who still haunt the alt-rock shows, and professors and professionals of indeterminate age. There's really something for everybody out there.

Second Saturdays

Once a month on **Second Saturdays** (www.2ndsaturdaysdowntown.com), the streets of downtown Tucson come alive, as thousands of Old Pueblo residents head to the city's traditional heart to meet and mingle. The event, which, as its name suggests, goes down on the second Saturday of every month, features street vendors, performers, food, bands, art shows and more, and all the downtown stores, bars, clubs, and restaurants along Congress Street are usually hopping with activity. This is the best time to see downtown Tucson at its most active and interesting.

Bars, Pubs, and Lounges

DOWNTOWN AND UNIVERSITY DISTRICT

The Tap Room (311 E. Congress St., 520/622-8848, www.hotelcongress.com, 11am-2am daily) has been around since 1919 and still packs them in, especially when there's a band playing at Club Congress, to which the Tap Room serves as a kind of hideout from the crush and noise. But if you belly-up here of an afternoon, or on a slow midweek night, you'll notice the details: the retro booths and stools; the scratchy juke in the corner; and especially the cowboy-life art of Pete Martinez, one of several lauded western artists who once called Tucson home. Martinez, who lived in Tucson from 1935 until his death in 1971, was neighbor to the painter and illustrator Maynard Dixon and friend to Ted DeGrazia, and he reportedly spent a good deal of his time drinking at the Tap Room. Martinez's art can be seen on the bar's walls. People always used to say that he would from time to time trade his work for his drinks, and that's how they got there. But the management says that's just a rumor, and that the artist gifted the paintings to his favorite bar.

The **Playground Bar & Lounge** (278 E. Congress St., 520/396-3691, http://playground-tucson.com, 4pm-2am Mon.-Fri., noon-2am Sat.-Sun.) is the premier downtown desert-hipster hangout with a lost childhood theme. The best thing about the Playground, besides its deep stylishness, is its spectacular rooftop patio with panoramic views of the city—the perfect place to sip a margarita or a martini while the sun dips away in the cool of the evening. Twentieth Century nostalgia and a kind of slacker-intellectual ethos pervade here: DJs playing only vinyl, "show and tell" lectures on local issues, scarf-wearing fans gathering to watch FIFA soccer games. Often there's a shoe-gazing local band playing on one floor while an energetic DJ entertains another. They offer cheap drinks during "recess" every weekday from 4pm to 7pm.

Scott & Co. (49 N. Scott Ave., 520/624-4747, www.47scott.com, 6pm-close Mon.-Sat.) is a tiny, outwardly nondescript "speakeasy-style" bar on downtown's Scott Avenue, and the emphasis here is on the drink in your hand. The expert bartenders at Scott & Co., which is connected to the excellent restaurant 47 Scott next door, take their jobs very seriously. The menu of unique and creative drinks, many of them updated twists on classic cocktails, changes often, but the ingredients are always top shelf and house-made. Don't pass up the chance to have the bartender make you a custom drink based on an interview about your preferences. This place is not appropriate for large, loud parties; it's more a romantic throw-back to the days when drinking cocktails was serious business.

At **Elliott's on Congress** (135 E. Congress St., 520/622-5500, http://elliottsoncongress.com, 11am-2am daily), a cozy and hip downtown bar and restaurant, they have dozens of house-infused vodka varieties with flavors that, at first, seem a bit nonsensical: jalapeno, habanero, green bell pepper, horseradish, etc. Always try it before you scoff, though; the best time to do so is during the daily happy hour from 4pm to 7pm, during which the unique concoctions are just $3.

Though it's not always open, **Borderlands Brewing Co.** (119 E. Toole Ave., 520/261-8773, borderlandsbrewing.com, 4pm-7pm Wed.-Fri., noon-4pm Sat., until 7pm during Second Saturdays) is the place to sample some of the best microbrews the Old Pueblo has to offer. The brewers here use local ingredients and follow in the footsteps of beer-loving Germans who settled in the Southwest in the 1800s.

They serve several different beers in a tasting-room setting, including a citrus IPA, a Prickly Pear wheat, and a rich vanilla porter. There's usually a food truck or two parked outside during the hours that the brewery is open for sampling, and there's often a band in residence.

Bar Toma at **El Charro,** one of the Old Pueblo's oldest and best-loved restaurants, 311 N. Court Ave., 520/622-1922, www.elcharrocafe.com, noon-9pm Sun.-Thurs., noon-10pm Fri.-Sat.) has patio seating and a small but stylish bar that is a laid-back and civilized place to drink a margarita or five.

The Shanty (401 E. 9th St., 520/623-2664, noon-2am Mon.-Sat., noon-midnight Sun.) is an old railroad bar turned Irish pub turned college kid hangout. It's on the edge of the Iron Horse neighborhood (where the railroad workers used to live) just off 4th Avenue. It has a large patio lined with greenery and is usually crowded on the weekends with, as in most Tucson bars, a mixture of the young and the not-so-young, all drinking together. They've got a lot of beers, between 80 and 100, with

most of the exotic stuff in bottles; they certainly pour a good Guinness. Several pool tables get heavy use. There's no food other than free bar-top popcorn. Though it has moved once since it opened, the Shanty holds the oldest liquor license in Tucson.

The **Surly Wench** (424 N. 4th Ave., 520/882-0009, www.surlywenchpub.com, 5pm-2am Mon.-Thurs., 2pm-2am Sat.-Sun.) is a cool 4th Avenue pub with a kind of punkabilly vibe. The holy trinity here is "booze, burlesque, and bands," but they also serve pretty good burgers, sandwiches, fried stuff, and a few Mexican dishes. This is the only place in town where you can see the tattooed and pulse-quickening bombshells that make up the Black Cherry Burlesque troupe (there's an up-to-date schedule of shows—and photos—on the website), and they are certainly something worth seeing.

Mr. Head's Art Gallery and Bar (513 N. 4th Ave., 520/792-2710, noon-2am daily) draws a mixed 4th Avenue-style crowd of college kids and frolicking urbanites with live

Mr. Head's Art Gallery and Bar

bands, curious, glorious and strange artwork, and a large selection of Arizona microbrews. The patio here is particularly nice.

Not exactly a hangout for revolutionaries in the Che Guevara mode, **Che's Lounge** (350 N. 4th Ave., 520/623-2088, noon-2am daily, www.cheslounge.com) is instead a small, inviting hangout for a vast array of 4th Avenue denizens, from college kids to forty-somethings. They don't charge much for their drinks, and if you're broke you can always find somebody with $1 to buy you a PBR or one of the round-robin of $1 drafts they serve nightly. Bands set up in the cramped corners most weekend nights, and there are a few classic arcade games scattered throughout and an excellent, fully stocked juke.

Next to Brooklyn Pizza on 4th Avenue, **Skybar** (536 N. 4th Ave., 520/622-4300, www.skybartucson.com, 9am-2am daily) is a "solar powered café by day" and an "astronomy bar by night." The open, airy bar, with a patio from which you can watch all the people sauntering along 4th Avenue, is ideal for kicking back with a drink and a slice of New York-style pizza from next door (which they'll bring to you). The "astronomy bar" title comes from the telescopes they set up come nightfall, allowing patrons to peer into the nearly always clear skies above Tucson. They also show deep space images on a big screen. From 5pm to 8pm daily the happy hour prices kick in, and throughout the week they offer theme nights (including a family night on Tuesday with pizza specials and a free astronomy show), as well as live jazz, DJs, open mic nights, and dance parties.

MIDTOWN

Smoke Cigar Patio and Bar (2959 N. Swan Rd., 520/327-7463, 11:30am-10pm daily) is a very comfortable and stylish climate-controlled smoker's patio-lounge at McMahon's Prime Steakhouse. If you're a smoker looking for fellow travelers and a high-end place to relax with a drink, an appetizer, and a clean ashtray at the ready, this is the place for you. It's a bit pricey all around, but they offer daily drink and food specials, and a half-price happy hour weekdays

from 3pm to 6pm. The cigar selection runs from as low as $2.50 to as high as $36, with most falling in the $8-15 range. While nearly all Tucson's bars have added enclosed, climate-controlled patios since an ordinance banned smoking in bars otherwise, this is by far the nicest.

The ancient recipe of fruit juice mixed with booze is at the heart of the retro-realistic **Kon Tiki** (4625 E. Broadway Blvd., 520/323-7193, www.kontikitucson.com 11am-10pm Mon.-Sat., 4pm-9pm Sun.), a favorite among the Arizona tiki-culture crowd since it opened way back in 1963. The drinks at Kon Tiki are a far cry from a red plastic cup full of "jungle juice" ladled out in some dorm room, however. Even if you claim to be a tough-guy shot-and-beer type, it's hard to resist escaping to Kon Tiki's cool dark interior to sip away a happy hour (when tasty pupus, with amazing booze-soaking power, are half price), trying something pink, something blue, something red, something frozen, something served in a Polynesian-style bowl bigger than your head. Make sure to say hello to the huge, languid iguana hanging out behind glass.

The Tucson Valley played a major role in the Cold War: For years ICBMs ringed the city, locked and loaded beneath the desert and aimed directly at various targets in the USSR. While there's a museum south of town where you can learn all about the Old Pueblo's Atomic Age bona fides, **The Shelter** (4155 E. Grant Rd., 520/326-1345, 3pm-1am daily) is the best place to celebrate, so to speak, the era and its two coolest cold warriors. It's dark and cool like a shelter should be, and there's plenty of good booze and always a campy cult film playing out silently on a TV in the corner. The walls are covered with Jack and Bobby, and the pinball machines ding and flap.

Named for the mountains where the Tohono O'odham believe their creator dwells, **Danny's Baboquivari** (2910 E. Fort Lowell Rd., 520/795-3178, 2pm-2am Mon.-Sat., 10am-2am Sun.), a near-dive bar near Ft. Lowell and Country Club, is the perfect place to hide out from the heat, or anything else you might be running from. It's cool and cozy and dark, with a low ceiling and big cushy Naugahyde booths along the wall. The juke box is excellent, the drinks are cheap, and there are a few pool tables in the back.

With folks behind Tucson's iconic restaurant El Charo in charge of the kitchen, **Sir Veza's** (699 E. Speedway Blvd., 520/323-8226, 220 W. Wetmore, 520/888-8226, www.sirvezas.com, 11am-midnight Sun.-Thurs., 11am-2am Fri.-Sat.), a retro-motorhead "Taco Garage," is definitely a fine place to fill up; but it's even better if you combine dinner with an evening of sampling cocktails both classical and unique in the bar and watching a game on the TVs. Try the "CerVezarita": a margarita with a bottle of Pacifico mixed in.

FOOTHILLS

The **Cascade Lounge at Loews Ventana Canyon Resort** (7000 N. Resort Dr., 520/299-2020, www.loewshotels.com, 2pm-10pm Mon.-Thurs. and Sun., Fri.-Sat. 2pm-midnight) is an eminently tasteful and upscale place to drink, with warm and earthy colors, thick and comfortable furniture, low, flattering lighting, and 30-foot windows offering commanding views from Ventana Canyon's high perch in the Catalina foothills. One of Tucson's most romantic night spots, Cascade offers a nightly happy hour with affordable drinks and small plates from 5:30pm to 7:30pm, music on Wednesday-Saturday.

Sipping a martini among stylish and stimulating surroundings while watching the desert city fade to black from high above the valley is just as much of a typical Tucson experience as scrambling up some rocky trail shadowed by saguaros. One of the best places to do the former is the **Azul Lounge** (3800 E. Sunrise Dr., 520/742-6000, www.westinlapalomaresort.com), a rather upscale but not forbidding lounge at the **Westin La Paloma Resort** in the Catalina Foothills. The lounge, decorated all in blue and washed by music that registers but doesn't get in the way, offers top-notch cocktails and delicious small plates, all complimented with a view that can't be beat. The

least expensive time to go is during happy hour, weekdays from 5pm to 7pm.

Live Music

Club Congress (311 E. Congress St., 520/622-8848, www.hotelcongress.com, 9pm-1am Sun.-Mon., 10pm-1am Tues.-Sat., cover varies), inside the historic Hotel Congress, is the city's premier spot for touring alternative rock and alt-country bands. Most nights if there's not a band playing there's a DJ and dancing. Music geeks and collegetown rock-n-rollers frequent the shows here, and it's a kind of headquarters for the thriving downtown music scene—the stage new local bands aspire to get to. If you're not in the mood for sweaty crowds, guitars, or break-beats, there's a somewhat quieter lounge in the lobby, but the music is the club's reason for being, and thank the gods for that. The nicest Quonset hut you've ever gotten drunk in, **The Hut** (305 N. 4th Ave., 520/623-3200, www.huttucson.com, 4pm-2am Mon.-Fri., noon-2am Sat.-Sun., cover varies) books in the

This tiki head greets you as you enter The Hut.

© TIM HULL

weird and the rocking in equal measure, with roots, rock, blues, reggae, and even spoken-word performance art filling the faux-tropical bar most nights. It has a kind of slum-tiki vibe, laid-back and beach-bound with a lot of frozen drinks on the menu. A three-story cement tiki head saved from a beloved but defunct miniature golf course in east Tucson was installed at the bar's entrance in 2008, adding one more reason to visit this classic watering hole.

A well-appointed, comfortable club frequented by downtown artists and musicians, hipsters, and students, **Plush** (340 E. 6th St., 520/798-1302, www.plushtucson.com, cover varies) is the place on 4th to experience Tucson's vibrant music scene, as well as nationally known alternative rock and alt-country acts. There are often acts playing in the front living-room area and on a stage in the back; there's also a patio for smoking.

When you see the two-story bottle of chianti near 1st Avenue and Prince, you'll know you've found **Boondock's Lounge** (3306 N. 1st Ave., 520/690-0991, www.boondockslounge.com, noon-2am Mon., 10am-2am Tues.-Sat.), a friendly place with lots of pool tables and dart boards, a cast of regulars, and a stage that welcomes roots-rock, reggae, and country bands throughout the week. The inhouse **Range Rider's Grille** serves good burgers, sandwiches, and finger foods, and five nights a week there's a dinner special for a mere $5-6 a plate. All around a fine place to spend your time.

The home of the best craft beer in the state, **Nimbus Brewing Company** (3850 E. 44th St. #138, 520/745-9175, www.nimbusbeer.com, 11am-11pm Mon.-Thurs., 11am-1am Fri.-Sat., noon-9pm Sun.) also books local and touring rock, folk, blues, and country bands into the same ultracasual brew-house setting from which they produce 22,500 barrels of delicious elixir every year. If you don't like beer, and you don' t like to rock, there's not much else to do here. But if you do like beer, especially European-style ales (Nimbus makes six different flavors), then you must go here. The bands are usually excellent and a lot of fun. They offer a small menu of tasty "munchies" to help soak up a few pints.

The **Skybox** (5605 E. River Rd., 520/529-7180, skyboxrestaurant.com, 11am-1am Sun.-Thurs., 11am-2am Fri.-Sat.) is a midscale bar and restaurant in the Catalina Foothills with spectacular views of the city and sports on all the televisions. It generally attracts 30- and 40-somethings who are happy to be out of the house with a buzz on and who aren't afraid to dance. Things reach a fever pitch on Friday nights around 9:30pm, when an after-work crowd, well-lubricated in the aftermath of happy hour (4pm-7pm weekdays), stays on to party with "80's And Gentleman," a 1980s-pop cover band—featuring a spot-on retro Madonna singer—that gets the whole place hopping and cheering. It's a campy, memorable good time.

Dancing

El Parador (2744 E. Broadway, 520/881-2744, www.elparadortucson.com, 4pm-9pm Mon.-Thurs., 4pm-2am Fri.-Sat., brunch 10:30am-2pm Sun.) has salsa dancing with a live band 10pm-2am and dance lessons every Friday beginning at 10:15pm. Every second and fourth Saturday of the month, a live salsa band performs 10pm-2am, and there is a disc jockey and dancing 10pm-2am on the first and third Saturdays.

One of the pinnacles of Tucson's rather modest club scene, the **Sapphire Lounge** (61 E. Congress St., 520/624-9100 or 520/306-8116, www.sapphiretucson.com, 6pm-2am daily) has all you'd expect from a high-end dance place (beautiful, dressed-up revelers, thumping beats and top-notch cocktails) with added attraction of the "Sky Deck Lounge," a rooftop patio with views of the city. Call ahead for VIP service and details on the dress code.

One of just a few dance clubs in the Old Pueblo, downtown's **Zen Rock** (121 E. Congress St., 520/306-8116, www.zenrocktucson.com, Mon.-Sat. 6pm-close) is a semi-swanky place with the usual Vegas-style club pretensions and a mostly college-age crowd of regular weekend revelers. The music is loud and exciting, the DJs deft and high-energy, and the crowd is generally sexy, slinky, and scantily clad. Call ahead for VIP service and dress codes.

THEATERS AND VENUES

From the 1930s to the 1970s, the **Fox Theatre** (17 W. Congress St., 520/624-1515, www.fox-tucsontheatre.org, box office open 11am-6pm Mon.-Fri., 11am-2pm Sat.) was the place to go in Tucson to see Hollywood's latest offering, and the theater's art deco style nearly matched the glamour on the screen. Along with many other once-famous and much-used buildings in downtown, the Fox fell into disrepair until the late 1990s, when a group formed to raise money to refurbish the old movie house. Now the theater, beautifully restored to its original grandeur, shows classic films several times a month and hosts concerts and events.

The **Rialto** (318 E. Congress St., 520/740-1000, www.rialtotheatre.com, box office open noon-6pm Mon.-Fri.) is a cool old theater with a balcony; its stage regularly hosts the best alt-rock and alt-country touring bands, acts like Ryan Adams, Son Volt, and Shooter Jennings. Across Congress Street from the Hotel Congress downtown, the theater originally opened in 1920 and served over the years as a vaudeville house, silent movie theater, and a porno theater, among other things. Now it operates as a nonprofit organization showing the best concerts in town.

The **Temple of Music and Art** (330 S. Scott Ave., 520/884-4875) is a beautiful old theater and playhouse built in 1927 downtown. It is the main stage for the Arizona Theatre Company and hosts concerts and shows throughout the year.

PERFORMING ARTS

The **Arizona Theatre Company** (330 S. Scott Ave., 520/622-2823) puts on an excellent season of plays September-May at the Temple of Music and Art, and the **Arizona Opera** (520/293-4336, www.azopera.org) presents some of the best regional opera in the country October-April at the TCC Music Hall

(260 S. Church Ave.). The **Tucson Symphony** (520/882-8585, www.tucsonsymphony.org) holds concerts September-May at the TCC Music Hall.

CINEMA

If you want to see the latest Hollywood blockbuster or just about any other film in wide release, try one of the 20 screens at midtown's **Century El Con** (3601 E. Broadway, 520/202-3343). The best theater in town is **The Loft Cinema** (3233 E. Speedway Blvd., 520/795-0844, www.loftcinema.com), which shows art-house foreign films, and free showings of classic films on Sunday afternoons and Monday nights. There's always something worth seeing at this remodeled old theater, and you can buy a beer and a slice of fancy pizza to go with all the soul searching on the big screen.

COMEDY

Touring stand-up comedians from around the country stop at **Laffs Comedy Club** (2900 E. Broadway, Ste. 154, 520/323-8669, www.laffscomedyclub.com), with show times at 8pm Thursday, 8pm and 10:30pm Friday, and 7pm and 9:30pm Saturday. It costs $7 to get in Thursday, and $10 Friday and Saturday.

CASINOS

The completely refurbished **Desert Diamond Casino & Hotel** on Tucson's south side (7350 S. Nogales Hwy., 520/294-7777 or 866/332-9467, www.desertdiamondcasino.com), operated by the Tohono O'odham tribe, has slot machines, blackjack, poker, keno, and bingo, as well as a grill and a Chinese restaurant, and a hotel that opened in late 2007. Take I-19 south to Pima Mine Road and you'll discover the other **Desert Diamond Casino** (520/294-7777, www.desertdiamondcasino.com) operated by the Tohono O'odham. It has slot machines, blackjack, poker, keno, and bingo, and serves home-style meals at an all-you-can eat buffet. **The Agave Restaurant** serves wonderful, eclectic lunches and dinners 11am-9pm daily. There's a constant stream of talent moving through Desert Diamond's

TUCSON

The Day of the Dead

© TIM HULL

In the Arizona borderlands it's difficult to find a boutique, gift shop, or gallery these days that doesn't sell calavera (skeletons doing human things) statues, paintings, T-shirts, and all manner of other consumer goods featuring the Day of the Dead aesthetic. Generally these art objects re-create the work, or at least the spirit of the work, of Posada, a late 19th-century-early 20th-century Mexican print maker and illustrator whose broadsides and newspaper illustrations employed the calavera and Day of the Dead traditions in social commentary. While Posada's work had the immediacy of journalism, it has outlasted its original intent and is more popular today than ever before. His style, and his overt political commentary, influenced the likes of Diego Rivera and other Mexican muralists of the first half of the 20th century.

To see Posada's famous broadsides in the original, as they were distributed on the streets of Mexico City, check out the University of New Mexico's collection at http://elibrary.unm.edu/cswr/posada.

The Day of the Dead, El Día de los Muertos, falls on November 2, but the celebrations begin on November 1 or even before that. It is roughly meant to coincide with the traditional Catholic holidays of All Saints Day and All Souls Day, but the tradition, most anthropologists believe, is far older than the Spanish conquest of Mexico. Indeed, it is, like most Latin American rites, a deep-time amalgam of pre-Columbian and Spanish traditions whose origins reach far back into the mist.

At its heart, the holiday is an explicit

intimate concert theater, which has hosted top-name acts like Willie Nelson and Bob Dylan.

West of I-19 on Valencia Road the Pascua Yaqui Tribe operates **Casino Del Sol** (800/344-9435, www.casinodelsol.com), a Mediterranean-influenced funland with poker, slots, bingo, blackjack, and keno. The complex has several places to eat and drink, including the delicious **Bellissimo,** which serves continental cuisine dinners daily 5pm-11pm. Stick around after the gaming for a concert in the casino's amphitheater, which regularly hosts major touring acts.

THE ARTS

The creative class is well represented in Tucson. Indeed, there are probably more artists and artisans living in or near the Old Pueblo than in any other Arizona locale save the Navajo and Hopi Reservations. Many of the top galleries in Tucson also have sister galleries in Santa Fe, New Mexico, or in Sedona in Northern Arizona. You don't have to appreciate the sometimes overly romantic depictions of the famed Old West to enjoy looking at art in Tucson. There are all kinds of galleries, especially those in the downtown area, that show art from a more experimental, contemporary Southwest, admittance that death and the dead have a profound influence on the living, and that the two camps coexist side by side always. The details of the celebrations vary from region to region, from town to town, from the big city to the outer rural areas. Generally they include feasts, often laid out in graveyards with a dead relative's favorite dishes prepared and set aside. There are parades and marches, candles and altars, sugar skulls, sweet breads shaped like skulls and skeletons, and, of course, calaveras galore.

For many years the Day of the Dead has been marching north, so much so that it now rivals Cinco de Mayo as the Southwestern Anglo's favorite Mexican import. The spectacles surrounding the holiday have always been a subject of fascination for tourists, especially those from the United States. As far back as the 1970s Mexican observers were complaining that in places like Mixquic and Patzcuaro, towns famous for their Day of the Dead celebrations "cameras had come to outnumber candles in the cemeteries."

What would those observers think today if they came to the borderlands and saw the proliferation of consumer goods featuring the Day of the Dead aesthetic? I can't say, but I for one am happy with this proliferation, to a degree.

To many, the Day of the Dead is not so much a holiday, but, as it is with many Mexicans, a year-round way of looking at the world. This way of looking at the world, for me, comes directly from Posada's work. The calavera, especially as it was presented by Posada, is a reminder that we are all mere skeletons; we are all the walking dead, and everything we do and say in this world will one day be forgotten. No matter how much money we have (and Posada's frequent target, along with those in political power, was the rich), no matter how much power we have, we are all equally bones underneath, and we will soon enough be gone. Death is not absent from your life until it comes for you. It is there walking beside you all the time, so you might as well give death its due, and a holiday too.

Usually, throughout November there's a traditional Day of the Dead altar at **Tolteca Tlacuilo** (186 N. Meyer, 520/623-5787, 10am-4pm Mon.-Sat., 11am-4pm Sun. June-mid-Sept., 9:30am-5:30pm Mon.-Sat., 11am-5pm Sun. mid-Sept.-May) in Tucson's Old Town Artisans complex, and the **Tucson Museum of Art** (140 N. Main Ave., 520/624-2333) typically celebrates the ancient rite with a family event on November 2, with the usual music, food, arts and crafts, an altar, and a parade and big-head puppets.

and there are few cowboys left these days. But if you do love Western and Southwestern art, from the conservative to the experimental, there are few better places to be. Head to the Foothills around Campbell and Skyline for galleries showing the best of the genre. Check with the **Tucson-Pima Arts Council** (www.tucsonpimaartscouncil.org) for a complete calendar of all the arts-related stuff going on in town at any given moment.

Galleries

For anyone enraptured by the classic art of the Southwest—from the photographs of Edward Curtis to the modernist illustrations of Maynard Dixon; from the ceremonial kachinas of the Hopi people to the elegant yellow-brown pottery of Nampeyo—**Mark Sublette's Medicine Man Gallery** (6872 E. Sunrise, 520/722-7798, www.medicinemangallery.com, 10am-5pm Mon.-Sat., 1pm-4pm Sun. Thanksgiving-Apr., 10am-5pm Tues.-Sat. May-Sept., 10am-5pm Mon.-Sat. Oct.-Thanksgiving) in the foothills is an absolute must-visit. The huge gallery also features the **Maynard Dixon Museum,** with a wide selection of often obscure paintings, illustrations, and ephemera from throughout the great artist's career. There's also a contemporary art gallery here featuring the best in new Western art by the likes of the fabulous Navajo artist Shonto Begay.

True to a long tradition of repurposing old buildings in downtown Tucson, **MOCA Tucson** (265 S. Church Ave., 520/624-5019, www. moca-tucson.org, noon-5pm Wed.-Sun., $8) used to be a fire station. MOCA puts on several exhibits each year, mixing paintings, photography, and installations, with a seeming preference for the latter. When they say contemporary here they really mean it: You will see art done this afternoon by working, struggling, and inspired artists confronting aesthetic and social themes in all kinds of interesting and confusing ways. Check the website before going for information on the most recent exhibits.

FESTIVALS AND EVENTS

In January the multicultural **Family Arts Festival** (Tucson Pima Arts Council, 520/624-0595, www.familyartsfestival.org) features exhibits, concerts, and performances. February is dominated by the biggest local event of them all, **Tucson Gem & Mineral Show** (520/322-5773, www.tgms.org), which brings thousands of visitors to the Old Pueblo. The busy month also welcomes the **La Fiesta de Los Vaqueros** (800/964-5662, www.tucsonrodeo.com), Tucson's famed rodeo and parade—the longest nonmechanized parade in the world. The **Southwest Indian Art Fair and Market** (520/621-6302, www.statemuseum.arizona.edu) in February brings the region's top jewelers, potters, weavers, and carvers from the Navajo, Hopi, Zuni, and other tribes.

In March Civil War enthusiasts re-create the Battle of Picacho Pass during the **Civil War in the Southwest** (www.azstateparks.com/Parks/PIPE). Also in March, the Tohono

O'odham hold their annual gathering at Mission San Xavier del Bac during the **Wa:k Powwow** (520/294-5727, www.powwows.com). Cinephiles file into town in April to catch the **Arizona International Film Festival** (520/628-1737, www.azmac.org).

The Tucson Kitchen Musicians put on their signature event, the always fun (and free) **Tucson Folk Festival** (www.tkma.org) in May. With the heat of June come prayers and dances for rain on **Día de San Juan,** a series of festivals and rituals celebrating John the Baptist and the saint's historical relationship with the desert's summer rainy season.

Ski Valley on Mount Lemmon celebrates **Oktoberfest on Mount Lemmon** (520/885-1181) a month early, in September. In October the **Tucson Culinary Festival** (www.tucsonculinaryfestival.com) features top local and national chefs and lots of good food. Also during the Halloween month, Old Tucson Studios hosts its popular annual horror show called **Nightfall** (520/883-0100, www.nightfallaz.com).

The **All Souls Procession** (www.allsoulsprocession.org), held the first weekend in November, has brought the artful traditions of the Day of the Dead to downtown Tucson since 1990. The celebration, organized by the nonprofit arts group Many Mouths One Stomach, culminates in a colorful and rather spooky nighttime parade through the downtown streets, featuring ghouls, ghosts, skeletons, big-headed puppets, and myriad other walking works of art. Throughout the weekend there are several related art shows and other events at various venues around the city—all celebrating the impermanence of life and the glory of human-made art. In recent years a concert by the world-famous Tucson-bred band Calexico has topped off the procession.

Shopping

David Puddy asked it on Seinfeld: "What can you get at the Gap in Rome that you can't get at the Gap on 5th Avenue?" Use this as your mantra while shopping in Tucson and Southern Arizona.

The Old Pueblo has all the chains, more so than most midsized cities. But if you spend your time at the Gap, you're going to miss a unique shopping experience—a chance to find that treasure that has eluded you, to return home with an authentic artifact.

You'll find merchants with Mexican imports, folk arts, Western Americana, and Indian jewelry; boutiques with clothes you'll find nowhere else, and galleries featuring the work of artists from Tucson and the rest of the world.

Take a short drive south to Tubac—an artist's village that caters to, or better yet exists for, the discriminating treasure hunter—then on across the border to Nogales, Sonora, and you'll find items you never knew you had to have. A brief scenic journey east and you're among the antique stores and artisan boutiques of old-town Bisbee.

Fear not, shopping in Southern Arizona isn't just for the moneyed (it helps, though). There are finds for everyone, and for every budget.

SHOPPING CENTERS AND DISTRICTS

Main Gate Square (University Blvd., 520/622-8613, www.maingatesquare.com) is right next to the University of Arizona and so is frequented by students. There are 52 stores and restaurants on this block, including Urban Outfitters and Landmark Clothing & Shoes. This is a good place to walk around and have lunch, and there's always something new opening or moving in. Be careful about parking; instead of braving the back-in-only metered parking, go to the **Main Gate Parking Garage** (815 E. 2nd St.) and leave your car in shade and safety.

The **Lost Barrio** (Park Ave. south of Broadway Blvd., 10am-6pm Mon.-Sat., noon-4pm Sun.) is a series of rustic old warehouses tucked away on Park Avenue just before you enter downtown from Broadway. Here you'll find nearly a dozen shops selling handcrafted and imported furniture, folk arts, antiques, and home decor. Several of the stores sell Mexican and colonial-style furniture and antiques, of course, while others offer treasures from Africa, Asia, and elsewhere. The oldest and best of the stores here is **Rustica,** which has gorgeous Mexican and Peruvian furniture and Talavera pottery.

Even if you don't have any room in your budget for pottery, Mexican folk arts, and turquoise jewelry, you should still find time to visit shady, historic **Old Town Artisans** (201 N. Court Ave., 520/623-6024, www.oldtownartisans.com, 9:30am-5:30pm Mon.-Sat., 11am-5pm Sun. Sept.-May; 10am-4pm Mon.-Sat.,

TUCSON

Old Town Artisans

© TIM HULL

11am-4pm Sun. June-Aug.) downtown across from the Tucson Art Museum. Six shops and galleries are gathered in the 150-year-old adobe structure, each one opening onto the verdant Mexican-style courtyard with a fountain and tables. There's a good restaurant here as well, and there are often festivals and live music going on in the courtyard, which is a fine place to sit and rest with a beer. The import shop **Tolteca Tlacuilo** (www.toltecatlacuilo.com) here sells some of the best Día de Los Muertos items in town. There are nearly 20 shops and restaurants at **Plaza Palomino** (southeast corner of Swan and Fort Lowell Rds., 520/320-6344, www.plazapalomino.com, 10am-6pm Mon.-Sat.), an upscale midtown shopping center, including purveyors of Native American arts and crafts, Southwestern-style items and home decor, furniture, jewelry, fine art, and high-style women's clothing. The best time for a visit is during the weekly **Saturday Morning Market** (10am-2pm summer, 9am-1pm winter), when there's a farmers market, artisans selling their creations, and live music.

There are a few shops worth visiting in the multicolored, Mexican-style **La Placita** (110 S. Church Ave., 520/903-9900, 6am-10:30pm daily) downtown, as well as several restaurants and the must-visit Tucson Visitors Center, which has all kinds of literature and information on what to do and how to do it in Southern Arizona. La Placita is a great place to sit back and enjoy an invariably beautiful Tucson day, and there's always something going on in the courtyard, whether it's a free lunchtime concert or a classic movie shown outdoors at night. Don't miss checking out the 1880s-era gazebo just off the grassy courtyard.

The ideal upscale shopping experience can be found in the foothills at Skyline Drive and Campbell Avenue. **La Encantada** (2905 E. Skyline Dr., Ste. 279, 520/299-3556, 10am-7pm Mon.-Wed., 10am-8pm Thurs.-Sat., 11am-6pm Sun.) has posh shops like Tiffany & Co., Louis Vuitton, Crate & Barrel, and dozens more in a lush, two-level outdoor setting. Also in the foothills but more for the value-minded shopper is the **Foothills Mall** (7401 N. La Cholla Blvd., 520/219-0650, www.shopfoothillsmall.com, 10am-9pm Mon.-Sat., 11am-6pm Sun.), with more than 90 stores, many of them designer outlets. Here you'll find the Nike Factory Store, Off 5th (Saks Fifth Avenue Outlet), a Levi's outlet, and many more. Plus, there's no city sales tax here. Take I-10 north to the Ina Road exit, and then head east to La Cholla Boulevard.

ANTIQUES

The **Grant Road Antique District** (Grant Rd. between Campbell Ave. and Craycroft Rd.) has more than half a dozen antique and resale shops on both sides of Grant Road between Campbell and Craycroft, the best of which is the **American Antique Mall** (3130 E. Grant Rd., 520/326-3070, www.americanantiquemall.com, 10am-5pm Tues.-Sat.). A visit here will give you a good idea of the kinds of antiques, collectibles, and generally interesting junk available at most of the Old Pueblo's resale places—a crowded mix of cowboy-life and Southwestern collectibles and kitsch; Native American jewelry and artifacts (not all of them authentic); furniture from the common to the rare, the handmade and Colonial, the retro and modern; old but not necessarily collectible books (*a lot* of Westerns); and all the varied possessions and ephemera left behind by several generations of snowbirds and retirees who spent their final days warm and content in the desert. Though not really recognized locally as such, there is a kind of **Speedway Antiques District** along both sides of busy Speedway Boulevard, roughly between Country Club and Wilmont, where you'll find half a dozen or more shops, both small and large, selling used furniture, antiques, and other used and historic treasures. The best of these is the sprawling **Copper Country Antiques** (5055 E. Speedway Blvd., 520/326-0167, www.coppercountryantiques.com, 10am-6pm Mon.-Sat., 1am-5pm Sun.), where you'll find a vast assortment of Western and Southwestern-themed treasures, along with mini-stores dedicated to Mid-Century Modern furniture, war memorabilia, old golf clubs, antique jewelry, and much more. Prepare to spend hours in here. Don't worry about missing lunch, though; there's a casual little bistro inside.

CLOTHES

Vintage clothing for New Bohemians is how the founder of **The Buffalo Exchange** (2001 E. Speedway, 520/795-0508, 10am-8pm Mon.-Fri., 10am-7pm Sat., 11am-6pm Sun.) describes her first store in Tucson. Now the chain has spread throughout the country to college towns and bohemian enclaves from Tempe to Brooklyn, but it all started in midtown Tucson in the early 1970s. This boutique, which has several Tucson locations including a store dedicated to children's clothes, offers some of the most unique used clothes you'll ever find.

NATIVE AMERICAN ARTS

First opened in 1952 by Tom Bahti, father of current owner Mark Bahti, **Bahti Indian Arts** (4330 N. Campbell Ave., Ste. 72, 520/577-0290, www.bahti.com, 9:30am-6pm Mon.-Sat., 9am-4pm Sun.), though no longer in its original location, is now the oldest shop of its kind in the Old Pueblo. The small shop at St. Philips Plaza, at River and Campbell, sells some of the finest examples of Navajo, Hopi, and Pueblo textiles, kachinas, jewelry, basketry, pottery, paintings, sculptures, and fetishes in the state, as well as an assortment of art and artifacts from tribes outside the Southwest. Mark himself is a noted expert on Native American arts, as his father was before him. He sells many useful books and guides at his store, including his own recent *Silver + Stone: Profiles of American Indian Jewelers.* An excellent Native American arts boutique at La Plaza Palomino, near Swan and Ft. Lowell, **Grey Dog Trading Company** (2970 N. Swan Rd., Ste. 138, 520/881-6888, www.greydog-trading.com, 10am-6pm Mon.-Sat.) carries an amazing array of kachinas, fetish carvings, sand paintings, basketry, pottery, and textiles (mostly by Hopis, Navajos, Zunis, and other Southwestern native artists), as well as a good assortment of books about the Indian arts past and present. **Morning Star Traders** (2020 E. Speedway Blvd., 520/881-2112, www.morningstartraders.com, 10am-6pm Mon.-Sat.) has a fabulous collection of the high-end Indian arts—kachinas, Navajo textiles, pots and baskets, carvings, and historical artifacts—from the Southwestern traditions and others as well.

The friendly, knowledgeable folks at **Mac's Indian Jewelry** (2400 E. Grant Rd., 520/327-3306, www.macsindianjewelry.com, 9am-5pm Mon.-Fri., 10am-5pm Sat.), longtime purveyors of Indian art and craft in Tucson, will help you find that playful kachina doll, that delicately wrought basket, or that substantial silver-and-turquoise heirloom you've always wanted.

FOLK ARTS

The Old Pueblo has its fair share of resident artists, and contrary to popular belief not all of them are struggling to find the most evocative pose for a sunset-lit cowboy atop his horse. A stop at midtown's **Bohemia** (2920 E. Broadway Blvd., 520/882-0800, www.bohemiatucson.com, 11am-4pm Sun.-Mon., 10am-6pm Tues.-Sat.)—selling handmade furniture, jewelry, home decor, fine art, gifts, and many items that are simply unclassifiable—will certainly disabuse one of any preconceived notions about what Southwestern art is. At Bohemia the entire inventory is made by Tucson artists and artisans (or at least Arizona-based artists), and it is astonishing in its variety, playfulness, and quality. **Native Seed Search** (526 N. 4th Ave., 520/622-5561, www.nativeseeds.org, 10am-5pm Mon.-Sat., noon-4pm Sun.) has uniquely Southwestern items, from heirloom seeds for nearly lost regional crops to one-of-a-kind gifts and videos and handmade crafts and soaps (yucca root soap, for example)—all with a link to the region and its past. A perfect gift to take back home is one of the gift baskets sold here, with all kinds of locally and regionally produced foods, soaps, and balms. This store also has an excellent selection of books about Tucson and the Southwest. The concept of "upcycling" is a relatively new one, but it makes a lot of sense in our cluttered world. The artists selling their wares at the charming 4th Avenue boutique

© TIM HULL

the Sacred Time Machine

Popcycle (422 N. 4th Ave., 520/622-3297, www.popcycleshop.com, 11am-6pm Mon.-Thurs., 11am-7pm Fri.-Sat., 11am-5pm Sun.) take old pop-culture artifacts—old record albums, found art, advertising, etc.—and create new and exciting items out of the detritus of the culture. You won't believe what a creative mind can come up with, given just a bit of time spent in the attic or thrift store.

The **Sacred Time Machine** (245 E. Congress St., Ste. 123, 520/777-740, www.sacredmachine.com, 6pm-9pm Wed.-Thurs., 5pm-9pm Fri., 4pm-9pm Sat., 3pm-6pm, Sun.) a small "museum and curiosity shop" on Congress St. downtown, showcases the mysterious, thrilling work and obsessions of world-famous Tucson artist Daniel Martin Diaz. They sell T-shirts, artwork and strange, unique craft items—often with that mixture of the sacred and profane that so typifies Diaz's work. This place is part gallery, part retail shop and part music performance space, and is definitely an essential stop for those looking for the cutting-edge in local culture.

BOOKS, MAPS, AND OUTDOOR SUPPLIES

Book lovers can't miss **Bookmans** (6230 E. Speedway Rd., 520/748-9555, 9am-10pm daily), a Southern Arizona original, which now has clones throughout the state. There are three Bookmans stores in Tucson, all of them featuring thousands of used books, CDs, videos, DVDs, and video games, but the relatively new Speedway location has become the firm's flagship store. Prices are cheap compared to smaller, boutique-style used bookstores, and the selection is absolutely without compare. This is one of the West's best used bookstores. **The Book Stop** (214 N. 4th Ave., 520/326-6661, www.bookstoptucson.com, 10am-7pm Mon.-Thurs., 10am-10pm Fri.-Sat., noon-5pm Sun.) is one of the last independent bookstores in Tucson. Open since the late 1960s, it's been on 4th Avenue since 2007. They have a decent selection of used and out-of-print books, including a substantial section on the Southwest. The books are a bit pricey in comparison to the bigger Bookmans, but when you're inside this classic store you feel a million miles away from the present and nestled deep in the heady world of dusty old books.

For books on Arizona's history and wild-lands, all the maps you could ever want, and the flags of every country in the world, go to **Tucson's Map & Flag Center** (3239 N. 1st Ave., 520/887-4234, www.tucsonmaps.com, 8am-5:30pm Mon.-Fri., 9am-5:30pm Sat.).

You'll find topographical maps and hiking guides, bedrolls, backpacks, outdoor cloth-ing, and everything else one needs while out-fitting for a desert adventure, including a large selection of mountaineering equipment, at **The Summit Hut** (5045 E. Speedway Blvd., 520/325-1554, www.summithut.com, 9am-8pm Mon.-Fri., 9am-6:30pm Sat., 10am-6:30pm Sun.).

Sports and Recreation

It's certainly true that Tucson is an active, out-doorsy, sunburned kind of place. On any given weekday, let alone during the crowded, busy weekends, you'll see Tucsonans decked out in colorful, skintight Lycra outfits, pedaling with all their might up and down the steep moun-tain roads and along the bike routes through the city; you'll also see them hiking on desert trails among the saguaro forests, and exploring the sky island mountain ranges that encircle the valley. If you're coming to Tucson to find some similar action, you won't have to look far.

PARKS

Some might say that there is neither river nor park at **Santa Cruz River Park** (south from Grant Rd. to 29th St.), but still it's as good a vantage as any other from which to view what remains. The Santa Cruz, like most Southwestern desert rivers, was never a deep, swollen river, but it at least had a perennial flow. It sustained a few different indigenous communities for eons, and was the green and cool home of beaver, otter, native fish species, and all manner of wild riparian life. Now look at it. It's not *all* our fault; the region is prone to long droughts, and most desert rivers have wildly fluctuating, even intermittent, flows. But it was largely the pumping of groundwa-ter throughout the region that sent the river underground for good a few generations ago. Every now and then, if the late-summer mon-soon comes on blessedly strong, the water rises and flows past this pleasant, man-made green

space just west of downtown, where you can ride your bike or take an early-morning jog, or just gaze at the dry, rocky bed.

A 131-acre greenscape on the southern end of midtown, **Gene C. Reid Park** (900 S. Randolph Way, 520/791-4873, www.tucsonaz.gov/parksandrec, 6am-10:30pm daily) is prob-ably the city's favorite non-desert playground, with plenty of imported tree-shade and cool Bermuda grass for lounging and forgetting. The park has, among dozens of other attrac-tions, two small duck-topped lakes (no swim-ming), a band shell and amphitheater for concerts under the stars, and an off-leash dog park. The playground equipment is all cool submarine-style passageways, twisting slides, fire poles and sky-reaching swing sets, and sev-eral layers of soft woodchips and some bouncy outdoor foam-floor provide for soft landings. Hi Corbett Stadium is located on the park's grounds, as are the Reid Park Zoo, a large, modern recreation and aquatics center, a tennis facility, and a golf course. Kids love the "splash pad" at **Brandi Fenton Park** (3482 E. River Rd., http://brandifentonmemorialpark.org), between River Road and the Rillito, and it's a worry-free good time for parents as well. Just push the button and for 15 minutes at a time cool water sprays out of fountains, falls from buckets, and bubbles and sprays up out of the ground, allowing water-resistant tykes to get the hang of a wet face before tackling the pool. The splash pad is open from mid-April until October 31, and it's free.

© TIM HULL

In the arid Southwest you can golf in short sleeves in December.

GOLF

It's not easy to justify the existence of golf courses in the arid Southwest, or anyway not from a perspective that recognizes the region's rather obvious resource deficiencies. It is, however, somewhat easier from the average golfer's point of view. For golfers, the region's primary deficiency—its aridity—is instead its greatest attribute, allowing them to play 36 holes on Thanksgiving morning with their envy-rotten visitors from Chicago. And so the courses proliferate. The City of Tucson operates five public courses in town, all of them excellent, though older and less dramatic than most of the resort and private courses invading the desert. The city's somewhat humbler courses come with the added benefit of being ecologically defensible: They are all irrigated with reclaimed water. The city maintains a helpful website (www.tucsoncitygolf.com) where you can see maps of all the courses and get rates (they are generally quite low, varying from $25-75 for 18 holes depending on premiums, season, time of day, and residency) and book tee times. All of the city courses have clubhouses, lighted driving ranges, carts, pros, and pro shops. The two most popular courses in Tucson's municipal system are **Randolph Golf Course and Dell Urich Golf Course** (600 S. Alvernon Way, 520/791-4161, www.tucsoncitygolf.com, daily 5am-7pm, $23-72 for 18 holes, price depends on season and residency), side-by-side courses at midtown's Reid Park. Randolph, the city's flagship course and the longest at 6,500 yards from the regular tees, has been the site of numerous PGA and LPGA tournaments, and is green and spacious and tree-lined. Dell Urich, a par 70 course a bit to the south of Randolph, opened in 1996 and is probably the most popular in town. Both make for easy-access, in-town, and relatively inexpensive play year-round.

HIKING

Tucson and its surrounding sky island ranges have hiking trails for all experience levels. Desert trails tend to be rather flat and rocky, while the mountain trails are steep and usually offer some spectacular views.

The Lemmon Rock Lookout

Arizona still has 72 active or semi-active fire lookouts, meaning they are staffed at least intermittently, especially during fire season or times of high risk and emergency. Only Oregon, with 106, and Florida, with 130, have more active fire lookouts than Arizona, according to the Forest Fire Lookout Association, a group that advocates for the preservation of lookouts and their traditions. What's more, Arizona has a higher ratio of active to standing lookouts than most states–72 active or semi-active out of 83 still standing. Contrast that with California, where 198 lookouts still stand but just 50 of those are active.

Only a small handful of lookouts classified as active are still staffed full time for the entire fire season, roughly April 1 to September 1, and one of these rare huts happens to be lashed to a rock overhang in the Santa Catalinas above Tucson, overlooking the Wilderness of Rocks and, beyond that, the unfurled basin and range territory as far as the urban haze will allow. The Lemmon Rock Lookout, at 8,820 feet, has been occupied for about five months a year since 1928. On the face of the 14-by-14 lookout shack, the side that stares down on the vast pine and boulder land below, someone stenciled long ago the words "No Diving," as if aware of the risks of so much war with oneself.

Fire lookouts like Lemmon Rock have been around, in one form or another, for a very long time, but they really started to proliferate in the 1930s with the advent of the Civilian Conservation Corps and the U.S. Forest Service's all-or-nothing suppression policy. Responding to several huge, unprecedented backcountry forest fires that plagued the nation during the first third of the 20th century, government foresters enacted the 10am policy, decreeing that every fire on public lands must be quelled by 10am the morning after its initial spark. The fire lookout was an integral component of that policy. There is still some debate, though not as much anymore, about the scientific efficacy of suppression, and we are, in many ways, paying for it now with overgrown, drought-ridden forests just waiting for a slash of dry lightning or a tossed cigarette to molt and be reborn, in the process ripping through the million-dollar homes we build in the forest hoping old Smokey the Bear will keep us safe from nature's cycles. Around the same time, the stock market crashed and so too the job market, hence the birth of the New Deal and the CCC, which put thousands of out-of-work Americans in the national forests building trails, fire breaks, and, in some of the most remote areas in the country, fire lookouts. Lemmon Rock was built by a CCC crew in the early 1930s, replacing a more primitive lookout on Mount Lemmon that had stood since 1913.

You can take a look at the Lemmon Rock Lookout for yourself and, during the summer months, sit down and have a high-altitude chat with the friendly current occupant of the little hut. To get there, drive up the **Sky Island Highway** to **Ski Valley** and park at the trailhead parking lot at the top of Mount Lemmon (keep going past the ski slopes and take the dirt road after the pavement ends). Once you park, pick up the short **Lemmon Rock Trail.**

The **Arizona Trail** (various trailheads around Southern Arizona, www.aztrail.org) is a nearly 800-mile network of mostly existing trails that one could follow on foot, horse, or mountain bike (if you want to carry your bike through the Grand Canyon and other federal wilderness areas along the way), from the border with Mexico to the border with Utah. There are 43 "passages" that make up the trail, each between 11 and 35 miles; more than a dozen of these are in Southern Arizona, within easy reach of Tucson. The trail through Southern Arizona traverses all of the region's biomes, from the scrubby desert to the dry grasslands to the cool, green mountains—it's a great way to get to know all of the natural wonders around Tucson. The nonprofit Arizona Trail Association is responsible for upkeep and trail building, and their website has a complete map and detailed descriptions of the trail.

Some of the best desert hiking in the region can be found at **Tucson Mountain Park** (www.pima.gov/nrpr/parks), a sprawling saguaro-crowded park west of the city. Here the trails are rocky and sandy, moderately flat, and thickly lined with desert vegetation. The nearly five-mile round-trip **Brown Mountain Trail** leads through a cactus forest along the sandy bottomlands between the mountains, then rises gradually to a ridgeline that looks out on the hard country all around. Keep an eye out for lazy desert tortoises, who are known to sun themselves on the trail early in the morning. You can access the trailhead at the Brown Mountain Picnic Area or the Juan Santa Cruz Picnic Area, both just southeast of the Arizona-Sonora Desert Museum off Kinney Road. Just before you reach the valley after the steep descent from Gates Pass, there's a parking lot and trailhead where you can pick up the 5.5-mile **David Yetman Trail,** named for the host of the PBS show *The Desert Speaks.* There's another trailhead at Camino de Oeste—and if you leave a car at both ends you won't have to do a more than 10-mile there-and-back trudge. Pima County's Natural Resources Department keeps a map of the trails around Tucson Mountain Park on their website.

The dozens of trails around and on 9,157-foot **Mount Lemmon and the Santa Catalina Mountains** (Coronado National Forest, 520/670-4522, www.fs.fed.us/r3/coronado, $5 per car), about an hour's drive up the winding Sky Island Highway from central Tucson and into another world entirely, are beloved among all those Tucsonans sweating away in the hot valley down there, dreaming of a weekend day spent scrambling around the evergreen forests and cool streams up on the mountain. Since there are so many trails to choose from (many of them lead into and branch off one another), consider the following eight-mile loop composed of portions of several trails, which is designed to take you through some of the best areas the mountain has to offer: At Summerhaven, turn onto the Sabino Canyon

Parkway and follow it down to **Marshall Gulch;** leave your car at the small streamside parking lot. Start on Trail #3 (Marshall Gulch Trail) behind the bathrooms and follow it up through the shady forest for 1.2 miles to Marshall Saddle, at 7,920 feet. At Marshall Saddle branch off on Trail #44, which will take you down about 700 feet into the beautiful **Wilderness of Rocks** for 1.7 miles. At the junction take Trail #12 (the Lemmon Rock Lookout Trail) as it rises and rises for about two miles to near the very peak of Mount Lemmon at 9,157, where you'll be among metal towers essential to life down below. Along the way you can stop off and look at the Mount Lemmon Lookout, which offers one the best views in the region. You'll see the ski lift near the top, but don't get on. Instead, hike along **Radio Ridge** using the Mount Lemmon Trail (Trail #5) for a mile or so to its junction with Trail #93 (The Aspen Trail), then follow that downhill for 1.3 miles, and you'll find yourself back at Marshall Saddle, where it's 1.2 miles back to the car. The climbs on this loop can be a bit brutal, but you're definitely rewarded for the effort. For information on other trails and more suggestions on which ones to try, stop by the Palisades Visitor Center on your way up the hill. There you can talk to rangers and pick up a map of the trail system.

Both sections of **Saguaro National Park** (Red Hills Visitor Center, 520/733-5153, www.nps.gov/sagu) offer superior desert hiking. In the **Tucson Mountains** district west of town, a strenuous but beautiful hike up to 4,687-foot **Wasson Peak,** the highest in the Tucson Mountains, is a great way to spend a Sonoran Desert morning. You can get there by picking up the **King Canyon Trail** just across Kinney Road near the Arizona-Sonora Desert Museum. It's about 3.5 miles to the top of the peak hiking on switchbacks through typical bajada desert; then you can make it a loop by heading down the **Hugh Norris Trail** to its junction with the **Sendero Esperanza Trail,** then take the **Gold Mine Trail** back to the car. The whole adventure is about 7.5 miles total. There are certainly easier and less steep trails around the

© TIM HULL

Both sections of Saguaro National Park offer superior desert hiking.

park as well. An easy one to take with kids is the half-mile **Signal Hill Petroglyphs Trail,** a modest climb to a collection of boulders with several petroglyphs on display. If you continue on from here on the flat, easy trail, you'll go through some wonderful desert with a good chance to see wildlife. In the park's eastern section, at the base of the **Rincon Mountains,** there are several three- to five-mile loop hikes that will take you through all of the best parts of the sprawling cactus forests; for a short, two-mile round-trip walk, the **Cactus Forest Trail** is an easy, mostly flat trail among the green-armed giants. The visitors centers at both the western and eastern sections have complete trail guides and rangers on duty who can help you decide the best routes, and the park's website has detailed maps and trail guides as well.

BIKING

The **3rd Street Bike Route** is an easy, flat way to get from midtown to downtown on a bike—it goes from Wilmont on the eastern edge of midtown all the way through the University of Arizona to downtown. The **Rillito Park Bike Route** is a flat and easy 11-mile route following the sandy-bottomed Rillito River, a great route for exercise and commuting across the north end of Tucson. Sure, the river is dry on top, but it's still a relatively green and shady path. The path runs from near I-10 all the way to Craycroft Road, and along the way it passes several parks, always hugging the parched riverbed, colored here and there with seeping lushness. The Rillito Park Bike Route is one of the more popular sections of an ambitious project called **The Loop** (www.pima.gov/TheLoop), which, when complete, will comprise some 130 miles of connected paths for bikers and walkers. At the time of writing, about 110 miles of The Loop were complete, connecting the Rillito River Park with Santa Cruz River Park downtown, and with other parks on the east and south sides. Pima County has a map of the entire Loop on its website, and hard-copy maps are available at most of the library branches and at the visitors center downtown.

Serious road cyclists proliferate in Tucson,

© TIM HULL

horseback riding on a desert trail

and a few teams even do their winter training here. One of their favorite rides on a warm weekend morning is the **Dan Yersavich Memorial Bikeway** along Old Spanish Trail from Broadway all the way to Saguaro National Park East. Another favorite route is the long, hard climb up the Catalina Highway, also called the **Brad P. Gorman Memorial Bikeway,** and into the cool heights of the mountains. The ride up and over Gates Pass and into the Tucson Mountains region west of downtown is another favorite.

Local mountain bikers love **Fantasy Island** (south end of Harrison where it intersects with Irvington), a system of trails on a swath of scrubby state trust land southeast of midtown. While none of the trails and loops is very long, they are all fun and relatively easy—a great place for beginners and novices to ride. There's a detailed trail map set up at the entrance. You need to purchase a permit to recreate on state trust land in Arizona, and you should always have it with you while you're riding, just in case. To purchase one ($15 for a year) go to www.land.state.az.us.

HORSEBACK RIDING

The horse has been an integral part of daily life in Tucson and Southern Arizona since the Spanish introduced the beast to the Southwest back in the 1500s. The useful new animal transformed the lives and cultures of the native peoples here virtually overnight, and still today there is a distinct subculture of "horse people" in the Old Pueblo whose lives are dedicated to the care and enjoyment of the equestrian kind. There are quite a few such people who will rent you a usually friendly, docile horse and guide you and your new friend deep into the desert on trails once traversed by conquistadores, cowboys, and Indians. Most places require that kids be at least six years old to ride, and most have a 230-pound maximum weight limit, but call ahead to make sure. Spring rides are the best, obviously, especially when the desert's in bloom. Summer is different—go early in the morning or book one of the fun evening or nighttime rides many places offer. Always wear long pants and closed-toe shoes, and always bring a hat, though it doesn't necessarily have to be the cowboy type.

In the northwest foothills of the Santa Catalina Mountains, about 20 miles north of town near Catalina State Park, **Pusch Ridge Riding Stables** (13700 N. Oracle Rd., 520/825-1664, www.puschridgestables.com, 8am-4pm daily, $40 one hour, $60 two hours, $50 sunset ride, $60 moonlight ride) offers fun desertland trail rides every hour on the hour 8am-3pm daily. During the busy spring season rides typically include about six to eight riders and a guide. The "moonlight rides" here are particularly enchanting, making one feel a bit like an outlaw on the run. These last 1.5 hours and cost $60 per person with a minimum of four riders. They also offer half-day ($100 pp) and full-day ($160 pp) rides, and private rides ($85 per hour). Call ahead for reservations, especially on the weekends.

About 13 miles southeast of town, out in the shaggy cactus-and-scrub desert not far from Saguaro National Park East, the friendly folks at **Pantano Riding Stables** (4450 S. Houghton Rd., 520/298-8980, www.horsingaroundarizona.com, 8am-5pm daily in winter, 8am-noon and 4pm-6:30pm daily in summer, $35 one hour, $45 1.5 hours, $65 two hours, $50 1.5-hour sunset ride) will take you out and make you feel like a real cowboy. Along with the usual one- to two-hour trail rides, they offer a fun "campfire ride," where you can dine under the stars as if you're working some kind of round-up. The desert out this way is beautiful and thick, and if you go when the cactus are blooming you are in for a spectacular show. It's a good idea to call ahead for a reservation.

SPECTATOR SPORTS

The biggest sports draw in the region are the teams of the **University of Arizona.** With perennial powerhouses in basketball, volleyball, and baseball, and a Pac-10 football team that is expected to hold its own in a tough division, there's always something to cheer for on campus. For ticket information call the UA's **McKale Center** (520/621-2287, www.arizonaathletics.com). Don't expect it to be easy.

In February, the PGA stops off in Tucson for the **Accenture Match Play Championships** (888/603-7600, www.worldgolfchampionships.com) at Dove Mountain, bringing along the world's top 64 golfers to battle it out for an oversized $8 million check.

The **Tucson Toros** (www.tucsontoros.com) are a minor league team in the Golden Baseball League. They play at **Hi Corbett Field,** in midtown, part of the Reid/Randolph Park complex. MLB spring training, once an important institution in Tucson, is now gone from the Old Pueblo, as the teams have all moved to Phoenix and elsewhere.

FC Tucson (Kino Sports Complex, Field No. 5, www.fctucson.com), Tucson's scrappy Premier Development League soccer team, is a lot of fun to watch. It's $12 to get into a game, which are played during a late-spring, early-summer season; you can buy your ticket at the gate. It's kind of a cross between MLS and AYSO, with a loud and dedicated group of chanters called the "Desert Pricks" adding big league atmosphere for a crowd of folks sitting on the sidelines in lawn chairs. A few vendors sell beer and soda and hot dogs, including the Sonoran variety. The action on the field is usually quite exciting, as promising young talents compete furiously for a future in the beautiful game.

TUCSON

Accommodations

There aren't a lot of inexpensive accommodations in Tucson worth taking a chance on. There is one hostel, in a clean and friendly house near downtown. It's the best choice for budget travelers. On the I-10 frontage road just west of downtown there is a long row of chain hotels, some of them inexpensive. This isn't the Old Pueblo's most charming district however. Throughout midtown and on to the east side there are dozens of big chain hotels to choose from, and of course there are dozens more around the south side near the airport.

For a truly memorable Tucson experience, consider staying in one of the small (though often relatively pricey) B&Bs and inns in one of the city's many historic neighborhoods. These include the beautiful Arizona Inn in midtown, and the very affordable Hotel Congress right in the center of the action downtown. There are also inns in the Sam Hughes Historic Neighborhood in midtown, and in the El Presidio District near downtown.

During the summer months, roughly from late May to late September, nearly all of the hotels, resorts, and inns in Tucson slash their prices—some by as much as 50 percent, but most by around 20 percent. If you're planning on coming to town during those torpid, quiet months, you might just be able to afford to live like a robber baron for a few days. Also, it pays to explore the websites of the larger chains listed below; most of them offer all kinds of different packages, one of which will likely save you some money. If you're coming to town in February or March, book early and plan to pay a bit more; those two perfect-weather months feature several very popular festivals, events, and conventions in the Old Pueblo, and most places are booked solid.

DOWNTOWN AND UNIVERSITY DISTRICT
$50-100

Built in 1919 and remodeled only slightly since then, **Hotel Congress** (311 E. Congress St., 520/622-8848 or 800/722-8848, www.hotelcongress.com, $89-149 d, about $10 less in summer beginning at the end of May) is a historic downtown hotel that offers charm and atmosphere; it's listed on the National Register of Historic Places and is right in the center of downtown's bar and music scene. Though the rooms are a bit creaky, the beds are comfortable and the historic atmosphere more than makes up for the lack sumptuous amenities (plus, it's the best value in town if you value personality in your sleeping quarters). There is noise some nights coming from the Club Congress downstairs (it's not too bad, but there is a slight thumping that comes through the walls). The club is a venue for alternative bands and alt-country bands from across the nation, and the Tap Room bar will make you feel like a cowboy on his day off. The Cup Café off the beautiful

the entrance to Tucson's Hotel Congress

© TIM HULL

old lobby has an eclectic mix of gourmet and Southwestern-style food for breakfast, lunch, and dinner.

The only hostel in Tucson, **The Roadrunner Hostel and Inn** (346 E. 12th St., 520/628-4709, cell tel. 520/940-7280, www.roadrunnerhostelinn.com), a block south of Broadway Boulevard downtown, is a clean and homey place to stay and offers the single best accommodations deal in the town ($20 for dorm, $40 for private room). They provide free linens and blankets, showers, laundry ($1 per load), and a large kitchen for guests to use. The four private rooms are small and a bit spare, but for the money they are perfect; the three dorm rooms (one for men, one for women, and one that's co-ed) each sleep six on the usual bunkbeds. They offer two computers hooked up to the Internet for guest use, plus free wireless throughout the place. There's a shady backyard patio for morning lounging with complimentary coffee or tea, and a living room with a big TV and lots of VHS and DVD movies to watch. They don't accept credit cards.

$100-250

The Catalina Park Inn (309 E. 1st St., 520/792-4541 or 800/792-4885, www.catalinaparkinn.com, $139-169) in the West University Historic District was built in 1927 and has beautiful mixed gardens with many native plants in a private, peaceful walled courtyard. There are six rooms, two of which are detached from the main house and open onto the lush courtyard. This inn is close to the UA, downtown, and midtown. Breakfast here is always an elegant, gourmet affair, and wireless Internet throughout the property makes it a great place for combining business and pleasure. Each individually decorated room has a private bath, cable television, a stereo with an iPod dock, big thick bathrobes, and more. The inn is popular with parents visiting their kids at the nearby University of Arizona; as such, in mid-May, during graduation, and in early October, for Parent's Day, they require a three-night minimum stay and raise the rates on their rooms by about $20-30 per night. This is true

during Gem Show (first two weeks in Feb.) as well. The inn is closed June 15-September 25.

The enchanting **El Presidio Inn Bed & Breakfast** (297 N. Main Ave., 520/623-6151), in the Julius Kruttschnitt House, built in 1886 and remodeled over the years in various architectural styles, is one of the city's best small inns. It's located in "Snob Hollow" in the historic El Presidio Neighborhood, the same block on which Tucson's wealthy pioneers used to live in their mansions. The inn has one of the finest garden courtyards I've ever seen, and it's so cool and lush and peaceful, with a babbling fountain, cobblestone walkways, and trees, that you may not get out of the inn to see the rest of Tucson. The inn has four rooms ($129, $139, and $160), two of which—the Carriage House and the Gate House—open onto the courtyard and have kitchenettes. There's also a heated pool and spa and immaculate grounds rooms. The rooms inside the house have private baths. **The Royal Elizabeth Bed and Breakfast Inn** (204 S. Scott, 877/670-9022, www.royalelizabeth.com, $155-285) is also in a historic home, this one known as the Blenman House, built in 1878 in Tucson's El Presidio District. There are six large rooms to choose from, all elegantly decorated in an old-world style, with big sweeping beds and footed stand-alone bathtubs. They only allow kids over 13 years old, and they don't allow pets or smoking. They require two nights minimum October-May.

MIDTOWN
$100-250

A charming Spanish-revival B&B in midtown's quiet, tree-lined Sam Hughes Neighborhood, the **Sam Hughes Inn Bed and Breakfast** (2020 E. 7th St., 520/861-2191, www.samhughesinn.com, $90-130) is within walking distance to the University of Arizona and is close to downtown. The inn has four distinctively decorated rooms with free wireless Internet and private bathrooms. The enclosed courtyard out back is something to see, green and cool and perfect for relaxing and watching the sun dip away.

Originally built in 1931, **The Lodge on the**

Desert (306 N. Alvernon Way, 520/325-3366, www.lodgeonthedesert.com, $65-370) changed hands in 2009 and underwent a major $15 million expansion and renovation. The hotel's new lobby and restaurant are beautiful and stylish, as are the hacienda-style rooms offering free wireless Internet, comfortable beds, and big cushy bathrobes. The grounds are green and private, and the patio lounge is one of the best in the city.

The **Double Tree Hotel at Reid Park** (445 S. Alvernon Way, 520/881-4200, www.doubletree.hilton.com, $119-139), at Broadway and Alvernon just east of Reid Park, is centrally located and close to the golf courses, bike paths, and zoo at Reid Park. It has a huge enclosed courtyard with a very nice outdoor pool. Many of the 295 rooms have balconies that look out on the central courtyard, and they all have free wireless Internet and big plasma TVs. This 14-acre hotel also has a fitness room, a whirlpool, and tennis courts. Pets are allowed. Rates go as low as $79 per night in the summer.

The big, beautiful **Aloft Tucson University** (1900 E. Speedway Blvd., 520/908-6800, www.starwoodhotels.com), right across Campbell Avenue from the University of Arizona, opened in 2013. Workers stripped the former Four Points Sheraton down to its husk and filled it up again with stylish, modern rooms and inviting lounges. The hotel is on par with other Aloft properties, which means it is upscale, comfortable and really, really cool.

The **Embassy Suites** (5335 E. Broadway, 520/745-2700, http://embassysuites.hilton.com, $139-159), a big chain-hotel compound at the Williams Center in east midtown (Broadway and Craycroft), is perfect for families. Each of the spacious suites has two rooms and two TVs, and has the option of coming with up to three beds. Every night the friendly staff passes out free drinks and popcorn during the Manager's Reception, and in the morning you can order up a complimentary big breakfast (no mere muffin and coffee here). They've got a great pool, and the lobby and lounge are decorated in an upscale, tasteful Southwestern style with big leather couches that you can just sink into. In summer the rates plummet, and you can get a suite for $109 or even lower.

Over $250

The historic ◀ **Arizona Inn** (2200 E. Elm St., 520/325-1541, www.arizonainn.com, $329-579, $195-309 in summer), a boutique hotel in central midtown founded in the 1930s by Arizona's first-ever congresswoman and still owned and operated by the same family, is the best place to stay in Tucson—as long as you have fairly deep pockets. They offer several different kinds of rooms, all of them decorated in the inimitable 1930s Southwestern style. The standard room has wireless Internet, a king-size bed, and a television and DVD player, while the larger suites have patios, dry bars, and sitting areas. But you probably won't be spending a lot of time in the room, as the grounds and lobby have so much charm to offer—there's a 60-foot pool, old-school tennis, and all kinds of little quiet corners in the verdant, retreatlike setting behind the high pink walls.

FOOTHILLS
$100-250

The **Windmill Inn** (4250 N. Campbell, 520/577-0007, windmillinns.com/tuc.htm, $111-239), a small chain hotel at St. Philips Plaza, at Campbell and River, is one of the few non-resort places to stay in the Foothills. The rooms are fantastic, with a mini-fridge, wet bar and cable TV, free wireless Internet, and continental breakfast. There's an exercise room, a heated outdoor pool and whirlpool, and bikes available for guests to use. The rooms are gathered around a poolside enclosed courtyard that feels private and serene even at this very busy intersection.

Resorts

Visitors and émigrés have sought healing in Southern Arizona since at least the early 19th century. Any tubercular patient lucky enough to flee the crowded, disease-ridden tenements of the Northeast or the malarial bottomlands of the South was invariably advised to seek the high and dry air of the Southwest.

Nineteenth-century medicine being what it was, physicians had little else but this general, somewhat specious advice to offer the scores of Americans who suffered from TB, fevers, dysentery, and other ailments of the chest and the blood.

Scholar Billy Jones, in his book *Health-Seekers in the Southwest 1817-1900,* estimates that some 20-25 percent of those who moved to the Southwest during the great migrations of the 19th and 20th centuries did so hoping to cure some ailment, creating a "Health Frontier" that, in Tucson, resulted in the haphazard construction of vast tent cities on the outskirts of town populated by consumptives and often destitute men and women not long for the world.

Medical science has since cured most of the diseases that once brought sickly travelers to the desert, but that hasn't stopped today's visitors from seeking health of a different breed. Tucson has long rivaled its ritzy northern neighbors Scottsdale and Sedona as a place where the afflicted, both physically and psychically, can find solace—usually very expensive solace.

Perhaps the valley's most famous resort, **Canyon Ranch** (8600 E. Rockcliff Rd., 520/749-9000 or 800/742-9000, www.canyonranch.com) is representative of what the other top resorts offer. Here you can not only pamper yourself silly with spa treatments (an activity sure to lead to optimum, albeit temporary, good health) but also schedule appointments with a staff nutritionist, chiropractor, acupuncturist, and internist. A personal trainer will work with you on keeping in shape long-term, while a meditation class will help you get in tune with your spirituality. After one of your three gourmet (but healthy) meals a day, you can attend lectures and classes on various topics in healthful living. For an experience so meaningful, it's not surprising that you're going to have spend accordingly. A minimum three-night stay at Canyon Ranch is going to set you back $2,600-5,020 per person depending on accommodations. That's all-inclusive, however. For that price you get three gourmet meals a day, spa treatments galore, consultations with all the medical professionals on staff, and unlimited activities. The high season at Canyon Ranch is September 23-June 7, after which, as it is with all Tucson's resorts, prices drop rather dramatically.

Founded in 1929 and displaying the elegant Spanish Colonial architecture of a more civilized age, ◖ **Hacienda del Sol Guest Ranch Resort** (5601 N. Hacienda del Sol Rd., 520/299-1501 or 800/728-6514, www.haciendadelsol.com) reflects more than any other local accommodations (save perhaps the Arizona Inn) the beauty and rustic chic of the high-style Southwest of yesteryear. Each of the rooms ($109-515 depending on the season) is distinctive, with custom-made furniture and a story all its own. There's even a "Spencer Tracy Casita," with two bedrooms, two bathrooms, and a kitchen, where Tracy and Katherine Hepburn used to stay ($300-515 depending on the season). The small, comparatively inexpensive Historic Rooms look out on the enchanting courtyard, with an inviting outdoor pool and hot tub. Like its younger Foothills neighbors, this resort has a full-service spa, an excellent New American restaurant, a wonderful patio bar, riding stables, and more.

One of the best things about **Loews Ventana Canyon Resort** (7000 N. Resort Dr., 520/299-2020 or 800/234-5117, www.loewshotels.com/hotels/tucson) is its view—anywhere you stand on the grounds you get a long, clear look beyond the sweeping golf course off to the valley below. With a fabulous restaurant, a top-notch spa, tennis courts, hiking trails, and one of the most scenic golf courses in the Southwest, it's no wonder this world-renowned hotel and spa ($345-495 depending on the season) was rated number 31 of the top 100 golf resorts in the nation by *Condé Nast* magazine. The resort also has a popular stargazing program and a desert setting you won't soon forget.

A young woman who spent three days and nights at **Miraval, Life in Balance Resort & Spa** (5000 E. Via Estancia Miraval, Catalina, 520/825-4000 or 800/232-3969, www.miravalresorts.com)—a favorite spot of no less an authority on living life to the fullest than Oprah Winfrey—said when she returned to the real world that henceforth her life would be divided into just two chapters: before Miraval and after Miraval. For what you pay ($798-1,300 minimum, probably more with added activities and such), one should expect some sort of life-changing experience. This world-famous resort, on 400 acres backed by the Santa Catalinas, has 118 rooms, a full-service (and then some) spa, a whirlpool, sauna, Olympic-size lap pool, a full gym, an obstacle course, climbing wall, yoga and Pilates centers, and much more. The rooms are very nice, but with all there is to do here you don't spend much time inside; still, most of the casita-style accommodations have TVs, DVD players, wireless Internet, and more.

Guests of **The Westin La Paloma Resort & Spa** (800 E. Sunrise Dr., 800/937-8461, www.westinlapalomaresort.com) are allowed to use the facilities of the nearby country club, which has a 27-hole Jack Nicklaus-designed golf course. The rooms here ($199-319, $109-159 in summer) are spacious and have private patios looking out over the desert, huge sink-in beds, wireless Internet, and some have fireplaces and sunken spa tubs. The nearby **Elizabeth Arden Red Salon and Spa** will pamper you silly after you play a few sets on one of 10 championship tennis courts. There are also indoor racquetball courts, a huge pool area, Pilates and yoga studios, and an exercise room.

First built as a private home in 1912, the hacienda-style **Westward Look Resort** (245 E. Ina Rd., 520/297-1151 or 800/722-2500, www.westwardlook.com) has Southwestern charm to

The Westin La Paloma Resort & Spa

spare. Though it has been built up and remodeled over time (including a multimillion-dollar facelift in 2008), the older, adobe portions still have the exposed vigas made from wood brought down from Mount Lemmon. The 241 guest rooms and suites ($139-339) have wireless and plasma TVs and all the usual high-end luxuries, and the resort offers horseback riding, tennis, spa treatments, and 80 acres of desert foothills grounds with nature trails, stargazing programs, and exhibits about the desert's natural history and native peoples.

Food

The Old Pueblo's culinary scene is famously dominated by the ranchland comfort food available at the dozens of Mexican eateries in town, most of them serving classic variations of a cuisine formed in Mexico's arid northern states and on the hot, dry coastlines of the nearby Sea of Cortez. While such homestyle Mexican food represents one of the most popular cuisines in America, in Tucson it has a kind of authenticity and diversity of taste that's available nowhere else—except perhaps just across the border, about an hour's drive from the city.

While you could spend a lifetime here eating carne asada, chiles rellenos, and enchiladas exclusively, you'd not only gain more weight than you'd like to but you'd miss out on sampling the work of some of the most creative, adventurous chefs and restaurateurs in the Southwest. The amorphous hodgepodge that is New American cuisine thrives in Tucson through an impressive array of mid- to high-end, locally owned "Tucson originals," many of which combine spices, flavors, ingredients, and crops common to the borderlands, with American, French, and other culinary traditions to create some new hybrid that goes by the inexact term *Southwestern.*

To be totally honest, though, when you've got year-round outdoor patio dining—with gentle heaters when it's chilly, and cold-water-spitting "misters" when it's hot—and the sky above that patio is ever blue and clear, and the views from that patio are of looming high mountains and sweeping desert valleys, the quality of the food in front of you often becomes a secondary issue. Whenever you can, barring something unlikely like rain or cold, ask to sit on the patio or in the Spanish-style courtyard—scores of restaurants here have them, and al fresco dining in, say, February is one of the great joys of desert living.

DOWNTOWN AND UNIVERSITY DISTRICT
Breakfast and Lunch

The B-line (621 N. 4th Ave., 520/882-7575, http://blinerestaurant.com, 7am-9pm Sun.-Thurs., 7am-10pm Fri.-Sat., $3.50-13.95) has huge breakfast burritos, a full coffee bar, and free wireless Internet. Make sure to check out the art on the walls. **Bison Witches Deli and Bar** (326 N. 4th Ave., 520/740-1541, 11am-midnight daily for kitchen, until 2am for bar, $2.75-7) has overstuffed sandwiches, soup in bread bowls, and good beers on tap. It gets a little crowded on the weekends but is worth the wait.

If you want a creative deli-style sandwich or a slice of stone-fired pizza try **Time Market** (444 E. University Blvd., 520/622-0761, 9am-8pm daily) between 4th Avenue and the university.

A cafe, bar, and market in the refurbished old Southern Pacific train depot downtown, **Maynards Market & Kitchen** (400 N. Toole Ave., 520/545-0577, www.maynardsmarket-tucson.com, 11am-10pm Sun.-Wed., 11am-midnight Thurs.-Sat., market, pastry, and coffee service 10am-7pm daily, $4-28) serves some excellent sandwiches—the Cuban pork with garlic mayo, cilantro, caramelized onions, and grilled jalapeños captures the pan-American chic of the place perfectly. The bar is cool and stylish and looks out on the railroad tracks. They serve their menu late into the night on the weekends.

American and Southwestern

The **C Cup Café** (311 E. Congress St., 520/798-1618, 7am-10pm Sun.-Thurs., 7am-11pm Fri.-Sat., $3.50-24) serves an eclectic blend of American food with a dash of several ethnic traditions. Inside the Hotel Congress downtown, the Cup is a popular weekend breakfast destination but is a perfect choice for lunch and dinner anytime.

The **Cushing Street Grill** (198 W. Cushing

TUCSON

© TIM HULL

Pasco Kitchen and Lounge

St., 520/622-7984, www.cushingstreet.com, 4:30pm-9pm Tues.-Thurs., 4:30pm-10pm Fri.-Sat., $3.50-18), on the edge of the Barrio Historico, has been operating out of its circa-1860s historic building since 1972. It's a nice space, with garden patio dining available when the weather permits, which is most of the time. The place is known for its carefully made mojito ($8), concocted with loads of fresh mint. Many of the entrees have a Southwestern flair—try the "gulf tacos" with fish fresh from the Sea of Cortez, just a couple of hundred miles south. Reservations are recommended.

A 4th Avenue institution, **Delectables** (533 N. 4th Ave., 520/884-9289, www.delectables. com, 11am-9pm Sun.-Thurs., 11am-11pm, Fri.-Sat., $8-20) serves light, fresh lunches and dinners in the gourmet mode. Consider the jalapeño BLT on freshly made French bread. There are vegetarian dishes, such as the awesome asparagus crepes, and bistro plates with all kinds of top-shelf meats and cheeses and fresh fruit. After 5pm they serve hearty dinners like rib eye, wild Pacific salmon, and chicken

picatta, and they have a wide range of pasta dishes. They serve a good selection of craft-brews and wine, and there's usually some fascinating, or at least intriguing, art on the walls, most of it by local artists.

Occupying a tastefully remodeled old building on shady Geronimo Plaza, along University Boulevard's Main Gate Square block, **Pasco Kitchen and Lounge** (820 E. University Blvd., 520/882-8013, http://pascokitchen.com, 11am-10pm Mon.-Wed., 7:30am-midnight Fri.-Sun., $8-20), charming New American restaurant and bar, serves "Urban Farm Fare." That means designer comfort food with an ever-present Southwestern attitude, made from ingredients supplied mostly by farms, ranches, and food-artisans in Arizona. Try the amazing "Sloppy Joe" sliders, spiced with various chilies and served with beans.

Chef Janos Wilder was among the first local chefs to focus on reforming and repurposing regional ingredients and styles in the 1980s. He's credited with reimagining Southwestern cuisine, infusing it with French mechanisms and a New American ethos. His influence can be seen in restaurants all over the Old Pueblo. These days, Janos, who is something of a local celebrity, serves a creative, seasonal menu heavy with local and regional ingredients and strong links to the various flavors of Mexico, Italy, and Asia at **Janos Downtown Kitchen and Cocktails** (135 S. 6th Ave., 520/623-7700, http://downtownkitchen.com, lunch 11am-2pm Mon.-Fri., dinner 5pm-10pm daily, $8-25). The stylish street-side patio and open, modernist interior make this restaurant and bar one of downtown's best places to kick back, sample unique dishes, and toss back a few expertly made cocktails.

Hidden away behind a nondescript storefront on downtown's Scott Ave., **47 Scott** (47 N. Scott Ave., 520/624-4747, www.47scott.com, 4pm-close daily, brunch 10am-4pm Sat.-Sun., $8-20) has a romantic, brick-walled patio that's lit subtly after dark. The menu is seasonally adjusted, but they generally serve a familiar but no less appetizing take on New American comfort food. To know what's going on here you need only order the phyllo-wrapped chicken—a juicy breast cased in toasted phyllo dough, stuffed with goat cheese and spinach, drizzled with a rich and hearty chicken jus, flanked by smashed potato cakes and sage carrots. It's a wonderful kind of deconstructed chicken pot pie.

The **Hub Restaurant and Ice Creamery** (266 E. Congress Street, 520/207-8201, www.hubdowntown.com, 11am-close Sun.-Wed., 11am-2am Thurs.-Sat.) has a hipster style and the soul of a great American diner. The food is certainly a few cuts above the usual countertop fare: fries smothered in prime rib and cheese sauce, shrimp and grits, chicken pot pie, warm lobster roll . . . So is the decor: white faux-leather booths, thick ropes like vines on the red-brick walls, upside-down house lamps hanging from the exposed rafters.

Asian

A popular Vietnamese eatery just east of the UA campus, **Miss Saigon** (1072 N. Campbell Ave., 520/320-9511, www.misssaigon-tucson.com, 10:30am-9:30pm Mon.-Sat., 11:30am-9:30pm Sun., $6.75-11.99) packs them in for the best pho in town. The traditional noodle soup is served with fresh herbs and bean sprouts and jalapeños on the side, and the spring rolls are light and delicious when dipped liberally in Miss Saigon's awesome peanut sauce. They also serve rich and decadent slushes with either coconut-jelly or tapioca, and other exotic desserts and drinks.

A cozy, art-filled spot upstairs from the American Apparel store at Main Gate Square, **Vila Thai** (972 E. University Blvd., 520/393-3489, www.vilathai.com, lunch 11am-5pm Mon.-Sat., noon-5pm Sun., dinner 5pm-9pm Mon.-Sat., $8.25-12.25) serves delicious pad Thai, a wonderful selection of curries, and all kinds of other Thai favorites. They have an excellent wine list, and serve a selection of Thai beers and other Asian brews. The art on the walls, mostly by local artists, changes monthly and can be challenging, inspiring, and infuriating.

Mexican and Latin American

Featured far and wide in gourmet and lifestyle magazines, **Cafe Poca Cosa** (110 E. Pennington St., 520/622-6400, www.cafepocacosatucson.com, 11am-9pm Tues.-Thurs., 11am-10pm Fri.-Sat., $13-27) is one of the Old Pueblo's top two or three eateries. Reservations are basically required, and the menu changes twice daily. That day's specials are printed in English and Spanish on a chalkboard that servers take around to each table. The food is usually an adventurous, learned, and creative hybrid—a kind of gourmet-Mexican food, created by Chef Suzanna Davila, a native of Guaymas, Sonora, Mexico, on the Sea of Cortez, that you won't find anywhere else in Southern Arizona. If you're looking for the usual enchiladas and burritos, this isn't the place. But if you want something on the far creative edge of Mexican cuisine—a much more varied style than most Americans are led to believe—then you must eat here. The interior is done up in a smooth, cool modernism with contemporary Hispanic art—including a print by the great Daniel Martin Diaz—peppered throughout.

El Charro Café (311 N. Court Ave., 520/622-1922, www.elcharrocafe.com, 11am-9pm Sun.-Thurs., 11am-10pm Fri.-Sat., $6-18) makes the city's most beloved Mexican food in a building once lived in by Julias Finn, a French stonemason who came to Tucson to work on the cathedral. The restaurant has a bar, **¡Toma!,** with half-price drinks and appetizers (delicious Mexican favorites like cheese crisps and quesadillas) 3pm-6pm daily.

Do you like loud music while you eat, waitresses who kiss and hug their customers, and a bit of attitude with your chiles rellenos? The food is so spectacular at **◖ Little Cafe Poca Cosa** (Stone Ave. at Alameda St., no phone, www.littlepocacosa.com, 7:30am-2:30pm Mon.-Fri., $5-10) you might be willing to put up with just about anything to get the simple Mexican and Latin American fare at this beloved lunch spot. The hugs and even the cheek-kisses from the waitresses are all right with a belly full of goodness. Make sure to tip big; a large percentage of everything made in this place goes to various causes. They only take cash, no exceptions.

The carne asada and the Mexican (also called Sonoran) hot dogs are the specialties of the house at **◖ El Guero Canelo** (5201 S. 12th Ave., 520/295-9005, www.elguerocanelo.com, 10am-11pm Sun.-Thurs., 10am-midnight Fri.-Sat., $4-7) and the 12th Avenue semi-outdoor location replicates better than any other Old Pueblo Mexican restaurant the atmosphere of casual eating south of the border. It has the feel of a taco stand, but with a huge menu and shaded patio seating. The beans here are different from many places, served whole instead of in the usual refried mash. If you're a fan of the hot dog, you really have to try the Mexican variation—a skinny, grilled dog hidden in a thick and rich, soft white bun, lathered with beans, mayo, salsa, and whatever else you want to add. It's amazing, but it rarely sparks ambivalence—people seem to either love it or hate it. The restaurant has two additional locations (North Midtown: 2480 N. Oracle Rd.,

520/882-8977; Eastside: 5802 E. 22nd St., 520/790-6000).

With so much Mexican food to choose from in the Old Pueblo, restaurants serving other Latin American cuisines tend to be forgotten, but not **Maya Quetzal** (429 N. 4th Ave., 520/622-8207, 11:30am-2pm and 5pm-8pm Mon.-Thurs., noon-9pm Fri.-Sat., $4.95-8.95). This colorful eatery on 4th Avenue has been serving delicious Guatemalan food since 1993. The small place opens up on to a shaded back patio with small fountains, and there's a mystic mural on one wall inside that conjures up the romance of Central America. The dishes are typically a mixture of rice, black beans, beef and chicken, corn tortillas, and vegetables from the exotic to the recognizable. The sauces here tend to be creamier and less spicy than their Mexican counterparts . . . make sure to try the cheesy "specialty rice."

Italian and Pizza

Magpies Gourmet Pizza (605 N. 4th Ave., 520/628-1661, www.magpiespizza.com, 11am-10pm Mon.-Wed., 11am-11pm Thurs.-Sat., $3-25) is a sure bet, having won the *Tucson Weekly*'s Best of Tucson poll every year since 1989.

There's nothing better than a greasy slice of authentic New York-style pizza after a night of hitting the bars, and **Brooklyn Pizza** (534 N. 4th Ave., 520/622-6868, www.brooklynpizzacompany.com, 11am-11pm Mon.-Sat., noon-10pm Sun.; slices served 11pm-2:30am Fri.-Sat.) serves late into the night (or rather, morning) on the weekends. The pizza here rivals anything you can find back East, and the meatball subs, calzones, and gelato are the best in town. What's more, the little pizza place has recently gone solar powered.

Caruso's (434 N. 4th Ave., 520/624-5765, www.carusositalian.com, 11:30am-11pm Tues.-Sun., $7.45-11.95) has been serving delicious Italian favorites on 4th Avenue since 1938. Sit on the shaded patio next to a trickling fountain and enjoy the pasta dishes and pizzas created

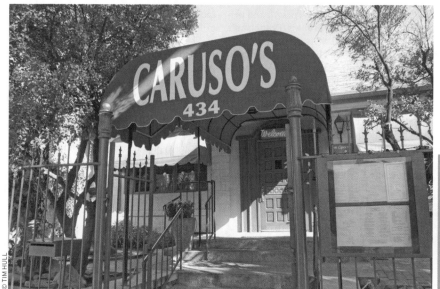

© TIM HULL

Caruso's, open since 1938

here. It's nothing fancy—just well-prepared Italian favorites in a laid-back atmosphere with, of course, checkered tablecloths and fat bottles of chianti. There's often a wait to be seated on weekend nights, and expect to be eating alongside a lot of families.

Some of the most toothsome pizza in town is served by **Reilly Craft Pizza and Drink** (101 E. Pennington St., 520/882-5550, www.reillypizza.com, 11am-11pm daily) out of a tastefully refurbished circa-1908 building that once housed a funeral home downtown. The restaurant kept the funeral home's name and sign but little else. With an urban-cool interior and sophisticated menu, Reilly is a standout in the ever expanding downtown culinary scene. The "craft pizzas" have a thick-but-light toasted crust and come with a variety of toppings far removed from the usual slice-on-the-corner variety (fennel pollen, truffle cheese, eggplant, fontina, etc.) Reilly's also serves pasta dishes, and extraordinary salads. Try the one with watermelon and goat cheese; it's truly something special.

VEGETARIAN
Café Desta (758 S. Stone Ave., 520/370-7000, http://cafedesta.com, 11am-9pm daily), a bright cafe on the southern edge of downtown, serves exceptional Ethiopian cuisine, much of it vegan, and has a full coffee bar. Bring your own bottle of wine and a few friends and try the "vegan signature plate" ($30, serves up to three people, a sampling of several spicy and exotic vegan dishes featuring mushrooms, lentils, cabbage, onions, collard greens, spinach, and more, served with rice and the spongy Ethiopian flatbread, injera (which is also vegan). If you have carnivores in tow, Desta also has flavorful dishes with beef, lamb, and fish.

MIDTOWN
Breakfast and Lunch
The **Rincon Market** (2513 6th St., 520/327-6653, 7am-10pm Mon.-Fri., 7am-8pm Sat., 8am-8pm Sun., $5-10) has delicious sandwiches and a nightly entrée, usually served to go. On the weekends there's a fabulous, but crowded, omelet bar.

The best greasy spoon in Tucson, and perhaps the greasiest, is ❰ **Frank's/Francisco's** (3843 E. Pima, 520/881-2710, 6am-2pm and 5pm-10pm Mon.-Thurs., 6am-2pm and 5pm-midnight Fri., 7am-2pm and 5pm-midnight Sat., 8am-2pm and 5pm-10pm Sun., $1.40-9), whose motto is "Elegant Dining Elsewhere." You can sit at a rickety table or belly up to the bar and watch your hash browns cook on the grill. The breakfast menu has all you'd expect, with the addition of Mexican favorites that come highly recommended. There's nothing like getting all spiced up early in the morning. At night Frank's becomes Francisco's and serves Michoacán-style Mexican food and gives away free slow-cooked pinto beans to go.

The locally beloved **Beyond Bread** (3026 N. Campbell Ave., 520/322-9965; 6260 E. Speedway Blvd., 520/747-7477; www.beyondbread.com, 6:30am-8pm Mon.-Fri., 7am-8pm Sat., $2.50-7.50) consistently scores Best Breakfast and Best Sandwich honors on the city's many Best of Tucson lists.

Huge and delicious omelets can be had at the **Blue Willow** (2616 N. Campbell Ave., 520/327-7577, 7am-9pm Mon.-Thurs., 8am-10pm Sat., 8am-9pm Sun., $8-12), serving out of a cute old house with a large covered patio in Campbell Avenue's busy commercial district. The emphasis here is on the fresh, homemade, and all natural. A gift shop sells funny stickers, buttons, and knickknacks about politics and gender issues.

American

The Dish Bistro (3131 E. 1st St., 520/326-1714, www.dishbistro.com, 5pm-9pm Tues.-Thurs., 5pm-10pm Fri.-Sat., $8-25) and wine bar inside The Rum Runner, a popular local wine and spirits shop, is famous for its mussels—a big steaming bowl of them floating in saffron broth with diced tomatoes and oregano. The "big plates" served in this very small bistro are all over $20 and include duck, salmon, and New York strip creations. The "small plates," best enjoyed with a glass of wine or two from Rum Runner's large inventory, run $8-15 and

include lobster tails and warm goat cheese with grilled bread. Reservations are a good idea.

The very definition of New American, **Pastiche Modern Eatery** (3025 N. Campbell Ave., 520/325-3333, www.pasticheme.com, 11:30am-midnight Mon.-Fri., 4:30pm-midnight Sat.-Sun., $7.50-26.50) an upscale, elegant eatery along Campbell Avenue, dips into culinary styles the world over and dribbles its findings on American-based dishes. The results are typically excellent, and the elegant atmosphere makes you want to stick around for a drink or two. If you're out on the town late, from 10pm until midnight every night Pastiche cuts the prices of its myriad creative appetizers—fried avocado, coconut shrimp, pot stickers, and much more—by half. If you're a Guinness drinker you might want to make a special trip to try the Guinness Steak ($15): ground steak marinated in Guinness, with porter cheddar, pepper bacon, Guinness gravy, and a fried egg on a grilled sourdough.

A local favorite for fresh and ingeniously prepared seafood, **Kingfisher** (2564 E. Grant Rd., 520/323-7739, www.kingfishertucson.com, lunch 11am-3pm Mon.-Fri., dinner 5pm-10pm daily, $8-24) has a thick oyster menu with something like 15 different varieties. For lunch, the pan-fried shrimp cakes are awesome, and the gulf shrimp is always fresh and sweet. For dinner there's a selection of fish, scallops, pasta, and meat dishes, including magnificent baby back ribs smothered in prickly pear barbecue sauce. The bar usually stays open until 1am or so, and there's a late-night menu of small plates. Reservations are recommended, especially on the weekends.

Feast (3719 E. Speedway Blvd., 520/326-9363 or 520/326-6500, www.eatatfeast.com, Tues.-Sat. 11am-9pm, Sun. 10am-9pm) a popular Midtown bistro, changes its menus every month to take advantage of the freshest local ingredients. The inimitable cuisine that results is generally bold and surprising.

Serving soul food with a pinch of Southwestern spice, **May's Counter** (2945 E. Speedway Blvd., 520/327-2421, http://mayscounter.com, 11am-10pm Mon.-Fri.,

8am-10pm Sat.-Sun.) can lay claim to one of the best meals in the Old Pueblo, whether it be morning, noon, or late at night: A few juicy pieces of peerless fried chicken on top of a rich, crisp waffle, all smothered in syrup and washed down with a Bacon Bloody Mary (with bacon-infused vodka).

With Executive Chef Ryan Clark, Tucson's reigning "Iron Chef," at the helm, the restaurant at **Lodge on the Desert** (306 N. Alvernon Way, 520/320-2000, www.lodgeonthedesert. com, breakfast 7am-10:30am daily, lunch 11am-2pm daily, dinner 5pm-9pm Sun.-Thurs., 5pm-10pm Fri.-Sat.) has become one of the city's most esteemed eateries. The midtown restaurant and bar, deep within the confines of the boutique hotel's property, exudes a kind of old-west, high-walled coziness that pairs perfectly with Clark's regional take on New American cuisine (e.g., mussels with grilled prickly pear cactus and shredded pork belly).

It's not in the most scenic part of Tucson, but the adventurous "Nahuan cuisine" and Southwestern comfort food served for breakfast and lunch at **Mother Hubbard's Café** (14 W. Grant Rd., 520/623-7976, www.motherhubbardscafe.com, 6am-2pm Mon.-Sat., 7am-2pm Sun.)—huevos rancheros, green corn waffles, and a host of less familiar Mexican-Native American hybrids—go far beyond the usual greasy-spoon fare. Don't worry if there's only one culinary adventurer in your party; Mother Hubbard's also serves more "traditional" breakfasts as well.

High-piled gourmet burgers in a casual setting—it's a rather simple concept that seems like a stroke of genius when you're trying to bite into your towering, inventive **Monkey Burger** (5350 E. Broadway Blvd., 520/514-9797, monkeyburgerrestaurant.com, 11am-9pm Mon.-Sat., noon-7pm Sun). They offer a dozen or so signature burgers and a few not-so-usual sides (fried pickles, sweet potato fries, roasted corn-on-cob), plus draft beer and thick shakes.

Asian

Karuna's Thai Plate (1917 E. Grant Rd., 520/325-4129, noon-3pm and 5pm-9pm Tues.-Thurs., noon-3pm and 5pm-10pm Fri.-Sat., 5pm-9pm Sun., $5-15) has a daily buffet and delicious, reasonably priced entrées.

Tucsonans, especially those who have recently migrated from the right and left coasts, are wont to complain about the city's paucity of good Chinese restaurants. Few are disappointed by the food at **Guilin Healthy Chinese Restaurant,** however (3250 E. Speedway Blvd., 520/320-7768, 11am-9pm Mon.-Thurs., 11am-10pm Fri., 11:30am-9:30pm Sat., 11:30am-9pm Sun., $4.95-12.95). It always tastes fresh and is never too greasy, and the menu is full of vegetarian options.

There are two reasons to visit **Sushi Garden** (15 N. Alvernon Way, 520/326-4700, www.sushigarden.com, 11am-11pm Mon.-Sat., noon-10pm Sun., $5-15): the sushi and the lunch buffet. The nigiri sushi and sashimi are always fresh and delicious, and the house ura maki rolls are typically outstanding. You can eat all that fits in your stomach for $20 per person. The lunch buffet ($9 per person, ends at 2pm) includes California rolls and usually a tempura roll of some kind, but the various Japanese noodle dishes, crunchy appetizers, chicken and beef dishes, and miso soup are the real draw. They serve a variety of Japanese beers and, of course, sake. It's a casual eatery with few frills, but the staff is friendly and there are several TVs staring down from the corners showing one sporting event or another.

The owners of **Yoshimatsu Healthy Japanese Eatery** (2660 N. Campbell, 520/320-1574, www.yoshimatsuaz.com, 11:30am-2:30pm and 5pm-9pm daily, $6.95-17) took a disused building along Campbell Avenue that was once a chain family dining joint and turned it into one of the most stylish and popular eateries in midtown. The interior of this casual place is all dark wood, framed Japanese pop-art images, and big, secluded booths for sake parties among friends. The staff is young and friendly, and the food—a variety of popular, traditional, and virtually unknown Japanese dishes unparalleled in Tucson—is fresh, light, and tasty. There's also a warm, wood-floored little sushi bar off the main dining room that's a great scene for couples and romance over half-priced happy hour sake and a tempura-fried "jalapeño seven" roll. And yes, of course, they have karaoke.

French

From a tucked-away space in a strip mall at Prince and Campbell, **Ghini's French Cafe and La Baguette Bakery** (1803 E. Prince, 520/326-9095, www.ghiniscafe.com, 6:30am-3pm Tues.-Sat., 8am-2pm Sun., $5.95-12.95) bring a bit of French taste to the desert city. Breakfast is the café's claim to fame, served all day on the weekend. The Ghini's Eggs Provencale, a fry-up of tomatoes and garlic and eggs on a crunchy baguette, is known far and wide, and their omelets are probably the best in town. The lunch menu includes a slew of unique Frenched-up sandwiches and salads, but my favorite is the simple, delicious *soupe à l'oignon*. Every Tuesday from 5pm to 7pm the café stays open after sundown for an "aperitif hour," during which they serve little plates of escargots, mussels, paté, and other French favorites, and offer discounts on glasses of wine from their smart collection. They also serve appetite-whetting pastis and various dark and decadent desserts from the bakery.

Mexican

Rosa's (1750 E. Fort Lowell Rd. #164, 520/325-0362, www.rosasmexicanfood.com, 11am-10pm daily, $2.50-10.50) is a favorite of Willie Nelson, who comes to town every now and again, and pictures of his visits are all over the walls. The familiar saucy and cheesy Mexican dishes here are the ideal comfort food for a road-weary traveler.

The airy, tropical interiors at **La Fuente** (1749 N. Oracle Rd., 520/623-8659, www.lafuenterestaurant.com, 11am-9pm Sun.-Thurs., 11am-10pm Fri., noon-10pm Sat., champagne brunch 11am-2pm Sun., $4.95-15.95), a popular Old Pueblo eatery since 1959, add to what always seems to be a busy, festive air in this popular Mexican restaurant on Oracle just north of downtown, but it's the loud and brassy mariachi band strolling among the tables

(Thurs.-Sun.) that really brings in the crowds. The food here is excellent, if a bit pricey; the fresh guacamole, prepared before your eyes right at the table, is among the best in town—and the atmosphere can't be beat.

A recognized leader among the Old Pueblo's many purveyors of the Sonoran hot dog, **BK Carne Asada & Hot Dogs** (2680 N. 1st Ave., 520/207-2245; Southside: 5118 S. 12th Ave., 520/295-0105; www.bktacos.com, 9am-11pm Sun.-Thurs., midnight at Southside location, 9am-midnight Fri.-Sat., 2:30am at Southside location), with a cozy midtown location, is the perfect place to have, say, 30 or so of the bacon-wrapped, bean-heaped dogs, and maybe a few dozen carne asada tacos, and an indeterminate number of cold beers. BK also serves awesome "caramelos." Apparently a local creation, they're a sort of grilled tortilla sandwich, usually overstuffed with meat, cheese, chilies and other staples.

The Arizona home of the Sonoran hot dog is **El Guero Canelo** (North Midtown: 2480 N.

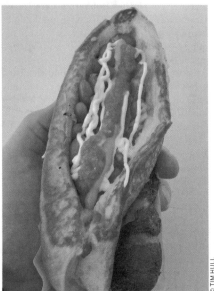

The Sonoran hot dog is Tucson's favorite street food.

© TIM HULL

Oracle Rd., 520/882-8977; Southside: 5201 S. 12th Ave., 520/295-9005; Eastside: 5802 E. 22nd St., 520/790-6000; www.elguerocanelo. com, 10am-11pm Sun.-Thurs., 10am-midnight Fri.-Sat., $4-7), which has been serving authentic and fast Mexican "street" food in the Old Pueblo for two decades. The restaurant's three locations serve what many believe to be city's best Sonoran dogs—a grilled beef hot dog wrapped in bacon and nestled deep in a thick, rich bun, and smothered in beans, onions, mustard, mayo and salsa. It's a decadent meal, especially because it's nearly impossible to have just one. Another must-try here are the carne asada tacos, and don't forget to wash it all down with a bottle of soda from Mexico, where the sodas are much, much tastier than they are north of the border. The Southside location has the feel and look of a Sonoran taco stand that grew out of all proportion, and has a lively atmosphere at night. You'll swear you somehow crossed the border without noticing it.

Steaks and Chops

The cowboy steaks at **Pinnacle Peak** (6541 E. Tanque Verde Rd., 520/296-0911, www. pinnaclepeaktucson.com, 5pm-10pm Mon.-Fri., 4:30pm-10pm Sat.-Sun., $4.95-18.95) are huge and served with delicious beans, and while you're waiting for your table you can look around the kitschy Old West town.

Middle Eastern

◖ **Ali Baba** (2545 E. Speedway Blvd. #125, 520/319-2559, 11am-8pm Mon.-Sat., noon-8pm Sun., $3-9) serves the city's best Mediterranean food in a casual atmosphere; the schwarma, falafel, gyros, hummus, and the like are all expertly prepared.

Vegetarian

Govinda's Natural Food Buffet (711 E. Blacklidge Dr., 520/792-0630, www.govindasoftucson.com, 11:30am-2:30pm Wed.-Sat., 5pm-9pm Tues.-Sat., brunch 11am-2:30pm Sun., $2-10) puts out a tasty, expertly prepared, and inexpensive all-you-can-eat vegetarian and vegan buffet. On Thursday nights everything is

vegan, and on Tuesdays authentic Indian food is served. Sundays they offer brunch from 11am to 2:30pm featuring pancakes, home fries, and scrambled tofu. The restaurant is located at the Chaitanya Cultural Center, its name referring to one of Krishna's many incarnations; you will be among Tucson's Hare Krishna community here, in a peaceful and always friendly atmosphere that may spark a meditative mood, postbuffet of course.

Not a few vegetarians in Tucson would like to take all their meals at **Lovin' Spoonfuls** (2990 N. Campbell, Ste. 120, 520/325-7766, www.lovinspoonfuls.com, 9:30am-9pm Mon.-Sat., 10am-3pm Sun., $5.75-11.25). For breakfast it'd be a Southwestern tofu scramble with soy chorizo and green chilies. For lunch, a portobello griller or maybe a soy burger with guacamole. Then, if they're still hungry, for dinner it'd be the lasagna with mock Italian sausage. The atmosphere here is calm and friendly and homegrown in the best possible sense, and if you go once, you will likely return again and again.

Fast Food

A homegrown enterprise, **Eegee's** (21 locations throughout Tucson, www.eegees.com) has been a favorite among Tucsonans since 1971. The most popular items on the menu are the frozen drinks—multiflavored shaved ice in a Styrofoam cup that goes down very easy on a hot summer day in the desert. My favorite is still the one they started with: lemon. They serve excellent deli-style sandwiches—many of them hot—and french fries and similar fare. The ranch fries, a heap of sliced and deep-fried potatoes smothered in ranch dressing and topped with bacon bits, are a delight if you can risk the coronary. There's one of these Tucson-only joints on a corner near you wherever you are in the Old Pueblo.

FOOTHILLS
American and Southwestern

An admirable restaurant in an incomparable setting, the **Flying V Bar and Grill** (7000 N. Resort Dr., 520/299-2020, www.loewshotels.

TUCSON

com/en/restaurants/flying-v-bar-grill, 5:30pm-9pm Mon.-Thurs., 5pm-10pm Fri.-Sat., 5pm-9pm Sun.) at Loews Ventana Canyon, a gorgeous Catalina Foothills destination resort, combines all the best elements of Tucson's dining scene in one place: awesome views, a romantic terrace, guacamole made to order tableside by a "guacamoliere," and inspired comfort food with a dollop of Southwestern flavor.

Perched in the Catalina Foothills and outfitted with big windows looking out over the sprawling desert city, **Acacia** (3001 E. Skyline Dr., 520/232-0101, www.acaciatucson.com, 11am-9pm daily) offers some of the best view-accompanied dining in Tucson. The seasonal dinner menus generally combine French technique, locally sourced ingredients, and a few regional nods. In the bar there's a host of surprising cocktails, and the long menu of small plates (from 2pm) reveals precisely what's going on in Acacia's kitchen for a bit less than you'd likely spend on dinner.

An upscale pub on the edge of the Foothills, **Union Public House** (4340 N. Campbell Ave., 520/329-8575, www.uniontucson.com, lunch 11am-4pm Mon.-Sat., dinner 4pm-close daily, brunch 10am-2pm Sun.) has outstanding food and one of the best patios in town, looking out on St. Philip's Plaza, with its shady trees and trickling fountain. The menu features creative variations on comfort classics—the pot pie, chicken and waffles, fish and chips, burgers and flatbread pizzas.

A delightful, upscale New American eatery in Casas Adobes Plaza, **Wildflower** (7037 N. Oracle Rd., 520/219-4230, www.foxrestaurantconcepts.com, 11am-3pm and 5pm-9pm Mon.-Thurs., 11am-3pm and 5pm-10pm Fri.-Sat., 5pm-9pm Sun., $9-29) has a charming patio and familiar but dressed-up lunches and dinners. Reservations are recommended.

For those who could exist on beef alone, and who believe that beef is best served ground, in patty form, and between two warm buns, there is **Zinburger** (1865 E. River Rd., 520/299-7799, www.foxrestaurantconcepts.com, 11am-10pm Sun.-Thurs., 11am-11pm Fri.-Sat., $8-13), a gourmet homage to the good old burger joint.

Not surprisingly the Kobe Burger (with cheddar cheese and wild mushrooms) is quite popular, as is the Samburger, with maple bacon, American cheese, and Thousand Island dressing—a kind of dressed-up Big Mac. The sides are worth a visit alone: sweet potato chips, zucchini fries, double truffle fries. Thick shakes, crème brûlée, and bananas foster are among the perfectly paired desserts offered in this sleek and bright burger house.

Tucson, especially its Foothills, is known for its year-round patio dining and sweeping views of the city, twinkling lights from the valley like signal fires in the darkness below. The best patio of them all is **Terraza del Sol** at the **Grill at Hacienda del Sol** (5601 N. Hacienda del Sol Rd., 520/529-3500, www.haciendadelsol.com, 5:30pm-10pm daily, brunch 10am-1:30pm Sun., $24-42), a charming, historic resort restaurant. The bar serves a relatively low-priced menu ($7-26) of creative small plates, and features live music Thursday-Sunday. The menu includes entrées on the order of pork osso bucco and Tasmanian ocean trout. Reservations are recommended.

Bluefin Seafood Bistro (7053 N. Oracle Rd., 520/531-8500, www.bluefintucson.com, 11am-9pm Sun.-Thurs., 11am-11pm Fri.-Sat., $9-29) has an enchanting patio bar that looks out on a courtyard with a fountain. They serve perfect fish and chips and clam chowder for lunch, and for dinner they bring out the Alaskan king crab, Maine lobster, and host of creative seafood creations.

A unique pairing of South-by-Southwest food styles, **The Parish** (6453 N. Oracle Rd., 520/797-1233, www.theparishtucson.com, 11am-midnight Sun.-Thurs., 11am-2am Fri.-Sat., $8-16) calls itself a "Southern fusion gastropub." That generally means New Orleans meets Tucson, and it's a meeting that anybody who loves food will want to be present for. Try the crawfish hushpuppies; you may end up eating a dozen or so. Or the housemade pork rinds, or the bacon popcorn . . . and that's just the appetizers. The entrées include various steaks, fish, and burgers, all prepared with Southern methods and just a dash of Southwestern spice.

The Parish in Tucson's Foothills neighborhood serves the best hushpuppies in the world.

The Parish also has a creative cocktail menu and a wide selection of beers on tap.

Steaks and Chops

El Corral Restaurant (2201 E. River Rd., 520/299-6092, www.elcorraltucson.com, 5pm-10pm Mon.-Thurs., 4:30pm-10pm Fri.-Sun., $8.95-18.95) is a charming, historic choice for prime rib, a thick steak, and big bowl of cowboy beans. In a low-ceiling, stone-and-wood-beam territorial ranch house with flagstone floors along River Road, it's been a Tucson institution since 1926. The setting is almost as inviting as the sizzling beef and barbecue ribs, with Technicolor portraits of movie-house cowboys on the walls and several rooms that offer romantic, fireside dining.

SOUTH OF DOWNTOWN

If you only have the time or inclination to eat at one of Tucson's famous Sonoran-style Mexican restaurants, consider **Mi Nidito** (1813 S. 4th Ave., 520/622-5081, www.minidito.net,

11am-10:30pm Wed., Thurs., Sun., 11am-2am Fri.-Sat., $2.50-10.90); Bill Clinton did. While on a short stopover in Tucson during his presidency, Clinton, known for his love of food (especially the comfort variety), stopped at Mi Nidito (My Little Nest), sampling pretty much one of everything. His order is preserved as a special on the menu still. It's difficult to say what it is about this bright South 4th Avenue restaurant, with its tropical decor and friendly albeit always harried staff, that sets it apart from the dozens of other similar eateries in the Old Pueblo. It is the best, that's all there is to it. *Tucson Weekly* readers invariably name it the top (or at least among the top) Sonoran joints in town in that publication's annual Best of Tucson poll, and you shouldn't be surprised to see a line of people waiting to be seated at 10:45am on a Wednesday. On a weekend night, figure on at least a half-hour on the porch, waiting anxiously for your name to ring out.

The distinctive fruit and chili concoction that gives **Taqueria Pico De Gallo** (2618 S. 6th Ave., 520/623-8775, 9am-9pm Mon.-Sat., 10am-5pm Sun., $4.95-8.95) its name is something to behold. Pico de gallo (beak of a rooster) in many places is a chunky mixture of tomatoes, peppers, onions, and lime heaped on tacos; here it's a cup of fresh fruit cut in big chunks and doused with salty chili powder. The tortillas, made fresh for each order, make whatever's stuffed inside them nearly moot. This is a good place to get takeout; the dining room is merely serviceable.

WEST OF DOWNTOWN
American and Southwestern

As you approach **Li'l Abner's Steakhouse** (8500 N. Silverbell Rd., 520/744-2800, 5pm-10pm Sun.-Thurs., 5pm-11pm Fri.-Sat., $6-25), you'll spot cord upon cord of mesquite stacked in the backyard, just waiting for the flame to turn it into flavor. The steaks and ribs and chickens here are cooked over a big open pit outside, and on the weekends there's often music and dancing. Ages of patron graffiti marks the walls inside, giving the place a friendly, casual air that could easily turn

TUCSON

celebratory with the right mix of meat, music, and alcohol.

The ideal place to refuel after exploring the desert in and around Tucson Mountain Park, Saguaro National Park, and the Arizona-Sonora Desert Museum, **Coyote Pause Café** (2740 S. Kinney Rd., 520/883-7297, www.coyotepausecafe.com, 7:30am-2:30pm Mon.-Thurs. and Sat.-Sun., 4pm-8pm Fri.) is a casual diner-style eatery serving classic American rib-stickers with a few nods to the territory. It's in a refurbished 1950s-era desert outpost called Cat Mountain Station and an easy drive from all of the main west-side attractions. The "Coyote Burger," with house-made prickly pear BBQ sauce (you might want to take home several dozen bottles) and thick, crunchy onion rings will restore any energy that you left out on the Saguaro-lined trails nearby.

Fast Food

Fans of the chili dog will want to try longtime local favorite **Pat's Drive-In** (1202 W. Niagara St. at Grande Ave., 520/624-0891, 11:30am-10pm Mon.-Sat., 11:30am-9pm Sun., $2.95-5.95), a throwback to the early days of fast food in both style and substance. It's usually busy here at lunchtime, there isn't a lot of parking, and the staff can get overwhelmed on occasion; but it's worth the trouble if you like hot, flavorful chili over a hot dog with mustard and onions. The fries and onion rings and burgers are pretty good too.

Information and Services

VISITORS CENTER

Make sure to stop by the **Metropolitan Tucson Convention and Visitors Bureau** (110 S. Church, Ste. 7199, 520/624-1817, 8am-5pm Mon.-Fri., 9am-4pm Sat.-Sun.). The bureau produces a helpful guide to the city you can pick up at the office or out in front during off hours. There are scores of tourist pamphlets for the perusing. Park in the metered parking on Church Avenue in front of the Technicolor **La Placita**, which houses the bureau and a few shops and cafés.

FOREST CONTACTS

Most of the public lands around Tucson and Southern Arizona are administered by **Coronado National Forest.** The forest's main office in Tucson (300 W. Congress St., 520/388-8300, www.fs.fed.us/r3/coronado, 8am-4:30pm Mon.-Fri.) can direct you to a specific field office.

The **Bureau of Land Management** (12661 E. Broadway, 520/258-7200, www.az.blm.gov, 8am-4pm Mon.-Fri.) monitors much of the public land that is not within the national forest.

If you have any trouble with wild animals or need to report a poaching incident, call the **Arizona Game & Fish Department** (555 N. Greasewood Rd., 520/628-5376, www.azgfd.gov, 8am-5pm Mon.-Fri.).

HOSPITALS

Dial 911 for emergencies anywhere in Southern Arizona. **University Medical Center** (1501 N. Campbell Ave., 520/694-0111) has the region's only Level 1 Trauma Center, so if you are seriously hurt anywhere in Southern Arizona, you are likely to be treated by the capable staff there.

MEDIA

The morning daily newspaper *The Arizona Daily Star* (www.azstarnet.com) has a local focus but isn't provincial by any means. The weekly alternative tabloid *Tucson Weekly* (www.tucsonweekly.com) is the place to go for news on arts, entertainment, politics, and local news. You'll find it free throughout the city.

Getting There and Around

AIR

Tucson International Airport (520/573-8000, www.tucsonairport.org) hosts 10 major airlines (including American, Delta, Frontier, Continental, Southwest and Northwest, and Alaska Airlines) making approximately 60 departures every day. It's a small but efficient airport, with free wireless Internet access and daily nonstop flights to Atlanta, Chicago, Minneapolis, Houston, Albuquerque, Denver, Salt Lake, Vegas, Seattle, San Francisco, L.A., and San Diego If you're coming in from or headed to a city not on this list, it's likely you'll stop first at the state's major airport, **Sky Harbor International Airport,** in Phoenix, and then desert-hop, as it were, for about 45 minutes south (probably after waiting more than an hour or so at the terminal). If you find yourself at Sky Harbor and don't feel like boarding an absurdly short flight, you can rent a car there and make the easy 1.5-hour drive down I-10 across the desert—though the scenery along the I-10 is certainly not representative of what you're in for when you get to Tucson. Or, you can call **Arizona Shuttle Service** (520/795-6771 or 520/795-6775, www.arizonashuttle.com), which offers 18 daily trips between Phoenix and Tucson.

If you're arriving or departing from TIA, remember that **Arizona Stagecoach** (520/881-4111 or 520/889-1000, www.stage-coach.com) runs a door-to-door 24-hour shuttle to and from TIA. You can park at the airport's long-term lot for a mere $4 per day, and a free shuttle runs from the terminal to the parking area, or you can walk it if you're so inclined. There are always cabs waiting just outside the main entrance; expect to pay about $20 for the ride to midtown. To get the airport from midtown, take Campbell; this turns into the Kino Parkway south of Broadway. Follow road signs to Benson Highway, which leads to Tucson Boulevard and the airport entrance.

CAR

A car is necessary to truly visit Tucson the way it deserves to be visited. To get out into the desert you need your own vehicle, though it need not be a four-wheel drive.

The main national route to and from Tucson is I-10, which acts as a kind of in-town freeway as well. Tucson is rather isolated from the east-west route to the north, I-40. It's a 4 hour, 263-mile drive from Tucson to Flagstaff, which is along I-40 and one of the best gateway cities for a visit to the Grand Canyon. Phoenix is just 100 miles or so up I-10, a drive of about two hours. The Old Pueblo is connected to its former owner, Mexico, via I-17, a straight one-hour shot (70 miles) south through the beautiful Santa Cruz Valley.

Car Rental

If you're flying into Tucson and don't have friends or relatives to chauffeur you around a typically sprawling Southwestern city, you'll need to rent a car. The airport has several counters from which to choose. If you're booking ahead, try the locally owned **Adobe Car & Van Rental of Tucson** (3150 E. Grant Rd., 520/320-1495 or 888/471-7951), which has free pickup service.

LONG-DISTANCE BUS

For bus service from Tucson to all points on the map, there's the **Greyhound Bus Station** (471 W. Congress, east of I-10, 520/792-3475, www.greyhound.com).

TRAIN

The **Amtrak Station** (400 N. Toole Ave., 520/623-4442, www.amtrak.com) is downtown.

PUBLIC TRANSPORTATION
Buses

The City of Tucson operates the **Sun Tran** (4220 S. Park Ave., 520/623-4301, www.

suntran.com) bus line. It has stops all over the Old Pueblo and operates 6am-7pm weekdays and 8am-5pm weekends. Full fare is $1.25, with children under five riding free.

Modern Streetcar

The **Sun Link Modern Streetcar** (www.tucsonstreetcar.com), a sleek rail system being constructed across several neighborhoods downtown, is expected to transform the Old Pueblo's downtown and entertainment districts when it opens in summer 2014.

The project will put seven brand-new railcars on the streets of downtown, 4th Avenue, Main Gate Square near the University of Arizona, and the so far mostly undeveloped Mercado District west of I-10—connecting all of the neighborhoods to each other. All told the route will comprise about 4 miles. The street cars, each with a 180-passenger capacity, will run the route every 10 minutes in daytime and every 20 minutes in evening, making 17 stops along the way.

Cabs and Shuttles

Cab rides can get expensive in Tucson because everything is so spread out. Expect to spend about $15 for a ride from midtown to restaurants and bars downtown or on 4th Avenue. There are plenty of rides to choose from. Try **AAA Yellow Cab Co./Fiesta Taxi** (520/624-6611 or 520/399-6062), or **All State Cab Company** (520/798-1111 or 520/887-9000). **Arizona Stagecoach** (520/881-4111 or 520/889-1000, www.azstagecoach.com) runs a door-to-door 24-hour shuttle to and from TIA, and **Arizona Shuttle Service** (520/795-6771 or 520/795-6775, www.arizonashuttle.com) offers 18 daily trips between TIA and Phoenix's Sky Harbor Airport.

The Santa Cruz Valley

Heading south out of Tucson on I-19 you enter the Santa Cruz Valley, a storied landscape through which the Spanish took some of their first steps into the vast north.

This is the land of the trailblazing Father Eusebio Kino, who in the later 1600s traveled through Pimeria Alta, the "land of the upper Pima," as the Spanish called this region, referring to one of the many native populations that called the valley home for eons before Europeans arrived. The Tohono O'odham also live here, formerly called the Papago, whose San Xavier Indian Reservation stretches out west of the interstate. Kino, a Jesuit with a penchant for roughing it, founded several missions in Pimeria Alta, two of which, on the Arizona side of the border, still stand and still hold masses. One of the oldest continually inhabited villages in North America can be found at Tubac, now an artist colony and tourist stop where they celebrate the legacy of the Basque adventurer Juan Bautista de Anza the younger, who attempted to tame the valley of its hostile Apaches and eventually led the expedition west that established San Francisco, California.

The valley has always been a ranching area, even during Kino's time, and after the Gadsden Purchase several Anglo ranches were established and thrived for generations. Much of the former ranchland has been sold to establish conservation areas and wildlife refuges in this rare ecosystem. During the Cold War, intercontinental ballistic missiles (ICBMs) were cocked and ready in underground missile silos throughout the valley, an era celebrated with a museum. The area has also long been home to large open-pit copper mines, and the towering tailings piles rise like ziggurats to the west of the retirement community of Green Valley. And in Ambos Nogales—the name meaning, roughly, "both Nogaleses"—you'll witness the teeming U.S.-Mexico border region in all its fascinating chaos.

The Santa Rita Mountains to the east attract subtropical birds on the move from Mexico and points farther south to their sky island heights,

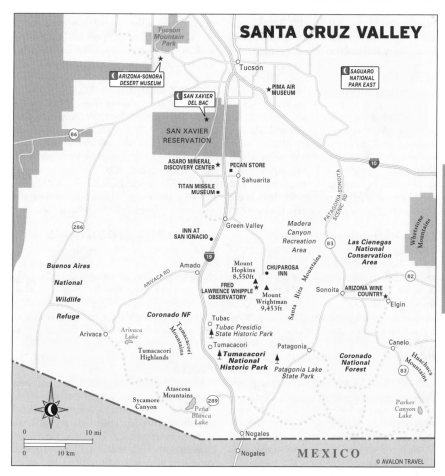

a fact that in turn attracts birding enthusiasts from around the world. You can hike to the top of 9,000-foot Mount Wrightson and see the whole world on a clear day, or stay in one of Madera Canyon's small lodges and take a tour of an observatory, where scientists are trying to discover the beginnings of the universe.

GREEN VALLEY/SAHUARITA

Sahuarita is a bedroom community about 15 miles south of Tucson, the site of the largest pecan-growing operation in the world. Green Valley is one of Arizona's best retirement communities, home to about 25,000 year-round residents and many more part-time snowbirds from the frozen north. Together the two towns make up a relatively large population center between the dry Santa Cruz River to the east and the copper mines to the west.

Asarco Mineral Discovery Center

Take exit 80 off I-19 and drive west of the casino to reach the **Asarco Mineral Discovery Center** (1421 W. Pima Mine Rd., Sahuarita, 520/625-8233, www.mineraldiscovery.com, 9am-5pm Tues.-Sat., exhibitions free, mine tour $6 adults, $4 children 5-12). This illuminating sight, using exhibits, old mining equipment, and films, explains how all the huge piles of dirt flanking the valley's west side got there.

The copper in the Santa Cruz Valley is of the porphyry variety, meaning it's very low grade and takes a lot of earth-moving to get at; a one-hour bus tour offered five times a day on Tuesday, Thursday, and Saturday will take you up into the hills to the sprawling Mission Mine to show you how it's done. From the bus you'll see the vast pit and the post-apocalyptic landscape created by large-scale copper mining, and you'll drive through a working mill. Back at the Discovery Center a gift shop sells souvenirs.

Titan Missile Museum

This deactivated missile site, one of several missile facilities staffed with underground-dwelling Cold Warriors in what was once referred to as the Titan Valley, had its Titan II aimed squarely at the USSR from 1963 to 1982. The site was decommissioned in 1986 and became a National Historic Landmark in 1994.

The one-hour tour of the **Titan Missile Museum** (1580 W. Duval Mine Rd., Sahuarita, 520/625-7736, www.pimaair.org, 9am-5pm daily, $8.50 adults, $5 children 7-12) takes you deep underground, and volunteer guides, some of them former crew members, explain what daily life was like working at the silo. The highlight of the tour for many is seeing an actual Titan II still waiting there in the launch duct. Guides also simulate the launch sequence that crew members hoped they would never have to complete. The visitors center provides context with a Cold War timeline and artifacts from the era, and a gift shop sells souvenirs and books.

Shopping

Drive east on Sahuarita Road past the pecan groves—roll down your windows and feel how much cooler the trees make the air—and you'll come to the **Pecan Store** (1625 E. Sahuarita Rd., Sahuarita, 520/791-2062 or 800/327-3226, www.pecanstore.com, 9am-5pm Mon.-Sat.), an outlet of Farmers Investment Corp.,

which operates the largest integrated pecan growing and packaging operation in the world (some 400,000 trees on 5,000 acres) and sells, of course, pecans and pecan accessories.

Accommodations

If you're staying a while in Green Valley, try the **Inn at San Ignacio** (1861 W. Demetrie Loop, Green Valley, 520/393-5700, www.innatsanignacio.com, $129-169), which has villa rooms and condo-style suites with kitchenettes, cable, and Internet access. The inn is near several golf courses and offers special deals for birders. There are also several chain hotels just off the interstate in Green Valley and Sahuarita.

SANTA RITA MOUNTAINS

Black bears, mountain lions, ring-tailed cats, deer, and too many birds to count call this sky island range home, where mining and logging once were legitimate pursuits but now outdoor recreation rules. The range's highest peak is 9,453-foot Mount Wrightson. Most visitors to the Santa Ritas head to Madera Canyon and its trails to the peak's summit.

Madera Canyon

Madera Canyon is the part-time home to many subtropical bird species that stop off on their migrations north to mate along a cool mountain creek in conditions not dissimilar from more tropical climes to the south. Consequently the canyon is a kind of mecca for serious birders fulfilling their life lists. It is one of a very few places in North America one can see the fat green-and-red elegant trogon, a relative of the quetzal and the source of much thrill and consternation for birders visiting from points far away. The great variety of hummingbird species flitting about the canyon also draws visitors from far and wide.

A paved two-lane leads from the desert floor up to about 6,000 feet, where well-used and relatively steep trails climb the slopes of **Mount Wrightson** all the way to its bare and rocky 9,453-foot peak. The most popular trail to the top is the 10.8-mile round-trip **Old Baldy Trail,** which is fairly steep but much shorter than the more gradual, 16-mile round-trip **Super Trail.** Both trails are well marked, heavily used, and start near the Mount Wrightson Picnic Area at the top of the canyon. Both trails also take you over **Josephine Saddle,** at about 7,000 feet, and **Baldy Saddle,** not far below the peak at more than 8,000 feet, which make good places to stop and rest. At Josephine Saddle make sure to look at the makeshift memorial to a group of Boy Scouts who got caught in a snowstorm on the mountain in the 1950s and never returned. If you're coming up the Super Trail, stop and rest at Sprung Spring just before you reach the saddle, which has delicious mountain water trickling from a spigot.

To see the lushness that a little trickling water can inspire hit the 5.8-mile **Bog Spring-Kent Spring Loop,** which leads over some old mining roads in the lower reaches of the canyon onto some fairly steep and skinny trails along a windswept ridge, providing some pretty spectacular views of the valley below. The trail eventually leads deep into the forest, where sycamores thrive on the edges of green and spongy clearings. Also try the 4.4-mile one-way **Nature Trail,** a fairly steep but relatively easy way to see the entire canyon, from the desert grasslands at its entrance at the **Proctor Parking Area,** where you can pick up the trail, all the way up to the woodlands at the top. Small signs along the way point out notable flora and fauna, and the highest point on the trail, high above the canyon floor, offers a unique perspective.

The average summertime temperature in the canyon is about 85°F, about 15-20°F cooler on any given summer day than it is down in the valley. It gets cold in the high country October-April, and it regularly snows up there in deep winter. Madera Canyon is an extremely popular day-use area and hiking destination for Tucson and Santa Cruz Valley residents, so expect to see quite a few people on the trails and using the three developed picnic areas, all of which have tables, bathrooms, and charcoal grills. You can pick up a trail map at any of the lodges in the canyon, or you can get one at the welcome station at the canyon's entrance, but it is staffed irregularly. There's a $5 per car user fee, or you can purchase a $20 annual pass.

Mount Hopkins Fred Lawrence Whipple Observatory

The Smithsonian Institution operates the **Fred Lawrence Whipple Observatory** atop 8,550-foot Mount Hopkins, where astronomers take advantage of the dark Southern Arizona sky to scan space for very faint objects. The MMT, the largest single-mirror telescope in North America, is one of four you can see up close during a six-hour tour of the facility offered Monday, Wednesday, and Friday, mid-March through November ($7 adults, $2.50 children 6-12, no children under 6). It's a good idea to call ahead for reservations far in advance. The **visitors center** (520/670-5707, http://cfa-www.harvard.edu/flwo, 8:30am-4:30pm Mon.-Fri.) near Amado has displays about the work being done on the mountain and the history of the telescope.

Accommodations and Camping

Madera Canyon used to be dotted with summer homes and getaway cabins, but beginning in the 1970s the U.S. Forest Service tore them down and converted the treasured ecosystem into a federal recreation area. Now only a scattered few homes remain on historic mining claims. Three of the lasting structures are lodges that welcome visitors year-round. As you're driving up the canyon's only road, first you come upon the **Santa Rita Lodge** (520/625-8746, www.santaritalodge.com, $110-165), offering several casitas and free-standing cabins with private decks. The lodge, the oldest in the canyon, has beautiful grounds along Madera Creek, where feeders attract birds and there are benches for viewing. There's also a gift shop, but no food, so bring your own or plan to eat in Green Valley about 12 miles away. March through May the lodge can fix you up with an experienced birding guide by appointment. Tours start early and last about four hours ($20 per person).

Next you'll see the A-frame **Madera Kubo** (520/625-2908, www.maderakubo.com, $95),

TUCSON

The Western Desert

© VISIONS OF AMERICA LLC/123RF.COM

Kitt Peak National Observatory

Southwest of Tucson, the vast desert homeland of the Tohono O'odham Indians stretches out, a hot wasteland where few dare to venture. You can head out to this 4,400-square-mile borderland reservation via Highway 286 west of Tucson, but there isn't much out here except gorgeous, mostly untouched desert. Straddling the border, the

which has four cozy cabins and a gift shop, but no food. Near the top of the canyon is the ◖ **Chuparosa Inn** (520/393-7370, www.chuparosainn.com, $150-200), with three beautiful rooms, a great bird-watching area, a barbecue, and friendly hosts. The Chuparosa serves a hearty continental breakfast, but you're on your own for lunch and dinner. If you prefer to rough it, the **Bog Springs Campground** (turn left off Madera Canyon Rd. at sign, 520/281-2296, www.fs.fed.us/r3/coronado) has campsites, $10 year-round, on a first-come, first-served basis.

Information
The area is managed by the **Coronado National Forest Nogales Ranger District** (303 Old Tucson Rd., Nogales, I-19 Ruby Rd. exit, then turn east, 520/281-2296, 8am-4:30pm Mon.-Fri.). The forest's main office in Tucson has information on this area as well.

BUENOS AIRES WILDLIFE REFUGE
This remote 118,000-acre refuge preserves large swaths of endangered semidesert grassland, home to the pronghorn. The refuge's flagship program was once the reintroduction of the rare masked bobwhite quail to the grasslands, but the program was transferred to a private organization in 2007. Its proximity to the U.S.-Mexico border has caused some trouble on the refuge, and portions are indefinitely closed to the public because of smuggling activity.

reservation is a popular, albeit deadly, corridor for illegal migrants heading north, and dozens die crossing the reservation every year. Only the O'odham know how to live out here. About 90 minutes west of Tucson along Highways 86 and 386 (follow the signs) you'll find another of Southern Arizona's famous observatories. **Kitt Peak National Observatory** (Hwy. 386, 520/318-8726, www.noao.edu, 9am-3:45pm daily, $2 suggested donation) operates 23 telescopes—the world's largest collection—atop the 6,875-foot peak in the reservation's Quinlan Mountains. Docent-led tours are available at 10am, 11:30am, and 1:30pm and last about an hour ($2 adults, $1 children over 6), or you can pick up a pamphlet and take a self-guided tour. The visitors center has exhibits on astronomy and a gift shop selling star- and planet-related items and O'odham baskets. Far off to the south look for 7,700-foot Baboquivari Peak, the home of I'itoi, the tribe's sacred "elder brother" god. The reservation capital, Sells, is a small outpost about 58 miles southwest of Tucson on Highway 86. There's a supermarket, a few businesses, offices, and a school. During the first weekend in February O'odham cowboys join in the All Indian Rodeo and Fair, during which locals set up food booths, play music, march in a parade, dance, and show off and sell their crafts. Continue through the thick desert west on Highway 86 and then north on Highway 85 and you'll hit Ajo, a copper mining community with a few restaurants and a good place to see the scars strip mining leaves open on the land. South of Ajo on Highway 85, past the tiny town of Why, you'll find **Organ Pipe Cactus National Monument.** This rugged, beautiful monument along the border protects what amounts to pretty much all of the Organ Pipe cacti in North America, along with many other species of cactus, and is a popular area for seeing spring wildflowers in bloom. It has in the past been named one of the most dangerous national monuments in the country. This area is a major drug-smuggling corridor and sees its share of illegal migrants, too. The **Kris Eggle Visitor Center** (520/387-6849), named for a ranger who was killed during a shootout with drug smugglers, is open 8am-5pm daily. There's a campground with 208 sites, drinking water, but no hookups or facilities ($12 per night). The 21-mile Ajo Mountain Drive, on a twisty dirt road that's usually passable, will take you into the monument's center, where you can see the many-armed cactus up close.

One the most accessible portions of the refuge is the **Arivaca Cienega,** a swamplike desert wetland just outside the tiny village of **Arivaca.** The easy two-mile loop trail includes boardwalks over the wetter portions, and birds, frogs, and snakes abound. Take Arivaca Road about 20 miles from I-19 Exit 48 until you see the sign for the Cienega, just east of Arivaca. At the western end of town turn at the Y and drive 2.5 miles to Arivaca Creek, also managed by the refuge, where there's easy creekside hiking among cottonwood and mesquite. Far off to the northwest in the Baboquivari Mountains is Brown Canyon, a riparian area accessible only with a guide and by appointment.

To get to **refuge headquarters** (520/823-4251, www.fws.gov/southwest/refuges/arizona/ buenosaires/index.html, 7:30am-4pm daily, closed weekends June 1-Aug. 15), go through Arivaca to Highway 286, head south four miles, then turn left at milepost 7.5. There's also a satellite office that's open intermittently in downtown Arivaca next to the mercantile.

TUBAC AND TUMACACORI

These two villages along the Santa Cruz River are steeped in the history of the Spanish adventures in Pimeria Alta. Padre Kino established the mission at Tumacacori in 1691, and Tubac, a Piman village, became a mission farm and ranch. By the 1730s Spanish colonists had arrived from the south to farm and ranch the fertile river valley. In 1751 the violent Piman revolt convinced the Spanish crown to establish the Presidio San Ignacio de Tubac, which was founded the next year. The famous Basque Juan Bautista de Anza II was the second commander of the presidio, and in 1776 he led the first of two overland journeys to establish a fort at San Francisco, California, taking along about 60 colonists from Tubac. In 1860 silver strikes nearby briefly made Tubac the largest town in the Arizona Territory. It eventually fell into obscurity, but was discovered again as an artists' colony during the second half of the 20th century, and today its many galleries and shops are a draw for tourists and locals alike.

Crowds flock to Tubac during the weeklong **Tubac Festival of the Arts** in February, during which artisans and artists from around the country set up booths. Music and the smell of greasy, delicious food fill the village.

Tubac Presidio
State Historic Park
Arizona's first state park, founded in 1959, **Tubac Presidio State Historic Park** (520/398-2252, www.azstateparks.com/parks/TUPR, 8am-5pm daily, $3 adults, $1 children 7-13) preserves the history and foundations of the Presidio San Ignacio de Tubac. You can see the fort's original foundation and peruse a museum that explains what life was like for the natives, settlers, and soldiers. Guided tours and hands-on interpretation programs are available on request. The park's annual **Anza Days** celebration around the third week of October honors the fort's most famous commander with historical re-creations, music, and food. The Tubaquenos, a historical reenactment society, put on living history demonstrations at the park 1pm-4pm Sunday, October-March.

Tumacacori
National Historic Park
Padre Kino founded **Mission San Jose de Tumacacori** in 1691, and much of it still stands today on 310-acre **Tumacacori National Historic Park** (three miles south of Tubac on the east-side Frontage Rd., 520/398-2341, www.nps.gov/tuma, 9am-5pm daily, $3 adults over 16). You can explore the mission

and its grounds, which include an old graveyard, an orchard, and a re-created Piman shelter. A museum tells the history of the mission and Pimeria Alta, and most days you can buy tortillas and refried beans made right before your eyes in the traditional fashion. A gift shop sells a wide assortment of books on local history.

The mission at Tumacacori still holds masses on holidays, but the two other missions protected by the park are mostly in ruins. The ruins of mission **San Cayetano de Calabazas,** normally closed to the public, can be visited on monthly guided tours for $10 per person. Reservations are required (520/398-2341).

Juan Bautista de Anza
National Historic Trail
There's a 4.5-mile portion of the route that was used to take colonists and their stock animals from Northern Mexico to Northern California in 1775-1776 between the presidio and the mission that makes for an easy and shady riverside hike, though there's often a lot of trash along the route as a result of illegal migration and seasonal flooding of the northward flowing Santa Cruz River. The route crosses private ranchland, and you're bound to see cattle. It leads from just outside the state park to just outside the national park, or vice versa, and is a route historically used to travel between the two landmarks.

Shopping
Tubac has more than 100 shops and galleries, many of them selling Mexican and South American imports. The village has two bookstores, a year-round Christmas gallery, and several little shops whose wares simply must be seen. Pick up an illustrated map of the shopping district at any of the shops or at the visitors center.

Accommodations
Tubac Golf Resort and Spa (1 Avenue de Otero, 520/398-2211, www.tubacgolfresort.com, $140-265) is a historic, upscale resort and golf course with casitas and rooms of various

© TIM HULL

Tumacacori National Historic Park

sizes and styles, two restaurants, a pool, hot tub, and other amenities. Once part of the sprawling Otero cattle ranch, the hotel and golf course opened on 500 lush acres along the Santa Cruz River in 1959. Bing Crosby was one of the original owners. New owners completed a $40 million restoration of the historic gem in 2007. Check the website for great package deals; prices drop considerably in summer. The **Tubac Country Inn** (12 Burruel St., 520/398-3178, www.tubaccountryinn.com, $90-175) is situated right in the heart of the village and offers suites with kitchenettes, TVs, and wireless Internet.

Food

Open since 1944 and still run by the same family, **Wisdom's Café** (1931 E. Frontage Rd., 520/398-2397, www.wisdomscafe.com, noon-3pm and 5pm-8pm Mon.-Sat. $5-12) may be the best restaurant in the Santa Cruz Valley, serving Mexican food from handed-down family recipes. Don't miss the famous fruit burrito for dessert. Head south on the Frontage Road toward the mission and look for the big chicken statue out front.

AMADO

You'll know you've made it to Amado, a former ranching center, when you see the building-sized cow skull on the west side of I-19 about 10 miles south of Green Valley, Exit 48. A statue of a Hereford announces the locally beloved **Cow Palace Restaurant** (520/398-1999, www.cowpalacerestaurant.com, breakfast, lunch, and dinner daily, $3-20), serving a wide variety of favorites from chicken fried steak to spaghetti; and if you hang out in the bar long enough, there's a pretty good chance you'll meet a real live cowboy.

Information

A good place to start your Tubac visit is the **Tubac-Santa Cruz Visitor Center** (4 Plaza Rd., 520/398-0007, www.toursantacruz.com, 9am-4pm Mon.-Fri., 10am-4pm Sat.-Sun.), just to the left as you enter the village by the big Tubac sign.

Tumacacori Highlands

This huge wilderness of semidesert grasslands, rugged mountains, and riparian canyons west of the valley can best be accessed using Ruby Road (I-19 Exit 12) just north of Nogales. West about 11 miles is **Peña Blanca Lake,** where bass and catfish can be lured in but not eaten because of high mercury content. There's a boat ramp and trail around the lake. Branch off on Forest Road 39 for the **White Rock Campground,** which has sites year-round, but no water ($5). Continue another five miles along Forest Road 39 to the trailhead for the **Atascosa Lookout Trail.** The popular, steep trail to the 6,255-foot peak, a six-mile round-trip, takes you to a decommissioned fire lookout which, for a

few months in 1968, was manned by writer **Edward Abbey.**

There's a sign pointing to the trailhead for the **Sycamore Canyon Trail** on Forest Road 39 about 10 miles in from Peña Blanca Lake. This trail leads deep into a watered canyon, with steep walls dotted with saguaro, white sycamore trees shading the creek bed, and jagged rocks jutting out from above. It's a five-mile hike one-way to the U.S.-Mexico border, marked by a barbed-wire fence. The trail isn't always well marked, as the creek often overtakes it, and you will certainly have to wade in parts. During the rainy season some sections may be impassable. The canyon is a major corridor for drug smuggling, and you are likely to see a lot of trash and other evidence of the trade.

The Border Region

Anywhere you are in Cochise or Santa Cruz Counties, you're never more than a few miles from Mexico, and small towns like Bisbee and Douglas each have a Mexican twin right across the line, and traffic between the two generally flows pretty easily (though they are fraternal twins; the Mexican-side counterparts are larger and more populous). But the easiest, and in a sense the safest, way to visit our neighbors to the south for the day is to walk across the border at the Mariposa Port of Entry in Nogales, Arizona, about an hour south on I-19 from Tucson. The Arizona side of what locals call Ambos Nogales (both Nogaleses) is a somewhat sleepy government and produce warehousing town with about 25,000 souls, while the sprawling industrial city just across the border teems with more than 500,000 residents. Most visitors stick to the tourist-friendly blocks just beyond the port of entry. A good portion of the nation's produce passes through the port of entry in Nogales, Arizona, as does a large amount of illegal drugs.

SIGHTS
Nogales, Mexico, Tourist District

Nogales, Sonora, Mexico, is a modern factory and produce shipping center, but it's also a very popular tourist destination. It's easy to get there: Just walk across the international border in downtown Nogales, Arizona, after parking at one of the many pay lots (about $4 per day) near the port-of-entry. There's a tourist area of about a square mile just south of the border, with restaurants, curio shops, and, if you want, drugstores. You can drive into Mexico, but the lines of cars driving north into the United States are long and slow. If you need to ride, there are cabs everywhere and the drivers speak English; they, like everyone else who deals with tourists, take U.S. cash.

In recent years more and more merchants in Nogales's tourist district are competing for fewer and fewer tourist dollars, making a slow, fun stroll along the narrow streets and souvenir-crowded shops an impossibility. Everybody puts on the hard sell these days; be prepared to be accosted at every step and begged repeatedly

© TIM HULL
Nogales, Mexico

to have a look at this or that shop, all of which contain similar if not identical items. There's lots of leather and silver, Mexican handicrafts, Day of the Dead items, ceramics, Mexican vanilla, and cheap booze, but is it worth putting up with the incessant barking of the increasingly desperate hawkers? Not really. But if you've never been to Mexico before, this is an easy and generally safe way to do so. There are *farmacias* on every block, and dentist and doctor offices everywhere, and their services are offered for a fraction of the price of their U.S. counterparts. Most of them have barkers standing outside, calling you to come in and spend your dollars.

Nogales, Arizona

This small town named, like its cross-border sister, for the walnut trees that once thrived in the area, has long been Santa Cruz County's seat, and the beautiful old neo-Classical, shiny-domed **Santa Cruz County Courthouse** (2150 N. Congress Dr.), built in 1904 out of stone quarried locally, lends it a historic feel that belies the constant comings and goings of a border town. The **Old City Hall** building, built in 1914, now houses the **Pimeria Alta Historical Society** (Grand Ave. and Crawford St., 520/287-4621, 10am-4pm Wed.-Sun.), with several interesting exhibits and artifacts on the history of the region. The town's historic downtown along **Morley Avenue** has a few stores that were established in the early 1900s and are still being run by descendants of pioneer merchants.

ACCOMMODATIONS

There are several chain hotels in Nogales, Arizona, along Mariposa Road and along Grand Avenue, both major thoroughfares. If you're looking for something special, there's the historic **Hacienda Corona de Guevavi** (348 S. River Rd., 520/287-6503, www.haciendacorona.com, $189-235), a historic inn along the Santa Cruz River that once hosted John Wayne and other stars. The inn features murals by Salvador Corona, a famous artist and bullfighter, and offers B&B-style rooms and stand-alone casitas. It has a swimming pool and offers horseback riding, stargazing, and many other activities.

FOOD
With dozens of authentic Mexican restaurants within an easy walk across the border, don't spend too much time eating on the Arizona side. If you insist on eating in Arizona, try the steaks and Sonoran-style food at **Las Vigas Steak Ranch** (180 W. Loma St. at Fiesta Market off Arroyo Blvd., 520/287-6641, 10:30am-8:30pm Tues.-Thurs., 10:30am-9:30pm Fri., 9am-9:30pm Sat., 8am-8pm Sun., $18.95-24.95), or the excellent Mexican food at **Cocina La Ley** (226 W. 3rd St., 520/287-4555, 8am-4:30pm Wed.-Mon., $1.35-9). Across the border, the main north-south street is Obregon, two blocks west of the border crossing station. Popular restaurants include **La Roca,** east of the railroad tracks in downtown; **El Toro,** a steak house, about two miles south of the border on Lopez Mateos; and **La Palapa,** a no-frills seafood place 1.5 miles south on Lopez Mateos. **The Oasis** has an outdoor balcony overlooking where two main thoroughfares, Lopez Mateos and Obregon, merge, reminiscent of Times Square, but much smaller. Sit there, enjoy shrimp in a warm cheese sauce, and watch the traffic. And yes, you can drink the water, but most restaurants will put a bottle of it on your table.

INFORMATION
For visitor information go to the **Nogales-Santa Cruz Chamber of Commerce** (23 W. Kino Park Pl., 520/287-3685, www.nogaleschamber.com, 9am-5pm Mon.-Fri.).

There's a **U.S. Consulate** (in Mexico tel. 01/631-311-8150 or 01/631-313-4797, from U.S. tel. 011-52/631-313-4820, 8am-5pm Mon.-Fri.) in Nogales, Sonora, on Calle San Jose, about five miles south of the border. If you get in trouble on the weekend, there's a

consulate officer who checks the Nogales, Mexico, jail daily—Monday through Friday.

Although it's hassle free to enter Mexico, coming back can present problems: Since 2009 U.S. citizens have needed a passport to return to the United States via land and sea. (A passport was already required for air travel from Mexico to the United States.)

THE MOUNTAIN EMPIRE: PATAGONIA, SONOITA, AND ELGIN
With an average elevation between 4,000 and 5,000 feet, and average annual rainfall around 20 inches, the grasslands and creek beds of the "Mountain Empire" on the eastern side of the Santa Rita range are much cooler than Tucson, and the landscape is unlike any other in Arizona. The towns here are tiny, but they serve an increasingly popular tourist spot, so little out-of-the-way inns are plentiful. In Patagonia, the largest town in the area with only about 800 people, there's a yellow train depot in the center of town, built in 1900, and a nearby butterfly garden. A few shops sell unique locally made items and other treasures.

Getting There and Around
There are two ways to get to the grassland seas and cottonwood forests of the Mountain Empire, a historic ranching and mining district between the Santa Rita, Patagonia, Mustang, and Huachuca Mountains. If you're coming from the Santa Cruz Valley, take Highway 82 from Nogales 19 miles northeast to Patagonia and then on to Sonoita, where Highway 83 branches off north to I-10. If you're coming from Tucson, take I-10 east to Highway 83.

Telles Grotto Shrine
Just southwest of Patagonia along Highway 82, near milepost 15.9, there's shrine built into the rock face of the mountain. It's worth taking a few minutes to climb the steps and take a peek inside, where there will likely be candles burning and messages written to the dead. The shrine was built in the 1940s by the Telles

family, whose matriarch vowed she would construct and keep up the shrine if her five boys returned safely from World War II. They did, and the shrine is still in use today.

Patagonia Lake State Park

About seven miles south of Patagonia on Highway 82 is Southern Arizona's largest lake, 2.5-mile-long **Patagonia Lake** (400 Patagonia Lake Rd., 520/287-6965, 8am-10pm daily), where you can fish for bass, bluegill, and catfish, and camp, rent a boat, swim, and lie around Boulder Beach, water-ski (though not on weekends), and hike around the 5,000-acre Sonoita Creek State Natural Area. The campground has 72 campsites and 34 hookups ($15 w/no hookup, $22 w/water and electric), and there are boat launches, restrooms, showers, a dump station, and a camp supply store. In March, crowds head to the park to see the annual Mariachi Festival. From Nogales head 12 miles northeast on Highway 82, then turn left at the sign and drive 4 miles to park entrance.

Patagonia-Sonoita Creek Preserve

The Nature Conservancy protects a Fremont cottonwood-Gooding willow riparian forest—one of the best and last remaining examples of this lush landscape in Arizona—on about 750 acres along perennial Sonoita Creek. A small green paradise, the **Patagonia-Sonoita Creek Preserve** (520/394-2400, www.nature.org/arizona, 7:30am-4pm Wed.-Sun. Oct.-March, 6:30am-4pm Wed.-Sun. Apr.-Sept., $5 per person) has six miles of easy trails leading through the forest, with its 100-foot tall, 130-year-old cottonwoods—the biggest and oldest in the country—and along the creek. The birding here is excellent, and it's not uncommon to see deer, bobcats, toads, and frogs in this verdant preserve. Friendly Conservancy volunteers lead nature walks every Saturday morning at 9am. This is an extremely rare ecosystem, one that was once abundant in Southern Arizona but now has all but disappeared.

Accommodations and Food

The Sonoita Inn (3243 Hwy. 82, Sonoita, 520/455-5935, www.sonoitainn.com) at the crossroads of Highways 82 and 83 has 18 rooms with Western ambience, all with great views of the grasslands and mountains.

The Velvet Elvis Pizza Co. (292 Naugle Ave., Patagonia, 520/394-2102, www.velvetelvispizza.com, 11:30am-8:30pm Thurs.-Sun.) serves fabulous pizza and interesting pictures of The King and the Virgin on the walls. The **Steak Out Restaurant & Saloon** (at the junction of Rte. 82 and Rte. 83, Sonoita, 520/455-5205, 5pm-9pm Mon.-Thurs., 5pm-10pm Fri., 11am-10pm Sat.-Sun.) has steaks and ribs.

Wine Country

With soil and growing conditions often likened to those in Burgundy, France, the Sonoita-Elgin grasslands are becoming a well-known and well-reviewed winemaking region. It's fun to drive through the open landscape sampling wines, but consider taking along a designated driver.

In Sonoita just east of the crossroads on the east side of Highway 82, the **Dos Cabezas Wineworks** (3248 Hwy. 82, 520/841-1193) is open for tasting 10:30am-4:30pm Thursday-Sunday. The tasting room and gift shop at **Sonoita Vineyards** (290 Elgin-Canelo Rd., 520/455-5893, www.sonoitavineyards.com), located three miles south of Elgin, is open 10am-4pm daily. Also along the Elgin Road is **Callaghan Vineyards** (336 Elgin Rd., 520/455-5322, www.callaghanvineyards.com, tasting room 11am-3pm Fri.-Sun.). The **Village of Elgin Winery** (471 Elgin Rd., 520/455-9309, www.elginwines.com) has tasting 10am-4pm daily, and the **Rancho Rossa Vineyards** (201 Cattle Ranch Ln., Elgin, 520/455-0700, www.ranchrossa.com) is open 10:30am-3:30pm Saturday-Sunday, and Friday as well from December to March. In April locals turn out in Elgin for the annual **Blessing of the Vine Festival.** Check www.elginwines.com for details.

TUCSON

The Cochise Trail

The small towns in Southern Arizona offer many sights and attractions, mostly of the Old West variety, and are good bases for exploring the spectacular natural areas around them, mostly of the riparian and mountainous variety.

Named after the indomitable Apache chief Cochise, who waged war against the United States in the 1860s and 1870s, the region was also home to probably the most famous Apache of them all, the warrior and medicine man Geronimo, who was the last of his kind to surrender to the reservation. Miners, ranchers, cowboys, outlaws, and even a few gunfighters lived here, too, and their brief reign is still celebrated in touristy Tombstone. But many people come for the vistas, the birds, and the trails that can be found in the accessible Huachuca and Chiricahua mountain ranges.

Getting There and Around

The Cochise Trail and its environs are best traveled by car. If you want to avoid the Interstate, a good road trip can be made by heading east

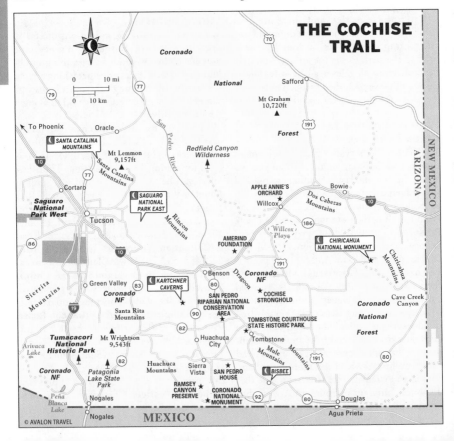

Southeast Arizona was once the favorite home and hideout of Cochise, the great Apache chief.

out of Tucson on I-10, then going south on Highway 83, which will take you through the grasslands of the Mountain Empire to the heights of the Coronado National Memorial (on some dirt roads), into the Huachuca Mountains, and then on to the San Pedro River Valley. Exit at Highway 90 or Highway 80, or Highway 191 to make loop drives to the all the best sights in the area.

Sierra Vista and Fort Huachuca

Much of the war against the Apaches was fought from Fort Huachuca, founded in 1877 in a canyon that had historically served as an escape route for the West's final holdout tribe. Currently the fort is a major center for military intelligence training. Both stories are told at two museums here. The **Fort Huachuca Museum** (Building 41401, 520/533-5736, 9am-4pm Mon.-Fri., 1pm-4pm Sat.-Sun., $2 suggested donation) has exhibits about army life on the Southwestern frontier, the famous battles with the Chiricahua Apaches, and the Buffalo Soldiers—African American cavalrymen whose story is one of the most fascinating of the West. The **U.S. Army Intelligence Museum** (9am-4pm Mon.-Fri., 1pm-4pm Sat., $5 suggested donation) tells the 200-year story of the army's underrated intelligence corps. The museum is located two doors down from the Fort Huachuca Museum.

The military town of Sierra Vista, while the largest town in the valley, the fort's host, and sitting at the base of the Huachuca Mountains, has little charm in and of itself. There are a lot of well-known U.S. chain hotels and restaurants, and it's close to the southern end of the San Pedro River. It makes a good base if you're planning on spending some quality time in the mountains, but otherwise it's just a drive-through.

ACCOMMODATIONS AND FOOD
There is no shortage of chain hotels and restaurants in Sierra Vista, especially along Fry Boulevard, the town's main drag. But if you want to stay in the mountains—and who wouldn't?—there are several bed-and-breakfasts nestled in the range's canyons. The riverside **Casa de San Pedro** (8933 S. Yellow Ln., Hereford, 520/366-1300 or 888/257-2050, www.bedandbirds.com, $149-175) is a territorial-style home with a central courtyard, a pool, hot tub, and all kinds of activities geared toward birders and nature lovers. **Ramsey Canyon Inn** (29 Ramsey Canyon Rd., Hereford, 520/378-3010, www.ramseycanyoninn.com, $130-150) just outside the Ramsey Canyon Preserve, has six rooms named for hummingbird species, delicious breakfasts, and a setting that can't be beat.

INFORMATION
Check out the **Sierra Vista Convention and Visitors Bureau** (3020 E. Tacoma St., 520/417-6960 or 800/288-3861, 8am-5pm Mon.-Fri., 9am-4pm Sat.) for information about this area.

TUCSON

TUCSON

© DERRICK NEILL/123RF.COM

snow on the Huachuca Mountains

Huachuca Mountains

Ranging in elevation from 3,934 feet at the base to 9,455 feet at the top of Miller Peak, the Huachucas are another of Southern Arizona's signature sky island ranges. You'll see the common transition from semidesert grasslands at the base, up into arid scrub, onto mixed oak forests, and all the way up to cool ponderosa pine forests in the higher reaches. There are dozens of trails in the range, and rough roads that lead deep into the outback. If you're looking to put together a backpacking or camping adventure in this range, talk to the staff at the **Coronado National Forest Sierra Vista Ranger District** (5990 S. Hwy. 92, Hereford, 520/378-0311).

Ramsey Canyon

You'll pass the ranger station as you head up to the 300-acre **Ramsey Canyon Preserve** (27 Ramsey Canyon Rd., 520/378-2785, www.nature.org, 8am-5pm daily Mar.-Oct., 9am-4pm daily Nov.-Feb.), an easily accessible, stream-influenced canyon protected by the Nature

Conservancy. This is a very popular area with birders, who come to see the more than 14 species of hummingbird and other avian species that stop over in the cool riparian canyon, fed by babbling Ramsey Creek, protected by high canyon walls, and crowded with sycamores, maples, and columbines.

The upper part of the canyon is within the **Miller Peak Wilderness Area.** Make sure you stop at the Nature Conservancy's visitors center, which has maps, trail guides, books, T-shirts, and helpful, friendly volunteers. It's a good idea to get there early; this area is very popular and the parking lot only has 23 first-come, first-served spaces.

To reach the preserve, take Ramsey Canyon Road west from Highway 92 south of Sierra Vista (six miles south of Fry Blvd.); the preserve is at the end of the road, four miles west of the highway.

Also along Ramsey Canyon Road, before you reach the preserve, you'll find the **Arizona Folklore Preserve** (520/378-6165, www.arizonafolklore.com), a quaint little theater along the creek where Arizona State Balladeer and nationally known folkie Dolan Ellis puts on acoustic folk concerts at 2pm on Saturdays and Sundays. The shows are popular, so call ahead for a reservation.

Coronado National Memorial

Named in honor of the Spanish conquistador Francisco Vásquez de Coronado, who trudged north in 1540 searching for the Seven Cities of Cibola—which turned out to be nothing more than a few hardscrabble pueblos—this beautiful landscape along the U.S.-Mexico border, on the southern end of the Huachuca Mountains, has a **visitors center** (Coronado Memorial Rd., 5 miles from Hwy. 92, 520/366-5515, www.nps.gov/coro, 9am-5pm daily) with exhibits about its namesake, local history, and natural history. Three miles west of the visitors center there's a scenic overlook at Montezuma Pass, with expansive, windswept views of the San Pedro and San Rafael Valleys and Mexico. You can have a picnic here and hike around on a number of trails leading to and from the lookout, but there's no camping allowed. To get there go south on Highway 92 about 20 miles to S. Coronado Memorial Drive; then it's 5 miles to the visitors center. (At the visitors center, you can purchase a map of the Huachucas with all the trails on it for $5.)

San Pedro Riparian National Conservation Area

This 58,000-acre preserve protects some 40 miles of the upper San Pedro River between St. David and the border. There are about 400 species of birds here, 82 mammal species, and 45 reptile and amphibian species, some of which you're likely to see if you stay vigilant and quiet while exploring. Beavers, once plentiful in the now nearly extinct riparian habitats of Southern Arizona, have been reintroduced here. The **Friends of the San Pedro River** have converted a 1930s-era ranch house—in the shade of a beautiful 120-year-old Fremont cottonwood tree—into the **San Pedro House** gift shop and bookstore (9800 Hwy. 90, 520/508-4445, 9:30am-4:30pm daily), where you can pick up information and pamphlets for a self-guided river walk and other trails, as well as get advice from the volunteers here. You'll also find the **Murray Springs Clovis Site and Trail,** a kind of stone-age butcher shop frequented by Clovis people 8,000-11,000 years ago. Scientists have dug up the fossils of several huge extinct mammals here, some of which are currently housed at the Museum of Natural History in New York.

◖ Kartchner Caverns

Kartchner Caverns (P.O. Box 1849, Benson, AZ 85602, 520/586-2283 for reservations, 520/586-4100 for information, www.azstateparks.com, 7:30am-6pm daily, free with tour reservation, $5 per vehicle up to four people, $2 each additional person) were discovered in the early 1970s by two cave-loving University of Arizona students. Gary Tenen and Randy Tufts knew right away that they had shimmied down a sinkhole in the Whetstone Mountains into caving immortality, because the small, wet cave—meaning that it is still forming drip by drip, in a very real sense "alive"—is one of the most spectacular water-on-rock formations of its kind. And yet the explorers managed to keep their find a secret for several years in an effort to protect it from cavers less responsible than themselves. They called it Xanadu, after the great English poet Samuel Taylor Coleridge's famous unfinished poem "Kubla Khan," a name given to the Throne Room's 58-foot main column, formed not so much by drips but by torrents of water flowing into the cave over millennia, and the largest cave column in Arizona.

Eventually Tenen and Tufts told the property owners what they'd found, and the Kartchner family quickly joined those who wanted to see the cave preserved. A pre-tour film in the park's **Discovery Center** tells the whole story and explains what makes this cave unique. There's also an interesting museum and a gift shop; just outside the Discovery Center a native-plant butterfly garden is worth a stroll.

There are two different tours you can take through the caverns. The **Big Room Tour** (1.5 hours, $23 adults, $13 children 7-13, no children under 7) is offered only October 15-April 15. During the summer months a large colony of bats returns to the big room, as they have likely done for eons, to give birth to and rear their single pups. The **Rotunda/Throne Room Tour** (1.5 hours, $19 adults, $10 children 7-13) is offered year-round and is more than enough to satisfy even the most discerning spelunker.

Because the cave is still "alive," much is made of its conservation. Visitors are warned repeatedly not to touch any of the formations, and guides are not shy about telling kids to stand back and keep their hands to themselves. The tour information is repetitive if you've just watched the pre-tour movie.

If a tour of the cave isn't enough, the park offers campsites with electric hookups, water, a dump station, and restrooms with showers ($22).

Benson

The **Horseshoe Café** (154 E. 4th St., Benson, 520/586-3303, 11am-9pm daily, $5-15) serves pretty good steaks, burgers, and Mexican favorites—including big, sloppy, and tasty burritos. It's been around since 1938 and is right on Benson's main drag; it's decorated with all kinds of portraits of horses and a few antiques. Author Neil Miller, in his recent history of the nearby caverns, reports that every time Gary Tenen and Randy Tufts would visit their secret cave during the many years they kept the discovery a secret, after rising out of the ground, they'd invariably stop at the Horseshoe for a bite to eat before returning to Tucson. For some reason, nobody in the restaurant seemed to think it was strange that the two spelunkers always came in covered in mud.

TOMBSTONE

Just outside the green and lush Mormon village of St. David, Highway 80 rises onto the dry scrubby plane where Ed Schieffelin struck silver in 1879, defying the soldiers who'd predicted he'd find only his own tombstone out there.

The town of the same name became one of the largest, rowdiest, and most deceptively sophisticated locales in the Southwest for a time, a place where legends were created daily by overheated newspapermen, and where a 30-second gunfight of dubious legality became a defining frontier myth. These days about 1,600 residents call Tombstone home, many of them retirees or working in some capacity for the town's tourism industry, which attracts visitors, many of them from Europe, year-round.

Boothill Graveyard

Reportedly, many of Tombstone's gunfighters, along with their victims, lie alongside prostitutes, settlers, and obscure passers-through in the hilltop **Boothill Graveyard** (7:30am-6pm daily, donations welcome). You can walk among the more than 300 uniformly bland and refurbished graves, and read short messages on some of them that illuminate what death was like on the frontier. It doesn't feel authentic in the least, despite claims to the contrary, but it is free. Boothill is just off Highway 80 at the north end of town.

Allen Street and National Historic District

Closed to cars and lined with wood-plank sidewalks, Western kitsch shops, and even a few genuine historical attractions, Allen Street *is* Tombstone to most. There are several saloons and restaurants here, and faux-gunfighters and saloon girls (some of them with somewhat anachronistic tattoos) mill about next to the working stagecoach replicas of **Old Tombstone Historical Tours** (520/457-3018, $10 adults, $5 children). The National Historic District includes several streets off of Allen, including Toughnut, Fremont, and 6th Streets.

Within this historic district you'll find the **Tombstone Epitaph Museum** (5th St., 520/457-2211, 9:30am-5pm daily), where you can see the original press used to print the perfectly named *Epitaph,* first published in 1880 and still going, and other printing-related exhibits. The **O.K. Corral and Historama** (Allen St., 520/457-3456, www.ok-corral.com, 9am-5pm daily, $7.50 with gunfight, $5.50 without) has all the information you'll need on the

© TIM HULL

Allen Street in Tombstone

famous, albeit short, gunfight between the Earps and Clantons. You can see a rather tired and dusty historical reenactment of the fight and watch a show, narrated by Vincent Price, on the major events in Tombstone history.

Among the saloons in the district, the **Crystal Palace Saloon** and **Big Nose Kate's Saloon** are worth a look, with Kate's being a fine place to knock back a few and look at all the pictures on the walls if you have the time. Both are on Allen Street. One of the best sights on Allen is the **Bird Cage Theatre** (Allen and 6th Sts., 520/457-3421, 8am-6pm daily, $6 adults, $5 children 8-18), an 1881 dance hall, brothel, saloon, theater, and casino that has been spectacularly preserved. A self-guided tour takes you through the building, which looks much as it did when it closed in 1889. On Fremont and 6th Streets the **Tombstone Western Heritage Museum** (520/457-3800, 9am-5pm Mon.-Sat., 12:30pm-5pm Sun., $5 adults, $3 children 8-18) has many relics of Tombstone's past, including a few personal items once owned by the Earps.

Tombstone Courthouse State Historic Park

A more sober treatment of Tombstone's history is presented inside the preserved 1882 **Tombstone Courthouse** (3rd and Toughnut Streets, 520/457-3311, 8am-5pm daily, $4 adults, $1 children 7-13). The museum features artifacts, pictures, and ephemera from the territorial days, and there's a rebuilt gallows in the building's courtyard. Particularly interesting are the two nearly forensic accounts of the gunfight, with slightly differing details.

Rose Tree Inn Museum

Planted way back in 1885, this Lady Banksia, sent all the way from Scotland to Tombstone as a gift, is believed to be the world's largest rose tree at 8,700 square feet and is listed in the *Guinness Book of Records*. The white blossoms are usually at their best in early April. The small **Rose Tree Inn Museum** (4th and Toughnut Sts., 9am-5pm daily, $3) exhibits photos and furniture owned by the tree's planter, who moved to the territory in 1880.

Events

In March, Tombstone celebrates its founder during **Ed Schieffelin Territorial Days.** In April the **Tombstone Rose Tree Festival** shines the light on the record-making rose tree, and in May, Tombstone's most famous citizen gets his own party during **Wyatt Earp Days.** The anniversary of that infamous gunfight warrants a celebration every year in October. Contact the Tombstone Chamber of Commerce (888/457-3929, www.tombstonechamber.com) for more information.

Accommodations

There are a few easy-to-locate chain hotels in Tombstone and a variety of bed-and-breakfasts. The **Tombstone Boarding House B&B** (108 N. 4th St., 520/457-3716 or 877/225-1319, www.tombstoneboardinghouse.com, $59-89) offers comfortable rooms in two adobe houses that date to the 1880s. The **Wild Rose Inn** (101 N. 3rd St., 520/457-3844 or 866/457-3844, $79-89, $109 with private bath) is in a Victorian home built in the early 1900s.

Food

Nellie Cashman Restaurant (5th and Toughnut Sts., 520/457-2212, 7:30am-9pm daily, $3.50-7.95), the oldest restaurant in Tombstone and named for the so-called "angel of the camp" Nellie Cashman, serves delicious and filling home-style breakfasts and burgers, sandwiches, and salads for lunch and dinner. Cashman was known throughout the mining camps of the American West for her work aiding sick and distressed miners. She opened a hotel and restaurant in Tombstone in 1882.

Information

Make sure to stop by the **Visitor Information Center** (4th and Allen Sts., 520/457-3929, 10am-4pm daily), where you'll find a nearly overwhelming amount of information about the town and its sights.

◖ BISBEE

The most charming town in Cochise County began life in the 1880s as a copper mining camp. Eventually several billion pounds of the useful ore would be taken out of the ground here, and by 1910 Bisbee was said to be the biggest city between the Midwest and West Coast.

Flooding in the 1,000-foot-deep tunnels and the boom-and-bust nature of the mining economy closed the mines by the 1970s, and the town, with its labyrinthine staircases and cozy little bungalows built precariously on the slopes of the Mule Mountains, was nearly moribund when it was discovered by hippies, artists, and artisans, a group that funkified the town into what it is today. Retired miners, retirees from elsewhere, county government workers, and sons and daughters of the pioneers also call Bisbee home. Old Town is stuffed full of shops, galleries, restaurants, historic landmarks, and some of the best old hotels in the West. Perhaps the most fun to be had in Bisbee comes from just walking around, climbing the scores of off-kilter steps, and exploring its back alleys and narrow streets.

Mining History Sights

Driving in on Highway 80, just after the intersection with Highway 92, you can stop at a turnout along the side of the road and witness the **Lavender Pit Mine** and the huge tailings surrounding the largest open-pit mine in the state, now closed.

Bisbee is still proud of its history as the queen of all mining towns, and you can learn all about it at the **Bisbee Mining and Historical Museum** (Copper Queen Plaza, junction of Main St. and Brewery Gulch, 520/432-7071, www.bisbeemuseum.org, 10am-4pm daily, $4 adults, $1 children 4-16), housed in the building formerly occupied by the headquarters of the Copper Queen Consolidated Mining Company. Now an affiliate of the Smithsonian Institution, the museum has exhibits on local history and culture during territorial days, with an emphasis on the history and science of copper mining.

You can see for yourself what it was like descending into the earth every day to coax the ore out of the mountain on the 75-minute **Queen Mine Tour** (478 N. Dart Rd., 520/432-2071 or 866/432-2071, www.cityofbisbee.com/queenminetours, 9am, 10:30am, noon, 2pm, and

TUCSON

© TIM HULL

shops in Bisbee

3:30pm daily, $12 adults, $5 children 4-15). Retired miners lead these tours and will regale you with stories of what it was really like underground, as you ride deep beneath the earth on an old mine car, wearing a yellow slicker, a hard hat, and a headlamp. It's about 47 degrees in the shaft, so think about taking something warm to wear. If you don't want to go under, consider going over on the 90-minute, 11-mile **Surface Tour** (departs from the Queen Mine Tour Office daily at 10:30am, noon, 2pm, and 3:30pm, $10), which takes you through the historic district and shows you the open pit while you sit back in a comfortable van.

Shopping

Old Town Bisbee has dozens of unique shops, and there always seem to be new ones opening. There are jewelry stores, shops selling local and Mexican folk art, a bookstore with both new and used tomes and a large section of books by local authors, a shop that sells only things made out of copper, and several multilevel antique and junk shops that you can get lost in for hours.

Accommodations

There are all manner of accommodations in

Bisbee, and bed-and-breakfasts proliferate along the narrow, twisty roads of Old Town.

The **Bisbee Grand Hotel** (61 Main St., 520/432-5900 or 800/421-1909, www.bisbeegrandhotel.net, $79-175) is in a Victorian building in Old Town. It offers small, well-decorated rooms with private baths, and a full breakfast is served on the veranda. It has wireless Internet and a saloon frequented by tourists and locals. **The Copper Queen Hotel** (11 Howell Ave., 520/432-2216, www.copperqueen.com, $114-176) is an institution in Bisbee, built in 1902 and still in beautiful shape, but almost certainly haunted, as anyone in Bisbee will tell you. It has a solar-heated pool, a saloon, and a restaurant.

For a truly unique experience rent one of the 1950s vintage trailers at **Shady Dell RV Park** (1 Old Douglas Rd. 520/432-3567, www.theshadydell.com, $45-145), each beautifully refurbished and decorated. Many have interiors of polished chrome and wood and include black-and-white TVs and phonographs complete with 45 singles from the era.

The oldest brick building in Bisbee now houses an elegant, friendly and truly memorable **Letson Loft Hotel** (26 Main St.,

© TIM HULL

the Bisbee Grand Hotel

520/432-3210, www.letsonlofthotel.com, $115-175). This small boutique hotel in the heart of Old Town offers romantic, high-end but affordable accommodations in a gorgeously remodeled and tastefully decorated space. All of the rooms have modern amenities and are quiet and cozy, despite being located right in the thick of the action along Bisbee's narrow, shop-lined main drag, onto which some of the rooms look down from on high, giving the dweller a bit of a sense of what the old town was once like in its busy urban heyday.

Food

Café Roka (35 Main St., Old Town Bisbee, 520/432-5153, www.caferoka.com, 5pm-9pm Wed.-Sat., $14-24) has some of the best Italian food around with a tasteful, elegant multilevel interior.

The best breakfast in town can be found at the **Bisbee Breakfast Club** (75 Erie St., Bisbee, 520/432-5885, www.bisbeebreakfastclub.com, 7am-noon Mon., 7am-2pm Thurs.-Sun., $4.99-8.99), serving huge American-style breakfasts, along with a bit of Mexican spice, of course, in a refurbished old building on the largely abandoned historic block next to the huge pit. You might have to wait to get a table, but the food is worth it. **Café Cornucopia** (14 Main St., 520/432-4820, 11am-4pm daily, $2-10) is a perfect place for lunch, with scrumptious sandwiches, soups, salads, and baked goods.

Santiagos (1 Howell Ave., 520/432-1910, santiagosmexican.blogspot.com, 11am-9pm Mon.-Thurs., 11am-10pm Fri.-Sat., 11am-9pm Sun.), a small, often busy Mexican restaurant in Old Town Bisbee, serves impeccable dishes in a new traditionalist style. Everything here is familiar (ceviche, chiles rellenos, enchiladas, etc.), but it's so well made—the ingredients fresh and local, the sauces soothing and surprising all at once—that you'll swear you never had its like before. They also make a huge, mean margarita.

Be warned: If you visit the **Old Bisbee Brewing Co.** (200 Review Alley, 520/432-2739, www.oldbisbeebrewingcompany.com, noon-10:30pm Mon.-Fri., 10am-10:30pm Sat.-Sun.), so well-situated in Bisbee's old "Brewery Gulch," and if it is pleasant out, which it so often is, and if you imbibe one or more of the several delicious and nutritious beers brewed on site, and if you are sitting there in the sun on

© TIM HULL

Santiagos

the patio looking out over the quaint old town when you do so, you probably aren't going anywhere for a while.

The **Bisbee Table** (2 Copper Queen Plaza, Bisbee Convention Center, 520/432-6788, 11am-9pm daily), a popular New American bistro in Old Town Bisbee, serves familiar (burgers, tacos, barbequed pork, fish and chips, mussels), well-made lunches, dinners, and desserts from locally sourced ingredients.

Events

Like most of the old mining towns in Arizona and Northern Mexico, much of Old Town Bisbee is perched rather precariously on the sides of a mountain, and the early residents installed steps all over town so folks could reach their homes. These days the steps are more atmospheric than useful; they contribute much to Bisbee's quaint character. Every October strange characters from all over the world gather in Old Town to run up and down these stairs during the **Bisbee 1000 Stair Climb** (Bisbee, www.bisbee1000.org, $55-100). Don't ask why. You too can join in, but the event fills up fast so register early.

Information

At the **Bisbee Chamber of Commerce & Visitor Center** (1 Main St., Copper Queen Plaza, 520/432-5421 or 866/224-7233, www.bisbeearizona.com, 9am-5pm Mon.-Fri., 10am-4pm Sat.-Sun.) you'll find brochures on self-guided walking tours and loads of information on what to do and see.

Parking isn't easy, especially on weekends, so it's a good idea to find a space, stick with it, and explore the town on foot.

WILLCOX AND VICINITY

Though the former railroad and ranching town has seen better days, the canyons, mountains, and grasslands around Willcox are worth the 80-mile drive east on I-10 from Tucson. Willcox today has a few boarded-up buildings and abandoned motels along its main thoroughfare, but its historic downtown holds some interest and is worth a mosey. The famous singing cowboy Rex Allen grew up in the area; a museum and an annual festival honor that fact. Willcox is also known as the place where Wyatt's brother, Warren Earp, met with a bullet in 1900, later to be buried in the Historic Willcox Cemetery.

Historic Downtown and Railroad Avenue

This area used to be where life in Willcox happened, and even today it's the most interesting part of town. There's a shady, grassy park with a big bronze statue of native son Rex Allen, and across the street on Railroad Avenue the singing cowboy's life and career are celebrated at the **Rex Allen Arizona Cowboy Museum** (150 N. Railroad Ave., 520/384-4583 or 877/234-4111, 10am-4pm daily, $2 single, $3 couple, $5 family), which also displays a **Cowboy Hall of Fame** honoring area ranchers and cowboys. Just down the sidewalk a bit is the **Willcox Commercial Store,** which claims to be the oldest continually operating store in the state. The **Willcox Rex Allen Theater** (520/384-4244), a 1935 art deco movie house, still runs new movies daily, and at the end of Railroad Avenue is the **Southern Pacific Depot,** built way back in 1880 and now used by the City of Willcox. The depot's lobby has exhibits on the history of the area and the railroad, and Rex Allen narrates a video played on a loop (8:30am-4:30pm Mon.-Fri.). The small town honors its most famous native with **Rex Allen Days** the first week in October every year.

Just around the corner from Railroad Avenue, the **Chiricahua Regional Museum** (127 E. Maley, 520/384-3971, 10am-4pm Mon.-Sat.) exhibits mining artifacts, weapons used by Native Americans and the cavalry, and rocks and minerals found in the region. There's also an excellent display on the history of the Apaches.

Apple Annie's Orchard

The Sulphur Springs Valley outside of Willcox has the perfect growing conditions for the apple, peach, pear, and Asian pear orchards at **Apple Annie's Orchard** (2081 N. Hardy Rd., Willcox, 520/384-2084, www.appleannies.com, 8am-5:30pm daily July 3-Oct. 31). From July to late October every year people flock to the "U-Pick" farm to pick and purchase

the Rex Allen Arizona Cowboy Museum

fruit by the bucketful. The farm also serves delicious hamburgers and cowboy beans for lunch, and you can buy all kinds of homemade preserves, sauces, condiments, and pies in the farm store. Take I-10 to exit 340, turn west on Ft. Grant Road and travel 5.5 miles to the Apple Annie's sign.

Amerind Museum

On your way east on I-10, get off at the Dragoon Exit (318) to visit the **Amerind Museum** (2100 N. Amerind Rd., Dragoon, 520/586-3666, www.amerind.org, 10am-4pm daily, closed Mon.-Tues. June-Sept., $4 adults, $3 children 12-18), an excellent little museum in beautiful Texas Canyon. Established in 1937, the Amerind Foundation (a contraction of American and Indian) preserves and studies Native American cultures from prehistory all the way to the Chiricahua Apache and beyond. It is commonly thought to hold one of the best private ethnological collections in the nation. The museum is fascinating, and the location, among the imposing boulders of Texas Canyon, makes it well worth the stop.

Cochise Stronghold

A bit farther east on I-10, Exit 331 takes you to the former hideout of Cochise and his band in the strange Dragoon Mountains. Head southeast on Highway 191, then west nine miles on Ironwood Road. The last four miles are on a dirt road. The great Apache chief is said to be buried somewhere out here, but nobody knows precisely where. As you look around, it seems an ideal place to hide, with plenty of bluffs from which to watch the plains for the oncoming army. There are a few easy trails at the Stronghold, including a short nature trail and a paved history trail with information about the Chiricahua Apache. A few campsites ($12) are sheltered by the same high boulders that once kept the Chiricahua hidden. If you want to hike deeper into the canyon, try the six-mile round-trip Cochise Stronghold Trail that veers off the nature trail.

◖ Chiricahua National Monument

This place simply has to be seen to believed. Precarious rock spires jut into the sky in this strange, wonderful landscape, called the "Land of Standing Up Rocks" by the Apache. About 38 miles southeast of Willcox (120 from Tucson) on Highway 186, the **Chiricahua National Monument** (520/824-3560, www.nps.gov/chir, 8am-4:30pm daily, $5 adults over 16) protects one of the most unusual areas in Arizona. There's a visitors center two miles from the monument entrance on Bonita Canyon Road, a paved two-lane road you can drive six gorgeous miles up to **Massai Point** and one of the most spectacular overlooks this side of the Grand Canyon. The visitors center has an excellent free guide with information on all the trails within the monument, their length, and how to find the trailheads, and there's a free hikers' shuttle available. You can camp at the Bonita Campground a half mile from the visitors center for $12 per night (no hookups). Bring your own food and water to this special place because none is available for miles in any direction. For information and advice on getting out into the less accessible regions of the Chiricahua range, contact the **Douglas Ranger District** (1192 W. Saddleview Rd., 520/364-3468, 8am-4:30pm Mon.-Fri.), 2.2 miles north of Highway 80 on Highway 191 in Douglas.

TUCSON

© TIM HULL

hoodoos in the Chiricahua National Monument, the "Land of Standing Up Rocks"

FLAGSTAFF AND NORTH-CENTRAL ARIZONA

Before and after the advent of air-conditioning, Arizona's north-central transition zones and coniferous mountain highlands made the long five-month summers livable for desert dwellers, who spent the hot months establishing "mountain clubs" in the cool pine forests of Prescott and Payson and the White Mountains.

HIGHLIGHTS

LOOK FOR ◖ TO FIND RECOMMENDED SIGHTS, ACTIVITIES, DINING, AND LODGING.

wonders of the Northern Sinagua golden age—800-year-old red-rock apartment buildings rising from the dry scrublands (page 209).

◖ **Walnut Canyon National Monument:** Hike above a diversely vegetated canyon, moving from desert to forest in one short walk, past high-wall ruins built of stacked and mortared stone. Far below, petrified sand dunes swirl and a ribbon of water flows through lush bottomlands (page 211).

◖ **Jerome:** Discover a haunted old mining town clinging to the side of a mineral-laden hill, now home to bed-and-breakfasts, hotels, eclectic restaurants, and one-of-a-kind boutiques (page 240).

◖ **Montezuma Castle National Monument:** See the mysterious ruins of the Southern Sinagua culture's highpoint—a cliff-wall castle molded out of limestone and cozy apartments clinging to the walls above a rare sinkhole (page 244).

◖ **Oak Creek Canyon:** Drive along a shady creekside with red-and-white-rock walls towering on each side, where birds, butterflies, and people flock to the babbling water sliding over pink slickrock (page 262).

◖ **The Mogollon Rim:** Sit on the very edge of the Colorado Plateau overlooking a deep-green sea of pine treetops, your legs dangling over the high cliff with all of lowland Arizona spread out before you (page 264).

◖ **Museum of Northern Arizona:** Don't miss the Colorado Plateau's premier museum, where you'll learn about the plants, animals, geology, and people that make the northlands such a fascinating landscape (page 208).

◖ **Sunset Crater Volcano and Wupatki National Monuments:** Explore the foothills of a silent black-rock crater and the architectural

FLAGSTAFF

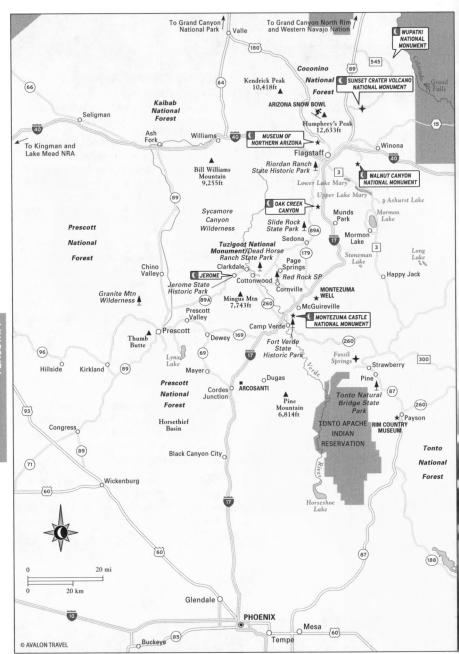

© AVALON TRAVEL

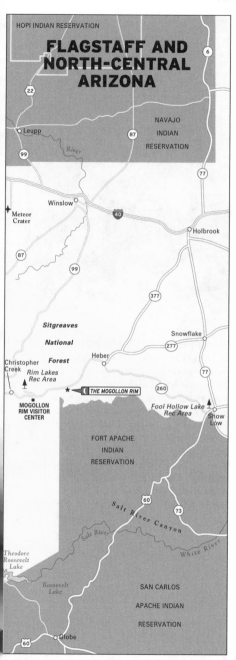

FLAGSTAFF

Between Prescott—a quaint, Midwestern-style town with a colorful Old West history—and Flagstaff—one of the Colorado Plateau's capital cities and the hub of the northland—you'll find the famed Red Rock Country, one of the world's most celebrated landscapes.

Posh Sedona sits at the center of a red, pink, and green-dotted geologic canvas, with the green bursts of Oak Creek Canyon and the often ignored but gorgeous Verde Valley right nearby. Just to the north is the Mogollon Rim, a 200-mile-long cliff that marks the southern border of the vast plateau. The Rim, as it's called locally, drops 2,000 feet in some places and provides some inspiring views. Those same views inspired the likes of the writer Zane Grey, who called the region home on occasion.

Exploring this region you'll find a different Arizona, one that most of the clichéd ideas about the state don't account for. Don't miss contemplating the ruins of the Sinagua culture scattered all over this land. And bring your hiking boots, mountain bikes, skis, canoes, kayaks, and tents; this is outdoor country at its best. But there are also cleaner and more comfortable things to do: Sedona, Flagstaff, Prescott, Jerome, and other towns in the region offer unique accommodations and dining, as well as a variety of shops and boutiques selling arts and crafts, antiques, and souvenirs of the arid West's high country, once the province of miners and lumberjacks, cattlemen and shepherds.

PLANNING YOUR TIME

This region attracts visitors regardless of the season, mostly because, unlike lowland Arizona, this region actually has a few seasons. In the summer, the pine forests of the transition zone are a cool respite from the desert: Prescott, the Verde Valley, and Rim Country on average are about 10 to 20°F cooler than the lower Sonoran life zones. Flagstaff and, to the east, the White Mountains, can seem like another country altogether; in these high places winter snowfall makes skiing and snow play a popular attraction. In the fall, the

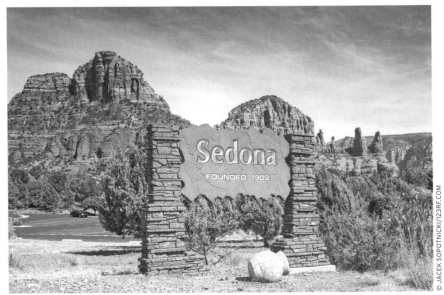

© JACEK SOPOTNICKI/123RF.COM

the red rocks of Sedona

turning leaves throughout the region are glorious; the orange and yellow of the scattered deciduous trees look like fire-flares among the dominant stands of ponderosa pine.

A comprehensive trip to the region, one touching on all its charms and sights and including backcountry hikes and off-the-track exploring, would take about two weeks. A week would suffice to see everything, indulge your sensual whims, and explore the pinelands, red rocks, and mountaintops a bit.

Flagstaff makes an ideal base for a visit to this region, as it is within a two-hour drive (often less) of all the sights to see and adventures to be had in North-Central Arizona. The quaint town of Prescott is good for a day trip from Flagstaff to Phoenix (it's about two hours each way from both), or a weekend if you're going to explore the pine forests that surround it. Sedona, a popular day trip from Phoenix (two hours each way), is only about an hour's scenic drive from Flagstaff and can be easily done in a long day from either. However, consider staying overnight or over a weekend in Sedona so you can explore the red rocks and riparian canyons. A visit to Payson and Rim Country is best done in a weekend or as a day trip from Phoenix or Flagstaff.

Flagstaff and Vicinity

The San Francisco Peaks, Arizona's tallest mountains and the Olympus of the Hopi kachina, watch over this highland hub, the long-ago waterless home of the Sinagua and the Colorado Plateau's Arizona-side capital. Cinder-rocks from centuries of volcanic activity crunch perpetually beneath your feet here, and the town's scent is a potpourri of pine sap, wet leaves, and wood smoke mixing with incense, patchouli oil, train smoke, and beer. The red-brick, railroad-era downtown sits at around 7,000 feet, and the whole area from mountains to meadows is covered under about 100 inches of snow every year. In the summer it's mild, in the 70s and 80s mostly, but it gets cool and then cold pretty fast from September to December, when, in wet years, the first snow falls. In the deep winter and on into early April, daytime temperatures are cold, and nighttime lows dip well below freezing.

Always a crossroads, it is especially so these days, thriving as a tourism gateway to the Grand Canyon, Indian Country, and the Colorado Plateau. It is also a college town attracting students from all over the world, and a major pull-off along I-40. Despite all that, it has managed to retain a good bit of its small mountain-town charm and Old West-through-Route 66 character. Its picturesque qualities, combined with its myriad opportunities for outdoor adventuring, make Flagstaff a major northland tourist draw in its own right.

Flagstaff's founding, including its rather literal naming legend, date to July 4, 1876. A group of New England émigrés, guided by one of those famous mountain men who had stalked the region for years already, camped nearby at a perpetual spring long known to wilderness loners and indigenous residents. In honor of the birthday happening back in the states, the Yankees stripped a skinny pine of its branches and attached a U.S. flag at the top, thus marking the spring and naming (as it was a flag-staff) a new stop along the trail. The outpost really didn't get going until the Santa Fe Railroad arrived in the 1880s, establishing the present-day downtown area and allowing for the ranching and lumber industries to exploit the surrounding forests and grasslands. Today Flagstaff is home to about 65,000 residents, and it's surrounded by nearly 2 million acres of the Coconino National Forest. Though tourism and the service industry are the town's major lifelines these days, the railroad is still very much a part of Flagstaff. As many as 80 trains a day chug through the heart of town, dividing it in two and often stopping traffic. The wail of train horns is so ubiquitous that many residents don't even notice it anymore. There's something romantic and evocative, almost emotional, about being in a warm bed on a cool, star-bright forest night and hearing the plaintive whine of a westbound train.

SIGHTS
Historic Downtown District
Flagstaff has managed to hold on to many of its historic downtown buildings, short red-brick high-rises and quaint storefronts that served the needs of the railway and its passengers, housed and kept Route 66's argonauts, and marked the social and commercial heart of the town for generations. These days few residents would have occasion to go downtown to purchase a staple, unless healing crystals or wind chimes are integral to their lifestyle. Recent upgrades, which thankfully didn't completely corporatize the downtown, have made the fact that the area remains vibrant only to draw tourists, eaters, drinkers, and strollers more explicit than ever. Such is the fate of many old railroad and territorial downtowns throughout the West, but it has largely been a happy fate for Flagstaff. On the National Register of Historic Places since the 1980s, many of the buildings in the downtown area date from the late 19th and early 20th centuries, including the Babbitt Brothers Building, which was constructed in

FLAGSTAFF

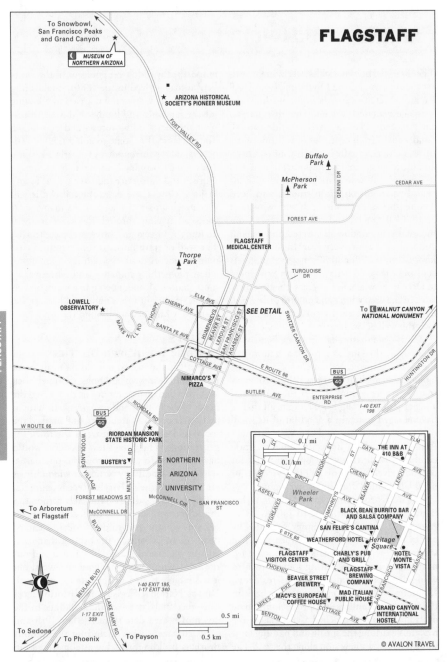

FLAGSTAFF

To Snowbowl, San Francisco Peaks and Grand Canyon

MUSEUM OF NORTHERN ARIZONA

ARIZONA HISTORICAL SOCIETY'S PIONEER MUSEUM

FORT VALLEY RD

Buffalo Park

McPherson Park

GEMINI DR

CEDAR AVE

FOREST AVE

FLAGSTAFF MEDICAL CENTER

Thorpe Park

TURQUOISE DR

ELM AVE

LOWELL OBSERVATORY

CHERRY AVE

SEE DETAIL

To WALNUT CANYON NATIONAL MONUMENT

THORPE RD

MARS HILL RD

SANTA FE AVE

HUMPHREYS

BEAVER ST

LEROUX ST

SAN FRANCISCO ST

AGASSIZ ST

SWITZER CANYON DR

HUNTINGTON DR

COTTAGE AVE

E ROUTE 66

BUS 40

NIMARCO'S PIZZA

BUTLER AVE

ENTERPRISE RD

I-40 EXIT 198

W ROUTE 66

BUS 40

RIORDAN RD

RIORDAN MANSION STATE HISTORIC PARK

KNOLES DR

NORTHERN ARIZONA UNIVERSITY

WOODLANDS VILLAGE

MILTON RD

BUSTER'S

FOREST MEADOWS ST

McCONNELL DR

McCONNELL CIR

SAN FRANCISCO ST

To Arboretum at Flagstaff

BEULAH BLVD

I-40 EXIT 195, I-17 EXIT 340

LAKE MARY RD

I-17 EXIT 339

To Sedona

To Phoenix

To Payson

0   0.5 mi
0   0.5 km

© AVALON TRAVEL

Detail inset

0   0.1 mi
0   0.1 km

PARK ST

KENDRICK ST

DATE ST

BIRCH AVE

CHERRY AVE

LEROUX ST

ELM AVE

THE INN AT 410 B&B

ASPEN AVE

SITGREAVES AVE

HUMPHREYS

BEAVER ST

Wheeler Park

BLACK BEAN BURRITO BAR AND SALSA COMPANY

SAN FELIPE'S CANTINA

E RTE 66

WEATHERFORD HOTEL

Heritage Square

HOTEL MONTE VISTA

FLAGSTAFF VISITOR CENTER

CHARLY'S PUB AND GRILL

FLAGSTAFF BREWING COMPANY

SAN FRANCISCO ST

AGASSIZ ST

PHOENIX AVE

BEAVER STREET BREWERY

MIKES PIKE

MAD ITALIAN PUBLIC HOUSE

MACY'S EUROPEAN COFFEE HOUSE

COTTAGE AVE

GRAND CANYON INTERNATIONAL HOSTEL

BENTON

© TIM HULL

Heritage Square is the heart of downtown Flagstaff.

1888, and the Coconino County Courthouse, built in 1894. Just across Route 66 from the downtown area is the old Santa Fe Depot, built in the Tudor Revival style in 1926.

Downtown is a pleasant place to be any time of year, and the traveler will find myriad places to eat and to drink and to hunt for all manner of artistic and handmade treasures. Take a half a day or so and walk along Humphreys Street, Beaver Street, Leroux Street, San Francisco Street, and Route 66 (also called Santa Fe) across from the train depot, ducking in and out of shops, galleries, watering holes, and eateries. **Heritage Square** (Aspen Ave. between Leroux and San Francisco Sts., 928/853-4292, www.heritagesquaretrust.org) hosts live music, outdoor movies, and arts and crafts fairs on weekends during the warmer months.

Southside Historic District

After exploring downtown, walk south of the tracks, where there are more shops, restaurants, and bars in the Southside Historic District, which is a bit shaggier than downtown and offers a look at Flagstaff's left-of-center scene. It's just south of downtown and bordered by Route 66 and the Santa Fe Railroad, the Rio de Flag, and Northern Arizona University. The neighborhood was added to the National Register of Historic Places in 2010. Check out the ruins of the **Historic Basque Handball Court** (east side of San Francisco) built in 1926 by tourist-home owner Jesus Garcia, who migrated to Flagstaff from Spain in 1912. The ruins of the 40-foot-high court, made of sandstone, are all that remains. It's said to be the last such court standing in Arizona and one of only a few in the nation.

Riordan Mansion State Historic Park

Here's a great American success story that would have come off perfect in Technicolor: Two brothers, Michael and Timothy Riordan, make it big on the Western frontier denuding the Arizona northland of its harvestable

© TIM HULL

the ruins of an old Basque handball court in Flagstaff's Southside Historic District

lumber. The boys are rich and powerful and run in Flagstaff's founding circles, helping to build a lasting American community out of a rough, arid wilderness. The close brothers marry close sisters, Caroline and Elizabeth Metz, and the two fledgling families get on so well that they decide to build a 40-room, 13,000-square-foot Arts and Crafts-style masterpiece and live in it together. They hire El Tovar Hotel designer Charles Whittlesey to design two mansions in one, each shooting off in separate directions like wings and linked by a pool hall and communal space. Then they decorate their majestic home with Stickley furniture, stained glass, and enough elegant details to draw crowds of visitors for the next 100 years. And everybody lives happily ever after.

The rock-and-log mansion, sprawling amidst a stand of pines in the middle of Flagstaff's commercial section and abutting the NAU campus, is now **Riordan Mansion State Historic Park** (off Milton Rd. at 409 W. Riordan Rd., 928/779-4395, www.azstate-parks.com/parks/RIMA, 9:30am-5pm daily,

$10 adults, $5 children 7-13, tours offered on the hour, 10am-4pm, reservations recommended). The park offers tours of the Arts and Crafts treasure, one of the best examples of the distinctive Anglo architecture that left a stylish stamp on the Southwest in the late 19th and early 20th centuries. Only a small portion of the structure is included in the tour, but it's full of original furniture and displays about the family and life in Flagstaff's formative years.

Lowell Observatory

The hilltop campus of **Lowell Observatory** (1400 W. Mars Hill Rd., 928/774-3358, www.lowell.edu, 9am-9:30pm Mon., Wed., and Fri.-Sat., 9am-5pm Tues., Thurs., and Sun. Mar.-May, 9am-10pm daily June-Aug., 9am-9:30pm Mon., Wed., and Fri.-Sat., noon-5pm Tues., Thurs., and Sun. Sept.-Oct., noon-9:30pm Mon., Wed., and Fri.-Sat., noon-5pm Tues., Thurs., and Sun. Nov.-Feb., stargazing starts at 7:30pm Wed., Fri., and Sat. Sept.-May, 8pm Mon.-Sat. June-Aug., $12 adults over 17, $5 children 5-17) just west of downtown, occupied by tall straight pines and a few small white-domed structures with round concrete bases, has had a good deal of influence over the science of astronomy since its founders began searching the clear rural skies over Flagstaff in 1894. The historic viewpoint has had something to do with contemporary ideas about the beginnings of the universe as well.

It was here between 1912 and 1914 that Vesto Slipher discovered that the universe's galaxies are moving away from the earth, a phenomenon measured by changes in the light spectrum called redshifts. This in turn helped Edwin Hubble and others confirm that the universe is expanding, thus providing the first observable evidence for the Big Bang. Another historic distinction came a few years later in 1930, when 24-year-old Clyde Tombaugh looked out from atop Mars Hill and discovered the former planet, now dwarf-planet, Pluto.

Today the campus welcomes the public with 45-minute tours offered on the hour, 10am-4pm in summer and 1pm-4pm in winter. The tours include a look through a solar telescope to view spots and flares on the sun, a duck into the Pluto Telescope building, and a look at some of fascinating historical documents and artifacts. The **Steele Visitor Center** (9am-9:30pm Mon., Wed., Fri., and Sat., 9am-5pm Tues., Thurs., and Sun.) shows a movie about the observatory and has interesting exhibits on astronomy. If you visit at night you can take part in galactic viewing sessions with staff astronomers.

Though smaller and less sleek and impressive than the more state-of-the-art telescopes in Southern Arizona, Lowell is worth the trip for its historical import (it's one of the oldest observatories in the nation, deemed a federal Historic Landmark in 1965), and for its picturesque location in the shadowy pines at the border of Flagstaff's Thorpe Park. Don't miss checking out **Percival Lowell's tomb,** a neo-classical, observatory-shaped mausoleum that honors the observatory's founder, whose popular writings led many Americans to suspect that there was a series of observable canals, and by implication life, on Mars.

© DERRICK NEILL/123RF.COM

Lowell Observatory's museum, on Mars Hill

Museum of Northern Arizona

A couple of well-educated and adventurous easterners, Mary and Harold Colton, an artist and a zoologist who first came to Northern Arizona to climb mountains on their honeymoon, founded the **Museum of Northern Arizona** (3101 N. Fort Valley Road, U.S. 180 three miles north of downtown, 928/774-5213, www.musnaz.org, 9am-5pm daily, $10 adults over 17, $6 children 10-17) in 1928 to preserve and encourage the indigenous arts and crafts of the Colorado Plateau. Since then this essential museum has become the cultural and scientific center of the Four Corners region, collecting, interpreting, and displaying the natural history, art, and artifacts of timeless landscapes and timeworn human cultures.

The museum's main building is itself a dark-wood and river-rock work of art set amidst the pines along the shallow Rio de Flag, with Arts and Crafts-era touches like the handmade Hopi-tile borders around the main entrance, fired on commission by the famous Hopi potter Sadie Adams in the 1930s. Inside there are comprehensive exhibits on the Four Corners region's ancient and current biomes and its buried and blowing strata, and one of the better introductions to Ancestral Puebloan and Puebloan cultures you'll find, with displays on the Basketmakers through the Anasazi and up to the Hopi of today. Volunteer docents stroll about and are eager to discuss and supplement any of the exhibits. The collection of Pueblo Indian pottery, jewelry, kachina, and basketry is the museum's high point, and the galleries showing contemporary Hopi and Pueblo art, including oil paintings, watercolors, and sculpture, tend to open one's eyes to the vibrancy of the great plateau's current cultural moment. Those who appreciate design should stroll into the **Branigar/Chase Discovery Center** lounge to see the Arts and Crafts flourishes in this cozy living-room setting.

Arizona Historical Society-Pioneer Museum

Stop at the **Arizona Historical Society-Pioneer Museum** (2340 N. Fort Valley Rd., 928/774-6772, www.arizonahistoricalsociety.org, 9am-5pm Mon.-Sat.) near the Museum of Northern Arizona to see how the early Anglo settlers lived in Flagstaff and Northern Arizona. It's rather fascinating, especially after just learning about the ancient plateau lifeways of the Hopi and other tribes, to see how a completely different culture adapted to the same relatively harsh conditions. The building is something to see in itself: It's the old Coconino County Hospital for the Indigent, which was built in 1908 out of native volcanic rocks. The museum has several displays on, among other things, frontier farming, education, transportation, and medicine, including a bedroom kept exactly as a hardworking nurse would have left it a century ago. There's also a retired steam train and various old farming implements parked on the beautiful forested grounds, where the museum puts on a host of events throughout the spring and summer.

Coconino Center for the Arts

Not a few artists and artisans lurk among the tall pines in Flagstaff, and many more sit atop the Hopi Mesas, carving kachinas out of cottonwood root, while others walk the wide empty roads of Navajoland and then recreate the wide empty land. Throughout the year the local arts group Flagstaff Cultural Partners gathers them together for a series of art exhibitions and concerts at the **Coconino Center for the Arts** (2300 N. Fort Valley Rd., 928/779-2300, www.culturalpartners.org, 11am-5pm Tues.-Sat.), a sleek, modern gallery that looks somewhat futuristic among the trees and contrasted with the historical architecture of the nearby Museum of Northern Arizona and the Pioneer Museum. Check the website for an up-to-date calendar of events at this, the "cultural hub of Flagstaff."

The Arboretum at Flagstaff

A 200-acre botanical garden and research station spotlighting the flora (and, if you're lucky, the fauna) typical of the Colorado Plateau, **The Arboretum at Flagstaff** (4001 S. Woody Mountain Rd., 928/774-1442, www.

thearb.org, 10am-4pm Wed.-Sun. May-Oct., $7 adults, $3 children 3-17) offers 45-minute guided walking tours daily at 11am and 1pm, and shows off sharp-taloned birds of prey at noon and 2pm. The forested property on the volcanic lands southwest of downtown Flagstaff has easy, winding trails, tall, shaggy trees, a pond, a tree-ring maze, and much more. A few hours here and you'll be able to recognize and appreciate the unique plants and animals that flourish in the high and dry plateau country. The arboretum is about four miles south of Route 66 on Woody Mountain Road, only the first mile of which is paved, though passenger cars will have no problems making it.

Elden Pueblo Heritage Site

The **Elden Pueblo Heritage Site** (Townsend-Winona Rd, off Hwy. 89, 928/527-3452, www.coconinoforest.us), a Sinagua ruin in the shadow of 9,280-foot Elden Mountain, on Flagstaff's eastern edge, was once a bustling trading center related to the more dramatic Wupatki and Walnut Canyon settlements to the north and east. These easily accessible volcanic-rock ruins were first studied in 1926 by the great Southwestern archeologist and ethnologist Jesse Walter Fewkes, who also supervised digs at Casa Grande in Southern Arizona and Mesa Verde in Southern Colorado. The settlement in its heyday, from about AD 1100 to 1275, had 60 to 70 rooms and hosted a fairly well-connected population: archeologists have found macaw skeletons and other evidence of trade with the far south. The site is still being studied and excavated today, often with the help of students and volunteers. Tall ponderosa pines guard the ruin along the 250-yard dirt path (ADA accessible) that circles the site. This is a perfect first stop on a daylong tour of the Sinagua ruins around Flagstaff. There's a sign for the parking lot on Townsend-Winona Road, one mile north of the Flagstaff Mall on the west side of Highway 89.

Sunset Crater Volcano and Wupatki National Monuments

Sunset Crater Volcano isn't really a volcano at all anymore, but a nearly perfectly conical pile of cinder and ash that built up around the former volcano's main vent. Sunset Crater erupted, probably several different times, between 1049 and 1100. The eruptions transformed this particularly arid portion of the not exactly lush Colorado Plateau, and now huge cinder barrens, as surprising as an alien world the first time you see them, stretch out along the loop road leading through these popular national monuments. You can't climb the crater-cone anymore—years of scarring by the crowds saw to that—but you can walk across the main lava field at the crater's base, a cinder field with scattered dwarfed, crooked pines and bursts of rough-rock-adapted flowers and shrubs, all the while craning up at the 1,000-foot-high, 2,550-foot-wide cone.

Along with turning its immediate environs into a scorched but beautiful wasteland, the volcano's eruptions may have inadvertently helped the Sinagua culture thrive for a brief time in this formidable environment, the subject and object of Sunset Crater's sister monument, Wupatki. The series of eruptions spewed about a ton of ashfall over 88 square miles, and closer to the source the ash created a kind of rich mulch that, combined with a few years of above average rainfall, may have stimulated a spike in population growth and cultural influence. Archaeological findings in the area suggest that the five pueblos in the shadow of the crater, especially the large Wupatki, were at the center of a trading crossroads and the most important population center for 50 miles or more, with about 2,000 people living within a day's walk from the sprawling red-rock apartment building by 1190. Times seem to have been good for about 150 years here, and then, owing to a variety of factors, everybody left. The Hopi and other Pueblo people consider Wupatki a sacred place, one more in a series of former homes their ancestors kept during their long migrations to Black Mesa. Today you can walk among the red and pink ruins, standing on jutting patios and looking out over the dry land, wondering what that waterless life was like, and marveling at the adaptive, architectural, and artistic genius of those who came before.

VISITING THE MONUMENTS

The monuments sit side by side on an arid, clump-grass sweep with humps of volcanic remains and colored with pine stands and, if you're lucky, blankets of yellow wildflowers,

about 12 miles north of Flagstaff along Highway 89. Turn onto the Sunset Crater-Wupatki Loop Road, which will lead you across the cinder barrens, through the forest, and out onto the red-dirt plains and the ruins, and then back to Highway 89. One ticket is good for both monuments.

Heading north from Flagstaff, you'll get to

Who Were the Sinagua and Where Did They Go?

The Sinagua left their architecture and masonry all over North-Central Arizona, from the red-rock apartment buildings rising from the cinder plains below the San Francisco Peaks, to the sandstone cliff hideouts of Walnut Canyon, to the limestone castles in the lush, easy-living Verde Valley, to the brick-stone rooms leaning against Sedona's red walls.

We don't really know what they called themselves, but we call them, according to tradition more than anything else, the Sinagua, Spanish for "without water"—a name that alludes to that given by early Spanish explorers to this region of pine-covered highlands still stuck somehow in aridity: *Sierra Sin Agua* (mountains without water).

Their cultural development followed a pattern similar to that of the Ancestral Puebloans in the Four Corners region. They first lived in pit houses bolstered by wooden beams and made a living from small-scale dry-land farming, hunting, and gathering piñon nuts and other land-given seasonal delicacies. They made strong and stylish baskets and pottery (though they didn't decorate theirs in the manner of the Anasazi and others); they were weavers, craftsmen, and traders.

Around AD 700 a branch of the Sinagua migrated below the Mogollon Rim to the Verde Valley and began living the good life next to fish-filled rivers and streams that flowed all year around; these migrants are now called the Southern Sinagua, and the ones that stayed behind are called the Northern Sinagua. When, around AD 1064, the volcano that is now Sunset Crater, northeast of Flagstaff, erupted, there were Sinagua villages well within reach of its

spewing ash and lava, though archaeologists have found evidence that nearby pithouses had been disassembled and moved just before the eruption, leading to the assumption that they probably knew the big one was coming.

The eruption would not be the end of the Sinagua—quite the contrary. Though the reasons are debated—it could have been that crops grew to surplus because a posteruption cinder mulch made the land more fertile; or it could be that the years following the big blow were wetter than normal; or it could be a bit of both—after the eruption Sinagua culture began to become more complex, and soon it would go through a boom time. From roughly 1130 to 1400 or so, Sinagua culture flourished as the Sinagualands became an important stop in a trade network that included Mexico to the south, the Four Corners to the north, and beyond. At pueblo-style ruins dating from this era, archaeologists have found shells, copper bells, and macaw bones, all from Mexico. Sinagua architecture became more Puebloan, and villages often had Mexican-style ball courts and kivas similar to those of the Anasazi. It is from this era that the famous ruins protected throughout this region date.

Then it all ended. Owing to drought, disease, war, civil strife, a combination of any one or all of these, or some other strange tragedy we will never learn about, by the early 1400s the Sinagua culture was on the run. By 1425, even the seemingly lucky farmers of the Verde Valley had abandoned their castles, the survivors and stragglers mixing with other tribes, their kind never to be seen again. Lucky for us they were such good builders.

Wupatki National Monument

the **Sunset Crater Volcano Visitor Center** (928/526-0502, www.nps.gov/sucr, 9am-5pm daily Nov.-Apr., 8am-5pm daily May-Oct., $5 for 7-day pass, children under 16 free) first, about two miles from the junction. Take a few minutes to look over the small museum and gift shop; there are several displays about volcanoes and the history of the region. Pick up the guidebook ($1 or free if you recycle it) to the one-mile loop **Lava Flow Trail** out onto the **Bonito Lava Flow** and head up the road a bit to the trailhead. This is an easy walk among the cinder barrens, a strange landscape with a kind of ruined beauty about it—only squat pines will grow, but there are surprising flushes of life throughout, small niches in which color can find a foothold. The trail skirts the base of the great crater-cone and takes about an hour or so.

Another 16 miles on the loop road and you're at the **Wupatki Visitor Center** (928/679-2365, www.nps.gov/wupa, 9am-5pm daily, $5 for 7-day pass, children under 16 free), a total of 21 miles from the junction, near the last of the five

pueblos, the titular Wupatki. The other pueblos are before Wupatki, reached by two separate short trails, each with its own parking lot along the loop road. At Wupatki, you can purchase a guidebook ($1 or free if you recycle it) to the half-mile **Wupatki Pueblo Trail,** which leads around the village complex and back to the visitors center. If you don't have time to see all five pueblos, head straight to Wupatki, the biggest and best of them all.

◖ Walnut Canyon National Monument

Not far from Wupatki, another group of Sinagua people farmed the forested rim and built stacked limestone-and-clay apartments into the cliffsides of Walnut Canyon, a 20-mile-long, 400-foot-deep gathering of nearly every North American life zone in one relatively small wonderland. Near the rim, a huge island of rock juts out of the canyon innards, around which residents constructed their cells, most of them facing south and east to gather warmth.

Depending on how much sunlight any one side of the island received, the Sinagua could count on several seasons of food gathering, from cactus fruit to piñon nuts to wild grapes. A creek snakes through the canyon's green bottomlands, encouraging cottonwoods and willows. The Sinagua lived in this high, dry Eden for about 125 years, leaving finally for good around 1250. This is an enchanting, mysterious place that should not be missed.

VISITING THE MONUMENT

Take I-40 east from Flagstaff for 7.5 miles to Exit 204, then it's 3 miles south to the canyon rim and the **Walnut Canyon Visitor Center** (928/526-3367, www.nps.gov/waca, 9am-5pm daily Nov.-Apr., 8am-5pm daily May-Oct., $5 for 7-day pass, children under 16 free), where there are a few displays, a small gift shop, and a spectacular window-view of the canyon. An hour or more on the **Island Trail,** a one-mile loop past 25 cliff dwellings (close enough to examine up close) and into several different biomes high above the riparian bottomlands, is essential to a visit here, but it's not entirely easy; you must climb down (and back up) 240 rock-hewn steps to get to the island, descending 185 feet. Once you're on the island, though, it's an easy, mostly flat walk, and one that you won't soon forget. There's also a short trail up on the rim with some great views.

ENTERTAINMENT AND EVENTS
Nightlife
BARS, PUBS, AND LOUNGES

Most of Flagstaff's favorite nightspots can be found in and around the Historic Downtown, the Southside Historic District, and on the edges of the Northern Arizona University campus. The nightlife here is naturally full of college students, but you'll find plenty of older locals and tourists in the mix.

The **Monte Vista Lounge** (100 N. San Francisco St., 928/774-2403) is a genial and historic place to sip cocktails or cry in your beer, with live music on the weekends and DJs on Thursdays and pool anytime. It's in what feels like the low-ceilinged basement of the Monte Vista Hotel, built way back in 1928. On entering this old-school little joint down the steps from the hotel lobby, you can smell four score years of spilled beer and general revelry imprinted deeply into the walls and floor. They say there are even a few ghosts still hanging around, unwilling to go home. Also off the Monte Vista's lobby is the more modern-minded **Rendezvous Coffee House and Martini Bar** (off the lobby of the Hotel Monte Vista, 928/779-6971, http://hotelmontevista. com, 6:30am-2am daily), a coffeehouse-cum-cocktail lounge with an impressive selection of spirits and creative cocktail creations. The coffee here is superior, but don't be surprised if you start drinking early after looking at all of those bottles as you sip your brew. The sleek, elegant interior and big windows that look out on bustling downtown Flagstaff encourage lounging and a "let's have another" attitude.

You're bound to see college kids dancing on the bartops at **San Felipe's Cantina** (103 N. Leroux St., 928/779-6000, www.sanfelipesflagstaff.com, happy hour 4pm-7pm), a Mexican beach-themed joint that serves beer buckets, huge margaritas and the deadly 24-ounce blue Cabo Wabo Fish Bowl ($15) that's understandably popular with the NAU party crowd.

More sedate and drawing a slightly older crowd is **Charly's Pub** (23 N. Leroux St., 928/779-1919, www.weatherfordhotel.com/entertainment.html), in the historic Weatherford Hotel downtown. One of the town's favorite spot for live blues, Charly's has live music most Friday and Saturday nights, trivia on Wednesdays, and karaoke on Thursdays.

The rooftop bar at the **Mad Italian Public House** (101 S. San Francisco St., 928/779-1820, www.maditalianpublichouse.com) should not be missed, and the pool tables, dart boards, beer pong, and happy crowds here are perfect for a highland weekend night.

The Southside's **Flagstaff Brewing Company** (16 E. Route 66, 928/773-1442,

© TIM HULL

the Rendezvous Coffee House and Martini Bar

FLAGSTAFF

© TIM HULL

Charly's Pub is one of downtown Flagstaff's favorite places to eat, drink, and listen to live music.

www.flagbrew.com) is the place to kick back a few finely crafted microbrews, play some pool, and talk to some locals. The restaurant here has excellent pizzas and burgers, but the **Brews and Cues** section stays open late, after the kitchen has closed and all the amateurs have gone home to bed.

If you're looking to kick up your cowboy boots and line-dance your way through an evening, check out the historic **Museum Club** (3404 E. Route 66, 928/526-9434, www.museumclub.com) east of downtown. At this venerable northland institution they offer trivia (Tues.), dime beer (Wed.), country-style dance lessons, and live acts every weekend. This legendary honky-tonk, built in 1931, looks like a log-cabin hunting lodge, and it has long been a Route 66 monument. It once served as trading post, taxidermy shop, and an actual museum, but now the attractions are the big wood dance floor and two beautiful wood bars. On the list of National Historic Landmarks, the Museum Club has hosted many American music luminaries over the years and still brings in both new acts and touring immortals like Robert Earl Keen and Billy Joe Shaver.

The Green Room (15 N. Agassiz St., 928/226-8669, http://flagstaffgreenroom.com) has a super-fun happy hour, a big dance floor, and a party vibe nearly every night. On the weekends this dance club and live music venue brings in local and touring bands, and they have a popular karaoke program as well.

Flagstaff is a ski town, and the Southside's **Altitudes Bar & Grill** (2 South Beaver St, 928/214-8218, www.altitudesbarandgrill.com, 11am-10pm daily) celebrates that fact with its snow-sports decor and "Skishots," a convivial way to get hammered quickly. A friendly bartender, perhaps with a full cold-weather beard and a wool cap, serves three or four shots of your favorite spirit affixed to an old ski. You and your drinking buddies must cooperate to sink them, a task that becomes increasingly futile as the night progresses. Altitudes also

Try the "Skishots" with a few friends at the Southside's Altitudes Bar & Grill.

offers a good selection of local beers and live music, and serves a sufficiently tasty American grill-style menu until 10pm.

Collins Irish Pub & Grill (2 N. Leroux St., 928/214-7363, www.collinsirishpub.com) downtown is a decent place to watch the game and sock back a few pints of Guinness. The emphasis here is on sports, and the menu of pub food is a strange amalgam (Irish Nachos?); but if you forget that it's supposed to be an "Irish pub," it turns instantly into a regular old American joint with a friendly crowd and all sorts of fun distractions.

Monsoon Downtown (6 E. Aspen Ave. No. 100, 928/226-8844, www.monsoondowntownflag.com), a Chinese and sushi restaurant with a sleek, upscale bar, is an after-dark haunt of NAU students and Flagstaff's modest crowd of beautiful party people: DJs spin, girls dance, intricate concoctions flow. A large patio looks out on the heart of downtown off Heritage Square, a fine place to enjoy a cocktail and a cool mountain-town night.

The scene is a bit more understated at **The Wine Loft** (17 N. San Francisco St., 928/773-9463, 3pm-midnight daily) downtown, while the end is same. This laid-back wine bar and shop downtown has a superlative selection of wines from all over the world, as well as a fairly substantial beer selection. A variety of cheeses and crackers, and oftentimes an acoustic ensemble jamming among the wine racks, contribute to a general air of relaxed sophistication. Another wine shop downtown, **Vino Loco** (22 E. Birch Ave., 928/226-1764, www.vinolocoflag.com, 11am-9pm Sun.-Wed., 11am-midnight Thurs.-Sat.), concentrates on small-vineyard wines, particularly those made in Arizona. They offer a $9 flight and other choices at their tasting bar, which also serves beer.

LIVE MUSIC

Flagstaff's a pretty laid-back town, and it has its share of mountain men, bohemians, and creative types. NAU's more than 20,000 students, many from abroad, help give the old frontier town a dash of do-it-yourself cosmopolitanism. It's not surprising, then, that the area attracts headlining acts and smaller indie favorites to its bars and theaters at a steady clip. If you're a fan of alternative pop, alt-country, classic country, bluegrass, classic rock, and just plain rock and roll, it's a good idea to check the websites of the following venues before making your travel plans. Odds are some funky act you love or have barely heard of will be playing during your visit.

The Orpheum (15 W. Aspen St., 928/556-1580, www.orpheumpresents.com), a retro-cool theater and bar that was Flagstaff's first movie house, hosts practitioners of modern music from Ozomatli to Rob Zombie and shows classic, neoclassic, and first-run movies on special nights each month. The **Pepsi Amphitheater** (2446 Fort Tuthill Loop, 928/774-0899, www.pinemountainamphitheater.com) out in the pines at Fort Tuthill Park is the region's best outdoor venue and attracts great bands from all over, many of the bluegrass and country persuasion. **Prochnow Auditorium** (Knoles Dr., North Campus, Northern Arizona University, 928/523-5638 or 888/520-7214) at NAU books national and international acts into an intimate setting.

Festivals and Events

Flagstaff hosts a variety of cultural events, mostly during its cool springs and warm summers. In May, world-renowned authors come to town for lectures, signings, readings, and panel discussions at the **Northern Arizona Book Festival** (928/380-8682, www.nazbookfest.org).

The **Museum of Northern Arizona Heritage Program** (928/774-5213, www.musnaz.org) puts on several important and well-attended cultural festivals each year, featuring native arts and crafts markets, food, history displays, and entertainment: the **Hopi Festival of Arts and Culture** in early July; the **Navajo Festival of Arts and Culture** in early August; and, in late October, **Celebración de la Gente,** marking Día de los Muertos (Day of the Dead). In late

FLAGSTAFF

The Orpheum, a retro theater still standing in downtown Flagstaff

May, the museum puts on the **Zuni Festival of Arts and Culture.** The second week in September, just before it starts to get cold in the north country, Flagstaff ushers in **Route 66 Days** (www.flagstaffroute66days.com), celebrated with a parade, a classic car show, and all manner of special activities along the downtown portion of the Mother Road. In October the **Flagstaff Mountain Film Festival** (www.flagstaffmountainfilms.org) screens the year's best independent films with an environmental, outdoor-adventure, and social-justice bent at the Orpheum.

If you find yourself in the northland on New Year's Eve, head over to the historic Weatherford Hotel downtown (23 N. Leroux) for the popular local party known as the **Pine Cone Drop.** Among rocking bands and general revelry, the hotel lowers a six-foot-tall lit-up pinecone from its roof as if this little railroad town in Arizona were Times Square. Thousands attend to meet the new year with cheer and watch the fireworks that attend the pinecone's fall. They do it twice: once at 10pm to coincide with the party on the East Coast, and again at midnight.

SHOPPING

The best place to shop for distinctive gifts, souvenirs, decorations, clothes, and outdoor gear is Flagstaff's historic downtown. You'll find Native American arts and crafts, Western wear, New Age items, art galleries specializing in handmade objects, antiques stores, and more.

Outfitters

Babbitt's (12 E. Aspen, 928/774-4775, http://babbittsbackcountry.com) sells top-notch outdoor gear from a famous old building with a famous old northland name. The knowledgeable staff here can help you plan a northland backcountry adventure and will recommend the best gear for the conditions; they also have an excellent map and book section. Another locally owned outfitter downtown, **Aspen Sports** (15 N. San Francisco St., 928/779-1935,

© TIM HULL

The famous Babbitt Brothers Building houses a wilderness outfitter.

http://flagstaffsportinggoods.com), sells the best in outdoor, hiking, skiing, snowboarding, and trekking gear, and has an experienced staff of experts, all of whom would likely rather be skiing the peaks or hurling themselves into a canyon somewhere nearby. In this wilderness those are the folks you want on your side.

Books
Bookmans (1520 S. Riordan Ranch Rd., 928/774-0005, www.bookmans.com), Arizona's original used-media supercenter, is the best bookstore in Northern Arizona bar none, with a huge selection of used books, CDs, vinyl records, DVDs, and musical instruments.

Galleries
Stop by the **West of The Moon Gallery** (14 N. San Francisco, 928/774-0465, http://westofthemoongallery.com) in Flagstaff's downtown to see the best work of contemporary painters, artists, and artisans from around the region, including both classic and experimental

work from Navajo artists. This is one of several places in Arizona to see and purchase the luminous, swirling, mysterious paintings of Shonto Begay, one of the best Native American artists working today. **Gallery 113** (113 E. Birch, 928/600-2113, www.galleryone13.com), also located within the quaint confines of the historic downtown, sells an eclectic, creative selection of fine art by local and national artists, and one-of-kind, handmade gifts and keepsakes.

SPORTS AND RECREATION
Hiking
Head north on Highway 180 eight miles to the San Francisco Peaks for the best hikes in the area. There are dozens of lesser hikes around the peaks, but the most memorable, essential hike in these sylvan, volcanic lands is the **Humphreys Peak Trail.** The tough hike leads to the highest reaches of Humphreys Peak at 12,633 feet—the very top of Arizona and nearby to the sacred realms wherein the Hopi kachina dwell and watch. The nine-mile

round-trip is very strenuous but beautiful and thrilling all the same. The trail moves through a shady aspen forest and then up above the tree line to a windy and rocky alpine stretch. Be careful of altitude sickness if you're a habituated lowlander. The trailhead is signed along Snow Bowl Road (Forest Road 516). The **Kachina Trail,** which begins at the dead end of Snow Bowl Road, is a less vertical walk and is popular with locals. It's a 10-mile round-trip stroll along mostly flat land—you're at 9,500 feet anyway . . . why go up any more?—through thick stands of conifers and aspens and sweeping views at every corner. This is a particularly beautiful route in the fall, with fiery yellows and reds everywhere.

Contact the **Coconino National Forest** (1824 S. Thompson St., 928/527-3600) for information on hiking in the peaks, and see www.fs.fed.us/r3/coconino for other hikes in the volcanic highlands.

Mountain Biking

Mountain biking is very popular in Flagstaff, and many of its trails are up-and-down exciting and technical to the point of mental exhaustion. Enthusiasts will want to head straight-away to the series of moderate-to-difficult interconnected trails of the **Mount Elden Trail System** northeast of town along Highway 89. There are enough loops and mountainside single-tracks in this area to keep you busy for a while.

Perhaps the most fun that can be had on two wheels in the Flagstaff area are the roller-coaster trails on and around the San Francisco Peaks and the Snowbowl ski resort, where mountain bikers abound during the spring and summer months.

The **Flagstaff Biking Organization** (http://flagstaffbiking.org) offers information on northland biking events and issues, and the experts at **Absolute Bikes** (202 E. Route 66, 928/779-5969, 9am-7pm Mon.-Fri., 9am-6pm Sat., 10am-4pm Sun. April-Dec., 10am-6pm Mon.-Sat., 10am-4pm Sun. Jan.-March), which also has a store in the nearby slickrock paradise of Sedona, keep a list of some of the best local trails at www.absolutebikes.net/visitor-info/flagstaff.

Snowbowl

On the slopes of the San Francisco Peaks, the **Snowbowl** (take Hwy. 180 north to Snow Bowl Rd., 928/779-1951, www.arizonasnowbowl.com) offers skiers and snowboarders over 2,300 feet of vertical drop and 32 scenic trails that cover 777 acres. In wet years the first snow usually falls in December, but in recent, drought-ridden years the snow has stayed away until late in the season. The resort recently prevailed in a dispute with Native Americans over man-made snow and has commenced building a system to make powder from reclaimed water when Mother Nature won't play along. The Hopi and other regional tribes consider the mountains sacred.

In the summer, the ski lift becomes the **Skyride** (928/779-1951, www.arizonasnowbowl.com, $15 adults over 12, $10 children 8-12), lifting passengers slowly up to 11,500 feet, where you need a jacket in July and the hazy flatland stretches out for eternity.

DISC GOLF

The Snowbowl also has a challenging high-mountain **disc golf** course that opens during the summer months (9am-5pm daily). It takes from three to five hours to complete and has some steep climbs and, of course, gorgeous scenery.

Flagstaff Nordic Center

A complex of trails and sledding hills, the **Flagstaff Nordic Center** (Hwy. 180 north 15 miles to mile marker 232, 928/220-0550, www.flagstaffnordiccenter.com) is a popular place for cross-country skiing, sledding, snow-shoeing, and all manner of snow play as long as there's snow on the Coconino National Forest at the base of the peaks. Equipment rental, lessons, and races are available.

Lake Mary and Mormon Lake

Several lakes dot the volcanic plateau south of Flagstaff, including **Mormon Lake,** the state's largest natural lake. Though shrinking and even sometimes dry altogether due to drought, Mormon Lake is sometimes a beautiful body of water set amidst the green pines and junipers of the plateau. In the winter, the plateau country is popular with cross-country skiers and snowmobile enthusiasts. There are also plenty of lakeside hiking trails and mountain bike routes nearby, and myriad opportunities for bird-watching and wildlife viewing, including herds of elk that call the plateau home.

To reach Flagstaff's lake district, head south out of town on Lake Mary Road. Along the way you'll pass several smaller lakes—**Lower and Upper Lake Mary, Marshall Lake,** and **Ashurst Lake**—before reaching Mormon Lake via Forest Road 209, about 30 miles from town. Most of the lakes in Northern Arizona are dependent on snowmelt and rainfall, both of which are often in short supply on this dry plateau, so don't be surprised if you find them dusty and small. The drive into the forest is worth it even if there's little water.

The **Dairy Springs and Double Springs Campgrounds** ($16 per night, open May through mid-Oct.) offer spots with drinking water and vault toilets. Nearby, **Mormon Lake Lodge** (928/354-2227, www.mormonlakelodge.com, $54-345) has comfortable log cabins of various sizes to rent and has a 74-spot RV park as well. There's a delicious steak house with an old-fashioned mesquite-pit, along with a saloon with rustic Western ambience that's been serving forest explorers since the 1920s. The lodge rents horses and mountain bikes, and even snowmobiles in the winter.

For more on hiking, biking, fishing, boating, and camping opportunities on the plateau, contact **The Peaks/Mormon Lake Ranger Districts** (5075 N. Hwy. 89, 928/527-3600, www.fs.fed.us/r3/coconino, 8am-4:30pm Mon.-Fri.).

ACCOMMODATIONS

Flagstaff, being an interstate town close to several world-renowned sights (not least the Grand Canyon), has all the chain hotels. A good value and a unique experience can

FLAGSTAFF

© TIM HULL

the Mormon Lake Lodge in the pines outside of Flagstaff

be had at one of the historic downtown hotels like the Weatherford or the Hotel Monte Vista. Along Route 66 as you enter town from the east, there are a large number of chain and locally-owned small hotels and motels, including several old-school motor inns, and a few places that are likely inexpensive for a reason. East Flagstaff, while it lacks the charm of the downtown area, is an acceptable place to stay if you're just passing through. If you're a budget traveler and don't mind students, hippies, and folks from other lands, try the hostels in Flagstaff's Southside Historic District.

Under $50

The **Grand Canyon International Hostel** (19 S. San Francisco St., 888/442-2696, www. grandcanyonhostel.com, $22-60) is a clean and friendly place to stay on the cheap, located in an old 1930s building downtown in which you're likely to meet some lasting friends, many of them foreign tourists tramping around the Colorado Plateau. The hostel offers bunk-style sleeping arrangements and private rooms, mostly shared bathrooms, a self-serve kitchen, Internet access, free breakfast, and a chance to join in on tours of the region. It's a cozy, welcoming hippie-home-style place to stay. The same folks operate the **DuBeau Hostel** (19 W. Phoenix St., 800/398-7112, www.grand-canyonhostel.com/dubeau, $22-48), a clean, homey hostel with a small dorm and eight private rooms. They offer a free breakfast, wireless Internet, and a "party room" with a juke box and pool and foosball tables.

$50-100

The **◖ Weatherford Hotel** (23 N. Leroux St., 928/779-1919, www.weatherfordhotel. com, $49-139) is one of two historic hotels downtown. It's basic but romantic, if you're into stepping back in time when you head off to bed. There are no TVs or phones in the rooms, and the whole place is a little creaky, but the location and the history make this a fun place to rest, especially with the bar and grill downstairs.

The **◖ Hotel Monte Vista** (100 N. San Francisco, 928/779-6971 or 800/545-3068, http://hotelmontevista.com, $70-175 April 15-Nov. 5, $50-175 Nov. 6-April 14), the other historic downtown hotel, is a bit swankier. The red-brick high-rise, built in 1927, once served high-class and famous travelers heading west on the Santa Fe Line. These days it offers rooms that have historic charm but are still comfortable and convenient, with cable TV and private bathrooms. There's a hip cocktail lounge downstairs, and like many of the grand old railroad hotels, there are lots of tales to be heard about the Hollywood greats who stayed here and the restless ghosts who stayed behind. Some of the cheapest rooms share a bathroom, and they cannot guarantee that you will find parking in the hotels' small parking lot, which is not reserved for guests. You may have to park in a metered space and get up early to move your car in the morning.

Over $100

The **Embassy Suites** (706 S. Milton, 928/774-4333, http://embassysuites.hilton.com,

© TIM HULL

the DuBeau Hostel

© TIM HULL

The historic Hotel Monte Vista is the place to stay in downtown Flagstaff.

$99-139) offers a cozy and tasteful compound in the center of commercial Flagstaff, with a pool and hot tub, free made-to-order breakfast, and a complimentary nightly cocktail hour in its leather-chair lounge. This place is perfect for families: A relatively inexpensive suite offers two large beds in one room, a hide-a-bed in another, TVs in both, and a refrigerator.

The Inn at 410 Bed and Breakfast (410 N. Leroux St., 928/774-0088 or 800/774-2008, http://inn410.com, $185-215) has eight artfully decorated rooms in a classic old home on a quiet, tree-lined street just off downtown. This is a wonderful little place, with so much detail and stylishness. Breakfasts are interesting and filling, often with a Southwestern tinge, and tea is served every afternoon. You certainly can't go wrong with this award-winning place, one of the best B&Bs in the state. Booking far in advance, especially for a weekend stay, is a must.

The stately **England House Bed and Breakfast** (614 W. Santa Fe Ave., 928/214-7350 or 877/214-7350, www.englandhousebandb.

com, $129-199) is located in a quiet residential neighborhood near downtown at the base of Mars Hill, where sits the famous Lowell Observatory. This beautiful old Victorian has been sumptuously restored and its rooms are booked most weekends. If you're just passing through, the innkeepers are happy to show you around, after which you will probably make a reservation for some far future date. They pay as much attention to their breakfasts here as they do to details of the decor. This is one of the best little inns in the region.

The same can be said of the **Aspen Inn Bed and Breakfast** (218 N. Elden St., 928/773-0295 or 800/999-4110, www.flagstaffbedbreakfast.com, $129-169), an inviting Arts-and-Crafts B&B a few blocks from downtown. Wyatt Earp's cousin, C. B. Wilson, built the house in 1912, and these days it offers four comfortable rooms with televisions, Wi-Fi and all the other comforts, plus a delicious breakfast and friendly atmosphere.

The sprawling **Little America** (2515 E. Butler Ave., 928/779-7900, http://flagstaff.

The sandstone England House is a charming bed-and-breakfast.

© TIM HULL

littleamerica.com, $119-204) is a huge hotel complex on 500 acres near the University of Northern Arizona and is popular with visiting parents. It has a pool, several restaurants and pine-studded grounds. This is a good, centrally located option for families.

Forest Inns

The **Ski Lift Lodge** (6355 N. Hwy. 180, 928/774-0729 or 800/472-3599, www.arizonasnowbowl.com/lodging, $75-95) has simple, rustic cabins and rooms with cozy fireplaces and a good restaurant. Best of all it's in the forest beneath the San Francisco Peaks, about seven miles northwest of downtown, right near the road up the peaks to the Snowbowl. It's dark out there, and you can see all the stars in the universe on many nights. This lodge is a good bet if you're skiing or engaging in other snow-related activities. Make reservations in advance for ski season, as there are few other places to stay in the immediate area. The drive from Flagstaff proper is about 10-20 minutes, longer in inclement weather.

The **Starlight Pines Bed and Breakfast** (3380 E. Lockett Rd., 928/527-1912 or 800/752-1912, www.starlightpinesbb.com, $135-189) is located about three miles northeast of town in the forest at the foot of Mount Elden, offering four rooms stuffed with antiques in a Victorian-era home. There's a porch swing, claw-foot bathtubs perfect for bubble baths, and fresh-cut flowers in every room, but no TVs. They'll even bring your breakfast to your room for you.

Tucked in the pines about six miles south of downtown Flagstaff, the **Abineau Lodge** (1080 Mountainaire Rd., 928/525-6212, http://abineaulodge.com, $139-179) has eight cozy rooms in a glorious wilderness location. The house itself is a stylish red-wood forest retreat built in 1997, with large decks for lounging in the cool highland air. The Abineau, located in the tiny little Flagstaff residential offshoot of Mountainaire, has a sauna and serves up delicious home-cooked breakfasts that will stick with you as you explore the forest surroundings.

For a touch of wilderness adventure with

all the comforts of an in-town hotel, try the **Arizona Mountain Inn** (4200 Lake Mary Rd., 928/774-8959, www.arizonamountaininn.com, $130-500), offering 17 rustic but comfortable cabins in the pines outside of town near Lake Mary, each with wood-burning stove, kitchen, and outdoor grill.

FOOD
American and Southwestern

There's something about drinking a dark, handcrafted pint of beer in the piney mountain heights that makes one feel as good as can be—maybe it's the alcohol mixed with the altitude. The best place to get that feeling is the **Beaver Street Brewery** (11 S. Beaver St., 928/779-0079, www.beaverstreetbrewery.com, 11am-11pm Sun.-Thurs., 11am-midnight Fri.-Sat., $7-18), where excellent beers are made on-site, and there's delicious, hearty food of the bar and grill variety, including excellent pizzas and burgers.

For the very best burgers in the northland head to **Diablo Burger** (20 N. Leroux St. #112, 928/774-3274, Mon.-Wed. 11am-9pm, Thurs.-Sat. 11am-10pm, $5.50-13.25), which serves a small but stellar menu of beef raised locally on the plains around Flagstaff. All the finely crafted creations, such as the "Cheech" (guacamole, jalapenos, and spicy cheese), or the "Vitamin B" (bleu cheese with bacon and a beet) come on Diablo's branded English muffin-style buns and a mess of Belgian fries. They also have a terrific veggie burger.

Brandy's Restaurant and Bakery (1500 E. Cedar Ave. #40, 928/779-2187, www.brandysrestaurant.com, 6:30am-3pm daily, $4.99-9.49) often wins the Best Breakfast honors from readers of the local newspaper, and those readers know what they're talking about. The homemade breads and bagels make everything else taste better. Try the Eggs Brandy, two poached eggs on a homemade bagel smothered in hollandaise sauce. For lunch there's crave-worthy sandwiches (Brandy's reubens are some of the best in the business) and burgers, including a bleu cheese and mushroom variety that won't let go of your soul anytime soon.

Buster's (1800 S. Milton Rd., 928/774-5155, www.busters-restaurant.com, 11:30am-10pm daily, $7.50-29) has been a local favorite for years, serving up good steaks and burgers and such, and offering the hangover-assuring Buster Bowl to any hard-drinking college student who happens in.

Josephine's Modern American Bistro (503 N. Humphreys St., 928/779-3400, www.josephinesrestaurant.com, 11am-2:30pm Mon.-Fri. and 5pm-9pm daily, $9.25-32.50) offers a creative fusion of tastes for lunch and dinner, such as the roasted pepper and hummus grilled-cheese sandwich and the chile relleno with sun-dried cranberry guacamole, from a cozy historic home near downtown.

Charly's Pub and Grill (23 N. Leroux St., 928/779-1919, www.weatherfordhotel.com, 8am-10pm daily, $6-24), inside the Weatherford Hotel, serves Navajo tacos, enchiladas, burritos, and a host of other regional favorites for breakfast, lunch, and dinner. Their Navajo taco, a regional delicacy featuring fry bread smothered in chili and beans, might be the best off the reservation. Try it for breakfast topped with a couple of fried eggs. Charly's also has more conventional but appetizing bar-and-grill food such as hot, high-piled sandwiches, juicy burgers, steaks, and prime rib.

Brix Restaurant & Wine Bar (413 N. San Francisco St., 928/213-1021, http://brixflagstaff.com, 5pm-close daily, $6-36) operates out of a historic building a few blocks north of downtown and serves creative and memorable food using regional ingredients. The menu here changes often based on what's new at Arizona's small farms, ranches, and dairies. The New American cuisine that results is typically spectacular. They also have fine selections of wine and cheese, a heavenly butternut squash soup, and desserts that should not be missed.

The **Tinderbox Kitchen** (34 S. San Francisco St., 928/226-8400, www.tinderboxkitchen.com, 5pm-9pm Sun.-Thurs., 5pm-10pm Fri.-Sat., Annex Cocktail Lounge 4pm-close daily, $10-30) in the Southside District serves a revolving menu of New American comfort food, and has an elegant lounge where you can wait

FLAGSTAFF

for your table with a martini. The chef uses seasonal ingredients to create variations on American favorites. There's always something new and exciting here—like venison served with bleu cheese grits, or bacon creamed corn, or jalapeno mac-and-cheese . . . you get the idea: It's one of those places—places that abound in Phoenix, Scottsdale, Tucson, and Sedona—where the chef is limited only by his ingredients and imagination. And the chef here is lacking in neither.

For the best sandwiches in the northland, head to **Crystal Creek Sandwich Company** (1051 S. Milton Rd., 928/774-9373, 9am-9pm daily, $4.99-7.99). A Flagstaff institution, this casual order-at-the-counter joint serves high-piled delights on fresh bread, and has a pool table too. Grab a couple of big sandwiches to go and head out into the pines for a picnic—the perfect way to spend a day in Flagstaff.

Diners

For a big breakfast of eggs, bacon, and potatoes,

The Downtown Diner is a great place for breakfast.

or an omelet stuffed with cheese, a hot cup of coffee, and friendly service, head over to the **Downtown Diner** (7 E. Aspen Ave., 928/774-3492, 6am-9pm Mon.-Sat., 7am-6pm Sun., $3-12) right across from Heritage Square. This clean little greasy spoon also has good burgers, shakes, and hot dogs. There's similar fare at local favorite **Miz Zip's Route 66 Diner** (2924 E. Route 66, 928/526-0104, 6am-9pm Mon.-Sat., 7am-2pm Sun., $5-15) on Flagstaff's eastside. Open since the 1950s, they are still serving the same diner classics of the golden age, such as hot opened-faced sandwiches smothered in rich gravy, big juicy burgers, and filling breakfasts. They only take cash.

At the **Crown Railroad Café** (3300 E. Rte. 66, 928/522-9237, 2700 S. Woodlands Village Blvd., Ste. 600, 928/774-6775, http://thecrownrailroadcafes.com, 6am-9pm daily, $5-10) they celebrate the golden era of the railroad. Sit among model trains, iron road memorabilia, and Navajo blankets, while enjoying the huge, three-egg "Route 66 omelet," expertly prepared huevos rancheros, and a fresh homemade biscuit.

Mexican and Latin American

A colorful Southside favorite, **Café Olé** (121 S. San Francisco St., 928/774-8272, 11:30am-3pm and 5pm-9pm daily, $4.95-10.95) serves delicious enchiladas, burritos, and tamales, has decent salsa, and offers an unusual selection of vegetarian and vegan options. Especially good here is the calabacitas, a traditional mixture of squash, onions, tomatoes, and corn served with rice and beans or stuffed in a tortilla. This charmingly decorated little café also has a patio that's ideal for sipping margaritas in the evening.

Criollo Latin Kitchen (16 N. San Francisco St., 928/774-0541, http://criollolatinkitchen.com, lunch 11am-4pm Mon.-Fri., dinner 4pm-9pm Mon.-Thurs., 4pm-10:30pm Fri.-Sat., brunch 9am-2pm Sat.-Sun., $5-22), in Flagstaff's historic downtown, creates an eclectic, ever-changing menu of gourmet, Latin-inspired dishes for brunch, lunch, and dinner,

© TIM HULL

Café Olé, a Southside favorite

from ingredients grown regionally on small farms and ranches. Try the beer-battered catfish tacos, and the wonderfully flavorful tortilla soup and carne asada. The sleek and refined interior, with eye-catching paintings and small tables that look out on downtown through a glass front, creates an urbane atmosphere that complements the creative food and somewhat belies the rural mountain setting.

Asian

About three miles southwest of downtown in the Wal-Mart shopping center, **Delhi Palace** (2700 S. Woodlands Village Blvd., 928/556-0019, www.cuisineofindia-az.com, 11am-3pm and 5pm-10pm daily, $3-17) serves all the exotic tastes of the subcontinent in a friendly, family-owned atmosphere. It's one of Flagstaff's favorite restaurants, popular for its fresh and delicious lunch buffet ($9.95).

Consistent with its role as a port-of-call for canyon-country visitors from all over the world, Flagstaff has two excellent Thai restaurants, both stars of this atypical small town's varied and cosmopolitan food scene. **Swaddee Thai** (115 E. Aspen Ave., 928/773-1122, http://swaddeethai.com, lunch 11am-3pm Tues.-Sun., dinner 5pm-9pm Tues.-Thurs., 5pm-9:30pm Fri.-Sat., $7.95-$15.95), in Flagstaff's historic downtown right across from the Weatherford Hotel, serves fresh and authentic Thai dishes in an elegant setting. It's a clone of a restaurant that opened in the Phoenix area in 2007 and has quickly become one of state's most acclaimed Thai eateries. The food here is unassailable: flavorful, consistent, and filling without being heavy. Just a short stroll south sits **Dara Thai** (145 San Francisco St., 928/774-0047, 11am-10pm Mon.-Sat., $10-25), in the Southside neighborhood. Part of small regional chain with sister-restaurants in Williams and Santa Fe, Dara Thai has been a beloved local institution since 1992. Close to campus, it's popular with students and locals for its rich, tasty, and perfectly spiced dishes. Both Dara Thai and Swaddee Thai offer a relatively wide range of vegetarian options.

Italian

Named Flagstaff's favorite pizza 10 years running, **Fratelli Pizza** (119 W. Phoenix Ave., 928/774-9200, 2120 N. 4th St., 928/714-9700, www.fratellipizza.net, 10:30am-9pm daily, $6.50-20) swears by its "stone deck oven" and eschews the "conveyer belt" mentality of the chains. The results are sublime. Try the pie called The Flagstaff, with basil pesto, sun-dried tomatoes, and artichoke hearts, reportedly popular with the town's vocal hippy minority. You can also build your own pie from among dozens of fresh toppings, or stop in for a huge slice ($2.95). They also serve salads, antipasto, and calzones, and offer a decent selection of beer and wine.

NiMarco's Pizza (101 S. Beaver St., 928/779-2691, http://nimarcospizza.com, 11am-9pm daily, $5-20), a Southside neighborhood mainstay for decades, serves a more than decent pizza pie in a casual space with picnic tables not far from campus. This is a dependable place to call for a delivery, as long as you are in the downtown or Southside area or near campus. The pizza is nothing fancy, just fresh, hot, and delicious. On the fancier side of the pizza street is the wonderful **Pizzicletta** (203 W. Phoenix Ave, 928/774-3242, pizzicletta.com, 5pm-close Tues.-Sun., $6-15), also in the Southside neighborhood. Here they offer soppressata rather than pepperoni, and prosciutto di Parma rather than ham. Among the carefully chosen, rather spare, list of toppings are almonds and charred kale. But it's the dough that makes the pizza here something like heaven sent. They also serve fantastic bread, beer, and wine, and house-made gelato.

Vegetarian

The **Morning Glory Café** (115 S. San Francisco St., 928/774-3705, 10am-2pm Tues.-Fri., $6.50-9.75) serves natural, tasty vegetarian eats from a cozy little spot on San Francisco Street. Try the hemp burger for lunch, and don't miss the blue corn pancakes for breakfast. With local art on the walls, free wireless Internet, and friendly service, this is an ideal place to get to know the laid-back Flagstaff vibe. There are a lot of vegan and gluten-free options here. They don't take credit cards so bring some cash.

Macy's European Coffee House (14 S. Beaver St., 928/774-2243, www.macyscoffee. net, 6am-10pm daily, $5-10) south of the tracks is the best place to get coffee and a quick vegetarian bite to eat, or just hang out and watch the locals file in and out, many of them dreadlocked.

INFORMATION

The **Flagstaff Visitor Center** (1 E. Route 66, 928/774-9541 or 800/379-0065, www.flagstaffarizona.org, 8am-5pm Mon.-Sat., 9am-4pm Sun.), located in the old train depot in the center of town, has all kinds of information on Flagstaff and the surrounding area.

GETTING THERE AND AROUND

Air

Flagstaff's small **Pulliam Airport** (928/556-1234, www.flagstaff.az.gov), located about five miles south of downtown, offers five flights daily to and from Sky Harbor in Phoenix through **US Airways** (800/428-4322, www.usairways.com). It's a roughly 50-minute flight, as opposed to a 2.5-hour drive from Phoenix, and generally costs $150-300. This is not your best option, as you must rent a car to explore the northland properly. If you are coming from Phoenix, it's best to rent a car there and make the scenic drive north.

Car

The best and, really, the only easy way to properly see Flagstaff and the surrounding country is by car. From Phoenix, take I-17 north for about 2.5 hours (142 miles) and you're in another world. The scenic route to Flagstaff from I-17 starts at Highway 260 in the Verde Valley, about 100 miles (1.5 hours) north of Phoenix near Cottonwood. Get off the interstate at Exit 287, heading west toward Cottonwood. About 12 miles on, take State Highway 89A north through Sedona and Oak Creek Canyon and all the way to the mountains and the pines. It's only about 50 miles from Cottonwood to Flagstaff, but it takes at least an hour and probably more to drive the scenic route through the verdant riverside valley and past the otherworldly red rocks of Sedona. You can also pick up Highway 89A at the Village of Oak Creek, which is 39 miles from Flagstaff, and take it straight north through Sedona and Oak Creek Canyon. This route is spectacular, as it includes about 8 miles of travel on Highway 179 past some the Sedona area's most famous eroded-rock attractions. Get off the interstate at Exit 298 (Hwy. 179) and pick up Highway 89A about 8 miles north at Sedona. From there, Sedona and Flagstaff are separated by about 30 slow miles of winding two-lane road with amazing views.

Once in "Flagg," as the locals sometimes call this mountain town, you're ideally situated to visit a long list of unique attractions. Chief among these is Grand Canyon National Park's South Rim, a mere 81 scenic miles away. Take Hwy. 180 north from downtown, driving through the pine forest in the shadow of the towering San Francisco Peaks. Pick up Hwy. 64 east at the tiny, windswept roadside stop known as Valle, about 50 miles from Flagstaff. From there it's a straight shot across a barren plain to the South Rim gate. The whole trip takes about 1.5 hours, making Flagstaff a logical place to base your Grand Canyon visit if you don't want to stay in the park. A trip to the North Rim from Flagstaff takes quite a bit longer. Take Hwy 89 north across the volcanic cinderlands, through the western edge of the vast Navajo Reservation, and into the lonely landscape near the Utah border known as the Arizona Strip. After about two hours, 123 miles, pick up U.S. Highway 89A going west at Bitter Springs. Cross the Colorado River at Marble Canyon, and skirt the edge of Vermilion Cliffs National Monument toward the Kaibab Plateau, climbing to the forested highlands and Jacob Lake, the center of plateau life. The 50-mile drive from Bitter Springs to Jacob Lake usually takes an hour or more. When you pass the hotel and restaurant at Jacob Lake, you have another 45 miles to go on State Highway 67, a drive that takes an hour or more through a mountain forest of evergreens and aspen, with patches blackened by fire. The whole gorgeous, unforgettable, 208-mile drive will take you at least four hours and probably longer. It's not a great idea for a day-trip from Flagstaff unless you want to spend all day in the car. It's a better idea to take two days and stay overnight in the park or at Jacob Lake.

The sights closest to town are Meteor Crater, 45 miles east on I-40; Sunset Crater and Wupatki, 14 and 39 miles, respectively, north on Highway 89; and Walnut Canyon, a quick, seven-mile drive east on I-40. These places attract visitors from around the world and are easy to find. You can't miss them if you follow the signs along the highway and the interstate. The Navajo Nation's reservation begins about 50 miles north of Flagstaff on Highway 89, and Lake Powell spreads across the hard land 136 miles to the north on the same route. The Petrified Forest and Painted Desert are about 115 miles east on I-40.

The 467-mile drive from Los Angeles to Flagstaff typically takes about seven hours, most of it along I-40. If you're starting from Las Vegas, take Hwy. 93 past Hoover Dam and over the Colorado River to I-40. The 252-mile drive takes about four hours.

CAR RENTAL

Most of the major car-rental companies have a presence at Flagstaff's small **Pulliam Airport** (928/556-1234, www.flagstaff.az.gov), about five miles south of downtown. **Avis Downtown Flagstaff Car Rental** (175 W. Aspen Ave., 928/714-0713, www.avis.com, 7am-6pm Mon.-Fri., 8am-4pm Sat., 9am-1pm Sun.) is located right in the middle of all the action at the corner of Aspen Ave. and Humphreys Street. **Budget** (www.budget.com) operates out of the same facility with the same hours and phone number. **Enterprise Rent-A-Car** is located on the eastern edges of town along I-40 (213 E. Route 66, 928/526-1377, www.enterprise.com, 8am-6pm Mon.-Fri., 9am-noon Sat.).

If you're looking for a mythic Southwestern experience, stop by **EagleRider Flagstaff** (800 W. Route 66, 928/637-6575, www.

FLAGSTAFF

route66rider.com, 8am-6pm daily, $159 per day, $931 per week) and rent a Harley-Davidson.

Long-Distance Bus
Flagstaff's **Greyhound Bus Lines** (800 E. Butler Ave., 928/774-4573, www.greyhound. com) station is located along the industrial wasteland that is E. Butler Ave. The company offers bus service to Flagstaff from most points on the map. **Arizona Shuttle** (800/888-2749, www.arizonashuttle.com, $45 per person, one way) offers several daily trips between Flagstaff's Amtrak station and Sky Harbor Airport.

Train
Amtrak's (800/872-7245, www.amtrak.com) Southwest Chief Route, which mirrors the old Santa Fe Railway's Super Chief Route of the grand Fred Harvey days, stops twice daily (one eastbound, one westbound) at Flagstaff's classic **downtown depot** (1 E. Route 66), the former Santa Fe headquarters and also the town's visitors center (800/842-7293). The route crosses the country from Chicago to L.A., dipping into the Southwest through northern New Mexico and northern Arizona.

Public Transportation
Flagstaff's city bus, the **Mountain Line** (928/779-6624, www.mountainline.az.gov, $1.25 per ride or $2.50 for day pass), runs 6am-10pm weekdays and 7am-8pm weekends to stops all over town.

Bike
Flagstaff is a relatively bicycle-friendly city with a well-established and active bike culture. You'll likely see a lot of people riding mountain bikes around town, even in the winter. It's pretty easy to get around most of the town on a bike following a network of trails of multi-use paths laid out in the **Flagstaff Urban Trails and Bikeways Map,** available for free at the **Flagstaff Visitor Center** downtown. You can pedal from downtown to the east side of town while avoiding the always busy traffic along Route 66 using the popular **Route 66 Trail.** The 4.4-mile paved trail runs along the south side of Route 66 east from downtown and is popular with bike commuters. The ambitious 42-mile **Flagstaff Loop Trail** is about half finished. The trail will someday circle the town and feed smaller, spoke-like paths to various points in town.

Prescott

Here you'll find the true transition zone, the no-man's-land between the high forests and the low deserts. Dry chaparral brushlands climb the rocky mountains to become dry ponderosa pine forests, and it's not surprising to see clumps of cactus the entire way up. The whole region, even its most forgotten outbacks, is crisscrossed by trails and roads left over from the old mining days. Head up and over the mountains and you'll find a lush river valley, fed by the perpetual Verde River, and the golden-age ruins of a lost tribe. There's a lot to do and see in the central transition zones, especially if the history of the Old West, highland outdoor adventuring, and

poking around for artistic treasures are of any interest to you.

President Abraham Lincoln signed the bill that created the Arizona Territory in 1863, separating Arizonaland from the vast frontier called New Mexico. Around the same time it was decided to found the administrative capital of the new territory in a clime more northerly than that Confederate hotbed down in Tucson, then one of the largest population centers in the region. A group of federal appointees headed out for the rocky, chaparral-clogged midlands and the skinny pine forests around a mile high, near placer-laden Hassayampa Creek and the Bradshaw Mountains, both objects of desire for

© CHRIS PUTNAM/123RF.COM

the historic Yavapai County Courthouse in Prescott

gold and silver miners who couldn't make a go of it in crowded California.

They eventually built the capital as a strange but functional Midwestern church town-meets-rowdy mining camp amalgam that today, long after the little mountain-nestled burg consciously turned from extraction and ranching to tourism for its supper, brings in droves of Phoenicians and other desert-dwellers on weekends and holidays, each of them looking for something that has been left behind and forgotten out in the unrecognizable valley sprawl. With more than 700 buildings on the National Register of Historic Places and a rough Old West history full of political chicanery and violence to back up its sometimes heavy-handed marketing, the town has much to recommend it to tourists, especially those fascinated by the 19th-century Anglo West and Victorian architecture. Thus Prescott has become "Everybody's Hometown," a slogan printed on signs and flags throughout the Middle-American-picturesque downtown. The town has a sizable population of well-off retirees and a hard-to-miss group of young back-to-nature bohemian residents, many of them students at Prescott College, a private liberal arts college specializing in environmental studies.

Prescott enjoys the further distinction of being "Arizona's Christmas City." Every year, just after Thanksgiving, the huge neoclassical courthouse downtown is decked in semigaudy Christmas decorations and illuminated during a crisp nighttime ceremony, attendance at which would make even a lifelong big-city resident nostalgic for small-town life.

Prescott's most lasting draw for those living down the hill and elsewhere is its four-season climate—warm in summer, perfect in spring, cool in fall, and cold, sometimes even snowy, in winter—which over the generations has prompted the desert folk to build getaway cabins and then dream homes in the cool piney hills around the town. The Prescott National Forest hugs the outskirts of town in a sappy embrace, traversed by hundreds of trails and

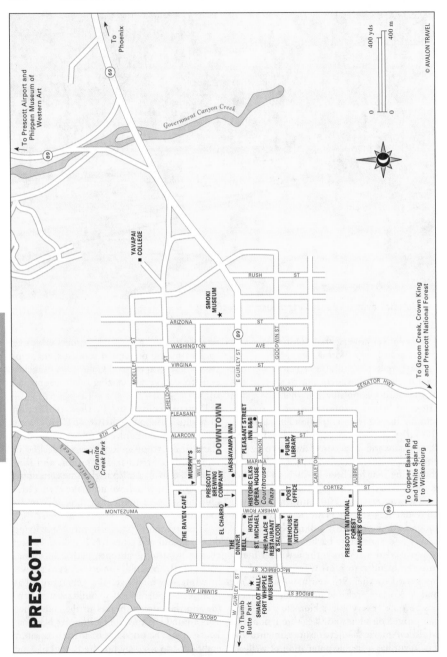

PRESCOTT

FLAGSTAFF

To Phoenix

To Prescott Airport and
Phippen Museum of
Western Art

Government Canyon Creek

© AVALON TRAVEL

400 yds

400 m

YAVAPAI
COLLEGE

SMOKI
MUSEUM

RUSH   ST

ARIZONA   ST

WASHINGTON   AVE

VIRGINA

MOELLER ST

SHELDON ST

PLEASANT

ALARCON

DOWNTOWN

BTH ST

Granite Creek

Granite
Creek Park

MURPHY'S

PRESCOTT
BREWING
COMPANY

HASSAYAMPA INN

WILLIS

PLEASANT STREET
INN B&B

E GURLEY ST

GOODWIN ST

MT VERNON AVE

SENATOR HWY

ST

ST

UNION

MARINA

PUBLIC
LIBRARY

ST

CARLETON

CORTEZ

AUBREY

ST

To Groom Creek, Crown King
and Prescott National Forest

To Copper Basin Rd
and White Spar Rd
to Wickenburg

THE RAVEN CAFE

EL CHARRO

MONTEZUMA

THE
DINNER
BELL

HOTEL
ST. MICHAEL

(WHISKEY ROW)

HISTORIC ELKS
OPERA HOUSE

Courthouse
Plaza

THE PALACE
RESTAURANT
& SALOON

FIREHOUSE
KITCHEN

POST
OFFICE

ST

PRESCOTT NATIONAL
FOREST
RANGER'S OFFICE

MCCORMICK ST

W GURLEY ST

SUMMIT AVE

GROVE AVE

SHARLOT HALL-
FORT WHIPPLE
MUSEUM

BRIDGE ST

To Thumb
Butte Park

How Prescott Got Its Name

Though not really a literary incubator of any note, Prescott is curiously named after an esteemed New England man of letters, historian William Hickling Prescott (1796-1859).

Though Prescott had died before the remote little camp in the Arizona's thirsty central mountains acquired his famous name, his work, especially his best-selling *History of the Conquest of Mexico*, published in 1843 to universal acclaim, was much on the minds of the party sent to found Arizona's territorial capital. While on the trail toward the territory, the officials, many of whom, like most learned men of their time, were fans of Prescott's work, passed the time reading the reports of Lt. Amiel Weeks Whipple, who'd trekked through the region with the railroad's 35th Parallel Survey about a decade earlier.

In his writings, the lieutenant suggests several times that what is now North-Central Arizona may actually be that vague land to the "northwest" from where, as Prescott had written, the ancient Aztecs hailed before they conquered the Valley of Mexico. Somehow the suggestion stuck, and so did the name. Likewise, two of downtown Prescott's main streets were given famous names from the conquest: Montezuma Street and Cortez Street.

Don't expect most native residents to know this little tale, though you can always tell a longtimer when he or she questions your pronunciation of their cryptically named hometown. "It's not Prescott, it's Preskit," goes the common corrective.

ideal for all manner of outdoor retreats and recreation.

SIGHTS
Downtown and the Courthouse Plaza

Most of Prescott's charm is centered on a few blocks in the downtown area (Gurley, Montezuma, Cortez, and Goodwin Streets), among dozens of shops, boutiques, antique stores, and art galleries (many of them with an Old West theme, and most in the middle to high end of the price range), and the town's best restaurants and bars, most of them frequented by visitors and locals alike. The whole scene surrounds the big, tall-pillared stone courthouse, built in 1916 out of locally quarried stone, and its grassy grounds lined by imported trees; there's always something going on—square dancing, craft shows, live theater, a few families or couples lounging on the grass with a picnic, kids playing with Frisbees and Hacky Sacks, and exercisers doing laps on the cobblestone walkways, led quickly by their dogs.

Large bronze statues grace three sides of the plaza: a cowboy supine fireside with his horse watching over him, a lifelike war memorial with sinewy soldiers, and a huge equestrian scene featuring Bucky O'Neill, frontier Renaissance man and Spanish-American War victim. This famous area landmark was sculpted by Solon Borglum, whose brother Gutzon sculpted Mount Rushmore. Downtown is definitely the place to be in Prescott, and you could spend an entire day and night just strolling around, shopping, eating, drinking, people-watching, looking at old buildings, and sucking in the clean mile-high air, never bothering to see the rest of the town, which is much bigger (population 40,000) than the quaint plaza and downtown suggest.

While no longer the capital of the entire territory, Prescott is seat of the Yavapai County, and as such the downtown's government buildings can get busy on weekdays. On weekends the road and foot traffic slow a bit, but not significantly. Tourists and day-trippers crowd the center of town, especially during summer and during the many festivals and shows held on the plaza throughout the year. There are

© TIM HULL

downtown Prescott

FLAGSTAFF

parking spaces all along the downtown streets, and a public garage just west of the plaza on Gurley Street. It's best to find a parking space and keep it as long as you can.

Sharlot Hall Museum

Named for its brilliant founder, Sharlot M. Hall, a writer, editor, poet, and historian in a time when Western women didn't usually do such things, the **Sharlot Hall Museum** (two blocks west of the plaza on Gurley St., 928/445-3122, www.sharlot.org, 10am-4pm Mon.-Sat., noon-4pm Sun., $7 adults, $3 children 13-17, children under 13 free) has beautiful grounds and interesting exhibits on the town's wild frontier days, balanced by a good portion of the quotidian details and artifacts of hard, complex daily life on the Southwestern edge of American civilization. The grassy complex, spread over three acres with rose gardens and re-creations of frontier-style structures, features the refurbished Victorian gem called the **Bashford House** and the log-cabin residence of the state's first governor. A rose garden honors

Prescott's pioneer women, the fascinating biographies of which are available for perusal in a file at the museum. It's an easy walk from downtown to the Sharlot Hall Museum, worth it if only to see the pretty green grounds and the mansions of another age.

Fort Whipple Museum

The Sharlot Hall Museum also operates the small **Fort Whipple Museum** (Bldg. 11, Veterans Administration campus, 500 N. Hwy. 89, 928/445-3122, 10am-4pm Thurs.-Sat., free) about four miles north of downtown on the tree-lined campus of the VA Hospital, formerly home to Fort Whipple, a major base for General Crook's war against the Apache. The museum, housed in an old Victorian house once used as officers' quarters, displays the memorabilia and daily items of frontier military life and puts on historical reenactments one Saturday a month.

Smoki Museum

For 70 years, from 1920 to 1990, the builders

of this little puebloesque building a few miles east of downtown off Gurley Street—a group of Prescott businessmen who called themselves the Smoki People—covered their half-naked bodies in a shade of brownish-red, and sold tickets to an annual fairground performance of dances and ceremonies based on Hopi religion, including even the famous Snake Dance with its live props. A corresponding museum preserved and displayed some excellent examples of Pueblo, Navajo, and Yavapai arts, crafts, and artifacts, and items from tribes throughout the West. Not exactly a politically correct organization, the Smoki People were protested out of existence in 1990 by the Hopi, who were fed up with having their sacred culture co-opted, and, as they saw it, mocked, by Anglos. The whole story is told through a fascinating and frank exhibit in the **Smoki Museum** (147 N. Arizona St., 928/445-1230, www.smokimuseum.org, 10am-4pm Mon.-Sat., 1pm-4pm Sun., $7 adults, children under 12 free), now dedicated to interpreting the Smoki phenomenon, which was extremely popular among locals for many years, and preserving some wonderful treasures collected over the years. This is a quirky and illuminating attraction, and the building itself should be seen by lovers of unique structures. The museum is part of the Prescott Armory Historic District, which includes nearby Ken Lindley Field, the old Prescott National Guard Armory, and the Citizens' Cemetery, each of which will be of at least passing interest to history buffs and old-building enthusiasts.

The Phippen Museum of Western Art

Prescott's only art museum, **The Phippen Museum of Western Art** (4701 Hwy. 89 North, 928/778-1385, www.phippenartmuseum.org, 10am-4pm Tues.-Sat., 1pm-4pm Sun., $7 adults, children under 12 free) is an essential stop for those who appreciate the Cowboy Artists of America school of painting and bronze sculpture. The museum's namesake, the artist George Phippen, was that famous group's cofounder and first president, and the collection features many of the luminaries

of the movement, as well as Native American arts and crafts and about four special Western-related exhibits every year. The drive out to the hilltop museum is as stimulating as all the oil paintings of cattle drives and bronze bucking broncos inside put together. The building overlooks a little dry-grass valley just past the strangely piled giant boulders of Granite Dells and the reedy confines of Watson Lake nearby, a scenic seven miles north from downtown.

ENTERTAINMENT AND EVENTS
Nightlife

Although these days there are more galleries and boutiques than saloons, gambling halls, and brothels along the short stretch of Montezuma Street known since territorial days as **Whiskey Row** (www.whiskeyrow.us), downtown is still the best place to party in Prescott.

Performing Arts

The **Historic Elks Opera House** (888/858-3557, www.elksoperahouse.com) is on Gurley Street downtown, on Elks Hill right across from the Hassayampa Inn. The stylish old opera house, which still has a good bit of its grandeur, books acts throughout the year.

Festivals and Events

The Courthouse Plaza hosts several large shows and festivals every year, including the **Mountain Artist Guild Spring Festival** in mid-May and the **Phippen Museum Western Art Show & Sale** over Memorial Day weekend, both big events in the regional Western art world. June brings the kooky and colorful **Tsunami on the Square** (www.tsunamionthesquare.org), a performance festival that has costumed characters and street theater taking over the downtown sidewalks. Also in June, major touring acts show up in town for the **Prescott Bluegrass Festival.** Prescott is famous, and used to be a bit infamous, for the wild public revelry of the Fourth of July weekend, when **Prescott Frontier Days and the World's Oldest Rodeo** puts the populace and the many visitors in the mood to party. In August the **Mountain**

Artists Summer Festival hits the plaza, and just up the road, literary cowpunchers get together and put on readings and performances at the Sharlot Hall Museum's **Annual Cowboy Poets Gathering.**

SHOPPING

Prescott is well known as a place to find antiques, art, and that unique, indescribable item you always knew you needed but never could find. Downtown is the best place to search for such treasures. The streets flanking the Courthouse Plaza (Gurley, Montezuma, Cortez, and Goodwin Streets) and continuing on for several blocks in every direction are crowded with shops and boutiques and galleries selling cowboy-style Western art, Mexican folk arts, handmade jewelry and crafts, gifts, Western clothing, and even high-style, contemporary furniture and home decorations. **Cortez Street** especially is a kind of antiques row, with several big stores stacked with the fascinating leftovers of past generations, the members of which usually constructed their daily-life items to last and to look beautiful and stylish while doing so. There's really no need to venture out of the downtown to shop for souvenirs, but if you're looking for the big chains, head north out of town on Gurley to Highway 69 toward Prescott Valley and you'll see a few large strip malls with all the usual conveniences, restaurants, and stores. A little farther on is the **Prescott Gateway Mall** (Gateway Blvd. and Lee Blvd., 928/442-3659, www.theprescottgatewaymall.com, 10am-8pm Mon.-Thurs., 10am-9pm Fri.-Sat., 11am-6pm Sun.), a large complex with major department stores and all kinds of mall shops and chain stores.

SPORTS AND RECREATION

The **Prescott National Forest,** more than a million acres of desert scrub, chaparral, piñon, juniper, and pine-carpeted rolling hills, dry-grass flatlands, and rocky mountains, is the western edge of the largest ponderosa pine forest in the world, the beginning of the great Arizona Pine Belt that stretches across and below the Mogollon Rim all the way to New Mexico.

Just a few miles from downtown, the forest around Prescott is a perfect place for a high-altitude hike over pine needle-strewn trails, an afternoon picnic, a cool-breeze glide across a tucked-away forest lake, or an overnight camping trip beneath the tall, sap-scented woods. The forest has long been used for small-scale mining, ranching, and outdoor recreation, and in some places it shows its wear and tear. There are more homes on this forest than one usually sees on federal land, mostly owing to the fact that owners of mining claims are allowed to build on public lands, and there are a lot of still-active mining claims in those mineraled mountains. Old mining and logging roads are now used by mountain bikers and hikers, and, in some areas, off-road vehicle enthusiasts.

The forest's **headquarters** (344 S. Cortez St., 928/443-8000, www.fs.fed.us/r3/prescott, 8am-4:30pm Mon.-Fri.) just outside downtown has a kiosk with free single-sheet descriptions and maps of every trail on the forest. It's really a good idea to stop here if you're going to be doing anything in the forest—there's simply too much information to pass up. Staff rangers at the office can help you with any questions.

Lynx Lake Recreation Area (day use 6am-8pm Apr.-Sept., 7am-6pm Oct.-Mar., $5 parking), just north of town off Highway 69, is a 55-acre lake surrounded by ponderosa pines and stocked with trout. You can float your own boat out on the lake and fish, or rent a craft and gear at the **Lynx Lake Store and Marina** (928/778-0720). The surrounding forest has several hiking and biking trails. The 4.3-mile hike to Salida Gulch will get you to the **Gold Pan Day Use Area,** where you can engage in the bent-over occupation that put the forest around Prescott on the map. The area has two basic campgrounds ($18 per night, no reservations).

In the forest just outside town along Senator Highway is **Goldwater Lake,** a popular place for picnicking, kayaking, and canoeing. Out along Highway 89, about five miles north of

Watson Lake

downtown, **Watson Lake** is surrounded by giant otherworldly boulder piles, an area called **Granite Dells.** The five-mile **Peavine Trail,** an old railroad right-of-way that takes you through the heart of the amazing rock piles, is a highlight of this area and can be hiked or biked with ease. If you didn't bring your mountain bike, you can rent one from **Ironclad Bicycles** (710 White Spar Rd., 928/776-1755, www.ironcladbicycles.com, 10am-5:30pm Mon.-Sat., 10am-2pm Sun., $12-16 per hour). If you forgot your canoe or kayak, or if you want to try either of these activities for the first time, call **Prescott Outdoors, LLC** (928/925-1410, www.prescottoutdoors.com, closed in winter).

Granite Basin Recreation Area ($5 parking fee) is a boulder-and-pine wilderness west of town off Iron Springs Road, the home of 7,600-foot-high Granite Mountain, the stained sheer-rock face of which is a preferred residence of peregrine falcons. The area has a small lake with fishing and a popular, basic campground ($18, no hookups or reservations), as well as miles of hiking and biking trails.

Hiking and Mountain Biking

You could spend years hiking and biking the Prescott National Forest and still not get to every trail and hidden, trickling-water canyon. If you've got years to spare, go down to the forest headquarters, pick up all of the handy free maps, and get hiking. If you have only a few days, however, try one of the popular and beautiful hikes described below. Most forest trails that aren't in a Wilderness Area are open to hikers, bikers, and horseback riders; all trails are closed to motorized vehicles unless expressly set aside for off-road recreation.

The five-mile Peavine Trail through Granite Dells near Watson Lake, north of town, is definitely a recommended hike if you only have time for one or two adventures, as is the steep but relatively easy two-mile hike up to a saddle at the base of **Thumb Butte,** providing awesome views of the town all nestled among the pines. Several trails around the popular **Thumb Butte Picnic Area** (three miles west of downtown on Gurley St., which becomes Thumb Butte Rd.) lead into the forest, along creeksides, and off to highlands from which you can see the San Francisco Peaks way up north. The **North Thumb Butte Trails** are all short, but a significant loop around the whole area can be cobbled together from the disparate routes. To reach other trails around Thumb Butte, or to take a scenic back-road tour of the area in your car (best if it's high clearance) or on your mountain bike, head past the picnic area and take the **Thumb Butte Loop Road,** a 20-mile route around the Thumb that ends up on White Spar Road, taking you through the high pine lands and past some amazing lookouts. The road has hiking trails and old jeep roads all along it, each of them leading deep into the shady forest.

The four-mile one-way hike up to the big boulders waiting atop **Granite Mountain** (three miles west of downtown off Iron Springs Rd., $2 parking fee) is highly recommended for those who don't mind a steep trudge. It's one of the most popular trails in the Prescott area, and for good reason. Peregrine falcons nest on the mountain's rock face, so bring binoculars. The trail winds up the mountain from a manzanita and piñon forest up through to the pine and on up to the rocky peak at 7,600 feet. It gets pretty cold in the early spring, fall, and winter, and there's likely to be snowpack in the higher regions in the winter. This is a Wilderness Area, so no mountain bikes are allowed, and some of the areas around the cliff face are closed in spring and winter so the falcons can go about their nesting in peace.

Probably the best all-around hike in the Prescott forest, the **Groom Creek Loop Trail** extends through the forest and up more than 1,000 feet to the top of Spruce Mountain, where there's a fire lookout and a few promontories from which you can just about see the top of every tree in the land. The winding single-track heading downhill makes this a wild ride on a mountain bike, nearly worth the difficult climb up. Head out Senator Highway via Mount Vernon Avenue, lined with intricate old Victorian homes, for about six miles until you see the sign for Groom Creek Horse Camp.

The trailhead parking lot is on the east side of the road.

ACCOMMODATIONS

A tourist haven, Prescott has many chain hotels, one or two of them nearly upscale, not a few smaller independents, and a growing number of bed-and-breakfast establishments. Most of the accommodations can be found along Gurley Street from one end of town to the other. The **Tourist Information Center** (800/266-7534, www.prescott.org) downtown has reams of pamphlets and brochures on various area accommodations. It's best to make reservations before arriving, especially in the summer.

Under $50

Pine View Motel (500 Copper Basin Rd., 928/445-4660, $45-55) is a great bargain just outside of the downtown area, along Copper Basin Road on the way out into the forest. The rooms are basic and clean, some of them with kitchenettes.

$100-200

The historic **Hotel St. Michael** (205 W. Gurley St., 928/776-1999, http://stmichaelhotel.com, $69-119) is right downtown on the corner of Whiskey Row and Gurley Street, a red-brick reminder of another era. Built in 1901 with gargoyles staring down from its facade, the hotel has an excellent bistro and coffeehouse on its street level and individually decorated rooms, cable TV, and air-conditioning. The comfortable old building still operates an elevator installed in 1925. A room comes with breakfast in the bistro.

The **Hotel Vendome** (230 S. Cortez St., 928/776-0900 or 888/468-3583, www.vendomehotel.com, $59-199) is a delightful, finely detailed place to stay in one of Prescott's central, tree-lined neighborhoods, with beautiful relics of the Victorian heyday on every lot. Within easy walking distance to downtown, the Vendome, a Registered Historic Landmark, offers rooms with big bathtubs and all the

Your Own Cabin in the Pinebelt

Ever dreamed of having your own secluded cabin deep in the woods, accessible only by an unmarked jeep-trail, watched over every dark wilderness night by a riot of smeared-sky stars?

The U.S. Forest Service in Arizona has a unique program called a **Room with a View** (877/444-6777, www.reserveusa.com for reservations), through which they rent out remote cabins and ranch houses, most of them former ranger residences, to anyone who wants to stay a few nights deep in the wilderness on a relatively comfortable bed. You bring your own dishes, utensils, sheets and blankets, but most of the cabins have running water, flush toilets, showers, stoves, and outside barbecue grills and picnic tables. This program provides a rare opportunity to see what it was like homesteading in the Southwestern pinebelt, only with a lot more comfort and convenience.

Listed below are the Room with a View properties in North-Central Arizona, each of them worth considering as your own personal hideout in the forest.

Horsethief Cabin ($109 per night, sleeps up to 6 people, available May 1-Nov. 30) is in the pine-covered Bradshaw Mountains above Prescott, near the old mining camp Crown King (where there's a saloon and a store). The cabin is next to small Horsethief Basin Lake, which is stocked with catfish and bass, and close to dozens of forest trails. The **Towers Mountain Cabin** ($109, sleeps up to 4 people, available Apr. 1-Nov. 30), in the Prescott National Forest sits at 7,628 feet above Crown King, right next to an active fire lookout tower. **Sycamore Cabin** ($109 per night, sleeps up to 8 people, available year-round), in the Prescott National Forest's Verde District, was built by the Civilian Conservation Corps in 1936 and has gas heating and a swamp cooler. There's a horseshoe pit out by the barbecue grill and picnic table, and cool Sycamore Creek, lined with cottonwoods, runs right behind. The **Crescent Moon Ranch** ($209 per night, sleeps up to 10 people, available year-round), in the Coconino National Forest near Sedona, sits at the base of Cathedral Rock on the banks of Oak Creek. It's a large three-bedroom, three-bath ranch house with an enclosed Arizona Room. There are hiking trails nearby, bass and trout in the creek, and rare birds—maybe even a beaver or a river otter—hanging around streamside. Up on the Mogollon Rim in the Coconino National Forest you'll find **Fernow Cabin** (928/526-0866, $75-100 depending on season, sleeps up to 8, available year-round), a cozy little log house with two bedrooms and a loft, tucked into the high forest, waiting . . .

FLAGSTAFF

comforts you could ever want and still feel good about yourself.

As historic Prescott hotels go, however, the ◖ **Hassayampa Inn** (122 E. Gurley St., 928/778-9434, www.hassayampainn.com, $104-244) is the star. Built in 1927 atop Elks Hill, a high-class gateway to downtown, the landmark hotel has a kind of red-brick, modified Spanish Colonial Revival style, with a bell tower and a covered passageway from the street to the lobby doors. Off the lobby there's a great restaurant, the Peacock Room, and a cozy dark-wood lounge where a jazz band often plays. The rooms are old, but classic; a little creaky, but comfortable and stylish. All the rooms have TVs and air-conditioning, which the likes of D. H. Lawrence and Greta Garbo lacked when they stayed here.

The **Prescott Pines Bed and Breakfast** (902 White Spar Rd., 928/445-7270, http://prescottpinesinn.com, $119-300) sits on the edge of the forest and offers Victorian country-style charm and some amazing breakfasts, surrounded by roses and grass and the color pink. The **Pleasant Street Inn Bed and Breakfast** (142 S. Pleasant St., 928/445-4774, www.pleasantbandb.com, $129-195), just a few blocks from downtown, is in a Victorian home built in 1906, a romantic reminder of the aesthetic and cultural origins of the Anglos who "civilized" North-Central Arizona after the railroad arrived.

FOOD
American

For the best breakfast in town, and a hearty lunch in the New American Diner style, head to **☾ The Dinner Bell** (321 W. Gurley St., 928/445-9888, 6:30am-2pm Mon.-Fri., 7am-2pm Sat.-Sun., $3-12, cash only), two blocks west of the plaza, a favorite with locals for generations.

The **Raven Café** (142 N. Cortez St., 928/717-0009, www.ravencafe.com, 7:30am-11pm Mon.-Thurs., 7:30am-midnight Fri.-Sat., 8am-3pm Sun. brunch, $5-22), with its dark-wood interior, decorative-tin ceiling, and fantastical local art on the walls, is a true Prescott original, and the center of café culture in this small, historic burg. All the food is fresh, and many of the ingredients are local or regional. The breakfasts here are amazing, with thick cuts of bacon, local eggs, and flavorful potatoes. They have an excellent beer selection, top-notch coffee, free wireless Internet, and patio for lounging around on a beautiful mile-high day.

If you love beer, don't miss the **Prescott Brewing Company** (130 W. Gurley St., 928/771-2795, www.prescottbrewingcompany.com, 11am-10pm daily, $7-20), right across Gurley on the Courthouse Plaza. While serving rib-sticking pub fare like bangers and mash and shepherd's pie, along with a wide assortment of lighter dishes, the "brewpub," as it's called locally, brews up some of the best beers in the territory. It's bound to get a little loud in there on the weekends, but nothing like it used to get during the wild days down at **The Palace Restaurant and Saloon** (120 S. Montezuma St., 928/541-1996, www.historicpalace.com, 11am-9:30pm Mon.-Thurs., 11am-10:30pm Fri.-Sat., lunch $9-13, dinner $13-30), though back then it was simply called the Palace, and it was known throughout the region as a rowdy and fun place to be on a weekend night (or a weeknight, for that matter). Though the old heavy-wood bar remains, and it can still get

a little rowdy with drunk tourists and locals mixing together, the Palace is today mostly a good restaurant with sandwiches, burgers, and salads for lunch, and steak, prime rib, fish, and other dishes for dinner. Everybody's partied at the Palace, from the Earp brothers to Steve McQueen. At least three-quarters of the fun of a visit is looking at all the artifacts and memorabilia on the walls of days much more exciting than our own.

The **Peacock Room** (122 E. Gurley St., 928/778-9434, http://hassayampainn.com, 7am-9pm Sun.-Thurs., 7am-9:30pm Fri.-Sat., lunch $5-13, dinner $12-35) inside the Hassayampa Inn is a great place for a long, lazy lunch or a romantic candle-lit dinner. Puffy booths line the walls, art-deco lines define the interior, and the chef serves up good steak, lamb, and fish dishes, along with Southwestern-tinged specials like Sonoran pork osso buco. **Murphy's** (201 N. Cortez, 928/445-4044, 11am-3pm daily, 4pm-10pm Sun.-Thurs., 4pm-11pm Fri.-Sat., lunch $8-15, dinner $17-46) is a local favorite for prime rib, seafood, and a slow drink in a cozy, private booth. The bar serves delicious pub-style eats (3pm-4pm).

Housed in a tastefully remodeled old fire station downtown, the **Firehouse Kitchen** (218 W. Goodwin St., 928/776-4566, http://firehousekitchen.dine.com, 11:30am-2pm and 5pm-8pm Wed.-Thurs., 11:30am-2pm and 5pm-9pm Fri.-Sat., noon-8pm Sun.) serves New American comfort food in the manner of baked mac-and-cheese with truffle sauce, beef stroganoff, and delectable Texas-style beef brisket. They offer intimate patio dining with heaters for the cool mountain nights, and a fun, relaxed bar as well.

Mexican

El Charro (120 N. Montezuma St., 928/445-7130, 11am-9pm daily, $6-13.50), a casual Mexican place downtown that's been serving great Sonoran-style food since 1959, is a favorite spot among locals for an inexpensive and delicious lunch or dinner, with maybe a few margaritas on the side.

INFORMATION AND SERVICES

The **Prescott Chamber of Commerce** (117 W. Goodwin St., 928/445-2000 or 800/266-7534, www.prescott.org, 9am-5pm Mon.-Fri., 11am-2pm Sat.-Sun.) has friendly volunteers and tons of free information on the area. A volunteer offers free guided historical tours of the downtown at 10am Friday-Sunday out of the Chamber building.

The Verde Valley

In the Verde Valley—an ancient oasis fed and greened by water falling headlong off the Mogollon Rim—you can't walk a mile without seeing some fallen ruin or artifact left behind by the conquistadores, miners, agriculturists, and speculators who've been drawn to this fertile valley and its surrounding mountains over the centuries. Most people came here after rumors of ore; others grew crops and orchards and raised livestock. The area continues to grow at a steady pace, as more and more refugees from the Phoenix sprawl hunt out the remaining rural enclaves. It's still rather quiet here, though that is likely to change in the next decade or so. The area has long been known for one ruin in particular, the spectacular, if misnamed, Montezuma Castle. This must be seen. There's a good bit of outdoor fun to be had in the valley, including tubing and boating down still-wild stretches of the Verde River, and hiking into beautiful Sycamore Canyon. But, even before you reach the valley, you'll get a chance to shop, eat, and stay in some memorable stores, restaurants, and hotels in Jerome, a former copper boomtown that is too cool to pass up.

MINGUS MOUNTAIN

The best way to start a tour of the Verde Valley is to drive up and over the mountain that watches over it from the west, 7,743-foot

A Northland Road Trip

This is ideal road-trip country, its scenic treasures nearly always represented not only deep in the wilderness but right there on the roadside, too. Starting from Phoenix, the most scenic road trip, and one on which you'll hit all the wonders and sights, goes first to Prescott, where you'll pick up State Highway 89A, twisting up and over Mingus Mountain through Jerome, then down the other side to the Verde Valley. After seeing the ruins and lush riverine spectacle of Verde country, continue on Highway 89A to Sedona, through Oak Creek Canyon, and up to Flagstaff, where it becomes U.S. Highway 89 and leads to Wupatki and Sunset Crater. Then head south to I-40 and east a little way to Walnut Canyon. Continue on the interstate to Winslow, where you'll pick up State Highway 87 south through the pines to Payson and Tonto Natural Bridge, just below the Mogollon Rim. After exploring below the rim, take Forest Road 300 (a dirt road but easily traversed) across the rim to State Highway 260 (if you want to skip the dirt road backcountry, pick up Highway 260 in Payson), which becomes the White Mountain Scenic Highway and leads through the high forest and meadow country to U.S. Highway 191, the Coronado Trail. Slowly twist and turn down the forest-lined, two-lane road, through the tiny mountain towns, down to the desert grasslands of southeastern Arizona. Then take I-10 west through Tucson and back to Phoenix. If you don't stop too long at any one place, such as a drive-through, best-of-the-region's scenery road trip makes for a memorable and busy long weekend.

Mingus Mountain, part of the Black Hills range. Take State Highway 89A from the mountain's base—either from the Verde Valley on the east side or Prescott Valley on the west—and slowly negotiate the switchbacked two-lane road, towered over by cliffs and overlooking deep, pine-swept draws. It's one of the most scenically stunning drives in the region, usually taking about an hour to go the 30 miles or so over the mountain, through the old mining metropolis of Jerome, and down the other side. The drive is understandably popular with motorcycle enthusiasts and sports-car pilots, so you might have to pull over and let some of the more hasty pass. Near the top of the mountain, you'll find **Mingus Mountain Recreation Area,** where there's a few high forest campgrounds (basic spots, $10, no reservations) and the eight-mile round-trip hike along the **Woodchute Trail** into the Woodchute Wilderness and up around to the north side of Woodchute Mountain, from which the long-ago boomtown Jerome got the wood to build itself. It's a pretty easy hike through an open pine and juniper forest that allows for some spectacular views. If you don't feel like hiking but still want to see the valley from way up high, head about three miles on the dirt road to the recreation area, where there's a promontory from which you can see mile after hazy mile spreading out in various shades of green and brown, as you sit high up in the clouds on a granite outcropping.

◀ JEROME

More than 1,000 years ago the Sinagua took minerals out of the cliffs Jerome would one day cling to, engaging in prehistoric small-scale mining for precious stones and paints. This established the primary use of Cleopatra Hill, where Spanish conquistadores, too, would dig for what was precious to their culture—gold and silver. But it wasn't until copper became one of the most useful metals of the modern age that the "Million Dollar Copper Camp" really got going. At its zenith in the 1920s, it would boast some 15,000 residents.

the town of Jerome

© CHRIS PUTNAM/123RF.COM

FLAGSTAFF

Throughout the late 19th and early 20th centuries, Jerome was known for its moral subjectivity; prostitution and other common territorial sins were tolerated, albeit regulated, well into the 1940s. Mining, no matter what mineral you're after, is always going to be a boom and bust enterprise, and by the 1950s the bust had descended and Phelps Dodge left, never to return. The town turned ghostly by 1953, when it had less than 50 full-time residents and a lot of abandoned and moldering homes, hotels, and shops. By the 1970s, however, hippies, artists, dropouts, and crafters had found the picturesque old town and began its resurgence as a colorfully populated hilltop village of creative people, the kind of funky tourist haven and hideaway one finds all over the old mining frontier. Today dozens of shops, many of them carrying one-of-a-kind creations made by Jerome's bevy of resident artists and artisans, line the narrow, twisting streets through town, and saloonesque bars, historic boutique hotels, and New American eateries occupy the old buildings that once served as saloons, hardware stores, hospitals, and hotels during the town's busy mining years, when the pits were worked around the clock. A couple of hours walking Jerome's streets, shopping for nowhere-else gifts and souvenirs, and eating at one of its excellent restaurants, is a fine way to spend an Arizona day.

Jerome Historical Mine Society Museum

The small **Jerome Historical Mine Society Museum** (200 Main St., 928/634-5477, www.jeromehistoricalsociety.com, 9am-5pm daily, $2, children free) has exhibits on Jerome's exciting and sometimes violent history. It has ephemera and artifacts from the town's various eras, from its boom days through the big bust in the 1950s and beyond. There's a hefty touch of the lurid here, with a lot about violence and illicit sex and the social consequences of each—the most fascinating displays in the building, naturally. There's also a small gift shop that sells books on the history of Jerome and souvenirs of the region.

Jerome State Historic Park

The Douglas family ruled mining in Jerome for decades, and in 1916 patriarch James "Rawhide Jimmy" Douglas built this palatial adobe house above his Little Daisy Mine, the better to welcome mine investors and company officials to town with the kind of style and comfort not always expected in western wildlands. The mansion is now **Jerome State Historic Park** (Douglas Rd. off Hwy. 89A, 928/634-5381, www.azstateparks.com/parks/JERO, 8:30am-5pm Thurs.-Mon., $5 adults, $2 children 7-13, children under 7 free), dedicated to Jerome's history, and it's worth a visit just to see the building; the library has been beautifully restored and evokes what it was like to live comfortably and richly in an otherwise rough mining town. There are also several interesting displays on Jerome's history, and a lot of rusty old mining equipment sitting around the grounds. A short video, narrated by a friendly ghost, tells the story of Jerome, and a cool 3-D model of the town shows what the tunnels looked like under it.

Shopping

There are dozens of shops, boutiques, galleries, and antique stores in Jerome, and there are always new ones opening up as the tourist traffic through town increases. Along with all the usual shops with gifts and crafts and a Southwestern flare, you'll find contemporary fine art, handmade wines, fudge, pottery, copper and turquoise jewelry, and all sorts of other treasures in Jerome, where shopping is really the primary activity. Make sure to check out the amazing collection of kaleidoscopes at **Nelly Bly** (136 Main St., 928/634-0255, www.nellieblyscopes.com). Stick to Main Street to find most of the shops, although others can be found on Clark Street, Hill Street, and Jerome Avenue.

Nightlife

Though these days it's nothing like it used to be back when Jerome was known as one of the "wickedest" places in the territory, and certainly far from what it was in the 1970s and

1980s, when, according to legend, illegal narcotics were regularly ingested from the town's bar-tops, Jerome's nightlife can still get a little rowdy, and therefore fun. The **Spirit Room Bar** (166 Main St., 928/634-8809, www.spiritroombar.com, 11am-1am daily) offers deep cocktails and live music Saturday and Sunday afternoons and into the night.

Accommodations

Jerome has several boutique hotels and bed-and-breakfast inns, most of them in refurbished historic buildings with at least one or two ghosts in residence.

[**Jerome Grand Hotel** (200 Hill St., 928/634-8200, www.jeromegrandhotel.net, $125-460) used to be a hospital, and from the outside has the character of an old sanatorium, perched on a hill and heavy with secrets; inside, the rooms are tastefully decorated and comfortable, with nice showers and tubs, TVs, and views of the valley below. The **Connor Hotel of Jerome** (164 Main St., 928/634-5006, www.connorhotel.com, $95-165) has been around in one form or another in the same location since 1898, a high-class establishment for boomtown visitors. Today it's a charming, comfortable place to stay in downtown Jerome, with 12 rooms, each with TV, mini-fridge, private bath, and wireless Internet. The **Mile High Inn** (309 Main St., 928/634-5094, www.jeromemilehighinn.com, $85-130), a comfy, historic, and friendly place occupying a red-brick storefront on Main Street, has five rooms individually decorated with a Southwestern-Victorian style, not all with private baths.

Food

Mile High Grill & Spirits (309 Main St., 928/634-5094, breakfast, lunch, and dinner daily, 11am-4pm Tues.-Thurs., 8am-9pm Fri.-Sat., $5-12.50) serves great breakfasts until noon, and steaks, prime rib, sandwiches, and salads for lunch and dinner. The bar has a great beer selection and serves some unique, locally inspired specialty drinks. The walls are decorated with the work of local artists. Sit at one of the window tables and watch people walk by while you kick back a few cold ones. Or you could sit at one of the candle-lit tables overlooking the Verde Valley at **[** **The Asylum** (200 Hill St., 928/639-3197, www.theasylum.biz, 11am-3:30pm and 5pm-9pm daily, lunch $10-15, dinner $20-32) up on a hill inside the Jerome Grand Hotel. The restaurant bills itself as "a restaurant on the fringe," meaning, one assumes, cooking on the cutting edge of New American cuisine. The menu has an interesting mix of the familiar and the exotic fused together to create some delicious meals, and the wine selection is as impressive as the elegant, view-centered interior.

Information and Services

Check out the **Jerome Chamber of Commerce** (928/634-2900, www.jeromechamber.com) for up-to-date information about all the goings-on in Jerome and environs.

CLARKDALE AND THE VERDE CANYON RAILROAD

Founded in 1912 by the United Verde Copper Company for workers at a nearby smelter, Clarkdale remains largely unreconstructed today, though the smelter and the company shut down long ago. It's said that the quiet town was the first master-planned community in Arizona, a state that would one day suffer from a surfeit of that breed. There's not much here save **The Verde Canyon Railroad** (300 N. Broadway, 800/582-7245, www.verdecanyonrr.com, $54.95-119), an excursion train that runs on tracks formerly used to bring ore from Jerome to the smelter in Clarkdale. The four-hour round-trip ride takes its passengers from Clarkdale to Perkinsville Ranch and back, snaking through Verde Canyon, an inaccessible, bald eagle-populated notch with ochre cliffs towering on one side and the green river meandering on the other. It's a slow but unforgettable route, at one point disappearing into a dark, 680-foot tunnel. There's a small café and a gift shop at the Clarkdale depot.

The least expensive fare is an adult coach ticket at $54.95, which is a basic and comfortable ride through the spectacular canyon. A

© TIM HULL

Tuzigoot National Monument

first-class ticket starts at $79.95 and includes open-air viewing cars, a complimentary glass of champagne, supremely comfortable seats, and a full bar. For $119 you can book passage on the Grape Escape Train, which includes a wine-tasting party featuring four or five different wines and foods to complement the varietals.

TUZIGOOT
NATIONAL MONUMENT

Just outside of Clarkdale, **Tuzigoot National Monument** (100 Main St., off Broadway between Clarkdale and Old Town Cottonwood, 928/634-5564, www.nps.gov/tuzi, 8am-6pm daily in summer, 8am-5pm daily in winter, $5 adults, children under 16 free), a 120-room, stacked-stone pueblo ruin on top of a hill overlooking the lush river valley, is the first of three federally protected sites in the Verde Valley that preserve what remains of the disappeared Sinagua culture. A museum has some good exhibits on Sinagua culture and the natural history of the area. You can walk up to the roof of the building and see the green valley with

Sinagua eyes. Not as dramatic as Montezuma Castle or Well, but a fascinating and important place nonetheless.

OLD TOWN COTTONWOOD

This pleasant and short stretch of State Highway 89A (Main Street) through downtown Cottonwood, just a few miles east of the road to Tuzigoot, was once the commercial and social heart of the valley. Some of the old buildings remain; others have been rebuilt and replaced several times over the generations. Along the clean, refurbished sidewalks there are a few shops, antique stores, cafés, and galleries, and a couple of really good restaurants. The Old Town area is on the National Register of Historic Places, and is worth a brief stroll and maybe a stop for lunch or dinner. The **Old Town Café** (1025 N. Main St., 928/634-5980, www.oldtownroaster.com, 8am-3pm Tues.-Sat., $4.50-9.50) has decadent European-style pastries, filling sandwiches, quiche, Greek salad, and excellent coffee.

The 1950s-style **Bing's Burger Station** (794

N. Main St., 928/649-1718, www.bingsburgers.com, 11am-3pm Tues.-Thurs., 11am-7pm Fri.-Sat., $6-9) is housed in a retro gas station in Old Town and serves some of the best burgers in the region. Fans of the old-school roadhouse diner should see this place, with its road-culture antiques and simple, filling, and well-prepared comfort food.

DEAD HORSE RANCH STATE PARK

The near-jungle of **Dead Horse Ranch State Park** (675 Dead Horse Ranch Rd., Cottonwood, 928/634-5283, http://azstateparks.com/Parks/DEHO/index.html, opens at 8am daily, $7 per car up to four people), just a few blocks from Old Town Cottonwood, provides easy access to the riparian wonders of the Verde River. Here you can walk streamside for miles, below weeping cottonwoods and hanging willows, and through all kinds of vines and branches teeming out of proportion. You'll completely forget that you are in the arid West here. If you want to camp and fish one of the man-made lagoons, there are dozens of spots with hookups, bathrooms, and showers ($12-20 per night). But the park is best used for a riverside day trip, a few hours spent exploring the source of all life in the valley, maybe with a picnic and some bird-watching. The best hike is the 1.5-mile loop along the **Verde River Greenway,** a six-mile stretch of lush life along the Verde between the Tuzigoot and Bridgeport bridges meant to preserve the riparian ecosystem, one of only a few remaining in the state. Unlike the park's creepy name, the Verde River Greenway's name is descriptive to perfection—that's exactly what it is, a greenway, and it is all the more beautiful for being so rare and threatened.

FORT VERDE STATE HISTORIC PARK

One of several outposts in the central highlands from which General Crook battled the Apache and others, **Fort Verde State Historic Park** (125 E. Hollamon St., Camp Verde, 928/567-3275, www.azstateparks.com/parks/FOVE, 9am-5pm Thurs.-Mon., $4 adults, $2 children 7-13, children under 7 free) will be of interest to history lovers and those wondering what a poor soldier's life was like serving on what must have felt like the very edge of the world. You can stroll the grounds and look into a few old buildings set up with original fort artifacts, furniture, and daily-life items that give one a feeling for late 19th-century Anglo-West life and a connection to the officers, surgeons, and enlisted men who must have wondered every day how they got all the way out here.

◀ MONTEZUMA CASTLE NATIONAL MONUMENT

If you have time to make only one stop in the Verde Valley, make it the **Montezuma Castle National Monument** (I-17 Exit 289, 928/567-3322, www.nps.gov/moca, 8am-5pm daily, 8am-6pm daily in summer, $5 for 7-day pass, children under 16 free). The five-story, 20-room limestone castle, built in about AD 1200, looks

Montezuma Castle National Monument

© TIM HULL

The Verde Backcountry

© TIM HULL

Verde Hot Springs

Forest Road 708, also known as the Fossil Creek Road, is a 26-mile dusty washboard of a road below the Mogollon Rim, deep in the river valley outback between Camp Verde and Strawberry. Take this out-of-the-way route to find deep collecting pools for swimming, warm smooth rocks for sunbathing, and a tough but beautiful semidesert hike. Or, detour off down to the banks of the Verde and take a short walk along the river past a decommissioned power plant to the ruins of an old resort, its hot springs still spilling and steaming out of the ground.

Fossil Springs: Take Highway 260 from either Camp Verde or Strawberry and then turn on Forest Road 708. About five miles from Strawberry look for the sign that says Fossil Creek Trail. It's a tough and steep, eight-mile round-trip hike that drops more than 1,300 feet, but once you see where it leads all will be forgiven. Fossil Springs flows interminably, at a constant 72°F, 20,000 gallons a minute into a series of inviting pools at the bottom of a deep canyon.

Verde Hot Springs: If you're looking for an easier hike, take Forest Road 502 off of Forest Road 708 (signed from the west but not the east), about 12 miles from Strawberry. Drive about 6.5 miles south to the Verde, where the old power plant molders, and take a short hike against the river flow along the road beyond the ruined plant. After about a mile you'll see the ruined baths of the old Verde Hot Springs Resort across the green river, now a hidden public art gallery decorated with generations of graffiti and wall-paintings. It's not likely that the baths are cleaned too often, and you might, on any given day, run into a few naked or nearly naked refugees from the world, drinking beer and enjoying the solitude of one of the stranger of the famous Verde Valley ruins.

down on Beaver Creek and the former farmlands of its builders from an improbable niche in the cliffside. It seems like it *was* a castle of some kind, the home of a ruler or a god; but it was more likely the apartment-style shelter for a group of Sinagua who found the creek and the sheltered cliffs to their liking. There's not much to do here other than walk along the short trail and look up at the ruin, but it is something that really should be seen. Imagine being the first explorer to come upon the abandoned castle—it's easy to do so; when you walk out of the small visitors center and behold the cliffside for the first time, it's a breath-catching moment.

Montezuma Well

The **Montezuma Well** (I-17 Exit 293, 928/567-4521, 8am-6pm daily June-Aug., 8am-5pm Sept.-May, free), a sister monument just up the interstate from the castle, is often overlooked, but it's a fascinating, quiet stop that will leave you in a bit of awe at nature's strangeness. The "well" is actually a sinkhole into which 1.5 million gallons of 74°F spring water has flowed daily for untold stretches of flowing time, ringed by rough cliffs into which the Sinagua built apartments. You can walk a short, twisting path down to the water's edge and explore the rock-wall rooms.

BEAVER CREEK RECREATION AREA

If you find the streamside red rocks of Sedona and Oak Creek too busy, try this rather out-of-the-way oasis at the dirt-road southern end of Forest Road 618 (I-17 Exit 298), about two miles from the interstate. Here red-rock banks and tree-shade await, lining Wet Beaver Creek. The warm red-rock slabs provide perfect jumping boards into the pools along the creek, great for splashing around and soaking your feet. There's a campground here with nice creekside spots if you can't bear to leave this beautiful spot (928/203-2900, $16 per night).

The red rocks shine along Wet Beaver Creek near Sedona.

V-Bar-V Ranch Petroglyph Site

Most of the hundreds of rock-carved symbols, animals, and mysterious beings at the **V-Bar-V Ranch Petroglyph Site** (I-17 Exit 298, www.redrockcountry.org/recreation/cultural/v-bar-v.shtml, 9:30am-3:30pm Fri.-Mon.) were created between AD 900 and AD 1300 by the Sinagua, the same people who built Montezuma Castle and other ancient sites around the Verde Valley. Here you can walk along an easy, level creek-side trail, shaded by cottonwoods and willows, and get up close to the strange rock carvings. There is usually a knowledgeable docent around to explain things, otherwise there are several information panels scattered around the site. Plan on spending an hour or more here and make sure to bring your own water. You need a Red Rock Pass to visit, which you can buy here for $5. To reach the site, which was the V-Bar-V Ranch until it was purchased by the Forest Service in the 1990s to preserve the astonishing petroglyphs, drive two miles south on Forest Road 618 from I-17 Exit 298 and cross over Wet Beaver Creek.

SPORTS AND RECREATION

Along with an aforementioned stroll along the Verde River Greenway, **hikers** should make it a point not to leave the valley before taking a jaunt into the **Sycamore Canyon Wilderness Area,** one of Arizona's most beloved and beautiful natural treasures, often called, as are other lesser canyons in the state, "the other grand canyon." It is the state's second largest canyon and one of the first to enjoy federal wilderness protection.

You can reach the southern rim of the canyon by taking the road to Tuzigoot and then turning left after the bridge on Sycamore Canyon Road, then heading about 10 miles to the rim.

The best day trip into the canyon from this end starts at the Parsons Trailhead on the rim. You descend about 500 feet into the bottomlands, where you'll walk along the creek, with cottonwood and willow and other water-loving flora all around, deep collector pools catching

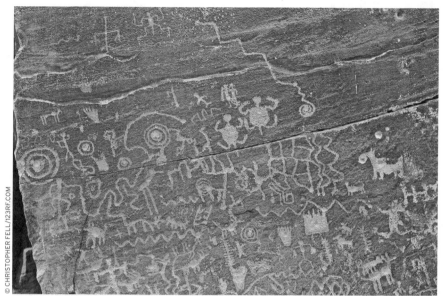

© CHRISTOPHER FELL/123RF.COM

rock carvings at the V-Bar-V Ranch Petroglyph Site

falling leaves in the fall, the riverside shade life-saving in the summer, and dark high walls towering over you, closing in ever tighter. You can backpack through the entire 11-mile canyon bottom, but the day-use portion of the Parsons Trail ends about four miles in at a deep pool—the spring that feeds the creek. From there, return the way you came, climbing back up to the rim. Expect to get your feet wet crossing the creek in a few places, and expect to not want to leave the canyon bottom and return to dry reality.

The **Verde River Scenic Area** is a wild stretch of the river that is popular with canoers, kayakers, and other **boating** types. The beautiful, sometimes rough and rapid stretch from Beasly Flat to Childs offers a true river adventure. The best way to prepare for a trip is to get a hold of the **Boater's Guide to the Verde River,** which you can download for free at www.fs.fed.us/r3/coconino. Or contact the **Verde Ranger District** (300 E. Hwy. 260, Camp Verde, 928/567-4121).

ACCOMMODATIONS AND FOOD

While the valley has some affordable and comfortable places to stay and a few great places to eat, its proximity to better dining and sleeping in Jerome and Sedona make it easy to skip over when it comes to food and accommodations.

That being said, the **Little Daisy Motel** (34 S. Main St., Cottonwood, 928/634-7865, www.littledaisy.com, $56-125) is a clean little place with basic rooms, friendly hosts, and a very agreeable bill at the end of your stay. If you feel like gambling and watching classic-rock reunion gigs, check out **The Lodge at Cliff Castle** (333 Middle Verde Rd., Camp Verde, 928/567-6711, www.cliffcastlecasino.net, $80-114) at Cliff Castle Casino in Camp Verde, just before the turnoff to Montezuma Castle, hence the name.

For lunch or dinner try **Nic's Italian Steak & Crab House** (925 N. Main St., Cottonwood, 928/634-9626, www.nicsaz.com, 5pm-9pm

Sun.-Thurs., 5pm-10pm Fri.-Sat., $10-31). Nic serves some tasty Italian dishes, as well as steaks and seafood, and offers homemade bread and a good wine list.

For those who have to have delicious mounds of Mexican food wherever they travel, try **La Casa Bonita** (991 S. Main St., Cottonwood, 928/634-7018, www.casabonitaaz.com, 9:30am-10pm Sun.-Mon., 11am-10pm Tues.-Thurs. and Sat., 11am-11pm Fri., $8-15).

Sedona

Second only to the Grand Canyon as a favorite Arizona destination, Sedona and its red rocks resemble the great gorge in several ways. Like the canyon, Sedona's rare beauty is the result of geologic circumstance—the slow work of wind, rain, trickling water, and the predictable restless rocking of the Colorado Plateau. The little resort town sits at the base of the plateau, and its red-rock monuments sit dramatically alone rising into the light-blue sky. The monuments were once a part of the plateau, the connection eaten away by erosion, that ingenious sculptor that makes all of Arizona its medium, over millions of years. High concentrations of iron-oxide, or rust, in the sediment layers stain the rock statues many shades of red as a finishing flourish. The result is one of the most beautiful and sought-after landscapes on earth.

Also like the canyon, this landscape seems so otherworldly that it's a struggle not to go a little beyond yourself here. For most, all other explanations fail, which can explain why the spiritual instincts come alive for many who visit, and why there are hordes of spiritual entrepreneurs ready to exploit those instincts. Here you can stay in extreme comfort, bordering on the decadent, or rough it to a certain degree. You can purchase a world-class work of art, and jostle through the backcountry in a pink jeep. There will be crowds—some four million tourists come to the red rocks every year, searching for one thing or another. It's easy to forget that, despite its international reputation as a life-list destination, Sedona is really just a small, somewhat rural town with only about 10,000 year-round residents. It just happens to be stuck in a geologic wonderland.

PLANNING TIPS

Sedona is only a two-hour drive from Phoenix, and is just an hour or so from Flagstaff. As such, it is a popular destination for day trips, and most people who visit this spectacular landscape spend only a brief time within it. Those who spend the most time here are either hiking or mountain-biking enthusiasts, spiritual seekers or guests at high-end resorts. In the summer, the cool waters of Oak Creek and Wet Beaver Creek call to desert dwellers, who then throng to their sandy red banks.

Sedona can be easily and somewhat thoroughly enjoyed in an unhurried day trip from Phoenix or Flagstaff. The best way to do it is to arrive by, say, mid-morning. Drive along the **Red Rock Scenic Byway** on your way into town from I-17, take a stroll on one of the trails around **Bell Rock**, stop at the **Chapel of the Holy Cross** and poke around Uptown before having lunch there or in west Sedona. After lunch, take the **Red Rock Loop Road** down to **Red Rock Crossing** too see the creek and the warm red rocks. Lastly, on your way back to Highway 179 and the interstate, drive up to **Airport Mesa** for one last look at the region. If you're visiting from Flagstaff you may want to skip the Red Rock Loop road and instead drive through Oak Creek Canyon on State Highway 89A.

It's easy to fit a visit to **Montezuma Castle** into a day trip to Sedona from Phoenix or Flagstaff. It's just 30 miles away along I-17 and doesn't take long to see. Ideally, you would see it before you arrive in Sedona; that way you are less likely to be tired and blow it off on the way home.

For those with more time and interest, a Sedona dream vacation would last from three days to one week, with plenty of time for

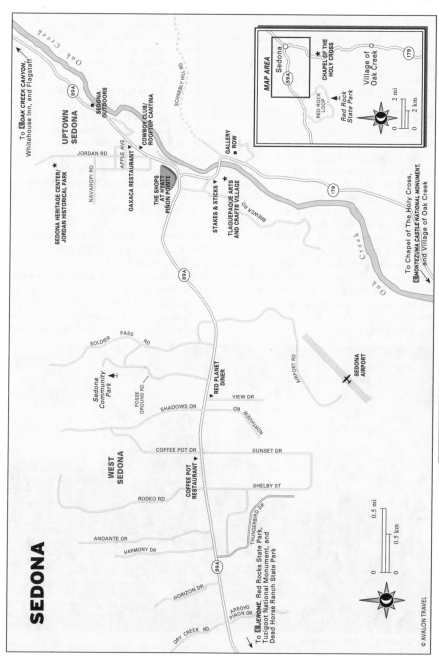

SEDONA

© AVALON TRAVEL

FLAGSTAFF

hiking, biking, and exploring the backcountry. If you're planning a long Southwestern road trip, Sedona is easy to include in your itinerary. Its highlights can be seen in a few hours, and it is less than an hour from Flagstaff and just 114 miles, or two hours, from the Grand Canyon.

SIGHTS

Nature is the main attraction here, but all of Sedona and its environs qualify as a "sight," so to speak. Still, you'll want to make sure you get a look at the famous **Chapel of the Holy Cross** (780 Chapel Rd., three miles south of the Y at Chapel Rd., www.chapeloftheholycross. com, 9am-5pm Mon.-Sat., 10am-5pm Sun., free), part of the Roman Catholic Diocese of Phoenix. The towering, cross-faced chapel appears to be emerging full born from a red-rock cradle southwest of town (and supposedly near a vortex). In keeping with the self-conscious spiritual vibe in Sedona, many visitors come here to quietly commune with the view, encouraging the emotion all that stained sandstone inspires.

To learn a little local history, at least from the Anglo point of view, check out the **Sedona Heritage Museum** (735 Jordan Rd., 928/282-7038, www.sedonamuseum.org, 11am-3pm daily, $3 adults, children under 12 free) in Uptown's **Jordan Historical Park,** where there's an old fruit orchard and a few disused artifacts from the agricultural past. The museum features a historic cabin, built in the 1930s by fruit growers, and now restored with some original furnishings, wherein is told the story of early Sedona from the 1880s on. The best exhibit is the **Movie Room,** all about the many films that have been made amid the red rocks (Zane Grey's *Call of the Canyon, Johnny Guitar,* etc.).

To see the whole strange landscape laid out before you in miniature, make the short drive up **Airport Mesa** (the end of Airport Road). On the side of the road leading to this small rural airport and lodge, some 500 feet above the town, there's a look-out spot that is simply breathtaking and a logical place to take a few pictures. You can park for free at a nearby lot.

the Chapel of the Holy Cross

What's a Vortex and Why Should You Care?

Bell Rock is one of Sedona's vortex sites.

Hanging around the Sedona Visitor Center in the summer, one hears more than once the suggestions of local volunteers trying to get out-of-towners, especially first-time visitors, interested in the little town's story beyond the famous vortexes. "But we came out here from Boston and we want to see the vortexes."

Well, you can't really see them. A vortex, they say, is a place with a special energy, a space in a landscape that gathers energy from all around it, concentrating it, perhaps to be manipulated by someone in touch with the earth's languages. The red rocks around Sedona are said to be rotten with them, and a hike or drive to a vortex site has become the most popular New Age activity here in recent years. Don't worry, you can still get your tarot cards read, have your aura photographed, your past

lives remembered, and your crystals recharged at storefronts all over town.

The vortex movement, according to Dwight Garner of the *New York Times*, began in 1987, "the year of the Harmonic Convergence when believers flocked to mystical places across the planet, hoping for a global awakening of harmony and love." Reportedly some 5,000 true believers descended on Sedona, obviously one of those "mystical places," probably owing more to its unique scenery than anything else, and many of them never left. These days there's no shortage of guides who will take you out into the red rocks and introduce you to the vortexes, and, perhaps, your spiritual self.

Suzanne McMillan and her staff at **Sedona Vortex Tours** (1385 W. Hwy. 89A, 928/282-2733, www.sedonavortextours.com, $75-130 per person, 3-5 hours) promise to "teach you how to feel the vortex energy." McMillan has been leading tours since 1988, taking seekers out in vans or on hikes to vortexes and on Medicine Wheel Tours. Linda Summers of **Sedona Spirit Journeys** (928/282-8966, $75 per person for 2.5 hours) has a degree in Native American Studies and guides a "Sedona Vortex Healing Journey," during which she shares the history of the vortex sites and offers "guided meditation, drumming, and a special crystal and Reiki healing energy in the beauty of nature." Cynthia Tierra of **Healing from the Heart** (928/821-0989, www.healingone.net, $100-500 per person, 1-3 hours) has 25 years of experience as a holistic health practitioner and Reiki master. She will guide you to both well-known and "secret" vortexes, and she gives psychic readings as well. **Sedona Spirit Yoga & Hiking** (928/282-9900 or 888/282-9901, www.yogalife.net, $85-155 per person, 3-6 hours), run by Johanna (Maheshvari) Mosca, who calls herself "Madame Vortex," offers guided vortex hikes that include yoga sessions on the red-rock buttes.

FLAGSTAFF

ENTERTAINMENT AND EVENTS
Nightlife

Sipping wine amid the scenery and doing all manner of things by candle- and starlight are the particular habits of nocturnal Sedona, mostly a couple's scene and romantic to an absurd degree.

If you're looking to be around people, have a few drinks and some conversation, try the **Rooftop Cantina** at Oaxaca (321 N. Hwy. 89A, 928/282-4179, www.oaxacarestaurant.com) in Uptown. The shaded patio bar, which looks down on Sedona's main tourist strip from on high, provides long romantic views of the red rocks that seem to get more beautiful with every round of margaritas. The crowd here is the typical northland mix of hometown locals, tourists from all over creation, canyon-and-river rats and spaced-out vortex hunters. It's likely to be crowded and noisy and fun on a weekend night in season.

The high-end sports bar atmosphere at **Steak & Sticks** (160 Portal Lane, 928/204-7849) fits right in to the sumptuous Los Abrigados Resort adjacent to Tlaquepaque. It has more than 20 flat-screen TVs and a separate billiards room. The bar and pool room are open daily 11am-11pm, and the restaurant serves a full menu of thick, tasty steaks and burgers, wings and nachos and pizzas, until 9pm. This is a fun place where you'll likely meet tourists from all over the world.

The **Oak Creek Brewery** (2050 Yavapai Dr., 928/204-1300, www.oakcreekbrew.com, call for hours) attracts a lot of locals and is an enjoyable place to hang out. The brewery offers some of the best microbrews in the state in a laid-back tasting-room atmosphere. This casual place, which is in west Sedona away from the more touristy sections of the town, should not be confused with **Oak Creek Brewery and Grill** (336 Hwy. 179, 928/282-3300, www.oakcreekpub.com, 11:30am-8:30pm daily, $7.95-22.95) at Tlaquepaque Village, which is also a fun place to kick back a few of the Oak Creek varieties. The brewery is a place to let loose and sweat a bit. Tuesday is "drum and dance" night.

Expect a whirling and friendly contingent of Sedona hippies. Irish music rings through the brewery on Mondays, and local and regional bands take the stage on Friday, Saturday, and Sunday. The cover for these shows varies, but the Friday event is usually free. When you get tired of dancing, you can sip a microbrew on the patio and try **Simon's Hotdogs** (www.simonshotdogs.net), which operates on-site and serves an awesome variety of delicious hot dogs, including a veggie dog.

The **Sedona Wine and Beer Company** (2575 W. Hwy. 89A, 928/554-4682, www.sedonawineandbeerco.com, 3pm-11pm Tues.-Thurs., noon-11pm Fri.-Sat., noon-9pm Sun., kitchen 3pm-10pm Tues.-Sat., $6-15) offers an impressive selection of wines, including many from Arizona. There is a special emphasis here on wines from the nearby Verde Valley. This relaxing, laid-back place attracts locals and tourists alike with its daily happy hour from 4pm to 6pm. You just might find here the truest Sedona experience: The cool, fragrant northland breeze ruffles your hair as you kick back on the patio, sipping a glass of wine made a few miles away and listening to the tinkle and twang of an acoustic band, as the waiter approaches with your tapas steaming on the plate.

Festivals and Events

The red rocks make a good backdrop for just about any kind of activity, and music bouncing off the sun-drenched buttes just seems to sound better. Each September since 1981 the best jazz artists in the world have gathered here to play the **Sedona Jazz on the Rocks** festival (928/282-1985, www.sedonajazz.com) and to prove that theory. September is a great time to be in the northland, like a second spring; if you are a jazz fan you should plan your life accordingly. The same applies to classical music lovers, who will appreciate the usually stellar lineup that late August brings to the **Red Rocks Music Festival** (602/787-1577 or 877/733-7257, www.redrocksmusicfestival.com) every year. Cinephiles will enjoy drinking wine with indie film stars during the **Sedona International Film Festival** (928/282-1177,

painting at the Sedona Plein Air Festival

www.sedonafilmfestival.com), five days in late February and early March filled with cutting-edge and independent films with discussions and workshops on the same. The plastic arts take over in October, with the renowned **Sedona Arts Festival** (928/204-9456, www. sedonaartsfestival.org) and the **Sedona Plein Air Festival** (928/282-3809 or 888/954-4442, www.sedonapleinairfestival.com).

SHOPPING AND GALLERIES

Contemporary eclectic, mid-to-high-end arts and crafts with a fetish for the Southwestern legendary, Native American jewelry and spiritual objects, Mexican colors and religious items, or a heavy-framed painting of a cowboy sleeping next to a campfire, his worn old hat pulled down a bit over his eyes. . . . This is pretty much what you'll find in Sedona's many shopping districts, though there are notable exceptions. After a while, one boutique, gallery, and fancy "trading post" tends to meld into the next. It's great fun, and probably the second most popular activity here, just below staring dumbfounded at the rocks. It's doubtless even more fun if you have the wallet to afford the best pieces, which, sadly, always cost the most, and sometimes even more than that.

Start at the **Uptown Shops** (N. Hwy. 89A), the original Sedona shopping district. Both sides of Highway 89 have several levels of little touristy shops, souvenir stands, boutiques, and jewelry stores. If you feel like going hiking and didn't plan for it, look for **Sedona Outdoors** (270 N. Hwy. 89A, Ste. 5, 928/282-0296, 9am-8pm daily), where you can get pretty much any gear you need and a lot you probably don't.

Next, head to the high-end **Shops at Hyatt Piñon Pointe** (at the Y, 928/204-8828, www. theshopsathyattpinonpointe.com), where shoe-loving shoppers can lose their minds at **Marchesa's Fine Shoe Salon** (101 N. Hwy. 89A, Ste. D21, 928/282-3212, www.marchesas.com). Don't miss what is arguably Sedona's best gallery, **Visions Fine Art Gallery** (101 N. Hwy. 89A, Ste. E24, 928/203-0022), which has a more varied collection than just about anybody in town.

After Piñon Pointe, it's on to Sedona's true shopping treasure, **Tlaquepaque Arts & Crafts Village** (336 Hwy. 179, 928/282.4838, www.tlaq.com), an enchanting collection of Mexican-style courtyards with all kinds of unique shops and the best restaurant in town, René at Tlaquepaque. There's even a little white stucco chapel in the "village," as if you're in an upscale version of Old Mexico, with beautiful stained glass and a mural above the altar. There are more than 40 shops and galleries among the courtyards and shade trees, including **Feliz Navidad** (928/282-2752, www.feliznavidadsedona.com, 10am-7pm Wed.-Sat., 10am-5:30pm Sun.-Tues.), dedicated to Christmas ornaments with a Mexican aesthetic.

Across the street from Tlaquepaque is **Gallery Row,** where you'll find the best Native American art. **Kopavi** (411 Hwy. 179, Garland Building upstairs, 928/282-4774, www.kopaviinternational.com, 10:30am-5pm Mon.-Sat., noon-5pm Sun.) has the best items made by Hopi artists. It is a good idea to call first to

FLAGSTAFF

© TIM HULL

Tlaquepaque Arts & Crafts Village

FLAGSTAFF

make sure they are open. Also check out the **Lanning Gallery** at Hozho Center (431 Hwy. 179, 928/282-6865, www.lanninggallery.com, 10am-6pm Mon.-Sat., 11am-5pm Sun.) for tasteful Southwestern styles.

The **Hillside Sedona** (671 Hwy. 179, 928/282-4500, www.hillsidesedona.net) complex is also in this area and deserves a look, especially the **Gallery of Modern Masters** (888/282-3313, www.galleryofmodernmasters.com, 10am-5pm daily), which has some spectacular pieces by some of the all-time greats.

Village of Oak Creek

If you haven't had enough shopping yet, head about five miles south on Highway 179 and explore the shops at the **Tequa Festival Marketplace** (7000 Hwy. 179, 928/284-4699, www.tequa.net) and, perhaps for the first and only time during your visit to Sedona, find a bargain at the **Oak Creek Factory Outlets** (6601 S. Hwy. 179, 928/284-2150).

ACCOMMODATIONS

There are dozens of hotels and resorts in Sedona, some of them like little towns themselves. There are a few bargains, but you could spend hundreds, even thousands, a night if you wanted to, and you generally get what you pay for. Some of the resorts are outlandishly well appointed, with golf courses and all kinds of spa treatments, workshops, and spiritual rituals. Rates tend to go up during holidays and special events, and are subject to some seasonal variation.

Some of the most romantic and secluded spots are about two to four miles north of Uptown Sedona on State Highway 89A, in Oak Creek Canyon along the small but verdant Oak Creek, which is stocked with trout.

$50-100

The **Whitehouse Inn** (2986 W. Hwy. 89A, 928/282-6680, www.sedonawhitehouse-inn.com, $60-99) is an affordable and basic place to stay, not sumptuous or anything, but a clean and central base for a realistic visit without the huge price tag, mud baths, or chakra healing.

The clean and relatively inexpensive **Sedona Village Lodge** (105 Bellrock Plaza, 800/890-0521, www.sedonalodge.com, $49-79) is a good choice for hikers and those who are more interested in red rocks than gift shops. It's across from Bell Rock, a name given to an eroded mound of rock that looks vaguely like a bell, about six miles south of downtown along Highway 179—close enough but also a bit far away, which is the ideal place to be. The rooms are comfortable, the hosts are friendly, and the Wi-Fi is free. It's a good idea to reserve a room far in advance.

Another great value is the **Sugar Loaf Lodge** (1870 W. Hwy. 89A, 928/282-8451 or 877/282-0632, www.sedonasugarloaf.com, $60-90), a little 15-room motel just a mile or so west of the junction of Highways 89A & 179. It's close to everything and offers a clean, comfortable room with a refrigerator and television. With its pool, hot tub and budget-friendly price, Sugar Loaf is one of the best deals in a town where they are often hard to find.

$100-200

The **Arroyo Pinion Hotel** (3119 W. Hwy. 89A, 928/204-1146 or 800/789-7393, www.ascend-collection.com, $100-179) is an excellent choice for hikers and mountain bikers. It's located in west Sedona, a bit away from the tourist bustle of Uptown and Tlaquepaque. The location provides easy access to backcountry roads that lead to the trails around Chimney Rock and Sugarloaf. The rooms are well-appointed with flat-screen TVs, refrigerators, and big comfortable beds perfect for resting your bones after a day in the wilderness.

Located right in the middle of all the action in Uptown Sedona, the **Matterhorn Inn** (230 Apple Ave., 800/372-8207, www.matterhorninn.com, $119-159) is one of the best places to stay if you're hoping to experience all that Sedona has to offer. The small hotel sits among dozens of shops and restaurants and yet still manages to provide amazing views of

COURTESY OF SEDONA CHAMBER OF COMMERCE

FLAGSTAFF

Many hotels can be found in Uptown Sedona.

the beautiful, exotic Sedona landscape. The Southwestern-style rooms offer comfort, free Wi-Fi and private balconies from which to stare at the red rocks. There's also a pool and hot tub next to a romantic outdoor sitting area with a fireplace.

The **Oak Creek Terrace Resort** (4548 N. Hwy. 89A, 928/282-3562 or 800/224-2229, www.oakcreekterrace.com, $99-250) is tucked into the greenery along Highway 89A just south of Slide Rock State Park in Oak Creek Canyon. Arizonans love Oak Creek Canyon because it is one of the last easily accessible riparian areas left in the state, and its green and shady nature is shocking for its rarity. It seems impossible that one could improve on the natural splendor of this place, but the folks at Oak Creek Terrace have made an honest and successful go of it. The little bungalows and cabins on this beautiful property have fireplaces, in-room hot tubs, outdoor barbecues, and kitchenettes. This is a perfect place for families looking to get out of the city and back to nature without giving up any of the comforts of home.

The **Orchards Inn** (254 N. Hwy. 89A, 928/282-2405 or 800/341-5931, http://orchardsinn.com, $99-200) has wonderful rooms, many with fireplaces and patios with views of the red rocks, a tasteful, cozy lobby, and a central location in Uptown that's hard to beat. Stay here and you can walk to all the shops and restaurants on the main tourist strip of 89A and leave your car parked.

The **Sky Ranch Lodge** (1105 Airport Rd., www.skyranchlodge.com, $80-145) offers something a little different: It's located on top of Airport Mesa, 500 feet above the red land, set next to the small Sedona Airport. Its best feature is its location high above the rest of Sedona, and the views, especially at sunrise and sunset, are spectacular and right outside your door. They offer a variety of rooms, including large ones with kitchens for families and cozy romantic hideaways with fireplaces. Don't worry about noise from planes. It's an airport, yes, but a very small one that serves mostly private planes, corporate jets, and air-tour

companies. The Sky Ranch Lodge also has a decent restaurant and bar, so it's conceivable that you could stay up here and never go down again.

The **Wildflower Inn** (6086 Hwy. 179, 928/284-3937 or 888/494-5335, www.sedonawildflowerinn.com, $99-159) in the Village of Oak Creek looks out at Bell Rock and offers rooms with fireplaces, and in-room whirlpool tubs—a little bit of decadence at a relatively affordable price.

Over $200

Amara Creekside Resort (310 N. Hwy. 89, 928/282-4828, www.amararesort.com, $189-409) is one of those Sedona places you've heard about; lovely beyond reason, intimidating yet tasteful, this retreat on the banks of Oak Creek has a full-service spa and all the other amenities you'd expect from a five-diamond hideaway.

The enchanting **Garland's Oak Creek Lodge** (8067 Hwy. 89A 928/282-3343, www.garlandslodge.com, $265-315) has 16 charming and comfortable cabins of various sizes set on 10 acres along Oak Creek, on the edge of the Red Rock Secret Mountain Wilderness. The lodge has a renowned restaurant, and the price of a room includes breakfast, dinner, and tea. This wonderful place is surrounded by orchards and a lush green lawn, on which they serve cocktails every evening. The lodge is open April 1 through Nov. 15 and has a two-night minimum. Some people love this place so much that they make a habit of returning year after year, so you have call far, far ahead of time to book a spot, and you might end up on a waiting list. Something to consider: There are no televisions or telephones in the rooms.

The Inn on Oak Creek (556 Hwy. 179, 928/282-7896 or 800/499-7896, www.innonoakcreek.com, $200-295), is a charming bed-and-breakfast that seems a world away. There are 11 rooms, each decorated in a theme and featuring all kinds of interesting collectibles, antiques, assorted knick-knacks, and ephemera. Some of the rooms have private patios overlooking the creek, whirlpool baths, and, of course, spectacular views. It's located on Oak

Creek, though not in Oak Creek Canyon. It sits along the creek as it flows along Highway 179, close to Tlaquepaque and not far from Uptown.

The **El Portal Sedona** (95 Portal Lane, 800/313-0017, www.elportalsedona.com, $179-399) is an amazing 12-room hacienda in the rustic-elegant style, with deep comfort, great food, and furniture you'll want to pack up and take home. Most of the rooms have private patios and fireplaces, and all of them have televisions and free Wi-Fi. This fabulous little inn is located next to the Los Abrigados Resort and Tlaquepaque Village, and if you stay at El Portal you are allowed to use the resort's pool and spa.

FOOD

A favorite with the locals, the **Coffee Pot Restaurant** (2050 W. Hwy. 89A, 928/282-6626, coffeepotsedona.com, 6am-2pm daily, $3-13) is great for breakfast and lunch, with filling home-style American and Mexican food in big portions. They serve breakfast all day, especially from their signature list of "101 Omelettes." It may be that a few of them were desperation choices: the final omelette on the list comes with peanut butter, jelly, and banana. Nonetheless, there are at least 70 others worth trying. Located in west Sedona along Highway 89A, not far from Coffeepot Rock, this popular restaurant also has a shaded patio and an eclectic gift shop. Expect a crowd and a bit of a wait on weekend mornings.

The sci-fi kitsch at the **Red Planet Diner** (1655 W. Hwy. 89A, 928/282 6070, 7am-11pm daily, $10-20) is something to see, and you won't mind sticking around for the diner-style fare. Spaceships, flying saucers, and free-flying aliens hang from a ceiling painted with stars and planets and infinite space. It's like a space geek took over a 1950s diner. In west Sedona along Highway 89A, the Red Planet is open relatively late, as all diners should be, and serves a large menu of omelets, burgers, sandwiches, soups, salads, and shakes.

The **Cowboy Club** (241 N. Hwy. 89A, 928/282-4200, www.cowboyclub.com,

11am-10pm daily, $11-37) in Uptown Sedona is a perennial favorite, a Western-style joint with buffalo meat and rattlesnake on the menu along with great burgers and steaks. Founding members of the Cowboy Artists of America used to hang out here long ago when it was called the Oak Creek Tavern, and that tradition continues in the many paintings by the group's famous members on display throughout the restaurant.

One of the better Mexican restaurants in the northland is **Oaxaca Restaurant** (321 N. Hwy. 89A, 928/282-4179, www.oaxacarestaurant.com, 11am-9pm Mon.-Fri., 8am-9pm Sat.-Sun., $6.75-21.25). This popular restaurant in Uptown Sedona has a spectacular patio and excellent food that's both pleasingly familiar and a bit off-kilter.

René at Tlaquepaque (336 Hwy. 179, 928/282-9225, www.rene-sedona.com, 11:30am-2:30pm and 5:30pm-8:30pm daily, lunch $11-16, dinner $22-42), with its Mexican courtyard ambience and outrageously tasty food, has long been one of Sedona's top spots to

© TIM HULL

René at Tlaquepaque

FLAGSTAFF

dine. Try the baked French onion soup and the sweet potato ravioli, or the venison, or the . . . just try the whole menu, and go back again and again if you can.

If you're headed up to Airport Mesa to view all of Sedona laid out before you, and you should be, stop by the **Mesa Grill** (1185 Airport Rd., 928/282-2400, www.mesagrillsedona.com, breakfast 7am-11am, lunch 11:30am-3pm, dinner 4pm-9pm daily, $5.25-$29.95) for a bite to eat or a drink (happy hour 3pm-6pm daily). The small, sleek restaurant and bar looks out on the airport's runway through large, view-framing windows. The eclectic menus feature pasta dishes, hamburgers, and seafood.

As the name says, **Nick's Westside** (2920 Hwy. 89A, 928/204-2088, www.nickswestside.com, 7am-9pm Mon.-Sat., 8am-2pm Sun., $2.75-$11.95) is a popular joint in west Sedona along Highway 89A, popular with locals for breakfast, lunch, and dinner. This place serves exceedingly satisfying homestyle food: ribs, brisket, burgers and sandwiches, burritos, tacos, and enchiladas. Nick's tends to be busy for breakfast on weekend mornings.

The **Oak Creek Brewery and Grill** (336 Hwy. 179 at Tlaquepaque Village, 928/282-3300, www.oakcreekpub.com, 11:30am-8:30pm daily, $7.95-22.95) serves excellent bar-and-grill-style fare, including fantastic barbecue ribs and fish-and-chips, not to mention a large selection of pizzas. Then there's the enchanting setting within the charming confines of Tlaquepaque Village. Sit on the patio if weather permits, and it usually will. The locally brewed beer on tap here is some of best in the state.

INFORMATION

The **Sedona Chamber of Commerce** has a very energetic and organized tourism bureau that operates a well-stocked and well-staffed visitor center. The **Visitor Information Center** (331 Forest Rd., 928/282-7722 or 800/288-7336, www.visitsedona.com, 8:30am-5pm Mon.-Sat., 9am-3pm Sun.) in the Uptown shopping area is easy to spot.

GETTING THERE AND AROUND

Since it's a small town with a huge transient population, driving and parking in Sedona can be an adventure; nonetheless, it's easy to find your way around. The first thing you have to know is that there are four distinct zones in and around Sedona, all of them accessible using just two connecting roads. State Highway 89A runs right through the heart of town and on north to Oak Creek Canyon and eventually to Flagstaff. The portion of this road north of its junction with State Highway 179, the town's main intersection, called the "Y" among locals, is called Uptown. The stretch of Highway 89A west of the Y is called West Sedona. Highway 179 heads southwest from the Y and continues through the red rocks, eventually intersecting with I-17. The stretch of Highway 179 between Schnebly Hill Road and Canyon Drive is called Gallery Row. The Village of Oak Creek is about five miles southwest of Sedona along Route 179.

By Car

You really must have a car to see Sedona and Red Rock Country right, and it would be ideal to have an SUV or a four-wheel-drive vehicle. A regular sedan will work just fine, though, and if you still want to explore the inaccessible backcountry you should book a jeep tour.

The best and quickest way to get to Sedona from Phoenix is to take I-17 north to State Highway 179, which will take you past some amazing scenery and right into the small town's heart. The 116-mile drive from Phoenix to Sedona, about 90 percent of it on the interstate, usually takes about two hours.

Coming from Flagstaff to the north, take State Highway 89A through Oak Creek Canyon, one of the most scenic routes in the state. Much of the road is slow and twisty, so expect the 44-mile drive to take at least an hour. You can also take I-17 south from Flagstaff to Hwy. 179, about 90 miles or 1.5 hours. This route, though longer, is probably the safest way to go during inclement weather.

A lot of travelers combine a visit to Sedona

NAVAJO AND HOPI COUNTRY

Here is the Arizona you often see on posters and in old films: Monument Valley, the Painted Desert, the railroad tracks, and Route 66. This is also the Arizona you rarely see unless you make a concerted effort to do so: the Navajo Nation, the Hopi Mesas, and the hidden, forgotten ruins of an ancient civilization. From the vast, arid grasslands of the high desert to the pink

Hwy., 928/468-6500, www.gerardosbistro. com, 11am-9pm Mon.-Sat., $8-25). The baked sandwiches, hand-tossed brick-oven pizzas, and classic pasta dishes are alone a fair excuse for heading to the pinelands.

The **Buffalo Bar & Grill** (311 S. Beeline Hwy., 928/474-3900, 11am-2am daily, $5-20) has a fun atmosphere, a friendly staff, plenty of locals hanging around, and all kinds of typical grill-style dishes that go perfectly with the rural forest location.

The chili and burgers at **Macky's Grill** (201 W. Main St., 928/474-7411, 10am-8pm Sun.-Wed., 10am-9pm Thurs.-Sat., $3.95-17.95) are excellent, and the menu is stocked with all kinds of other dishes, including a vegetarian burger and other options. This place is popular with locals and has a fun, kitschy cowboy decor. The patio here is the place to eat on a cool high-country afternoon.

The Mexican food at **La Sierra Mexican Restaurant** (800 N. Beeline Hwy., 928/468-6711, 11am-9pm Mon.-Fri., 10am-9pm Sat.-Sun., $5-15) is delicious, and the enchanting, folk-art atmosphere is just the thing to slow you down to a reasonable, healthy pace as you inhale your cheesy enchilada.

ACCOMMODATIONS

Payson and the Rim work best as a drive-through or a day-trip, but if you want to stay longer, there are several chain hotels along Highway 87, the main drag through town. You can't go wrong staying at the small **Majestic Mountain Inn** (602 E. Hwy. 260, 800/408-2442, www.majesticmountaininn.com, $69-150), which has nice, clean rooms, Internet, a heated pool, and more. Just west of Highway 87 on Highway 260 you'll pass **Kohls Ranch** and **Christopher Creek,** tiny forested burgs with

cabins to rent. Try the **Kohl's Ranch Lodge** (202 S. Kohl's Ranch Lodge Rd., 928/478-4211, $120-350), with its bucolic mountain-forest setting and creekside cabins.

GETTING THERE AND AROUND
By Car

Payson and the Mogollon Rim are easy to visit by car from Phoenix. It's only 90 miles from Phoenix to the pine forests below the Rim. The best route is State Highway 87, also called the Beeline Highway. It usually takes about 1.5 hours to make the trip, but it can take much longer; traffic can be slow on weekends in the summer, when everybody gets the same idea to head to mountains out of the heat. Fill up before you leave Phoenix, as gas is likely to be more expensive along the road.

To reach this region from the Verde Valley and Sedona, take State Highway 260, east from Camp Verde 36 miles to Strawberry, then it's 30 miles south on the dual-designated Highway 260/Highway 87 to Payson, or only a few yards to Forest Road 300, which leads across the Rim to the White Mountains.

From Flagstaff, head south to the Verde Valley on State Highway 89A, through Sedona, then take Highway 206 to Payson from Camp Verde. Another scenic way to go is to take Forest Road 209, also known as Lake Mary Road, out of Flagstaff, through the forest, past Happy Jack and Clints Well to Highway 87 near the Rim Road. The incredibly beautiful forest drive is about 100 miles long and takes more than two hours. The road sometimes closes in winter.

To reach the White Mountains region from Payson, simply take Highway 260 east for 90 miles to Show Low.

FLAGSTAFF

FLAGSTAFF

Tonto Natural Bridge State Park

rocks, watching water drip off the bridge's arch high above. A visit here typically takes about an hour, but could go much longer.

Pine and Strawberry

Tucked just below the rim north on Highway 87 about 20 miles from Payson, the tiny towns of **Pine** and **Strawberry** have a few antique stores, small inns and restaurants, and a historic, rural atmosphere.

Pine comes first as you drive north from Payson on Highway 87. The **Pine-Strawberry Museum** (15 miles north of Payson on Hwy. 87, 928/476-3547, www.pinestrawhs.org, 10am-2pm Mon.-Thurs., 10am-4pm Fri.-Sun. May 15-Oct. 15, 10am-2pm Mon.-Sat. Oct. 16-May 14, $1, children under 11 free) is located here and is worth a short stop. Housed in a former Mormon chapel that dates from 1917, the museum has an interesting collection of information and artifacts on the area's prehistoric cultures and its later settling by several tough Mormon families in the 1880s.

Strawberry is located just three miles north of Pine along Highway 87. About a mile into town is the **Fossil Creek Road,** which leads to the Verde Valley from the Rim Country. About two miles to the west on Fossil Creek Road from Highway 87, you'll find Arizona's "Oldest Standing Schoolhouse," a pine-log cabin called the **Strawberry Schoolhouse** (10am-4pm Sat., noon-4pm Sun. May 15-Oct. 15; also open Mon. and Fri. June 15-Aug. 6). Built in 1882 to serve a few pioneer families in the area, the small pine-plank, one-room school house has been preserved and restored by locals and now presents a 19th-century frontier school room as it would have looked to the kids filing in from the forest trails so long ago.

FOOD

There are a lot of chain restaurants and hotels around Payson to serve Phoenicians escaping the heat, as it's a mere 1.5-hour drive from Phoenix. Most of the services are along the main route through town.

You'll find some of the top-rated Italian food in the state at **Gerardo's** (512 N. Beeline and take food and water with you; there's little but beautiful views along the way.

Drive north out of Payson on State Highway 87 (also designated as State Highway 260 westbound) for 29 miles until you see the sign for Forest Road 300 on the right side of the road, not far after Highway 260 separates and continues west. Turn east on Forest Road 300 and drive all the way across the Rim to the visitors center, where there's a paved trail and some breathtaking views right at the edge of the White Mountain region, near an eastern portion of Highway 260. You can make a loop back to Payson by taking Highway 260 from the Mogollon Rim Visitor Information Center southwest 34 miles back to town. You could also start the trip from Payson going northeast on Highway 260 eastbound and then drive west on Forest Road 300 across the rim to Highway 87.

Along the Rim Road you'll see the effects of the huge wildfires that have threatened this region repeatedly over the last few decades. Blackened stands of deadwood and new green growth are everywhere along the escarpment, and the whole region is generally bone dry and drought-ridden, and is usually subject to campfire restrictions in the summer.

Rim Lakes

In the forest just north of the Rim along Forest Road 300 there are several small, pine-encircled man-made lakes that are stocked with trout and bass and offer camping spots and plenty of easy trails to the Rim's edge.

The best of these is **Woods Canyon Lake,** a gorgeous little 55-acre lake not far from the Rim Visitor Center. There are four **campgrounds** (Apache-Sitgreaves National Forests, Black Mesa Ranger District, Overgaard, 928/535-7300, www.fs.fed.us/r3/asnf, $16-24 per night) near the lake, offering a total of about 150 sites, some of which can take trailers up to 32 feet long. There's also a country store that sells all kinds of supplies, a dump station, picnic tables, and bathrooms, and there's a company that rents boats. The lake is open April 1-October 15 and is quite popular. The easiest way to reach Woods Canyon Lake and the other nearby rim lakes, is to take Highway 260 northeast from Payson 30 miles to Forest Road 300, which is paved on this stretch. Then drive about four miles west and turn right on Forest Road 105. The lake is a mile farther on.

INFORMATION

For more information on the Rim and its lakes and trails, try the **Apache-Sitgreaves National Forests, Black Mesa Ranger District** (Overgaard, 928/535-7300, www.fs.fed.us/r3/asnf). Another good source for information about hiking, biking, and camping in this region is the local website, www.rimcountry.com.

Zane Grey Cabin

Even if you've never read any of Zane Grey's more than 130 books, a look at the **Zane Grey Cabin** (700 Green Valley Pkwy., 928/474-3483, www.zanegreycabin.org, 10am-4pm Wed.-Mon., $5) is a must when you're in the small town of Payson. The famous, beloved writer of Westerns loved this area, which he called the Tonto Rim, and came here to write and hunt often between 1918 and 1929. The original cabin burned down in the 1990 Dude Fire, but a local group rebuilt it exactly and furnished it according to surviving pictures. There's also a small **Rim Country Museum** next door with exhibits on Grey and what life was like for the Anglo pioneers who settled this piney area below the great rim.

Tonto Natural Bridge State Park

The **Tonto Natural Bridge State Park** (11 miles north of Payson on Hwy. 87, 928/476-4202, www.azstateparks.com/parks/TONA, 8am-6pm daily, last entry at 5pm, $5 over 14, $2-7) is the major stop in Rim Country other than the rim itself. The world's largest natural travertine bridge, the strange and wondrous sight can be hiked to or over on short trails. Though the trail going to the dripping, moss-covered inner bridge is steep going back up, it's short and should really be taken to get the full experience. Hike down and sit on the wet

FLAGSTAFF

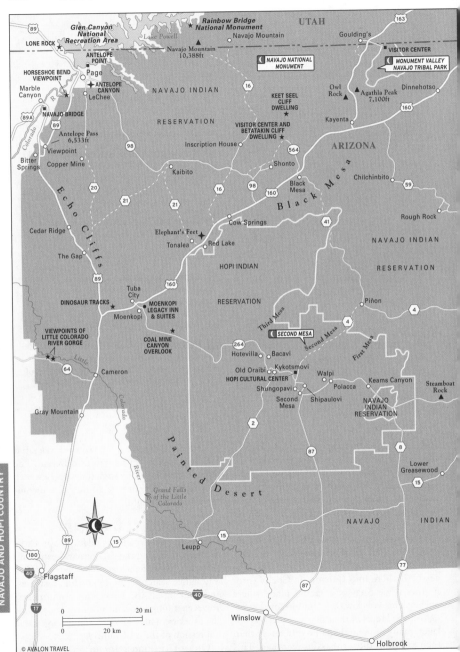

HIGHLIGHTS

LOOK FOR ◖ TO FIND RECOMMENDED SIGHTS, ACTIVITIES, DINING, AND LODGING.

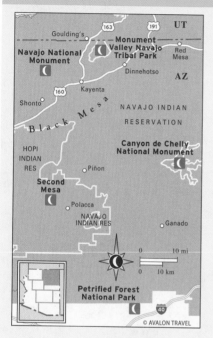

© AVALON TRAVEL

◖ **Navajo National Monument:** Stand on the edge of sacred Tsegi Canyon and gaze at an ancient city rising out of the flaking, reddish-pink rock, hidden and forgotten (page 276).

◖ **Monument Valley Navajo Tribal Park:** Drive the red-dirt loop around a barren valley populated by jutting, crumbling stone giants, an awe-inspiring landscape rooted deeply in the American imagination (page 279).

◖ **Canyon de Chelly National Monument:** Hike to the White House Ruin along a precipitous rock trail hewn out of the cliffside, circled endlessly by ravens and silence (page 287).

◖ **Second Mesa:** Take a quiet walk through the oldest continually inhabited village on the continent, where past and present bleed together and thousand-year-old traditions are a part of everyday life (page 295).

◖ **Petrified Forest National Park:** Walk among the slickrock remains of a swampy forest, now a parched land strewn with reminders of the earth's unfathomable age (page 297).

and red sandstone guardians of Indian Country, the scenery here gets top billing, but there are also comforts to be had in this region that was once an exotic, longed-for destination for generations of Americans and still is a major draw for those looking for something just a bit off the beaten path.

Here you can gaze at weather-formed canyons with rock features that seem deliberately molded according to a strange, thrilling aesthetic; hike into Canyon de Chelly (pronounced "de Shay"), a sacred place where pueblo ruins sit below sheer, multicolored walls; or visit the Hopis in their remote mesa-top villages, many of them living no differently than their ancestors did a thousand years ago. This place is not for the lazy, easy-come traveler, but for those looking for something different. The region's challenges, its sometimes foreign feel, only make a trip out here all the more memorable and meaningful.

PLANNING YOUR TIME

You could easily spend five days to a week in this region, hiking the canyons and exploring the ruins, following native guides to out-of-the-way sights, searching for handmade treasures, and touring all the parks and monuments; however, a long weekend would suffice to hit all of the essentials and to gain an unforgettable impression of Indian Country.

One of the most important things to

remember while traveling in Indian Country is that the Navajo Nation recognizes **daylight saving time,** unlike the rest of Arizona. That means that from March through November, the reservation observes Mountain Daylight Saving Time, while the rest of Arizona observes Mountain Standard Time (MST) all year.

GETTING THERE AND AROUND

It's relatively easy to navigate Indian Country, as long as you have a steady vehicle and a good map. Remember that the distances between stations, much as it was in the old days of the territory, are far, for the most part, so it's important to take advantage of off-road respite when it presents itself.

To reach the high-desert railroad towns and the sights nearby, stick to I-40, which is well signed for tourist sights. To reach the Navajo and Hopi Reservations from the west, take U.S. Highway 89 north from I-40 at Flagstaff to Cameron, at the entrance to the Navajo Nation. Past Cameron, turn east on U.S. Highway 160, which will take you through Tuba City and Kayenta, past the Navajo National Monument and Monument Valley Navajo Tribal Park. Take Highway U.S. 191 south from Highway 160 east of Kayenta to reach Chinle and Canyon de Chelly National Monument. From there take Highway 191 farther south to Ganado and the Hubbell Trading Post, and then head east on State Highway 264 to Window Rock, the Nation's capital.

If you're entering the Nation from the east, take Indian Road 12 north to Window Rock from I-40 and then go north and west to hit the sights.

Hopiland can be reached from the west by way of State Highway 264 from Highway 160 at Tuba City and Moenkopi; from the east, pick up State Highway 264 at Window Rock.

The best map of this area is the American Automobile Association's (AAA) Indian Country Guide Map.

Monument Valley

The Navajo Nation

Though it has been visited by tourists regularly for more than a century, the 27,000-square-mile Navajo Nation still feels like the American outback. This is one of the most isolated, undeveloped regions in the country, a land of red-dirt roads, scrubby gray-green sweeps of arid plane, and pink-rock spires reaching for the persistent, glaring blue-white sky. To visit "Indian Country" one must enter without expectations, and be open and ready for sudden bolts of strange beauty and spiritual recognition.

The appeal of the sprawling Nation is primarily scenic. Understanding this, the Diné have not exploited their homeland for the sake of more dollars and euros. The comforts are few and far between, and the landscape is all the better for it. Moreover, the land here is sacred in a very real sense to the Diné: This is where they live; it is not a tourist attraction

but a homeland, a birthright, and a cathedral. Respectful visitors will find this seemingly empty land to be full of wonder.

But then again the Nation isn't as remote as it seems. Just as it was before paved highways traversed the land, a trip to the reservation today is a journey between springs. The few population centers have all grown up naturally where stores of cool water flow beneath the otherwise parched high desert—semigreen places like Tuba City, Kayenta, Chinle, and Window Rock, the Nation's capital on the eastern border. These towns, while not much to look at—they are no more than dusty accumulations of houses and businesses along the highway, the minor accomplishments of humans dwarfed even more in this land of great rock giants—offer the usual chain hotels (though nearly all rooms are on the expensive side) and some

© TIM HULL

rock spires and blue sky of the Navajo Nation

homegrown restaurants serving foods unique to the region.

There are rare opportunities here to go beyond—beyond time when you contemplate the abandoned cities hanging from the cliffs of Navajo National Monument and Canyon de Chelly, and beyond reality as you watch the sun set over Monument Valley, surrounded by an alien but all too familiar beauty.

For shoppers, collectors, and treasure hunters, the Nation probably has the most working artists this side of Santa Fe. The best and most memorable items—famous Navajo rugs and overlay jewelry, Hopi baskets and pottery—can be found at trading posts, co-op stores and sometimes even purchased on the artist's doorstep—but you have to keep your eyes open for homemade signs out in all that vastness.

As guests of the Diné, tourists are expected to be respectful and follow a few simple but nonnegotiable rules of the reservation. One should not, however, overreact to these rules in a way that keeps you from interacting with the friendly and fascinating Navajo people. If you simply remember that you are not in a living diorama—that these are real people with real lives to live—then you should be fine. Think about how you'd feel if strangers showed up and started photographing your house. It is never appropriate to photograph Diné individuals or their property without first obtaining permission. The federal parks and monuments are an exception, though there are farms in Canyon de Chelly that you can't photograph. This is a hard-and-fast rule, so don't even try it. If you do, expect to have your camera gear confiscated. Also, even though the reservation may seem wild and open at times, it's not appropriate to drive off-road or across the land. The land here provides many a Diné family's livelihood, and it should not be disturbed by visitors. If you are invited to witness a religious ceremony of some kind, all due respect is expected—take off your hat and watch silently, as you would a Catholic mass. Drugs and alcohol are not allowed anywhere on the reservation.

The Diné

The Diné (the name the Navajo give to themselves, meaning "The People") are the largest and most populous Native American nation. They migrated down from Canada, with their Apache brethren, to the Colorado Plateau about a century before the Spanish arrived from the south, and lived a seminomadic life of hunting, gathering, and raiding that sometimes had them at odds with their neighbors, who were sedentary, pueblo-dwelling farmers.

After contact with the Spanish and the Pueblos, the Diné also became pastoralists and farmers, one of many occasions when these resilient people borrowed from another culture to expand their own. As the anthropologist Edward T. Hall explains: "In their natural state all people are highly adaptable, but the Navajos seem to be the most adaptable people on earth—not simply in adapting to new technologies… but in their ability to live with, even absorb into their society, people who are different."

The Nation's modern story is largely one of survival in the face of government antagonism and neglect. In 1863, Col. Kit Carson was sent in to exert government control over the Navajo, loosing a brutal campaign to round up what remained of the tribe and forcibly march them some 300 miles toward isolation and death at Fort Sumner, New Mexico Territory. This event, called the "Long Walk" in Navajo lore, remains an indelible scar on the collective heart of the Diné, a before-and-after dividing line in the Nation's modern history. About 8,000 Navajo were interned at Fort Sumner; four years later, when the tribe returned to Navajoland, some 5,000 remained.

After years of extreme privation, they eventually returned to their adapting ways, becoming very successful pastoralists, weavers, and artists. They were encouraged and helped by the white traders who found worldwide markets for high-quality Navajo crafts and brought modern goods to the remote reservation. The Diné have thrived and reproduced more than any other Native American group, and now, less than 150 years after the Long Walk, they number 298,000 (about 180,000 of whom live on the reservation).

Still, today, despite the presence of large mineral and energy mining operations on their lands, nearly half of all Diné families live below the federal poverty line, and many still live without modern conveniences most of us take for granted. For some this economic reality comes about because they choose to live a traditional Navajo existence; for others it is more about the lack of jobs and opportunity on the reservation, whose economy is often compared to that of a developing nation. Those who leave the reservation often do so to attend college in Flagstaff, Tempe, Tucson, and Albuquerque. Education remains one of the best future hopes for the Nation and a source of pride and advocacy for Navajo leaders. According to a Comprehensive Economic Development Strategy for the Navajo Nation released in 2007, more than 75 percent of female and 69 percent of male Navajo high school students graduate annually. There are some 5,000 Navajo women and 2,340 Navajo men enrolled in college.

CAMERON

If you're heading north on U.S. 89 from Flagstaff to the Nation, the **Cameron Trading Post** (877/221-0690), while usually crowded with folks on their way to the Grand Canyon, makes for a handy first stop for gas and snacks and a look at the beautiful old bridge that crosses Little Colorado Gorge. There's also a restaurant, a hotel, shops, and a gallery to browse.

TUBA CITY AND VICINITY

The Navajo call it *Tonaneesdizi* (Weaving Water or Water Scattered), due to its many life-giving underground natural springs that coax greenery out of the rocky ground and make this small town a kind of dusty oasis. For centuries an agricultural center for the Hopi (who would run from the mesas to nearby Moencopi to tend their corn), in the late 1800s the area was settled by Mormons. They named their town after a Hopi leader called Tuuvi, who had become a Latter-day Saint and invited others to settle here. In 1903 the federal government sent off the settlers because the town was on part of the expanded Navajo Reservation. Today Tuba City, with a population of about 9,000 residents, serves as the administrative and cultural center of the western portion of the reservation. Its location at the junction of Highway 264 and U.S. 160 and proximity to the essential Navajo National Monument (about 65 miles to the northeast) makes it a natural stop for travelers. Nearby you can witness the marks ancient beasts have left on the landscape. Tuba City may not look like much—it isn't, really—but there are a few places to eat and stay, and, of course, trading posts to browse.

Sights

Approaching Tuba City from the west (from U.S. Highway 89 north from Flagstaff to U.S. 160 east), you'll drive through a wondrous stretch of **Painted Desert,** red, dusty-orange, and gray mounds rising above the ruins of washes, like the humped, craggy backs of buried dinosaurs, with not a shrub in sight. There are several natural turnoffs along the road to take pictures of this strange landscape. In downtown Tuba City, you'll find the **Explore Navajo Interactive Museum** (Main St. and Moenave Rd., 928/640-0684, www.explore-navajo.com, 8am-6pm Mon.-Sat., noon-6pm Sun., $9 adults, $6 children 7-12). The museum offers interesting displays on Navajo history and culture, created with the assistance of Navajo scholars and artists, that explain the various stages of a traditional Navajo life. It's expensive, but worth it if you have a particular interest in the tribe's traditions. The museum is next to the Quality Inn and the Tuba City Trading Post.

About five miles west of Tuba City on U.S. 160 look for a sign that says **Dinosaur Tracks.** Turn north onto the dirt road and expect to be greeted by one of several Navajo guides who hang around the area, especially during the busy summer season. You can follow one of the friendly guides onto a great red-rock sandstone slab, where eons ago running raptor dinosaurs and other ancient monsters populated this land, back when it was swampy and fertile. Their birdlike tracks were sealed forever in the stone, and the guides, many of whom learned details about the tracks from Northern Arizona University archaeologists working in the area, will spray water on the dozens of claw-prints to bring them out of the red rock while explaining exactly what you're seeing. Expect to tip $10-20 for the tour (it seems a bit excessive, but think about sitting out on that hot high desert all day). Off to the northeast look for the lush green hillsides of **Moenave,** where several Navajo families live off the natural springs for which this area is known. This is also where Mormon farmers settled in the 1870s, and was for eons prior to that a Hopi farming area.

Shopping

The **Historic Tuba City Trading Post** (Main St. and Moenave Rd., 928/283-5441, 8am-6pm daily) in downtown Tuba City has been selling native crafts and a vast array of staples since the 1870s. It's still open, offering a great assortment of handmade jewelry, rugs, and other popular Indian Country souvenirs and collectibles. **Van's Trading Post** (928/283-5343, 8am-8pm daily) along Highway 160 is like a lesser Wal-Mart, half grocery store and half other merchandise like clothing and furniture. There's a coin laundry next door, and a pawn shop is also operated on-site.

Events

The **To'Nanees'Dizi Diné Fair** (a.k.a. the Western Navajo Fair, 928/283-3284), held once a year in mid-October, is the social event of the season in this corner of the reservation. It's not easy to secure reservations over the three-day fair, which brings hundreds of Navajo families to Tuba City from around the reservation for a rodeo, parade, traditional food and ceremonies, live bands, cutest baby and Miss Western Navajo pageants, and sporting events. It's a fun and illuminating time to be in Tuba City.

NAVAJO AND HOPI COUNTRY

Accommodations and Food

The nicest hotel in Tuba City is the **Quality Inn Navajo Nation** (Main St. and Moenave Rd., 928/283-4545, www.qualityinntubacity.com, $92-127), right next to the Historic Tuba City Trading Post. The two-story hotel has clean rooms decorated in a soft Southwestern style, a gift shop, and wireless Internet. On the same property is the **Hogan Restaurant** (928/283-5260, 6am-10pm daily, $5-15), a diner-style place that serves decent food for breakfast, lunch, and dinner daily, everything from burgers and fries to Navajo tacos and mutton stew, as well as a few Mexican favorites. Next door you can get a cappuccino or a latte and check your email at **Hogan Espresso** Internet cafe (928/283-4545 ext. 309, 7am-9pm Mon.-Thurs., 7am-7pm Fri., 9am-7pm Sat.-Sun., $2-10) The inn, restaurant, and the on-site museum are all operated by the Navajo Nation Tribal Council's **Navajo Nation Hospitality Enterprise,** so while they seem like chains, the money you spend generally stays on the reservation.

The **Greyhills Inn** (Hwy. 160 and Warrier Dr., 928/283-6271, ext. 142, $56) is a hostel-style inn located next to Greyhills High School (just east of the junction off Highway 160), and is operated by students as part of a hotel management training program. For about $56 you can get a clean room with two queen beds in a remodeled dormitory. All rooms have TVs and are nonsmoking. You share bathrooms, a kitchen, and a lounge.

A note about reserving a room: Every room in town is booked weeks before the Western Navajo Fair, and expect to pay extra if you manage to book one.

Elephant Feet

On the north side of Highway 160 at mile marker 345, about 24 miles east of Tuba City near Tonalea, you'll see two sandstone spires, side by side and similarly eroded with wide, red-banded bases tapering up to slender, flat peaks. They really do look like elephant feet; perhaps they are the last remains of some great mammoth turned to stone. Probably not, but

you might pull over and take a few pictures anyway. They are improbable landmarks, yes, but merely two of the hundreds of rock formations you will soon see that will have you wondering whether some design sneaked into the seemingly random, though no less artistic, forces of erosion that formed this strange, thrilling land.

◖ NAVAJO NATIONAL MONUMENT

Though it's within the Navajo Reservation, beautiful **Tsegi Canyon,** an eroded pink-rock landscape carpeted with gray-green piñon pine and juniper forests, was once home to the *Hisatsinom,* ancestors of the Hopi. These Ancestral Puebloans (commonly called Anasazi) are credited with building the three cliffside villages in the canyon—some of the best-preserved and most awe-inspiring ruins in the Southwest. The Hopi, Navajo, Zuni, and Paiute cultures still consider this a sacred place, so only a few short hikes to promontories above the canyon are open to the general public. If you want to explore the area deeper, you can sign up to take guided hikes to two of the ruins with a park ranger.

Only the ruins of the village called Betatakin by the Navajo and Talastima by the Hopi are visible from the canyon rim, tucked in a south-facing natural rock alcove that kept the village cool in the summer and warm in the winter; just below the village is a white-and-green aspen forest. Deeper in is Keet Seel, an older and larger village than Betatakin and one of the largest cliff dwellings in the Southwest. It's called Kawestima by the Hopi. **Inscription House,** or Tsu'ovi, is also perched in the canyon, but has been closed to the public since the late 1960s.

Archaeologists believe that the Kayenta Anasazi (one of three Ancestral Puebloan subgroups, along with the Chaco Anasazi and the Mesa Verde Anasazi) lived in the canyon as early as AD 950, with major building projects getting under way around AD 1250. But by AD 1300, for reasons only guessed at, all of the villages had been abandoned.

Navajo National Monument

Visiting Navajo National Monument

The park is about 50 miles northeast of Tuba City and some 20 miles southwest of Kayenta. Approaching from either way on U.S. 160, take Route 564 nine miles to the park entrance. Unlike most parks and monuments off the reservation, admission here is free. The **Visitor Center** (928/672-2700, www.nps.gov/nava, 9am-5pm daily, free) has a gift shop that sells books, T-shirts, hats, and small water bottles, as well as an interesting museum featuring items used in everyday life by the Puebloans and found in their left-behind villages.

Just outside the visitors center there are three short hiking trails that allow for optimum viewing of the canyon. The one-mile round-trip **Sandal Trail** is paved and leads to an overlook perfect for viewing the village of Betatakin/Talastima sleeping in its alcove. It's steep going back up and should not be treated lightly just because it's short. Take water, especially in the summer. The 0.8-mile round-trip **Aspen Forest Overlook** descends about 300 feet to provide a good look at the forest below the village, but you can't see the ruins; the **Canyon View Trail** leads 0.6 mile round-trip to a nice view of the ruins near the **Canyon View Campground.**

Hiking

If viewing Betatakin from the ridgetop isn't enough for you, you can sign up to take one of two hikes into the canyon to explore the ruins up close. The hike to Betatakin is five miles round-trip and takes three to five hours to complete. A ranger guides you 700 feet down into the canyon and then on to the ruins. It is a mildly strenuous hike, but memorable for its scenery and not its difficulty. Two hikes are available daily in the summer May-September, leaving from the visitor center at 8:20am and 11:30am. During the rest of the year one hike leaves from the center daily at 10am. It's required that you sign up beforehand with the rangers at the visitor center if you want to take the hike.

The trek to **Keet Seel** (which roughly

NAVAJO AND HOPI COUNTRY

translates to "shattered house") is a bit more involved. One of the best preserved ruins in the Southwest, Keet Seel was "discovered," for the Anglo world anyway, by the famous Southwestern ruin-hunter Richard Wetherill while he was chasing a runaway burro.

Reaching the ruin involves a 17-mile round-trip trudge through the canyon bottomlands along a meandering stream—with several small waterfalls—that you have to cross dozens of times. You will get your feet wet early and often on this hike; there's no way to avoid it. Many hikers take along a sturdy pair of hiking sandals and change into them after descending 1,000 feet into the canyon along a rock-hewn trail. When you arrive at the primitive campground within sight of the ruin, a volunteer ranger who lives in a hogan-shaped log cabin nearby will take you on an hour-long tour of the ruin, which you reach by climbing a steep ladder into a cliffside rock alcove. He explains all about the Anasazi who once lived in this hidden canyon, and usually shows off a few astounding items found at the site from the everyday lives of the stone village's builders and residents. This is as close as you're likely to get to the ancients.

If you are some kind of world-champion hiker, you could go in and out in the same day, but a stay overnight at the campground, with the ruins dark and mute just across the wash, is a memorable experience. (There is no water available at the campground, nor are fires allowed; but there is a compost toilet.) You have to attend a short orientation meeting either the morning of your hike at 8am or the afternoon prior at 4pm. It's best to arrive the day before so you can get an early start. Though there's a small hotel near the entrance road to the monument, the best place to stay is at one of the chains in Kayenta, about a half-hour drive from the monument. It's a good idea to purchase and pack all your backpacking supplies before arriving on the reservation, as there aren't any good places to do so nearby.

Reservations and a backcountry permit are required for Keet Seel and are limited to 20 persons per day. Call ahead for best results (928/672-2700). The hike is offered daily in the summer, May-September, but after September 15 it's offered every second weekend of the month only.

Accommodations

The monument has two small campgrounds, free and open year-round, with spaces available first-come, first-served. Spaces have charcoal grills, but open campfires aren't allowed. The closest place to gear up is the rather spare **Black Mesa Trading Post** at the junction of Highway 160 and Route 564. It's a good idea to get supplies in either Tuba City or Kayenta before traveling to the monument for an overnight visit.

The **Anasazi Inn** (Hwy. 160, 928/697-3793, www.anasaziinn.com, $66-109), 10 miles west of Kayenta at the mouth of Tsegi Canyon, is just a short drive from the monument. It's not as nice as some of the chains in Kayenta, but it is clean and basic and is the closest hotel to the Keet Seel trailhead—a good choice for those planning to get an early start.

KAYENTA AND VICINITY

Called *Tohdineeshzhee* (Water Going in Different Directions) by the Diné, Kayenta is the reservation town nearest to Monument Valley and is a good base for a visit to the northern reservation. John Wetherill, who with his brother Richard was one of the first Anglos to explore (and exploit) the Ancestral Puebloan ruins of Mesa Verde and Chaco Canyon, opened a trading post here in 1910. Today it's the only town on the reservation with a U.S.-style township government, home to about 5,000 people, mostly workers in the tourism industry and employees of the Peabody Coal Company, which operates the nearby Kayenta Mine on Black Mesa.

Shopping

The Navajo Arts and Crafts Enterprise has a retail store at Kayenta (928/697-8611, www.go-navajo.com, 9am-5pm Mon.-Fri.) at the junction of Highways 160 and 163. Operated by Navajos, the company sells all kinds of local handmade arts and crafts, curios, rugs, silver jewelry, concha belts, bolo ties, pottery, and more.

Accommodations and Food

Because it is so close to Monument Valley, there are several nice chain hotels in Kayenta, most of them along Highway 160 as you enter town. The **Hampton Inn** (928/697-3170, $100-150) is very comfortable and offers free wireless Internet, a pool, a gift shop, a restaurant, and free continental breakfast. The **Best Western Wetherill Inn** (U.S. 163, 928/697-3231, www.gouldings.com, $59-108) has a pool, wireless Internet, a gift shop, and a complimentary breakfast.

One of the best restaurants on Navajoland, the **Blue Coffee Pot Café** (0.25 mile east of U.S. 160 and 163 junction, 928/697-3396, $4-12) in Kayenta serves outstanding home-style Navajo, American, and Mexican food in a hogan-shaped building just off Hwy. 160. The Navajo taco here is simply fantastic, as are the beef ribs. The staff is friendly, if a bit harried in this busy place, and you might find yourself sitting at a table next to a 90-something Navajo woman dressed like it's the 19th century.

The **Amigo Café** (U.S. 163, 928/697-8448, $5-10) just north of the junction serves Mexican, Navajo, and American food and is popular with the locals. The **Burger King** (928/697-3534) on Highway 160 (near the Hampton Inn) has the usual, with the added feature of a **Navajo Code Talkers** exhibit, which you can view as you chow down on your french fries.

MONUMENT VALLEY NAVAJO TRIBAL PARK

The drive north 22 miles from Kayenta along U.S. Highway 163 to Monument Valley Navajo Tribal Park is almost as dramatically scenic as the destination itself. About a third of the way along the paved route you'll see the aptly named **Owl Rock** to the west, and the hulking, jagged **Agathla Peak** to the east (also known

The Blue Coffee Pot Café in Kayenta is one of the best restaurants on the Navajo Reservation.

© TIM HULL

NAVAJO AND HOPI COUNTRY

as El Capitan), which tribal lore says marks the center of the world.

If there was any question that this is one of the most celebrated and enticing landscapes in the world, listen to the conversations around you as you visit Monument Valley—and you must visit Monument Valley, if only to prove that all the images you've seen are real. It sounds like "It's a Small World" out on this arid, dusty valley. Italian, German, British, and various Eastern European visitors gather at every lookout, looking for something distinctly Western, or American, in the iconic jutting red rocks.

It was the director John Ford who brought this strange, remote place to the world and made it a stand-in for the West's dueling freedom and danger, most memorably in *The Searchers*. Now, to drive around the park is to enter a thousand car commercials, magazine layouts, road films, and Westerns, a landscape that's comfortably, beautifully familiar even if you're seeing it for the first time.

The Navajo have thankfully not overdeveloped this sacred place—some would argue it's underdeveloped for its potential—so the only way to see the park without a Navajo guide is to drive the 17-mile unpaved loop road (6am-8:30pm daily May-Sept., 8am-4:30pm daily Oct.-Apr., $5), which has 11 pullout scenic views of the rock spires and lonely buttes. Upon entering the park you'll get a map of the drive with the names of each "Monument"—names like Wetherill Mesa, John Ford's Point, and The Thumb. If you can, it's worth arriving about an hour or so before sundown to see sunset over the valley—you'll wonder how you got here, and you'll stay until the lights go out. Be warned, though, that with the constant stream of cars driving the dry, dirt road, the air tends to get dusty.

You're allowed to take photographs here, but only of the natural wonders. Remember to ask permission before taking pictures of any Navajos or their private property.

Visitors Center

The park's **Visitor Center** (435/727-5874 or 435/727-5870, www.navajonationparks.org/htm/monumentvalley.htm, 6am-8pm May-Sept., 8am-5pm Oct.-Apr.), perched on a promontory overlooking the valley and the dirt road that snakes through it and around the eroded-sandstone sculptures, is an obvious place to start your visit. There's a small museum with displays on Navajo culture and history, as well as the history of Hollywood's use of this iconic landscape, and a wall or two showing contemporary Navajo art. Staff here can set you up with a guide if you want to go deeper into the valley and learn about the tribe's religious, cultural, and economic ties to the valley. There's a small patio outside the visitors center, which is right next to the View Hotel, restaurant, and trading post-gift shop, where you can sit and contemplate the natural art before you.

The Valley Drive

The best way to see the valley and its monuments up close and on your own time is to head out into the hazy red lands via the 17-mile, self-guided Valley Drive. The route, which is all dirt and a bit rough in some spots, has 11 pull-outs for longer views of some of the more famous mesas, buttes, and spires. At many of these numbered stops, which otherwise have no services, you'll find Navajo families selling jewelry and souvenirs. Plan to spend at least two hours exploring the valley. If dust bothers you, so too will the Valley Drive, but try not to let that stop you: This is one of the most scenic, inspirational, and absolutely essential drives in the Southwest. Take water and food along, and check your tires before you head out. The roughest part of the drive is at the start, going down a steep hill into the valley, but the rest is easy and flat. Don't follow too close behind other cars; you'll be buried in red dust if you do. The tribe does not allow motorcycles or RVs on the Valley Drive.

The road into the valley starts just past the visitors center parking lot and has two lanes until Camel Butte, where it becomes a one-way loop around **Rain God Mesa.** The first stop, just as you enter the valley, provides a classic, much-photographed view of the "mittens,"

West Mitten Butte and **East Mitten Butte,** named so because of the spires that rise from the side of each butte to form what looks like a hand in a mitten. Just a short scoot up the road is **Merrick Butte,** named, according Richard Klinck in his classic history of the valley, *Land of Room Enough and Time Enough,* for James Merrick, a soldier turned prospector who was killed near the butte for trespassing on a Navajo silver mine. The huge mesa opposite Merrick Butte is called **Mitchell Mesa,** for it is said that at its base died Ernest Mitchell, Merrick's partner in trespass and violent death.

The second stop on the drive, **Elephant Butte,** is supposed to look like the titular pachyderm. The third and fourth numbered stops, **The Three Sisters** and **John Ford's Point,** are two of the best. The sisters are side-by-side spires on the edge of Mitchell Mesa, and the point is named for the famous director who revealed this valley to the world through his Westerns. The fifth stop is **Camel Butte,** named for the stone-frozen ungulate that to many it resembles. Just a bit up the road from

the fifth stop, a ramshackle hut and corral provides **horseback tours of the backcountry** (30-minute to 6-hour tours, $45-165, credit cards accepted). You can also stop here and take pictures of the horses, but make sure to ask first and be prepared to pay $5.

The sixth numbered stop on the drive provides a view of the formation called **The Hub,** which looks somewhat like the hub of a wagon wheel, and of huge **Rain God Mesa,** marking the center of the valley. Here the road turns to loop around Rain God Mesa, with pull-offs at **Thunderbird Mesa** and the edge of **Spearhead Mesa.** Here you'll see red sand dunes and, far off in the valley beyond the road, the impossibly delicate spire called the **Totem Pole,** which rises next to a gathering of thicker spires the Navajo call **Yei Bi Chei**—"dancers emerging from a Hogan." The ninth stop is at the far tip of Spearhead Mesa, where there's a short, easy trail out to **Artist Point Overlook.** The view here is spectacular, and it's easy to see how the promontory got its name. Continuing on around the other side of Rain God Mesa, you'll

© TIM HULL

one of the Valley Drive's 11 numbered stops, The Three Sisters

© TIM HULL

Rent a horse and head out on a Monument Valley backcountry tour with a Navajo guide.

see **Cly Butte,** at the base of which is buried "Old Cly," a beloved Navajo medicine man who died in 1934. Cly Butte is the last numbered stop, seen from a short side road up to the penultimate stop, the **North Window Overlook,** which provides a breathtaking view of the valley's northern section. The loop ends at Camel Butte, behind which rises a spire called **The Thumb.** Then it's back to the visitors center along the two-lane route from Camel Butte. You'll pass the same monuments on the way back, obviously, and feel free to stop at them again.

Wildcat Trail

The only hiking you can do in the absence of a hired Navajo guide is along this 3.2-mile loop trail around **West Mitten Butte.** It's an easy, quiet walk along a red-dirt path among gray-green scrub and sagebrush, the spires and buttes looming close, lizards whipping over red rocks. The trail starts 0.4 mile north of the visitors center. It's easy enough for kids, but there's no shade, and it can get windy out there. Take

water with you, and plan on being out for two hours or more.

Tours

As impressive as the buttes and jutting rock castles along the main road around the valley are, they are but a small sampling; many more hulking, crumbling buttes, as well as wondrous arches, delicate spires, petroglyphs, and traditional Navajo homesteads are scattered throughout this vast, remote land, accessible only with a hired guide at your side.

There is no shortage of Navajo guides, and you can easily hire one inside the park at the visitors center. Also, the **Navajo Parks and Recreation Department** has a list of reputable, Navajo-owned guide companies on its website (www.navajonationparks.org). Prices vary slightly between the different companies, but you can generally expect to pay about $65 for a 1.5 hour ride in an open jeep around the main road, to about $115-165 for an all-day backcountry immersion tour. You have to book a 2.5-hour tour or longer (generally around

$75 per person) to go anywhere you can't go on your own.

It's a good idea to call ahead and book in advance for an all-day tour, as these are usually subject to minimums. If you really want to go deep into the traditional Navajo world, guide Roy Black of **Black's Jeep** (928/429-0637, www.blacksmonumentvalleytours.com), which also offers various jeep and horseback tours, will take you on a three-hour horseback ride that includes an overnight stay in a Navajo hogan ($140 per person; call far in advance).

Serious photographers should definitely consider booking a guide, lest they return home with images not considerably different from those snapped by a teenage tourist with a cell phone. Guide Tom J. Phillips of **Keya-Hozhoni Tours** (928/674-1960, www.monumentvalley.com), which also offers regular jeep and horseback tours, charges $30 an hour to show photographers the best shots outside the mainstream; the tour lasts for four or five hours in the morning, and starts before the sun rises, and then picks up again for four or five hours in the later afternoon.

Accommodations and Food

For all its fame, Monument Valley is still a considerably remote place, and there aren't a lot of services out here. Don't come hungry; eat in Kayenta before you head out, or bring your own food with you. That's not to say that there's nothing to eat at all. The **View Restaurant** (435/727-3468, www.monumentvalleyview.com, 7am-2pm and 5pm-8pm daily, $5-25) inside the park has decent Navajo, Mexican, and American food for breakfast, lunch, and dinner. In between meals there are only packaged sandwiches, fruit, and snacks available. At the junction of Highway 163 and the park entrance road, there's a small shopping center where you can get snacks and fry bread, and there are a few gift shops selling local crafts and curios.

When the tribe developed **The View Hotel** (435/727-5555, www.monumentvalleyview.com, $390 and above), the only in-park, noncamping accommodations available at Monument Valley, they probably could have thrown up a few trailers and a kiddy pool and charged $100 per night. The location alone is the attraction; everything else just gets in the way. But they didn't do that, thankfully. The View is instead a complement to the landscape, a low and tucked-away line of rooms near the Mitten Buttes, with patios facing east over the valley where the sun comes alive in the morning. The color of the hotel fairly merges with that of the buttes and monuments and vast red dunes, making it appear inevitable. The rooms are just a few years old, very comfortable and decorated in a generic Southwestern style. It's the view that you're paying for, obviously, and you will pay much, if you can get a reservation. There are no cheap rooms, especially during the spring and summer high season.

CAMPING

Campsites are available at the **Mitten View Campground** ($10 per night up to 6 people, $20 for up to 13, half price Oct.-Apr.) year-round, first-come, first-served. Each site has a table, grill, ramada, and trash can, and there are restrooms and coin-operated showers. No hookups are available, but a dump station is open during the summer. Check in at the visitors center to get a campsite.

GOULDING'S LODGE

This compound just outside the park features a hotel with luxury amenities, a campground, a museum, and a trading post selling Navajo crafts. It keeps the name of the first trader to settle in the valley, Harry Goulding, who opened a trading post here in 1928, exchanging staples for Navajo jewelry and rugs. The story goes that in the late 1930s Goulding himself went to Hollywood to convince Ford to come to Monument Valley to film *Stagecoach*.

Goulding's Lodge (435/727-3231, www.gouldings.com, $175-187 summer, $73-95 winter) has 62 rooms and 8 family-friendly, multi-room suites with cable TV and DVD players. There's an indoor swimming pool and exercise room, and you can even rent one of the many classic Westerns available and watch it in your room. The **Stagecoach Dining Room**

serves American and Navajo food (such as lamb stew, Navajo tacos, and fry bread) for breakfast, lunch, and dinner. The well-equipped **Goulding's Campground** offers tent sites for $22 per night and full hookup sites for $36 per night. A camping cabin with a TV, kitchen, and bathroom is available for $69 per night. There's also a convenience store, gas station, coin laundry, car wash, and an indoor pool at the campground.

Goulding's offers tours of the monument with Navajo guides for $35 (everyone over 8 years old) for 2.5 hours, $45 for 3.5 hours, and $80 per person for an all-day excursion, which includes a cookout lunch.

MEXICAN HAT, UTAH

This very small town on the San Juan River is just 27 miles north of Monument Valley along Highway 163, about 40 minutes from the tribal park. As such, Mexican Hat, named for a precariously balanced rock near town that looks like a sombrero, is an excellent place to base your visit, especially if you are approaching from the north or the east rather than from Phoenix. Another virtue of Mexican Hat is that it lacks the Navajo Reservation's prohibition on alcohol. The tiny conglomerate of buildings stretches out along Highway 163 near the San Juan for a mile or so, and there really isn't much to it. There are, however, a few places to stay and eat, and a few scenic sites to whet your appetite for a tour of the red sandstone monuments just to the south.

The vista at **Goosenecks State Park,** about eight miles or 15 minutes north of Mexican Hat, provides a jaw-dropping, head-scratching look at the San Juan River wrapping around large buttes from 1,000 feet above. The park is nothing more than the vista, and has no services save for bathrooms. Take Highway 163 east out of town, turn left on Utah State Highway 261 and then left on State Highway 316, following the signs. Along the way look for the eponymous rock wearing a sombrero off to the east along Highway 163.

Another place near Mexican Hat worth a visit is the remote **Valley of the Gods,** a kind of

© TIM HULL

This is the rock that gave Mexican Hat its name.

The San Juan River winds through the strange Goosenecks, just a few miles from Mexican Hat.

© TIM HULL

lesser Monument Valley. You can drive through the valley and view its buttes and mesas along a 17-mile dirt road, which is a bit rough but safe for most passenger cars. There are no services out here so bring your own water and food and make sure you have enough gas. There is a gas station in Mexican Hat along Highway 163. From Mexican Hat take Highway 163 east of town eight miles to Valley of the Gods Road and turn left, then it's another five miles from there.

Accommodations and Food

The few accommodations in Mexican Hat are generally less expensive than the chain hotels in Kayenta, and are much less expensive than the View Hotel in Monument Valley. Moreover, a few restaurants here serve alcohol, which is prohibited on the reservation.

The **San Juan Inn and Trading Post** (Hwy. 163 and the San Juan River, 800/447-2022, www.sanjuaninn.com, summer $88-104, winter $65-78) is right on the banks of the beautiful San Juan River and next to the bridge that spans it, offering basic rooms, comfortable and clean, with air conditioning, TV, and spotty Wi-Fi. Perhaps the best thing about this place, which is the best place to stay and eat in Mexican Hat, is the **Old Bridge Bar & Grill** (7am-9pm daily, $5-20). This rustic little place in middle of nowhere serves a big, filling breakfast, tasty Mexican food and Navajo tacos, plus burgers and all the other grill-style mainstays. It also has a full bar and pool tables, and strikes one as a place where a lot of backcountry adventurers hang out when they are not running rivers or scaling mesas. The decidedly unique **Mexican Hat Lodge** (Hwy. 163 across from the Shell Station, 435/683-2222, $84-175) has basic rooms with TVs and phones, with a fun, laid-back and friendly vibe that is more akin to a bed-and-breakfast than a regular motel. The restaurant here is called **The Swinging Steak** ($13-40), and it has a pleasant patio where you can watch your steak being cooked over a swinging grill. They

The San Juan Inn and Trading Post is the best place to stay in Mexican Hat.

serve wine and beer, but it's the low-alcohol Utah variety.

Four Corners Monument

About 70 miles east on Highway 160 from Kayenta is the **Four Corners Monument** (928/871-6647, 8am-5pm daily Sept.-May, 7am-8pm daily June-Aug., $3), the only place in the United States where, if you do a little bit of Twister-style contorting, you can exist briefly in four states at once—Arizona, Colorado, New Mexico, and Utah. You're not likely to stay long after you take the obligatory picture. In the summer months there are usually Navajos and others set up selling crafts.

CHINLE AND VICINITY

Like most town names on the arid Navajo Reservation, Ch'inlih refers to moisture, in this case "Water Flowing." There isn't much here for the tourist save a few chain hotels and the gateway to Canyon de Chelly. Chinle has been a center for canyon visitors since the early 20th century, when the famous trader Lorenzo

Hubbell operated a stagecoach from the train stop at Gallup to bring tourists to see the ancient cliff dwellings and the other wonders of the canyon.

Accommodations and Food

Chinle is the best place to base a multi-day visit to Canyon de Chelly National Monument. The town's not much to look at, but it does have two comfortable, long-established chain hotels, both with good restaurants, where most overnight visitors stay.

The **Best Western Canyon de Chelly** (928/674-5875, www.canyondechelly.com, $66-109), about four miles from the canyon, has clean and comfortable rooms with cable television and Wi-Fi, as well as a good restaurant serving American, Navajo, and Mexican dishes for breakfast lunch, and dinner. The hotel also has heated indoor pool, and staff here can help you arrange a tour of Canyon de Chelly.

The **Holiday Inn Canyon de Chelly** (928/674-5000, www.holiday-inn.com,

$100-150 d) has nice, comfortable rooms and a restaurant that serves excellent American, Navajo, and Mexican dishes for breakfast, lunch, and dinner. There's an outdoor pool here and pleasant courtyard, as well a trading post-gift shop.

Near the visitor center on Canyon de Chelly National Monument is the **Thunderbird Lodge** (3.5 miles east of U.S. 191 on Indian Route 7, 928/674-5841, $110-163 summer, $63-94 winter) offers Southwestern-style rooms with Navajo flourishes, a cafeteria-style restaurant, Internet, and tours of the canyon with Navajo guides. Also on the monument is the **Cottonwood Campground,** a free, first-come, first-served campground with running water and flush toilets in the summer only.

◖ CANYON DE CHELLY NATIONAL MONUMENT

The most visually impressive wind- and water-worn notch in the Colorado Plateau save for the one they call Grand, Canyon de Chelly (pronounced "de Shay"; the name is a Spanish approximation of the Navajo word for canyon, *tsegi*), is a labyrinth of eroded sandstone mesas, buttes, and spires, washed in pink and red and varnished with black and purple. The canyon's fertile bottomlands and safe, hidden alcoves, seemingly designed beforehand to host stone cliff dwellings, have drawn people here for some 4,000 years. The greatest among the Southwest's ancients, the Anasazi, built several hanging villages against the red-rock cliffs, the remains of which are still slowly crumbling in their shady alcoves.

There are about 40 Navajo families who call the canyon and its rimlands home. You'll pass some of their homesites and hogans as you drive the two scenic roads along the rim. There are also many free-roaming horses who like to munch on the grasses and weeds that grow along the side of the road; they will generally ignore you until you get out of your car for a photo, when they will promptly turn and trot away. The federal monument comprises about 84,000 acres of the canyon; however, like the other federal parks on the reservation, the

© TIM HULL

Canyon de Chelly National Monument

Navajos' interests trump all others here. Nearly all of the canyon is off limits without a hired Navajo guide.

Visitors Center

The **visitors center** (928/674-5500, www.nps. gov/cach, 8am-5pm daily, free) is a good place to start your visit. Here you can find out about guided tours (a ranger will give you a long list if you ask), learn about the history and science of the canyon, and browse a small bookstore stocked well with volumes on the Southwest and the Colorado Plateau. A map of the park's scenic drives is available here for free.

White House Ruin Trail

The short but steep hike (2.5 miles round-trip) down a skinny trail hewn out of petrified pink sand dunes to the **White House Ruin** is the only route to the sandy, shady canyon bottomlands that you can take without a guide, and it is one of the highlights of a visit to Indian Country. The trail offers a rare chance to see Anasazi ruins up close and on your own. Once on the canyon bottom, you pass a traditional Navajo hogan and farm, and the canyon walls, streaked with purple, black, and orange, rise hundreds of feet. Hawks and ravens circle overhead, black and brown dots high in the bright blue sky. Cavelike hideouts built by natural forces in sandstone alcoves call for you to rest and sit back in their cool shade. Cottonwoods, willows, and peach trees grow in the bottomlands, while piñon pine, juniper, scrub oak, cholla, and prickly pear cling to the sides of the precipitous trail, a dusty-green set against the reddish-pink of the de Chelly sandstone. Although you can also take two scenic drives to see all the canyon's wonders, there is no substitute for hiking in. Pick up the trailhead at the **White House Overlook,** the fourth signed stop along the South Rim Drive, about six miles from the visitors center. If you're on the hunt for Navajo arts, take some cash with you on the hike; there are often artists sitting beneath the shady trees near the White House Ruin, offering their creations for sale.

Scenic Drives

Two paved scenic rimside drives offer the most comprehensive look at Canyon de Chelly without hiring a guide. The visitors center has a free map of the easy drives, and both can be done in a regular car. The 37-mile round-trip **South Rim Drive** will take you to the **Spider Rock Overlook,** where you can see the eponymous 800-foot red-rock spire, a must-see of any visit to the canyon. The south drive has seven overlooks, while the 34-mile round-trip **North Rim Drive** has three: **Antelope House Ruin, Mummy Cave Overlook,** and **Massacre Cave Overlook,** each with a view of ruins. Many of the lookouts are at the end of a short walk.

Tours

You need a Navajo guide with you to travel deep into the canyon, and there are many available for hire throughout the year. Expect to pay about $50-60 per hour for one to three people for a private jeep tour along the canyon bottom to some of the out-of-the-way ruins, caves, and rock-art sites. **Canyon de Chelly (Unimoq)**

Spider Rock

Tours (Chinle, 928/674-5433 or 928/349-1600, $40-66 per person) offers a three-hour group tour in a big four-by-four (you ride with about 10 other passengers in the open bed) for about $60 per adult that will take you from Antelope Ruin to White House Ruin. **Antelope House Tours** (Chinle, 928/674-5231, www.canyon-dechelly.net) offers jeep tours of all the ruins, and hiking tours for about $30-90 depending on the size of your group, with guides versed in the lore and culture of the Navajo and the other peoples that lived in this spectacular place before them. It's a good idea to call ahead for reservations.

Tasalie and Diné College

At the end of the scenic drive along the Canyon de Chelly's north rim (Indian Rte. 64), past the last established lookout, you'll come to Diné College, a Navajo-run junior college that has been educating tribal members and preserving tribal traditions since 1968. The circular, hogan-shaped campus is designed to reflect traditional Navajo philosophy, which the **Ned Hatathli Museum and Gallery** (Diné College Tasalie campus, 1 Circle Dr., Indian Rte. 12, 928/724-6600, 8am-5pm Mon.-Fri., closed for the lunch hour, free)—itself housed in a six-story glass hogan—interprets, as well as showing off historic tribal artifacts and contemporary Navajo arts and crafts.

HUBBELL TRADING POST NATIONAL HISTORIC SITE

When you walk into the rustic building in **Ganado** that has housed the **Hubbell Trading Post** (928/755-3475, www.nps.gov/hutr, 8am-6pm in summer, 8am-5pm in winter, $2 adults over 16 for Hubbell Home Tour) since 1876, you expect to enter a museum or a typical visitors center. Instead, you enter the "bull pen," a working trading post that looks much like it did 100 years ago, still selling jewelry, rugs, and staples, still an important commercial spot to the Diné. The area has a fascinating history, and this is the best place to learn about the impact white traders—J. L. Hubbell and his family the most famous and beloved among

the Hubbell Trading Post

them—had on Navajo lifeways and the reservation economy. You can tour the homestead with a ranger or with a self-guided tour book, and peek into the Hubbell Home, laden with Navajo rugs, old books, and original paintings by the famous artist E. A. Burbank. There's also a small museum and bookstore operated by the National Park Service.

WINDOW ROCK

The capital of the Navajo Nation is a lot like the other population centers on the Navajo Reservation: small, utilitarian, and surrounded by scenery that dwarfs the man-made buildings. The town of about 4,000 persons is right on the Arizona-New Mexico border and just 27 miles northwest of Gallup, New Mexico, a fairly large city (with about 25,000 persons) by the standards of this remote, rural corner of the world. At nearly 8,000 feet, Window Rock has a cooler climate than the lower western reservation, and in winter the ponderosa pine and piñon-juniper forests that decorate the artfully eroded sandstone buttes and spires

© TIM HULL

Navajo Code Talker Memorial at the Window Rock Navajo Tribal Park, by sculptor Oreland Joe

around the town are often dusted with a thin layer of snow.

Sure, it's a long drive to get here from Phoenix (300 miles) or Tucson (355 miles) or the Grand Canyon (234 miles), but it is a scenic drive, and one that must be undertaken by anyone truly interested in what the Navajo Nation is all about. It has the best museum on the reservation in the Navajo Nation Museum, and is a fun stop for families with small kids for its free zoo featuring the reservation's most famous and prevalent creatures.

Sights

The famous **Window Rock** that gives the town its name—a 200-foot-high red sandstone monument with an unlikely 47-foot-diameter wind- and water-chipped hole in it (called *Tseghahodzani* by the Navajo, roughly translating to "the rock with the hole in it")—is at the **Window Rock Navajo Tribal Park,** just a short drive north on Indian Route 12 from its intersection with State Highway 264. It stares down like an oracle. You can't climb it or anything,

but it is a ready-made photograph: pink-red and towering against the usually bright blue sky, with gnarled, deep-green junipers and piñons and little yellow wildflowers stretched out in front of it. There's also an evocative statue here of a Navajo soldier kneeling with a radio to his ear and a look of serious intensity on his face. It is the centerpiece of a **memorial to the Navajo Code Talkers** of World War II and is instantly recognizable as a depiction of those celebrated men.

Window Rock has been the center of the Navajo Nation government since the 1930s, when the Civilian Conservation Corps built the rough-hewn but stylish native-stone and pinewood **Navajo Nation Council Chambers** and its surrounding buildings, which sit in the shadow of the one-eyed red rock and are used intermittently when the council is in session.

About three miles west of Window Rock in St. Michaels (a small town along Hwy. 264), you'll see the **St. Michael's Mission,** a Franciscan mission established in 1896 by St. Katherine Drexel. The **St. Michael's**

the Navajo Nation Museum

Historical Museum (3 mi. west of Window Rock on Hwy. 264, 928/871-4171, 8am-5pm Mon.-Fri. Memorial Day-Labor Day) on the mission grounds has a small, interesting museum about Navajo and Catholic interactions and the history of the mission.

NAVAJO NATION MUSEUM

The tribal members could charge $10 per person or more for a look around the sleek and informative **Navajo Nation Museum** (Hwy. 264 and Loop Rd., 928/871-7941, www.navajonationmuseum.org, 10am-5pm Mon.-Sat., free), but instead they let everybody in for free. That's just the first of many surprises here. Another is that there is plenty of space dedicated to contemporary reservation life—a subject that many tourists tend to overlook in favor of the romantic, story-filled past. The museum's art gallery hosts revolving shows featuring Navajo artists and photographers, and throughout the museum there are examples of silverwork and weaving by many living artists. The museum reaches into the past to tell the story of the harrowing Long Walk and the tribe's near fatal exile at Fort Sumner in the 1860s, showing actual artifacts and ephemera related to the events that help make the traumas suffered seem recent, as they still are from the Navajo perspective. There is also a fascinating display that explains the traditional Navajo way of life. This is simply the best museum on the reservation, and one that should be visited by anyone with an interest in the Navajo Nation. And even if you have no interest before entering, it's likely that you will upon exiting. Just outside the museum's front entrance, there's a traditional hogan that you are allowed to enter and examine up close; it's surprising how cool it is inside, even at the height of summer.

NAVAJO NATION ZOOLOGICAL AND BOTANICAL PARK

Tall, fat cylinders of beige-colored sandstone stand just to the north of the museum. They are called, for reasons that will be obvious to anyone who sees them, **The Haystacks.** These photo-worthy monoliths watch over a tiny zoo run by the tribe. The **Navajo Nation Zoological and Botanical Park** (Hwy. 264 and Loop Rd., 928/871-6574, www.navajozoo.org, 10am-5pm Mon.-Sat., free) houses examples of many of the animals that share these wild, open lands with the Navajos, most of which occupy a sacred place in the traditional Navajo belief system. A short, easy trail leads around a small open area overlooked by the Haystacks, past fenced-in habitats with raccoons, bobcats, a cougar, a black bear, prairie dogs, and other common Colorado Plateau wildlife. Along the trail there are interpretive signs naming the animals and various native plants, and explaining their presence and use in traditional Navajo life. You really get up close to the often playful animals, and the kids will love it here. The zoo is just a short walk across from the entrance to the museum.

Events

The population of Window Rock swells every year during the first week of September as the **Navajo Nation Fair** (www.navajonationfair.com, $5) brings Navajos and others to one of largest Native American cultural fairs anywhere. The weeklong event features a rodeo, horticulture contests, pageants for babies, teens, and Miss Navajo, a parade, a midway and carnival, native foods and arts and crafts, drumming and dancing, and myriad other events. Don't count on getting a hotel room in town, or even in nearby Gallup, New Mexico, unless you call far ahead of the fair.

Shopping

The headquarters of the **Navajo Arts and Crafts Enterprises** (928/871-4090, 9am-5pm Mon.-Fri.) and a well-stocked outlet are located east of the junction of Highway 264 and Indian Route 12, just across from the Quality Inn, as is the **Chi Hoo Tso Indian Market**

(928/871-5443), where there's a flea market on the weekends.

Accommodations and Food

The **Quality Inn Navajo Nation Capital** (48 W. Hwy. 264, 928/871-4108, $64-83) offers wireless Internet and a full breakfast. It has comfortable, clean rooms decorated in a generic Southwestern style, and the staff is very friendly and helpful. This is definitely the best place to stay in town. The **Diné Restaurant** inside the Quality Inn (928/871-4108, $10-14) serves American and Navajo food for breakfast, lunch, and dinner and is a popular spot with the locals. Guests of the inn may partake in the restaurant's breakfast buffet at no additional cost, but the price is its most attractive feature.

Some visitors choose to stay in nearby Gallup, New Mexico, about 27 miles to the southeast, which, as an I-40 stop, has loads of hotels and restaurants.

INFORMATION AND SERVICES
Tourist Information

Contact the **Navajo Tourism Department** (P.O. Box 663, Window Rock, AZ 86515, 928/810-8501, www.discovernavajo.com) for advice and information about traveling in this region.

Hospitals

The **Navajo Area Indian Health Service** (Hwy. 264 & St. Michael Rd., St. Michael, 928/871-4811, www.ihs.gov/Navajo/index.cfm) operates six hospitals on the vast Navajo reservation. In Arizona, the **Fort Defiance Indian Hospital** (928/729-8000), eight miles north of Window Rock on the eastern reservation, has a Level 2, 24-hour emergency room; on the western reservation, the **Kayenta Health Center** (928/697-4000), in Kayenta, has the same.

Hopi

When you visit Hopi, you step out of normal time into a kind of sacred time in which the *Hisatsinom* still speak to their modern-day descendants, the "People of Peace," and the lessons and stories of the ancients still guide and rule life in the 21st century, the dawning of which has mostly been ignored around Hopi.

The Hopi are a very religious, conservative people on the whole, and what many of them want, it seems, is to be left alone to mark their sacred time and grow their small plots of corn in their washes and valleys—which is a Hopi religious rite in itself. Signs are everywhere on Hopi pleading with visitors to show respect for the present in this land that seems so rooted in the past. Go to Hopi if you want to have a quiet, spiritual experience touring crumbling villages occupied for centuries, interacting with the friendly and creative people whose direct and well-remembered ancestors built and lived in most of the spectacular Pueblo ruins around Indian Country, and searching for artistic treasures built on patterns and narratives laid down before time began.

The Hopis do not allow any photography, sketching, or recording on Hopi land, and they don't like it when you enter their villages without first asking a village leader or at least someone at a craft store or gallery. Talk to the folks at the **Hopi Cultural Center** on Second Mesa or the **Moenkopi Legacy Inn & Suites** in Moenkopi if you have any questions about the rules. Be respectful, and remember, as it is with the Navajos, the Hopi people are living their lives, not participating in an anthropological experiment. Don't bring any drugs or alcohol onto the reservation, and don't take any pottery shards off of it.

MOENKOPI

Since opening the **Moenkopi Legacy Inn & Suites** (junction of Hwy. 160 and Hwy. 264, Tuba City, 928/283-4500, www.experiencehopi.com) a few years ago, the Upper Village

of Moenkopi, at the junction of Highway 160 and Highway 264 near Tuba City, has become the gateway to visiting Hopi. The all-Hopi staff at this gorgeous hotel and visitors center can help you book a guide to take you on an unforgettable tour of the Hopi mesas. It makes sense, now that the Moenkopi Legacy Inn is open, to start any tour of Hopi from the west and head east along Highway 264, which will take you to each of the mesas.

HOPI MESAS

Many Hopis live on three remote mesas on the southern tip of **Black Mesa,** a separate reservation carved out of the southwest portion of the Navajo Nation. There are 10 villages on the mesas, which are numbered east to west.

You can drive yourself up and over the mesas, and enter many of the villages, but this is not an ideal, or even a very interesting, way to visit Hopi. Without a bit of historical and cultural context, many of the mesa villages simply look like rundown rural outposts. But with a guide, a whole ancient, hidden world that exists beneath the rather hardscrabble surface opens up, and the mesas become sacred, mysterious ground.

About 15 miles from Moenkopi along Highway 264, look for milepost 336 and a dirt road that leads to **Coal Mine Canyon,** a spectacular gorge with magnificently eroded, multicolored hoodoos that's worth a few hundred snapshots from a sitting area near the rim.

Tours

It's essential to call ahead to book a tour. The Hopi religious calendar is rather full, and often one village or another will close to outsiders for days at a time. Weather on the remote mesas can also cancel tours. The best place to book a tour is through the **Moenkopi Legacy Inn & Suites** (junction of Hwy. 160 and Hwy. 264, Tuba City, 928/283-4500, www.experiencehopi.com) or the **Hopi Cultural Center**

© TIM HULL

Moenkopi Legacy Inn & Suites

(928/734-2401, www.hopiculturalcenter. com, 8am-5pm daily) on Second Mesa. The Moenkopi Legacy Inn's website, www.experiencehopi.com, has a comprehensive list of approved guides and their prices.

Left-Handed Hunter Tour Company (Second Mesa, 928/734-2567, $120-195 per person for 4-8 hours) offers exceedingly informative and memorable tours of the Taawaki Petroglyph Site, Moenkopi, Old Oraibi, Hotevilla, Bacavi, Kykotsmovi, Sipaulovi, and Musangnuvi, as well as visits with local artists. The **Ancient Pathways Tours** (Second Mesa, 928/797-8145, $15-165, 1-6 hours) offers tours of Old Oraibi and the Dewa Park petroglyph site, from one hour to all day. The Village of Sipaulovi on Second Mesa offers **Hopi Sipaulovi Tours** (Second Mesa, 928/737-5426, www.sipaulovihopiinformationcenter. org); a one-hour walking tour costs $15 per person.

Third Mesa

The first of the mesa villages along Highway 264, and the first you reach on the road from Moenkopi, are **Hotevilla, Bacavi,** and **Kykotsmovi.** All are a mix of mostly ramshackle homes next to ancient, stacked-rock half-ruins hundreds of years old. The best place to stop on Third Mesa is **Oraibi,** also called Old Oraibi, which sits on what is considered to be the oldest inhabited ground in North America. Twenty-four families still live in the village, which sits at the edge of the mesa and looks out over the hazy flatland sea below. There's no electricity, no running water. "Our elders want no webbing above us and nothing buried in the ground," a Hopi woman who had been born and raised in the village explained. Some villagers have installed solar panels on the roofs of their small homes—each one built next to or on top of the ruin of an older one—to bring a little modern comfort. There are several kivas in the village that look exactly like those seen in the *Hisatsinom* ruins, with their rough ladders sticking out of their trap-door entrances, except these are still in use. A walk around this village, in which people have made lives since at least AD 1100, is a strangely humbling experience. You may come away from it wondering why most of us think we need so much stuff to live that elusive good life. Stop in at **Hamana So-o's Arts and Crafts** (928/206-6392) at the entrance to the village before walking around. The friendly couple there will tell you about the history of the village and give you a few rules of etiquette.

Second Mesa

The **Hopi Cultural Center** (928/734-2401, www.hopiculturalcenter.com, 8am-5pm daily) on Second Mesa has a small museum ($3) featuring blown-up photographs of Hopi taken in the 19th and early 20th centuries, and displays on Hopi culture as well as many artifacts from around the mesas. It provides one of the few stops along the road through Hopi that can be enjoyed without a guide. The museum is an essential stop for anyone interested in Hopi culture. The center also has a restaurant serving traditional Hopi dishes, a hotel, and the **Hopi Arts and Crafts Co-Op Guild** (928/734-2463), a good place to shop for Hopi arts. The village of **Shongopavi** on Second Mesa is believed to have been the first Hopi village, and the village of **Sipaulovi** on Second Mesa offers walking tours and other information about visiting Hopi.

First Mesa

Polacca, just below First Mesa, is one of the younger villages on Hopi, founded in 1890. There are many Hopi and Tewa potters living in Polacca. If you're interested in buying direct from the artists, keep a look out for handmade signs outside of homes. Next you'll come to **Hano,** founded in 1680 after the Pueblo Revolt by Tewas from New Mexico. The Hopi said the fleeing Tewas could stay in exchange for their vigilance in keeping enemies and attackers off the mesa trails. Hano is the home of the famous Tewa potter **Nampeyo;** in the early 1900s, Fred Harvey convinced Nampeyo to move to the Grand Canyon to demonstrate pottery making for tourists, living in a kind of live diorama at the famous Mary Colter-designed

"Hopi House." The area is still a center of pottery making, and artists directly related to Nampeyo—who is credited, even as a Tewa, with beginning a renaissance in Hopi pottery and thus creating a major modern art form and economy—still reside and work here, selling pottery out of their homes.

Just above Hano is **Sichomovi,** founded in 1750 by citizens of **Walpi.** This village has running water and electricity, unlike Walpi, a traditional village at the very edge of the mesa founded in the 1600s when villagers moved up the mesa from their village below to escape the predations of their neighbors.

Walpi Guided Walking Tour

If you have time for just one tour, make it of Walpi, a traditional Hopi village where the old ways live on. You will also meet several Hopi artists on the tour of Walpi, sitting on the steps in front of their rock-carved homes, carving katchina dolls from Cottonwood root. The people here are so friendly—everybody says hello and smiles, welcoming and inviting you into their homes to show you their art. If you are at all interested in Hopi art, this is the place to buy it. Not only will the price be significantly less than at a museum store or trading post, but you'll also get to meet the artist—and maybe even watch the final stages of creation. Take cash with you. Your Hopi tour guide will take you on a slow walk around the clifftop village, a time warp on the edge of the world. You'll learn all about the traditions and history, both temporal and spiritual, of this ancient place. It's a fascinating and memorable experience.

You should book a tour a day in advance if you can, and don't be surprised if the village is closed due to weather or for religious reasons. Tours run through **First Mesa Consolidated Village Office** (928/737-2670, 9am-3pm, last tour at 2pm daily in winter, in 8am-4:30pm daily in summer, $20 adults, $10 children under 18), about 71 miles from Moenkopi in Polacca at the base of First Mesa, where you must stop and check in before heading up to Walpi. Take Highway 264 west to mile marker

390.8, turn north at the stop sign and go a quarter of a mile to the office, which is next to the post office.

Shopping

The Hopis are world renowned for their pottery, baskets, overlay jewelry, and kachina dolls. There are dozens of artists on the Hopi Reservation making and selling collectible, museum-quality crafts for much, much less than you are likely to pay in a museum store or trading post. Look for homemade signs advertising crafts for sale at homes in most villages, and take lots of cash with you.

In recent years many Hopi artists have banded together to form the **Hopi Arts Trail,** a marketing campaign that has made it easier than ever to meet and buy art from Hopi artists living on and below the mesas. A free pamphlet-guide to the trail is available online at www.hopiartstrail.com or at the Moenkopi Inn. The guide features eight galleries spread out around Hopi in 12 villages along Highway 264, and lists the name, phone number, and specialty of 18 different Hopi artists. An artist will typically invite you into his or her home, where you can view the work and learn about the process.

Another great way to meet artists on Hopi is by taking the **Walpi Guided Walking Tour** on First Mesa. The **Hopi Arts and Crafts Co-Op Guild** (928/734-2463) and the Hopi Cultural Center on Second Mesa also have art for sale.

PRACTICALITIES

There are few services on Hopi, but it isn't far from any of the Navajo towns, and it's close to the high-desert towns as well.

The **Moenkopi Legacy Inn & Suites** (junction of Hwy. 160 and Hwy. 264, Tuba City, 928/283-4500, www.experiencehopi.com, $141-196 summer, $97-141 winter) set a new standard for accommodations on Hopi when it opened a few years ago. It has luxury rooms with big, comfortable beds, tastefully decorated with photographs of Hopi and with a patio door that opens to a heated, saltwater pool and spa. There is a small eating area where a continental breakfast is served in the morning, or there's a café at the gas station across the street (also operated by the Hopi) that serves diner-style fare and some Hopi dishes. Each room has free wireless and a flat-screen TV, and there are some excellent examples of Hopi arts throughout the beautiful lobby. This is the best hotel in Indian Country for the price.

The **Hopi Cultural Center on Second Mesa** is a hotel ($95-100 Mar.-Oct., slightly cheaper in winter) and restaurant (6am-9pm daily in summer, 7am-8pm in winter) that serves American and Hopi food for breakfast, lunch, and dinner. The **Hotevilla Village Co-Op Store** on Third Mesa (928/734-2350) has a convenience store with a gas station, and **The Kykotsmovi Village Store** on Third Mesa (928/734-2456) has a deli and a gas station.

The High Desert

HOLBROOK AND VICINITY

Long ago, by most accounts, Holbrook was a rough and violent cowboy town; then it profited, like everything else in this region, from the railroad and Route 66, back when tourists would necessarily stay a while. These days it's not much more than a convenient gateway and stopover for those visiting the nearby Petrified Forest National Park and Indian Country, offering several chain hotels and mostly fast food.

For those interested in the history of both the old and the modern West, a trip to the **Navajo County Historical Society's Museum** (100 E. Arizona St., 928/524-6558 or 800/524-2459, 8am-4pm, free) in the 1880s Navajo County Court House is a must. Donations are encouraged and rewarded with free chips of petrified wood. It's a strange, crowded place without a lot of context—you feel like you're wandering around an abandoned government building after the population has died out. Sitting in the old jail, used until the 1970s and still decorated with the graffiti and sketches of its former inmates, is an eerie, almost thrilling experience.

Accommodations and Food

American popular architecture like that employed at the **Wigwam Motel** (811 W. Hopi Dr., Holbrook, 928/524-3048, www.galerie-kokopelli.com/wigwam, $56-62) had its postwar heyday along Route 66, and, like the route itself, it is mostly gone from the landscape these days in favor of cookie-cutter chains. But the kitschy tradition still has a hold on these dry high-desert plains at the Wigwam Hotel in Holbrook, one of the last of many similarly designed motor courts that once lined the Mother Road. It's clean and comfortable and has all the updated amenities, but a stay here is mostly about its retro appeal. It should not be missed by Route 66 enthusiasts, road-trip scholars, chroniclers of fading Americana, and the like.

There are a number of chain hotels off I-40 in and around Holbrook, most of them located on Navajo Boulevard, the town's main drag, including a comfortable **Holiday Inn Express** (1308 E. Navajo Blvd., 928/524-1466, $99-119) with a small indoor pool, wireless Internet, and continental breakfast.

█ PETRIFIED FOREST NATIONAL PARK

What once was a swampy forest frequented by ancient oversized reptiles is now a blasted scrubland strewn with multicolored, quartz-wrapped logs some 225 million years old, each one possessing a smooth, multicolored splotch or swirl seemingly unique from the rest. You can walk among the logs on several easy, paved trails and view a small ruin and petroglyph-covered rocks (best with binoculars, but there are viewing scopes provided). Then, driving through the pastel-hued badlands of the **Painted Desert,** which, seen from a promontory along the park's 28-mile scenic drive, will take your breath away, stop at the **Painted Desert Inn Museum.** The historical interest in this Pueblo Revival-style structure is

more modern than primordial. Redesigned by Mary Colter, the great genius of Southwestern style and elegance, the inn was a restaurant and store operated by the Fred Harvey Company just after World War II, and before that it was a rustic, out-of-the-way hotel and taproom built from petrified wood. There's a gift shop and bookstore at the inn now, and you can walk through it and gaze at the evocative, mysterious murals, full of Hopi mythology and symbolism, painted by Fred Kabotie, the great Hopi artist whom Colter commissioned to decorate the inn's walls. The park's proximity both to a major railroad stop at Winslow and Route 66 have made it a popular Southwestern tourist attraction since the late 19th century, and the lore and style of that golden age of tourism pervades the park with a pleasant nostalgia, adding an extra, unexpected dimension to the overwhelming age all around you.

Visiting the Park

Approaching the **Petrified Forest National Park** (928/524-6228, www.nps.gov/pefo, 7am-6pm in summer until Oct. 27, then 8am-5pm daily, $10 per vehicle for 7 days) from the west, take I-40 to U.S. Highway 180 from Holbrook to the south entrance, past numerous shops featuring all things petrified. A paved road leads 28 miles north through the park, past several pull-over points of interest, back to I-40. From the east take I-40 Exit 311 to the north entrance, then head south through the park.

There are two **visitors centers,** one at the south entrance and one at the north, both showing a short movie about the park and passing out free maps of all the stops. At the south entrance there's a █ **Fred Harvey Company** restaurant that serves delicious fried chicken, Navajo tacos, and other road-food favorites in a cool Route 66 retro dining room.

WINSLOW AND VICINITY

Stop at this small, ex-Route 66, ex-railroad town if you happen to be in the area. Much of its historic downtown remains intact, if not too busy, and there are a few off-track treasures to be found if you have time to walk

© RYAN DEBERARDINIS/123RF.COM

Petrified Forest National Park

around. The town seems committed to celebrating the fact that its name appeared in the song "Take It Easy," an Eagles hit co-penned by Jackson Browne. There are reminders in nearly every business, and there's even **Standin' on the Corner Park** along the town's main street, featuring a statue of a man doing just that. The primary reason to stop in Winslow is to see **La Posada,** Southwestern architect Mary Colter's masterpiece and a place where Fred Harvey-style outback elegance is kept alive.

Sights

The **Old Trails Museum** (212 Kinsley Ave., 928/289 5861, www.oldtrailsmuseum.org, 10am-4pm Tues.-Sat., free) in downtown Winslow is a treasure trove of strange and thrilling artifacts, photographs, and stories about life in the high desert, with a special emphasis on the region's Route 66 past and its connection with the stylish railroad era of the Fred Harvey Company. The museum also has a fine collection of Navajo arts and crafts, and

all kinds of weird and forgotten items that take on new historical meaning and emotional color simply by virtue of being old and saved. It's a small museum, but definitely worth a stop for anyone interested in Route 66, the railroad, and Fred Harvey, and one that should be paired with a look around the restored Harvey House, **La Posada.**

Accommodations

There are several chain hotels and fast-food places off the interstate at Winslow for those in a hurry.

People travel to this lonely, ramshackle high-desert town just to stay at (**La Posada** (303 E. 2nd St., Winslow, 928/289-4366, www.laposada.org, $119-169) and eat at the **Turquoise Room,** so it's essential to call ahead for a reservation. Built in 1929 and obsessively restored by its current owners, the hacienda-style hotel is truly an Arizona treasure. The rooms all have that rare touch of retro style, and each is named for some famous person who visited the hotel back in the golden

La Posada:
The Last of the Fred Harvey Railroad Hotels

© TIM HULL

Now owned by Allen Affeldt and his wife, the brilliant painter Tina Mion (whose paintings fill the arched hallways of the hotel), **La Posada** (303 E. 2nd St., Winslow, 928/289-4366, www.laposada.org, $119-169) has been beautifully restored and is a reminder of the days when traveling to Indian Country was a chic journey taken by the rich and famous and anybody else who could afford it.

This was largely the result of the genius of Fred Harvey. He and his "Harvey Girls"—well-trained professional young women imported to the West to serve train passengers at Harvey's restaurants along the Santa Fe Railroad's right-of-way—made a trip to this barren, underdeveloped high desert, an experience quite beyond merely comfortable. The Harvey Company lunch counters and hotel restaurants offered fine dining and fresh, gourmet food prepared by European chefs, and the unmatched service of the Harvey Girls, many of whom ended up marrying their customers. Using the talents of Mary Colter, the Southwest's greatest designer and architect, Harvey built fine hotels in decidedly out-of-the-way places, allowing passengers on the Santa Fe's popular Los Angeles-to-Chicago line to live well even when stopping in Needles, California, and Winslow, Arizona.

Harvey also hired attractive, educated young women who knew their history, anthropology, ethnology, and art as tour guides. Intrepid tourists who could pay, in 1936, about $45 per person were packed into tough but comfortable limousines, along with gourmet box lunches, and driven in style deep into Indian Country. These trips were famously called "Indian Detours"—three days of adventure and exoticism billed, according to surviving marketing pamphlets, as "the most distinctive motor cruise service in the world...off the beaten path in the Great Southwest."

The crowning achievement of the Harvey-Colter partnership came just before the stock market crash with the construction of La Posada (The Resting Place) at Winslow, the headquarters of the Santa Fe Railroad and the gateway to Arizona's Indian Country. Howard Hughes, Frank Sinatra, Albert Einstein, Bob Hope, and the Crown Prince of Japan all stayed in Colter's masterpiece, along with many other luminaries of American and world culture. They'd hop off the train right outside the hotel, tour the Hopi Mesas and Navajoland, and then return to the comfort of the Spanish Hacienda-inspired hotel and supreme comfort in a land that knew little of that luxury.

Eventually train travel fell off, and Route 66 gave way to the interstate, and not long after that everything was the same, and the interstate became the province of chain hotels and those restroom machines that blow hot air on your hands. La Posada closed in the 1950s and sat disused until a few years ago when Affeldt and Mion saved it. Now the old hotel has been restored beyond even its original glory, and it's booked up often with guests from all over the world. The hotel is especially popular these days with Europeans, many of whom rent motorcycles and ride the remainders of Route 66, searching for some lost version of the "America Road." Affeldt said recently that the irony of this phenomenon was not lost on a modern-day celebrity visitor to La Posada: the "Easy Rider" himself, Peter Fonda.

Standin' on the Corner Park in Winslow

age of train travel; but they also have up-to-date amenities, including deep tubs and heavenly beds. Never mind that there's still not much to see in Winslow: You could spend two full days exploring this hotel—walking its tiled and arched corridors and its lush green grounds, looking at co-owner and artist Tina Mion's gallery of strange and thrilling paintings, eating locally sourced, Fred Harvey-inspired meals at the Turquoise Room, or just sitting outside on the back platform, watching the trains go by.

At **Earl's Motor Court** (512 East 3rd St., 928/289-0188, www.earlsmotorcourt.com, $49.95-59.95) they are consciously attempting to resurrect the style, friendliness, and comfort once offered along the route, and doing a pretty fair job of it too. Earl's is the best place to stay in town, besides La Posada of course.

Food

The independently operated **C Turquoise Room** (928/289-2888, breakfast, lunch, and dinner, $15-40, reservations required for dinner), just off La Posada's main lobby, serves "Fred Harvey-inspired" meals like prime rib and steak, and a wild blend of gourmet dishes under the heading "Native American-inspired nouvelle cuisine." Interesting, creative, and delicious is what that means. This is the best restaurant in the region and one of the best in the state.

The **Casa Blanca Café** (1201 E. 2nd St., 928/289-4191, 11am-9pm daily) serves decent Mexican and American food in a casual setting.

Information and Services

The **Winslow Chamber of Commerce** (101 E. 2nd St., 928/289-2434) offers tourist information and advice on the region.

METEOR CRATER

Meteor Crater (I-40 and Meteor Crater Rd., 928/289-4002, www.meteorcrater.com, 7am-7pm in summer, 8am-5pm the rest of the year,

© TIM HULL

Earl's Motor Court in Winslow has a bit of retro-Route 66 charm.

$15 adults, $14 seniors, $8 children 6-17), though impressive, is perhaps best viewed prior to a visit to, say, Canyon de Chelly or the Grand Canyon. Compared to those nearby attractions, built over eons by wind and water, this pockmark has trouble looking like more than the hole in the ground it is, isolated on the plain off I-40.

But an interesting hole nonetheless, being born from the collision of an asteroid with the high-desert grasslands about 50,000 years ago. A small museum examines this and other meteor sites, and the role the crater and its owner played in the study of meteors and in the U.S. space program. There's a 10-minute film about the crater, and rangers offer short interpretive hikes, but insist that you have closed-toe shoes to tag along. A Subway on-site sells sandwiches and drinks. Unlike most of the outdoor sights in Arizona, Meteor Crater is run by a private corporation. The $15 adult entrance price is, truthfully, a bit steep for what you get.

HOMOLOVI RUINS STATE PARK

Here in the grasslands south of the Hopi mesas, along the banks of the Little Colorado River, the *Hisatsinom* (Anasazi) settled for a time in the 1200s and 1300s before moving on northward to Black Mesa. A few crumbling rock aggregations and beds of shattered pottery, what remains of decades of looting, sit on dry promontories. It's a beautiful place, windy and desolate, but the ruins aren't as impressive as others nearby. This is a good place to start a trip to Indian Country and its ancient castles; afterward, it pales in comparison to what you've already seen. The **visitors center** (I-40 to U.S. 87 North at Winslow, 928/289-4106, 8am-5pm daily, $5 per car) has one of the best selections of books on Southwestern archaeology in the region and offers a chance to converse with Hopi artists. There are picnic tables and trails on the park, and a 53-site campground ($10-20) with hookups and showers.

THE WHITE MOUNTAINS AND THE GILA VALLEY

Though still the domain of a few real cowboys and not a few Apache Indians, the high pine forests of eastern Arizona's White Mountain region have for generations been a cool summer getaway for the state's lowlanders and city dwellers. It was in these still largely unbroken stands of evergreens, high on the Colorado Plateau, that the idea of wilderness for its own sake began

© TIM HULL

HIGHLIGHTS

LOOK FOR ◀ TO FIND RECOMMENDED SIGHTS, ACTIVITIES, DINING, AND LODGING.

◀ White Mountain Trail System: Hike, bike, or ride a horse through the thick, cool green forests of the White Mountains on this renowned series of trails (page 309).

◀ Apache Cultural Center and Museum: Learn about the lifeways and history of the Western Apache at this small but fascinating museum and cultural center (page 312).

◀ Sunrise Park Resort: In the winter bring your skis and snowboards and slide down dozens of ski runs on three high, forested peaks. In the summer, do the same on a mountain bike (page 313).

◀ Casa Malpais Indian Ruins and Archaeological Park: Explore a basalt-rock village built by the ancestors of the Hopi and the Zuni tribes on a tour of this thrilling ruin (page 317).

◀ The Coronado Trail: Drive one of the most isolated, traffic-free roads in the state: 120 miles of twisting, two-lane switchbacks from the desert to the high pine forests (page 320).

◀ Gila Box Riparian National Conservation Area: See the remains of the once mighty Gila River and hike beside the slow, lazy flow, watching wildlife hiding out in the cool shade (page 329).

in America with the great conservationist and writer Aldo Leopold. He arrived in Springerville in 1909, a young man just starting out in the newly created U.S. Forest Service. Years later and still moved by these mountains, forests, and meadows, he would write about them in his 1949 classic *A Sand Country Almanac,* one of the prime movers of a then nascent campaign to preserve the West's wild places. Leopold predicted the fate of Arizona as a state and its slow, ongoing changeover from an extractive economy to one that is, today, largely based on tourism, when he wrote of the predator control

agent who killed the last known grizzly bear in the state, around 1910: "He did not foresee that within two decades the cow country would become tourist country, and as such would have greater need of bears than of beefsteaks."

Now, just over a century since Leopold rode these forests on horseback, his observations still ring true. For the White Mountains are known today as a wilderness playground, a place where the real Old West—the Old West not of gunfights and card sharps, but of wilderness, solitude, and natural beauty—lives on. The region still lacks grizzlies, but the wolf has returned.

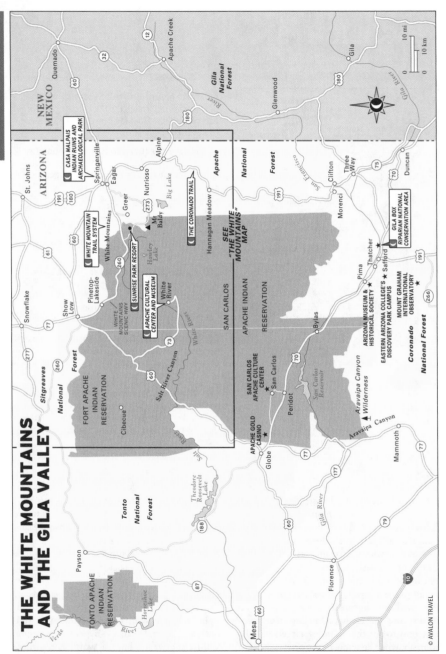

THE WHITE MOUNTAINS AND THE GILA VALLEY

© AVALON TRAVEL

On a dark, quiet night in these ancient forests, all snuggled up and safe in your rented-cabin bed, you might happen to hear a long-forgotten howl-at-the-moon from deep in the rural darkness. And then you'll know why you came here, and you will never forget again.

PLANNING YOUR TIME

Unless you're a snow-lover, the best time to visit the White Mountains is during the summer months, when the cool, green highlands offer respite from the desert heat. May through September you'll find gorgeous, temperate days and nippy nights in the high country, and you won't be alone. The campgrounds, cabins, and lakesides of the region are a big draw for campers, hikers, hunters, and anglers, so it's best to plan ahead. The snow starts falling (ideally) around December and can last until March or thereabouts. During these months skiers and snowboarders crowd the region, mostly on the weekends.

If you're coming from Phoenix or Tucson, a weekend is enough to see the glorious mountains and forests of the region; this is the perfect destination for a road trip—cruising slowly along twisty mountain roads, taking in the scenery and keeping a sharp eye for wildlife.

The Gila Valley's charms are less obvious. It's hot in this desert river valley in the summer, but cool and temperate in the fall and winter. The best way to see the Gila Valley is to drive through it on your way to the mountains along the Coronado Trail. It's a slow, winding route, but one that won't be forgotten soon.

If you have more time, say, five days to a week, consider renting a cabin beside one of the high-country lakes, or setting up a camp deep in the forest, and sampling the White Mountains' many trails for hikers and mountain bikers. Or grab your kayak or canoe and float down the remaining wild sections of the Gila River. If you're interested in seeing the huge telescopes that scan the heavens from the heights of the Gila River Valley's Mount Graham, make sure you reserve a spot far in advance and plan to be in the region for at least one full day and night.

GETTING THERE AND AROUND

You really must have your own car to visit this out-of-the-way mountainous playground. Pinetop-Lakeside, the capital village of the White Mountains region, sits about 200 miles northeast of Phoenix, the capital city of Arizona, but it is a scenic 200 miles that stretches from the desert to the cool mountain pines. Plan on the drive taking at least 3.5 hours, longer on the weekends. Take U.S. Highway 60 east to Mesa, then pick up State Highway 87 north to the Mogollon Rim and then east on State Highway 260 to Show Low, which is right near Pinetop-Lakeside.

The White Mountains

The Hopi and Zuni have ancient ties to these mountains, the highest of which is Mount Baldy, at 11,400 feet the second highest peak in Arizona. Mormons settled the region from the north along the Little Colorado River in the 1870s, and still have a major presence in the area. The towns are all small but set up for tourists. Bring your hiking boots, your fishing rod, your mountain bikes, your skis, your snowboard, and your kayak, and don't forget your binoculars and your camera.

SHOW LOW

The largest town in the White Mountains region with about 11,000 residents, Show Low stretches out along Highway 60, which becomes Deuce of Clubs as it passes through the one-strip town. Surrounded by the Apache-Sitgreaves National Forests and sitting at 6,400 feet above sea level, Show Low has average temperatures running 25-30 degrees lower than those on the desert 175 miles to the south. It's a popular place for summer homes

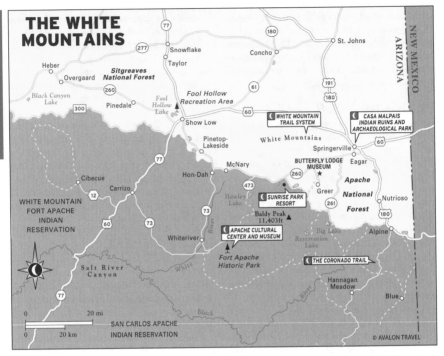

THE WHITE MOUNTAINS

and getaway cabins. It makes a good base for a White Mountains excursion, but the resort town of Pinetop/Lakeside just 10 miles to the southeast along the White Mountain Road (AZ 260) has a greater diversity of accommodations.

The town, founded in 1870, got its unique name from a card game played for its spoils. Two early settlers, the story goes, decided that the townsite wasn't big enough for both of them, and so played a hand of Seven-Up to decide who would stay and who would move on. Whoever could "show low," that is, the lowest card, would win the site. There's a sculpture depicting the card game at the **Festival Market Place** (Deuce of Clubs and E. Cooley, between 9th St. and 11th St.).

Festivals and Events

The **Show Low Main Street Farmers' Market & Art Walk** showcases local artists, artisans, horticulturists, and ranchers every Saturday between late May and early October. Locally grown produce, locally raised beef, and all manner of folk art and the typical farmers market wares are sold from more than 60 booths set up at the **Festival Market Place** (Deuce of Clubs and E. Cooley, between 9th St. and 11th St., www.showlowmainstreet.org, 9am-1pm).

Accommodations

Just 10 miles southeast of Show Low in Pinetop-Lakeside there are several excellent motels, hotels, and cabins available, so there's really no reason to stay in Show Low, which doesn't have a lot of accommodations. If you're staying overnight, try the **Best Western Paint Pony Lodge** (581 W. Deuce of Clubs, 928/537-5773, $79-110), which has 50 standard rooms, free Wi-Fi, and a free continental breakfast.

Food

Most of the accommodations and restaurants in Show Low can be found along the town's short main drag, Deuce of Clubs.

The **Branding Iron Steakhouse** (573 Deuce of Clubs, 928/537-5151, brandingironsteakhouse.com, 11am-9pm Mon.-Thurs., 11am-10pm Fri., 4pm-10pm Sat., $4-26) at the junction of Deuce of Clubs and White Mountain Road claims to have the best prime rib ($13-23) in the White Mountains. While there hasn't to my knowledge been an official prime rib-off among the region's various red-meat purveyors, I don't think this old-school western kitsch saloon and steak house is doing any bragging that it can't back up. The food and atmosphere here are the perfect complement to the high-elevation forest. They serve hearty breakfasts (breakfast burritos, chicken-fried steak and eggs, biscuits and gravy, etc.) and excellent sandwiches, salads, steaks, burgers, and surf and turf for lunch and dinner. The saloon offers live entertainment of the jazz, honky-tonk, and country-rock variety and has pool, darts, and shuffleboard, and you're likely to meet a few cowboy-hat-wearing locals hanging out. On summer days, the patio is the ideal place for a leisurely lunch.

Café Bocado (4551 White Mountain Blvd., 928/537-8190, www.cafe-bocado.com, 11am-3pm Tues.-Sat., 5pm-8pm Fri.-Sat., $3-10) is a fabulous cafe, open for lunch daily and dinners Friday and Saturday, as well as excellent coffee drinks and a juice and smoothie bar. This charming little place has a comfortable, laid-back coffeehouse atmosphere, with a menu that includes roast beef gyros, sandwiches from pastrami to portobello, a delightful kielbasa hot dog, and selection of pleasing soups and salads.

Information and Services

There's a well-stocked **Visitor Center** (81 E. Deuce of Clubs, 928/537-2326, 9am-5pm Mon.-Fri.) on the main drag that has a lot of information on the White Mountains region.

Summit Healthcare Regional Medical Center (2200 Show Low Lake Rd., 928/537-4375, www.nrmc.org) has a 24-hour emergency room with a Level IV trauma center.

FOOL HOLLOW LAKE RECREATION AREA

Fool Hollow Lake Recreation Area (1500 Fools Hollow Rd., Show Low, 928/537-3680, 5am-10pm daily, $7 per vehicle up to three people, $3 for individuals on bikes in the spring and summer, $3 per vehicle and $2 for bikers Oct.-March; ranger station open 8am-4:30pm daily April-mid-Oct., 8am-11am and 3:30pm-4:30pm daily mid-Oct.-March) offers fishing, camping, picnicking, swimming, and hiking in and around a jewel-like blue highland lake surrounded by tall pines. A dam at the meeting of Show Low Creek and Fool Hollow Wash (named so because people said the original settlers were fools to attempt to farm here) created the 150-acre lake in 1957, and it has since become a popular spot for outdoor types, especially in the summer months. There's a short, 1.5-mile, trail along the south and west sides of the lake that's worth a stroll. This is a family-oriented place with a playground and interpretive programs on natural history and wildlife. There always seem to be a lot of parents and kids fishing together for rainbow trout, large- and smallmouth bass, sunfish, catfish, and other species. Only nonmotorized boats are allowed. Canoe and kayak rentals are available at the **East Dock** (928/892-9170, 9am-5pm Mon.-Thurs., 8am-6pm Fri.-Sat., 8am-4pm Sun., $20-25 per hour).

Camping

Fool Hollow is an ideal spot for car campers ($17-30, electricity available, make reservations at https://azstateparks.itinio.com), as it's just a few miles from Show Low and only 15 miles from Pinetop-Lakeside and the area's best trails and restaurants. There are 31 tent sites tucked among the evergreens, with fire rings and picnic tables, and 92 RV spots for rigs up to 40 feet long. All the sites have water and are just a short walk from relatively clean restrooms and showers.

SNOWFLAKE

Founded in 1878 by Mormon pioneers sent south from Utah by Brigham Young to establish colonies throughout the arid west, this small roadside village 18 miles north of Show Low on State Highway 77 is home to the Latter-day Saints' 108th temple (there are 133 total) and Arizona's only pulp and paper mill. The **Stinson Pioneer Museum** (102 N. 1st East, 928/536-4881, 10am-4pm Tues.-Sat.) offers a tour of some of the restored homes of the early settlers and other historic sites, and has some interesting artifacts from the pioneer period on display. The town is in the foothills of the White Mountains at 5,600 feet and enjoys a more moderate climate than those higher up.

Festivals and Events

Saturdays from May through October the **Snowflake-Taylor Farmers Market** (Heritage Square on Main St., 9am-1pm) offers locally grown produce, folk arts, and live music.

Accommodations and Food

A stay at the **Heritage Inn Bed and Breakfast** (161 N. Main St., 928/536-3322 or 866/486-5947, www.heritage-inn.net) is reason enough to stop in Snowflake. The charming pioneer-Victorian home rents 10 rooms ($110-140, $95-130 winter), each decorated with antiques and frontier elegance. Three of the rooms have Jacuzzi tubs, and all come with Wi-Fi, TV, and DVD players. Frequented by Mormons visiting the local temple, this is a very friendly place with excellent breakfasts.

PINETOP-LAKESIDE

This small resort village marks the beginning of the **White Mountain Scenic Road,** otherwise known as State Highway 260. Pinetop-Lakeside, one incorporated community, stretches out along the highway at more than 7,000 feet, a high-forest getaway with just 4,000 year-round residents. When the snow melts, however, more than 35,000 call this place home, mostly on summer weekends. This is the White Mountain region's tourism capital, and there are quite a few distinctive forest resorts, shops, and restaurants here; it is, indeed, the region writ small: mountain village charm, forest-and-meadow trails beside glimmering

lakes, country comfort food, and adorable little antique shops run by friendly senior citizens and big-city runaways. Pinetop-Lakeside is an essential stop if you're on a short schedule, and it should be your base if you're planning to spend a few days in the White Mountains.

Events

In summer, weekend desert refugees crowd the stretch of Highway 260 running through this scattered roadside village, in search of cool air and a thick steak. In winter, skiers and snowboarders chain up and head up, in search of snow. In the midst of all this bustle, deep back in the woods, huddled in cabins and trailers, a legion of hermit artists makes jewelry, wood carvings, wildlife paintings, and other strange and wonderful objects. Over the 4th of July every year they sneak into town and sell their creations at the **Northeastern Arizona Fine Arts Association Arts & Crafts Show** (July 3-5, 480/816-4165, www.highcountryartgallery.com, 9am-5pm). The long-running juried festival features more than 75 booths with unique arts and crafts, live music, and food from Charlie Clarks, a legendary local bar and grill. The artisans set up in The Orchard, a cool, grassy area behind the restaurant and saloon, to which those who are averse to craft fairs can retire for a cool one.

There's nothing quite like buying a work of Arizona-bred Native American art directly from the artist. It tends to add a layer of personal meaning to an artifact already prestacked with notions and narratives. At the summertime **White Mountain Native American Art Festival** (exact dates change, usually mid-June or July, 928/367-4290, www.pinetoplakesidechamber.com, 9am-5pm, free) more than 50 artists from many of the state's tribes offer their best work for sale, and they're usually eager to talk about their process and cultural influences. The juried show of handmade blankets, jewelry, paintings, pottery, and other items takes place at the **Pinetop-Lakeside Chamber of Commerce** (102 W. White Mountain Blvd.) and includes American Indian performers and food.

In fall the quaking aspen and other deciduous minorities of the mountain pinelands turn red and yellow, flashing like flames from their evergreen surroundings. This inspiring time of year brings the **Pinetop-Lakeside Fall Artisans Festival** (late September, 800/573-4031, www.pinetoplakesidechamber.com, 9am-5pm) to the **Mountain Meadow Recreation Complex** (1101 S. Woodland Rd.), with more than 150 artists and artisans selling their unique wares. The festival includes the **Run to the Pines Car Show** and antique and quilt shows, all around a great weekend to be in Pinetop.

Shopping

There are a number of antique stores, boutiques, gift shops, and galleries scattered along Highway 260 through Pinetop-Lakeside, one of the sure signs that you're in a resort community. As such, the scene here tends to be seasonal; if you're planning a visit in the dead of winter you could find some places closed; many stores are open from April until October.

Stop at the **High Country Art Gallery and Gift Shop** (592 W. White Mountain Blvd., 928/367-3916, www.highcountryartgallery.com, 10am-5pm Tues.-Sun.) to check out paintings, jewelry, clothing, pottery, and other arts and crafts for sale by local artist. At **Harvest Moon Antiques** (392 W. White Mountain Blvd., 928/367-6973, 10am-5pm Tues.-Sat.) you'll find some of the best Native American and Historic Old West pieces in the region. The **Red Door Consignment Shops** (2701 N. Porter Mountain Rd., 928/368-2477, 10am-5pm Tues.-Sat.) has 6,000 square feet of resale furniture, antiques, clothes, jewelry, and all manner of treasures waiting to be found. There's also a coffee bar and hot dog stand inside. The **Orchard Antiques** (1664 White Mountain Blvd., 928/368-6563, 10am-5pm Tues.-Sat.) is one of the oldest and best of the area's many antique stores and has a fairly representative sampling of what you'll find in most of the area's shops: high-quality furniture, glass, knickknacks, art, and other staples, many with a Western influence. If you're up for something

truly unique, have the "master chainsaw artist" at **The Burly Bear** (1545 S. Adair, at White Mountain Blvd., 928/367-2327, Mon.-Sat., 10am-5pm, www.theburlybear.com) carve you a 15-foot-high cuddly-faced wood bear or some one-of-a-kind furniture.

Recreation

Surrounded by the Apache-Sitgreaves National Forests, Pinetop-Lakeside offers a pine needle-paved antidote to hikers and mountain bikers who are sick of saguaros, creosote, and unrelenting sunshine. About 180 miles of single-track trails and old mining and logging roads wind through the wrinkled, rocky forest of tall ponderosa pine, Douglas fir, and quaking aspen.

From the highland town's strip of hotels and resorts it's a scenic 30-mile drive east along Highway 260 to **Sunrise Park Resort,** the center of the region's winter recreation scene with its 65 ski runs. The resort is also a popular summer recreation destination, drawing mountain bikers to its steep, roller-coaster descents, and offering fishing, trail rides, and other high-country pursuits.

WHITE MOUNTAIN TRAIL SYSTEM

Closer to town, the White Mountain Trail System organizes 19 trails into loops that run through some of the most beautiful areas of the forest around Pinetop-Lakeside and Show Low, and there's always a chance you'll see a deer or two bounding through a meadow. The trails are heavily used by mountain bikers, horseback riders, and hikers, especially in the summer. They can get muddy during the later summer rainy season, turning a ride into a chore. The trails run from 1.5 miles to 14 miles, and several of them wind along babbling brooks with spongy green banks and up highland ridgeways overlooking the pine tops.

The heroic local group that organized the trail system in response to encroaching development on the forest keeps a guide to the trails at **www.tracks-pinetop-lakeside.org.** The **Lakeside Ranger District** (W. White Mountain Blvd., 928/368-5111, www.fs.fed.

us/r3/asnf/recreation/trails) sells a paperback guide to the trail system for $2; the guide has detailed directions on how to get to the trail-heads, and the rangers are usually easy with the advice. **Cycle Mania** (100 N. White Mountain Rd., Show Low, 928/537-8812) has bike equipment, repairs, and rentals.

WOODLAND LAKE PARK

This small park (Pinetop-Lakeside Parks and Recreation, 928/368-6700, sunrise-10pm April-Oct., sunrise-sunset Nov.-March, free) offers the best of the White Mountains in miniature, and it's an ideal place to hike around and get a deep impression of the forest if you don't have the time or inclination to mount a major expedition. The little reservoir attracts wildlife and anglers, and the trails are easy—especially the 1.25-mile **Lake Loop Trail,** a paved route around the lake that's perfect for families with young children. Hiking the two-mile **Hitching Post Loop Trail** is an excellent way to introduce yourself to the forest, and there's a side trail off the loop that leads to the marshy meadow of the **Big Springs Environmental Study Area.** The park has bathrooms, picnic tables, and charcoal grills. To get there take Highway 260 south to Woodland Lake Road.

Accommodations

There are more than 40 hotels, motels, and country-cabin resorts in this tiny sylvan burg—so many that it seems like the whole town is for rent by the night. Rates fluctuate somewhat according to season, with the prices highest during the summer months (roughly mid-May-Sept.), and the ski season (late Dec.-Mar.). It's a good idea to make reservations long in advance, especially for cabin rentals.

One of the least expensive options is the **Executive Inn** (1023 E. White Mountain Blvd., 928/367-4146, www.executiveinnpinetop.com, $69-99), a regular motel-style place that looks better with the forest around it—a good choice for families on a budget.

The **Econo Lodge Inn & Suites Woodland** (458 E. White Mountain Blvd., 928/367-3636, www.econolodge.com, $78-109) has clean and comfortable rooms with flat-screen TVs, refrigerators, microwaves, and free Wi-Fi. The hotel offers a free hot breakfast and has an indoor spa.

At the **Moonridge Lodge** (596 W. White Mountain Blvd., 928/367-1906, www.moonridgelodge.com, $35-199) you can rent your own one-, two-, or three-bedroom cabin, a few of which also have lofts. The three-bedroom can hold groups or families of up to 12 people. They also let two small "sleeping rooms" with bathrooms for a mere $35 per night. The cabins have pinewood interiors and comfy old chairs and couches and TVs; many have covered porches and picnic tables, and all are surrounded by the whispering forest and are close to restaurants, shopping, and trailheads. Pets are allowed for a fee.

The **Hidden Rest Resort** (3448 White Mountain Blvd., 928/368-6336, www.hiddenrest.com, $119-169) rents 11 country-quaint and comfortable knotty-pine-paneled cabins on a forested property along Highway 260. Four of the cabins have in-room whirlpool tubs, and most will sleep up to four people. All the cabins have private bathrooms, a gas or a wood fireplace, and a stocked kitchen. Pets are allowed for a fee.

The **Lake of the Woods Resort** (2244 W. White Mountain Blvd., 928/368-5353, www.lakeofthewoodsaz.com, $99-299) has rustic but generally clean fishing cabins around a 12-acre lake stocked with trout. This is a great place to introduce kids to fishing. The resort rents tiny studio cabins and cabins with one to five bedrooms, all with kitchens or kitchenettes. Some of the cabins are very close to the noisy highway, and there's usually a four-night minimum stay for those with lake views and a three-night minimum for those without. The resort has two hot tubs, a recreation center, a playground, and boat rentals, and the lake is an excellent spot for bird-watching.

Lazy Oaks Resort (1075 Larson Rd., 928/368-6203, http://lazyoaks.com, $109-239) rents 11 rustic but comfortable log cabins around **Rainbow Lake,** which has excellent trout fishing. The two-room cabins can sleep

6 to 10 people. The cabins have fireplaces, stocked kitchens, and televisions. Lazy Oaks is the "sister resort" to Lake of the Woods, and has most of the same minimum-stay requirements.

Food

More and more varied restaurants are opening in Pinetop-Lakeside all the time it seems, and the area certainly has more food choices than any other White Mountain community. You'll find Italian food and pizza, Thai food, seafood, fast food, and just about any other style (within reason) that you're in the mood for as you drive slowly through the one-strip town spread out along Highway 260. The places listed below are the leading lights of this moderately bustling food scene—local favorites, many of which have been serving the townies and tourists alike for generations.

The oldest continually operating restaurant in the White Mountains, **Charlie Clark's Steakhouse** (Hwy. 260, 928/367-4900, www.charlieclarks.com, lunch 11am-3pm daily, dinner 5pm-10pm daily, $7-25) serves up some of the best steaks, barbecue beef, and prime rib in the area on a site that disguised a distillery during prohibition. A casual Western-style place that's popular with tourists and locals alike, Charlie's has been open in one form or another since the late 1930s. Lunch is served daily in the saloon and enclosed log cabin patio, and there's a garden-style outdoor bar out back called **The Orchard.** For lunch they serve a full menu of sandwiches and salads, and some really excellent fish tacos and other specials. Sitting in the saloon, you'll hear regulars and cowboys joshing each other; make sure to check out all the cartoon caricatures that line the walls depicting favored customers throughout the years.

The **Christmas Tree Restaurant** (455 N. Woodland Rd., 928/367-3107, www.christmastreerestaurant.com, lunch 11am-3pm, dinner 4pm-close Wed.-Mon., $5-24) is a famous country-style place with soul-warming, full-plate entrées perfect for the elevation, with legendary chicken and dumplings and beef stroganoff and the kind of nostalgic decor

you'd expect from the name. The soups and fresh-cut salads are excellent, and the pasta, steak, and seafood dishes are expertly prepared. If you take your restaurant-going seriously, don't miss this small-town gem.

Darbi's Café (235 E. White Mountain Blvd., 928/367-6556, $5-10) is a favorite among locals for big American-style breakfasts and burgers, sandwiches, soups, and salads for lunch, all at a fair price. There's usually a wait for breakfast, especially on the weekends.

El Rancho Restaurant (1523 E. White Mountain Blvd., 928/367-4557, www.elranchopinetop.com, 11am-9pm Mon.-Sat., 11am-8:30pm Sun., $5-19) serves reliably tasty and filling Mexican favorites like enchiladas, burritos, and fajitas, and has a fairly extensive selection of tequila and brain-freezing margaritas. This has been a favorite spot for locals since the early 1960s.

Information and Services

The **Pinetop-Lakeside Chamber of Commerce Visitor Center** (102-C W. White Mountain Blvd., 800/573-4031, www.pinetoplakesidechamber.com, 8:30am-4:30pm Mon.-Fri., 8:30am-2:30pm Sat.-Sun.) has all the information you will need on visiting this area.

WHITE MOUNTAIN APACHE INDIAN RESERVATION

The homeland of the White Mountain bands of the Western Apache, who call themselves the Ndee (the People), comprises some 2,600 square miles of tall pines and lush green, flower-strewn meadows in and below the White Mountains. Established in the 1880s, the reservation is home to about 12,000 of the tribe's more than 15,000 members. There's not much to see save for beautiful high-elevation forests, and a few scattered, often dilapidated homes and trailers, most of them with a corral and several perfectly posed horses peeking through the screen of pine trees along the highway. The tribe operates two of the region's top stops—**Hon-Dah Resort and Casino** and **Sunrise Park Resort.** The reservation is also home to **Salt River Canyon,** a 2,600-foot-deep wild mountain gorge, and the sacred 11,400-foot-high Mount Baldy, the second highest mountain in Arizona. The reservation begins just south of Pinetop along Highway 260, and its capital is the tiny roadside village of **Whiteriver,** along State Highway 73 about 30 miles south of Pinetop.

Apache Cultural Center and Museum

The Western Apache preserve and interpret their history at the Apache Cultural Center and Museum (928/338-4625, www.fortapache-arizona.org, 8am-5pm, Mon.-Sat., 11am-3pm Sun. in summer, closed weekends in winter, $5 adults, $3 children) in Whiteriver (Indian Rte. 46, about 5 miles south of Whiteriver), part of **Fort Apache Historical Park** (7am-sunset).

Called *Nohwike' Bágowa* (the House of Our Footprints), the cultural center and museum has a fascinating collection of Apache artifacts and historic photographs, and features revolving exhibits on Apache history and culture. Apache artists-in-residence show their work here, and a gift shop sells locally made baskets, beadwork, Crown Dancer figures, and books about the tribe. You'll come away from this small but well-managed museum with an introductory understanding of the tribe's hard-fought and often tragic history, especially if you spend some time perusing the exhibit "Ndee Biké'/Footprints of the Apache," which traces the tribe's epic journey from creation to the present day.

The surrounding 288-acre historical park is a National Register Historic District; a self-guided tour reveals something of what it was like to be a soldier at this far-flung mountain outpost of the Apache wars of the 1870s. The oldest building here is the 1871 log cabin called "General Crook's Cabin," where the exhibit **The Fort Apache Legacy** explains the history of the fort. There's even an old cemetery here, and a 1.4-mile loop trail through a small canyon that goes past an old scout camp. About four miles west of the park, the **Kinishba Ruins National Historic Landmark** preserves a small Pueblo ruin occupied until about 1400. Admission to the historic park includes the ruin. Apache tour guides are sometimes available to take you around if you call in advance.

Scenic Drive

Highway 73 through the reservation's western section becomes the **Whiteriver Scenic Road** as it winds through the lumpy green landscape and hooks up with U.S. Highway 60/State Highway 77 south through **Salt River Canyon** toward Globe and the desert. This is the most scenic route out of the region, and a stop at the pullout about an hour south of Whiteriver provides a breathtaking view of Salt River Canyon. Make sure to gas up and fill up first, though. There are no gas stations until Globe after Whiteriver (almost 100 miles), where gas is expensive, and there's nothing much to eat past the casino. One of the more impressive roadside natural wonders in a state chock-full of them, the canyon was once used as a hideout by the Apache during the Indian wars. The 2,600-foot-deep jagged desert gorge is where the Salt River runs free and wild. There's a parking area before the bridge where you can learn about the canyon and take pictures, and easy paved trails lead down to the flowing river. If you've got a four-wheel drive, you can head off on a riverside jeep trail and explore the canyon in more depth. The traffic along Highway 77 near the canyon bridge can get heavy and frustrating, especially on the weekends. The canyon is about 40 miles north of Globe and about 60 miles from Whiteriver.

Events

In late August, the Southwest's bluegrass aficionados gather at the Hon-Dah Resort and Casino's festival grounds in Pinetop for the **Tall Pines Bluegrass Festival** (800/573-4031, www.pinetoplakesidechamber.com, 9am-5pm, $15), featuring more than a dozen bands and performers, kids' music workshops, food, and other fun stuff; the bands are usually top-notch and drift toward the cowboy/Western side of the genre.

Thousands head to the tiny town of Whiteriver in late August and early September for the **White Mountain Apache Fair and**

Rodeo at the White Mountain Apache Rodeo Grounds (S. Chief Ave. and Mint Rd., 928/338-4346, $3-5), which started in 1925. Apaches of all ages compete in and watch bull riding, roping, barrel racing, and other rodeo events, and there's a fry-bread-making competition, traditional dancing, food, and handmade local arts and crafts.

Recreation

Elk, deer, black bears, bobcats, wild turkeys, and a host of other beasts share these coniferous mountains with the Apaches, and hunters from all over the Southwest fill the region's campgrounds in all seasons. As do anglers, for the reservation has 12 stocked lakes and some 800 miles of cold-water trout streams renowned for giving up various river-monsters, including the Apache trout, Arizona's official state fish.

The tribe operates the Southwest's largest ski resort at Sunrise Park, where the temperate summer months find mountain bikers whipping down the runs and hikers and horseback riders taking a slower tack through the highland forests and meadows. The still and the patient have a reasonable chance of seeing a group of deer, heads lowered to graze in some flowery meadow, and maybe, if you're really lucky, a chubby black bear waddling toward the tree line. If you do see a bear, take your obvious good luck and your hard-earned money straight to the tribe's Hon-Dah Resort and Casino and see how the one-armed bandits and the blackjack tables react.

PERMITS

You must purchase a recreation permit from the tribe to do just about anything within the boundaries of the reservation (fishing $9 per day; camping $8 per day; boating $5; hiking, mountain biking, and sightseeing $15 per day; rafting $20). **White Mountain Apache Wildlife & Outdoor Recreation** (100 West Fatco Rd., 928/338-4385, www.wmatoutdoors.org) in Whiteriver controls outdoor recreation on the reservation and issues the permits; state fishing and hunting licenses hold no authority here. You can secure a permit online (www.

wmatoutdoors.org) or at the **Hon-Dah Ski and Outdoor Sport** (787 Hwy. 260, 928/369-7669, www.hon-dah.com/sos.html), where you can also rent and buy equipment and get some local advice. The shop also organizes rafting and canyoneering trips deep into Salt River Canyon and other remote corners of the reservation. Hunters should contact the tribe's recreation department or check the website for detailed information on elk, deer, small game, and predator hunt permits. The tribe offers guided hunts, but you can also go out on your own.

Permits are available throughout the region, including at **Pinetop Sporting Goods** (747 E. White Mountain Blvd., 928/367-5050). City dwellers can purchase reservation permits before heading for the hills at **Sportsman's Warehouse** locations in Phoenix (19205 N. 27th Ave., 623/516-1400) and Tucson (3945 W. Costco Dr., 520/887-4500).

Sunrise Park Resort

Like drunken migratory birds, skiers and snowboarders from the desert flock north to the White Mountains every winter to slide down the 65 high-mountain (10,700-11,100 ft.) ski runs scratched into Sunrise, Cyclone, and Apache Peaks. **Sunrise Park Resort** (Hwy. 273 four miles south of Hwy. 260, 30 miles east of Pinetop, 928/735-7669, http://sunriseskiparkaz.com), which is usually at least ankle deep in snow by January, has a separate **Terrain Park** for snowboarding, with a half-pipe, wood and metal rails and jumps. The trails, the longest of which is the 1.2-mile "Sidewinder" from 10,700-foot Sunrise Peak, are somewhat diverse, with about 20 percent strictly for the expert skier. There are a fair number of runs for beginners and a few just for kids, and there are cross-country trails through the high pine forests for those strange folks who prefer a cardio workout to a whooshing rush. The park has 10 ski lifts running up the peaks (tickets $23-49). If you are willing to throw yourself down a mountain but lack the necessary equipment, there are rentals available at the Sunrise Park Lodge, or you can go to the folks at **Hon-Dah Ski and Outdoor Sport** (787 Hwy. 260,

928/369-7669, www.hon-dah.com/sos.html) at the casino for your gear.

The lifts creak to life on summer weekends from Memorial Day to Labor Day after a brief snow-melt hiatus (the season typically ends by March). A slow cool-breeze ride up one of the three peaks, high above the green-carpeted land on a summer's day, is a romantic and relaxing way to spend an hour or so (10am-4pm Sat.-Sun., $10 adults, $5 children). Also on summer weekends, the park welcomes **mountain bikers** for about the most fun you can have on two wheels. Sunrise is one of the few places in Arizona where the obvious benefits of going down can be had without a lot of heart-pounding ground work: Bikers can attach their rides to the lift chairs for an easy ride up the peaks and a high-speed roller-coaster ride down (10am-4pm Sat.-Sun., $20 for an all-day pass).

Summer also finds anglers vying for a spot along the shore of **Sunrise Lake,** the state's largest cold-water lake, stocked with big fat trout and other species and the only lake on the reservation that allows gas-powered motorboats (10hp or less). The park's **Snowy Mountain Stables** offer horseback rides (928/205-760, $22-180, half-hour-all day) through the cool forests and meadows during the summer months.

Hon-Dah Resort and Casino

On a rainy day in the White Mountains **Hon-Dah Resort and Casino** (junction of Hwy. 260 and Hwy. 73, 928/369-0299, www.hon-dah.com) can seem a bit dour, with dead-eyed RV-gypsies and chain-smoking octogenarians watching emotionless as a bleeping and blinking machine takes their retirement money. Other times it seems a bit brighter, but it rains quite a bit here. Hon-Dah, which means "welcome" in the Apache language, has a good restaurant (with a casino-style buffet Thurs.-Sun.), a store and gas station, an RV park, and a lodge with clean, basic rooms, but in truth it offers little for those not drawn to games of chance. It's relatively clean, and features the usual slot machines, poker, and blackjack.

Middling Las Vegas-style music acts, many of them with a country-western bent, play to the dance floor at the **Timbers Lounge and Showroom** Tuesday-Saturday.

Accommodations and Food

Hunters and anglers, the reservation's primary block of annual visitors, prefer to rough it in fishing cabins, tent camps, and RVs. For a comprehensive list of the reservation's **camping** options, talk to the tribe's recreation department (928/338-4385, www.wmatoutdoors.org). Camping permits cost $8 per day, and most sites on the reservation are first-come, first-served. Ice fishing is somewhat popular on reservation lakes in the winter, but not all the campgrounds are open and accessible during the snowy months.

The **Hawley Lake Recreation Area** (928/369-1753) rents out rustic but reasonably comfortable cabins along the shores of the reservation's highest lake. At 8,200 feet the 300-acre mountain lake is stocked with trout and is a popular spot for serious solitary anglers and families alike. The tribe rents 20 cabins that sleep from 2 to 14 people ($125-300), as well as a few two-person motel rooms ($65). There's also a large campground around the lake and an RV park. There are no phones, TVs, or microwaves in the cabins, but they are fully furnished with dishes, pans, and utensils, coffee makers and toasters. There's a small store and gas station on site, but it's best to come prepared with food and drinks just in case. To reach Hawley Lake from Pinetop-Lakeside, take Highway 260 through McNary to State Highway 473, then turn right on State Highway 473/Hawley Lake Road. Then it's about 9 miles to the lake.

The nicest accommodations on the reservation are at **Hon-Dah Resort and Casino** (junction of Hwy. 73 and Hwy. 260, www.hon-dah.com, $104-175 Sun.-Thurs., $124-195 Fri.-Sat.), which offers standard, clean, and comfortable rooms with free wireless, room service, and a swimming pool. Check the website for special ski and fishing packages. The rooms, though nothing special, are a half-notch above the region's decidedly midrange knotty-pine rental cabins, and the **Indian Pine Restaurant** (928/369-0299, 7am-9:30pm daily, breakfast $1.25-5.95, lunch and dinner $3.95-7.25) puts out a decent Vegas-style buffet ($7.25-17.95 Thurs.-Sun.), with succulent prime rib on Saturdays, crab legs, shrimp, and other fruits of the far-off sea on Friday, and champagne brunch on Sundays. The Indian Pine serves a fair plate of eggs, potatoes, and bacon for breakfast, as well as omelets and other staples, and sandwiches, pizzas, calzones, salads, and, of course, Indian fry bread for lunch. At dinner, the menu features tasty pizzas and calzones, prime rib, burgers, and ribs.

The tribe's **Sunrise Park Lodge** (928/735-7669 or 800/772-7669, www.sunriseskipark.com, $69-215 weekdays in winter, $124-295 weekends in winter) at the base of the three-peaked skiscape has basic, clean rooms that in the summer go for as low as $69-89. Some of the more pricey rooms have Jacuzzis. Though the accommodations are underwhelming and in need of remodel, the mountains, forests, and ski runs at Sunrise Park are not, so you're probably not going to spend too much time in your room. There's nothing like rolling out of bed onto the slopes. Otherwise you waste precious downhill time driving 30 icy-road miles from Pinetop. The lodge has two decent restaurants, and there are several snack bars and other eateries on-site.

GREER

Turn south off Highway 260 onto Highway 273 to reach the little village of Greer (www.greerarizona.com), a log-cabin hamlet (elevation 8,300 feet) nestled in the forest and green meadows around 7,000-9,000 feet, below the peaks of the White Mountains, through which flows the Little Colorado River. The area is outlandishly beautiful and picturesque. It could just as well be nestled and snuggled in the Alps, and the babbling forks of the river support a lush riparian belt with overgrowing greenery and flat skinny trails along the moss-covered waterway. There are four seasons in Greer, each spectacular. In spring and summer it's perfect for hiking, horseback riding, and lying around

in highland meadows, surrounded by colorful wildflowers. In winter the snow comes, and Greer makes a good base for trips to the ski hills and for cross-country expeditions into the forest.

Sights

While the forests and meadows tend to push everything else of interest off the radar, the strange and quaint **Butterfly Lodge Museum** (Hwy. 373 and County Road 1126, 928/735-7514, http://butterflylodgemuseum.org, 10am-5pm Thurs.-Sun. Memorial Day weekend-Labor Day weekend, $2 adults, $1 youth 12-17, children under 12 free) is worth a look if you're in Greer during the summer. The little log house was once the hunting lodge of James Willard Schultz, an early 20th-century writer of adventure stories about the West for magazines, known primarily for his 1907 book *My Life as an Indian*. The home was later used as a studio by Schultz's equally interesting son, Hart Merriam Schultz, or Lone Wolf, a famous Indian painter and artist. The home is set up with all kinds of artifacts and everyday items that show what life was like in this remote green mountain valley years ago. There are several of Lone Wolf's paintings on display, and a gift shop selling the elder Schultz's nostalgic writings.

On a guided tour of the **Little House Museum** (928/333-2286, www.xdiamondranch.com, $12) and the **Little Bear Archaeological Site,** you'll get an entertaining course on the whole long history of human habitation in the White Mountains region, from the proto-Pueblo inhabitants to the tough pioneers, cattlemen, and cattle rustlers. The museum, a cluster of restored pioneer-style buildings filled with all kinds of strange and wonderful Old West and pioneer-era furniture, household items, and collectibles, is on the grounds of the **X Diamond Ranch** and is only accessible with a reservation. The museum tour includes a jaunt out to the Little Bear site, where the rubble of several dwellings dates back to AD 500. A tour of the museum is $8 without the ruins.

Sports and Recreation

The best hiking in Greer is along the forks of the Little Colorado River. Pick up several trailheads where Main Street enters the National Forest on the south end of Greer. Head south until the end of the main road and follow the well-worn footpaths along the river. In some places the ground is so spongy and overgrown with greenery that it seems like you're in a rain forest. But walking is so lowland. Here, not 20 miles from where John Wayne himself raised prize Hereford cattle on the 26 Bar Ranch, consider letting a mountain-bred horse take you deep into the pines.

The **X Diamond Ranch** (928/333-2286, www.xdiamondranch.com, $25-150) offers guided rides ranging from one hour to all day, and they'll on occasion let a greenhorn do some ranch work à la *City Slickers*. The historic ranch, started by White Mountain pioneers John and Molly Butler in the early 1900s, also operates a catch-and-release fly fishery on the Little Colorado ($30 per person half day, $40 for full day).

Accommodations and Food

There are several lodges in Greer, and a host of cabins for rent, whether for the night or the season. For a complete list check out the official Greer, Arizona, website at www.greerarizona.com.

The historic ◖ **Molly Butler Lodge** (109 Main St., 928/735-7226 or 866/288-3167, www.mollybutlerlodge.com, $95-295) rents cabins for multiple people, great for families; the cabins are a little rustic but comfortable and clean and perfect for the setting; there are no TVs or phone in the rooms, but they have them at the lodge, where there's also a fantastic restaurant that's been serving hearty mountain food since 1910. It's open for dinner daily (5pm-9pm, $13-30), serving excellent fish, steaks, chili, prime rib, and more. The restaurant is open for lunch in the summer, 11am-3pm daily.

The equally historic **X Diamond Ranch** (928/333-2286, www.xdiamondranch.com, $110-300 Apr.-Oct., $95-275 Nov.-Mar.),

where Molly Butler once lived and raised cattle in the early 1900s, rents out seven comfortable and scenically placed cabins along the Little Colorado River. Each cabin is a unique structure surrounded by the outlandish grandeur of the area; all sleep up to four people and can accommodate eight, and they all have kitchens and fireplaces.

SPRINGERVILLE-EAGAR

The Round Valley opens up at the base of the mountains near the junction of U.S. Highways 191 and 60; nestled there at about 7,000 feet are the sister villages of Springerville and Eagar. The ancestors of the nearby Zuni and Hopi found this Little Colorado River valley to their liking in the 1250s, and Basque settlers arrived in 1870 and gave the area its moniker, *Valle Redondo.* By 1879 ranchers and farmers from New Mexico and Utah had trickled in to homestead and raise cattle and crops to supply nearby Fort Apache. A dramatic reminder of the frontier beginnings of these rural Arizona towns is the **Madonna of the Trails** statue, dedicated in 1928 and located on Main Street in Springerville across the street from the post office. John Wayne was famously a partial owner of the 26 Bar Ranch in Eagar, where the Duke and his partners raised high-quality Herefords in the 1960s and 1970s. The Hopi purchased the ranch in the late 1990s in a campaign to reclaim their ancestral lands in the Little Colorado River region.

A short drive north of Springerville on Highway 191/180 leads to the vast and lonely **Springerville Volcanic Field.** Covering some 1,200 square miles of basaltic badlands, the field, whose activity dates from more than 3 million to just about 13,000 years ago, has 405 vents, some of which look like giant anthills rising out of the sweeping plains strewn with black rocks. A pamphlet-guide for a driving tour of the volcanic field, the third largest in North America, is available at the **Springerville-Eagar Regional Chamber of Commerce** (318 Main St., 928/333-2123, www.springerville-eagarchamber.com).

◖ Casa Malpais Indian Ruins and Archaeological Park

The volcanic badlands around Springerville and Eagar were once home to several stone-built villages occupied by the ancestors of New Mexico's Zuni and Arizona's Hopi people. The upper Little Colorado River region was occupied on and off from at least AD 900 until about 1400, with the largest villages constructed during the Pueblo IV period from about 1275 to 1400. The remains of one of these basalt outposts overlooking the river are preserved by the City of Springerville at **Casa Malpais Indian Ruins and Archaeological Park** (418 E. Main, 928/333-5375, tours offered at 9am, 11am, and 2pm Tues.-Sat. year-round, weather permitting, $10, you must call in advance to reserve a spot). The "house of badlands" had about 50 rooms, a square kiva (a structure used for rituals), and even an observatory. It was constructed in the late 1270s and early 1280s and was occupied for about 50 years. Archaeologists believe that most of its residents had left the area by about 1400 and settled at Zuni, about 140 miles to the northeast, while some moved to the Hopi villages, about 180 miles to the northwest. When Coronado came through the area in 1540 searching for the Seven Cities of Cibola, the river valley had no permanent residents. Today both the Zuni and the Hopi consider the Little Colorado River region to be an integral part of their historic homelands. The tour is a fascinating and memorable way to learn more about the early settlers of this beautiful, harsh land, and the museum preserves some of the artifacts that they left behind.

Recreation

A popular site for fishing, boating, and camping, the **Big Lake Recreation Area** is open May-November and has several campgrounds around the 400-acre **Big Lake** and nearby **Crescent Lake,** about 19 miles southwest of Eagar off Highway 261. At 9,000 feet, the highlands here can get cold, even in the summer. Still, it's one of the most popular fishing and camping areas in the region and is often crowded with families during the summer months. Big Lake Tackle and Supply (at the junction of US 191 and 180, Alpine, 928/339-4338, www.biglakeaz.com) has all the bait, tackle, and other supplies you'll need for a day fishing on Big Lake. They also rent four- and five-person rowboats and motorboats ($16-53 per hour).

Hikers should check out the 7.5-mile **Indian Springs Trail** leading up to the **Big Lake Lookout,** where you can get a stunning overview of the blue-and-green landscape. Kids will like the 0.5-mile **Big Lake Nature Trail,** a short and easy self-guided tour of the area's natural wonders. There's a pamphlet available at the **Big Lake Visitor Center.** For more information about camping, hiking, and fishing at Big Lake, contact or stop by the **Springerville Ranger Station** of the Apache-Sitgreaves National Forests (418 E. Main, 928/333-4301, www.fs.fed.us/r3/asnf). The station gives away a booklet with detailed descriptions of the best trails in the area; the descriptions are also available on the website.

Serious hikers should not miss a trek up Arizona's second-highest mountain, 11,403-foot **Mount Baldy.** The high peak is sacred to the Apaches, and the actual tip-top of Mount Baldy is closed to the public. You can, however, make it to within a quarter mile or so of the peak, which most agree is good enough once they see the sweeping views from the near-top. There are a couple of routes up the mountain, but the most scenic is the 13.5-mile round-trip **West Fork Trail,** which follows the Little Colorado River for several miles through thick old-growth forests and high green meadows. The grade is mostly moderate, though you climb more 2,000 feet from the bottom to the top, which is above the tree line and rocky and cold, with short and gnarled subalpine trees and a blasting wind. To reach the trailhead, drive 3.1 miles west on Highway 260 from Eagar, then south on Highway 261 for 18.2 miles to Highway 273. Then head 7.2 miles northwest on Highway 273, cross the river, and drive 1 mile to Mount Baldy Wilderness Trailhead. From Pinetop-Lakeside, take Highway 260 26

fishing at Big Lake

miles east to Highway 273 (toward Sunrise Ski Resort), turn right on Highway 273, and head south for about 11 miles.

CAMPING

There are five campgrounds in the **Big Lake Recreation Area** (www.fs.usda.gov/asnf), which offer hundreds of sites for everything from monster RVs to pup tents and can be reserved at www.recreation.gov. **Apache Trout Campground** ($26 per vehicle per night, $38 with hookup) has full hookups and can handle big RVs while **Rainbow Campground** ($18-20 per vehicle per night) and **Grayling Campground** ($20 per vehicle per night) can hold small RVs and cars but don't have hookups. The campgrounds offer bathrooms and showers a short walk from your site, and there's a store nearby in case you forgot some supplies. **Brookchar Campground** ($14 per vehicle per night), with 12 sites right on the water, is for tent camping only, as is **Cutthroat Campground** ($14 per vehicle per night).

At most of the campgrounds on Big Lake you can rent an old-school white canvas tent cabin, just like the ones homesteaders in the area used while they built their cabins, complete with cots, lanterns and a stove, all for $60 per night (Springerville Ranger Station, 928/333-6200, www.fs.usda.gov).

Shopping

At the retro-rural **Western Drug & General Store** (106 E. Main St., 928/333-4321, www. westerndrugstore.com, 9am-7pm Mon.-Fri., 9am-6pm Sat., 9am-5pm Sun.) on Springerville's main drag you can buy a deer rifle, pick up a bag of chips and a soda, and fill a prescription. Even if you need none of these things, this 1934 precursor to Wal-Mart is worth a stop, if only to wonder at the bagged-and-stuffed menagerie featuring a mountain lion, an elk, a bighorn sheep, and other Arizona wildlife frozen in mid-grandeur by some loving taxidermist.

Accommodations and Food

There are a few small motels along the main

route through Springerville and Eagar. You could do worse for a base, as the Round Valley is just 23 miles east of Sunrise Park, 17 miles from Greer, and is situated at the junction of U.S. Highways 60 and 191.

Reed's Lodge (514 E. Main St., 928/333-4323, www.k5reeds.com, $51-70) has been welcoming travelers since 1949, and, reportedly, the Duke played cards here on occasion back when he owned the nearby 26 Bar Ranch. You probably won't see any celebrities these days, but there's a gallery featuring work by local artists and lots of Old West memorabilia, collectibles, and books. There's a big fireplace in the lobby, the rooms have free wireless, microwaves, and refrigerators, and outside there's a hot tub in which to soak your road-weary bones.

The patio and bar at **Java Blues Coffee House & Bistro Bar & Grill** (341 E. Main St., 928/333-5282, www.javabluesaz.com, 6am-7pm Mon.-Sat., 7am-3pm Sun., $5-25) could get you stuck in Springerville for the night if you can't be bothered to get up after a few hours of eating the wonderful bistro-style creations, drinking coffee or cocktails, and basking in the mountain air. They have tasty salads and sandwiches and excellent coffee, plus free Wi-Fi.

Booga Red's Restaurant and Cantina (521 E. Main St., 6am-9pm daily, cantina open 10am-11pm daily, $5-13) has been family owned since the 1970s and serves delicious, familiar Mexican fare from passed-down recipes.

The chef at the **Rusty Cactus Restaurant** (318 E. Main St., 928/333-3334, www.rusty-cactusrestaurant.com, lunch 11am-3pm, dinner 5pm-8pm Tues.-Sat., $7.95-22.95) has a talent for creating Southwestern variations on classic cuisine. Here they use the best local and regional ingredients to create dishes you'll find only in Arizona. Steaks and burgers, fish and even pasta dishes all submit to a thorough spicing up, and green chilies and agave and jalapeños and nopalitos are applied liberally to many dishes that wouldn't think would have them. This is a fine place to spend a few hours if you find yourself in these lonely highlands.

Services
The **White Mountain Regional Medical Center** (118 S. Mountain Ave., 928/333-4368, www.wmrmc.com) in Springerville has a 24-hour emergency room.

LYMAN LAKE STATE PARK
North of Springerville-Eagar along U.S. Highway 191/180, the landscape flattens out and opens wide as the crumpled mountains begin to give way to high desert. About 11 miles south of the small town of St. Johns, 1,500-acre **Lyman Lake,** a reservoir formed by the damming of the Little Colorado River, is stocked with bass and catfish and is one of the only lakes in the region with no boat restrictions. The lake is the centerpiece of the large **Lyman Lake State Park** (928/337-4441, http://azstateparks.com/Parks/LYLA/index.html, $7 per vehicle) where you can camp lakeside in a round canvas yurt ($40 per night, available Mar. 15-Nov. 15, sleeps up to six people) or in one of a few small log cabins ($55 per night), both of which have electricity and air-conditioning. There are also regular campsites and RV spots available ($20-30, electric, water, and sewer hookups available).

At a mere 6,000 feet above sea level, Lyman Lake State Park has a more temperate climate than the mountain towns, and it gets relatively hot here in the summer. The **Visitor Center** (8am-5pm daily May-Sept., 9am-4pm daily Oct.-Apr.) has lots of information and a few displays about the prehistory of the area and its natural history. A small store in the park sells ice, snacks, and fuel, but you should bring all your food with you.

One of the former highlights of a trip to Lyman Lake was the ranger-guided tour of **Rattlesnake Point Pueblo,** but state budget cutbacks have recently suspended the tours indefinitely. Still, you can check out the small ruin, which housed the ancestors of the Zuni and Hopi from about 1325 to 1390, on your own, and there's a booklet available on the website and at the visitor center with information on what you're seeing. There are also a number of ancient, mysterious petroglyphs etched into boulders throughout the park, some of which can be seen on the quarter-mile self-guided **Peninsula Petroglyph Trail** near the campground. You'll need a boat to reach the spectacular **Ultimate Petroglyph Trail,** a half-mile trail on the lake's eastern shore, but it's worth the trip over to see the rocks covered with those cryptic figures.

Apache County Historical Museum

Wooly mammoth tusks, frontier fashions, pioneer-era farming equipment and household items, rock slabs covered in petroglyphs, refurbished historic log cabins, and all manner of other artifacts and ephemera from prehistory to the near present are preserved at the **Apache County Historical Museum** (180 W. Cleveland, St. Johns, 928/337-4737, 8am-4pm Mon.-Fri.). It's worth a stop to learn about the people's history of northeastern Arizona—from proto-Pueblos to Mormon homesteaders and beyond. St. Johns has just 3,000 residents, but it has an outsized historical presence in the state because it's the hometown of the Arizona Udall clan, Mormon Democrats who produced two national politicians: congressman (1961-1991) and presidential candidate (1976) Mo Udall, and secretary of the interior (1961-1969) Stewart Udall.

Food

The atmosphere at **Iggy's Country Cooking** (160 Commercial St., 928/337-4447, 7am-7pm Mon., 5am-9pm Tues.-Thurs., 7am-8pm Fri.-Sun.) is as memorable as the hearty American and Mexican fare, with cluttered and eye-catching walls decorated in a beach and Route-66 theme and cozy, roofed booths and a friendly staff. If you are camping at nearby Lyman Lake and get sick of eating camp food, Iggy's is the ideal spot for a culinary escape. They take the term "country cooking" very seriously here, and the extensive menu has something home-cooked and tasty for everyone, including chili, catfish, and hushpuppies, and prime rib on Friday and Saturday.

◖ THE CORONADO TRAIL

When Francisco Vazquez de Coronado spurred his prancing mount north from Compostela, Mexico, in 1540, he had reason to believe that the vast unknown northern lands into which he would lead his crowded retinue held riches and glory quite beyond those even of Mexico itself. A few years later he returned, after having traversed what is now the great American Southwest, with nothing but saddle sores and a secure place in the history of North American exploration and conquest.

Nobody knows for sure the exact route that the Coronado expedition took on its way north in search of the sadly nonexistent Seven Cities of Cibola, but scholars believe that he passed through, or at least nearby, the White Mountains, perhaps following the San Francisco River drainage along what is now the border between Arizona and New Mexico. And they aren't just guessing: Ranching families, homesteaders, and other longtime residents of the region have been digging up and tripping over left-behind and discarded items from the Spanish colonial era for generations.

So it is not wholly unreasonable, as you slowly negotiate the switchbacks and hairpins along the twisty two-lane U.S. Highway 191 from the desert grasslands to the high pinelands, to feel a certain connection to the hardbitten Spanish explorer. And the 120-mile route from the copper mines of Clifton to the Highway 60 junction near Springerville, which takes from three to five hours to complete, is often as deserted as it must have been when there was no road at all, the haunt of more wildflowers than vehicles.

Along the way you'll pass the tiny settlements of **Alpine, Nutrioso,** and **Hannagan Meadow,** and to the east, between Clifton and Hannagan Meadow, is the vast **Blue Range Primitive Area,** a coniferous wildland cut through by the Blue River. The scenery is really the attraction here; it's best to take it slow, stopping often at the lookouts and pullouts set up along the route, marveling at the deep green meadows splashed with yellow, red, and purple in the spring and summer. With so much

The Wolves of the White Mountains

"We reached the old wolf in time to watch the fierce green fire dying in her eyes," wrote renowned conservationist and author Aldo Leopold in his classic *A Sand Country Almanac.* Leopold, a founding hero of the wilderness movement in America, did his first tour of duty as a U.S. Forest Ranger in the White Mountains in 1909, back when the only good wolf in Arizona was a dead wolf.

"I was young then, and full of trigger itch;" Leopold continued. "I thought that because fewer wolves mean more deer, that no wolves would mean hunters' paradise. But after seeing that green fire die, I sensed that neither the wolf nor the mountain agreed with such a view."

Though ahead of his time in the early 20th century, Leopold's hard-learned lesson—that a healthy ecosystem needs predators as well as prey to remain so—is today an accepted scientific fact (though there are still a few rural ranchers who would disagree). And the wolves, gone from these mountains and forests since the 1970s, have returned.

In 1998, several Mexican Gray Wolves were reintroduced into the White Mountains region in the Blue Range Wolf Recovery Area, near Hannagan Meadow along the Coronado Trail, and in a nearby New Mexico wilderness. According to the U.S. Fish and Wildlife Service, as of the end of 2007, there were 12 known wolf packs in the reintroduction area, 6 in Arizona and 6 in New Mexico—about 32 total wolves—plus 4 known single wolves in New Mexico. And the most exciting news is that "approximately 75 percent of the radio-collared individuals and 90 percent of all documented wolves (in the recovery area) were born in the wild."

---

beauty it's hard to keep your eyes on the road, so be careful, and look out for motorcycles; the route is understandably quite popular with that growing tribe.

Don't take this route if you're in a hurry to hit the lakes or the slopes (indeed, don't take it in winter at all), or if you are an impatient driver, or susceptible to car sickness.

Sports and Recreation

Most of the Coronado Trail is surrounded by the **Apache-Sitgreaves National Forests.** As you drive along Highway 191 you'll see a number of trailhead signs on both sides of the road. The helpful folks at the **Alpine Ranger Station** (42634 Hwy. 191, Alpine, 928/339-5000, www.fs.fed.us/r3/asnf) give away a handy 66-page guide to the hiking, mountain biking, and equestrian trails along the Coronado Trail and environs that has detailed descriptions of nearly 20 different trails, and information on the area's many lakes.

The best hike in this section of the White Mountains, and one that serious hikers should not miss, is the **Escudilla National Recreation Trail** to the top of **Escudilla Mountain,** a storied regional landmark and the state's third highest peak. The six-mile round-trip hike takes you through aspen groves and deep stands of fir and spruce, through wide green mountain meadows and into the Escudilla Wilderness Area (no bikes allowed here). The hike is relatively easy, especially compared to the monumental trek up Mount Baldy, Escudilla's big-sister peak to the west. When you reach the top, at about 10,900 feet above sea level, you'll see the **Escudilla Lookout,** a fire lookout that offers an even higher view of the green land spreading out below. To reach the trailhead, take Highway 191 north from Alpine for 5.5 miles to Forest Road 8056, then turn right and drive 3.6 miles to Terry Flat. Take the left fork past Toolbox Draw about a half mile to the trailhead.

Just three miles east of Alpine on Highway 180, the 154-acre **Luna Lake** is stocked with trout and is a popular camping, fishing, hiking, and biking spot. A few loop trails around the lake, which attracts bald eagles and other

THE WHITE MOUNTAINS

the Blue Range Primitive Area along the Coronado Trail

© TIM HULL

exotic wildlife to its shores, offer easy hiking and biking for families with children.

If you're dead set on seeing some of the region's abundant but typically shy wildlife, the best place to do so is at the **Sipe White Mountain Wildlife Area** (928/367-4281, www.azgfd.gov/outdoor_recreation/wildlife_area_sipe.shtml, visitors center open 8am-5pm daily, mid-May-mid-Oct.). Two miles south of Eagar off the Coronado Trail, this 1,362-acre former Hereford ranch has been converted by the Arizona Game and Fish Department into a prime wildlife-viewing area with several easy trails and developed lookouts. Bring your binoculars to spot elk, deer, bald eagles, hawks, wild turkeys, and other wildlife. This is another ideal place to bring the kids, as the trails are relatively flat, easy, and short, and everybody knows that kids love animals. The visitors center, which is open only in the summer months, has displays about the area's natural history. It's all free, and you can bring your horse or your bike along if you want, but the best way to see wildlife is to sit still and quiet, waiting.

Accommodations and Food

Most of the services along the Coronado Trail are in the tiny mountain village of **Alpine,** about 94 miles north of the scenic byway's beginnings in Clifton. If you're headed up the trail from the desert, there isn't much in the way of food or even gas between Clifton and Alpine, a drive that could conceivably take three hours. But once you reach the tiny highland settlement, at 8,050 feet and near the headwaters of the San Francisco River, there are several excellent restaurants to choose from for a leisurely lunch or dinner after a long day of driving and forest-play. Alpine, which is just six miles or so west of the New Mexico border, has a few rustic rural hideaways, and there are dozens of cabins for rent throughout the area. Some of the restaurant owners in Alpine also rent cabins, and the **Alpine Area Chamber of Commerce** (928/339-4330, www.alpinearizona.com) has information about rentals on its website. Many of the businesses in Alpine have seasonal hours, and are often closed in the deep winter.

About four miles north of Alpine off Highway 191, the **Tal-Wi-Wi Lodge & Saloon** (40 County Rd. 2220, just off Hwy. 191, 928/339-4319, www.talwiwilodge.com, $90-120) has nice rooms with blond knotty-pine interiors and some with whirlpool tubs next to the bed. There's free wireless in all the rooms. Tal-Wi-Wi is popular with car and motorcycle clubs traveling the trail. The staff is friendly and helpful, and the convivial **Longhorn Saloon** is a good spot for a drink, conversation and watching sports, with live music on weekends in season.

Hannagan Meadow Lodge (Hwy. 191 near mile marker 232, 22 miles south of Alpine, 928/339-4370, www.hannaganmeadow.com, $65-200) is a historic, cozy forest getaway with a backcountry atmosphere and antique country-style decor. It's been open since 1926, and sits right off the trail about 22 miles south of Alpine, lost to the mad world down below. The rates change according to the season, varying by about $5-10 per night, lowest in winter (early Nov.-Apr.) and fall (mid-Aug.-early Nov.), slightly higher in spring (May-early June), and highest in summer (early June-mid-Aug.). The lodge rents seven suites named for figures from Arizona history, and there are cabins named for luminaries of local history. The lodge's country-comfort dining room is open 8am-8pm daily.

Foxfire at Alpine (42661 Hwy. 180, 928/339-4344, foxfireatalpine.com, 11am-8pm daily, $9-15) serves delicious burgers, sandwiches, salads, soups, pasta, and pizza, all with a homemade touch and care for details. It's a pleasant little place, relatively new, close to the junction of Highway 180 and the Coronado Trail at Alpine.

A fellow named Anderson Bush was the first pioneer to settle in the Alpine area, in 1876, and some residents still call this green mountain pass the Bush Valley, including the proprietors of the adorable little white-and-blue house along Highway 191 wherein the **Bush Valley Café** (42661 Hwy. 191, Alpine, 928/339-4493) serves delicious pizza, salads, pasta, and elk and bison burgers. The café also has great coffee and a full bar.

© TIM HULL

Hannagan Meadow Lodge

A few miles north of Alpine in Nutrioso, **Bistro Escudilla** (41633 Hwy. 191, Nutrioso, 928/339-1150, lunch 11am-4pm Thurs.-Sun., dinner 5pm-9pm Thurs.-Sat., lunch $4.50-14.50, dinner $4.50-27) has a prime rib dip for lunch that melts in your mouth, and the White Mountain Philly Cheesesteak twists the classic sandwich a bit with tasty results. For dinner, only served three nights a week (reservations recommended), try the "Sonoran" gumbo, and you can't go wrong with the grilled salmon.

The Gila Valley

There are only about 40,000 people living in the Gila Valley (pronounced "Hee-la"), a meeting ground of the Sonoran and Chihuahuan Deserts near Arizona's border with New Mexico. Tiny towns, many of them moribund long ago, stand dusty and forgotten along the Old West Highway (Hwy. 70). Former Supreme Court Justice Sandra Day O'Connor grew up near Duncan, the last station before New Mexico, on the Lazy B Ranch. The whole lonely region is watched over by the largest of Southern Arizona's sky islands, Mount Graham, where telescopes scour the heavens for signs and wonders. Hot springs bubble up from beneath the hot sand, and the Gila River, a once mighty Southwestern river now dammed to oblivion and sucked mostly dry, still runs year-round here in a few lush, riparian oases.

SAFFORD AND VICINITY

Safford, a rural town with about 8,000 persons near the Gila River, has been a farming, mining, and ranching area since the 1870s. Cotton is still grown in this hot desert valley, and a mighty chunk of the nation's copper is ripped from the ground just to the northeast. While Safford still has a quaint downtown strip, an old courthouse building, and some residential neighborhoods with historic bungalows, most of the town is a jumble of chain stores, restaurants, hotels, and strip malls strung out along U.S. Highway 70 between the New Mexico border (about 45 miles east) and the San Carlos Apache Reservation (about 60 miles west). Safford is the bright light of the upper Gila Valley, to which all the outliers, holding tight to something in the nearly empty old communities of Pima and Thatcher to the west, and Solomon, Duncan, and Clifton-Morenci to the east, look toward for company and supplies. As such, it makes a good base for your Gila Valley adventures.

Sights

Not even the dust kicked up by all that uninterrupted open-pit mining less than 50 miles to the northeast can spoil the clear and dark rural skies here, and the 10,720-foot sky island peak that hems the valley to the southwest, Mount Graham, holds a few of the world's most powerful telescopes. **Eastern Arizona College's**

© TIM HULL

the Gila River

© TIM HULL

downtown Safford

Discovery Park Campus (1651 W. Discovery Park Blvd., Safford, 928/428-6260, www.eac.edu/discoverypark, 8am-5pm Mon.-Fri., 4pm-9:30pm Sat., free) celebrates and explains the area's astronomical benefits, and the science of astronomy, the beginnings of life, and the mysteries of the universe, at its **Gov Aker Observatory.** It costs nothing to take a look at the sun through a telescope equipped with eye-saving filters, or to listen to the eerie sounds of space. The highlight of a visit is a ride on the **Space Shuttle Polaris** simulator, in which you tour the solar system after buzzing Mount Graham. This is a great place to take kids. The grounds have several trails along which the public can stroll at will during business hours; the campus shows off the desert at its best, with a restored riparian area alive with birds and, if you are patient, maybe a few other animals. You can also book an all-day tour of the Mount Graham International Observatory here.

For a more down-to-earth, human-centric view of the valley, visit the **Eastern Arizona Museum and Historical Society** (2 N. Main, Pima, 928/485-9400, www.easternarizonamuseum.com, 10am-3pm Thurs.-Sat.), which preserves relics and stories from the valley's long history of habitation, from hunter-gatherer tribes to the Apaches, Mormon pioneers to cotton farmers and cattle ranchers.

An even deeper look at the valley's history is offered on the **Graham County Historic Walking and Driving Tour,** a self-guided tour of Highway 70 through Solomon, Safford, Thatcher, and Pima. Along the way you'll see just about every old building of note in the tiny, empty little towns, as well as Safford's 1916 neo-Colonial courthouse and several historic homes. The **Graham County Chamber of Commerce** (1111 Thatcher Blvd., Safford, 928/428-2511 or 888/837-1841, www.visitgrahamcounty.com) has a free 11-page booklet describing the tour, along with a plethora of other information about the area.

Events

The whole valley celebrates its Mexican restaurants and heritage with **SalsaFest** (www.

salsatrail.com) in late September, during which local chefs compete in salsa-making competitions, eaters try to outdo one another in a jalapeño-eating contest, children bounce around in castles, and bands play to crowds stuffed with food and fun.

Accommodations

The **Cottage Bed & Breakfast** (1104 S. Central, Safford, 928/428-5118 or 800/814-5118, www.cottagebedandbreakfast.com, $90-110) in Safford has the most distinctive and drive-worthy accommodations in town: adorable house-rooms decorated in the country style with a shared bathroom, and cottages with kitchenettes and private bathrooms. The red-brick Western Colonial Revival home is on the National Register of Historic Buildings and has a pleasant kind of Old West ambience. There's also a wonderful bakery on-site that serves homemade treats, espresso, and tea.

But nothing beats Duncan's **Simpson Hotel** (116 Main St., Duncan, 928/359-3590, www.simpsonhotel.com, $80-105), about 40 miles east of Safford on Highway 70, for that rural-West atmosphere. The owner has beautifully restored an old hotel first opened in 1915 and decorated its small, cozy rooms with a tasteful country simplicity. Plus the breakfasts are worth waking up for, made as they are with all-natural and often local ingredients.

The **Essence of Tranquility Natural Hot Spring** (6047 S. Lebanon Loop, Safford, 928/428-9312, www.azhotmineralspring.com), in the shadow of 10,720-foot-high Mount Graham, offers private, clothing-optional hot spring baths in which you can soak away all your stress and troubles. The baths are charmingly decorated and private; a bigger communal bath requires clothing. Though a bit on the rustic side, Essence of Tranquility is a wonderful place to visit if you love hot springs and want to meet like-minded soakers. If you want to stay the night or longer at the baths, you can camp for $15 per night, which includes use of a communal kitchen and barbecue area and unlimited use of the tubs. Rustic but comfortable "casitas" are also available for $50-70 per night.

You can make a reservation for ear coning (an alternative-medicine method of cleaning and detoxifying the ears), shiatsu and Swedish massage, or a detoxifying sweat wrap. If you're just going for the day, expect to pay $10 per person for use of the baths. While most of the baths are clothing optional, the owners don't allow any "open nudity." They also discourage bringing children along.

Food

The Gila Valley has some of the finest Mexican food restaurants in Arizona, most of them small, casual family-owned spots along Highway 70 and frequented by locals. About a decade ago 15 valley restaurants grouped together to form **The Salsa Trail,** a marketing campaign to draw visitors and diners to this lonely region. One can hardly imagine a more worthy public service. Uniformly first-rate, the Trail's member eateries serve up fresh and familiar Mexican fare with local and familial twists, and many of them offer American dishes as well. There is really no reason to eat anywhere else, and that's a good thing because the non-Mexican choices in Safford are for the most part chains and fast food. A brochure and map of the Salsa Trail are available at the **Graham County Chamber of Commerce** (1111 Thatcher Blvd., Safford, 928/428-2511 or 888/837-1841, www.visitgrahamcounty.com) or at any of the eateries listed below.

In Safford's retro and quiet old downtown, **El Coronado** (409 W. Main St., Safford, 928/428-7755, 7am-8pm Mon., Wed., Thurs. and Fri., 7am-5pm Sat.-Sun., $3-8) has superlative breakfasts: big fat burritos stuffed with egg, potato, cheese, and peppers, legendary huevos rancheros, or a simple plate of eggs and bacon if you're not into early morning spice. The Mexican dishes here are delicious and, of course, filling. Indeed, it's easy to fill up on chips and salsa: Owner Mary Coronado won a local salsa competition among Salsa Trail restaurants two years running (2007-2008).

For tortillas that might convince you to buy a trailer in Safford, just to be nearby, visit the famed **Mi Casa Tortilla Factory** (621 S. 7th

Ave., Safford, 928/428-7915, www.micasatortilla.com, 8am-5:30pm Mon.-Fri.). Fresh and hot, simple and handmade, the tortillas made here are known far and wide. Get a few dozen to chomp on in the car as you head out to the river or up to Mount Graham.

Valley locals love **El Charro** (601 W. Main St., Safford, 928/428-4134, 11am-8:30pm Mon.-Thurs., 11am-9:30pm Fri.-Sat., $3-10) in downtown Safford because they've been open, and serving pretty much the same food, since 1955. It's the oldest restaurant in the region. Their enchiladas, red- and green-chile burros, and other standard dishes are tasty and fresh, and their special chalaca, a fried masa bowl stuffed with beans and chile meat, is worth a try if you're in the mood for something slightly different.

About 10 miles west of Safford along Highway 70, **Bush & Schurtz** (232 E. 300 S. Old Hwy., Pima, 928/485-0679, 10:30am-8pm Mon.-Sat., $3-7) is housed in a circa-1905 building that used to be a hardware store of the same name. Stop in and try their chicken enchiladas and green-chile flautas. This is a good place to bring those who aren't overly enamored by beans, corn, and cheese, as they serve a mean burger and fries. To the east along Highway 70 a few miles, the family-owned and operated **La Paloma** (5185 Clifton St., Solomon, 928/428-2094, 10:30am-8pm Mon.-Thurs., 10:30am-9pm Fri.-Sat., $5-9) has superior Mexican food, cold and delicious margaritas, and friendly service in a laid-back atmosphere. About 40 miles farther along Highway 70, just before the New Mexico border, **Hilda's Kitchen & Meat Market** (115 Railroad Blvd., Duncan, 928/359-1771, 9am-6pm Mon.-Sat., 10am-3pm Sun., $5-8) has homemade Mexican food worth the drive, served in an ultracasual grocery-store setting; and you can take a couple of quarts of red and green chili home with you.

Services

The **Mount Graham Regional Medical Center** (1600 S. 20th Ave., Safford, 928/348-4000, www.mtgraham.org) in Safford has a full-service, 24-hour emergency room with 17 treatment bays.

ROPER LAKE STATE PARK

Desert-valley **Roper Lake State Park** (101 E. Roper Lake Rd., Safford, 928/428-6760, www.azstateparks.com/parks/ROLA, $7 per car) has decent fishing in a 30-acre reservoir and rents small but comfortable (more so than a tent anyway) log cabins that sleep up to six people ($55-65 reservations required). The lake is stocked with trout and bass, and there are clean shower facilities and both electric ($25) and nonelectric ($15) campsites.

But Roper Lake is also a fun spot to stop for a day of swimming from its sandy swimming beach, and soaking in its stone-lined hot tub filled by underground hot springs. There are about five miles of mostly flat, easy desert trails around the park, including a nearly two-mile loop trail at nearby **Dankworth Pond** (a unit of the park three miles south on Hwy. 191) that winds around a re-created village from the Paleo-Indian and Mogollon periods.

HOT WELL DUNES RECREATION AREA

Another developed hot spring bubbles up deep in the desert about 35 miles southeast of Safford in the middle of 2,000 acres of shifting sand dunes at **Hot Well Dunes Recreation Area**. This is a stark and hot landscape popular with off-road vehicle enthusiasts, who crowd the dunes in fall, winter, and spring to tear around on their sandrails and ATVs. The recreation area is often quite busy for being so remote, and if you're just looking to soak in the three developed, fenced-in tubs fed by a warm artesian well, it's not a good idea to go out on the weekends during the beautiful months. During summer it's blistering hot out here and not too welcoming. There's no electricity, drinking water, food, gas, or phones, so bring all your own supplies. There are several developed camping spots with fire rings and picnic tables, or you can camp in undeveloped spots. There are toilets on site. If you're planning to rip around the dunes, you need an OHV decal

© DERRICK NEILL/123RF.COM

the Pinaleno Mountains

($25); regardless, a recreation use fee of $3 per day is required.

Despite the distance to and isolation of the dunes, if you're a natural hot spring enthusiast, you should make the effort. The artesian well, discovered in 1928 by workers drilling for oil (you can still see the ancient drilling equipment nearby), spews out more than 250 gallons of 106-degree water every minute. It fills two developed tubs and overflows into a pond and mixes with other water to make a cooler third pool.

For more information contact the **Safford BLM office** (711 14th Ave., 928/348-4400, www.blm.gov/az/st/en/fo/safford_field_office.html). You can purchase an OHV decal at www.servicearizona.com.

PINALENO MOUNTAINS AND MOUNT GRAHAM

The largest of Southern Arizona's sky islands, the Pinaleño range guards the upper Gila Valley from the west, an often snow-capped Olympus for the lowlanders in the desert scrub below to ponder and worship. The range has

seven peaks, all of them over 7,000 feet but none as high as 10,720-foot Mount Graham, which residents here often use to refer to the entire range, its influence over the valley below being that strong.

Mount Graham, atop which astronomers scan the universe with some of the most powerful telescopes in the world, can be reached by just about any vehicle via the Civilian Conservation Corps-constructed **Swift Trail Parkway.** The steep, twisting two-lane road rises from the scrubby desert floor at just under 3,000 feet, to more than 9,000 feet near the top of Mount Graham, and along the way it passes through most of the state's major ecosystems, finally reaching the high evergreen forest, the air cool and thin. The road (State Hwy. 366, off Hwy. 191 about 8 miles south of Safford) is 35 miles one way, a trip that typically takes about two hours. You'll twist past old summer cabins, trailheads, campgrounds, lookouts, and picnic tables, and it's essential to stop along the way and take your time, noticing as the scrub gives way to oak woodlands, which give way to tall and thin pines, which pass on to majestic stands of fir and spruce. Snow usually closes the Swift Trail by November 14; it opens for the driving season on April 15. Most passenger cars can make it; 21.85 miles of the route are paved, and 13.35 miles are graded dirt. At the end of the trail you'll see **Riggs Lake,** a small highland fishing hole stocked with trout. The **Safford Ranger Station** (711 14th Ave., Ste. D, Safford, 928/428-4150, 8am-4pm Mon.-Fri.) has a lot of information on traveling, hiking, and camping in the mountains, including a booklet on driving the Swift Trail. The folks at the **Columbine Visitor Information Station,** about three quarters of the way toward the end of the road, are also helpful.

Operated by the University of Arizona in Tucson, the **Mount Graham International Observatory** sits near the top of Mount Graham, its powerful telescopes pointed at the heavens. Indeed, the **Vatican Advanced Technology Telescope** may be literally aimed heavenward. Also scanning the galaxy and beyond are the **Heinrich Hert Submillimeter Radio Telescope** and the **Large Binocular Telescope,** humankind's strongest eye on the great unknown. **Eastern Arizona College's Discovery Park Campus** (1651 W. Discovery Park Blvd., Safford, 928/428-6260, www.eac. edu/discoverypark) organizes infrequent tours of the observatory complex on Fridays and Saturdays, May-October, when the mountain weather cooperates. The tour, in groups of six or more, lasts all day (9am-4:30pm, $40 per person, no children under 8) and includes a sack lunch and a fair bit of the natural and human history of the area as well as an in-depth look at the observatory. You ride in a van along the Swift Trail to the top, and the guide points out all the interesting sights along the way. The tour begins in Safford at Discovery Park. It's a good idea to call far ahead to make a reservation.

GILA BOX RIPARIAN NATIONAL CONSERVATION AREA

Of course you can't visit the Gila Valley without at least a glimpse at the sad river that drew, in turn, Apaches, trappers, and Mormon farmers to this area long ago. The Gila was once a mighty desertland river, but you can't build the fifth largest city on the continent without a lot of water. Phoenix's thirst, along with the irrigation needs of the valley's farmers, has dammed and sucked the Gila to death, but in a few places it still runs wild and free through wilderness that isn't too different from that seen by the natives and pioneers. One of those places is the BLM-monitored **Gila Box Riparian National Conservation Area** (BLM Safford Field Office, 711 14th Ave., 928/348-4400, www.blm.gov/az/st/en/prog/blm_special_areas/ncarea/gbox.html), a 23,000-acre nature preserve off U.S. Highway 70 just 20 miles northeast of Safford.

A popular spot for kayakers and other river runners, the Gila Box offers streamside hiking, cool riparian coves, and a chance to see a few bighorn sheep clinging to rocky cliffs. Cottonwood stands, mesquite bosks, and sandbars line the mud-brown flow, hemmed by high, beige cliffs. The best way to see the river and possibly some wildlife is to take Sanchez Road off Highway 70, about five miles east of Safford (you'll see signs) to the **Spring Canyon Picnic Area** (it's about nine miles from the turnoff; along the way you'll pass an entrance kiosk). From there you can walk along the river on the two-mile loop **Cottonwood Trail** through the **Riverview Campground** and past the **Kearny Monument,** a tribute to General Stephen Watts Kearny, who led 300 soldiers along the Gila, camping nearby at Bonita Creek, to California during the Mexican-American War. Then it's on to the **Bonita Creek Watchable Wildlife Area,** which has interpretive signs about the area's animals. You can also drive all through the area on dirt roads, and there are two developed campgrounds ($5 per day). If you're a floater, make sure to check out the website for more information. There's a $3 per day recreation fee.

A rugged and scenic alternative route to the river is the **Black Hills Back Country Byway,** a 21-mile bumpy dirt road that passes over the river at the **Old Safford Bridge,** a historic

THE WHITE MOUNTAINS

Built in 1918, the Old Safford Bridge spans the Gila River.

© TIM HULL

concrete bridge built in 1918. You don't reach the river until 17 miles in, but along the way the dry scrublands provide some sweeping, lonely views, including of the post-apocalyptic Morenci Mine. There's a picnic area and campground with a bathroom below the bridge, and this is also a popular place for boaters to put in. The byway ends just outside of Morenci on Highway 191, and makes a good scenic detour.

CLIFTON AND MORENCI

These two small towns along U.S. Highway 191, bisected by the lazy San Francisco River and marking the start of the Coronado Trail into the White Mountains, were founded in the late 1800s as a copper mining complex, and they remain so today: Freeport-McMoran's Morenci Mine is the nation's largest, producing around 800 million pounds of the useful metal every year. There's a turnout about five miles north of town from which to view the monumental hole in the ground that is the result.

Clifton, with only about 2,000 residents, is full of boarded-up old buildings from the late-19th and early-20th centuries. Drive around slowly and wonder at the fix-up potential of these grand old structures. There's a small local-history museum and some really cool old buildings in the old downtown, and several across the bridge on the east side of the river. The town's old jail, chunked out of the cliffside, is still visible along the highway, and on the east side of the bridge there's a huge old digger that helped open up the pit. Up the hill a few miles in **Morenci,** the modern mineworks moan all day and night; about two thirds of the approximately 4,500 residents of the two towns work for the mine. Driving up or down the twisting road through Morenci at night, while the lit-up mine works on, is an unsettling—and thrilling—experience.

Sights

You can see for yourself the toll paid for cell phones and computers, both of which use a lot of copper, on a tour of the huge **Morenci Mine** (4521 U.S. Hwy. 191, Morenci). During the tour (call 877/646-8687), which lasts about

© TIM HULL

Clifton and Morenci were copper mining towns.

2.5 hours, you'll ride around the dusty mine site in a bus as a tour guide explains the mining process and peppers you with staggering statistics. Reservations are required, and the tours are only offered Friday-Saturday at 9am and 1pm.

Food

The northernmost stop on the Salsa Trail, **P.J.'s** (307 S. Coronado Blvd., Clifton, 928/865-3328, 5am-8pm Mon.-Fri., 5am-2pm Sat.-Sun., $5-20) in Clifton makes delectable Mexican and American food from local recipes, and has been doing so since the 1980s. Try the green chile omelet for breakfast, and anything smothered in enchilada sauce and melted cheese for lunch and dinner.

SAN CARLOS APACHE RESERVATION

Before 1871, the Western Apache bands that call this 1.8-million-acre reservation along the Gila River northwest of Safford home used to live and migrate across the valley's desert grasslands, streamsides, and oak woodlands, hunting game and gathering the land's many edibles. These days the San Carlos Apache Tribe welcomes visitors to recreate on their sparsely populated lands, and they operate a casino-resort complex with a golf course. To hike, fish, swim, and drive the backcountry here you need to purchase a permit from **San Carlos Apache Tribe Recreation & Wildlife Department** (Hwy. 70 and Geronimo Rd., San Carlos, 928/475-2343 or 888/475-2344, www. scatrw.com, $10 per day). Permits are also sold at the Apache Gold Casino's convenience store and at the Express Stop in Globe.

The **San Carlos Apache Culture Center** (Hwy. 70, milepost 272, 928/475-2894, www. sancarlosapache.com, 9am-5pm Mon.-Fri.) has interesting displays about the tribe's history and culture. Here you can also see and purchase examples of the locally made peridot jewelry. The world's largest deposit of the August birthstone is located near the reservation capital of **San Carlos,** and there are a few places in the small town that sell jewelry, Apache burden

The Western Apache and the Settlers

All over southern and central Arizona, where the Western Apache once wandered unchallenged according to a seasonal schedule held deep in their cultural memories, there is food: acorns, agave, wild spinach, wild onions, mesquite beans, cactus fruit, and more–all foods integral to the once diverse Apache larder.

Once settlers–Spanish then Mexican then American–began claiming this land as their own, the Western Apache found it increasingly difficult to gain unfettered access to their traditional gathering grounds, and they drew the unending ire of the new arrivals when they stole livestock, which many Apache saw as little different from hunting any other ungulate grazing in the desert.

Really the Western Apache never had much of a chance. Their lifeways were about thin-line subsistence, living lightly so as to conserve the relative abundance of the desert for future generations. The capitalist settlers couldn't have been more different; they wanted wealth, surplus, and the power that comes with it. Furthermore, settlers never really got the fact that not all Apaches were the same. The Western

Apache, one of the few agricultural-minded bands in Apacheria, were often blamed for the depredations of the less sedentary Chiricahua Apache, which claimed Geronimo as one of their leaders.

Thus we have the general circumstances, building over generations, that led to the Camp Grant Massacre in 1871, an infamous slaughter of more than a hundred Western Apache, mostly women and children, who were peacefully camped close to a U.S. Army fort near Aravaipa Canyon (south of San Carlos Lake on the San Carlos Apache Reservation).

The outrage was planned and perpetrated by the leading lights of Tucson's business community, and justified by the half-mad screeds of *Tucson Citizen* editor John Wasson. In the aftermath of the largely unprovoked massacre, Tucson's murderous elite didn't even bother to attempt to name the victims for the laughable trial that saw all the perpetrators acquitted; instead, they listed them as John Doe Apache, or Mary Doe Apache–names that reveal just how unknown the Western Apache were to their new neighbors.

baskets, cradle boards, and other local arts and crafts. The culture center has a good gift shop selling all of these items and more, as does the Apache Gold Casino.

Apache Gold Casino

Apache Gold (5 miles east of Globe on Hwy. 70, 800/272-2438, www.apache-gold-casino. com) is the center of activity on the reservation, offering the usual Indian casino-style slots, blackjack, poker, bingo, and live entertainment. The **Apache Stronghold Golf Course** is lovely and affordable, and the resort's rooms ($89-109 for basic room) and restaurants offer the best accommodations and meals on the reservation. The resort has a gift shop that sells local Apache crafts, and **Wickiup Buffet** ($5.95.-17.95) lays out prime rib on Saturdays, seafood on Fridays, and brunch on Sunday.

The always-open **Apache Grill** serves native and Southwestern dishes along with standard American fare.

San Carlos Lake

Formed by the damming of the Gila, this large reservoir, with 158 miles of desert shoreline and surrounded by the jagged Gila, Mescal, and Santa Teresa Mountains, has good fishing, and there's a tackle shop with snacks and other supplies on-site. The nearby **Coolidge Dam,** dedicated by its namesake commander-in-chief in 1930, is a feat of engineering that's worth seeing. Follow the signed road south off of Highway 70 at Peridot, to the **San Carlos Reservoir Recreation Area,** where you can boat and swim, water-ski, fish, camp, and walk around the rocky scrublands.

THE GRAND CANYON AND THE ARIZONA STRIP

There's a reason why Arizona's official nickname is "The Grand Canyon State." Any state with one of the true wonders of the world would be keen to advertise its good luck.

The canyon must simply be seen to be believed. If you stand for the first time on one of the South Rim's easily accessible lookouts and don't have to catch your breath, you might need

© TIM HULL

HIGHLIGHTS

LOOK FOR 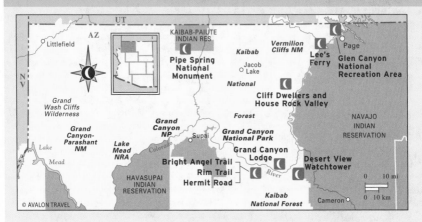 TO FIND RECOMMENDED SIGHTS, ACTIVITIES, DINING, AND LODGING.

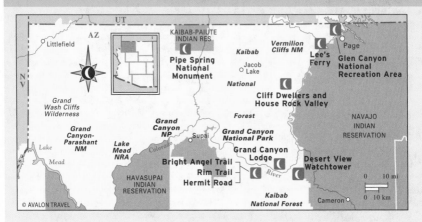

THE GRAND CANYON

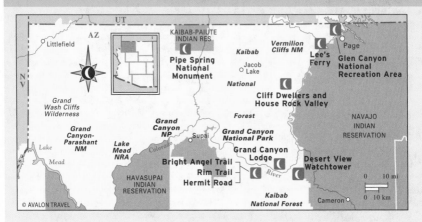 **Hermit Road:** Make your way west along the forested rim to the enchanting stone cottage called Hermit's Rest, stopping at different viewpoints to see the setting sun turn the canyon walls into fleeting works of art (page 349).

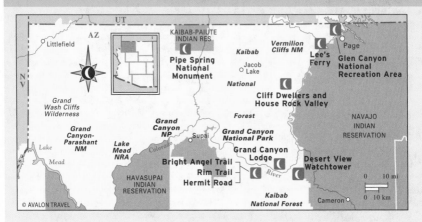 **Desert View Watchtower:** See one of architect Mary Colter's finest accomplishments—a rock tower standing tall on the edge of the canyon, its design based on mysterious Anasazi structures (page 357).

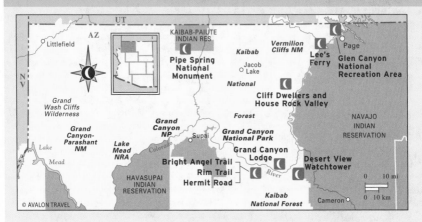 **Rim Trail:** Park your car, grab a bottle of water, and walk along the rim on this easy, accessible trail, past historical buildings, famous lodges, and several of the most breathtaking views in the world (page 357).

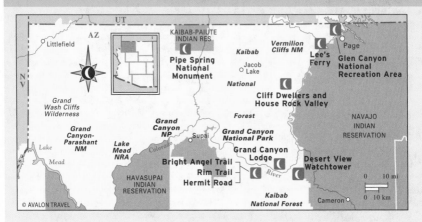 **Bright Angel Trail:** Don't just stand on the rim and stare—hike down the most popular trail on the South Rim, its construction based on old Native American routes. Or choose one of several additional trails to see the arid grandeur of the inner canyon (page 358).

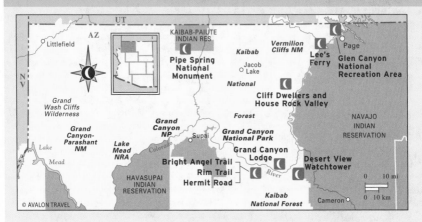 **Grand Canyon Lodge:** Even if you're not staying the night at the North Rim, make sure to step inside this rustic old lodge balancing on the edge of the gorge, where you can sink into

a chair and gaze out the picture windows at the multicolored canyon (page 368).

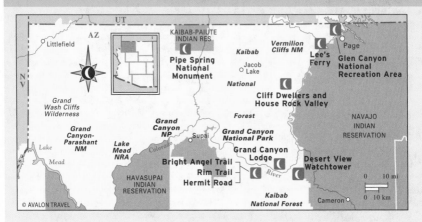 **Pipe Spring National Monument:** Learn the history of the Latter-day Saints that settled the isolated Arizona Strip in the 19th century at this wisely preserved ranch and homestead, where guides will show you what life was really like on the lonely frontier (page 388).

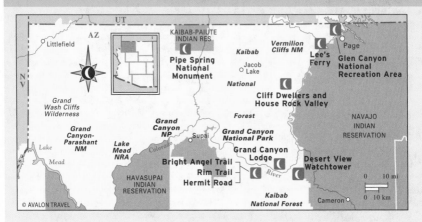 **Cliff Dwellers and House Rock Valley:** Stop along the highway and walk among these strange, thrilling little structures built of red rock (page 393).

 Lee's Ferry: One of the few places in the canyonlands where you can dip your toes in the mighty Colorado River without first hiking deep into the Grand Canyon, Lee's Ferry is Mile 0 to river runners; to everybody else it's an ideal place to sit on the beach and watch the river roil and rush (page 393).

 Glen Canyon National Recreation Area: Rent a houseboat or fish the waters of Lake Powell, a man-made lake formed by the Glen Canyon Dam, a grand engineering feat that has drawn the unending ire of environmentalists (page 398).

© TIM HULL

mules in the Grand Canyon

to check your pulse. Staring into the canyon brings up all kinds of existential questions; its brash vastness can't be taken in without conjuring some big ideas and questions about life, humanity, God. Take your time here—you'll need it.

The more adventurous can make reservations, obtain a permit, and enter the desert depths of the canyon, taking a hike, or even a mule ride, to the Colorado River, or spending a weekend trekking rim-to-rim with an overnight at the famous Phantom Ranch, deep in the canyon's inner gorge. The really brave can hire a guide and take a once-in-a-lifetime trip down the great river, riding the roiling rapids and camping on its serene beaches.

There are plenty of places to stay and eat, many of them charming and historic, on the canyon's South Rim. If you decide to go to the high, forested, and often snowy North Rim, you'll drive through a corner of the desolate Arizona Strip, which has a beauty and a history all its own.

Water-sports enthusiasts will want to make it up to the far northern reaches of the state to

the Glen Canyon Recreation Area to do some waterskiing or maybe rent a houseboat, and anyone interested in the far end of America's engineering prowess will want to see Glen Canyon Dam, holding back the once-wild Colorado.

PLANNING YOUR TIME

The ideal South Rim-only trip lasts three days and two nights (with the first and last days including the trip to and from the rim). This amount of time will allow you to see all the sights on the rim, to take in a sunset and sunrise over the canyon, and even do a day hike or a mule trip below the rim. If you just have a day, about five hours or so will allow you to see all the sights on the rim and take a very short hike down one of the major trails. If you include a North or West Rim excursion, add at least one or two more days and nights. It takes at least five hours to reach the North Rim from the South, perhaps longer if you take the daily shuttle from the south instead of your own vehicle. The West Rim and the Hualapai and

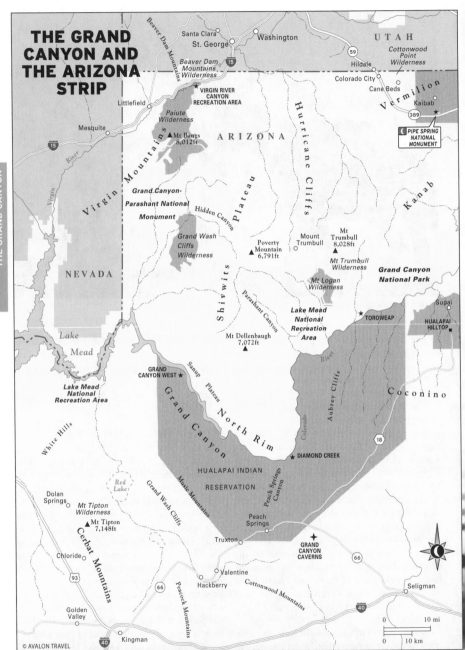

THE GRAND CANYON AND THE ARIZONA STRIP

THE GRAND CANYON

Beaver Dam Mountains

Santa Clara
St. George
Washington
UTAH

Cottonwood Point Wilderness

Beaver Dam Mountains Wilderness

Hildale

Colorado City
Cane Beds

VIRGIN RIVER CANYON RECREATION AREA

Littlefield
Paiute Wilderness

Kaibab
Vermilion

Mesquite

▲ Mt Bangs 8,012ft

ARIZONA

Hurricane Cliffs

PIPE SPRING NATIONAL MONUMENT

Virgin Mountains

Grand Canyon-Parashant National Monument

Hidden Canyon

Shivwits Plateau

Kanab

Grand Wash Cliffs Wilderness

Poverty Mountain 6,791ft

Mount Trumbull

Mt Trumbull 8,028ft

Mt Trumbull Wilderness

Grand Canyon National Park

NEVADA

Parashant Canyon

Mt Logan Wilderness

Lake Mead National Recreation Area

Supai

Lake Mead

Mt Dellenbaugh 7,072ft

★ TOROWEAP

HUALAPAI HILLTOP

Lake Mead National Recreation Area

GRAND CANYON WEST ★

Sanup Plateau

Grand Canyon

North Rim

Colorado River

Aubrey Cliffs

Coconino

White Hills

Red Lake

Grand Wash Cliffs

Music Mountains

★ DIAMOND CREEK

HUALAPAI INDIAN RESERVATION

Peach Springs Canyon

18

Dolan Springs

Mt Tipton Wilderness

▲ Mt Tipton 7,148ft

Peach Springs

Chloride

Cerbat Mountains

Truxton

93

Valentine

GRAND CANYON CAVERNS

66

Golden Valley

66

Hackberry

Cottonwood Mountains

Peacock Mountains

Seligman

40

Kingman

© AVALON TRAVEL

0   10 mi

0   10 km

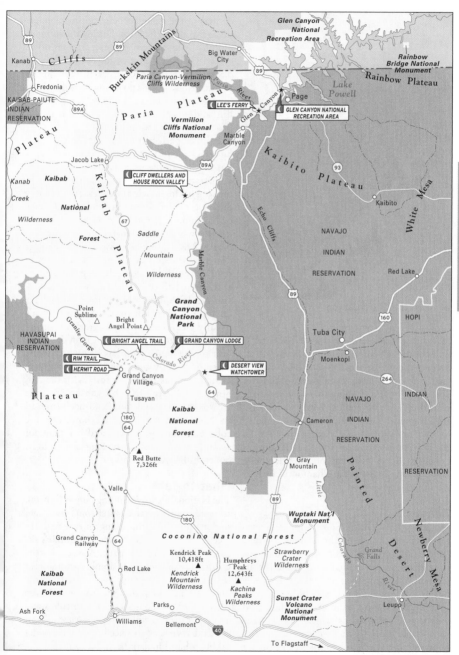

winter at the Grand Canyon

corners of the globe become legitimate enterprises if you're so inclined. During the summer months (May-September) temperatures often exceed 110°F in the inner canyon, which has a desert climate, but cool by 20-30°F up on the forested rims. There's no reason for anybody to hike deep into the canyon in summer. It's not fun, and it is potentially deadly. It is better to plan a marathon trek in the fall.

Fall is a perfect time to visit the park: It's light-jacket cool on the South Rim and warm but not hot in the inner canyon, where high temperatures during October range 80-90°F, making hiking much more pleasant than it is during the infernal summer months. October or November are the last months of the year during which a rim-to-rim hike from the North Rim is possible, as rim services shut down by the end of October and the only road to the rim is closed by late November, and often before that, from winter snowstorms. It's quite cold on the North Rim during October, but on the South Rim it's usually clear, cool, and pleasant during the day and snuggle-up chilly at night. A winter visit to the South Rim has its own charms. There is usually snow on the rim January-March, contrasting beautifully with the red, pink, and dusty green canyon colors. The crowds are thin and more laid-back than in the busy summer months. It is, however, quite cold, even during the day, and you may not want to stand and stare too long at the windy, bone-chilling viewpoints.

What to Take

The National Parks, including Grand Canyon, stopped selling bottled water some time ago, so don't forget to bring along an easy-to-carry receptacle to refill at the water fountains situated throughout the park. A water bottle, Camelback or canteen is simply required gear for a visit; you are going to get thirsty in the high, dry air along the rim. You might even consider taking along a cooler with cold water and other drinks, which you can leave in your car and revisit as the need arises. Consider taking a hat, binoculars, and a camera along

Havasupai Indian Reservations are some 250 miles from the South Rim over slow roads, and a trip to these remote places should be planned separately from one to the popular South Rim. The most important thing to remember when planning a trip to the canyon is to plan far ahead, even if you're just, like the vast majority of visitors, planning to spend time on the South Rim. Six months' advance planning is the norm, longer if you are going to ride a mule down or stay overnight at Phantom Ranch in the inner canyon.

Seasons

At about 7,000 feet, the South Rim has a temperate climate, warm in the summer months, cool in fall, and cold in the winter. It snows in the deep winter and often rains in the late afternoon in late summer. Summer is the park's busiest season—and it is *very* busy—four or five million visitors from all over the world will be your companions, which isn't as bad as some make it out to be. People watching and hobnobbing with fellow tourists from the far with your water bottle. The canyon's vastness can only be considered for so long before you start to notice the details hidden in plain sight; binoculars or a camera come in handy in such circumstances.

Even in summer bring along a light jacket, for the nights at 7,000 feet can turn somewhat chilly. In the winter, when it is 70-something in Phoenix, the South Rim is cold, and often snowy. Several easily-shed layers of cold-weather clothing will serve you well from October to May.

Gateways to the Canyon

Grand Canyon National Park, especially its South Rim, has some of the best accommodations in the entire national park system, but it's not always possible to get reservations. The park's lodging rates are audited annually and generally compare favorably to those offered outside the park, but you can sometimes find excellent deals at one of several gateway towns around canyon country. Using one of these places as a base for a visit to the canyon makes sense if you're planning on touring the whole of the canyonlands and not just the park. Besides offering affordable and even a few luxurious places to stay and eat, these gateways are often interesting in their own right and deserving of some attention from the traveler, especially those interested in the history of this hard and spacious land.

Flagstaff, 79 miles southeast of the park's main South Rim entrance, was the park's first gateway town, and it's still in many ways the best. The home of Northern Arizona University is a fun, laid-back college town with a railroad and Route 66 history. In the old days, Eastern tourists detrained at Flagstaff and then faced an all-day stagecoach trip across the forest and the plains, just for a glimpse at the canyon and a few nights in a white canvas tent. These days you just hop in your rental or your family road-trip wagon and take U.S. Highway 180 northwest for about an hour and a half and there you are. The route is absolutely (with apologies to desert rats who prefer the eastern Desert View approach) the most scenic of all the approaches to the canyon, passing through Coconino National Forest and beneath the San Francisco Peaks, the state's ruling mountain range.

CAMERON

About 50 miles north of Flagstaff along Highway 89, near the junction with Route 64 (the route to the park's east gate), the nearly 100-year-old **C Historic Cameron Trading Post and Lodge** (800/338-7385, www.camerontradingpost.com, $59-159) is only about a 30-minute drive from the Desert View area of the park, a good place to start your tour. Starting from the east entrance you'll see the canyon gradually becoming grand. Before you reach the park, the Little Colorado drops some 2,000 feet through the arid, scrubby land, cutting through gray rock on the way to its marriage with the big river to create the **Little Colorado Gorge.** Stop here and get a barrier-free glimpse at this lesser chasm to prime yourself for what is to come. There are usually plenty of booths set up selling Navajo arts and crafts and a lot of touristy souvenirs at two developed pull-offs along the road.

The Cameron Lodge is a charming and affordable place to stay, and is a perfect base for a visit to the Grand Canyon, Indian Country, and the Arizona Strip. It has a good restaurant (6am-9:30pm daily summer, 7am-9pm daily winter, $2.99-26.99) serving American and Navajo food, including excellent beef stew, heaping Navajo tacos, chili and burgers. There's also an art gallery, a visitors center, a huge trading post/gift shop, and an RV park ($25 full hookup, no bathroom or showers). A small grocery store has packaged sandwiches, chips, and sodas. The rooms are decorated with a southwestern Native American style and are very clean and comfortable, some with views of the Little Colorado River and the old 1911 suspension bridge that spans the stream just outside the lodge. There are single-bed rooms, rooms with two beds, and a few suites that are perfect for families. The stone-and-wood buildings and the garden patio, laid out with stacked sandstone bricks with picnic tables and red-stone walkways below the open-corridor rooms, create a cozy, history-soaked setting and make the lodge a memorable place to stay. The vast, empty red plains of the Navajo Reservation spread out all around and create a lonely, isolated atmosphere, especially at night; but the rooms have cable TV and free Wi-Fi, so you can be connected and entertained even way out here.

If you're visiting in the winter, the lodge drops its prices significantly during this less crowded touring season. In January and February, you can get one of the single-bed rooms for about $59 d.

WILLIAMS

This small historic town along I-40 (what used to be Route 66), surrounded by the Kaibab National Forest, is the closest interstate town to Route 64, and thus has branded itself "The Gateway to the Grand Canyon." It has been around since 1874 and was the last Route 66 town to be bypassed by the Interstate (not until 1984). As a result, and because of a resurgence over the last few decades owing to the rebirth of the Grand Canyon Railway, Williams, with about 3,000 full-time residents, has a good bit of small-town charm—the entire downtown area is on the National Register of Historic Places. It's worth a stop and an hour or two of strolling about, and there are a few good restaurants. It's only about an hour drive to the South Rim from Williams, so many consider it a convenient base for exploring the region. The drive is not as scenic as either Route 64 from Cameron or U.S. 180 from Flagstaff. This is the place to stay if you plan to take the **Grand Canyon Railway** to the rim, which is a highly recommended way of reaching the South Rim. It's fun, it cuts down on traffic and emissions within the park, and you'll get exercise walking along the rim, or renting a

downtown Williams

© ELIZABETH JANG

bike and cruising the park with the wind in your face.

Williams Historic District

On a walk through the **Williams Historic Business District** you'll see how a typical pioneer Southwestern mountain town might have looked from territorial days until the interstate came and the railroad died. Williams wasn't bypassed by I-40 until the 1980s, so many of its old buildings still stand and have been put to use as cafés, boutiques, B&Bs, and gift shops. Walk around and look at the old buildings, shop for Native American and Old West knickknacks, pioneer-era memorabilia, and Route 66 souvenirs you don't need, and maybe stop for a beer, cocktail, or a cup of coffee at an old-school, small-town saloon or a dressed-up café. The district is bounded on the north by Railroad Avenue, on the south by Grant Avenue, and on the east and west by 1st and 4th Streets, respectively. About 250 acres, the district has 44 buildings dating from 1875-1949, and an array of Route 66-era business signs and midcentury commercial architecture worth a few snapshots. Old Route 66 is variously termed Bill Williams Avenue, Grand Canyon Avenue, and Railroad Avenue, and splits into parallel one-way streets through the historic downtown before meeting up to the west and east.

Bearizona Wildlife Park

Don't be surprised if a big fat brown bear, gone lazy from living the easy life in beautiful pine-covered **Bearizona Wildlife Park** (1500 E. Route 66, I-40 Exit 165, 928/635-2289, www.bearizona.com, 8am-5pm daily, $10-20), decides to lounge on his back in front of your car; it's best to drive around the old beast, one of the many rescued animals that call this family-friendly drive-through wildlife park home. Along the two-mile drive through the forested park, which the park insists be done with windows up, you'll see many brown and black bears wrestling and lounging in the meadows, as well as wolves, bison, big horn sheep, and other classic animals of North America.

A walk-through section at the end of the drive called **Fort Bearizona** features adorable baby animals frolicking with innocence and wonder, along with a few regal birds of prey that would probably like to eat all those fuzzy little morsels. A snack bar and gift shop here will gladly take even more of your money. Indeed, it's a bit pricey, especially for large families; kids under 13 pay $10, and most others pay $20. That being said, kids absolutely love this place, and it makes for an easy side-trip on the way to the Grand Canyon: it's located just outside of Williams near the junction of I-40 and Route 64, right on the route to the South Rim. Allow about two hours to visit this fun park; many of the animals here have a bit of personality, and you might get hooked if you stay *too* long. Bearizona is busiest in the summer, but the park is open year-round. The hours may vary according to season and weather, so call before driving out there just to make sure. As always, bring your own water no matter the season.

Shopping

There's a gathering of boutiques and gift shops in Williams's quaint, historic downtown area, between Railroad and Grant, and 1st and 4th Streets.

The **Turquoise Tepee** (114 W. Route 66, 928/635-4709, 10am-5pm daily) has been selling top-shelf Native American arts and crafts, Western wear, and regional souvenirs for four generations. There's a lot to see in this store. The same goes for **Native America** (117 E. Route 66, 928/635-4600, 8am-10pm in summer, 8am-6pm winter), a Native American-owned shop with Hopi and Navajo arts and crafts.

Recreation

The alpine ski runs at the Arizona Snowbowl in the San Francisco Peaks are only a quick hour's drive from downtown Williams, so it's easy to overlook the more modest **Elk Ridge Ski and Outdoor Recreation Area** (Ski Run Rd., 928/814-5038 or 928/814-5027, www.elkridgeski.com, 10am-4pm, lift tickets are $25-35 adults, $25-20 children) in the Kaibab National

Forest about five miles from town. More laid-back and kid friendly than the big mountains to the north, Elk Ridge allows skiing, snowboarding, and tubing whenever there's snow to slide on. They also rent equipment here—skis, tubes and boards—and there's a decent café for warming up and resting.

Events

In mid-August, perfectly preserved classic cars and low-hung Harleys crowd Williams's narrow downtown streets for the **Cool Country Cruise-In** (928/635-1418, www.route66place.com), a celebration of the town's prominent place along the Mother Road. The two-day festival features a car show, vendors, live music, and the **Miss Route 66 Pageant.**

Northland kids wait all year for the Grand Canyon Railway's celebration of author Chris Van Allsburg's classic holiday story *The Polar Express.* The always sold-out **Polar Express and Mountain Village Holiday** (800/848-3511, www.thetrain.com, nightly departures at 6:30pm and 8pm, $29 adults, $19 children 2-15, mid-Nov.-early Jan.) features a one-hour nighttime pajama-party train ride, complete with cookies and hot cocoa, to a lit-up Christmastown that kids ooh and ahh at from their train seats. Riders dressed up like characters in the book read the story as kids follow along in their own copies. Then Santa boards the train and gives each kid some individual attention and a free jingle-bell like the one in the famous book. On the return trip, everybody sings Christmas carols, while the younger tykes generally fall asleep. Needless to say, this annual event is *very* popular with kids and their families from all over Northern Arizona, and tickets generally sell out early (even as early as August).

Accommodations

Williams has some of the most affordable independent accommodations in the Grand Canyon region, as well as several chain hotels.

It's difficult to find a better deal than the clean and basic **El Rancho Motel** (617 E. Route 66, 928/635-2552 or 800/228-2370, $75-82), an independently owned, retro motel on Route 66 with few frills save comfort, friendliness, and a heated pool open in season.

The **Canyon Country Inn** (442 W. Route 66, 928/635-2349, www.thecanyoncountryinn.com, $84-104) is an enchanting little place, home to a whole mob of stuffed bears and right in the heart of Williams's charming historic district. Its country-Victorian decor is not for everyone, but it's a comfortable and friendly place to stay while exploring the canyon country.

The **Grand Canyon Railway Hotel** (235 N. Grand Canyon Blvd., 928/635-4010, www.thetrain.com, $169-349) stands now where Williams's old Harvey House once stood. It has a heated indoor pool, two restaurants, a lounge, a hot tub, a workout room, and a huge gift shop. The hotel serves riders on the Grand Canyon Railway and offers the highest-end accommodations in Williams.

The original █ **Grand Canyon Hotel** (145 W. Route 66, 928/635-1419, www.thegrandcanyonhotel.com, $67-185) opened in 1891, even before the railroad arrived and made Grand Canyon tourism something not just the rich could do. New owners refurbished and reopened the charming old red-brick hotel in Williams's historic downtown in 2005, and now it's an affordable, friendly place to stay with a lot of character and a bit of an international flavor. Spartan single-bed rooms go for $67 a night with a shared bathroom, and individually named and eclectically decorated double rooms with private baths are $80 a night—some of the most distinctive and affordable accommodations in the region.

The **Red Garter Bed & Bakery** (137 W. Railroad Ave., 928/635-1484, www.redgarter.com, $135-160) makes much of its original and longtime use as a brothel (which didn't finally close, as it was with many similar places throughout Arizona's rural regions, until the 1940s), where the town's lonely, uncouth miners, lumberjacks, railway workers, and cowboys met with unlucky women, ever euphemized as "soiled doves," in rooms called "cribs." The 1897 frontier-Victorian stone building, with its

GATEWAYS TO THE CANYON

comfortable rooms, each named and inspired by English counties. They also have delicious breakfasts, a pool table, a cool old juke box, and antique bar-style shuffleboard game that may just keep you from exploring the pinelands and sitting out under the dark, star-smeared skies.

Food

A northland institution with some of the best steaks in the region, (**Rod's Steak House** (301 E. Route 66, 928/635-2671, www.rodssteakhouse.com, 11am-9:30pm Mon.-Sat., $11.50-35) has been operating at the same site since 1946. The food is excellent, the staff is friendly and professional, and the menus are shaped like steers. The **Pine Country Restaurant** (107 N. Grand Canyon Blvd., 928/635-9718, pinecountryrestaurant.com, 6:30am-9:30pm daily, $5-10) is a family-style place that serves good food and homemade pies. Check out the beautiful paintings of the Grand Canyon on the walls. **Twisters '50s Soda Fountain and Route 66 Café** (417 E. Route 66, 928/635-0266, 10am-9pm daily, $5-15) has 1950s music and decor and delicious diner-style food, including memorable root-beer floats. It has a full bar, excellent burgers, and friendly, upbeat staff. Even if you're not hungry, check out the gift shop selling all kinds of road-culture memorabilia.

You'll find comforting Mexican and Southwestern food at **Pancho McGillicuddy's** (141 Railroad Ave., 928/635-4150, www.vivapanchos.com, 11am-10pm daily, $10-17). They serve satisfying burritos, enchiladas, and Navajo tacos, carne asada, New York strip, and fish and chips in an 1893 building that used to be the rowdy Cabinet Saloon, on Williams's territorial-era stretch of iniquity known as "Saloon Row." They mix a decent margarita, but beer is the drink of choice in this high-country burg, and they have a great selection on tap. **Cruiser's Route 66 Bar & Grill** (233 W. Route 66, 928/635-2445, www.cruisers66.com, 11am-9pm Mon.-Thurs., 11am-10pm Fri.-Sun., $5.95-19.95) offers a diverse menu, with superior barbecue ribs, burgers, fajitas, pulled-pork

It's easy to find Rod's Steak House.

wide arching entranceway, has been beautifully restored with a lot of authentic charm, without skimping on the comforts—like big brass beds for the nighttime and delightful, homemade baked goods, juice, and coffee in the morning. Famously, this place is haunted by some poor unquiet, regretful soul, so you might want to bring your night-light along.

The Lodge on Route 66 (200 E. Route 66, 877/563-4366, http://thelodgeonroute66.com, $89-159) has stylish, newly renovated rooms with sleep-inducing pillow-top mattresses; it has a few very civilized two-room suites with kitchenettes, dining areas, and fireplaces—perfect for a family that's not necessarily on a budget. The motor court-style grounds, right along the Route of course, has a romantic cabana with comfortable seats and an outdoor fireplace. No pets.

If you want to get away from Route 66 and into the pine forests around Williams, check out the three-story **FireLight Bed and Breakfast** (175 W. Mead Ave., 928/838-8218, $160-250), which rents four eminently sandwiches, and homemade chili. They have a full bar and offer live music most nights.

The vegetarian's best bet this side of downtown Flagstaff is the **Dara Thai Café** (145 W. Route 66, 928/635-2201, 11am-2pm and 5pm-9pm Mon.-Sat., $3.50-$9.95), an agreeable little spot in the **Grand Canyon Hotel.** They serve a variety of fresh and flavorful Thai favorites and offer quite a few meat-free dishes.

Information and Services

Stop at the **Williams-Kaibab National Forest Visitor Center** (200 W. Railway Ave., 928/635-1418 or 800/863-0546, 8am-6:30pm daily spring and summer, 8am-5pm daily fall and winter) for information about Williams, the Grand Canyon, and camping and hiking in the Kaibab National Forest.

TUSAYAN

About a mile outside Grand Canyon National Park's south gate, along Route 64/U.S. 180, Tusayan is a collection of hotels, restaurants, and gift shops that has grown side by side with the park for nearly a century. The village makes a decent, close-by base for a visit to the park, especially if you can't get reservations at any of the in-park lodges. Although there are a few inexpensive chain hotels here, a stay in Tusayan isn't on the whole cheaper than lodging in the park; there are many more places to eat here than there are inside the park, but the culinary scene is relatively bleak nonetheless.

Sights

Tusayan is perhaps best known as the home of the **National Geographic Grand Canyon Visitors Center** (Rte. 64, 928/638-2468, www.explorethecanyon.com, 8am-10pm Mar.-Oct., 10am-8pm Nov.-Feb., IMAX movie tickets are $13 over age 10, $10 children 6-10, children under 6 free), which has been a popular first stop for park visitors since the 1980s. Truth be told, even with the recent addition of the corporate logo-clad **Grand Canyon Base Camp #1,** an interactive display of canyon history, lore, and science, the center wouldn't be worth a stop if not for its **IMAX Theater.** The

colossal screen shows the 35-minute movie, *Grand Canyon—The Hidden Secrets,* every hour. The most popular IMAX film ever (some 40 million people have reportedly seen it), the movie is quite thrilling, affording glimpses of the canyon's more remote corners that feel like real time, if not reality. If you can afford the admission price, this is a fun way to learn about what you're about to see in the park. It's also a convenient place to book tours—everything from jeep rides to helicopter tours to river rafting adventures. If you're going budget, skip it and drive a few miles north, where you're likely to forget about both movies and money while staring dumbfounded into that gorge.

Accommodations

Most of Tusayan's accommodations are of the chain variety, and though they are generally clean and comfortable, few of them have any character to speak of and most of them are rather overpriced for what you get. Staying in either Flagstaff or Williams is a better choice if you're looking for an independent hotel or motel with some local color, and you can definitely find better deals in those gateways.

Before you reach Tusayan you'll pass through Valle, a tiny spot along Route 64/U.S. 180, where you'll find one of the better deals in the whole canyon region. The **Red Lake Campground and Hostel** (8850 N. Rte. 64, 800/581-4753, $20 per person, per night), where you can rent a bed in a shared room, is a basic but reasonably comfortable place sitting lonely on the grasslands next to a gas station; it has shared bathrooms with showers, a common room with a kitchen and a TV, and an RV park ($25) with hookups. If you're going super-budget, you can't beat this place, and it's only about 45 minutes from the park's south gate.

The **Red Feather Lodge** (300 Rte. 64, 928/638-2414, www.redfeatherlodge.com, $86-159), though more basic than some of the other places in Tusayan, is a comfortable, affordable place to stay with a pool, hot tub, and clean rooms in separate hotel and motel complexes. The **Grand Hotel** (149 Rte. 64, 928/638-3333, www.grandcanyongrandhotel.com, $116-299), resembling a kind of Western-themed ski lodge, has very clean and comfortable rooms, a pool, hot tub, fitness center, and a beautiful lobby featuring a Starbucks coffee kiosk. The **Best Western Grand Canyon Squire Inn** (74 Rte. 64, 928/638-2681, www.grandcanyonsquire. com, $119-229) has a fitness center, pool and spa, salon, game room, a bowling alley and myriad other amenities—so many that it may be difficult to get out of the hotel to enjoy the natural sights.

Food

Nobody would go to Tusayan specifically to eat, but it makes for a decent emergency stop if you're dying of hunger. With one exception: We Cook Pizza would be good in any town, and it is a bright spot in this rather drab and chain-happy commercial parasite of the park. A lot of tour buses stop in Tusayan, so you may find yourself crowded into waiting for a table at some places, especially during the summer high season. Better to eat in the park, or in Flagstaff or Williams, both of which have many charming and delicious local restaurants worth seeking out. It's only about an hour's drive to either

place, so you might be better off having a small snack and skipping Tusayan altogether.

One of the better places in Tusayan is the **Canyon Star Restaurant** (928/638-3333, 7am-10am and 11:30am-10pm daily, $10-25) inside the Grand Hotel, which serves Southwestern food, steaks, and ribs, and features a saloon in which you can belly up to the bar on top of an old mule saddle (it's not that comfortable). **The Coronado Room** (928/638-2681, 5pm-10pm daily, $15-28) inside the Grand Canyon Squire Inn serves tasty steaks, seafood, Mexican-inspired dishes, and pasta.

If you're craving pizza after a long day exploring the canyon, try **We Cook Pizza & Pasta** (125 E. Rte. 64, 928/638-2278, www. wecookpizzaandpasta.com, 11am-10pm daily Mar.-Oct., 11am-8pm daily Nov.-Feb., $10-30) for an excellent, high-piled pizza pie. It calls you just as you enter Tusayan coming from the park. The pizza, served in slices or whole pies, is pretty good considering the locale, and they have a big salad bar with all the fixings, plus beer and wine. It's a very casual place, with picnic tables and an often harried staff. It gets really busy in here during the high summer season.

The South Rim

The reality of the Grand Canyon is often suspect even to those standing on its rim. "For a time it is too much like a scale model or an optical illusion," wrote Joseph Wood Krutch, a great observer and writer of the Southwest. The canyon appears at first, Krutch added, "a man-made diorama trying to fool the eye." It is *too big* to be immediately comprehended, especially to those visitors used to the gaudy, lesser wonders of the human-made world.

Once you accept its size and you understand that a river, stuffed with the dry rocks and sand of this arid country, bore this mile-deep, multicolored notch in the Colorado Plateau, the awesome power of just this one natural force—its greatest work here spread before you—is

bound to leave you breathless and wondering what you've been doing with your life heretofore. If there is any sacred place in the natural world, this is surely one. The canyon is a water-wrought cathedral, and no matter what beliefs or preconceptions you approach the rim with, they are likely to be challenged, molded, cut away, and revealed like the layers of primordial earth that compose this deep rock labyrinth, telling the history of the planet as if they were a geology textbook for new gods. And it is a story in which humans appear only briefly, if at all.

Visitors without a spiritual connection to nature have always been challenged by the Grand Canyon's size. It takes mythology, magical thinking, and storytelling to see it for what it

© ERIC SNYDER

view of the South Rim

really is. The first Europeans to see the canyon, a detachment of Spanish conquistadores sent by Coronado in 1540 after hearing rumors of the great gorge from the Hopi, at first thought the spires and buttes rising from the bottom were about the size of a man; they were shocked, upon gaining a different perspective below the rim, that they were as high or higher than the greatest structures of Seville. Human comparisons do not work here. Preparation is not possible.

Never hospitable, the canyon has nonetheless had a history of human occupation for around 5,000 years, though the settlements have been small and usually seasonal. It was one of the last regions of North America to be explored and mapped. The first expedition through, led by the one-armed genius John Wesley Powell, was completed at the comparatively late date of 1869. John Hance, the first Anglo to reside at the canyon, in the 1880s explored its depths and built trails based on ancient native routes. A few other tough loners tried to develop mining operations here, but soon found out that

guiding avant-garde canyon tourists was the only sure financial bet in the canyonlands. It took another 20 years or so and the coming of the railroad before it became possible for the average American tourist to see the gorge.

The black and white statistics—repeated *ad nauseam* throughout the park on displays and interpretive signs along the rim and at the various visitor centers—though impressive, do little to conjure an image that would do the canyon justice. It is some 277 river miles long, beginning just below Lee's Ferry on the north and ending somewhere around the Grand Wash Cliffs in northwestern Arizona. It is 18 miles across at its widest point, and an average of 10 miles across from the south to the north rim. It is a mile deep on average; the highest point on the rim, the north's Point Imperial, rises nearly 9,000 feet above the river. Its towers, buttes, and mesas, formed by the falling away of layers undercut by the river's incessant carving, are red and pink, dull brown and green-tipped, though these basic hues are altered and enhanced by the setting and rising of the sun,

The Canyon and the Railroad

Musing on the Grand Canyon in 1902, John Muir lamented that, thanks to the railroad, "children and tender, pulpy people as well as storm-seasoned travelers" could now see the wonders of the West, including the Grand Canyon, with relative ease. It has always been for storm-seasoned travelers to begrudge us tender, pulpy types a good view. As if all the people who visit the canyon every year couldn't fit in its deep mazes and be fairly out of sight. Muir came to a similar conclusion after actually seeing the railway approach the chasm: "I was glad to discover that in the presence of such stupendous scenery they are nothing," he wrote. "The locomotives and trains are mere beetles and caterpillars, and the noise they make is as little disturbing as the hooting of an owl in the lonely woods."

It wasn't until the Santa Fe Railroad reached the South Rim of the Grand Canyon in 1901 that the great chasm's now-famous tourist trade really got going. Prior to that travelers faced an all-day stagecoach ride from Flagstaff at a cost of $20, a high price to pay for sore bones and cramped quarters.

For half a century or more the Santa Fe line from Williams took millions of tourists to the edge of the canyon. The railroad's main concessionaire, the Fred Harvey Company, enlisted the considerable talents of Arts and Crafts designer and architect Mary Colter to build lodges, lookouts, galleries, and stores on the South Rim that still stand today, now considered to be some of the finest architectural accomplishments in the entire national parks system. Harvey's dedication to simple, high-style elegance and Colter's interest in and understanding of Pueblo Indian architecture and lifeways created an artful human stamp on the rim that nearly lives up to the breathtaking canyon it serves.

The American love affair with the automobile, the rising mythology of the go-west road trip, and finally the interstate highway killed train travel to Grand Canyon National Park by the late 1960s. In the 1990s, however, entrepreneurs revived the railroad as an excursion and tourist line. Today, the Grand Canyon Railway carries more than 250,000 passengers to the South Rim every year, a phenomenon that has reduced polluting automobile traffic in the cramped park by some 10 percent.

THE GRAND CANYON

changed by changes in the light, becoming throwaway works of art that astound and then disappear.

It is folly, though, to try too hard to describe and boost the Grand Canyon. The consensus, from the first person to see it to yesterday's gazer, has generally amounted to "You just have to see it for yourself." Perhaps the most poetic words ever spoken about the Grand Canyon, profound for their obvious simplicity, came from Teddy Roosevelt, speaking on the South Rim in 1903. "Leave it as it is," he said. "You cannot improve on it; not a bit."

EXPLORING THE SOUTH RIM

The South Rim is by far the most developed portion of **Grand Canyon National Park**

(928/638-7888, www.nps.gov/grca, open 24/7, $25 per car for 7-day pass) and should be seen by every American, as Teddy Roosevelt once recommended. Here you'll stand side by side with people from all over the globe, each one breathless on his or her initial stare into the canyon and more often than not hit suddenly with an altered perception of time, human history, even God. Don't let the rustic look of the buildings fool you into thinking you're roughing it. The park's easy, free shuttle service will take you all over if you don't feel like walking the level rimside trails. The food here is far above average for a national park. The restaurant at El Tovar offers some of the finest, most romantic dining in the state, and all with one of the great wonders of the world just 25 feet away.

Visitors Centers

Canyon View Information Plaza (9am-5pm daily) near Mather Point, the first overlook you pass on entering the park's main South Entrance, is the perfect place to begin your visit to the park. You get there by walking the short path from the Mather Point parking lot or by hopping off the free shuttle, for which the plaza serves as a kind of central hub. Throughout the plaza there are displays on the natural and human history of the canyon and suggestions on what to do, and inside the **South Rim Visitor Center,** the park's main welcome and information center, there are displays on canyon history and science, and rangers on duty who are always around to answer questions, give advice, and help you plan your visit. Head to the visitors center's 200-seat theater and watch the thrilling *Grand Canyon: A Journey of Wonder,* a 20-minute orientation film that takes you on a daylong journey through the canyon and around the park and explains the basics of the canyon's natural and human histories. The movie is free and starts on the hour and half hour.

Another information center, **Verkamp's Visitor Center** (8am-5pm daily) sits near the El Tovar Hotel and Hopi House in Grand Canyon Village, and sits near the El Tovar Hotel and Hopi House in Grand Canyon Village. Verkamp's was a souvenir shop, the park's first, from 1906 to 2008.

The farthest-flung of all the park's South Rim information centers, **Desert View Visitor Center and Bookstore** (9am-5pm daily), sits on Desert View Point about 25 miles east of Grand Canyon Village. It is staffed by helpful rangers and has information and displays on visiting the canyon; this is the natural place to stop for those entering the park from the quieter East Entrance.

As you enter the park you'll get a copy of *The Guide,* a newsprint guide to the South Rim that is indispensable. Make sure you read through it; it's pretty comprehensive and will likely answer most of your questions.

Entrance Stations

Unless you choose to ride the chugging train from Williams, there are only two ways, by road, in and out of the park's South Rim section. The vast majority of visitors to Grand Canyon National Park enter through the **South Entrance Station** along Route 64 from Williams. U.S. Highway 180 from Flagstaff meets up with Route 64 at Valle, about 30 miles south of the South Entrance; it's about 55 miles along scenic Highway 180 from Flagstaff to Valle. Route 64 from Williams to the South Entrance is 60 miles of flat, dry-grass and windswept plain, dotted with a few isolated trailers and manufactured homes and gaudy for-sale signs offering cheap "ranchland." Entering through the busy South Entrance will assure that your first look of Grand Canyon is from **Mather Point,** which is as a result one of the most iconic views of the river-molded gorge.

A lesser used but certainly no less worthy park entrance is the **East Entrance Station,** in the park's **Desert View** section. About 25 miles east of Grand Canyon Village and all the action, this route is a good choice for those who want a more leisurely and comprehensive look at the rim, as there are quite a few stops along the way to the village that you might not otherwise get to if you enter through the South Entrance. To reach the East Entrance Station take U.S. Highway 89 for 46 miles north of Flagstaff, across a wide big-sky landscape covered in volcanic rock, pine forests, and yellow wildflowers, to Cameron, on the red-dirt Navajo Reservation. Then head west on Route 64 for about 30 miles to the entrance station.

Tours
MOTORCOACH TOURS

Xanterra, the park's main concessionaire, offers in-park **Motorcoach Tours** (888/297-2757, www.grandcanyonlodges.com $21-60). Sunrise tours are available, and longer drives to the eastern and western reaches of the park are offered. This is a comfortable, educational, and entertaining way to see the park, and odds are you will come away with a few new friends—possibly even a new email pal from abroad.

Only pay for a tour if you like being around a lot of other people and listening to mildly entertaining banter from the tour guides for hours at a time. It's easy to see and learn about everything the park has to offer without spending extra money on a tour; as it is in most of the national parks, the highly-informed and friendly rangers hanging around the South Rim's sites offer the same information that you'll get on an expensive tour, but for free. Also, if you like being on your own and getting out away from the crowds, a tour is not for you.

AIRPLANE AND HELICOPTER TOURS
Three companies offer helicopter tours of the canyon of varying lengths. One of the better operators is **Maverick Helicopters** (888/261-4414, www.maverickhelicopter.com, $264 for a 45-minute fly-over, $399 for 3.5 hour tour from Las Vegas). Though not ideal from the back-to-nature point of view, a helicopter flight over the canyon is an exciting, rare experience, and by most accounts is well worth the rather expensive price—a chance to take some rare photos from a condor's perspective.

Maverick, and four other plane and helicopter tour operators operate out of **Grand Canyon Airport** (www.grandcanyonairport.org) along Route 64 in Tusayan. They all prefer reservations.

Driving Tours
◖ HERMIT ROAD
March through November the park's free shuttle goes all the way to architect and Southwestern-design queen Mary Colter's **Hermit's Rest,** about seven miles from the village, along the park's western scenic drive, called the Hermit Road. It takes approximately two hours to complete the loop, as the bus stops at eight viewpoints along the way. On the return route, buses stop only at Mohave and Hopi Points. A few of the Hermit Road viewpoints are some of the best in the park for viewing the sunsets. To make it in time for such dramatic solar performances, get on the bus at least an hour before sunset. There is often a long wait at the **Hermit's Rest Transfer Stop** just west

of the Bright Angel Lodge. The bus drivers will always be able to tell you when sunset is expected, and the times are also listed in *The Guide* newspaper handed out as you enter the park. In the winter the route is open to cars, and you can drive to most of the viewpoints and stare at your leisure.

Each of the Hermit Road lookouts provides a slightly different perspective on the canyon, whether it be a strange unnoticed outcropping or a brief view of the white-tipped river rapids far, far below. The first stop along the route is the **Trailview Overlook,** from which you can see the Bright Angel Trail twisting down to and across the plateau to overlook the Colorado River. The next major stop along the route is **Maricopa Point,** which provides a vast, mostly unobstructed view of the canyon all the way to the river. The point is on a promontory that juts out into the canyon over 100 feet. To the west you can see the rusted remains of the Orphan Mine, first opened in 1893 as a source of copper and silver—and, for a few busy years during the height of the Cold War, uranium. Consider taking the 10- to 15-minute hike along the Rim Trail west past the fenced-off Orphan Mine and through the piney rim world to the next point, **Powell Point.** Here stands a memorial to the one-armed explorer and writer, John Wesley Powell, who led the first and second river expeditions through the canyon in 1869 and 1871. The memorial is a flat-topped pyramid, which you can ascend and stand tall over the canyon. You can't see the river from here, but the views of the western reaches of the gorge are pretty good, and this is a strong candidate for a sunset-viewing vantage point. About a quarter of a mile along the rim trail from Powell Point is **Hopi Point,** which offers sweeping and unobstructed views of the western canyon. As a result, it is the most popular west-end point for viewing the sun dropping red and orange in the west. North from here, across the canyon, look for the famous mesas named after Egyptian gods—Isis Temple, off to the northeast, and the Temple of Osiris to the northwest. The next viewpoint heading west is **Mohave Point,** from which you can see the Colorado River and a few white-tipped rapids. Also visible from here are the 3,000-foot red-and-green cliffs that surround the deep side-canyon, appropriately named **The Abyss.** Right below the viewpoint you can see the red-rock mesa called the Alligator. The last viewpoint before Hermit's Rest is **Pima Point,** a wide-open view to the west and the east, from which you can see the winding Colorado River and the Hermit Trail twisting down into the depths of the canyon.

DESERT VIEW DRIVE

One more Mary Colter construction—arguably her greatest—and a Puebloan ruin are located along Desert View Drive, the 25-mile eastern drive from the village. The viewpoints along this drive, which one ranger called the "quiet side of the South Rim," gradually become more desertlike and are typically less crowded. The free shuttle goes only as far as **Yaki Point,** a great place to watch the sunrise and near the popular South Kaibab Trailhead. Yaki Point is at the end of a 1.5-mile side road two miles east of Highway 180. The area is closed to private vehicles. Along Desert View Drive, make sure not to miss the essential **Grandview Point,** where the original canyon lodge once stood long ago. From here the rough Grandview Trail leads below the rim. The viewpoint sits at 7,400 feet, about 12 miles east of the village and then a mile on a side road. It's considered one of the grandest views of them all, hence the name; the canyon spreads out willingly from here, and the sunrise in the east hits it all strong and happy. To the east, look for the 7,844-foot monument called the Sinking Ship and to the north below look for Horseshoe Mesa. This is a heavily wooded area, so for the best view hike a bit down the Grandview Trail. The steep and narrow trail is tough, but if you're prepared to hike, you can descend three miles to Horseshoe Mesa.

Moran Point, east of Grandview, is just eight miles south of Cape Royal (as the condor flies) on the North Rim and offers some impressive views of the canyon and the river. The point is named for the great painter of the canyon, Thomas Moran, whose brave attempts

to capture the gorge on canvas helped create the buzz that led to the canyon's federal protection. Directly below the left side of the point you'll see Hance Rapid, one of the largest on the Colorado. It's three miles away, but if you're quiet you might be able to hear the rushing and roaring. Farther on the Desert View Drive you'll come to **Lipan Point,** with its wide-open vistas and the best view of the river from the South Rim. At Desert View, from the top of the watchtower, you'll be able to catch a faraway glimpse of sacred Navajo Mountain near the Utah-Arizona border, the most distant point visible from within the park.

SIGHTS

Though you wouldn't want to make a habit of it, you could spend a few happy hours at **Grand Canyon Village Historical District** with your back to the canyon. Then again, this small assemblage of hotels, restaurants, gift shops, and lookouts offers some of the best viewpoints from which to gaze comfortably at all that multicolored splendor. Here is a perfect vantage from which to spot the strip of greenery just below the rim called **Indian Gardens,** and follow with your eyes—or even your feet—the famous **Bright Angel Trail** as it twists improbably down the rim's rock face. Here you can also see some of the most interesting and evocative buildings in the state, all of them registered National Historic Landmarks. If you're just visiting for the day, you can drive into the village and park your car in the El Tovar parking lot or at a rather large, mostly dirt lot near the train depot. More often than not, especially in the summer, the lot at El Tovar will be full. You can also park at the large lot at Market Plaza and then take the shuttle bus around the park. The **Backcountry Information Center** (928/638-7875) also has a rather large parking lot, the southern portion of which can accommodate RVs and trailers.

The Bright Angel Lodge

The village's central hub of activity, this rustic lodge was designed in 1935 by Mary Colter to replace the old Bright Angel Hotel, built by

John Hance in the 1890s, and the tent-city Bright Angel Camp that sat near the trail of the same name. The lodge resembles a rough-hewn hunting lodge constructed of materials found nearby and was meant to welcome not the high-toned traveler, but the middle-class tourist.

In a room off the lobby there's a small museum with fascinating exhibits about Fred Harvey, Colter, and the early years of Southwestern tourism. Here you'll see Colter's "geologic fireplace," a 10-foot-high re-creation of the canyon's varied strata. The stones were collected from the inner canyon by a geologist and then loaded on the backs of mules for the journey out. The fireplace's strata appear exactly like those stacked throughout the canyon walls, equaling a couple billion years of earth building from bottom to rim. The lodge includes a collection of small cabins just to the west of the main building, and the cabin closest to the rim was once the home of **Bucky O'Neill,** an early canyon resident and prospector who died while fighting with Teddy Roosevelt's Rough Riders in Cuba.

El Tovar

Just east of the lodge is the South Rim's first great hotel and the picture of haute-wilderness style. Designed in 1905 by Charles Whittlesey for the Santa Fe Railroad, El Tovar has the look of a Swiss chalet and a log-house interior, watched over by the wall-hung heads of elk and buffalo; it is at once cozy and elegant. This Harvey Company jewel has hosted dozens of rich and famous canyon visitors over the years, including George Bernard Shaw and presidents Teddy Roosevelt and William Howard Taft. On the rim side, a gazebo stands near the edge. While it is a wonderfully romantic building up close, El Tovar looks even more picturesque from a few of the viewpoints along the Hermit Road, and you can really get a good idea of just how close the lodge is to the gorge seeing it from far away. Inside you'll find two gift shops and a cozy lounge where you can have a drink or two while looking at the canyon. El Tovar's restaurant is the best in the park. And it's quite pleasant to sink into one of the arts-and-crafts leather chairs in the rustic, dark-wood lobby.

Hopi House

A few steps from the front porch of El Tovar is Colter's Hopi House, designed and built as if it sat not at the edge of the Grand Canyon but on the edge of Hopiland's Third Mesa. Hopi workers used native materials to build this unique gift shop and Native American arts museum. The Harvey Company even hired the famous Hopi-Tewa potter Nampeyo to live here with her family while demonstrating her artistic talents, and by extension Hopi life ways, to tourists. This is one of the best places in the region for viewing and buying Hopi, Navajo, and Pueblo art (though most art is quite expensive), and there are even items on view and for sale made by Nampeyo's descendants.

Lookout Studio

Mary Colter also designed the Lookout Studio west of the Bright Angel Lodge, a little stacked-stone watch house that seems to be a mysterious extension of the rim itself. The stone patio juts out over the canyon and is a popular place for picture taking. The Lookout was built in 1914 exactly for that purpose—to provide a comfortable but "indigenous" building and deck from which visitors could gaze at and photograph the canyon. It was fitted with high-powered telescopes and soon became one of the most popular snapshot scenes on the rim. It still is today, and on many days you'll be standing elbow to elbow with camera-carrying tourists clicking away. As she did with her other buildings on the rim, Colter designed the Lookout to be a kind of amalgam of Native American ruins and backcountry pioneer utilitarianism. Her formula of using found and native materials stacked haphazardly works wonderfully. When it was first built, the little stone hovel was so "authentic" that it even had weeds growing out of the roof. Inside, where you'll find books and canyon souvenirs, the studio looks much as it did when it first opened. The jutting stone patio is still one of the best places from which to view the gorge.

THE GRAND CANYON

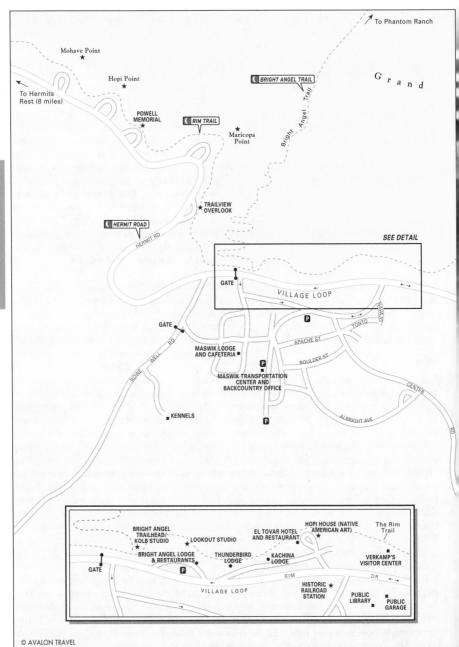

To Phantom Ranch

★ Mohave Point

★ Hopi Point

To Hermits
Rest (8 miles)

POWELL
MEMORIAL

(**BRIGHT ANGEL TRAIL**

G r a n d

Bright Angel Trail

(**RIM TRAIL**

★ Maricopa
Point

★ TRAILVIEW
OVERLOOK

(**HERMIT ROAD**

HERMIT RD

SEE DETAIL

GATE

VILLAGE LOOP

ROWE WELL RD

GATE

NAVAJO

TONTO

P

APACHE ST

MASWIK LODGE
AND CAFETERIA ●

P

BOULDER ST

MASWIK TRANSPORTATION
CENTER AND
BACKCOUNTRY OFFICE

CENTER RD

■ KENNELS

P

ALBRIGHT AVE

BRIGHT ANGEL
TRAILHEAD/
KOLB STUDIO
★

LOOKOUT STUDIO

EL TOVAR HOTEL
AND RESTAURANT

HOPI HOUSE (NATIVE
AMERICAN ART)
★

The Rim
Trail

BRIGHT ANGEL LODGE
& RESTAURANTS

THUNDERBIRD
LODGE

KACHINA
LODGE

VERKAMP'S
VISITOR CENTER

GATE

P

RIM

DR

VILLAGE LOOP

HISTORIC
RAILROAD
STATION ★

PUBLIC
LIBRARY

■ PUBLIC
GARAGE

© AVALON TRAVEL

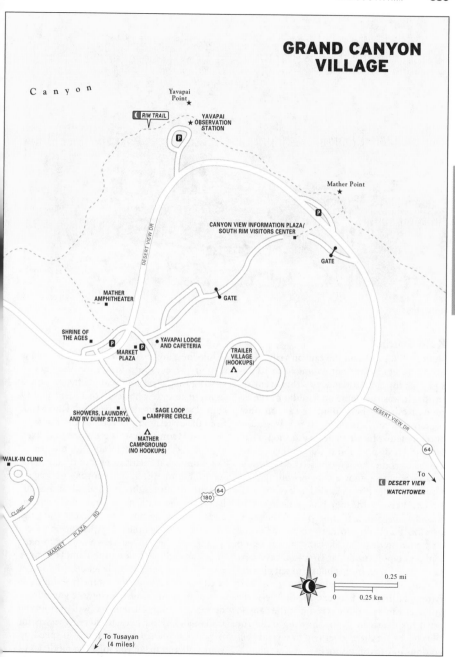

GRAND CANYON VILLAGE

Canyon

Yavapai Point ★

◖ RIM TRAIL

YAVAPAI ★ OBSERVATION STATION

Ⓟ

Mather Point ★

Ⓟ

CANYON VIEW INFORMATION PLAZA/ SOUTH RIM VISITORS CENTER ■

DESERT VIEW DR

● GATE

● GATE

MATHER AMPHITHEATER ■

SHRINE OF THE AGES ■

Ⓟ

MARKET PLAZA

Ⓟ

● YAVAPAI LODGE AND CAFETERIA

TRAILER VILLAGE (HOOKUPS) Λ

SHOWERS, LAUNDRY, AND RV DUMP STATION ■

SAGE LOOP ■ CAMPFIRE CIRCLE

Λ MATHER CAMPGROUND (NO HOOKUPS)

DESERT VIEW DR

64

WALK-IN CLINIC ■

CLINIC RD

MARKET PLAZA RD

180 64

To ◖ *DESERT VIEW WATCHTOWER*

0   0.25 mi
0   0.25 km

To Tusayan (4 miles)

© TIM HULL

Hopi House

Kolb Studio

Built in 1904 right on the canyon's rim, Kolb Studio is significant not so much for its design but for the human story that went on inside. It was the home and studio of the famous Kolb Brothers, pioneer canyon photographers, moviemakers, river rafters, and entrepreneurs. Inside there's a gift shop, a gallery, and a display about the brothers, who, in 1912, rode the length of the Colorado in a boat with a movie camera rolling. The journey resulted in a classic book of exploration and river running, Emery Kolb's 1914 *Through the Grand Canyon from Wyoming to Mexico*. The Kolb Brothers were some of the first entrepreneurs at the canyon, setting up a photography studio, at first in a cave near the rim and then in this house, to sell pictures of tourists atop their mules as early as 1902. After a falling out between the brothers, the younger Emery Kolb stayed on at the canyon until his death in 1976, showing daily the film of the brothers' river trip to several generations of canyon visitors.

The Viewpoints

While the canyon's unrelenting vastness tends to blur the eyes into forgetting the details, viewing the gorge from many different points seems to cure this; however, there are some 19 named viewpoints along the South Rim Road, from the easternmost Desert View to the westernmost Hermit's Rest. Is it necessary, or even a good idea, to see them all? No, not really. For many it's difficult to pick out the various named buttes, mesas, side-canyons, drainages, and other features that rise and fall and undulate throughout the gorge, and one viewpoint ends up looking not that different from the next. To really get the full experience, the best way to see the canyon viewpoints is to park your car and walk along the Rim Trail for a few miles, if not its whole length (if you get tired you can always hop on the free shuttle at any of its many stops), seeing the gorge from developed points all along, as well as from the trail itself. Driving to each and every viewpoint is not that rewarding and tends to speed up your visit and make you miss the subtleties of the different views. Consider really getting to know a few select viewpoints rather than trying to quickly and superficially hit each one. Any of the viewpoints along the Hermit Road and Desert View Drive are ideal candidates for a long love affair. That being said, the views from just outside El Tovar or the Bright Angel Lodge, right smack in the middle of all the bustling village action, are as gorgeous as any others, and it can be fun and illuminating to watch people's reactions to what they're seeing. In reality, there isn't a bad view of the canyon, but if you have only so much time, it's never a bad idea to ask a ranger at Canyon View Information Plaza or Yavapai Observation Station what their favorite viewpoint is and why. Everybody is going to have a different answer, but it stands to reason that those who actually *live* at the canyon are going to have a more studied opinion. The shuttle bus drivers are also great sources of information and opinions. Whatever you do, try to get to at least one sunset and one sunrise at one or more of the developed viewpoints; the canyon's colors and details can get a bit monotonous after the initial thrill wears off (if it ever does), but the sun splashing and dancing at different strengths and angles against the multihued buttes, monuments, and sheer, shadowy walls cures that rather quickly.

As most South Rim visitors enter through the park's south entrance, it's no surprise that the most visited viewpoint in the park is the first one arrived at along that route—**Mather Point,** named for the first National Park Service director, Stephen T. Mather. Mather Point, while crowded, offers a typically astounding view of the canyon and is probably the mind's-eye view that most casual visitors take away. It can get very busy here, especially in the summer. If you're going to the park's main visitors center, **Canyon View Information Plaza** (and you should), you'll park near here and walk a short paved path to the information plaza. At the viewpoint, you can walk out onto two railed-off jutting rocks to feel like you're hovering on the edge of an abyss, but you may have to stand in line to get right up

to the edge. A good way to see this part of the park is to leave your car at the large parking area at Mather (which is often full, of course) and then walk a short way along the Rim Trail west to **Yavapai Point** and the excellent, newly refurbished **Yavapai Observation Station,** the best place to learn about the canyon's geology and get more than a passing understanding of what you're gazing at. It's a good idea to visit the Yavapai Observation Station before you hit any of the other viewpoints (unless you are coming in from the east entrance).

Yavapai Observation Station

First opened in 1928, **Yavapai Observation Station** (8am-6pm in the winter and 8am-7pm starting April 15 daily, free) is the best place in the park to learn about the canyon's geology—this limestone-and-pine museum and bookstore hanging off the rim is a must-see for visitors interested in learning about what they are seeing. The building itself is of interest; designed by architect Herbert Maier, the stacked-stone structure, like Colter's buildings, merges with the rim itself to appear a foregone and inevitable part of the landscape. The site for the station, which was originally called the Yavapai Trailside Museum, was handpicked by canyon geologists as the very best for viewing the various strata and receiving a rimside lesson on the region's geologic history and present. Inside the building, you'll find in-depth explanations and displays about canyon geology that are fascinating and easily understood. Too much of the introductory geology found in guidebooks and elsewhere is jargon-laden, confused, and confusing and not very useful to the uninitiated. Not here: Many of the displays are new and use several different approaches, including maps, photographs, and three-dimensional models—coupled with the very rocks and cliffs and canyons and gorges they're talking about right outside the windows—to create fascinating and easy-to-grasp lessons. Particularly helpful is the huge topographic relief map of the canyon inside the observation center. Spend some time looking

THE GRAND CANYON

© TIM HULL

the entrance to Hermit's Rest

over the map in detail and you'll get a giant's-eye view of the canyon that really helps you discern what you're seeing once you turn into an ant again outside on the ledge.

Hermit's Rest

The final stop on the Hermit Road is the enchanting gift shop and resthouse called Hermit's Rest. As you walk up a path through a stacked-boulder entranceway, from which hangs an old mission bell, the little stone cabin comes into view. It looks as if some lonely hermit came out here and stacked rock upon rock until something haphazard but cozy rose off the rim; it is a structure familiar more to the world of fairy tales than to the contemporary world. Inside, the huge yawning fireplace, tall and deep enough to be a room itself, dominates the warm, rustic front room, where there are a few seats chopped out of stumps, a Navajo blanket or two splashing color against the gray stone, and elegant lantern-lamps hanging from the stones. Outside, the views of the canyon

and down the Hermit's Trail are spectacular, but something about that little rock shelter makes it hard to leave.

Tusayan Museum and Ruin

The **Tusayan Museum** (9am-5pm daily, free) has a small but interesting exhibit on the canyon's early human settlers. The museum is located near an array of 800-year-old Ancestral Puebloan ruins with a self-guided trail and regularly scheduled ranger walks. Since the free shuttle doesn't extend this far east, you have to drive to the museum and ruin; it's about 3 miles west of Desert View and 22 miles east of the village. It's worth the drive, though, especially if you're going to be heading to the Desert View section anyway (which you should). Though it hasn't been overly hospitable to humans over the eons, the oldest human-made artifacts found in the canyon date back about 12,000 years—little stick-built animal fetishes and other mysterious items. The displays in this museum help put human life on the rim and

© TIM HULL

the Desert View Watchtower

the South Rim's highest viewpoint, the whole arid expanse opens up, and you feel something like a lucky survivor at the very edge of existence, even among the crowds. Such is the evocative power, the rough-edged Romanticism, of Colter's vision.

RECREATION
Hiking

Something about a well-built trail twisting deep into an unknown territory can spur even the most habitually sedentary canyon visitor to begin an epic trudge. This phenomenon is responsible for both the best and worst of the South Rim's busy recreation life. It is not uncommon to see hikers a mile or more below the rim picking along in high heels and sauntering blithely in flip-flops, not a drop of water between them. It's best to go to the canyon prepared to hike, with the proper footwear and plenty of snacks and water. Just figure that you are, in all probability, going to want to hike a little. And since there's no such thing as an easy hike into the Grand Canyon, going in prepared, even if it's just for a few miles, will make your hike infinitely more pleasurable. Also, remember that there aren't any loop hikes here: If you hike in a mile—and that can happen surprisingly quickly—you also must hike out (up) a mile, at an oxygen-depleted altitude of 6,000 to 7,000 feet.

in the gorge in context, and the little ruin is fascinating. Imagine living here along the rim, walking every day to the great gorge, tossing an offering of cornmeal into the abyss, and wondering what your hidden canyon gods were going to provide you with next.

【 Desert View Watchtower

What is perhaps the most mysterious and thrilling of Colter's canyon creations, the Desert View Watchtower is an artful homage to smaller Anasazi-built towers found at Hovenweep National Monument and elsewhere in the Four Corners region, the exact purpose of which is still unknown.

The tower's high, windy deck is reached by climbing the twisting steep steps winding around the open middle, the walls painted with visions of Hopi lore and religion by Hopi artist Fred Kabotie. Pick up *The Watchtower Guide* free in the gift shop on the bottom floor for explanations on the meanings of the paintings and symbols. From the top of the watchtower,

【 RIM TRAIL

- Distance: 12.8 miles
- Duration: all day
- Elevation gain: about 200 feet
- Effort: easy
- Trailhead: Grand Canyon Village east to South Kaibab Trailhead or west to Hermit's Rest

If you can manage a 13-mile, relatively easy walk at an altitude of around 7,000 feet, the Rim Trail provides the single best way to see all of the South Rim. The trail, paved for most of its length, runs from the South Kaibab

THE GRAND CANYON

Hiking the Grand Canyon... the Easy Way

One of the first things you notice while journeying through the inner canyon is the advanced age of many of your fellow hikers. It is not uncommon to see men and women in their 70s and 80s hiking along at a good clip, packs on their backs and big smiles on their faces.

At the same time, all over the South Rim you'll see warning signs about overexertion, each featuring a buff young man in incredible shape suffering from heat stroke or exhaustion, with the warning that most of the people who die in the canyon—and people die every year—are people like him. The point here is this: You need not be a wilderness expert or marathon runner to enjoy even a long, 27-mile, rim-to-rim hike through the inner canyon. Don't let your fears hold you back from what is often a life-changing trip.

There are several strategies that can make a canyon hike much easier than a forced march with a 30-pound pack of gear on your back. First of all, don't go in the summer; wait until September or October, when it's cooler, though still quite warm, in the inner canyon. Second, try your best to book a cabin or a dorm room at Phantom Ranch rather than camping. That way, you'll need less equipment, you'll have all or most of your food taken care of, and there will be a shower and a beer waiting for you upon your arrival. Also, for about $50 you can hire a mule to carry up to 30 pounds of gear for you, so all you have to bring is a day pack, some water, and a few snacks. This way, instead of suffering while you descend and ascend the trail, you'll be able to better enjoy the magnificence of this wonder of the world.

trailhead area on the east, through the village, and all the way to Hermit's Rest, hitting every major point of interest and beauty along the way. The trail gets a little tough as it rises a bit past the Bright Angel Trailhead just west of the village. The trail becomes a thin dirt single-track between Powell Point and Monument Creek Vista, but it never gets too difficult. It would be considered an easy, scenic walk by just about anybody, kids included. But perhaps the best thing about the Rim Trail is that you don't have to hike the whole 13 miles—far from it. There are at least 16 shuttle stops along way, and you can hop on and off the trail at your pleasure.

Few will want to hike the entire 13 miles, of course. Such an epic walk would actually require twice the miles, as the trail is not a loop but a ribbon stretched out flat along the rim from west to east. It's better to pick out a relatively short stretch to walk, starting from the village and ending back there after turning around. Toward the west, try walking the roughly 2.2-mile stretch from the village to

Hopi Point. This would be an ideal hike toward the end of the day, as Hopi Point is a famed spot for viewing the sunset. You could then hike back in the dark, provided you have a flashlight, or take the free shuttle bus. Eastward, hike the Rim Trail from the village to Yavapai Point, a distance of about 2 miles one way. This route will take you past stunning views of the canyon to the Yavapai Observation Station, where you can learn all about that which you are gaping at.

◖ BRIGHT ANGEL TRAIL

- Distance: 1.5-9.6 miles
- Duration: a few hours to overnight
- Elevation gain: 4,380 feet
- Effort: moderate to difficult
- Trailhead: Grand Canyon Village, just west of Bright Angel Lodge

Hiking down the Bright Angel, you quickly leave behind the twisted greenery of the rim and enter a sharp and arid landscape, twisting down and around switchbacks on a trail that is sometimes all rock underfoot. Step aside for the many mule trains that go down and up this route, and watch for the droppings, which are everywhere. Because this trail is so steep, it doesn't take long for the rim to look very far away, and you soon feel like you are deep within a chasm and those rim-top people are mere ants scurrying about.

The most popular trail in the canyon owing to its starting just to the west of the Bright Angel Lodge in the village center, and considered by park staff to be the "safest" trail owing to its resthouses, water, and ranger presence, the Bright Angel Trail was once the only easily accessible corridor trail from the South Rim. As such, a $1 hikers' toll was charged by Ralph Cameron, who constructed the trail based on old native routes. The trail's general route has always been a kind of inner canyon highway, as it is blessed with a few springs. The most verdant of these is Indian Gardens (for centuries exactly that), a welcome slip of green on an otherwise red and rocky land, about 4.5 miles down from the trailhead. Many South Rim visitors choose to walk down Bright Angel a bit just to get a feeling of what it's like to be below the rim.

If you want to do something a little more structured, the three-mile round-trip hike to the **Mile-and-a-Half Resthouse** makes for a good introduction to the steep, twisting trail. A little farther on is **Three-Mile Resthouse,** a six-mile round-trip hike. Both resthouses have water seasonally. One of the best day hikes from the South Rim is the nine-mile round-trip to beautiful **Indian Gardens,** a cool and green oasis in the arid inner canyon. This is a rather punishing day hike, and not recommended in the summer. Same goes for the just-over-12-mile round-trip trudge down to **Plateau Point,** from which you can see the Colorado River winding through the inner gorge. Unless you have somewhere you absolutely have to be, you'll want to consider getting a backcountry permit and camping below the rim rather than trying to do Plateau Point or even Indian Gardens in one day.

SOUTH KAIBAB TRAIL

- Distance: 1.5-7 miles
- Duration: a few hours to all day
- Elevation gain: 4,780 feet
- Effort: moderate to difficult
- Trailhead: near Yaki Point

Steep but short, the 7-mile South Kaibab Trail provides the quickest, most direct South Rim route to and from the river. It's popular with day hikers and those looking for the quickest way into the gorge, and many consider it superior to the often-crowded Bright Angel Trail. The trailhead is located a few miles east of the village near Yaki Point; it can be easily reached by shuttle bus on the Kaibab Trail Route. The 1.8-mile round-trip hike to **Ooh Aah Point** provides a great view of the canyon and a relatively easy hike along the steep switchbacks. **Cedar Ridge** is a three-mile round-trip hike down the trail, well worth it for the views of O'Neill Butte and Vishnu Temple. There is no water provided anywhere along the trail, and shade is nonexistent. Bighorn sheep have been known to haunt this trail, and you might feel akin to those dexterous beasts on this rocky, ridgeline route that seems unbearably steep in some places, especially on the way back up. If you are interested in a longer haul, the six-mile round-trip hike to **Skeleton Point,** from which you can see the Colorado, is probably as far along this trail as you'll want to go in one day, though in summer you might want to reconsider descending so far. Deer and California condors are also regularly seen along the South Kaibab Trail.

HERMIT TRAIL TO DRIPPING SPRINGS

- Distance: 6.2 miles
- Duration: 5-6 hours
- Elevation gain: 1,400 feet

© TIM HULL

along the Hermit Trail

- Effort: moderate
- Trailhead: just west of Hermit's Rest

Built by the Santa Fe Railroad as an antidote to the fee-charging keeper of the Bright Angel Trail, the Hermit Trail just past Hermit's Rest leads to some less visited areas of the canyon. This trail isn't maintained with the same energy as the well-traveled corridor trails are, and there is no potable water to be found. You could take the Hermit Trail 10 miles deep into the canyon to the river, where the first-ever below-rim camp for canyon tourists was built by Fred Harvey 10 years before Phantom Ranch, complete with a tramway from the rim, the ruins of which are still visible. But such a trudge should be left only to fully-geared experts. Not so the 6.2-mile round-trip hike to the secluded and green **Dripping Springs,** which is one of the best day hikes in the canyon for midlevel to expert hikers. Start out on the Hermit Trail's steep, rocky, almost stairlike switchbacks, and then look for

the **Dripping Springs Trailhead** after about a mile and a half, once you reach a more level section dominated by piñon pine and juniper. Veer left on the trail, which begins to rise a bit and leads along a ridgeline across Hermit Basin; the views here are so awesome, and so barrier free, that it's difficult to keep your eyes on the skinny trail. Continue west once you come to the junction with the Boucher Trail after about a mile; then it's about a half mile up a side canyon to the cool and shady rock overhang known as Dripping Springs. And it really does drip: a shock of fernlike greenery hangs off the rock overhang, trickling cold, clean spring water at a steady pace into a small collecting pool. Get your head wet, have a picnic, and kick back in this out-of-way, hard-won oasis. But don't stay too long. The hike up is nothing to take lightly: The switchbacks are punishing, and the end, as it does when one is hiking up all of the canyon trails, seems to get farther away and not closer as your legs begin to gain fatigue-weight. There's no water on the trail, so make sure to bring enough along and conserve.

GRANDVIEW TRAIL

- Distance: 8.4 miles to the river
- Duration: a few hours to overnight
- Elevation gain: 4,792 feet
- Effort: difficult
- Trailhead: Grandview Point, 12 miles east of Grand Canyon Village

A steep, rocky, and largely unmaintained route built first to serve a copper mine at Horseshoe Mesa, and then to entice tourists below the forested rim, the Grandview Trail should be left to midlevel hikers and above. Though you can take the trail all the way to the river and Hance Rapid, more than eight miles in, for day hikers the 6.4-mile round-trip trek to Horseshoe Mesa, where you'll see the remains of an old copper mine, is probably as far as you'll want to go. This trail is definitely not safe for winter hiking. Hiking back up, you won't soon forget the steep slab-rock and cobblestone switchbacks, and hiking down will likely take longer than planned, as the steepest parts of the route are quite technical and require heads-up attention. Park staff are not exactly quick to recommend this route to casual hikers. Don't be surprised if you meet a ranger hanging out along the trail about a mile and half in, who may very well tell you to turn around if he or she doesn't think you have the proper gear or enough water to continue on.

Biking

Some of us who love the Grand Canyon, its innards and its rimlands alike, look forward to the inevitable day when all cars will be banned from the park. Long leaps have already been made toward this goal: the Grand Canyon Railway is as popular as ever, and a fleet of natural gas-powered shuttles moves thousands of visitors around the park every day. In 2010, the National Park Service took a further stride in the green direction by awarding a long-awaited permit to a bike rental vendor. Of course, you don't have to rent. Bring your own bike: Strap it on the back of your SUV, park that gas guzzler, and pedal the rim and the forest at your own pace. There is no better way to get around the park, and you'll be helping keep emissions, traffic, and frustration to a minimum.

Bright Angel Bicycles and Café (928/814-8704, www.bikegrandcanyon.com, 6am-8pm daily April-Nov., 7am-7pm daily Dec.-March, $12 per hour, $30 for 5 hours, $40 for 24 hours) rents comfortable, easy-to-ride KHS bikes, as well as trailers for the tots and safety equipment. They also offer guided bike tours of the South Rim's sights for $40 per person ($32 children under 17). If you get tired pedaling through the 7,000-foot air, you can strap your bike to a shuttle and have a rest. The friendly staff members here are quick to offer suggestions about the best places to ride. The little café serves an excellent brew and sells premade sandwiches and other snacks (same hours as rentals). Bright Angel Bicycles is located right next to the **Grand Canyon Visitor Center** near the southern entrance and Mather Point.

MOUNTAIN BIKING ON THE RIM

The **Tusayan Bike Trails** are a series of single-track trails and old mining and logging roads organized into several easy-to-moderate loop trails for mountain bikers near the park's south entrance. The trails wind through a forest of pine, juniper, and piñon, and there are usually plenty of opportunities to see wildlife. The longest loop is just over 11 miles, and the shortest is just under 4 miles. At the beginning of the trails there's a map of the area showing the various loops. Pick up the trails on the west side of Route 64 north of Tusayan, about a mile south of the park entrance.

LECTURES AND PROGRAMS

The staff at the South Rim does an above-average job keeping guests comfortable, informed, and entertained. Rangers seem to be always giving lectures, leading walks, and pointing out some little-known canyon fact—and such activities at the Grand Canyon are typically far more interesting than they are at other, less spectacular places. It will be worth your time to attend at least one of the regularly illuminating lectures held most nights at the **Shrine of the Ages** during your visit to the South Rim. Check *The Guide* for specific times and topics. Every day prior to late October there are at least 10 ranger programs offered at various sites around the rim. Typically these programs last between 15 minutes and an hour and are always interesting.

SHOPPING

There are more than 16 places to buy gifts, books, souvenirs, supplies, and Native American arts and crafts at the South Rim. Nearly every lodge has a substantial gift shop in its lobby, as do Hermit's Rest, Kolb Studio, Lookout Studio, and the Desert View Watchtower.

For books, the best place to go is **Books & More** at the Canyon View Information Plaza, operated by the nonprofit Grand Canyon Association. Here you'll find all manner of tomes about canyon science and history for both adults and children. All of the gift shops have a small book section, most of them selling the same general selection of popular canyon-related titles. If you're in need of camping and hiking supplies to buy or rent—including top-of-the-line footwear, clothes, and backpacks—try the general store at the **Canyon Village Market Plaza.** Here you'll also find groceries, toiletries, produce, alcoholic beverages, and myriad other necessities, like "I hiked the Grand Canyon" T-shirts and warm jackets in case you forgot yours.

Whether you're a semi-serious collector or a first-time dabbler, the best place on the South Rim to find high-quality Native American arts and crafts is inside Mary Colter's **Hopi House,** where pottery, baskets, overlay jewelry, sand paintings, kachina dolls, and other treasures are for sale. Don't expect to find too many great deals here though—most of the best pieces are priced accordingly.

ACCOMMODATIONS

There are six lodges within Grand Canyon National Park's South Rim confines. Over the last decade or so most of the rooms have been remodeled and upgraded, and you won't find any of them too much more expensive than those outside the park, as the rates are set and controlled by an annual review comparing the park's offerings to similar accommodations elsewhere.

A stay at **El Tovar** (303/297-2757, $183-440), more than 100 years old and one of the most distinctive and memorable hotels in the state, would be the secondary highlight—after the gorge itself—of any trip to the South Rim. The log-and-stone National Historic Landmark standing about 20 feet from the rim has 78 rooms and suites, each with cable TV. The hotel's restaurant serves some of the best food in Arizona for breakfast, lunch, and dinner, and there's a comfortable cocktail lounge off the lobby with a window on the canyon. A mezzanine sitting area overlooks the log-cabin lobby, and a gift shop sells Native American art and crafts and canyon souvenirs. If you're looking to splurge on something truly exceptional, a honeymoon suite overlooking the canyon is available for about $321-440 per night.

When first built in the 1930s, the **Bright Angel Lodge** (303/297-2757, $72-362) was meant to serve the middle-class travelers then being lured by the Santa Fe Railroad, and it is still affordable and comfortable, while retaining a rustic character that fits perfectly with the wild canyon just outside. Lodge rooms don't have televisions, and there is generally only one bed in each room. The inexpensive "hikers" rooms have shared bathrooms, so if that bothers you make sure to ask for a room with a private bath. It's the perfect place to stay the night before entering the canyon's inner depths. You just roll out of bed on the Bright Angel Trail. The lodge's cabins just west of the main building are a little better equipped, with private baths, TVs, and sitting rooms. There's a gift shop; drinking and dining options include a small bar; a family-style restaurant serving breakfast, lunch, and dinner; and a more up-scale eatery that serves lunch and dinner.

Standing along the rim between El Tovar and Bright Angel, the **Kachina Lodge** (303/297-2757, $170-180), a more recent addition to the canyon's accommodations list, offers basic, comfortable rooms with TVs, safes, private baths, and refrigerators. There's not a lot of character here, but its location and modern comforts make the Kachina an ideal place for families to stay. The **Thunderbird Lodge** (303/297-2757, $180-191) is located in the same area and has very similar offerings.

Maswick Lodge (303/297-2757, $92-160) is another nonhistorical lodging option, located on the west side of the village about a quarter mile from the rim. The hotel has a cafeteria-style restaurant that serves just about everything you'd want and a sports bar with a large-screen television. The rooms are basic and comfortable, with TVs, private baths, and refrigerators. **Yavapai Lodge** (303/297-2757, $125-166) is east of the village and is another of the nonhistoric facilities that offers nice rooms with all the comforts but little character or artistic value, though you don't really need any of that when you've got the greatest sculpture garden in the world a few hundred yards away.

Camping

【**Mather Campground** (877/444-6777, www.recreation.gov, $18 per night reservations up to six months ahead through Nov. 20, thereafter, first-come, first-served, $15) is located near the village and offers more than 300 basic campsites with grills and fire pits. It has bathroom facilities with showers, and laundry facilities are offered for a fee. The campground is open to tents and trailers but has no hookups and is closed to RVs longer than 30 feet.

Even if you aren't an experienced camper, a stay at Mather is a fun and inexpensive alternative to sleeping indoors. Despite its large size and crowds, especially during the summer, the campground gets pretty quiet at night, and there's nothing like sitting back in a camp chair under the dark, starry sky and talking around the campfire—even in summer the night takes on a bit of chill, making a campfire not exactly necessary but not out of the question, and camp without a campfire is missing something. Bring your own wood, or you can buy it at the store nearby. You don't exactly have to rough it at Mather; a large, clean bathroom and shower facility is located within walking distance from most of the campsites, and they even have blow dryers. Everything is coin operated, and there's an office on site that gives out change. Consider bringing your bikes along, especially for the kids. The village is about a 15-minute walk from the campground on forested, paved trails, or you can take the free tram from a stop nearby.

About 25 miles east of the village, near the park's east entrance, is **Desert View Campground** ($12 per night, first-come, first-served, closes mid-Oct. depending on weather), with 50 sites for tents and small trailers only, no hookups. There's a bathroom with no showers, and only two faucets with running water. Each site has a grill but little else.

If you're in a rolling mansion, try **Trailer Village** near the village, next to Mather Campground (888/297-2757, www.xanterra.com, $35 per night), where you'll find hookups.

FOOD

【**El Tovar Dining Room** (928/638-2631 ext. 6432, breakfast 6:30am-11am, lunch 11:30am-2pm, dinner 5pm-10pm daily, lunch $6.35-15.95, dinner $6.35-35, reservations required) is truly carrying on the Fred Harvey Company traditions on which it was founded more than 100 years ago. A serious, competent staff serves fresh, creative, locally inspired dishes in a cozy, mural-clad dining room that has not been significantly altered from the way it looked back when Teddy Roosevelt and Zane Grey ate here. The wine, entrées, and desserts are all top-notch and would be mightily enjoyed anywhere in the world—but they always seem to be that much more tasty with the sun going down over the canyon. Pay attention to the specials, which usually feature some in-season native edible and are always the best thing to eat within several hundred miles in any direction.

THE GRAND CANYON

THE GRAND CANYON

The Arizona Room (928/638-2631, lunch 11:30am-3pm daily Mar.-Oct., dinner 4:30pm-10pm daily Mar.-Dec., lunch $7-12, dinner $12-25), next to the Bright Angel Lodge, serves Southwestern-inspired steak, prime rib, fish, and chicken dishes amidst a stylish, but still casual, atmosphere. There's a full bar, and the steaks are excellent—hand cut and cooked just right with unexpected sauces and marinades. The Arizona Room is closed for dinner in January and February and closes to the lunch crowd November-February.

If you only have one nice dinner planned for your trip, think about choosing El Tovar over the Arizona Room (but make sure to make a reservation in advance). The food is great at both places, but El Tovar has so much atmosphere and is not that much more expensive than the Arizona Room, which doesn't have the historical and aesthetic interest that's all over El Tovar—although thinking about the Arizona Room's baby back ribs with prickly pear barbecue sauce makes one question such a recommendation.

Bright Angel Restaurant (928/638-2631, 6:30am-10pm daily, $3-12) just off the Bright Angel Lodge's lobby is a perfect place for a big, hearty breakfast before a day hike below the rim. It serves all the standard, rib-sticking dishes amidst decorations and ephemera recalling the Fred Harvey heyday. At lunch there's stew, chili, salads, sandwiches, and burgers, and for dinner there's steak, pasta, and fish dishes called "Bright Angel Traditions," along with a few offerings from the Arizona Room's menu as well. Nearby is the **Bright Angel Fountain,** which serves hot dogs, ice cream, and other quick treats.

Maswik Cafeteria (928/638-2631, 6am-10pm daily, $3-9) is an ideal place for a quick, filling, and delicious meal. You can find just about everything here—burgers, salads, country-style mashed potatoes, french fries, sandwiches, prime rib, chili, and soft-serve ice cream, to name just a few of the dozens of offerings. Just grab a tray, pick your favorite dish, and you'll be eating in a matter of a few minutes. There's a similar cafeteria-style restaurant at the Yavapai Lodge to the east of the village.

GETTING THERE
By Car

The majority of Grand Canyon visitors drive here, reaching the South Rim from either **Flagstaff** or **Williams** and entering the park through the south or east gates. The south entrance is usually the busiest, and during the summer, traffic is likely to be backed up somewhat. The quickest way to get to the south gate by car is to take Route 64 from Williams. It's about a 60-mile drive across a barren plain; there are a few kitschy places to stop along the way, including Bedrock City, a rather dilapidated model of the Flintstones' hometown with an RV park and a gift shop.

From Flagstaff take U.S. Highway 180 through the forest past the San Francisco Peaks. The road merges with Route 64 at Valle, for a total distance of about 80 miles from Flagstaff to the park gate. Or, to reach the east entrance, take U.S. Highway 89 north from Flagstaff to Cameron, then take Route 64 west to the entrance. This longer route is recommended if you want to see portions of Navajo country on your way to the canyon, and entering through the east entrance will put you right at Desert View, the Desert View Watchtower, and Tusayan Museum and Ruin—sights that otherwise you'll have to travel 25 or so miles east from Grand Canyon Village to see.

The Grand Canyon's South Rim is 224 miles from **Phoenix,** which has in Sky Harbor International Airport the closest major airport to the park. The best way to reach the canyon from out-of-state is to fly in to Phoenix, rent a car, and drive north on I-17. Once you reach the northland, you can either take the route through Williams along Route 64, or the Flagstaff route along U.S. Highway 89 and Route 64. Both will lead you to the canyon's edge within about an hour from their respective towns, though the latter is more scenic. Expect the drive from Phoenix to take about 3.5 hours, barring heavy traffic on the interstate.

The roughly five-hour drive from **Las Vegas** to the South Rim—a very popular trip—is a relatively short one by Southwestern standards. Even if you get a late-morning start and make a few stops along the way, you're still likely to arrive at the park by dinner time. If you feel like stopping overnight—and perhaps it is better to see the great canyon with fresh morning-eyes—do so in Williams. It's just an hour or so from the park's south entrance, has a bit of Route 66 charm, and offers several distinctive and memorable hotels and restaurants, all of which you'll miss if you breeze through town in a hurry. Stick to I-40 after leaving Kingman. The speed limit on most sections of I-40 in Arizona is 75 mph, so all that highland forest scenery flashes by unless you stop a few times to take it in. Most summer weekends you'll find the route crowded but manageable. At all times of the year you'll be surrounded by 18-wheelers barreling across the land.

If you are inclined to visit the **Hualapai Reservation's Skywalk**, remember that it's only 125 miles from Las Vegas (about a 2.5-hour drive), so it makes sense to include this remote side-trip if you're headed to the South Rim from Vegas anyway. A visit to the Skywalk, however, should not be substituted for the South Rim. You have not truly seen the Grand Canyon unless you have seen it its South or North Rim. The Skywalk is certainly not recommended to those seeing the Grand Canyon for the first time. It will add at least a full day to your trip, and the view from the South Rim is infinitely better, and cheaper. There's a $43 entrance fee to enter Grand Canyon West, on top of $32 for the Skywalk, and you'll probably have to ride a shuttle bus part of the way. You can purchase tickets to the Skywalk and to any of the other attractions at Grand Canyon West when you arrive.

To reach Grand Canyon West from Las Vegas, take U.S. Highway 93 out of the city, heading south for about 65 miles to mile marker 42, where you'll see the Dolan Springs/Meadview City/Pearce Ferry exit. Turn north onto Pearce Ferry Road. About 30 miles in,

turn east on Diamond Bar Road. Then it's about 20 miles, 7 or so miles of it unpaved, to Grand Canyon West.

To continue on to the South Rim, head to Peach Springs along Old Route 66. You can stop here for the night, at the **Hualapai Lodge**, or continue on for about an hour east on Route 66 to **Seligman**, which has several small hotels and a few good restaurants. Then head east on Route 66 to Ash Fork, where you can pick up I-40 east to Williams, the gateway to the South Rim.

Grand Canyon National Park's South Rim is 494 miles from Los Angeles, the capital of the American West. Most of the 7- or 8-hour drive is along I-40. It's an approximately 2-hour drive north on I-15 from L.A. to Barstow, where I-40 begins (or ends, if you're coming from the east), but it's sure to take considerably longer on the weekends and during the morning and evening rush hours, which in Southern California tend to be interminable. Expect snarls and delays around Barstow as well.

By Air

The Grand Canyon Airport at Tusayan, just outside the park's south entrance, has flights from Las Vegas, Nevada, daily and from other major Southwestern airports as well. Both Flagstaff and Williams have small airports, but most visitors fly into Sky Harbor in Phoenix, rent a car, and drive about 3.5 hours north to the South Rim. You can rent a car at Tusayan, and there are rental places in Flagstaff and Williams as well. A shuttle runs hourly between Tusayan and Grand Canyon Village.

By Bus

Arizona Shuttles (928/226-8060, www.arizonashuttle.com) offers comfortable rides from Flagstaff to the Grand Canyon three times daily ($58 round-trip for adults, March 1-October 31). The company also goes to and from Phoenix's Sky Harbor Airport ($39 one way) several times a day, as well as from Flagstaff to Sedona, the Verde Valley, and Williams ($22-29 one way).

Grand Canyon Railway

A fun, retro, and environmentally conscious way to reach the park, the **Grand Canyon Railway** (800/843-8724, www.thetrain.com, $59-199 round-trip for single adult, depending on accommodations) re-creates what it was like to visit the great gorge in the early 20th century. It takes about 2.5 hours to get to the South Rim depot from the station in Williams, where the **Grand Canyon Railway Hotel** (928/635-4010, www.thetrain.com, $89-179) and restaurant just beyond the train station makes a good base, attempting as it does to match the atmosphere of the old Santa Fe Railroad Harvey House that once stood on the same ground.

During the trip, one is always wondering when the train is going to speed up, but it never really does, rocking at about 60 mph through pine forests and across a scrubby grassland shared by cattle, elk, pronghorn, coyotes, and red-tailed hawks, all of which can be viewed from a comfortable seat in one of the old refurbished cars. Along the way, there are ruins of the great railroad days, including ancient telegraph posts still lined up along the tracks.

A trip to and from the Grand Canyon on the old train is recommended for anyone who is interested in the heyday of train travel, the Old West, or the golden age of Southwestern tourism—or for anyone desiring a slower-paced journey across the northland. Besides, the fewer visitors who drive their vehicles to the rim, the better. Kids seem to especially enjoy the train trip, as comedian-fiddlers often stroll through the cars, and on some trips there's even a mock train robbery complete with bandits on horseback with blazing six-shooters.

GETTING AROUND
Shuttles

The park operates an excellent free shuttle service with comfortable buses fueled by compressed natural gas. It's a good idea to park your car for the duration of your visit and use the shuttle. It's nearly impossible to find parking at the various sights, and the traffic through the park is not always easy to navigate—there

are a lot of one-way routes and oblivious pedestrians that can lead to needless frustration. Make sure you pick up a copy of the free park newspaper, *The Guide,* which has a map of the various shuttle routes and stops.

Pretty much anywhere you want to go in the park a shuttle will get you there, and you rarely have to wait more than 10 minutes at any stop. That being said, there is no shuttle that goes all the way to the Tusayan Museum and Ruin or the Watchtower near the east entrance. Shuttle drivers are a good source of information about the park, and they are generally very friendly and knowledgeable, and a few of them are genuinely entertaining. The shuttle conveniently runs from around sunup until about 9pm, and drivers always know the expected sunrise and sundown times and seem to be intent on getting people to the best overlooks to view these two popular daily park events.

By Bike

You are free, and strongly encouraged, to bring your bike along on your visit to the South Rim. There are several excellent routes for bikes to the west and east of Grand Canyon Village, along which you can generally avoid the crowds and traffic. You'll have to get off and push through the heart of the village, but just to the west and east it's generally pretty easy to navigate.

Bright Angel Bicycles and Café (928/814-8704, www.bikegrandcanyon.com, 6am-8pm daily April-Nov., 7am-7pm daily Dec.-March, $12 per hour, $30 for 5 hours, $40 for 24 hours) rents comfortable, easy-to-ride KHS bikes, as well as trailers for the tots and safety equipment. They also offer guided bike tours of the South Rim's sights for $40 per person ($32 children under 17). If you get tired pedaling through the 7,000-foot air, you can strap your bike to a shuttle and have a rest. The friendly staff members here are quick to offer suggestions about the best places to ride. The little café serves an excellent brew and sells premade sandwiches and other snacks (same hours as rentals). Bright Angel Bicycles is located right next to the **Grand Canyon Visitor Center** near the southern entrance and Mather Point.

The North Rim

Standing at Bright Angel Point on the Grand Canyon's North Rim, crowded together with several other gazers as if stranded on a jetty over a wide, hazy sea, blurred evergreens growing atop great jagged rock spines banded with white and red, someone whispers, "It looks pretty much the same as the other rim."

It's not true—far from it—but the comment brings up the main point about the North Rim: Should you go? Only about 10 percent of canyon visitors make the trip to the North Rim, which is significantly less developed than the South; there aren't as many activities, other than gazing, unless you are a hiker and a backcountry wilderness lover. The coniferous mountain forests of the Kaibab Plateau, broken by grassy meadows painted with summer wildflowers, populated by often-seen elk and mule deer, dappled with aspens that turn yellow and red in the fall and burst out of the otherwise uniform dark green like solitary flames, are themselves worth the trip. But it is a long trip, and you need to be prepared for a land of scant services and the simple, contemplative pleasures of nature in the raw.

EXPLORING THE NORTH RIM

It's all about the scenery here at 8,000 feet and above, and the often misty canyon, and the thick, old-growth forest along its rim, command all of your attention. Some of the people you'll meet here are a bit different from the South Rim tourists, a good portion being hardcore hikers and backpackers, waiting for early morning to hit the North Kaibab Trail for a rim-to-rim trek.

That's not to say that there's nothing to do on the North Rim. Spend some time on the lodge's back porch, have an overpriced beer at the cantina, and hike through the highland forest on easy trails to reach uncrowded viewpoints. There are similarly lonely lookouts (at least compared to the often elbow-to-elbow scene at some the South Rim's spots) at the end

of a couple of scenic drives. Only a rare few see the North Rim covered in snow, as it often is past November. The park here closes in mid-October and doesn't open again until mid-May.

Visitors Centers

The **North Rim Visitor Center and Bookstore** (8am-6pm daily May-Oct.) near the Grand Canyon Lodge, has information, maps, and exhibits on North Rim science and history. The nonprofit Grand Canyon Association operates the well-stocked bookstore. Rangers offer a full program of talks and guided hikes throughout the day, and night programs around the campfire. The North Rim edition of *The Guide* has an up-to-date list of topics, times, and meeting places. Try to attend at least one or two—they are typically interesting and entertaining for both kids and adults, and it tends to deepen your connection with this storied place when you learn about its natural and human history from those who know it best. For the kids, the visitors center has the usual super-fun and educational Junior Rangers Program.

Driving Tours
CAPE ROYAL SCENIC DRIVE

You can reach Point Imperial and several other lookout spots on the Cape Royal Scenic Drive, one of the most scenic, dramatic roads in the state. From the lodge to Cape Royal it's about 30 miles round-trip on a paved road that wends through the mixed conifer and aspen forests of the **Walhalla Plateau.** There are plenty of chances for wildlife spotting and lots of stops and short trails to viewpoints offering breathtaking views of the canyon off to the east and even as far as Navajoland. Plan to spend at least half a day and take food and water. Go to **Point Imperial** first, reached by a three-mile side road at the beginning of the Cape Royal Road. The best way to do it would be to leave the lodge just before sunrise and watch the show from Point Imperial, and then hit the scenic drive

© TIM HULL

Angel's Window is at the end of the North Rim's Cape Royal Scenic Drive.

for the rest of the day, stopping often along the way. Binoculars would be of use on this drive, as would, of course, a camera. Along the way, **Vista Encantadora** (Charming View) provides just that, rising above Nanokoweap Creek. Just beyond that is **Roosevelt Point,** where you can hike the easy 0.2-mile loop trail to a view worthy of the man who saved the Grand Canyon for all of us. When you finally reach the point of the drive, **Cape Royal** at 7,865 feet, you'll walk out on a 0.6-mile round-trip paved trail for an expansive and unbounded view of the canyon—one of the very best, from which, on a clear day, you can spot the South Rim's Desert Watchtower way across the gorge and the river far below. Along the short trail you'll pass **Angel's Window,** an unlikely rock arch that seems designed by some overly ambitious god trying to make an already intensely rare and wonderful view even more so.

SIGHTS
◖ Grand Canyon Lodge
Even if you aren't staying at the Grand Canyon

Lodge, a rustic log-and-stone structure built in 1927-1928 and perched on the edge of the rim at the very end of the highway, don't make the trip to the North Rim without going into its warm Sun Room to view the gorge through the huge picture windows. You may want to sink into one of the comfortable couches and stare for hours. At sunset, head out to the Adirondack chairs on the lodge's back patio and watch the sun sink over the canyon; everybody's quiet, hushed in reverence, bundled up in jackets and sweaters, and wondering how they came to such a rare place as this. Right near the door leading out to the patio, check out sculptor Peter Jepson's charming life-size bronze of **Brighty,** a famous canyon burro whose story was told in the 1953 children's book *Brighty of the Grand Canyon,* by Marguerite Henry. A display nearby tells the true-life aspects of Brighty's story, and they say if you rub his bronze nose you'll have good luck. The book, along with a movie based on the story, is available at gift shops and bookstores on both the North and South Rims.

© TIM HULL

the Grand Canyon Lodge

Viewpoints

There are three developed viewpoints at the North Rim, each of them offering a slightly different look at the canyon. **Bright Angel Point,** about a half-mile round-trip walk outside the lodge's back door, looks over Bright Angel Canyon and provides a view of Roaring Springs, the source of Bright Angel Creek and the freshwater source for the North Rim and the inner canyon. **Point Imperial,** at 8,803 feet, is the highest point on the North Rim and probably has the single best view from the rim, and **Cape Royal,** a view toward the south rim, is a 15-mile one-way drive across the Walhalla Plateau.

RECREATION
Hiking

It's significantly cooler on the high, forested North Rim than it is on the South, making hiking, especially summer hiking, and even more so summertime hiking below the rim, much less of a chore. There are a few easy rim trails to choose from, and several tough but unforgettable day hikes into the canyon along the North Kaibab Trail.

Easy trails lead to and from all the developed scenic overlooks on the rim, their trailheads accessible and well marked. *The Guide* has a comprehensive listing of the area's trails and where to pick them up. The three-mile round-trip **Transept Trail** is an easy hike along the forested green rim from the Grand Canyon Lodge to the campground that provides a good overview of the park. Hiking along the rim is an excellent way to see the canyon from many different points of view.

UNCLE JIM TRAIL

- Distance: 5 miles round-trip
- Duration: 3 hours
- Elevation gain: about 200 feet
- Effort: easy
- Trailhead: North Kaibab Trail parking lot

© TIM HULL

the Transept Trail

(3 miles north of Grand Canyon Lodge on the main park entrance road)

Take this easy, flat trail through the pine forest from which you can watch backpackers winding their way down the North Kaibab Trail's twisting switchbacks, and maybe see a mule train or two along the way. The trail winds through old stands of spruce and fir, sprinkled with quaking aspen, to Uncle Jim Point, where you can let out your best roar into the side notch known as Roaring Springs Canyon.

WIDFORSS TRAIL

- Distance: 10 miles round-trip
- Duration: 5-6 hours
- Elevation gain: negligible
- Effort: easy
- Trailhead: 4 miles north of the lodge, look for sign

This mostly flat and easy trail leads along the

rim of the side canyon called Transept Canyon, and through ponderosa pine, fir, and spruce forest, with a few stands of aspen mixed in, for five miles to Widforss Point, where you can stare across the great chasm and rest before heading back.

NORTH KAIBAB TRAIL

- Distance: varies; 9.4 miles to Roaring Springs
- Duration: a few hours to overnight
- Elevation gain: 5,961 feet from Phantom Ranch
- Effort: moderate to difficult
- Trailhead: North Kaibab Trail parking area

The North Kaibab starts out among the coniferous heights of the North Rim, a forest trail that soon dries out and becomes a red-rock desert, the trail cut into the rock face of the cliffs and twisting down improbable routes hard against the cliffs, with nothing but your sanity keeping you away from the gorge. Sooner than

© TIM HULL

quaking aspen

leaves every morning from the lodge at 5:45am and 7:10am.

North Rim Mule Rides
The mules at the North Rim all work for **Canyon Trail Rides** (435/679-8665, www.canyonrides.com, May 15-Oct. 15), the park's northside trail-riding concessionaire. Guides will take you and your friendly mule on a one-hour rimside ride for $40, or a half-day ride to Uncle Jim's Point for $80. You can also take a mule down into the canyon along the North Kaibab Trail to the Supai tunnel for $80. Kids have to be at least 7 years old to take part in a one-hour ride, at least 10 for the half-day, and 12 for the full-day rides. There's a 220-pound weight limit. Call ahead for a reservation if this is something you're set on doing; if you're not sure, you might be able to hop on last-minute, though probably not in June, which is the busiest time at the North Rim.

ACCOMMODATIONS
Built in the late 1930s after the original lodge burned down, the **Grand Canyon Lodge** (928/638-2611 or 888/297-2757, $116-192) has the only in-park accommodations on the North Rim. The rustic but very comfortable log-and-stone lodge has a large central lobby, a high-ceilinged dining room, a deli, a saloon ($6 for a beer), a gift shop, a general store, and a gas station. There are several small, comfortable lodge rooms, and dozens of cabins scattered around the property, each with a bathroom and most with a gas-powered fireplace that makes things very cozy on a cold night. The lodge is open from mid-May through mid-October. You must book far in advance (at least six months), though there are sometimes cancellations that could allow for a last-minute booking.

The **Kaibab Lodge** (928/638-2389, www.kaibablodge.com $95-175) is a small gathering of rustic, cozy cabins behind the tree line at the edge of a meadow along Route 67, about five miles north of the park boundary. You can rent cabins of varying sizes and

you realize, the walls close in and you are deep in the canyon, the trees on the rim just green blurs now. A good introduction to this corridor trail and ancient native route is the short, 1.5-mile round-trip jog down to the **Coconino Overlook,** from which, on a clear day, you can see the San Francisco Peaks and the South Rim. A four-mile round-trip hike down will get you to **Supai Tunnel,** blasted out of the red rock in the 1930s by the Civilian Conservation Corps. A little more than a mile on and you'll reach **The Bridge in the Redwall** (5.5 miles round-trip), built in 1966 after a flood ruined this portion of the trail. For a tough, all-day hike that will likely have you sore but smiling the next morning, take the North Kaibab five miles in to **Roaring Springs,** the source of life-giving Bright Angel Creek. The springs fall headlong out of the cliffside and spray mist and rainbows into the hot air. Just remember, you have to go five miles up and out, too. Start hiking early and take plenty of water. The trailhead is a few miles north of the lodge. A hiker's shuttle ($7)

© TIM HULL

cabins at the Grand Canyon Lodge

enjoy the lounge, gift shop, and warm fireplace in the lobby. The lodge closes in early November.

There is also a comfortable lodge at Jacob Lake, on the Kaibab Plateau about 50 miles from the park entrance.

Camping

The in-park **North Rim Campground** (877/444-6777, www.recreation.gov, $18-25 per night) has basic camping spots near the rim, with showers and coin-operated laundry. South of Jacob Lake about 25 miles on Route 67 is the **DeMotte Campground,** operated by the U.S. Forest Service ($18 per night, May-Oct., no reservations), about 20 miles north of the park entrance. It has 38 sites with tables and cooking grills, toilets, and drinking water. Tents, trailers, and motor homes are allowed, but there are no utility hookups or dump stations available. **Kaibab Camper Village** (Rte. 67, just south of Jacob Lake, 928/643-7804 or 800/525-0924, www.kaibabcampervillage.

com) has full hookup sites for $36 per night, and basic tent sites for $17 per night. The village also has cabins for $85 per night and offers fire pits, tables, toilets, and coin-operated showers.

FOOD

The **Grand Canyon Lodge Dining Room** (928/638-2611, breakfast 6:30am-10am, lunch 11:30am-2:30pm, dinner 4:45pm-9:45pm daily, $8-25, reservations required for dinner) is the only full-service restaurant in the park on the North Rim, serving fish, pasta, and steaks for dinner, and soups, sandwiches, and salads for lunch. It's not great and is even less so toward the end of the season (late October), but it is the only thing going for several miles around.

Kaibab Lodge Restaurant (breakfast, lunch, and dinner daily, $6.95-24.95) serves well-made, hearty fare perfect for the high, cool country—much better than the in-park eatery.

THE GRAND CANYON

© TIM HULL

the North Rim Country Store

GETTING THERE AND AROUND

Although it's only an average of about 10 miles across the canyon from points on the South Rim to points on the North Rim—but only if you're a hawk or a raven or a condor—it's a 215-mile, five-hour drive for those of us who are primarily earthbound. The long route north is something to behold, moving through a corner of Navajoland, past the towering Vermilion Cliffs, and deep into the high conifer forests of the Kaibab Plateau. On the plateau, which at its highest reaches above 9,000 feet, Route 67 from Jacob Lake to the North Rim typically closes to vehicles by late November until May. In the winter, it's not uncommon for cross-country skiers and snowshoe hikers to take to the closed and snow-covered highway, heading with their own power toward the canyon and the North Kaibab Trail.

Between the hotel, restaurant, and gas station at Jacob Lake on the Kaibab Plateau and the entrance to Grand Canyon National Park on the North Rim, there's not much more than high mountain forest scenery. However, in case you forget anything before venturing into this relative wilderness, you can always stop at the well-stocked **North Rim Country Store** (Hwy. 67, mile post 605, 928/638-2383, www.northrimcountrystore.com, 7:30am-7pm daily mid-May-early Nov.), about 43 miles along Highway 67 from Jacob Lake. The store has just about anything you'll need, from snacks to gas to camping supplies. There's also a small auto shop here in case you're having car troubles or catch a flat that you can't fix yourself. The store closes for winter, as does the whole region, around the beginning of November.

The **Trans Canyon Shuttle** (928/638-2820, $70 one way, $130 round-trip, reservations required) makes a daily round-trip excursion between the North and South Rims, departing the North at 7am and arriving at the South Rim at 11:30am. The shuttle then leaves the South at 1:30pm and arrives back at the North Rim at 6:30pm.

To get from the Grand Canyon Lodge—the park's only accommodations on the North

Rim—to the North Kaibab Trailhead, take the **Hikers Shuttle** ($7 for first person, $4 for each additional person), which leaves the lodge twice daily first thing in the morning. Tickets must be purchased the day before at the lodge.

If you paid your $25 park entrance fee at the South Rim, this will be honored at the North as long as you go within seven days. If not, you'll have to pay an additional $25. A North Rim edition of the park's helpful newspaper *The Guide* is passed out at the North Rim entrance.

The Inner Canyon

Inside the canyon is a desert, red and pink and rocky, its trails lined with cactus and scrub. It's not down at the ground that you're usually looking, though. It's those walls, tight and claustrophobic in the interior's narrowest slots, that make this place a different world altogether. A large part of a canyon-crossing trudge takes place in Bright Angel Canyon along Bright Angel Creek. As you hike along the trail beside the creek, greenery and the cool rushing of water clash with the silent heat washing off the cliffs on your other flank.

On any given night there are only a few hundred visitors sleeping below the rim—at either Phantom Ranch, a Mary Colter-designed lodge near the mouth of Bright Angel Canyon, or at three campgrounds along the corridor trails. Until a few decades ago visiting the inner canyon was something of a free-for-all, but these days access to the interior is strictly controlled; you have to purchase a permit ($10 plus $5 per night per person) to spend the night, and it's not always easy to get a permit—each year the park receives 30,000 requests for a backcountry permit and issues only 13,000.

No matter which trail you use, there's no avoiding an arduous, leg- and spirit-punishing hike there and back if you really want to see the inner canyon. It's not easy, no matter who you are, but it is worth it; it's a true accomplishment, a hard walk you'll never forget.

EXPLORING THE INNER CANYON

If you want to be one of the small minority of canyon visitors to spend some quality time below the rim, consider staying at least one full day and night in the inner canyon. Even hikers in excellent shape find that they are sore after trekking down to the river, Phantom Ranch, and beyond. A rim-to-rim hike, either from the south or from the north, pretty much requires at least a day of rest below the rim. The ideal inner canyon trip lasts three days and two nights: one day hiking in, one day of rest, and one day to hike out.

River trips generally last a minimum of three days to up to three weeks and often include a hike down one of the corridor trails to the river. Depending on how long you want to spend on the river, plan far, far in advance and consider making the river trip your only activity on that particular canyon visit. Combining too much strenuous, mind-blowing, and life-changing activity into one trip tends to water down the entire experience.

Permits and Reservations

The earlier you apply for a permit, the better, but you can't apply for one prior to the first of the month four months before your proposed trip date. The easiest way to get a permit is to go to the park's website (www.nps.gov/grca/planyourvisit/overnight-hiking.htm), print out a backcountry permit request form, fill it out, and then fax it first thing in the morning on the date in question—for example, if you want to hike in October, you would fax (928/638-2125) your request on June 1. Have patience; on the first day of the month the fax number is usually busy throughout the day—keep trying. On the permit request form you'll indicate where you plan to stay. If you are camping, the permit is your reservation, but if you want to stay at Phantom Ranch, you must get separate reservations, and that is often a close-to-impossible task. For more information on obtaining a backcountry permit, call the **South Rim Backcountry Information Center** (928/638-7875, 8am-5pm daily).

HIKING

A classic Grand Canyon backpacking journey begins at either the Bright Angel Trailhead or the South Kaibab Trailhead on the South Rim. Consider going up the one you don't use going down, mostly for variety's sake. Via the Bright Angel Trail, it's a 9.5-mile hike to the Bright Angel Campground, which is just a short walk from the Colorado River and also from Phantom Ranch. Ideally, spend at least two days—the hike-in day and one full day after that—and two nights in the Phantom Ranch area, hiking up the North Kaibab a short way to see the narrow and close walls, talking to the rangers, sitting on the beach watching the river-trippers float by, and generally losing yourself to the calm, quiet soul of the wilderness.

When it's time to leave the oasis that is Bright Angel Campground and Phantom Ranch, a question arises: Should you rise headlong to the rim (7 miles up on the South Kaibab or 9.5 miles up on the Bright Angel), or move on leisurely to the next oasis? Those inclined to choose the latter should consider staying an extra night below the rim at the campground at Indian Gardens, a green and lush spot 4.7 miles up the Bright Angel Trail from the Bright Angel Campground. The small campground here is primitive but charming, and the area around it is populated by deer and other creatures. After setting up camp and resting a bit, head out on the flat, 3-mile round-trip hike out to Plateau Point and a spectacular view of the canyon and river, especially at sunset. When you wake up beneath the shady trees at Indian Garden, you face a mere 4.9-mile hike to the rim.

There are lesser-known routes into and through the canyon, but most hikers stick to the corridor trails—Bright Angel, South Kaibab, and North Kaibab. The Bright Angel Trail from the South Rim is the most popular, but the South Kaibab is shorter, though much steeper. The North Kaibab is the only trail to the river and Phantom Ranch from the North Rim. For an epic, 20-plus-mile rim-to-rim hike, you can choose, as long as the season permits, to start either on the north or south. Starting from the South Rim, you may want to go down the Bright Angel to see beautiful Indian Gardens; then again, the South Kaibab provides a faster, more direct route to the river. If you start from the north, you may want to come out of the canyon via the South Kaibab, as it is shorter and faster, and at that point you are probably going to want to take the path of least resistance. Remember though, while it's shorter, the South Kaibab is a good deal steeper than the Bright Angel, and there is no water available.

It doesn't matter who you are or what trail you prefer, the hike out of the Grand Canyon is, at several points, a brutal trudge. It's even worse with 30-40 pounds of stuff you don't really need on your back. But when you finally gain the rim, and you *will* get there, a profound sense of accomplishment, nearing on glory, washes away a least half of the fatigue. The other half typically hangs around for a week or so.

Day Hikes Around Phantom Ranch

Some people prefer to spend their time in the canyon recovering from the hard walk or mule ride that brought them here, and a day spent cooling your feet in Bright Angel Creek or drinking beer in the cantina is not a day wasted. However, if you want to do some exploring around Phantom Ranch, there are a few popular day hikes from which to choose. When you arrive, the friendly rangers will usually tell you, unsolicited, all about these hikes and provide detailed directions. If you want to get deeper out in the bush and far from the other hikers, ask one of the rangers to recommend a lesser-known route.

© ERIC SNYDER

a bighorn sheep on the River Trail inside the Grand Canyon

RIVER TRAIL

- Distance: 1.5 miles round-trip
- Duration: 1-2 hours
- Elevation gain: negligible
- Effort: easy

A highly recommended and rather short hike is along the precipitous River Trail, high above the Colorado just south of Phantom Ranch. The Civilian Conservation Corps (CCC) blasted this skinny cliffside trail out of the rock walls in the 1930s to provide a link between the Bright Angel and the South Kaibab Trail. Heading out from Phantom it's about a 1.5-mile loop that takes you across both suspension bridges and high above the river. It's an easy walk with fantastic views and is a good way to get your sore legs stretched and moving again. And you are likely to see a bighorn sheep's cute little face poking out from the rocks and shadows on the steep cliffs.

CLEAR CREEK TO PHANTOM OVERLOOK

- Distance: about 1.5 miles
- Duration: 1-2 hours
- Elevation gain: 826 feet
- Effort: easy to moderate
- Trailhead: about 0.25 mile north of Phantom Ranch on the North Kaibab Trail

Another popular CCC-built trail near Phantom is the 1.5-mile **Clear Creek Loop,** which takes you high above the river to Phantom Overlook, where there's an old stone bench and excellent views of the canyon and of Phantom Ranch below. The rangers seem to recommend this hike the most, but, while it's not tough, it can be a little steep and rugged, especially if you're exhausted and sore. The views are, ultimately, well worth the pain.

RIBBON FALLS

- Distance: 11 miles round-trip

© TIM HULL

riding mules into the canyon

- Duration: 5-6 hours to all day
- Elevation gain: 1,174 feet
- Effort: easy to moderate
- Trailhead: look for the sign 5.5 miles north of Phantom Ranch on the North Kaibab Trail

If you hiked in from the South Rim and you have a long, approximately 11-mile round-trip day hike in you, head north on the North Kaibab from Phantom Ranch to beautiful **Ribbon Falls,** a mossy, cool-water oasis just off the hot, dusty trail. The falls are indeed a ribbon of cold water falling hard off the rock cliffs, and you can scramble up the slickrock and through the green creekside jungle and stand beneath the shower. This hike will also give you a chance to see the eerie, claustrophobic "Box," one of the strangest and most exhilarating stretches of the North Kaibab.

MULE RIDES

For generations the famous Grand Canyon mules have been dexterously picking along the skinny trails, loaded with packs and people. Even the Brady Bunch rode them, so they come highly recommended. A descent into the canyon on the back of a friendly mule—with an often taciturn cowboy-type leading the train—can be an unforgettable experience, but don't assume because you're riding and not walking that you won't be sore in the morning. A day trip down the Bright Angel to Plateau Point, from which you can see the Colorado, costs $139 per person and includes lunch. One night at Phantom Ranch, meals included, and a ride down on a mule costs $447 per person or $790 for two. Two nights at Phantom, meals, and a mule ride costs $626 per person or $1,043 for two. For reservations call 888/297-2757 or visit www.grandcanyonlodges.com. Call six months or more in advance.

RIVER TRIPS

People who have been inside the Grand Canyon often have one of two reactions—they either can't wait to return, or else they swear never to return. This is doubly true of those intrepid souls who ride the great river, braving white-water roller coasters while looking forward to a star-filled evening camped—dry, and full of gourmet camp food—on a white beach deep in the gorge. To boat the Colorado, one of the last explored regions of North America, is quite simply one of the most exciting and potentially life-changing trips the West has to offer.

Because of this well-known truth, trips are not cheap and not exactly easy to book. Rafting season in the canyon runs from April to October, and there are myriad trips to choose from—from a 3-day long-weekend ride to a 21-day full-canyon epic. An Upper Canyon trip will take you from River Mile 0 at Lee's Ferry through the canyon to Phantom Ranch, while a Lower Canyon trip begins at Phantom, requiring a hike down the Bright Angel with your gear on your back. Furthermore, you can choose between a motorized pontoon boat, as some three-fourths of rafters do, a paddle-boat, a kayak, or some other combination. It all depends on what you want and what you can afford. If you are considering taking a river trip, the best place to start is the website of the **Grand Canyon River Outfitters Association** (www.gcroa.org), a nonprofit group of about 16 licensed river outfitters, all of them monitored and approved by the National Park Service, each with a good safety record and relatively similar rates. After you decide what kind of trip you want, the website links to the individual outfitters for booking. If you are one of the majority of river explorers who can't wait to get back on the water once you've landed at the final port, remember that there's a strict one trip per year per person rule enforced by the Park Service.

ACCOMMODATIONS AND FOOD

Designed by Mary Colter for the Fred Harvey Company in 1922, **Phantom Ranch** (888/297-2757, www.grandcanyonlodges.com, $42 per person for dormitory), the only noncamping accommodation inside the canyon, is a shady, peaceful place that you're likely to miss and yearn for once you've visited and left it behind. Perhaps Phantom's strong draw, like a Siren wailing from the inner gorge, is less about its intrinsic pleasures and more about it being the only sign of civilization in a deep wilderness that can feel like the end of the world, especially after a 17-mile hike in from the North Rim. But it would probably be an inviting place even if it were easier to get at, and it's all the better because it's not.

As such, it is very difficult to make a reservation. Some people begin calling a year out and still can't get a room, while others show up at the South Rim, ask at the Bright Angel Lodge, and find that a cancellation that very day has left a cabin or bed open. This strategy is not recommended, but it has been known to work. Phantom has several cabins and two dormitories, one for men and one for women, both offering bathrooms with showers. The lodge's center point is its cantina, a welcoming, air-conditioned, beer- and lemonade-selling sight for anyone who has just descended one of the trails. Two meals a day are served in the cantina—breakfast, made up of eggs, pancakes, and thick slices of bacon ($19.63), and dinner, with a choice of steak ($41.68), stew ($26.10), or vegetarian ($26.10). The cantina also offers a box lunch with a bagel, fruit, and salty snacks for $12.39. Reservations for meals are also difficult to come by.

Most nights and afternoons, a ranger based at Phantom Ranch will give a talk on some aspect of canyon lore, history, or science. These events are always interesting and always well attended, even in the 110°F heat of summer.

Phantom is located near the mouth of Bright Angel Canyon, within a few yards of clear, babbling Bright Angel Creek, and is shaded by large cottonwoods planted in the 1930s by the Civilian Conservation Corps. There are several day hikes within easy reach, and the Colorado River and the two awesome suspension bridges that link one bank to the other are only about a quarter mile from the lodge.

Camping

There are three developed campgrounds in the inner canyon: **Cottonwood Campground,** about seven miles from the North Rim along the North Kaibab Trail; **Bright Angel Campground,** along the creek of the same name near Phantom Ranch; and **Indian Garden,** about 4.5 miles from the South Rim along the Bright Angel Trail. To stay overnight at any of these campgrounds you must obtain a permit from the **South Rim Backcountry Information Center** (928/638-7875, $10 for permit plus $5 per person per night). All three campgrounds offer bathrooms and a freshwater spigot, picnic tables and food storage bins to keep the critters out. There are no showers or any other amenities.

The best campground in the inner canyon is Bright Angel, a shady, cottonwood-lined setting along cool Bright Angel Creek. Because of its easy proximity to Phantom Ranch, campers can make use of the cantina, even eating meals there if they can get a reservation, and can attend the ranger talks offered at the lodge. There's nothing quite like sitting on the grassy banks beside your campsite and cooling your worn feet in the creek.

Guides

You certainly don't need a guide to take a classic backpacking trip into the Grand Canyon along one of the corridor trails. The National Park Service makes it a relatively simple process to plan and complete such a memorable expedition, and, while hikers die below the rim pretty much every year, the more popular regions of the inner canyon are as safe as can be expected in a vast wilderness. Then again, having some friendly, knowledgeable and undoubtedly badass canyonlander plan and implement every detail of your trip sure couldn't hurt. Indeed, it would probably make the whole expedition infinitely more enjoyable. As long as you're willing to pay for it—and it is never cheap—hiring a guide is an especially good idea if you want

Bright Angel Creek shines near Phantom Ranch.

to go places where few tourists and casual hikers dwell.

There are more than 20 companies authorized, through a guide permit issued by the National Park Service, to take trips below the rim. If your guide does not have such a permit, do not follow him or her into the Grand Canyon. For an up-to-date list, go to www.nps.gov/grca/planyourvisit/guidedtours.htm.

The **Grand Canyon Field Institute** (928/638-2481, www.grandcanyon.org, $560), which is operated by the nonprofit Grand Canyon Association, offers several three- to five-day guided backpacking trips to various points inside the canyon, including trips

designed specifically for women, for beginners, and for those interested in the canyon's natural history. Operating out of Flagstaff, **Four Season Guides** (1051 S. Milton Rd., 928/779-6224, www.fsguides.com, $799-1,450) offers more than a dozen different backpacking trips below the rim, from a three-day frolic to Indian Gardens to a weeklong, 45-mile expedition one some of the canyon's lesser known trails. The experienced and friendly guides tend to inspire a level of strength and ambition that you might not reach otherwise. These are the guys to call if you want to experience the lonely, out-of-the-way depths of the canyon but don't want to needlessly risk your life doing it alone.

Grand Canyon West

Since the Hualapai Tribe's Skywalk opened to much international press coverage in 2007, the remote western reaches of the Grand Canyon have certainly gotten more attention than in the past. Though as remote as ever, there has been an uptick in tourism to the Hualapai's portion of the rim, which is about two hours of dirt-road driving from the Hualapai Reservation's capital, Peach Springs, located along Route 66 east of Kingman. All that press has at the same time led to a little confusion. At the South Rim visitors center, one can usually hear the question, "How do we get to the Skywalk?" a few times an hour, followed by moans of disbelief and the cancellation of plans when the answer comes that it's about 250 miles away. If you want to experience Grand Canyon West, it's a good idea to plan a separate trip, or else carve out at least two extra days to do so. Along the way, you can drive on the longest remaining portion of Route 66, and, if you have a few days on top of that, hike down into Havasupai Canyon and see its famous, fantastical waterfalls.

HAVASUPAI INDIAN RESERVATION
Havasu Creek is heavy with lime, which turns the water an almost tropical blue-green. It

passes below the weathered red walls of the western Grand Canyon, home these many centuries to the Havasupai (Havasu 'Baaja), the "people of the blue-green water."

The creek falls through the canyon on its way to join the Colorado River, passing briefly by the ramshackle, inner-canyon village of Supai, where it is not unusual to see horses running free in the dusty streets, and where reggae plays all day through some community speaker, and where the supply helicopter alights and then hops out again every 10 minutes or so in a field across from the post office. Then, about two miles on from the village, the creek plunges 120 feet into a misty turquoise pool, and it does it again after another mile, but not before passing peacefully through a cottonwood-shaded campground.

Thousands of people from all over the world (the tribe says 20,000; other sources say half that) visit **Havasupai** (928/448-2731, www.havasupai-nsn.gov, $35 per person entry fee plus $5 environmental-care fee) every year just to see these blue-green waterfalls, to swim in their pools, and to see one of the most remote hometowns in America. The trip is all the more enticing and memorable because it's rather an expedition, or near to it. Still, there are those who return year after year, as if going home.

Getting There

A visit to Havasupai takes some planning. It's unbearably hot in the deep summer, and you can't hike except in the very early morning; the best months to visit are September, October, April, May, and June. If you aren't a backpacker, you can hire a packhorse to carry your essentials or yourself, or both ($187 both ways), or you can take the helicopter ($85 one way). A popular way to visit is to hike in and take the helicopter out. It's a five-minute thrill-ride through the canyon to the rim, and the helipad is only about 50 yards from the trailhead parking lot.

Most visitors stay the night at one of the motels along Historic Route 66 the night before hiking in. You'll want to get an early start, especially during the summer, and it's a 60-mile drive to the trailhead at Hualapai Hill from Route 66. The closest hotel is the Hualapai Lodge ($100 d; see below) in Peach Springs, about 7 miles west of Indian Route 18, which leads to the trailhead. You'll find cheaper accommodations in Seligman, about 30 miles to the east. The tribe requires a reservation to visit Supai and the falls; call at least six months in advance.

The eight-mile one-way hike to the Village of Supai from Hualapai Hilltop is actually one of the easier treks into the Grand Canyon. A few miles of switchbacks lead to a sandy bottomland, where you're surrounded by eroded humps of seemingly melted, pockmarked sandstone. This is not Grand Canyon National Park: You'll know that for sure when you see the trash along the trail. It doesn't ruin the hike, but it nearly breaks the spell. When you reach the village you'll see the twin rock spires, called Wii'Gliva, that tower over the little farms and cluttered-yard homes of Supai.

Accommodations and Food

Here, you can stay at **Havasupai Lodge** (928/448-2111 or 928/448-2201, $145 up to four people), which has air-conditioning and private bathrooms. The village also has a small café that serves decent breakfast, lunch, and dinner, and a general store. Most visitors pack in and stay at the primitive campground not far from the main waterfall, which is another 1.5 miles from the village ($17 per night, first-come, first-served).

The Waterfalls

What used to be Navajo Falls, just down the trail from the village, was destroyed in a 2008 flash flood. Now there's a wider set of falls and a big pool that sits below a flood-eroded hill. Perhaps the most famous of the canyon's falls, **Havasu Falls** comes on you all of a sudden as you get closer to the campground. Few hikers refuse to toss their packs aside and strip to their swimming suits when they see Havasu Falls for the first time. The other major waterfall, **Mooney Falls,** is another mile down the trail, through the campground. It's not easy to reach the pool below; it requires a careful walk down a narrow rock-hewn trail with chain handles, but most reasonably dexterous people can handle it. **Beaver Falls,** somewhat underwhelming by comparison, is another two miles of creek-sloshing toward the river, which is seven miles from the campground.

HUALAPAI INDIAN RESERVATION

Although Peach Springs is the capital of the Hualapai (WALL-uh-pie) Reservation, there's not much there but a lodge and a few scattered houses. The real attractions are up on the West Rim about 50 miles and two hours away. Peach Springs makes an obvious base for a visit to the West Rim, which has several lookout points, the famous Skywalk, and a kitschy Old West-style tourist attraction called Hualapai Ranch. The tribe's **Hualapai River Runners** (928/769-2219) will take you on a day trip on the river, and there are several all-inclusive package tours to choose from. Check out the tribe's website (www.grandcanyonwest.com) for more information.

© TIM HULL

Havasu Falls

Tour Packages

To visit Grand Canyon West, the Hualapai Tribe requires you to purchase one of its rather overpriced **Legacy Packages** ($43-86 per person), and only the most expensive "Gold" package includes the Skywalk. The lesser packages allow you to ride a shuttle from **Eagle Point,** where the Skywalk juts out, to **Guano Point,** an unobstructed view of the western canyon, and **Hualapai Ranch,** where fake cowboys will entertain you with Old West clichés, take you on a ride in a wagon, or on a horseback ride in a corral or to the canyon rim ($10-75). You can stay the night in one of the ranch's rustic cabins for $100 per night. A couple of the packages include a meal, or you can add one for $14.95 per person. You can also add the Skywalk to your package for $30 if you get up there and decide you really must try it. Frankly, the packages that don't include the Skywalk are definitely not worth the price or the drive. The views from the South and North Rims are much more dramatic and memorable, and it costs only $25 to see those.

The Skywalk

The Skywalk (928/769-2636, www.grandcanyonwest.com) is as much an art installation as it is a tourist attraction. A horseshoe-shaped glass and steel platform jutting out 70 feet from the canyon rim, it appears futuristic surrounded by the rugged, remote western canyon. It's something to see for sure, but is it worth the long drive and the high price tag? Not really. If you have time for an off-the-beaten-path portion of your canyon trip, it's better to go to the North Rim and stand out on Bright Angel Point—you'll get a somewhat similar impression, and it's cheaper. There is something of the thrill ride to the Skywalk, however. Some people can't handle it: They walk out a few steps, look down through the glass at the canyon 4,000 feet below, and head for (seemingly) more solid ground. It's all perfectly safe, but it doesn't feel that way if you are subject to vertigo. Another drawback of this site is that they won't let you take your camera out on the Skywalk. If you want a record of this adventure, you have to buy a "professional" photo taken by somebody

The Hualapai

Before the 1850s, northwestern Arizona's small Hualapai Tribe didn't really exist. It was the federal government's idea to group together 13 autonomous bands of Yuman-speaking Pai Indians, who had lived on the high dry plains near Grand Canyon's western reaches for eons, as the "People of the Tall Pines."

Before the colonial clampdown and the Hualapai Wars of the 1860s, the Pai bands were independent, though they "followed common rules for marriage and land use, spoke variations of one language, and shared social structures, kin networks, cultural practices, environmental niches, and so on," according to Jeffrey Shepherd's *We Are an Indian Nation: A History of the Hualapai People*, which the scholar spent 10 years researching and writing.

The U.S. Army nearly wiped out the bands during the land wars of the 1860s, and the internment of the survivors almost finished the job. But the bands persisted, and in 1883 the government established the million-acre Hualapai Reservation, with its capital at Peach Springs. Then it spent the next 100 years or so trying to take it away from them for the benefit of white ranchers, the railroad, and the National Park Service.

These days the Hualapai Nation, though still impoverished, is a worldwide brand—Grand Canyon West. How did this happen?

The small, isolated tribe has always been willing to take economic risks, one of the many ways, as Shepherd argues, that the Hualapai have twisted colonial objectives for their own survival. A few years ago they partnered with Las Vegas entrepreneur David Jin and built the Hualapai Skywalk, a 70-foot-long glass walkway hanging from the Grand Canyon's western rim. Now you can't walk two steps along the Vegas strip without a tour guide offering to drive you to one of the most isolated sections of Arizona.

Throughout their relatively short history as a nation proper, the Hualapai have consistently tried to make their windy and dry reservation economically viable, sometimes with the assistance of the government but often in direct contradiction to its goals. For generations they were cattle ranchers, but they could never get enough water to make it pay. They successfully sued the Santa Fe Railroad over an important reservation spring in a landmark case for indigenous rights. For a time in the 1980s they even hesitantly explored allowing uranium mining on their reservation. Now, they have bet their future on tourism.

else. You have to store all of your possessions, including your camera, in a locker before stepping out on the glass, with covers on your shoes like a surgeon entering the operating room.

Recreation

Though the Skywalk may not be worth the high price of admission and the long drive to reach it, the Hualapai Tribe offers one adventure that is worth the steep price tag: the canyon's only **one-day river rafting experience** (928/769-2636, www.grandcanyonwest. com, May-Oct.). It generally takes up to a year of planning and several days of roughing it to ride the river and the rapids through the inner gorge, making a Colorado River adventure something that the average tourist isn't likely to try. Not so in Grand Canyon West. For about $330 per person, Hualapai river guides will pick you up in a van early in the morning at the Hualapai Lodge in Peach Springs and drive you to the Colorado via the rough Diamond Creek Road, where you'll float downstream in a motor boat over roiling white-water rapids and smooth and tranquil stretches. You'll stop for lunch on a beach and take a short hike through a watery side canyon to beautiful Travertine Falls. At the end of the trip, a helicopter picks you out of the canyon and drops you on the rim near the Skywalk. It's expensive, yes; but if you want to ride the river without a lot of preplanning

The Skywalk is 4,000 feet above the canyon.

© ROBERT WILSON/123RF.COM

and camping, this is the way to do it. Along the way the Hualapai guides tell stories about this end of the Grand Canyon, sprinkled with tribal history and lore.

You can drive to the river's edge yourself along the 19-mile **Diamond Creek Road** through a dry, scrubby landscape scattered with cactus. The road provides the only easy access to the river's edge between Lee's Ferry, not far from the North Rim, and Pearce Ferry, near Lake Mead. The route is best negotiated in a high-clearance SUV; they say you can do it in a regular sedan, but you have to cross Diamond Creek six times as the dirt road winds down through Peach Springs Canyon, dropping some 3,400 feet from its beginning at Peach Springs on Route 66. The creek is susceptible to flash floods during the summer and winter rainy seasons, so call ahead to check road conditions (928/769-2230). At the end of the road, where Diamond Creek marries the Colorado, there's a sandy beach and an enchanting, lush oasis, and, of course, there's that big river rolling by.

Accommodations and Food

The **Hualapai Lodge** (900 Route 66, 928/769-2230 or 928/769-2636, www.grandcanyonwest.com, $75-105) in Peach Springs has a small heated saltwater pool, an exercise room, gift shop, 57 comfortable, newish rooms with soft beds, cable, free wireless, and train tracks right out the back door. The lodge is a good place to stay the night before hiking into Havasupai, as it's only about six miles west of the turnoff to Hualapai Hill and the trailhead.

The lodge's restaurant, **Diamond Creek** (6am-9pm daily, $6.99-16.99), serves American and Native American dishes. They offer a heaping plate of delicious spaghetti if you're carbo-loading for a big hike to Havasupai; the Hualapai taco (similar to the Navajo taco, with beans and meat piled high on a fluffy slab of fry bread) and the Hualapai stew (with luscious sirloin tips and vegetables swimming in a delicious, hearty broth) are both recommended. They also have a few vegetarian choices, good chili, and pizza.

For more food and accommodations along

Old Route 66 in the vicinity of Peach Springs and Grand Canyon West, try Kingman and Seligman.

GETTING THERE AND AROUND

The best way to get to **Grand Canyon West** is to take I-40 to the Ash Fork exit and then drive west on Route 66. Starting at Ash Fork and heading west to Peach Springs, the longest remaining portion of Route 66 moves through **Seligman,** a small roadside town that is a reminder of the heyday of the Mother Road. The route through Seligman, which stands up to a stop and a walk around if you have the time, is popular with nostalgic motorcyclists, and there are a few eateries and tourist-style stores in town. Once you reach Peach Springs, take Antares Road 25 miles, then turn right on Pearce Ferry Road for 3 miles, then turn east onto Diamond Bar Road for 21 miles, 14 of it

on dirt. Diamond Bar Road ends at the only entrance to Grand Canyon West. The 49-mile trip takes about two hours. For park-and-ride reservations, call 702/260-6506.

To reach **Havasupai Canyon,** turn north on Indian Route 18 just before Peach Springs and drive 68 miles north to a parking area at Hualapai Hilltop. From there it's an eight-mile hike in to Supai Village and the lodge, and another two miles to the campground. The trail is moderate and leads through a sandy wash with overhanging canyon walls. For the first two miles or so, rocky, moderately technical switchbacks lead to the canyon floor, then it's easy and beautiful the rest of the way. If you don't want to hike in, you can arrange to rent a horse (928/448-2121, 928/448-2174, or 928/448-2180, www.havasupaitribe.com, $120 round-trip to lodge, $150 round-trip to campground), or even hire a helicopter (623/516-2790, $85 per person one way).

The Arizona Strip

If there is any wild loneliness left in America, it is holed up on the Arizona Strip. This five-million-acre wilderness of crumbling red-rock walls, fallen boulders, and long sagebrush sweeps, humpbacked by the evergreen Kaibab Plateau, has only been accessible by highway from within Arizona since 1929 and the opening of the old Navajo Bridge across the Colorado River. Before that, only Latter-day Saints and Paiutes made a go of it here on any serious scale. The region is still inhabited primarily by polygamists and hermits, river guides and a few residents of the Kaibab Paiute Indian Reservation.

Think of the "strip" as exactly that: a narrow band of Arizona territory hemmed on the north by Utah's southern border, the south by the Grand Canyon, on the east by the Colorado River, and on the west by Nevada's eastern border. Within that band are several semidesert grassland valleys; the long red-rock southern escarpment of the Paria Plateau, a vast tableland

protected as the Vermilion Cliffs National Monument; a green and meadowy forest, smothered by deep snow come winter; and a historic human crossing-point where the Paria River washes into the Colorado, the only rest in the great river's canyon-cutting ways for hundreds of miles.

The first Europeans to enter the strip were the path-finding priests of the Dominguez-Escalante expedition in 1776, looking for a northern route from New Mexico to California. In the later 1800s Mormon pioneers from Utah were encouraged by their church leaders to settle in the region; some found the isolation of the strip to their advantage after the official LDS church outlawed polygamy in the 1890s; others raised cattle and cut wood and fought with the Navajo and Paiute over the land's scant resources. When construction on a Mormon temple began in St. George, Utah, to the west, the fruits of the Mormon ranch at Pipe Spring, now a national monument, and the conifers growing atop Mount Trumbull were used to feed the workers and build the temple. In the years before the railroad, the red-dust wagon road across this territory was known as the "Honeymoon Trail," as it was beaten and smoothed by a stream of LDS couples making the long journey from settlements along the Little Colorado River to St. George, where their unions would be officially sealed in the temple.

These days the strip isn't that different from the way it was before the bridge put Lee's Ferry out of business and any Arizonan with a sedan and a canteen could explore it. It remains lonely, isolated, and unpaved, for the most part. There are a few exceptions, of course; about 15 miles upstream from the Lee's Ferry crossing, Glen Canyon Dam has stopped the old warm and muddy Colorado and impounded its water in a 186-mile, canyon-flooding reservoir, where millions of boaters, anglers, and water lovers play year-round. The river that trickles out the other side of the dam is far from what it was in the old days, now running mostly clear and cold and predictable through its great, sculpted canyons.

A place of outlander history, desolate beauty, and long, quiet spaces, the Arizona Strip isn't for everyone. But for those who take the time and effort to explore it, it can become a haunting landscape, magnetic and well remembered in both dream and waking life.

PLANNING TIPS

This is classic road-trip territory, and if you're already in-state with a rental car or your own vehicle, consider taking time to at least drive the **Vermilion Cliffs Highway,** a paved two-lane route that runs, more or less, from St. George, Utah, to Lee's Ferry and Marble Canyon, using Route 59 in Utah, Arizona Highway 389, and U.S. 89A. Along the way you'll pass through the entire strip, ascending and coming back down the Kaibab Plateau and crossing the Colorado River. This can be done in one long day from either the west or the east, but if you want to stop and really see the landscape, take at least two days. If you're heading west to east, you might want to stay the night

in Fredonia or in Kanab, Utah; St. George, Utah; or even Mesquite, Nevada, near the Virgin River Gorge. If you're heading east to west, the Cameron Trading Post and hotel on U.S. 89, near the Little Colorado River and the eastern entrance to Grand Canyon National Park's South Rim, makes a good stopping destination. The most logical way to see the strip is to fold it into an excursion from the South Rim to the North Rim. Leave the South Rim early in the morning, cross the eastern strip, spend the night and the next day at the North Rim, then keep heading west down the Kaibab Plateau to Pipe Spring National Monument and on to St. George. From there it's easy to go on and explore Western Arizona and the Lower Colorado.

If you plan on doing more than road-tripping, such as hiking the empty spaces of the Vermilion Cliffs or standing on the unfenced edge of the Grand Canyon at Toroweap, it's best to plan ahead and to have at least a high and tough SUV, if not a four-wheel drive.

THE VERMILION CLIFFS HIGHWAY

Don't think of this scenic journey in terms of political boundaries, for it clips two other states. Rather, it is a journey over a landscape, through a region with a history that cannot be understood without seeing the formidable barriers thrown up by nature. If you begin your drive of the highway from the west, the best place to start is Mesquite, Nevada, along I-15. (From the east start at Cameron). Mesquite is a small but accommodations-packed town full of gambling senior citizens and cheap but nice casino-hotels on the order of Laughlin. It's common to find a comfortable room in the **Virgin River Casino** (100 Pioneer Blvd., Mesquite, NV, 877/438-2929, www.virginriver.com) for $25-50, especially on a weekday, and there is a good buffet, a pool, a movie theater, and a lot more. From Mesquite, head north on I-15 toward St. George, Utah. Just outside of town, you'll enter a corner of Arizona through which the Virgin River flows, cutting through the rocks to create the spectacular Virgin River Gorge.

© CHEE-ONN LEONG/123RF.COM

the Vermilion Cliffs Highway

Virgin River Gorge

The Virgin River, the strip's only perennial stream other than the Colorado River, cuts a dramatic rock maze through the Virgin and Beaver Dam Mountains in the far northwest corner of Arizona on its way toward Lake Mead and the lower Colorado. For several miles along I-15 between Mesquite and St. George, the views are towering and car crash-inducing: high and dry rock mountains, rough and jagged and molded haphazardly by the river, covered with holdout Mojave Desert vegetation, tripped over by desert bighorn and mountain lions. Few sections of the speedy interstate move through such precipitous, wild scenery, and it's best to stop and look around at one of the several pull-outs along the slipstream rather than craning your neck while trying to keep your eyes on the road. A good place to stop is Exit 18 (the Cedar Pocket Interchange) at the **Virgin River Canyon Recreation Area** (435/688-3200, www.blm.gov/az/outrec/camping/vrcg.htm), about 20 miles south of St. George and halfway through the gorge. This Mojave Desert riparian scene has a few easy and sandy trails that lead down to the river—its flows highly susceptible to the season—and great views of the cliffs and mountains. It is snugged in between two of the wildest wildernesses anywhere—the 19,600-acre **Beaver Dam Wilderness Area** and 84,700-acre **Paiute Wilderness Area**—and has about 75 campsites for $8 per night.

St. George to Pipe Spring

Interstate travel ends at St. George, the capital of Mormon expansion into southern Utah and Northern Arizona. Here you can visit the beautiful white **LDS temple** (250 E. 400 S., 435/673-5181, 9am-9pm daily, free), dedicated in 1877 and built using supplies and wood gathered on the strip. Continuing east out of St. George, you can either take the northeast route along Route 9 to swing by the otherworldly **Zion National Park** (435/772-3256, www.nps.gov/zion, $25 per car), or head straight to the heart of the strip southeast on Route 59, past the tiny polygamist town of Colorado City-Hilldale on the Arizona-Utah border, and on

THE GRAND CANYON

Warren Jeffs and Colorado City

Just west of Pipe Spring National Monument, the polygamist community of Colorado City-Hilldale, with a population of about 6,000 persons, sits in the jagged shadow of the Vermilion Cliffs. These sister towns, stretching across the Utah border, are little more than a collection of large homes that appear to have been built in stages and never quite finished, tri- and quad-plexes with little attention paid to finish carpentry, as if new wings had to go up quickly and cheaply all the time.

These isolated towns have been the subject of a lot of lurid media interest over the last several years thanks to the arrest and conviction of Warren Jeffs, erstwhile leader of the Fundamentalist Church of Jesus Christ of Latter-day Saints. Nearly all the property here, and all those sprawling homes, used to be owned by the church's financial arm, the United Effort Plan, which was controlled by Jeffs. Most FLDS members were born into the sect, the

descendants of a splinter group of Mormons who never accepted the mainstream LDS church's giving up of polygamy in 1890, and who migrated to this dry and windy, off-track place in the 1920s and 1930s.

Jeffs became the hereditary leader of the FLDS, Colorado City, and all the people in it in 2001. Jeffs was by many accounts a fickle and cruel leader, expelling community members for perceived lapses in morality while forcing underage girls into sexual relationships and into marriage with much older men. After several complaints were filed in Utah and Arizona, in 2005 a grand jury indicted Jeffs on two counts of sexual conduct with a minor and conspiracy. Jeffs left Colorado City and became a fugitive. A yearlong manhunt ensued, which saw Jeffs named to the FBI's Ten Most Wanted List. In 2006 he was captured near Las Vegas. He was tried and sentenced in Utah to five years to life for rape as an accomplice.

to Highway 389 and **Pipe Spring National Monument.**

C Pipe Spring National Monument

A shady, watered spot on an otherwise dry and windy red-dirt and sagebrush plain, **Pipe Spring National Monument** (928/643-7105, www.nps.gov/pisp, 7am-5pm daily June-Aug., 8am-5pm daily Sept.-May, $5) is the strip's best historic site. A museum and visitors center fronts a well-preserved fortified ranch house and a few historic outbuildings, a compound built in the 1860s and 1870s by Mormon pioneers intent on keeping the titular spring—a rare predictable water source in an otherwise arid landscape—to themselves and out of the hands of the Kaibab Paiute (on whose reservation the monument now sits) and Navajo, who had used it for centuries prior to the Anglo arrival. This and other conflicts led to a short war and regular scuffles between the natives and the Mormons, who raised cattle for meat

and cheese here, much of which was taken west weekly to feed temple workers in St. George.

An excellent museum inside the visitors center has several displays that tell the history of both Native American and Mormon settlement on the strip and shows artifacts of both cultures. For an in-depth introduction to the history and politics of the strip, this museum can't be beat. After looking over the displays and the bookstore and gift shop, you can head out to the fort for a personal tour by a volunteer (about every half hour in the busy season). The guide will take you through each room in the fortified home, called **Windsor Castle,** each furnished with period furniture and still displaying the open notches in the walls through which a rifle could be pointed to stop any outside attack. The tour also takes you into the factory-like rooms where cheese and other provisions were prepared and recalls the hardscrabble life on the 19th-century strip. The fort had the first telegraph in Arizona, part of which is still here. There is also a trail that

© GARY WHITTON/123RF.COM

Pipe Spring National Monument

extends about half a mile up a rise behind the fort that provides an expansive view of the vast plain stretching out toward the lonely Mount Trumbull to the south. A beautiful, isolating view, quiet except for the wind and the crunch of your feet on the rocky red ground. The rangers at Pipe Spring are excellent sources of information about touring the strip.

Grand Canyon-Parashant National Monument and Toroweap

Way off to the south and west of Pipe Spring rises the Shivwits Plateau and the huge, almost inaccessible **Grand Canyon-Parashant National Monument** (BLM Arizona Strip District, 345 East Riverside Dr., St. George, Utah, 435/688-3200, www.blm.gov/az/st/en/fo/arizona_strip_field.html, www.nps.gov/archive/para/visit.html, 7:45am-5pm Mon.-Fri., 10am-3pm Sat.). There are no paved roads within this million-acre wilderness, no visitors centers, well-stocked campgrounds, or concessionaires—truthfully, no services of any kind. There are, however, opportunities for the

intrepid and well-prepared visitor to see nature in its rawest state.

The plateau, rising to heights between 6,000 and 7,000 feet and covered by semidesert sweeps, short piñon forests, and stands of ponderosa pine on its mountains, marks the transition from the Mojave Desert basin and range province to the Colorado Plateau and is home to one of the loneliest and most inspiring Grand Canyon views anyone with a tough vehicle and several hours of hard travel in them can see. In the monument's western reaches, southwest of Pipe Spring, the Toroweap Valley stretches out toward the rim and **Toroweap Point** (sometimes both are called Tuweap, after an abandoned town nearby), a hard-won but amazing viewpoint, without fence or crowd, from which to see the canyon and the Colorado rushing by about 3,000 feet below. There are a few campsites right on the unhemmed rim, and more at a campground nearby, which are free but have no water or much of anything else. The mighty Lava Flow Rapids stir up the river just below the point, and nearby Vulcan's

Throne, a volcanic remnant, rises 50 feet or more from the plain. There is a ranger station near the viewpoint, and a few short trails run along the rim. While this is a truly wondrous place to visit, it's not easy getting here.

There are a few different ways to get to Toroweap Point (which is technically within Grand Canyon National Park), all of them rough, washboarded, and possibly impassable during inclement weather. Make sure you take supplies and tools with you, and a map as well. The most popular route to the viewpoint is nine miles west of Fredonia off Highway 389, road 109. It's about 60 miles of rough, slow travel from there following signs. This is an all-day, if not multiday, trip that should not be taken lightly or on a whim.

Also within the monument are the conifer-topped mountains, Trumbull and Logan, both reaching around 8,000 feet and in the old days supplying the only source of lumber on the strip. Both rise within federal Wilderness Areas in the scrub south of Pipe Spring; you'll pass by them on the way to Toroweap, and you can take a side trip to hike the short trails to both mountaintops or to walk to the half-mile trail to **Nampaweap,** a petroglyph site. For practical, local advice on visiting these areas, talk to a ranger at the **North Kaibab Ranger District** (430 S. Main St., Fredonia, 928/643-7395), one of the rangers at Pipe Spring National Monument, or the folks at the BLM office in St. George.

KANAB, UTAH

About seven miles north of the Arizona border along 89A in Utah, Kanab is the pleasant, relatively bustling capital of the Arizona Strip. Here you'll find varied accommodations, including several chain hotels and restaurants. It's a tiny, rural burg, far flung from the real world, isolated out here on the western end of the Colorado Plateau, home to only about 4,000 year-round residents. It is nonetheless well set up for travelers and tourists, as Kanab makes an ideal base for visiting Grand Canyon National Park's North Rim, just 80 miles, or about two hours away; Zion National Park,

just 40 miles to the northwest; Bryce Canyon National Park, 77 miles to the northeast; and Lake Powell, which is 70 miles off to the east.

Accommodations and Food

The **Quail Park Lodge** (125 N. 300 W., 435/215-1447, www.quailparklodge.com, $89-189), along Highway 89 as it rolls through Kanab, is clean, affordable and has a freshly painted, retro motor lodge look to it that draws in the fan of American road culture and popular architecture like some kind of mid-century siren. A small pool, tasteful motel-style rooms with TVs and Wi-Fi, and a location that can't be beat conspire to the make this one of the best places to stay on the Arizona Strip. Right next door and owned by the same folks, the **Canyons Lodge** (236 N. 300 W., 435/644-3069, www.canyonslodge.com, $59-219) is less nostalgic than its sister, choosing instead a nattier, posh-wilderness look that is as warm as it is stylish. There's also a small pool here, and the comfortable rooms offer flat-screens, Wi-Fi and crisp, relaxing beds for the end of a hard day of outdoor play.

The **Rocking V Café** (97 W. Center St., 435/644-8001, www.rockingvcafe.com, noon-8pm daily, $10-30) serves fresh and delicious food, and there's an interesting art gallery upstairs. They make a good burger, including a Boca burger, as well as tasty chicken and pasta dishes, veggie enchiladas, creamy mac-and-cheese, and more. They also have a decent selection of beer and wine, including microbrews.

FREDONIA

Fredonia is a small settlement of about 1,000 residents at the junction of State Highway 389 and U.S. Highway 89A, about seven miles south of Kanab. It's a former polygamist holdout, these days a mostly tumbledown, friendly village offering brief respite and gear storage for river guides and canyonland explorers. The name means "free woman" in Spanish. It is Arizona's northernmost town, just four miles south of the border with Utah. It was originally settled by residents of Kanab. Though it has fewer services than Kanab, it is a fine place to base your visit to the Arizona Strip, Southern Utah, and the Grand Canyon's North Rim.

Accommodations and Food

The **Grand Canyon Motel** (175 S. Main St., 928/643-7646, www.grand-canyon-motel.com, $20-44) is just the kind of place you'd expect to find way out here in the sagebrush wilderness; its romantic rusticity fairly enchants the lonely Strip voyager. The little compound offers 12 cabins, six with kitchens, plus a hostel where you can get a bed for $20. The cabins are clean and charming, and there's a quaint, grassy courtyard with barbecues.

Within walking distance of the Grand Canyon Motel, the **Cowboy Butte Grill & Steakhouse** (165 N. Main, 928/643-6848, call for hours, $8-23) serves good burgers and sandwiches, chicken fried steak smothered in rich gravy, excellent french fries and fried chicken, pork ribs and steaks and more—superior, home-style comfort food to fill you up and warm your soul after exploring the landscape.

THE KAIBAB PLATEAU

After Fredonia, U.S. Highway 89A begins to rise into a piñon-juniper woodland that quickly becomes a ponderosa pine forest as the highway climbs the massive upsweep in the land known as the Kaibab Plateau. This islandlike highland, surrounded by arid valleys and giving way on its southern edge to the Grand Canyon, measures about 60 miles from north to south and roughly 45 miles east to west, ranging in height, and so climate and flora, from 3,000 to 9,200 feet. In the plateau's highest ranges, viewed easily by driving Route 67 from Jacob Lake to the North Rim, lush mixed-conifer forests with intermittent aspens crowd the edges of green subalpine meadows. One of the state's best forest landscapes, the Kaibab has long been logged and hunted; there are old logging and jeep trails crisscrossing the tableland, which make backcountry exploring relatively easy, though only in a four-wheel drive and not in the winter. After November you are likely to find Route 67 to the North Rim closed, but U.S. 89A usually stays open year-round, even when the plateau is covered in a thick blanket of white.

While negotiating the steep and twisty highway on the west side of the plateau—or descending it if you're coming from the east—look for the sign for the **Le Fevre Overlook** and stop at the pull-out for a great view.

Accommodations and Food

The primary services area for the Kaibab Plateau is the **Jacob Lake Inn** (junction of U.S. 89A and Rte. 67, 928/643-7232, www.jacoblake.com, $94-133 for rooms, $86-135 for cabins, 6:30am-10pm), about 40 miles from the North Rim. The complex has a small, relatively new hotel building with television and Wi-Fi, plus several rustic (though not necessarily in a good way) cabins, a restaurant, gift shop, small general store, bakery, and a gas station. They may have variable hours in winter; call ahead before planning on a stop. The restaurant serves good comfort food, warm and filling, and is especially good for breakfast.

Information

Next to the Jacob Lake Inn, the rangers at the **Kaibab Plateau Visitors Center** (Rte. 67 and U.S. 89A, Jacob Lake, 928/643-7298, 8am-5pm daily May-Sept., 8am-1pm Sat.-Sun. Oct.-Dec.) can give you advice on hiking and exploring the plateau, and there's a good selection of books for sale and a few displays on the area's flora and fauna.

VERMILION CLIFFS NATIONAL MONUMENT

Most Arizona Strip visitors see only the southern escarpment of the Paria Plateau as they cut through the valley along Highway 89A. It is that edge's high crumbling sandstone cliffs that give this national monument of swirling slickrock and narrow, high-walled river canyons its name. The cliffs are best viewed from an established viewpoint about 10 miles east of Jacob Lake, as the highway begins to descend to the House Rock Valley.

The Paria River cuts through the northeast portion of the 294,000-acre monument,

© TIM HULL

the Vermilion Cliffs

creating Paria Canyon, one of the most popular canyonland backpacking trips (38 miles, about five days, reserved $5 permit required), with high, red and purple and black sandstone cliffs rising above narrow slots of sand and water. There aren't any services or visitors centers on the remote monument, and much of it is within the **Paria Canyon-Vermilion Cliffs Wilderness Area** and so can't be accessed by car. The area is best explored from the north, along Highway 89 in Utah between Kanab, Utah, and Page, Arizona. From Page, head west on U.S. 89 for about 30 miles to reach the BLM's **Paria Canyon-Vermilion Cliffs Wilderness Ranger Station,** where you can get advice on visiting the area; it serves as a kind of visitors center and crossroads for backpackers and day hikers. This is really the kind of place you have to plan ahead for; most of the best areas require a permit, and those are given out on a lottery system for some of the most popular attractions. You can also access the monument from the west on the compacted-dirt House

Rock/Coyote Valley Road (BLM Road 1065), off the south side of U.S. 89A at House Rock, which leads to the **Coyote Buttes Permit Area.** Coyote Buttes has a north and south section—the north is best gained via U.S. 89 in Utah. This is a world-famous trekking area where there are several trails that lead through a strange rock world of twisted, undulating, multicolored sandstone formations, often appearing as if rough red, yellow, and pink water was held up and petrified. Along these trails you'll see all the sandstone arches, alcoves, spires, domes, amphitheaters, and buttes that make the canyonlands so exotic and enticing. A limited number of people are allowed in each day, even for day hiking, so make sure to get a permit (www.blm.gov/az/asfo/paria/coyote_buttes/permits.htm, $5) before traveling. For more information on the monument, talk to the folks at the BLM's **Arizona Strip Field Office** (345 E. Riverside Dr., St. George, UT, 435/688-3200) or the **Kanab Field Office** (435/644-4600).

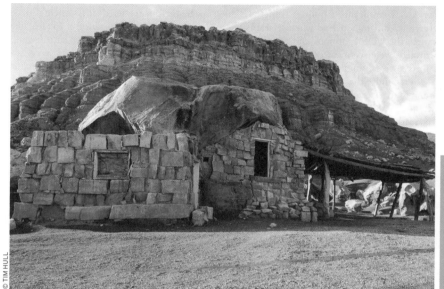

You can explore the Cliff Dwellers house, but remember it is private property.

CLIFF DWELLERS AND HOUSE ROCK VALLEY

U.S. Highway 89A continues on through the red-dirt and sagebrush House Rock Valley at the base of the Kaibab Plateau, looked over by the Vermilion Cliffs. Just after passing the lodge in the wide spot in the road known as Cliff Dwellers—so named not for some mysterious Pueblo ruins nearby but simply because those who dwell here dwell near cliffs—you'll see a little sandstone-brick structure tucked beneath a fallen boulder, like some kind of canyon-country Hobbit house, the red-rock slabs and the sculpted boulder as indistinguishable from the cliffs as the chipped light-blue trim paint is from the ever-empty sky. This little rock house, nearly melding into the vermilion scenery, is one of the most enchanting structures in all of Arizona. There's usually a Navajo or two selling jewelry here, and you can walk around and duck in and out of the strange rock hovels, as long as you realize that this is private property and should be treated as such. The house and the other little shelters were built

by Blanche and Bill Russell, the area's original homesteaders, who operated a trading post out of the rock house. The Russells also catered to the needs of Mormon travelers moving through the valley on their way to the St. George temple.

LEE'S FERRY

One of the strip's signature stops is **Lee's Ferry** (www.nps.gov/glca/planyourvisit/lees-ferry.htm), which is technically within the Glen Canyon National Recreation Area but rather far from Lake Powell. Reached via paved road past high red buttes just east of Cliff Dwellers (look for the sign), Lee's Ferry is the only spot in hundreds of miles of canyonland where you can drive down to the Colorado River. It's named for a man who occupied the area rather briefly in the early 1870s, Mormon outlaw John D. Lee, one of the leaders of the infamous Mountain Meadows Massacre in Utah. Lee was exiled to this lonely spot after he and others attacked and murdered more than 100 westbound

Arkansas emigrants moving through Utah Territory during a period when relations between the Utah Mormons and the U.S. government were strained, to say the least. One of Lee's wives, Emma Lee, ended up running the ferry more than Lee ever did; he soon lit out and lived as a kind of fugitive until he was finally, in 1877, recalled home and sentenced to death. The proclamation was carried out by firing squad on the very ground where the massacre had taken place. To the end and in a published memoir, Lee insisted that he was a scapegoat for the higher-ups, and many believe the massacre occurred on the orders of the prophet Brigham Young.

The Lee family operated a small ranch and orchard near the crossing, the remnants of which can still be seen on a self-guided tour of the **Lonely Dell Ranch Historic Site,** which includes the rusting remains of a mining operation, several old boat ruins, and a graveyard. There are a few rocky hiking trails around the area, but one of the best things to do here is to simply sit on a soggy beach and watch the river flow by the sun-spattered cliffs. There's a nice campground ($12, no hookups) if you feel like staying, and a ranger station and launch ramp as well.

For long before and after Lee lent his name to the crossing, this two-mile break in the Colorado River's canyon-digging, near the mouth of the Paria River, was one of the very few places to cross the river in southern Utah and northern Arizona; in fact, it remained so until the bridging of the Colorado at Marble Canyon in 1929. Today, the area is the starting block for thousands of brave river-trippers who venture into the Grand Canyon atop the Colorado every year. It's also a popular fishing spot, though the trout here have been introduced and were not native to the warm muddy flow before the dam at Glen Canyon changed the Colorado's character. For guides, gear, and any other information about the area, try **Lee's Ferry Anglers** (928/355-2261 or 800/962-9755, www.leesferry.com) located at the Cliff Dweller's Lodge.

Lee's Ferry is also significant because it

historic buildings at Lee's Ferry

© GARY WHITTON/123RF.COM

© TIM HULL

Lee's Ferry Lodge at Vermilion Cliffs

provides the dividing line between the upper and lower states of the Colorado River's watershed, inasmuch as they were divided by the compact that divvied up the river's water for human use. This has made Lee's Ferry "river mile 0," the gateway and crossroads to both the upper and lower Colorado, and the place where its annual flows are measured and recorded.

Accommodations and Food

The small **Cliff Dweller's Lodge** (928/355-2261 or 800/962-9755, www.cliffdwellerslodge.com, $75-85) is nearly drowned by the scenery around it, tucked beneath the base of the red cliffs. This lodge offers charming, rustic-but-comfortable rooms with satellite television, and the restaurant serves good breakfasts, lunches, and dinners ($10-25), everything from fajitas and ribs, to falafel and halibut. They also serve the hard stuff, beer and wine, which you can sip on the little patio here at what seems like the very end of the world. There's also a gas station here.

The **Lee's Ferry Lodge at Vermilion Cliffs** (U.S. Hwy. 89A near Marble Canyon, 928/355-2231 or 800/451-2231, www.leesferrylodge.com, $63) has romantic little rooms in a retro-West little rock-built structure that blends into the tremendous background wonderfully, and a delicious restaurant serving hearty fare perfect after a long day of outdoor play, and its beer selection (more than 100 different bottles) is outrageously diverse for such an out-of-the-way place. The steaks are hand cut, and the ribs are outstanding, smothered in the lodge's special homemade sauce. The lodge serves breakfast, lunch, and dinner daily ($10-20).

The trading post first established by Lorenzo Hubble at **Marble Canyon Lodge** (U.S. Hwy. 89A near Marble Canyon) had been open for business since 1920—it said so right on its sign. That's nearly 100 years of waiting for the odd customer under the ever blue sky, which is the only thing bigger than this wide-open landscape. The historic store and restaurant burned down in 2013, but it will likely be rebuilt and open again someday.

Navajo Bridge over the Colorado River

NAVAJO BRIDGE AND MARBLE CANYON

A few miles before U.S. Highway 89A runs into U.S. Highway 89 south toward Navajoland and the Grand Canyon, two bridges span Marble Canyon, where the Colorado River digs deep again after its surfacing at Lee's Ferry. This is the exit from or the entrance to the heart of the strip, depending on which way you're headed. The original Navajo Bridge was opened in 1929, the first bridge to cross this part of the Colorado, putting Lee's Ferry out of business for good. By 1995, a new bridge had opened, as the original was not up to the increased traffic along Highway 89A. The original bridge is now kept open for sightseers, and you can walk over it and look down at the river flowing through magnificent Marble Canyon, here at the very start of the Grand Canyon. The **Navajo Bridge Interpretive Center** (928/355-2319, www.nps.gov/glca/historyculture/navajobridge.htm, 9am-5pm daily Apr.-Oct.) has a book shop and displays about the bridge, and

there are usually several booths selling Native American arts and crafts.

PAGE AND LAKE POWELL

The town would not exist without the lake, and the lake would not exist without the dam: such is the symbiotic chain of existence here in the slickrock lands around sunken Glen Canyon, where water lovers come to play among the red and pink sandstone labyrinths.

Page is a small, tidy town with a higher-than-normal number of churches for its size; they are all lined up along one long block at the beginning of this resort burg's main drag. The population here was once composed primarily of dam builders and their families, for the town was founded in 1957 as a government-run camp for Glen Canyon Dam workers, built on land formerly owned by the Navajo but traded for a slice of property in Utah. These days Page has sizable Latter-day Saint and Navajo communities, and the population swells with boaters, water skiers, swimmers, and houseboat loungers in the spring and summer. The business life of Page is now dedicated to that influx, so there are plenty of chain hotels and restaurants here if you don't want to stay and eat at Wahweap Marina, the lake's largest marina and the center of most Arizona visits to the lake, most of which is in Utah.

Sights
JOHN WESLEY POWELL MUSEUM AND VISITOR INFORMATION CENTER

Just off Page's main drag is the **John Wesley Powell Museum and Visitor Information Center** (6 N. Lake Powell Blvd., 928/645-9496 or 888/597-6873, www.powellmuseum.org, 9am-5pm Mon.-Fri., $5 adults over 12, $1 children 12 and under), named, as is the nearby man-made lake, for the one-armed Civil War veteran, scientist, writer, and explorer who led the first two river expeditions through the Grand Canyon. The center has an excellent bookstore, and the friendly staff can help you book boat and air tours, but the museum itself takes a little more effort to enjoy. There is a lot of information on Powell and the river runners

Lake Powell

who followed in his path, but most of the displays are made up of long articles that you have to stand there and read. Children will likely be impatient, though there's a small interactive display on the natural science of the area.

HORSESHOE BEND

As you drive into Page from the south along Highway 89, look for milepost 545 (about four miles south of town), where you can walk an easy trail (0.75 mile one way) to a viewpoint above the famous, much-photographed Horseshoe Bend, where the Colorado River curves horseshoelike around a lonely pink butte far below.

ANTELOPE CANYON
NAVAJO TRIBAL PARK

A color-swirled, water-worn slot in a mesa on Navajoland, **Antelope Canyon Navajo Tribal Park** (928/698-2808, 8am-5pm daily Apr.-Oct., $6 admission, guided tours extra) is a few miles outside Page on Highway 98. This popular crevice of twisting and twirling slickrock

requires a Navajo guide, but it's easy to find one. You pile into a big four-wheel drive with your guide and others and ride several bumpy miles down a sandy wash to the slit in the rocks rising up out of the ground—the entrance to a wonderland. The guide then takes you through the short slot canyon and out the other side, and then back again. It's an easy walk along a sandy bottomland, with the canyon walls rising 130 feet and impossibly narrow in some stretches. It's a strange, fantastic, and very memorable stroll, and one that is highly recommended despite the relatively high cost of a tour. The tours are staggered, so you are never crammed in there with too many other people. The earlier you go the better; the light and the colors are said to be at their best between 10am and noon. However, during these hours the guides usually charge $40 or more—nearly twice that charged at other times. It's really only important for serious photographers to go at these ideal times of the day.

The slot canyon's unique undulations and warm reds and pinks, especially in the summer

Antelope Canyon is one of the most photographed slot canyons in the world.

with the sun high in the sky and shining in laserlike shafts through small gashes high above, makes it one of the most photographed in the canyonlands, if not the world. It is a very popular attraction, and you'll find no shortage of guides in Page. Still, it's a good idea to make a reservation. The price to get in the park is generally wrapped into what you pay the guide. You can also go to the park yourself and hire a guide there.

Antelope Canyon Navajo Tours (928/698-3384, http://navajotours.com, tours offered at 9am, 11am, 2pm, 3pm, and 4pm, $25-40) in Page will take you out in one of its big four-wheelers for a 1.5-hour general tour or a 2.5-hour photographer's tour.

Antelope Canyon Tours (22 S. Lake Powell Blvd., 928/645-9102, www.antelopecanyon.com, $35-46) offers two different tours every day, all year round, departing from Page. The 1.5-hour general tour leaves at 8am, 9:30am, 11:30pm, 1:30pm, and 3:30pm.

One of the better photography tours of

Antelope Canyon is offered by **Adventurous Antelope Canyon Photo Tours** (Hwy. 98, mile post 302, 928/1380-1874, www.navajoantelopecanyon.com, $86-186), and they will also take you out to a few other, though lesser, slot canyons that aren't as well-known and heavily visited as Antelope Canyon. This company is recommended for serious amateur and professional photographers.

ANTELOPE POINT MARINA

The Navajo tribe's **Antelope Point** (537 Marina Pkwy., Navajo Rte. N22b, 928/645-5900, www.antelopepointlakepowell.com) has a tasteful sandstone welcome center and offers a variety of services, as well as access to Lake Powell in a starkly beautiful setting. The **Ja'di' Tooh Restaurant** (11am-9pm daily, $5.95-24.95) serves decent American food (burgers, sandwiches, steaks, salads) and looks out over the stark, red land and the glowing blue lake. A hotel is planned for the future. You can rent houseboats and other water craft, and get flicked across the water at the wakeboarding park, and there are slips to park your boat and a store to purchase supplies. The marina is located about 9 miles outside Page on Navajo land. Take Route 98 east to Navajo Route 222. It's not far from Antelope Canyon Tribal Park.

◀ Glen Canyon National Recreation Area

Sprawling over the Arizona-Utah border and some 1.25 million acres, **Glen Canyon National Recreation Area** (928/608-6200, www.nps.gov/glca, $15 per car for seven-day pass) is a popular boating, fishing, and hiking area centered on **Lake Powell,** the continent's second largest man-made lake. Created by the damming of the Colorado River and the destruction of the river-sculpted Glen Canyon, the lake is 186 miles long and has more than a thousand miles of meandering desert shoreline. Its waters run through a red-rock maze of skinny side canyons, like canals around an ornate, abandoned city sculpted out of sandstone. During the spring and summer months the lake is crowded with sometimes rowdy Jet

© TIM HULL

You must hire a guide to see Antelope Canyon.

Skiers, water-skiers, and houseboat residents, but one could visit the area and never get wet— the canyon-country scenery is enough to draw and keep even the most water-averse visitors. The whole area resembles one vast, salmon-pink sand dune frozen and petrified at once—it is a desolate, lonely place sometimes, beautiful and sacred, but also a reminder of how humans can change a seemingly unalterable landscape at their will.

Probably the most popular activity on Lake Powell is houseboating. The floating mansions chug among the buttes and spires, while their residents shoot water cannons at each other and stop at night for parties on the beaches around the lake. As it is on the nearby Navajo Reservation, some places around Lake Powell are an hour off of Arizona time during daylight savings time.

GLEN CANYON DAM
Looking out at the dam through large picture windows in Glen Canyon's **Carl Hayden Visitor Center** (928/648-6404 or 928/608-6072,

www.nps.gov/glca, 8am-5pm daily, free tours offered), it's difficult not to be impressed. The great concrete slab shimmed into the narrow Navajo-sandstone channel allows for the storage of some 27 million acre-feet of water (an acre-foot of water is roughly the amount that a family of four uses in a year); it's a brash reclamation feat if there ever was one. But it is also difficult to see Lake Powell, the man-made reservoir turned water playground created by the dam, and not feel that something was lost in the flooding of once-spectacular Glen Canyon and the irrevocable alteration of the Colorado River's ecosystem.

The writer and desert-country anarchist Edward Abbey, whose famous 1975 trickster-novel *The Monkey Wrench Gang* envisions the destruction of Glen Canyon Dam by a group of eco-warriors, described the long-lost canyon, waiting silent about 300 feet below Lake Powell's glassy surface, as a "once lovely wonderland of grottoes, alcoves, Indian ruins, natural stone arches, cottonwood groves, springs and seeps and hanging gardens of ivy,

© TIM HULL

Houseboating and camping are popular at Lake Powell.

columbine, and maidenhair fern—and many other rare things."

Along with the sinking of this natural wonderland, the dam severely altered the character of the Colorado River downstream. A sediment-laden river—a characteristic of the mighty flow that allowed it to carve those famous canyons—the Colorado River once ran warm and muddy, filled with native fish and lined by beaches, sand bars, and groves of cottonwood and willow. Now that the flow is stopped at the dam and impounded, the once sediment-heavy river runs cool and clear coming out of the other side, which has encouraged exotic, invasive plant and fish species to thrive to the detriment of the native flora and fauna. Beaches that are eroded don't come back so easily because of the lack of sediment in the river flow, and a controlled flow has replaced the natural flood cycle of the river, leading to the disappearance of an entire ecosystem.

Many people, including some who once supported the dam's construction, now believe that too much was lost for what was gained. The dam is surely an awesome sight, and it will either draw your admiration for the brave and tough men who built it from 1957 to 1964, or your disgust for the loss of a once-wild river that it changed forever. More likely, you'll feel a little bit of both, and you will agree with Abbey, who conceded that "though much has been lost, much remains."

Since the 1990s the river below the dam has been purposely flooded several times with timed releases of flows from the reservoir. An army of scientists then moves into the canyon along the river to determine the flood's effects on the ecosystem. While these experiments have been helpful, many scientists believe they happen too infrequently to make much of a difference in combating the dam's negative influence downriver.

WAHWEAP MARINA AND LAKE POWELL RESORT

The largest marina in the recreation area and the center of Arizona-side visits to Lake

© TIM HULL

The Glen Canyon Dam formed Lake Powell by stopping the Colorado River.

Powell, the **Wahweap Marina** (928/645-2433, www.lakepowell.com) offers lodging, food, boat and other watercraft rentals, camping, RV parking, tours, and shopping all within one area. Aramark is the main concessionaire at the marina, running the **Lake Powell Resort and Marina** (100 Lakeshore Dr., 928/645-2433, $94-198), where you can rent the equipment to do just about anything on the lake. The hotel has two heated pools, a sauna, a hot tub, and a workout room. The marina's **Rainbow Room** (100 Lakeshore Dr., 928/645-2433, 6am-2pm and 5pm-10pm daily in season, 7am-1:30pm and 5pm-9pm daily in winter, $6-16) at the Lake Powell Resort has lakeview tables and serves delicious fish, steak, pork chops, and pasta for dinner and a buffet at lunch. The hotel also has a stylish, relaxing bar, the **Driftwood Lounge,** inside with good drinks and tasty tapas. The marina also has a sandy beach with chairs, cabanas, and offers guided fishing tours and waterskiing instruction, among myriad other activities.

BOATING ON LAKE POWELL

If you make the drive to these remote corners of the Colorado Plateau, crossing Indian lands and canyonlands just to see the drowned landscape, and fail to get out on the water, you are indeed missing something.

Many otherwise landbound folks who visit Lake Powell have their own boats, including a large contingent of locals and near-locals from the surrounding region. Others become laketop locals for a week ever year, conspiring with friends and friends of friends to raise a lesser king's ransom to lounge in houseboat luxury under the relentless sun, blushed in a more or less permanent buzz. Most of the houseboats available for rent here sleep up to 12 people and have all the comforts of a land-loving home and then some. On average, expect to pay about $100-150 per person per day for a houseboat, which you can rent from three days up to seven days. You can rent a boat at **Wahweap Marina** (www.lakepowell.com/houseboats), and it's best to plan far ahead and make a reservation (888/896-3829).

The boat rental facility at Wahweap (8am-6pm daily Arizona time), which is just a short drive from the resort along Lake Shore Drive, also rents Jet Skis ($180 for two hours, $375 all day, plus $500 deposit) and powerboats ($200-250 for two hours plus, $400-584 all day, plus $500 deposit). While pricey and a bit obnoxious, exploring the canyons and alcoves of Lake Powell on a speedy boat or Jet Ski seems otherwise ideal. There's no easier, or faster, way to see the whole lake and to explore its mysterious corners and beaches.

A more peaceful and contemplative activity, which also has the virtue of being great exercise, is kayaking on Lake Powell. It's even better with a loved-one; the double sit-upon kayak here is perfect for couples, especially if one of the pair is not inclined to do much paddling ($28 for two hours, $43 all day, plus $100 deposit). Make sure to take some water and food along with you. You can buy groceries in Page, and they sell a small selection of snacks and drinks at a store near the rental office, which also has bathrooms. Two or three hours is more than enough time to paddle across the lake to one of the white beaches spreading out from sheer white rock faces nearby, have a picnic and climb into the shallow caves in the rock-face, and paddle back again. Don't forget the sunscreen.

Between April and October, the marina offers several boat tours of the lake, including dinner and breakfast cruises and day trips to Rainbow Bridge and elsewhere. The red rocks grow warm and flash their deep hidden colors during sunrise and sunset, and a boat tour is a great way to experience this. There are night-time tours of the lake for a view of the city of stars that emerges from the huge, clear sky. Depending on their length and destination, boat tours from Wahweap run $41-125. There's a booking desk inside the Lake Powell Resort at Wahweap Marina.

RAINBOW BRIDGE NATIONAL MONUMENT

Rainbow Bridge, the world's largest arched-rock span and one of the true wonders of the natural world, is a sacred site to the Navajo, who call it *Nonnezoshi* (rainbow turned to stone). An improbable arch of reddish-orange sandstone 290 feet high, the "bridge" is one of the most popular sites within the recreation area, even with the difficulty in getting there and the admonitions against walking under it in deference to Navajo beliefs. While you can gear up for a multiday backpack trip across the hot, rugged land to reach the wonder on foot, most visitors take a 50-mile, all-day boat tour from Wahweap Marina, or take their own boat to the well-signed port of call. **Aramark** (800/528-6154, www.lakepowell.com, $125 per person) is in charge of tours. The trip includes an easy two-mile round-trip hike from the dock to the arch.

Events

Every year on the first weekend in November, about 50 hot-air balloonists bring their colorful crafts to Page for the **Page Balloon Regatta** (928/645-2741, www.pagechamber.

© TIM HULL
Lake Powell is perfect for kayaking.

com). The highlight of the event is the Balloon Glow, when the balloonists light up their balloons on the ground, creating dozens of glowing orbs. There's also a street festival and other events that attend this busy weekend near Lake Powell.

Accommodations

Most of the chain accommodations outside the marinas are midrange. There's a very affordable and clean **Motel 6** (637 S. Lake Powell Blvd., 928/645-5888, $55-81) with a pool and interior corridors, and the **Best Western at Lake Powell** (208 N. Lake Powell Blvd., 928/645-5988, $106-210) serves a good continental breakfast and offers wireless Internet. The bed-and-breakfasts fill up fast, so call ahead several months in advance for high-season reservations.

Canyon Colors B&B (225 S. Navajo Dr., 928/645-5979, www.canyoncolors.com, $125) rents two bright and homey rooms in Page, and has an outdoor barbecue area and a pool, friendly hosts, and big, delectable breakfasts. The **Dreamkatcher Lake Powell Bed & Breakfast** (66 S. American Way, Big Water, UT, 435/675-5828, www.dreamkatcherslakepowell.com, $109-129) is about 20 minutes from Page on the Utah side of the recreation area. There are three pleasant rooms with private baths, a library with views of Lake Powell, and a hot tub with a spectacular view of the canyonlands.

Food and Nightlife

Millions of tourists drive through Page every season to see Lake Powell and the canyonlands, and as a result the area has all the usual chain hotels and several chain restaurants—more than is usual for a small town in the middle of nowhere. You'll find most of Page's services along Lake Powell Blvd., the main drag through town.

The Dam Bar & Grille (644 N. Navajo, 928/645-2161, www.damplaza.com, 11am-10pm daily, $2.99-24.99) is the small resort town's slick entertainment complex, featuring

a surf-and-turf restaurant (with well-made baby back ribs, steaks, prime rib, sandwiches, and salads), and the **Gunsmoke Saloon** (7pm-2am daily), a nightclub with a strobe-dappled dance floor, live bands, pool tables, and other bar games.

For dinner or lunch try **Strombolli's Italian Restaurant & Pizzeria** (711 N. Navajo Dr., 928/645-2605, 11am-close Mon.-Sat., noon-close Sun., $6.95-18.95) for toothsome Italian entrées like baked ravioli with meat sauce, calzones, New York-style pizza, chicken parmigiana, stuffed eggplant parmigiana, burgers, steaks, and salads, and a decent wine list. This is the best restaurant in the area.

Information and Services

The **Page Lake Powell Tourism Bureau** (647-A Elm St., 928/660-3405, www.pagelakepowelltourism.com) has all kinds of information on Page, Glen Canyon, and the rest of the region, and the staff there can help you book tours.

Getting There and Around

The best and really the only practical, freewheeling way to travel to and explore the Lake Powell region is by car. If you're flying into Phoenix, it's a long, lonely five-hour drive from the teeming metropolis northward to poor, drowned Glen Canyon, now called Lake Powell. Take I-17 out of the valley to Flagstaff, about a two-hour drive from the desert to the forest; then take Highway 89A from Flagstaff north across the western edge of the Navajo Reservation to Page, a total of 327 miles that passes through Arizona's three great landscapes—the Sonoran Desert, the pine forest, and the Colorado Plateau.

A trip north to Lake Powell can easily be folded into a visit to the Grand Canyon's South Rim, but it's a bit closer to the North Rim, which is just as spectacular in its way but without the crowds. Lake Powell is 187 miles from the South Rim. Take Highway 64 east through the Desert View gate to Cameron, about 60 miles, then head north on Highway 89 for 45 miles to Page. The total distance is 136 miles and will take about three hours. The North Rim is 154 miles from Lake Powell along Highway 89A. It will likely take you just as long as the drive from the South Rim; figure on three hours without stops.

If you're visiting the North Rim along with Zion National Park and Bryce Canyon National Park, consider a side-trip to Lake Powell, especially if you're staying in Kanab, Utah, a central basecamp for visiting all of the Arizona Strip and Southern Utah. Kanab is 74 miles from Lake Powell along Highway 89, just to the north of the Arizona border. The drive across the vast sagebrush plain takes about 1.5 hours. From Kayenta and Monument Valley on the Navajo Reservation, east of Lake Powell, take U.S. 160 west to Highway 98 for about 100 miles, a two-hour drive. You'll reach the region right near Antelope Canyon, one of its top sights to see.

THE LOWER COLORADO RIVER

The great river is the chief draw of this region, and there's always much to see and do in the small resort communities along its banks, especially if you like getting wet.

Here you can marvel at the engineering audacity of Hoover Dam, which sought to tame the Colorado and bring hydroelectricity, irrigation, and predictable flows to the desert. Spend

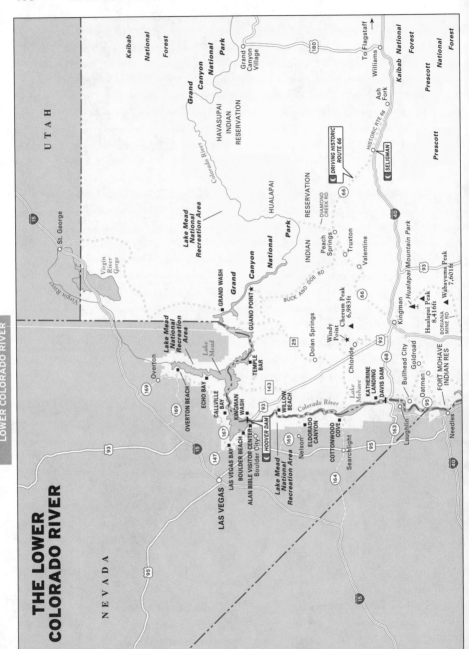

LOWER COLORADO RIVER

THE LOWER
COLORADO RIVER

N E V A D A

U T A H

Kaibab National Forest

Grand Canyon National Park

Grand Canyon Village

To Flagstaff →

Williams

Ash Fork

Kaibab National Forest

Prescott National Forest

Prescott

HAVASUPAI INDIAN RESERVATION

HISTORIC RTE 66

DRIVING HISTORIC ROUTE 66

SELIGMAN

St. George

Virgin River Gorge

Virgin River

Colorado River

HUALAPAI

Lake Mead National Recreation Area

Grand Canyon National Park

INDIAN RESERVATION

DIAMOND CREEK RD

Peach Springs

Truxton

Valentine

Hualapai Mountain Park

GRAND WASH

GUANO POINT ★

BUCK AND DOE RD

Cherum Peak 6,983ft

Overton

Lake Mead National Recreation Area

Lake Mead

Dolan Springs

Windy Point ★

Chloride

Kingman

Hualapai Peak 8,416ft

Wahayuma Peak 7,601ft

BORIANA MINE RD

ECHO BAY

CALLVILLE BAY

KINGMAN WASH

TEMPLE BAR

Bullhead City

Goldroad

Oatman

LAS VEGAS

LAS VEGAS BAY

BOULDER BEACH

ALAN BIBLE VISITOR CENTER

Boulder City

HOOVER DAM

WILLOW BEACH

Colorado River

Lake Mohave

KATHERINE LANDING

DAVIS DAM

FORT MOHAVE INDIAN RES

Lake Mead National Recreation Area

Nelson

ELDORADO CANYON

COTTONWOOD COVE

Searchlight

Laughlin

Needles

Overton Beach

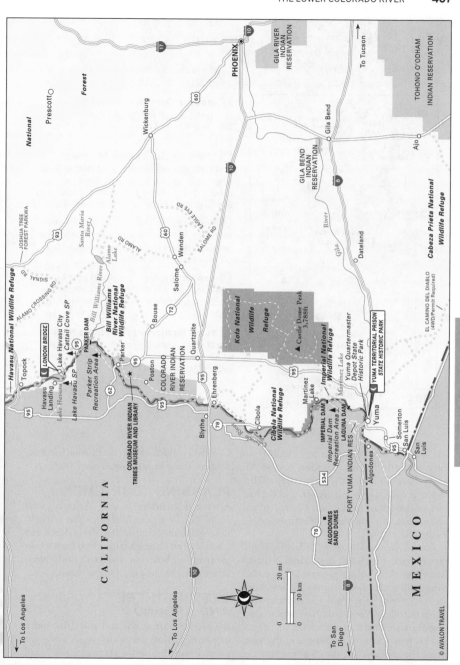

© AVALON TRAVEL

HIGHLIGHTS

LOOK FOR ◖ TO FIND RECOMMENDED SIGHTS, ACTIVITIES, DINING, AND LODGING.

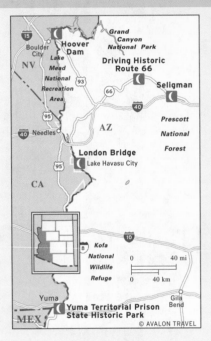

◖ **Hoover Dam:** Tour one of the largest concrete dams in the world, holding back the Colorado River in a barren desert canyon (page 410).

◖ **Driving Historic Route 66:** Drive the longest remaining stretch of the old Mother Road, where nostalgia for a long-gone American road culture rules and there's something fascinating and forgotten around every bend (page 416).

◖ **Seligman:** This small town is a throwback to the Route 66 era and one of the models for the forgotten town of Radiator Springs in the hit Disney-Pixar film *Cars* (page 423).

◖ **London Bridge:** This picturesque bridge that once spanned the Thames in London now reaches across the Lake Havasu channel (page 430).

◖ **Yuma Territorial Prison State Historic Park:** Witness how the rapscallions and outlaws of Arizona's wild territorial days lived in this legendary Old West prison (page 436).

hot, lazy days by the water at Lake Havasu City, and stroll across London Bridge, rebuilt here in the desert in the 1970s. Discover the Old West in Yuma, and the history of American road culture in Kingman, Seligman, and along the lonely remains of old Route 66.

Several river-and-desert wildlife refuges and the red-rock stretches of Lake Mead National Recreation Area offer a glimpse at the power nature still wields over us, no matter how much we try to control it. And the shifting sand dunes outside of Yuma will make you wonder if you've wandered into the Sahara.

This region is often the hottest in the state, if not the country, but the cool waters of the Colorado make it a resort destination for thousands of water-loving visitors every year.

PLANNING YOUR TIME

A week is sufficient to tour "Arizona's west coast" (a half-serious nickname that refers to the region's river-centric lifestyle) in depth, but a scenic drive-through with a stop for a dip in the river, or a boat tour, and a visit to all the essentials can be done in a long weekend.

GETTING THERE AND AROUND

It's best to start at one end and drive south or north, hitting towns and sights along the river. From the north, start at Lake Mead

National Recreation Area (or in Las Vegas, just an hour or so to the northwest) and move south on U.S. Highway 93 to Kingman. Along the way, visit the recreation area and Hoover Dam, an absolutely essential stop in this region. From Kingman, take Historic Route 66 over Sitgreaves Pass and through the little Old West reenactment town of Oatman, with its friendly semiwild burros. If you want to gamble or splash in the Colorado, from Oatman head west to State Highway 95 and Bullhead City-Laughlin; if you want to skip Route 66 altogether and head straight back to the river, take Highway 68 west from Kingman. If you're more interested in desolate stretches than riverplay, you can keep south on Route 66 from Oatman to Topock and the Havasu National Wildlife Refuge. A brief tug east on I-40 and then south through the seemingly empty land along Highway 95 will take you right into Lake Havasu City, where you can stroll beneath London Bridge and maybe rent a boat or book a cruise up to wild Topock Gorge. Keep heading south through the sparse, jagged desert around Parker and Quartzsite and then on to Yuma, the southern end of the tour. A short drive west into California on I-8 will take you to the strange and thrilling Algodones Dunes, where you can imagine that you're floating above the Dune Sea in *Return of the Jedi*. Just west of U.S. Highway 95 north of Yuma you'll find Martinez Lake, where you can book a boat tour into the Imperial National Wildlife Refuge. To reach the refuge on your own, take I-10 from Quartzsite to Blythe, California, then Highway 78 south. Also just a bit north of Yuma along Highway 95 you'll pass the huge Kofa National Wildlife Refuge, where you can take a short hike into Palm Canyon to see the state's only native palm trees. If you're starting from Yuma in the south, which makes sense if you're coming from either Tucson or Phoenix, reverse the route, taking Highway 95 north across the desert, then Route 66 northeast, then Highway 93 northwest to Hoover Dam.

Lake Mead National Recreation Area

Water spreads like exploring fingers over the dry, scrubby land, molding a wet playground out of the necessities of industry and progress. It wasn't enough for those reclaimers of the 1930s to stop the Colorado River dead in its tracks and impound all the water the imagined Southwestern empire would need. Why not create a boating and fishing empire while we're at it? And so we have this 290-square-mile, 2.5-million-acre national recreation area, the nation's first.

There are two desert lakes here: Mead, at 112 miles long the continent's largest man-made body of water, and the smaller Mohave (pronounced "Mo-hah-vee"), 67 miles downriver. Two dams hold the waters back: Hoover, some 70 stories high, keeps Lake Mead in check, while the smaller Davis Dam has its back to Mohave. The placid waters lap at more than 700 miles of Mojave Desert shoreline in two states and stretch north toward a third. The Mojave Desert is named after the desert tribe that lived along the Colorado River—the word means something like "alongside the water." The folks that established Mohave County in 1864 used a variant spelling of the word. Throughout this region you'll see the word spelled both ways.

Millions of waterborne and sun-stained revelers find this place every year, flocking from nearby Las Vegas and the Arizona cities. There is excellent fishing here no matter the season, and boating, swimming, scuba diving, sunbathing, and houseboat touring. If you're not a water type, a tour of Hoover Dam or a slow drive along Lake Mead's scenic North Shore Road—the sun igniting the red-rock cliffs of the Bowl of Fire, bighorn sheep picking along the rough rock spines along the road—are enough to justify a visit.

© KOBBY DAGAN/123RF.COM

Hoover Dam

Due to prolonged drought in the Southwest, the recreation area has been plagued in recent years by low water levels—in some places it is 60 feet below normal levels—causing the closure of a few areas. It's a good idea to call the **Lake Mead National Recreation Area headquarters** (601 Nevada Way, Boulder City, NV, 702/293-8907, www.nps.gov/lame) or check the website before making your travel plans.

◖ HOOVER DAM

Once the largest dam of its kind just about anywhere, Hoover Dam is still one of the nation's greatest engineering and construction feats and stands today as a testament to the brawn and ambition of a people set on taming a wild river. The Southwest as we know it simply would not exist without this dam. At the same time, the Colorado River will never be the same, and we may have traded an entire native river ecosystem for a more predictable flow than that allowed by the natural flood and drought cycles that ruled the wild river. In

the process, an epic human story played out, with thousands of men climbing the sheer rock walls of an overheated canyon in the middle of nowhere, holding back a river with concrete and will. Some say more than 700 men died during the dam's construction (a number higher than the official estimates), which took five years and about 3.2 million cubic yards of concrete to complete.

Not only is Hoover Dam an engineering audacity of the highest order, it's a rather stylish one at that. Heading northwest out of Kingman along U.S. Highway 93, suddenly the walls of Black Canyon close in and the huge concrete slab of the dam comes into view. You have to drive over the dam to reach Nevada and the **Parking Garage** (8am-6pm daily, $7 cash only), passing sculptor Oskar J. W. Hansen's soaring *Winged Figures of the Republic*, two 30-foot-high bronze man-angels with arms bearing the strained and hard muscles of the long-gone dam builders attached to up-stretched wings, meant to symbolize, according to the artist, "the enormous power of trained physical strength, equally enthroned in placid triumph of scientific accomplishment."

The **Hoover Dam Visitor Center** (702/494-2517 or 866/730-90979, www.usbr.gov/lc/hooverdam/service/index.html, 9:30am-5pm daily, $8 without tour) has numerous exhibits on the building of the dam and the scientific and social justifications behind the enormous undertaking. There's a short movie, and an elevator to the roof and the best overview of the dam complex and the river flowing beyond it on down to Lake Mohave. If you're here already, it's worth it to take one of two tours offered. The **Powerplant Tour** ($11 adults, $9 children 4-16) lasts about two hours and gives a comprehensive view of the dam and an explanation of how it works. The **Hoover Dam Tour** ($30, no children under 8 allowed) lasts about 1.5 hours and goes deep into the dam and reveals the inner workings of the huge complex. This tour is highly recommended and is worth the extra money; it includes a booklet about the dam for each participant. You get to walk the rounded and brightly lit low-ceilinged corridors inside the damworks, and view the lazy band of river from high up in the dam. This tour also provides a chance to see all the beautiful art deco touches folded into the design of the dam complex in the 1930s, an arguably more stylish era than our own. The entire inner complex is floored with a gray Italian marble flecked with reds and yellows, and there are stylized Native American-inspired designs etched into the floor in even the most out-of-the-way corners. In summer, the first tour begins at 9am, and the last tour begins at 5:15pm. In winter, the last tour begins at 4:15pm. The last tickets are sold an hour before the last tour. There's a standard gift shop near the parking garage and a little café that serves good hamburgers, sandwiches, hot dogs, and other tasty eats.

Hoover Dam Bypass/ Colorado River Bridge

Unless you're in a hurry to get to Vegas, or you hate slow traffic and security checkpoints, there's no reason to skip the scenic drive along U.S. Highway 93 over Hoover Dam. It's one of the most spectacular sights in the region, and the dam itself should not be missed. That being said, there's a new attraction in Black Canyon that provides a pretty awesome view of the river and the dam itself. In October 2010, after years of planning and construction, the Hoover Dam Bypass opened to much fanfare. The main draw of this new segment of U.S. 93—which is meant to ease traffic congestion over the dam and provide an alternative route for commercial trucks—is the Colorado River Bridge. The bridge spans Black Canyon about 900 feet above the Colorado River just south of Hoover Dam. Officially named the **Mike O'Callaghan-Pat Tillman Memorial Bridge** (after Nevada governor Mike O'Callaghan and Pat Tillman, a former Arizona Cardinals player and Army Ranger killed by friendly fire in Afghanistan), it's the nation's first concrete-steel composite arch bridge and has the longest concrete arch in the Western Hemisphere. There's a sidewalk and viewing area where you can stop and look at the dam and the river rushing by far below.

LAKE MEAD

The larger of the two lakes in the recreation area is Lake Mead. When full (which it hasn't been since the early 1980s because of drought), the lake is 112 miles long, some 500 feet deep, and has 247 square miles of surface area. It is very hot here in the summer, despite all the splashing and frolicking going on in the water. There is little shade in the Mojave, and the sun is incessant and unforgiving. The vegetation is sparse—nothing but rocks, scrub, and barren red, pink, and blue hills, sharp and jagged. The native terrain seems out of touch with the man-made oases around the lake, with their imported palm trees and other assorted lush touches, creating a contradictory atmosphere that is strange and thrilling. Throngs flood the lake country, with speedboats, sailboats, and fishing boats in tow, on any given spring or summer weekend. From April through October the high temperatures are generally in the 80s, then the 90s, then up to the triple digits in deep summer, then back down to the 90s and then 80s. By November and through

March the weather is cooler, though certainly not cold during the day. Water temperatures range from 45°F in winter to 85°F in the summer. One of the least crowded times of year to visit is January and February, though you might not want to get in the water during this time. The best place to start is the **Alan Bible Visitor Center** (U.S. 93 and Lakeshore Scenic Dr., four miles southeast of Boulder City, NV, 702/293-8990, www.nps.gov/lame, 8:30am-4:30pm daily, $10 per vehicle, good for seven days, boats and other vessels $16) just west of Hoover Dam along U.S. 93. Here you'll find helpful rangers and volunteers with all the information and maps you'll need for your visit.

NORTHSHORE ROAD

If you're only going to be in the area for a day or so, or if you're not the water-sports type, the best way to see the recreation area's natural wonders is to take a slow, scenic drive along Lake Mead's Northshore Road. From the entrance station near the Alan Bible Visitor Center, head north on Lakeshore Scenic Drive, which turns into North Shore Road. You'll pass all the major west- and north-end bays and beaches, and you can turn off at any point and stop. The road extends more than 50 miles along the shore and eventually becomes Route 169 near Overton, Nevada. Try to make it as far as the spectacular **Bowl of Fire** at the base of the Muddy Mountains, about 25 miles from the entrance. The Bowl of Fire is so named for the deep red rocks jutting up off the desert, which light up as if ablaze, especially as the sun is dropping in the west. Climb up about half a mile to the overlook on the **Northshore Summit Trail** (it's well signed at the trailhead) for one of the best views in the region. Keep your eyes open along the rocky spines of the mountains on both sides of the road, for you're likely to see a few bighorn sheep negotiating the rugged terrain.

RECREATION
Hiking and Biking

One of the longer hikes in the recreation area will take you to natural hot springs in a slot canyon below Hoover Dam. The hike to **Arizona Hot Springs,** in White Rock Canyon, is a six-mile round-trip moderately rough trek to the Colorado River and into a side canyon with nearly vertical walls and the spare and rocky landscape typical of this inhospitable but strangely beautiful land. This isn't for the weak, though—you have to climb down a 20-foot ladder stuck in the rocks to reach the best pools, and the walk back to the car can be a tough trudge even for well-worn hikers. To reach the trailhead go east from the visitors center about eight miles, four miles past Hoover Dam on U.S. 95 to a dirt parking lot, which is at the head of White Rock Canyon (the trailhead is on the map you'll get when entering the recreation area). Just outside the visitors center is the trailhead for the **Railroad Tunnel Trail,** which leads along the disused right-of-way built during the construction of Hoover Dam and through five spooky old train tunnels. From the visitors center to the entrance to the fifth tunnel is just over two miles one way. A hike from the visitors center through all five tunnels to the dam is just over three miles one way. The recreation area's newspaper, **Desert Views,** has a comprehensive listing of the trails around Lake Mead, most of which are quite short and lead to some overlook or scenic feature. Be careful hiking here, especially in the summer, when you probably won't want to do much walking, let alone long hard desert trekking.

There are more than 800 miles of backcountry dirt roads through the Mojave Desert in the recreation area, perfect for touring on a mountain bike. Ask at the visitors center for a map of the backcountry roads. Also try the Railroad Tunnel Trail for biking.

Boating

You can rent boats for fishing, exploring, waterskiing, and living the easy laketop life at **Las Vegas Boat Harbor** (702/293-1191) and **Lake Mead Marina** (which, due to low water levels in early 2008 moved permanently from its original location at Boulder Harbor two miles south to become part of Las Vegas Boat Harbor and Marina in Hemenway Harbor) and **Callville**

Bay Resort (702/565-8958)—everything from 16-foot fishing crafts to big patio cruisers to 18-foot speedsters. Prices range $50-95 per hour for wakeboard boats, pontoon boats, and Jet Skis.

A leisurely sightseeing cruise around Lake Mead, with some trips attended by either breakfast or dinner, is a popular way to take in the scenery. **Lake Mead Cruises** (702/293-6180, www.lakemeadcruises.com, $22-58) offers several different options.

You can rent a **houseboat** for three days or up to a week ($750-4,000); most sleep between 6 and 14 people and come with all kinds of extras depending on how much you want to pay. Contact **Seven Crown Resorts** (800/752-9669, www.sevencrown.com) or **Forever Houseboats** (800/255-5561, www.forever-houseboats.com).

If you're more about floating and skimming by your own power, look into **Black Canyon/Willow Beach River Adventures** (in Hacienda Hotel on Hwy. 93, 702/494-2204, 10:30am-5pm Mon.-Fri., or call 702/293-8204, www.blackcanyonadventures.com). They rent kayaks and canoes at the Willow Beach Marina (928/767-4747, $10-20 per hour, minimum two hours, plus $45-85 deposit).

They also offer five-hour group raft trips through the starkly beautiful Black Canyon at the base of Hoover Dam to Willow Beach, with several stops at beaches for swimming and frolicking and a waterside box lunch ($87.95 per person).

Boulder City Riveriders (1631 Industrial Rd., Boulder City, NV, 702/293-1190, www.bouldercityoutfitters.com, $210 plus $17 for permit) provides all-day (8 hours) guided kayak tours of the same area with lunch.

Those with their own paddle craft need to get a permit ($12, plus $3 entrance fee) to launch at Black Canyon; you can get one through Black Canyon/Willow Beach Adventures in its office at the Hacienda Hotel just west of Hoover Dam.

Swimming and Scuba Diving

The best place to swim and scuba dive is around **Boulder Beach,** not far from the visitors center, which has a cordoned swimming area that's popular with families. The area has been lately adversely affected by low water levels, but swimming there remains viable. There's a **Dive Park** at North Boulder Beach that's a great place for beginners and experts alike, and a few watercraft have been deliberately submerged here for exploring and pretending. **Boulder Islands,** large concrete tanks that were used to store water during the construction of the dam, is also a popular area for scuba enthusiasts. More experienced and adventuresome scuba divers have many options around the two lakes. Check out the website (www.nps.gov/lame/planyourvisit/scuba.htm).

Fishing

Sport anglers launch on Lake Mead in search of striped and largemouth bass, rainbow trout, channel catfish, and others. The biggest striped bass in Lake Mead have been known to weigh up to 50 pounds. Each of the marinas has fishing gear for sale and rent, boats for rent, fishing guides, and information. The recreation area's website has an up-to-date fishing report at www.nps.gov/lame/fishrpt.html.

ACCOMMODATIONS AND FOOD

There's just one lakeside lodge left within the Lake Mead portion of the recreation area. The **Temple Bar Resort and Marina** (928/767-3211, www.templebarlakemead.com, $60-130) near the eastern part of the lake, offers standard rooms, fishing cabins, and suites with kitchens, some with lake views and some with desert views.

There are hundreds of **camping** spots around Lake Mead, each offered at $10 per night and obtained on a first-come, first-served basis. The campgrounds—with showers and tables and grills and all the other amenities a camper needs—are at **Boulder Beach** (154 sites), **Callville Bay** (80 sites), and **Temple Bar** (153 sites), and **Las Vegas Bay** (89 sites). Visitors with RVs will find sites with full hookups at **Callville Bay Resort** (702/565-8958).

LOWER COLORADO RIVER

LAKE MOHAVE

This lake doesn't really seem like a lake at all but more like the river it's filled with. Mohave is thin and runs long through Black Canyon as if it were the untamed Colorado, widening at Arizona Basin and Cottonwood Basin to seem more lakelike. The scenery around Mohave is similar to that around Mead, spare and rocky, ruled by creosote and other scrub, with sandy beaches and hidden coves. The recreation opportunities are similar as well—fishing and waterskiing, houseboating and floating in the calm, warm water. To rent a boat or to hire a guide to take you on a tour of Mohave, try **Desert River Outfitters** (2649 Hwy. 95, Bullhead City, 888/529-2533, www.desertriver-outfitters.com, $25-80 for kayak rental, $35 for 3-4-hour guided trip on Lake Mohave).

A boat launch and placid waters ringed by ragged rock cliffs make **Willow Beach** a fine place for an easy day on the water with your canoe, fishing near a fish hatchery, or just lounging and picnicking on the hot desert beach. Waterfowl and other birds abound. Take U.S. 93 west toward Hoover Dam and turn at the sign for Willow Beach.

Accommodations and Food

Lake Mohave has two major marinas, both with small hotels with basic and clean lakeside rooms, stores, restaurants, bars, and boat and watercraft rentals (including houseboats)—everything you'll need for a perfect time on the water.

Cottonwood Cove Resort & Marina (702/297-1464, www.cottonwoodcoveresort.com, $65-115) is on the Nevada side and has a nice little lodge and campground, and a great swimming beach popular with kids. On the Arizona side just outside of Bullhead City is **Lake Mohave Resort at Katherine Landing** (2690 E. Katherine Spur Rd., Bullhead City, 928/754-3245, www.sevencrown.com, $95-250), close to Davis Dam.

Kingman and Vicinity

Spread across a dry desert basin below pine-topped mountains and cut through by I-40, Kingman and its environs have long been a stopover for those traveling the two famous American trails along the 35th Parallel: the Santa Fe Railroad and Route 66. Indeed, the town, mostly a transportation hub and county government center these days, has secured its place in Americana, along with a few other Arizona towns, by appearing in the song *Route 66*, certainly one of the most frequently covered tunes of all time, written in 1946 by Bobby Troup and first recorded by the great Nat King Cole.

Kingman's identity, at least for the sake of tourism, is all wrapped up in being the "Heart of Route 66," and there are a few nostalgic sights here harking back to a time when cross-country travel was slower and, in a sense, more meaningful than it is today. The town, which isn't much to look at, sits near the junction of two scenic drives that will show you an unvarnished Arizona, rolling through large swaths of left-alone desert and old mining ghost towns taken over by artisans and actors, up over mountain passes held together by strange cacti, across bridges swaying high above dry arroyos, and past abandoned outposts and tourists traps, the rusted shells of long-dead vehicles, and all those tiny white roadside crosses remembering road-weary tragedies.

SIGHTS

Here you can peruse museums and stores featuring the artifacts and stories of the heyday of Route 66 travel, and hop in your car and drive the rough and lonely remains of the Mother Road, through squat cactus forests and old lost towns still pining for the region's long-gone gold- and silver-mining days.

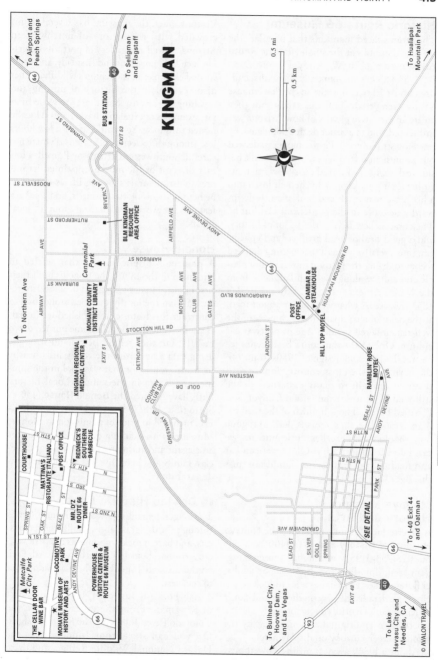

KINGMAN

To Airport and Peach Springs

To Seligman and Flagstaff

To Hualapai Mountain Park

0.5 mi

0.5 km

BUS STATION

EXIT 53

TOWNSEND ST

ROOSEVELT ST

BEVERLY AVE

RUTHERFORD ST

BLM KINGMAN RESOURCE AREA OFFICE

AIRFIELD AVE

ANDY DEVINE AVE

To Northern Ave

AIRWAY AVE

BURBANK ST

Centennial Park

HARRISON ST

MOHAVE COUNTY DISTRICT LIBRARY

MOTOR AVE

CLUB AVE

GATES AVE

FAIRGROUNDS BLVD

POST OFFICE

DAMBAR & STEAKHOUSE

HUALAPAI MOUNTAIN RD

STOCKTON HILL RD

HILL TOP MOTEL

EXIT 51

KINGMAN REGIONAL MEDICAL CENTER

DETROIT AVE

ARIZONA ST

WESTERN AVE

RAMBLIN' ROSE MOTEL

COUNTRY CLUB DR

GOLF DR

BEALE ST

ANDY DEVINE AVE

GREENWAY DR

N 7TH ST

N 5TH ST

PARK ST

SEE DETAIL

GRANDVIEW AVE

To I-40 Exit 44 and Oatman

LEAD ST

SILVER ST

GOLD ST

SPRING ST

EXIT 48

To Bullhead City, Hoover Dam, and Las Vegas

To Lake Havasu City and Needles, CA

© AVALON TRAVEL

Detail inset:

THE CELLAR DOOR WINE BAR

Metcalfe City Park

COURTHOUSE

MATTINA'S RISTORANTE ITALIANO

POST OFFICE

REDNECK'S SOUTHERN BARBECUE

SPRING ST

OAK ST

BEALE ST

N 1ST ST

N 2ND ST

3RD ST

4TH ST

N 5TH ST

MR. D'Z ROUTE 66 DINER

MOHAVE MUSEUM OF HISTORY AND ARTS

LOCOMOTIVE PARK

ANDY DEVINE AVE

POWERHOUSE VISITOR CENTER & ROUTE 66 MUSEUM

Historic Route 66 Museum

The serious-faced manikins that populate the life-size dioramas at the small **Historic Route 66 Museum** (120 W. Andy Devine Ave., 928/753-9889, 9am-5pm daily, $4 adults, children under 13 free, upstairs in the Powerhouse Visitor Center) are a bit unsettling, but they create an evocative picture of how Arizona was influenced, and to a major degree populated, by one long strip of road. Plastic pioneers, decked out in authentic frontier-era outfits, walk beside real wagons, while sad dust-bowl migrants gather their possessions and their children into a broken-down truck and look plaintively toward a new life in the gardens of California. The curators here have stuffed a lot of history, and a good deal of local artifacts and ephemera, into a relatively small space, using detailed scenes to depict the historic movement of people and culture along the 35th Parallel—from the Native Americans to Lt. Edward Beale's 1857 trek across what was then a wagon road, at the helm of a company of 25 camels, to the well-remembered Golden Age of postwar car culture. One of the museum's best scenes recreates the style and design of 1950s Route 66, the heyday of the cross-country family road trip that brought so many easterners to the still-wild West to see the Grand Canyon and Petrified Forest. Though much of the road romance found in those eras is dead and gone now, thanks to this excellent little museum, we can relive it all just a bit. Old American car and road culture enthusiasts should not miss this sight.

Mohave Museum of History and Arts

A diverse local history museum, the **Mohave Museum of History and Arts** (400 W. Beale St., 928/753-3195, www.mohavemuseum.org, 9am-5pm Mon.-Fri., 1pm-5pm Sat., $4 adults, children under 12 free) has a lot to look at, including a detailed display on the life and career of Kingman's favorite son, actor Andy Devine (there are even original *telegrams* sent by the famous screen cowboy on display here).

About a block away from the Powerhouse Visitor Center, the museum has several rooms crowded with the history of northwestern Arizona, as well as a gallery of portraits depicting each U.S. president and first lady, and some stuffed examples of the region's wildlife. Other displays explain the history of mining and ranching in the area, and there are some first-rate examples of Hualapai basketry and locally mined turquoise. You could spend a few hours lost among the eclectic collections if you're not careful. Southwestern artist Roy Purcell, a former director of the museum, painted its impressionistic murals showing life as it used to be here in this forgotten frontier, and a gallery features the work of a rotating group of local artists.

Bonelli House

A pioneer Mormon family that settled in Kingman in the 1890s, the Bonellis built their first home of materials a good deal less fire-resistant than the locally quarried stone used to construct this historic, refurbished territorial-era home. The first Bonelli home burned down in 1915, but they rebuilt better and stronger, using tufa stone from the rocky hills nearby to create an interior that was cool in the summer and warm in the winter. Local history buffs have restored the **Bonelli House** (430 E. Spring St., 928/753-1413, 11am-3pm Mon.-Fri., included in price of admission to Mohave Museum) with exacting detail, giving visitors an elegant and authentic look at what middle-class family and home life was like on the high-desert frontier.

◖ Driving Historic Route 66

The longest remaining stretch of Route 66 runs through the dry grasslands, cholla-choked deserts, and barren rocky mountains of northwestern Arizona, about 165 miles between Ash Fork on the east and Topock on the Colorado River to the west.

Ash Fork sits just off I-40, 94 miles east of Kingman. From there head west to the Colorado River, following the Route 66 signs. Or, you can start from Topock, near the Havasu National Wildlife Refuge, and drive

DRIVING HISTORIC ROUTE 66

east, ending at Ash Fork. Either way, you'll pass through sleepy Peach Springs, capital of the Hualapai Indian Reservation, and the nearly abandoned Truxton and Valentine, a few buildings dating from the 1930s to the 1950s moldering along the road. You'll pass Hackberry and the famous and much-photographed Hackberry General Store, and climb up a scrubby, rocky mountain, where the road gets washboarded, and steep and curvy beyond reason, passing old ghost homes and mine shafts and a few sprawling junkyard compounds before climbing up over Sitgreaves Pass and down the other side of the mountain to Oatman, home of the wild burros of Route 66, each descended from the beasts of burden

that helped prospectors fight these desert hills more than a century ago.

HACKBERRY GENERAL STORE

Try *not* to stop at this picture-ready old store and junkyard museum. It can't be done. Maybe it's the cherry, 1957 Corvette parked conspicuously out front. Maybe it's because it's the only sign of life for miles in either direction along this forgotten stretch of the old Mother Road. Maybe it's the root beer.

Cluttered with Route 66 and American road culture memorabilia, including several rusting old cars that once made their way along the Route, the **Hackberry General Store** (11255 E. Hwy. 66, Hackberry, 928/769-2605, www.

© MIROSLAV LISKA/123RF.COM

Grab a root beer at the Hackberry General Store.

hackberrygeneralstore.com, 9am-6pm daily) looks like it belongs to another era. Inside you'll find cold sodas, snacks, souvenirs, and a lot to look at, including some really cool road-map murals on the walls by artist Bob Waldmire. The owners, who bought the place on a whim years ago while driving Route 66, encourage visitors to walk around the property, examine the memorabilia, and take pictures. The store is 28 miles east of Kingman and 60 miles west of Seligman.

COOL SPRINGS STATION

Twenty miles west of Kingman and 16 miles east of Oatman, the original gas-station model for the photogenic gift shop **Cool Springs Station** (8275 W. Oatman Hwy., 928/768-8366, www.coolspringsroute66. com, 10am-5pm Tues.-Sun.), on the way up over the Black Mountains, was blown up in the 1990s for the film *Universal Soldier.* New owners rebuilt a detailed replica of the old station, which was first built in the 1920s, and now it's a small museum and gift shop

worthy of a stop. The museum features a fantastic collection of signed Rolling Stones album covers.

OATMAN

Between 1904 and 1931 about $36 million in ore, mostly gold and silver, came out of these dry rocky hills. At its peak, the town of Oatman had some 10,000 residents. It went ghostly for a while after the mines shut down, but, as it was with so many mining towns in the Southwest, Oatman was rediscovered in the 1960s and 1970s as a tourist stop along one of the roughest stretches of Historic Route 66. There are a few resale shops and gift boutiques here, a restaurant or two, and a saloon. Some latter-day gunfighters will stage duels in the street on most days, and you can check out the old **Oatman Hotel,** where Clark Gable and Carol Lombard spent their honeymoon. But the real fun in Oatman—which is a touch kitschy and has few genuinely authentic buildings left anymore—is to feed and commune with wild burros. They're not really

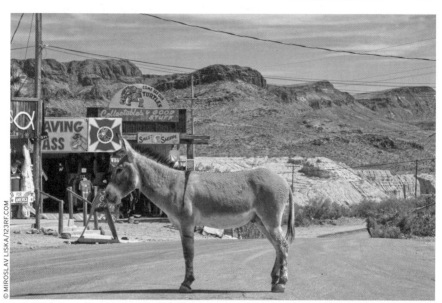

a stubborn burro on an Oatman street

"wild" anymore—they'll walk right up and say hello, letting you pet their heads and feed them snacks sold by various vendors in town. There are usually a few baby burros milling around too.

Leaving Oatman and descending along Route 66 to the desert floor just east of the river, the foothills are covered with cholla, which blooms, along with a few dormant wildflowers, in the spring and adds a bit of bright shocking color to the landscape, making those warm and clear months the perfect time for a visit.

Keepers of the Wild Nature Park

Though tawny cougars are known to occasionally haunt these windy high-desert plains, and some stretches of Historic Route 66 could perhaps stand in for a sweeping African savannah, one doesn't expect to encounter a shaggy-maned lion here, or for that matter a flitting lemur or a thoughtful baboon. Except perhaps at this hospital, retirement home, and haven for abused, neglected,

and abandoned exotic animals. **Keepers of the Wild Nature Park** (13441 E. Hwy. 66, milepost 87, www.keepersofthewild.org, 9am-5pm Wed.-Mon., $18 for all-day pass, $12 children over 12) has tigers, several lazy cougars, a chubby black jaguar named Hope, and a whole village full of squealing, playful monkeys. The animals live in large, fenced-in habitats, with big boulders and pools and mostly native trees and shrubs. The paths are easy, but there isn't a lot of shade, so bring a hat. The whole park is wheelchair accessible, and there's a gift shop with snacks and drinks. They encourage picnicking, so feel free to bring a basket. The last tickets are sold at 4pm. For $10 more per person, a guide will take you on a driven "safari" tour of the park that lasts about an hour and a half (9:30am, 11:30am, and 3:30pm). This is an ideal stop for families with kids, most of whom might not find the barren spaces along Route 66 particularly scintillating. Most of the animals here have cute names and sad life stories, so you run the risk of falling in love.

Who Is Andy Devine?

Kingman's favorite son was one of those great American character actors that most of us recognize but often can't name. His strained, gravelly but high voice, the result of a childhood accident that permanently damaged his vocal chords, and his size—a former football star, he was corpulent his entire adult life—make Andy Devine (1905-1977) stand out more than most.

While film buffs will remember Devine as the driver in John Ford's 1939 Western classic *Stage Coach*, John Wayne's breakout film, made partly in Monument Valley, or as one of the soldiers in John Huston's *The Red Badge of Courage* in 1951, his career was long and diverse, encompassing radio, both B- and A-grade movies, and television. He started out as a bit player in silent films during the 1920s and went on to entertain several generations.

Those of us who grew up in the 1970s and 1980s will likely remember Devine by his voice alone, which became that of the gentle and funny Friar Tuck in Disney's animated *Robin Hood* in 1973. Those who grew up in the 1950s and 1960s, on the other hand, remember Devine as "Jingle Jones" from the Western television series *Wild Bill Hickok*, or as the host of the Saturday morning show *Andy's Gang*. And, if you remember the 1930s and 1940s, you'll recognize that voice again as a regular on the Jack Benny radio show, where his greeting "Hiya, Buck!" made him famous, and of course you'll know Devine as the funny sidekick in many Roy Rogers Westerns.

Though Devine was born in Flagstaff a couple hours northeast of Kingman, where his father worked for the railroad, he moved to Kingman when he was just one year old. An on-the-job accident had taken the elder Devine's leg and a settlement with the railroad helped the family buy the Beale Hotel in Kingman, where Devine grew up and is celebrated in the local museum and during an annual festival and parade.

EVENTS

The month of May brings thousands of Route 66 nostalgics and classic-car lovers to the old stretch of the Mother Road from Seligman to Topock for the **Historic Route 66 Fun Run** (928/753-5001, www.azrt66.com). Far-flung drivers in a riot of old and new vehicles—many of them gorgeous and classic, and many of their owners in some kind of recycled 1950s-wear—gather in Seligman for the kickoff of this popular regional event. After eating and dancing to the live bands, a host of roaring two- and four-wheelers makes its slow way along Historic Route 66 west to Kingman, where they park en masse for show-and-tell in the parking lot of the Powerhouse Visitor Center. In downtown Kingman there's more eating, bands and other entertainment, and vendors. Come Sunday morning, hangover or not, everybody gets up and climbs back behind the wheel and heads east to Topock and the end of the road, stopping of course to give some love to the burros in Oatman.

In late September Kingman celebrates itself and its favorite son during **Andy Devine Days Parade & Community Fair** (928/757-7919), which features food vendors, arts and crafts, and entertainment in the town's historic, if usually a bit desolate, downtown.

SHOPPING

There are two shops in the **Powerhouse Visitor Center** (120 W. Andy Devine Ave., 928/753-6106, 9am-6pm daily in spring and summer, 9am-5pm Dec.-Feb.) where you'll find items you might not be able to get too many other places. For Route 66 and American road-culture gifts and souvenirs check out the **Historic Route 66 Association of Arizona Gift Shop** inside the Powerhouse.

If you're into finding the treasures that other people have given up, there are a few antique and resale shops along East Beale Street in the historic old town area that are definitely worth wandering through.

RECREATION
Hiking and Camping

If you missed North-Central Arizona's pinebelt, head to northwest Arizona's answer at **Hualapai Mountain Park** (6250 Hualapai Mountain Park, 928/681-5700, www.mcparks.com), about 12 miles from Kingman. This sap-and-campfire-scented 2,300-acre mountain park is high in the pines overlooking the scrub valley. The titular mountain range rises from the plain southeast of town to heights between 5,000 and nearly 8,500 feet, cloaked in the conifers typical of such elevations in Arizona. There are 19 cabins for rent through the **Mohave County Parks Division** (877/757-0915, www.mcparks.com/hualapai_mt_park.htm, $60-125), built of stacked stone and wood by the Civilian Conservation Corps in the 1930s and sleeping 2-12 people, most with rustic old fireplaces—but also with kitchens and electricity. You can camp here, too, or park your RV among the pines ($15-25); most of the camping spots don't have water and are obtained on a first-come, first-served basis.

The park's trail system leads high into the mountains for some inspiring views. The trails are well worn and forested, with huge slabs and half-buried outcroppings of granite dropped in everywhere like there was a rock fight among giants here long ago. The 8,417-foot **Hualapai Peak** is the highest point in the park and in the region. The 4.3-mile round-trip **Potato Patch Loop Trail** is a moderate and representative hike, running through ponderosa pines, aspens, and high stands of spruce and fir, strewn with needles and cones and watched over by boulders covered in dry lichen. Start out on the switchbacks of the **Aspen Springs Trail** and then meet up with the loop at the Aspen Springs-Potato Patch Junction after about a mile. You go up about 800 feet in the first mile and half, but it levels out on the loop. A map of the entire system, which has about 16 miles of developed and undeveloped trails, is available at the park office. There's really no time of year to stay away from this pleasant, heavily used mountain park (there will be ATV riders here, so be forewarned if you like wilderness only).

It's hot in the summer, but with the breezy moderation that its elevation allows; it's cold and sometimes snowy in the winter, but not to any uncomfortable degree.

ACCOMMODATIONS

There are several very affordable, basic hotels located on Andy Devine Avenue, Route 66, in Kingman's downtown area, some of them with retro road-trip neon signs and Route 66 themes. There are a good many chain hotels in town as well.

The **Ramblin' Rose Motel** (1001 E. Andy Devine Ave., 928/753-4747, $35-42) doesn't look like much, just another roadside place to park and snooze. It's inexpensive, for one thing, and it's clean and has big, comfy beds. And you can check your email using the free Wi-Fi, chill your soda in the mini-fridge, and warm up a burrito in the microwave. You can't ask for much more for the price.

The 🍴**Hill Top Motel** (1901 E. Andy Devine Ave., 928/753-2198, www.hilltopmotelaz.com, $47-55) has character. Its 1950s-era neon sign calls out to all Route 66 road trippers, clicking something far back in the American memory, convincing them to stop and stay. This small, affordable motel, near the top of a hill looking out on the Hualapai Mountains, has a connection to the dark side of American culture as well: Oklahoma City bomber Timothy McVeigh stayed here for a few nights in 1995 while planning his attack on the Alfred P. Murrah Building for April of that same year. The bombing killed 168 people. Built in the 1950s but refurbished since then, the Hill Top has standard, comfortable rooms with refrigerators and microwaves, and free wireless. Outside there's a stylish pool and a well-kept cactus garden.

Along Hualapai Mountain Road on the way up to the piney mountains, the **Hualapai Mountain Resort** (4525 Hualapai Mountain Rd., 928/757-3545, $79-159) rents eight rustic but comfortable and clean rooms in a quiet, secluded setting. They have a decent restaurant on site (11am-8pm Wed.-Thurs., 11am-10pm Fri., 8am-10pm Sat., 8am-8pm Sun., $6-22), serving steaks and burgers, salads, sandwiches, and other standard American fare.

At **Upton's Hidden Pines Bed & Breakfast** (935 S. DW Ranch Rd., 928/279-7394, www.uptonhiddenpines.com, $125) you can rent one of three small, tasteful, cozy rooms with big beds and cedar-lined wardrobes. Just east of town off I-40, within sight of the Hualapai Mountains, this friendly spot, on five acres and decorated with an Old West ranching theme, has a comfortable living room for chatting and lounging, and a big wraparound porch for staring off into the vast distance. There's also an entertainment room and library, and an aqua massage machine.

FOOD

The **Dambar & Steakhouse** (1960 E. Andy Devine Ave., 928/753-3523, 11am-10pm daily, $10-30) is local favorite that serves great steaks, prime rib, lobster, cowboy beans, and burgers. The bar has excellent regionally brewed beers, and the sawdust on the floor, the cowboy kitsch, and Route 66 memorabilia add a bit of character this popular place. They offer patio seating in the summer and live country music on the weekends.

The best restaurant for miles in any direction is (**Mattina's Ristorante Italiano** (318 E. Oak St., 928/753-7504, www.mattinasristorante.com, 5pm-10pm Tues.-Sat., $13-25), where you can get perfectly prepared Italian food, including outstanding beef medallions and rack of lamb. It's difficult to choose from the diverse and outlandishly appetizing selection of pasta dishes, but it's equally difficult to pass up the lobster ravioli or the thick, creamy fettuccini Alfredo. Don't leave without trying the tiramisu or the key lime pie, and consider sampling liberally from their well-stocked wine cellar.

Redneck's Southern Barbecue (420 E. Beale St., 928/757-8227, 11am-8pm Mon.-Sat., www.redneckssouthernpitbbq.com, $3-10) in Kingman's small, often quiet downtown serves some of the best Southern-style barbecue this side of Memphis, with delicious baked beans and coleslaw on the side. The pulled pork and the brisket should not be missed by connoisseurs of those heaven-sent dishes.

It is widely known throughout this flat and windy region that the retro Route 66 drive-in **Mr. D'z Route 66 Diner** (105 E. Andy Devine, 928/718-0066, www.mrdzrt66diner.com, $2.95-$16.95) serves the best burger in town, but they also have a large menu with all manner of delectable diner and road food, like chili dogs, pizza, hot sandwiches, baby back ribs, chicken-fried steak, and a big plate of spaghetti. Plus, breakfast is served all day. The portions are big, but save room for a thick shake or a root-beer float. Don't leave your camera in the car; the turquoise-and-pink interior and the cool old jukebox here are snapshot ready.

A focal point of Kingman's downtown, **The Cellar Door Wine Bar & Bottle Shop** (414 E. Beale St., http://the-cellar-door.com, 4pm-10pm Wed.-Thurs., 4pm-midnight Fri.-Sat.) adds a bit of urban class to this decidedly rural region. They offer about 120 different wines, 25 beers, and a small menu with a cheese plate, hummus, and olives. You can sit at the tasteful wine bar and listen to a laid-back local musician, or take your bottle with you.

Next door, **Beale Street Brews Coffee Shop** (418 E. Beale St., 928/753-4004, http://bealestreetbrews.net, 7am-9pm Mon.-Fri., 7am-3pm Sat.-Sun.) has free-trade coffee drinks, pastries, free wireless, poetry readings, local art on the walls, local music in the air, and a few tables outside, perfect for relaxing the day away.

INFORMATION AND SERVICES
Visitors Center

Built in 1907 to supply power to the region's mines, the **Powerhouse Visitor Center** (120 W. Andy Devine Ave., 928/753-6106, 9am-6pm daily in spring and summer, 9am-5pm Dec.-Feb.) has information on all the sights, accommodations, and attractions in Kingman and environs, plus a model train circling the inside perimeter.

Hospital

Kingman Regional Medical Center (3269

Stockton Hill Rd., 928/757-2101, www.az-krmc.com) has a full-service emergency room.

◖ SELIGMAN

This tiny roadside settlement 87 miles east of Kingman holds on tight to its Route 66 heritage. There are fewer than 500 full-time residents living in this old ranching hub, railroad center, and Route 66 stop, but there is often, especially on summer weekends, twice that number of tourists driving through and stopping for a bite to eat and a look around the gift shops. Tour buses and large gangs of motorcycling Europeans even stop here and crowd up the one-strip town on occasion, as Seligman has become in recent years one of the top stops for a burgeoning subculture of classic car nuts, forty-something *Easy Rider* role players, and lovers of mid-20th-century commercial architecture and road culture, all of whom prefer to eschew the interstate and take to the back roads.

John Lasseter, codirector of the 2006 Disney-Pixar film *Cars,* has said that he based the movie's fictional town of **Radiator Springs** partly on Seligman, which, like Radiator Springs, nearly died out when it was bypassed by I-40 in the late 1970s.

Sights

Stop in at the **Route 66 Gift Shop & Visitor's Center** (217 E. Route 66, 928/422-3352, www.route66giftshop.com, 8am-5pm daily) to buy a Route 66 souvenir and learn about the history of the area from Angel and Vilma Delgadillo, longtime residents who are largely responsible for keeping Seligman on the map.

In 2005 Seligman's commercial center, a three-block area off of Chino Street (Historic Route 66) that's hemmed by First Street on the west, Lamport Street on the east, Picacho Street on the north, and Railroad Avenue on the south, was placed on the National Register of Historic Places as "an important reminder of how transportation systems influenced the development of communities in the American West." Pick up a pamphlet for the self-guided tour of the **Seligman Historic District** at the Historic Seligman Sundries

© JOERG HACKEMANN/123RF.COM

LOWER COLORADO RIVER

historic Seligman

and other places in town, and walk the district with your camera, snapping shots of all the retro signs and buildings from the pre-interstate era.

About 22 miles west of Seligman along Historic Route 66, **Grand Canyon Caverns** (Mile Marker 115, Route 66, 928/422-3223, www.gccaverns.com, 8am-6pm in summer, 10am-4pm in winter, $18.95 per person) offers guided underground tours of North America's largest dry cave, where crystals and other strange rock formations hide in the weatherless darkness. The main tour lasts about 45 minutes and takes you about three quarters of a mile through the limestone cavern, but not before you descend 21 stories (210 feet) beneath the earth in an elevator. There's a lot of history here, too: During the Cold War the cavern served as a bomb shelter-in-waiting, packed with enough food and water to sustain hundreds of blast-weary survivors if the unthinkable occurred. The friendly folks here at this old-school combination Route 66 tourist trap (in the best sense of the phrase) and motel also

offer an off-trail tour for $69 that goes much deeper into the caverns. And they'll be happy to take you out into the nearby ranchlands on horseback or in a jeep.

Shopping

Inside the turquoise-and-pink 100-year-old **Historic Seligman Sundries** (22495 Historic Route 66, 928/853-0051, www.seligmansundries.com, 8am-7pm daily, closed Nov.-Mar.), you'll find a plethora of Route 66 memorabilia, as well as motorcycle- and car-culture items, Native American jewelry, cowboy kitsch, and really good coffee and malts. There's a small museum, and the walls are covered with old advertisements and other reminders of the mid-20th-century heyday of American popular culture.

That sprawling building with all the dressed-up manikins standing around on the roof, and Elvis kicking back on the bumper of a classic pink roadster, is **The Rusty Bolt** (115 E. Route 66, 928/422-0106, www.rustybolt66. com, 8am-4pm daily), where they sell the usual

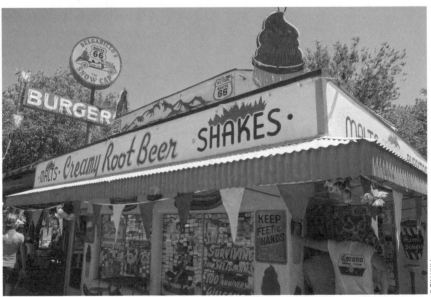

Delgadillo's Snow Cap Drive-In

local Route 66 memorabilia and a large selection of items for motorcyclists.

Food

A majority of the Route 66 Argonauts who slide through Seligman stop at **(Delgadillo's Snow Cap Drive-In** (301 E. Chino Ave., off Route 66 on the east end of town, 928/422-3291), a famous food shack whose family of owners have been dedicated to feeding, entertaining, and teasing Route travelers for generations. They serve a mean chili burger, a famous "cheeseburger with cheese," hot dogs, malts, soft ice cream, and much more, but the food's not really the point. Originally built in 1953 out of found lumber, the Snow Cap has become one of the stars of the back-to-Route-66 movement. There's a lot to look at outside: a 1936 Chevy and other old cars (all of them with big eyes on their windshields, à la Disney-Pixar's 2006 homage to Route 66, *Cars*), railroad junk, and several very silly signs; and inside, the close walls are covered with the business cards of customers from all over the world. Don't go here if you're grumpy: There will likely be a stand-up wait, especially on summer weekends, and you *will* be teased, especially if you have a question that requires a serious answer.

The **Roadkill Café** (502 W. Hwy. 66, 928/422-3554, www.route66seligmanarizona. com, 7am-9pm daily, $4.95-23.95) is more than just a funny name, it's a popular place for buffalo burgers, steaks, sandwiches, and other typical Old West-themed bar-and-grill-style eats. Have a few drinks in the **OK saloon** and a look around at the cluttered interior.

The majestic, if stuffed, mountain lion that watches over diners at **Westside Lilo's Café** (415 W. Chino Ave., 928/422-5456, 6am-9pm daily, $4.99-22.99), a popular diner-style eatery (complete with counter service), was shot not far from the restaurant by a member of the owners' family. It's just one of the backcountry touches that add to the ambience here, where they serve good burgers, excellent homemade potato salad, and other standard American fare. They are famous for their carrot cake, which is moist and flavorful.

Accommodations

There are several small, locally owned motels in Seligman, many of them with historic, retro signs and, of course, a Route 66 theme. The accommodations here are nothing special, though they are typically quite affordable.

The **Supai Lodge** (134 W. Chino, 928/422-4153, $48-52), named for the nearby Grand Canyon-bottom village inhabited by the Havasupai tribe, has clean and comfortable rooms at a fair price. The **Historic Route 66 Motel** (928/422-3204, www.route66seligmanarizona.com, $57-62) offers free wireless and refrigerators in clean, comfortable rooms, and the **Canyon Lodge** (114 E. Chino Ave., 928/422-3255, www.route66canyonlodge.com, $55) has free wireless in its themed rooms (which means posters on the walls of James Dean, Marilyn Monroe, John Wayne, and other pop-culture icons), along with refrigerators and microwaves. They also serve a free continental breakfast.

U.S. HIGHWAY 93

Though not as popular as Route 66, U.S. Highway 93 between Wickenburg, an hour north of Phoenix, and Hoover Dam, about an hour northwest of Kingman, has 200 miles of spectacular desert scenery. Just north of Route 71 before the town of Wikieup, U.S. 93 becomes the **Joshua Tree Forest Parkway.** Look out your window and you'll see why. A few miles north of Kingman, Mohave County Road 125 leads to **Chloride** (four miles east from U.S. 93), an old mining town turned tourist trap in the foothills of the Cerebat Mountains. Here you can browse through some shops and galleries, explore the ruins of mine shafts and a brothel; watch gunfights (high noon the first and third Sat. July-Aug., and every Sat. Sept.-June); and look at all the artwork and found-art in town, including famous rock-face murals by renowned Southwestern artist Roy Purcell.

Food

As you pass through the wide spot in the road known as Wikieup, stop at **Luchia's** (15797 S. Hwy. 93, Wikieup, 928/765-2229, 9am-5pm

Sun.-Fri., $4.95-13.95), where they serve tasty American and Mexican dishes on a lush and shady outdoor patio. They are known for their homemade pies (when in doubt, get the apple, $4.25 per slice, $15.35-16.45 whole pie), and they sell Indian jewelry, rugs, pottery, kachinas, and baskets.

The out-of-the-way **Yesterdays Restaurant** (9827 N. 2nd St., 928/565-4251, 11am-8pm Mon.-Fri., 8am-8pm Sat.-Sun., $3-22) in Chloride is a fun place to visit, with live music on occasion, a historic building, and a menu that features superior burgers and a few unique dishes, including some with Spam as the main ingredient. Though probably not worth a special trip, if you're in Chloride for a look around already, this is the obvious place to stop.

Bullhead City and Laughlin

You pretty much have to be interested in either river games or games of chance to get anything out of a visit to Laughlin or Bullhead City, often two of the hottest spots in the nation during the summer months. On August 11, 1983, at 2:21pm, the shade temperature in Bullhead City reached 132°F—the hottest on record. However, if you'd like nothing more than to skim and spray around the river on a Jet Ski during the day and play poker and slots when the unforgiving sun finally dips away, then you'll want to follow the many Arizona families from Phoenix and elsewhere who head for this desert playground several times a year, with their kids, speed boats, and Jet Skis in tow. Bullhead City, which has little to offer otherwise, is also a good choice for river rats, though without the gambling and Vegas aesthetic. (It has more of a strip-mall aesthetic, unfortunately.) It borders the Lake Mead National

walking along the river in Laughlin

Recreation Area and is right near Lake Mohave, with its marinas and boat rental shops, and has one of the best river parks in the region at Davis Camp.

CASINOS

There are 9 resorts and 13 casinos in Laughlin, most of them relatively affordable. The best of the bunch stretch out along the river's west bank, and there's a riverside walkway between them with street lights, public art, and boat docks. Room prices vary, but you can often find a relatively nice bed on the river for under $50. Prices generally go up on holidays. Most of the resorts offer a variety of packages that include meals and river cruises. These aren't the Indian casinos that you've seen in Arizona; Laughlin's gambling halls are pure Vegas clones. What with the heat and the desert and all, it's possible to forget you're not in Sin City, especially if you've been head-down at the blackjack table for two days straight. But then you look out the window and see that blue river, and you know exactly where you are.

© TIM HULL

"River Rick," of the Pioneer Hotel and Gambling Hall

The **Pioneer Hotel and Gambling Hall** (2200 S. Casino Dr., 800/634-3469, www.pioneerlaughlin.com, $35-170) has some of the most affordable rooms in Laughlin, many of them looking out over the riverwalk and the river with the hotel's landmark "River Rick" sign looking down from high above. (You can buy a stuffed version of the local cowboy icon in the gift shop.) The Pioneer is a step or two down from the likes of the Aquarius and the other newer luxury places in town, but the rooms are just fine, some of them decorated in a kind of Victorian-cowboy style. The casino has the usual slots, poker, blackjack, roulette, and more. This is a good choice for folks with boats and other watercraft because you can park close to your room. In the high-rise hotels, you generally have to park your rig in a big parking lot far from your door.

The **Riverside Resort Hotel and Casino** (1650 S. Casino Dr., 800/227-3849, www.riversideresort.com, $50-115) was the first casino built in Laughlin, way back in 1966. Of course, it's been built up mightily since then. It has a movie theater, a classic car collection, a bowling alley and game room, and two swimming pools. The rooms, many of them high in the sky and overlooking the dry land and the river, are standard, clean, and comfortable. The 80,000-square-foot casino has slots, blackjack, table games, and more, and a concert venue hosts music, comedy, and burlesque shows.

The **Colorado Belle Hotel and Casino** (2100 S. Casino Dr., 877/460-0777, www.coloradobelle.com, $59-130), a nonfloating replica of a 19th-century Mississippi paddlewheel, is a wonder of popular architecture. It has a swimming pool and spa, a huge casino with the usual games, and nice rooms that overlook the river. It's right on the riverwalk and you can look down from your room and watch the crowds go by and the water-skiers go down.

The **Aquarius Casino Resort** (1900 S. Casino Dr., 800/662-5825, www.aquariuscasinoresort.com, $50-170) has slots, blackjack, poker, keno, and a variety of table games, brings in entertainers for frequent concerts in its pavilion (Foreigner, ZZ Top, and the like), and has a fun nightclub called the **Splash Cabaret**. It's one of the newer places in town, and it has elegant rooms with river views and an adults-only tower. There's a big pool on the roof with cabanas and some amazing views of the stark desert cut through by that shining band of blue river. They make you pay for wireless, but don't do it; the Starbucks in the lobby has it for free.

EVENTS

In late April thousands of Harley-Davidson enthusiasts gather in the desert along the river for the **Laughlin River Run** (714/694-2800 or 800/357-8223), which includes concerts and festivals and all sorts of general revelry.

SHOPPING

Nearly all of the casino resorts in Laughlin have several different retail shops and gift shops selling local souvenirs and T-shirts with silly slogans, cowboy gear, and the necessities of river play.

If you're more inclined to drop your money at the shoe store than in a slot machine, check out the **Laughlin Outlet Center** (1955 S. Casino Dr., 702/298-3650, 9am-8pm Mon.-Sat., 10am-7pm Sun.). The 68 outlet stores in this air-conditioned mall across the street from the Aquarius will keep bargain hunters busy and out of the heat and sun.

SPORTS AND RECREATION

The recreation scene in Laughlin and Bullhead City is all wet, of course, and has a deep, painful sunburn. People come here for the river, to float on it, speed over it, and swim in it. Every other Ford F-150 barreling down the melting blacktops around here tows a speed boat, and the river-rat kids walk around in their life vests because they are rarely out of the water long enough to care.

Davis Camp

If you're not staying in one of the casino resorts, the best place to spend a day playing in the river and seeing if your boat still floats is at **Davis Camp** (2251 Hwy. 68, Bullhead City, 928/754-7250, www.mcparks.com/davis_camp.htm, $5 per day, dawn-dusk) in Bullhead City, which was built in the 1940s to house workers building nearby Davis Dam. You can fish here, ride your Jet Ski (or rent one), and swim and lounge in the sun on the park's sandy beaches, which all have charcoal grills and picnic tables. There's a mile and half of shoreline here, and it's the easiest and most convivial way to get a taste, though hopefully not a mouthful, of the Colorado. Just east of the park's boat dock **BestJetz** (702/208-0333, www.bestjetz.com, 8am-11pm daily, $189-279) rents Jet Skis.

Boat Tours

Along the riverwalk in Laughlin and in many of the casino resorts, you can book speed-boat tours of the river. One of the best is **London Bridge Jet Boat Tours** (888/505-3545, http://laughlinboattours.com, $70). The fully enclosed boats run 58 miles downriver to London Bridge in Lake Havasu City, passing through spectacular **Topock Gorge,** with its bighorn sheep dancing on the cliffs above, along the way. The trip takes all day—two hours each way and a two-hour layover at the bridge for lunch and sightseeing—but is worth the time away from the casino for all the beautiful scenery.

ACCOMMODATIONS
Laughlin

In Laughlin, your best bet for accommodations is the casinos.

Bullhead City

There are several chain hotels in town, but you can probably find a better deal and a nicer, more entertaining place to stay just across the river. **Davis Camp** (Hwy. 68, Bullhead City, 928/754-7250, www.mcparks.com/davis_camp.htm) on the river rents rustic 1940s-era two- and three-bedroom bungalows ($105-145) that are perfect for a weekend family getaway, and also has dry camp spots ($15) and an RV park ($20-25). Reservations for a bungalow are recommended far in advance.

© TIM HULL

A boat tour is a great way to see the area.

FOOD

Laughlin

Most of the casinos have chain restaurants, but the Vegas-style buffets are really where it's at. Typically one night of the weekend is prime rib night and one night offers seafood, and your dinner usually comes with a free drink or two. Three of the best in town are the **Windows on the River Buffet** at the Aquarius, **Riverside Buffet** at the Riverside, and the **Gourmet Room** at the Riverside. For nonbuffet eating, try the **Pints Brewery and Sports Bar** (11am-11pm daily, late night breakfast and lunch 3am-11am daily, $3.95-16.95) at the Colorado Belle, which has well-crafted beers and serves appetizing and tasteful pub eats, including pizza, buckets of deep-fried shrimp, and amazing onion rings. Their motto here? "Vegetarian: an old Indian word for bad hunter." Better

still is **Mark Twain's Chicken, Ribs and Steak** (4pm-9pm Fri.-Tues., $11.99-23.99) also at the Colorado Belle, a Sam Clemens-themed steak house with a fun ambience and rib-sticking ribs, steaks, and other hearty fare.

Bullhead City

The **Black Bear Diner** (1751 W. Hwy. 95, 928/763-2477, www.blackbeardiner.com, 6am-10pm Sun.-Thurs., 6am-11pm Fri.-Sat., $6-16) has good breakfasts.

INFORMATION AND SERVICES

Stop in at the **Laughlin Visitor Information Center** (1555 Casino Dr., 702/298-3321, www.visitlaughlin.com, 8am-4:30pm Mon.-Fri.) for information on Laughlin and the surrounding area.

Lake Havasu City and Vicinity

This riverside haven for snowbird retirees and boat-cruising vacationers sprang up from the hot and sandy desert in 1963. A few years later, Havasu's developer, Robert McCulloch Sr. secured the master-planned community's place in history by bringing a bit of history to its brand-new shores. He purchased the London Bridge and shipped it to Arizona, where he installed it brick by brick across the channel at Pittsburgh Point, a peninsula now referred to locally as "the island." McCulloch also hired a former Disneyland designer to help create an "English Village" in the bridge's shadow, and the whole package has been a popular tourist draw ever since. These days, the state parks and walkways and beaches along the reservoir are crowded most weekends in spring and even in summer— when the triple digits rule for three months or more—with boaters, anglers, and Jet Ski enthusiasts. During the college universe's annual Spring Break bacchanalia, hordes of bikini- and board short-clad students descend on the town, while at other times it seems as though everyone is over 60.

Lake Havasu City, like many other once-sleepy communities along the state's west coast, has grown immensely over the last decade or so, and there are more and more working families living here now, and so more chain-stores and restaurants. For the visitor, however, it is still Lake Havasu—born from the building of Parker Dam and holding water that travels across the desert in canals to Phoenix and Tucson—that is the main draw. If you're not into water sports and if you wilt easily in the sun, consider spending no more than an afternoon here, strolling over and beneath the bridge and along the walkway next to the channel, watching the ducks dip and bob. If you want to get to know the reservoir, though, there are all manner of wet and cool things to do here, and there are several excellent restaurants as well.

SIGHTS AND RECREATION

If you're not boating or fishing or swimming or generally worshiping the sun here, you may find things a bit dull. The water is the place to be, but you can easily get on it without getting wet. All along the main walkway under the bridge you'll find boat rentals, fishing guides, excursion cruises, and even a singing gondola ride. There are also unique shopping opportunities near the lake, and a few great places to eat. This is where you'll want to head first— just follow the signs to London Bridge, where the parking is generally free.

❰ London Bridge

London Bridge (928/453-8883, free) began its long life in 1831, spanning the Thames River in London. First, horses pulled carriages across it, and then the first cars chugged its length, and then, inevitably, the modern world caught up with it. By the early 1960s the old bridge no longer had what it takes to serve such a busy crossing, so the City of London sold it to Robert McCulloch, a chainsaw manufacturer just then entering the lucrative trade of master-planned retirement and resort communities. Now it spans a man-made channel of the Colorado River, walked and driven over by millions of sun-baked tourists every year. It's a strange sight, this old-world urban structure stuck out here in the middle of the desert. The best views are from below, where the scene has a bit of a picturesque old London look to it— but not quite. The bridge's seeming incongruity isn't as strange as it appears, however. In the 19th century, the lower Colorado and the Arizona Strip, not too far north of this region, were settled by Mormon pioneers from Salt Lake City, many of whom were English. That has little to do with the bridge's travels, though. Take a half hour or so to walk across and under it, and read the plaques placed at either end that explain how these bricks from the north Atlantic wound up stacked here in the desert.

© 12FISH/123RF.COM

London Bridge over the Colorado River

Lake Havasu State Park

Popular **Lake Havasu State Park** (99 London Bridge Rd., 928/855-2784, www.azstateparks.com/Parks/LAHA, sunrise-10pm, $10 per car, $15 on weekends and holidays, camping $14-25) stretches along the river north and south of the bridge and includes **Windsor Beach** ($10 per car, camping $15), an excellent riverside campground and sunning spot. Jet Ski rentals are available at the park through **Windsor Beach Rentals** (928/453-4792, www.windsorbeachrentals.com, $55 per hour). If you're looking to laze around on the beach for a while and watch the people and the waterfowl, Windsor Beach is the place to do it.

Cattail Cove State Park

About 15 miles south of the bridge along Route 95 the tell-tale cattails that give **Cattail Cove State Park** (Rte. 95, 928/855-1223, www.azstateparks.com/Parks/CACO, sunrise-10pm daily, $10 per car, $15 on weekends and holidays, camping $20-26) its name rise up out of the water. Here you'll find camping, boating,

and fishing opportunities just a bit outside the main town area, including several primitive campsites along the shores accessible only by boat. There's a nice beach and good swimming here—a perfect place for a laid-back day or overnight riverine outing with the family. The nearby **Sand Point Marina** (7952 S. Sandpoint Rd., 928/855-0549, www.sandpointresort.com) rents fishing boats ($40-90, 4-24 hours), pontoon boats ($200-375, 4-24 hours), and personal watercraft for up to three people ($100-745, 2-72 hours); most require a $500 deposit. The marina also has a good restaurant and a general store in case you forgot your supplies.

Havasu National Wildlife Refuge

Havasu National Wildlife Refuge (317 Mesquite Ave., Needles, CA, 760/326-3853, www.fws.gov/southwest/refuges/arizona/havasu) protects 30 river miles of Colorado River habitat from Needles, California, to Lake Havasu City, Arizona, where one of the last remaining natural sections of the lower Colorado

River flows through the 20-mile-long spectacle that is **Topock Gorge,** where you'll see bighorn sheep and other native animals. There are several concessionaires beneath the London Bridge in Lake Havasu City that offer guided tours of Topock Gorge.

Watercraft Rentals

One of the better outfitters is **London Bridge Watercraft Tours and Rentals** (928/453-8883, lakehavasubestboatandjetskirentals.com), which operates out of **Crazyhorse Campgrounds** (1534 Beachcomber Blvd., 928/855-4033, www.crazyhorsecampgrounds.com) on "the island" on the west side of the bridge. There are any number of other rental places along the walkway beneath the bridge, offering all-day and dining excursions, fishing trips, expeditions into the Lake Havasu Wildlife Refuge upriver, and paddleboats and canoes for sticking closer to the shore. The rental prices may change according to the season, with Spring Break and other crowded times ushering in higher fees. All of the rental places are going to require some kind of deposit, typically taken care of by handing over your credit card number.

EVENTS

Not surprisingly, most of Lake Havasu's annual events have something to do with the water. The biggest event of the year is probably Spring Break, which happens throughout March and April. The population skews young during this time of year, and if you're not looking for a party and crowds, you might want to stay away. In late February the **Mark Hahn Memorial Havasu 300 APBA National Team Endurance Race** (www.pwcfun.com/markhahn300.asp) brings together the nation's best Jet Ski pilots for a big race. Mid-March brings the **Lake Havasu Marine Associations Annual Boat Show** (928/453-8833), a three-day event featuring the best in watercraft, food, concerts, and all sorts of other fun. Later in March anglers come to town for the **U.S. Angler's Choice Fishing Tournament** (800/360-7112, www.usanglerschoice.net) and

the **New Horizons' Pro-Am Bass Tournament** (928/854-9378).

SHOPPING

Stick around the water to find distinctive gifts and souvenirs at the **English Village** (1477 Queens Bay, 928/855-0888, www.amdest.com/az/lhc/ev/engv.html), and under the bridge and across the channel you'll find the **Island Mall & Brewery** (1425 McCulloch Blvd., 928/855-6274), a two-story enclosed mall. Away from the bridge and water area, the **Main Street in the Uptown District** (upper McCulloch, 1 mile east of London Bridge) has more than 200 shops, including Shambles Village, which has all kinds of antique galleries.

ACCOMMODATIONS

Though you could definitely do it, it is not necessary to spend a lot of money to find a nice place to stay on the lake.

The **Island Inn Hotel** (1300 McCulloch Blvd., 928/680-0606 or 800/243-9955, $49-275) has basic, affordable rooms available near the water and right in the middle of all the fun. The most popular place in town is the **London Bridge Resort** (Rte. 95, 928/855-0888, www.londonbridgeresort.com, $99-519), right near the bridge and overlooking the lake, which endeavors to look "English" and offers several different room choices with bridge and channel views, a good restaurant, and a lot of extras. If you're camping or have an RV, the state parks are a good bet, as is the **Sand Point Marina and RV Park** (7952 S. Sandpoint Rd., 928/855-0549, www.sandpointresort.com, $40-45, no tent camping).

FOOD

Juicy's River Café (25 N. Acoma, 928/855-8429, www.juicysrivercafe.com, 7am-8pm Mon.-Sat., 7am-2pm Sun., $8-15) serves delectable breakfasts, sandwiches, and homemade comfort fare such as ribs and fish and chips, for those who've worn themselves extra-hungry playing on the river. The **Barley Brothers Brewery and Grill** (1425 McCulloch Blvd., 928/505-7837, www.barleybrothers.com,

11am-1am daily, $8-20), makes the best microbrew in the region and serves up tasty desert pub-style meals and wood-fired pizza and a great riverview atmosphere. A bit more fancy is **Krystal's Restaurant** (460 El Camino Way, 928/453-2999, 4pm-10pm daily, $10-25), which has perfect prime rib and is a great place for seafood and steaks, while **Shugrue's** (1425 McCulloch Blvd., 928/453-1400, www.shugrues.com, 11am-9pm Sun.-Thurs., 11am-10pm Fri.-Sat., $8-28) has a great view, delicious seafood and burgers, and homemade pastries and bread.

INFORMATION AND SERVICES

The **Lake Havasu City Convention and Visitors Bureau** (314 London Bridge Rd., 928/453-3444 or 800/242-8278, www.golakehavasu.com) can help you with all your questions and provide plenty of literature on sights and events in Lake Havasu.

PARKER AND THE PARKER STRIP

The small resort town of Parker looks out on about 16 miles of swift-flowing Colorado River called the Parker Strip, where retirement and vacation homes line the banks between the town and Parker Dam to the north. Most of the land below and around Parker comprises the **Colorado River Indian Reservation,** 270,000 acres that include the beautiful 16,400-acre **Swansea Wilderness Area,** about 25 miles northeast of town. This is one of the best stretches of the lower Colorado, and it's packed with boaters and other river lovers most weekends in season. Again, though, if you're not a river-rat or trying to be one, there's not much of an incentive to stop.

Sights and Recreation

The small **Colorado River Indian Tribes Museum and Library** (Hwy. 95 at 2nd and Mohave, 928/669-9211, 8am-5pm Mon.-Fri., 10am-3pm Sat.) has some interesting exhibits and artifacts of these often overlooked tribes. **Buckskin Mountain State Park** (5476 Hwy.

95, 928/667-3231, www.azstateparks.com/Parks/BUMO, $10 per car) and its **River Island Unit** (5200 Hwy. 95, 928/667-3386), about 12 miles north of Parker, have excellent camping, fishing, and boating opportunities. You can also drive over **Parker Dam** (760/663-3712) just north of the town; it's open to passenger vehicles only 5am-11pm. On the California side of the dam, there's a rough but scenic drive that will take you along the river and past a few historic sites and shoreline oases.

Just north of Parker the Bill Williams River flows from the east into the Colorado River. A beautiful thin ribbon of water moving through a marshy forest of cattails announces the **Bill Williams River National Wildlife Refuge** (60911 Hwy. 95, Parker, 928/667-4144, www.fws.gov/southwest/refuges/arizona/billwill.html), which protects a thick cottonwood-willow forest and has excellent bird-watching and kayaking opportunities. The refuge is located between mileposts 160 and 162 on State Highway 95, about 17 miles south of Lake Havasu City.

Accommodations and Food

The place to be in the Parker area is the Colorado Indian Tribe's **Blue Water Resort & Casino** (Hwy. 95, 928/669-7000, www.bluewaterfun.com, $45-139), which has affordable, clean, chilly rooms that look out over the river and the marina, where you can rent boats and Jet Skis and park your own craft if you have one. Inside the hotel there's a buffet; slots, blackjack, and poker; and a multi-tiered pool and water slide that the kids won't want to leave behind. There's also a movie theater and a sports bar, among other amenities.

QUARTZSITE

This quiet desert spot on Highway 95 between Parker and Yuma, right off I-10, is nearly deserted in the summer, when temperatures can and do reach 120°F fairly regularly. When the mercury dips, however, this wide spot in the road becomes crowded with itinerant retirees and roaming bands of gem and mineral dealers and other assorted swap-meet entrepreneurs.

LOWER COLORADO RIVER

The Naked Bookseller of Quartzsite

Paul Winer, the 64-year-old, nearly nude proprietor of the **Reader's Oasis** (690 E. Main St., 928/927-6551) in Quartzsite, has been selling books along the tiny desert town's main drag since the 1990s.

"I used to wear very brief shorts," he said. "I didn't drop them and feel free to be who I am until I had 180,000 books; then I thought I could do it."

Winer spent 25 years back East playing boogie-woogie piano, nude, under the name "Sweet Pie." He fought a protracted public indecency battle and eventually prevailed, he said. In lieu of recompense he chose to settle a rather large IRS bill free and clear, and then headed out to Arizona to see his parents. He started selling his mom's paperbacks at the big swap-meet gem shows that give Quartzsite one of the largest populations in Arizona for a few weeks every winter, when the desert becomes a tent

city and there are all manner of strange and interesting itinerant merchants around. Paul is here to stay, however; he's open year-round, he said, even when the heat reaches 120°F, which it is wont to do here in the summer. Arizona, he said, "is one of the few states that would tolerate someone like me on the main street of a town. It has a history of having the most obstinate, stubborn, off-the-wall people. There is still quite a tolerance for outsiders."

He has a lot of good books for sale, including an excellent selection of used books about the Southwest and children's books. Book lovers who might otherwise be put off by Winer's lack of clothing—he usually wears a small thong-style loincloth and not much else on his thin and tanned frame—will want to think twice about missing this unique store. Winer is a smart, friendly fellow, and he won't hesitate to tell you his crazy story and recommend a book.

Throughout January and February, the streets in town are lined with booths and tables selling all manner of gems and jewelry and just about anything else you can think of, and on through the winter the RV tribe of retirees makes Quartzsite a temporary boomtown.

Even if it's summer and 110°F in the shade, if you happen to be passing through this settlement around lunch or dinnertime, make sure you stop at the ◖**Grubstake Social Club** (725 N. Central, Hwy. 95, 928/927-4485,

11am-2am daily, $7-16), where you can get the best plate of fish-and-chips in the state and a cool glass of Boddingtons' Ale (way out here in the middle of the desert!). The Grubstake also makes a great fried-shrimp po' boy and a plate of supposedly mini "slider" hamburgers that are actually three regular-size burgers on top of a huge pile of fries. The portions here are large to say the least, but you'll be happy you had to take some on the road with you.

Yuma and Vicinity

Yuma has long been an important place. For centuries the area where the once wild Colorado and Gila Rivers found each other and merged was a natural crossing point for Native Americans, and during the great gold rush of 1849 the riverside desert became a crucial crossing and lifeline for all those prospectors and adventurers going to California. For

a time steamboats chugged up and down the Colorado, docking at Yuma to load and unload supplies important to the settling of the Southwest. Some of the Wild West's most despicable characters found themselves sweltering in the hell of the Yuma Territorial Prison. In the era of reclamation Yuma became an important agricultural center, and it still is,

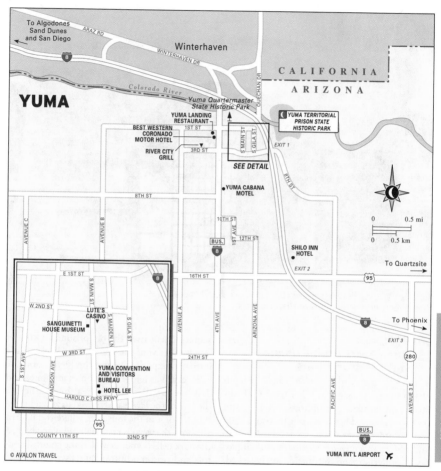

producing winter lettuce and other crops. In 1915 Yuma became an important link in the nation's commercial scene with the opening of the famous Ocean-to-Ocean Highway Bridge over the Colorado. To most Arizonans who don't live near the state's western border, Yuma is known mostly as a place to stop and get gas on the way to the cool ocean breezes of San Diego.

Today Yuma is a growing city of about 105,000 people with an economy based largely on agriculture and the service industry. From about November through March the city's population swells by some 90,000 people, many of them retirees and snowbirds seeking the easy life in one of Yuma's more than 80 RV and mobile home parks. While the town boasts sunny skies 95 percent of the year, and winter temperatures are often in the 70s and even the 80s, it is not a place that you want to visit during the height of summer. You'll find the temperature hovering many days around 110°F, cooling off very little at night. Consequently, some businesses and attractions have truncated hours or shut down altogether when the heat reigns.

© TIM HULL

Yuma Territorial Prison State Historic Park

LOWER COLORADO RIVER

SIGHTS
◖ Yuma Territorial Prison State Historic Park

They say Yuma Prison wasn't as bad as its reputation suggests, that the more than 3,000 outlaws, polygamists, gunfighters, robbers, and murderers housed here between 1876 and 1909 were afforded three squares a day, health care, and education, conveniences many of their pioneer counterparts on the outside sorely lacked. But spend a little time exploring popular **Yuma Territorial Prison State Historic Park** (100 Prison Hill Rd., 928/783-4771, www.azstateparks.com/Parks/YUTE, 9am-5pm daily, $6 adults, $3 children 7-13) and you'll likely come to a different conclusion: This wasn't a place where you'd want to spend any time, especially in an era long before air-conditioning. If you think it's hot in Yuma today, just imagine being confined to a dark airless cell, the heat as incessant as the din from the cell block, full of half-mad prisoners and constant tubercular coughing.

There's not a lot left of the original buildings;

Yuma citizens used the old prison as a kind of free lumber yard for years before it was made into a state park. During the Depression the cells served as temporary homes for hobos and destitute families. But the real interest here is the lore of the lawless territorial days, and there is much of it in the museum, where you'll learn all about the various characters who once called the dark cells home, as well as the colorful doctors and prison administrators who managed the place. You can climb up to the large guard tower and look over the slowly meandering Colorado as it snakes through wetlands below, and feel what it was like (sort of, anyway) to be confined to a prison cell way out here in the middle of the desert, far from home and grace. Plan on spending at least an hour or two here, as there is much to discover in the stories and artifacts of crime and punishment on the Southwestern frontier.

Yuma Quartermaster Depot State Historic Park

A small historic park on Yuma's main drag,

Yuma Quartermaster Depot State Historic Park (201 N. 4th Ave., 928/329-0471, www.azstateparks.com/Parks/YUQU, 9am-5pm daily, $4 adults, $2 children 7-13) preserves the history of the U.S. Army's presence in Yuma from 1864 to 1883, when riverboat steamers brought supplies up from the mouth of the Colorado to serve army outposts throughout the region. Before the railroad entered the Southwest, a six-month supply of food, clothing, ammunition, and other staples was quartered here for distribution to forts in Arizona, Utah, Nevada, and New Mexico. At the park you can see the old commanding officer's quarters and a few other historic buildings and artifacts related to the army's long occupation of the wild open West.

The most interesting story told at the park, which until the summer of 2007 was called Yuma Crossing Historic Park, is about the construction of the audacious Yuma Siphon, an engineering project that would sound ambitious even today. Using old Captain Nemo-style diving gear, workers built a concrete tunnel underneath the Colorado River in order to divert the river for use in agriculture, changing the fate of Yuma forever and, really, securing the town's survival beyond being a way station for goods and people headed to California. At the park there are some excellent displays on the project, and a few of the old diving suits and other artifacts of this incredible reclamation feat.

Sanguinetti House Museum

The history of Yuma is on display at the **Sanguinetti House Museum** (240 S. Madison Ave., 928/782-1841, www.arizonahistorical-society.org, 10am-4pm Tues.-Sat., $3 adults, children 12 and under free) in the city's quiet historic downtown. Named after the home's former owner, pioneer merchant E. F. Sanguinetti, the little adobe house has informative displays on the history of the lower Colorado region from prehistory through modern times, with period rooms and a shady garden patio and aviary with talking birds in cages. If you're really interested in the history of the region, make sure to converse with one of

the volunteer docents who staff the main desk; they are usually longtime residents or natives of the area and can provide personal context to the historical displays. A separate adobe next door, formerly the residence of a riverboat captain, houses an excellent local- and regional-history bookshop.

Historic Downtown

Yuma's downtown has been going through a planned rebirth for a few decades now, and there are some cool old buildings from various eras still standing, including the art deco **Yuma Theatre** built in 1936. It has been restored and now shows movies, and nearby, the **Yuma Downtown Art Center** has four galleries showing the work of local and regional artists. Other buildings show the influence of Spanish Colonial Revival style, and there are even a few old adobes still standing from the territorial days. It's easy to walk around the downtown. Start at **Main Street Plaza** and just explore—there are a few shops, antique stores, galleries, and boutiques along the narrow streets, and on the edges of the downtown you'll see a few old historic homes. That being said, on most days the downtown is a bit quiet and deserted, especially in the summer. Still, it's a good place to get a feel for what Yuma used to be.

Algodones Dunes

Desert country neophytes might be a little disappointed with the relative lushness of the typical Arizona desert landscape, which defies with its diversity the daydream of Saharaesque dunes with nothing but white sand for miles and miles. If you were hoping for a "real desert," something on the order of Luke Skywalker's home planet of Tatooine, head across the bridge into California for a look at the southeastern end of the great shifting stretch of sand known as the Algodones Dunes, also called the Imperial Dunes. About 17 miles west on I-8 outside of Yuma take the Gray's Well exit to a parking lot on the edge of the dunes near the Midway campground, part of the **Imperial Dunes Recreation Area.** Here you can park your car and witness the

© TIM HULL

Algodones Dunes

45-mile by 6-mile dunes—but don't go far. There is literally nothing out here but sand, and then more sand. If you think it looks like Tatooine, that's because it is: George Lucas filmed portions of *Return of The Jedi* near here in the 1980s. These days the dunes are popular with motorcycle and ATV enthusiasts, who tear around nearby Glamis on holiday weekends in a great rumbling and rolling party. A few miles west on the frontage road from Gray's Well (follow the signs) you can see what remains of the old **Plank Road**, a movable highway of wooden planks once placed on top of the dunes so early car travelers could pass without sinking into the sand, this before highway technology advanced enough to build the interstate that now bisects the area. It's not recommended that you go here in the summer, nor should you take off across the dunes on foot. Just look, or maybe scamper up a tall dune near the parking lot and see what an expanse of nothing looks like—it's preternaturally beautiful, and a good place for meditating on, well . . . nothingness.

ENTERTAINMENT AND EVENTS

For Vegas-style entertainment and games of chance, head over to **Quechan Paradise Casino** (I-8 to 4th Ave. exit, then north on Imperial County Route S-24, 888/777-4946, www.paradise-casinos.com), where popular bands of yesteryear play often, and there are slots, blackjack, poker, and lots of food and drinks.

In early January Yuma's historic downtown hosts the **Old Town Jubilee,** with artisans, entertainment, and activities for the whole family. If you're in town in mid-February, when the weather in Yuma is perfect, don't miss **Yuma River Daze** and the **Yuma Crossing Days Festival,** three days celebrating local history and culture that includes river races, swimming, and a block party downtown.

RECREATION

About 35 miles north of Yuma on U.S. Highway 95 is **Martinez Lake,** where you can fish, boat, and view wildlife, among other activities. The Imperial National Wildlife Refuge is just north of the lake and extends for 30 miles upriver, teeming with water-loving birds and other wildlife.

A popular and fun way to see the river and the refuge is to take a boat tour with **Yuma River Tours** (1920 Arizona Ave., 928/783-4400, www.yumarivertours.com). Make sure to call ahead in summer as they have limited hours during the hot months. The best tour is the 4-5-hour, 32-mile boat trip to **Norton's Landing** ($75 per person, includes lunch), an old steamboat port and mining ghost town. The tour takes you deep into the refuge, and the guides are expert at spotting and pointing out birds and mammals along the way. Reservations are required. Yuma River Tours also offers day and dining cruises on an old stern-wheeler ($48-63 per person), and overnight guided kayak and canoe trips.

At **Fisher's Landing** (928/782-7049, www.fisherslandingresort.com) on Martinez Lake you can rent a boat for the day ($50). You can also rent or buy fishing gear and book a guide to show you the best hideouts of bass, crappie, bluegill, stripers, and flathead catfish. There's a restaurant serving burgers, sandwiches, fish, and steaks ($4.95-17.95) and a general store.

Wildlife Refuges

While the many dams built along the Colorado River during the era of reclamation in the 1930s and 1940s made it possible for the Southwest to grow and thrive as a habitat for humans, the loss of the river's natural and wild flow ruined much of the essential riparian habitat downstream. In an effort to restore what was lost and hold on to what remains, the U.S. Fish and Wildlife Service has established a number of wildlife refuges in western Arizona. These are wild and rugged places, not for the unprepared or the uninitiated. But for those looking for something far off the track, these protected lands provide some of the best bird-watching, wildlife viewing, and nature communing—especially of the desert and riverine kind—in the entire state.

Two of the refuges—Imperial and Havasu—feature well-established tour companies that will take you along the river and point out all there is to see.

Just north of Yuma along U.S. 95, the ruggedly beautiful **Kofa National Wildlife Refuge** (356 W. 1st St., Yuma, 928/783-7861, www.fws.gov/southwest/refuges/arizona/kofa) includes 665,400 acres of rough desert landscape, home to the dexterous bighorn and legions of reptiles who couldn't live anywhere else but this dry and sharp-rock land. Within the refuge is **Palm Canyon,** in the west end of the Kofa Mountains, where grow the only native palm trees in Arizona—a state that probably has more than its fair share of palms imported to its city streets. The half-mile hike into Palm Canyon to see the trees is one of the region's best. Along U.S. 95 north of Yuma, watch for the Palm Canyon sign, then follow the dirt road east for nine miles toward the mountains and the trailhead.

Heading west to the river, you will find the 25,768-acre **Imperial National Wildlife Refuge** (Martinez Lake, 928/783-3317, www.fws.gov/southwest/refuges/arizona/Imperial/index.

© DESIGNPICS/123RF.COM

Kofa National Wildlife Refuge

html), a 30-mile desert-meets-wetland landscape that is renowned as a stop for various migratory bird species and that is full of desertland mammals like bighorn sheep, mountain lions, bobcats, deer, wild horses, and burros. There's a visitors center here, a rough-and-tumble scenic drive that takes you through an unvarnished Sonoran Desert stretch, and a few awesome lookouts with views of the river valley. The 1.3-mile **Painted Desert Trail** leads to a grand view as well. **Yuma River Tours** (1920 Arizona Ave., 928/783-4400, www.yumarivertours.com) offers boat tours into the refuge.

Farther upriver is the **Cibola National Wildlife Refuge** (66600 Cibola Lake Rd., Cibola, 928/857-3253, www.fws.gov/southwest/refuges/CibolaNWR), where you'll find some of the best birding in the region. Just outside the visitors center there's a short scenic drive (called Canada Goose Drive), along which you can stop and hike the one-mile loop nature trail, moving through a beautiful riparian habitat of cottonwood, willow, and mesquite forests. In winter, thousands of Canada geese, snow geese, ducks, and sandhill cranes are usually visible from an observation deck here.

The **Cabeza Prieta National Wildlife Refuge** (1611 N. 2nd St., Ajo, 520/387-6483, www.fws.gov/southwest/refuges/arizona/cabeza.html), about 90 miles east of Yuma, is a forbidding landscape hugging the U.S.-Mexico border. If you're looking for the Sonoran Desert in the raw, you'll find it here. The Cabeza Prieta (meaning "Dark Head" in Spanish, for the area's volcanic coloring) is a hot and sparse land, covered in cacti and creosote (and wildflowers and other blooming desert show-offs in the spring). The refuge provides 860,010 acres of habitat for desert creatures to roam, including bighorn sheep and the cactus-pollinating lesser long-nosed bats. There's a small visitors center and short interpretive trail at the refuge office, where you have to stop first to pick up a permit to explore the refuge. Most of the refuge is within the airspace of the Barry M. Goldwater Air Force Range, so there are often low-flying aircraft

in the area, crossing the refuge on their way to the bombing ranges to the north. Somewhere out in that sublimely wild swath of Sonoran Desert, that great advocate of wild desert, the author Edward Abbey, is said to be buried in an unmarked grave.

ACCOMMODATIONS

Yuma has all the chain hotels and motels a town its size would ever want, and many of them are located just off I-8 or along 4th Avenue, the town's main commercial thoroughfare.

An affordable and clean place to stay is the **Yuma Cabana Motel** (2151 S. 4th Ave., 928/783-8311, www.yumacabana.com, $45-73), where amenities include free Wi-Fi, a swimming pool, and a continental breakfast. The rooms are small and can seem a bit bleak with their concrete walls, but this is a fine place, especially for those on a budget, and the retro sign is picture-worthy. The best hotel in town is the **Best Western Coronado Motor Hotel** (233 4th Ave., 928/783-4453, $79-129), which has comfortable rooms and a friendly staff and is right in the center of everything. It has a pool and offers a free, full breakfast every morning.

The **Shilo Inn Hotel** (1550 S. Castle Dome Ave., 928/782-9511, www.shiloinns.com, $122-200) is a bit more upscale, offering a free breakfast buffet, free Internet, a nice pool area, and comfortable rooms. For something a little more historic and distinctive, head to Yuma's sleepy downtown to the **Hotel Lee** (390 S. Main St., 928/783-6336, www.hotellee.com, $49-99), built in 1917 and renovated with a Victorian touch. The hotel is charming, and the rooms are all individually decorated and have a historic ambience without sacrificing modern comforts.

FOOD

The must-visit restaurant in Yuma is **Lute's Casino** (221 S. Main St., 928/782-2192, www.lutescasino.com, 9am-8pm Mon.-Thurs., 9am-9pm Fri.-Sat., 10am-6pm Sun., $5-15) downtown, a place popular with locals and visitors alike. Even if you aren't hungry you'll enjoy sitting at one of the tall tables and drinking a brew, your neck craning to look at all the strange and hilarious—and even a bit bawdy—pictures covering the walls. The menu offers everything from burgers and hot dogs to burritos and tacos, all served up in huge portions. If you like hot dogs, don't miss Bob's Polish Kraut Dog ($4.50)—it's awesome. Lute's is also a good place to enjoy some nightlife with the locals.

The **Yuma Landing Restaurant** (195 S. 4th Ave., 928/782-7427, www.yumalanding.com, 6am-9pm Sun.-Thurs., 6am-midnight Fri.-Sat., $5-15) is on the site where the first airplane landed in Yuma, and it has all sorts of memorabilia about that and other town history on the walls. It serves an eclectic mix of salads, sandwiches, steaks, prime rib, and Mexican dishes and has a bar with a good happy hour. The **River City Grill** (600 W. 3rd St., 928/782-7988, www.rivercitygrillyuma.com, lunch 11am-2pm Mon.-Fri., dinner 5pm-10pm daily, $7-22) serves top-notch seafood, sushi, lamb, beef, chicken, and vegetarian dishes in a cool contemporary setting, with a great patio for dining in the warmth of winter.

GETTING THERE AND AROUND

Yuma International Airport (2191 E. 32nd St., 928/726-5882, www.yumainternationalairport.com) offers a few flights each day to L.A. and Phoenix, but you really need a car to explore this region and to get around Yuma. The main line in and out of the city is I-8, and if you're going north along the river use U.S. Highway 95.

INFORMATION AND SERVICES

The **Visitor Information Center at Yuma Quartermaster Depot State Historic Park** (201 N. 4th Ave., 928/783-0071 or 800/293-0071, www.visityuma.com, 9am-5pm daily Oct.-May, closed Mon. June-Sept.) downtown has all kinds of pamphlets and advice for enjoying Yuma and the Lower Colorado River region.

BACKGROUND

The Land

The Arizona landscape is more varied than most, changing, with rises in elevation, from hot, cactus-choked **deserts** to scrubby bushlands to open **ponderosa pine forests** to coniferous, snowy highlands. Dry **grasslands** and long stretches of sagebrush plains spread across the higher deserts.

While it snows and rains much more in the high country than it does in the desert belt, the entire state is subject to what Lawrence Clark Powell called a "wrinkled dryness." Aridity is a constant no matter where you go. Spread thinly across the land, a few life-giving river ways and **riparian areas** are treasured as oases and predictably exploited.

Arizona has 114,000 square miles, making it sixth in size among the states. Large tracts of wild, open land remain, and likely always will.

GEOGRAPHY AND GEOLOGY

When dinosaurs roamed the earth, this desert was a swampy and wet place. Over the eons different portions of Arizona were covered by shallow seas that flowed in, flourished, and then dried up and retreated. Eventually the Arizona you see took shape—mountains rose, volcanoes burst and created new land, and plates

© TIM HULL

the view from Mount Humphreys

important international observatories on their high reaches, and the cities and towns around them, Tucson included, are encouraged to keep their street lights and other "light noise" to a minimum so as to keep the sky dark and clear. These southern ranges are often referred to as sky islands because they are exactly that: islands of biological diversity surrounded, and isolated, by vast seas of harsh, hot desert. In these sky islands can be found flora and fauna that exist in few other places in North America. Subtropical birds and other animals use these mountains as the northern reaches of their ranges, so it's not uncommon to find quetzal-like birds and even jungle-loving jaguars flitting and stalking around the misty creeksides of these forested ranges.

The central and north-central region of Arizona is also very mountainous, though the ranges here are somewhat smaller and older than those in the south. Around Prescott the Bradshaws and the Sierra Prieta reach to about 9,000 feet and are covered in pine. They were once, and perhaps still are, strewn with the precious minerals that became the impetus for one of the state's first mining booms. Throughout the state there are several other ranges and many detached, lonely peaks, many of them high and timbered and others midsized and rocky, covered in cactus and creosote and old mining tunnels.

slid apart and crashed into each other, creating upland plateaus and digging deep canyons with the erosional help of rivers, wind, and aridity.

Mountains

Few places have such extremes in elevation: You could travel from sea level along the lower Colorado to the 12,600-foot peak of **Mount Humphreys,** part of the volcanic San Francisco Mountain range above Flagstaff, in a matter of a day or so. The White Mountains in the central-eastern part of the state tower higher than 10,000 feet and are often snowcapped. The Santa Catalinas, north of Tucson, rise to similar heights and feature the nation's southernmost ski run. A bit south of Tucson toward the U.S.-Mexico border, the Santa Rita Mountains tower above the Santa Cruz Valley, and just to the east the Huachuca Mountains do the same over the San Pedro Valley. Farther east the Pinaleño Range rises above 10,000 feet, with towering Mount Graham watching over the Gila Valley. Many of these high Southern Arizona mountain ranges have

The Colorado Plateau

The plateau country dominates the northern portion of the state, covering about two fifths of its area; its nearly 200-mile southern edge, the **Mogollon Rim,** borders the scrub-and-pine belt of the transition zone. Below that is the **basin and range province** of the desert country, stretching from the western to the eastern border and south to Mexico. The elevations in the basin and range swing from sea level to about 4,000 feet above it, though several large mountain ranges dot the lowlands and rise beyond 9,000 feet. In the uplands of the plateaus, deep canyons plunge into the layers of ancient rock. The bottom of the Grand Canyon, which is cut into the Colorado Plateau, is a low, hot desert. The highest points in the plateau country reach above 12,000 feet and are dominated by tundra and bare cold boulders.

It is the contrast between the plateau and the basin and range provinces that makes Arizona such a rare landscape. Both have their origins deep in geologic time. The plateau country began to form in its current shape around 600 million years ago, when the continent was relatively flat and layer after layer of limestone, sandstone, siltstone, and shale were deposited by tropical seas moving in and then receding, leaving behind dunes and stream deposits and eroding the older layers for some 300 million years. Then the dune deposits started to harden and petrify, creating the strange swirling rock-dune sandstone one sees all over the plateau region. Volcanic eruptions around the plateau added to the great piling of sediment, while rivers and lakes and inland seas flushed in and then dried up or receded. But the plateau itself, while it was eroded and cut and sculpted and formed, remained relatively stable in contrast to the other lands around it, which changed mightily. About 70 million years ago the land all around the Southwest began to rise, pushing the plateau from about sea level to more than 10,000 feet above it. Great mountains were thrust up out of the ground all around the region, and the earth stretched with underground tension to create the basin and range province to the west and south of the plateau. According to the U.S. Geological Survey, about 20 million years ago a "great tension developed in the [earth's] crust . . . and the basin and range province broke into a multitude of down-dropped valleys and elongated mountains" similar to what we see today in Arizona's desertlands. But the Colorado Plateau remained stable and eventually rose nearly a mile higher than the basin and range. The Colorado River fell through the plateau and cut deep into the rock, carving the Grand Canyon—a process that started less than six million years ago.

The Grand Canyon

A visit to Grand Canyon reveals much of the story of the continent's geologic formation. The top layers of rock, through which the Colorado first cut, called the Kaibab Formation, are around 270 million years old, while the gneiss and schist of the inner canyon are about 1.8 billion years old. Many geologists believe that the lower 2,000 feet or so of the canyon was cut and eroded just in the last 750,000 years—the blink of a geologist's eye. The canyon was formed by the great cosmic need of all water to return to the sea from whence it came: Water falls—that's its sole mission in life—and huge torrents of water carrying loads of dry, rocky sediment fall hard and fast and cut deep into the rocks of an uplifted plateau. As the cuts get deeper, the land around it gives way and falls apart, thus creating the deep, wide, and wonderful hole in the plateau that has made Arizona famous.

Deserts

Arizona is the only state where three major deserts converge: The **Sonoran Desert** stretches across the southern portion of the state and includes the Phoenix and Tucson areas, while the **Mojave Desert** dominates on the western reaches. The **Chihuahuan Desert** of Mexico stretches north into southeastern Arizona.

The Sonoran Desert comprises about 120,000 square miles across the southwestern and south-central parts of Arizona. It is a woody desert, full of mesquite and paloverde trees, creosote, and, of course, the famous saguaro cactus. A small portion of the Mojave Desert dominates northwestern Arizona, and is marked by creosote and other small bushes, cholla, and Joshua trees. The Chihuahuan Desert spreads out through southeastern Arizona and into Mexico, dominated by arid grasslands.

Rivers

The state's rivers, though many of them are dry for much of the year these days, have made human culture possible in Arizona. The **Gila River,** nearly dead today, was the main east-west waterway, stretching from the mountains of New Mexico all the way to the lower Colorado, which forms the western border. The banks of the Gila's tributaries, the Verde, the San Pedro, the Salt, and the Santa Cruz, saw the rise of several complex and creative cultures over the centuries, including the Hohokam, the Salado, the Sinagua, and the Mogollon. The state's main river, the **Colorado River,** drains the vast Colorado Plateau and stretches from Wyoming all the way to Mexico. Much of the river through Arizona, about half of its total length, has historically been difficult to access because it flows deep within intricately carved canyons. Tributaries of the Colorado, like the Little Colorado in the northeastern portion of the state and the Bill Williams River in the central-west, have also been important to human settlement in Arizona. The Little Colorado provided a reasonable water supply for the Ancestral Puebloan cultures that settled on the high plains and, much later, was the source of life for Mormon pioneers in the 19th century.

Most of the state's rivers are no longer wild, having been dammed and controlled, a process that started, on a major scale, in the late 19th and early 20th centuries with the era of reclamation. Because wild desert rivers like the Gila, Salt, and Colorado were subject to intense flooding and severe drought, it was difficult for European settlers to rely on their quirky flows for agriculture. The federal government was also eager to harness the rivers' power to create hydroelectricity and to build vast reservoirs of water that could be sent to the growing agricultural and urban areas of Arizona, California, and elsewhere. Beginning at the turn of the 20th century with the building of Roosevelt Dam on the Salt, which helped make Phoenix and the Valley of the Sun first an agricultural boomtown and then an urban megalopolis, the era of reclamation saw most of the state's rivers dammed, ending with the damming of the Colorado River at Glen Canyon in the mid-20th century. Earlier, the biggest dam of them all, Hoover, was constructed in Black Canyon on the Colorado at the Arizona-Nevada border, creating the world's largest man-made lake, **Lake Mead,** and making the agricultural blunder called the Imperial Valley, in California, possible. The damming of any

© TIM HULL

the Colorado River in Yuma

river changes that river irrevocably; the damming of the Colorado at Glen Canyon altered the stretch of the West's greatest river that created the Grand Canyon so much that it is unrecognizable from its previous form. Even the color of the river is different. The Colorado River, the red river, used to flow muddy and warm through the canyon, hence its name, because it was full of the sediment that helped cut the great gorge. Since the dam was built, most of that sediment is deposited behind the dam in the reservoir known as **Lake Powell,** and the river flows cool and green through the inner gorge. This has led to a complete change in the river's downstream ecosystem, as the ancient cycles of flood and drought have changed to a predictable, constant flow, thus changing the very character of the river and making it difficult for native species to survive.

CLIMATE

Contrary to popular belief, many regions of Arizona experience four seasons. Even on the desert, while summers are long and hot below 5,000 feet or so, the sky island mountain ranges experience little pockets of seasonally based weather.

Spring is the best time to be on Arizona's lowland deserts. From late February until May temperatures typically hang around the high 70s and 80s from the lower Colorado River region across the desert belt to the New Mexico border.

The highland summer is warm—even hot—during the day and cool at night, ranging from the mid to high 80s to the low 60s at night. In late summer the smell of wet pine needles precedes each late-afternoon "monsoon" rainstorm, and a mist rises when the cold raindrops hit the warm rocks.

While it also rains during the late summer on the deserts, during the beloved "monsoon" season, the storms only serve to make an already unbearable heat humid as well. Summers in the desert are intensely hot and listless. The daytime highs range from the high 90s to 110°F or even 120°F at their worst, while at night the lows rarely fall below the 80s. In

Tucson and Phoenix it is not uncommon to experience several months straight of 100°F or higher temperatures with little or no rainfall.

The monsoon season, which, to be strictly correct, should be called simply the summer rainy season, occurs when shifting winds from the south encourage late-afternoon downpours, often attended by thunder and lightning, nearly every day from July into September. During this time of year the dry washes and riverbeds throughout the state are subject to flash flooding, as torrents of rain flow through the channels from the uplands to the desert. Never stop or park in a dry wash during this time of year—it could become a raging river rather quickly, even if the sun is shining overhead. Monsoon storms are highly localized—so much so that it is sometimes raining in the backyard and not in the front yard. Hiking up a canyon during this time of year can be dangerous and sometimes deadly; you never know if it's raining in the mountains above you, and that water could show up anytime, falling off the mountain and rushing through the canyon and taking hikers with it. Also, washes fill up quickly during the rainy season and often trap drivers trying to cross them, necessitating rescues that are expensive and dangerous for first responders. Never venture into a flooded wash, no matter how shallow it appears. Unless you visit Arizona during the two months or so of the summer rainy season, or during the couple months in winter when it may be snowing in the highlands and raining intermittently on the deserts, you're not likely to experience anything but sunshine.

In the highlands during spring you'll encounter cool days and cold nights, and it has even been known to snow across the pine belt in April or later. Depending on the length and strength of the winter, there will typically be snow in the north-central high country in February and even into March.

Fall (Oct.-Dec. or Jan.) comes on cold and barren in the highlands, and the ground crunches with fallen leaves. The "second spring" begins on the desert. The weather gets perfect again, from the high 60s to the 80s,

The Desert at Risk

Many scientists in Arizona these days are busy researching how climate change and prolonged drought will affect the region's arid life zones over the long term. One of these scientists is Travis Huxman, director of the Biosphere 2 lab and an associate professor of ecology and evolutionary biology at the University of Arizona in Tucson. Huxman is interested in how plants translate climate into ecosystem behavior—how plants respond to temperature fluctuation, carbon dioxide concentration, animals, and microbes, and how a plant's interaction with all these elements affects how an ecosystem processes water, which is probably the single most important question here in the arid, thirsty Southwest.

"Plants can tell us a lot about ourselves, especially here in the desert," Huxman says. "Deserts are very sensitive to change; you see big impacts in deserts before you might see them somewhere else."

Huxman and others argue that, because of climate change, big, representative species of the Sonoran Desert, most notably the mighty saguaro, are living under a very real threat.

We could lose the saguaro and other celebrities of the desert because of fires sparked by invasive grasses, the spread of which is a direct impact of global climate change. It's happening in North America's other deserts as well. In the Mojave Desert to the west, the great Joshua tree is similarly threatened, according to Huxman.

"I don't have a projection for how long it would take, but you can hardly drive a freeway through the North American deserts and not see this change and the impact of fire on these landscapes," Huxman says. "It's fairly obvious."

So far in Arizona, such changes are most evident in the high deserts of the state's north-central pinebelt. There, the largest ponderosa pine forest in North America is on the verge of total collapse. The conifers are stressed due to drought, and that stress allows bark beetles and other killers to dig in, which in turn leaves this typically fire-resistant species ready to burn. And once they're gone, will they grow back, or has the ecosystem changed irrevocably?

But that's not even the biggest problem, Huxman says. What we don't know yet is how the water cycle will react if a single dominant species like the ponderosa pine is no longer part of the ecosystem. "That's the big research question," he says. "How will all this affect water?"

And that, according to Huxman, points to the most important fact we can learn from plants: what he calls the water-energy problem.

"Plants take up carbon dioxide in order to grow, but to do so they have to lose water to the atmosphere," he explains. "That's our problem on many different scales: How water and energy are related; so the most important thing we can do now is to remember that when we are thinking about energy efficiency, we are also thinking about water efficiency at the same time."

---

with cool, light-jacket nights. This is the time of year when the snowbirds arrive from the Midwest to set up camp until it starts to get hot. After December, the winter rains come to the desert and it starts to snow in the high country, and for a very brief couple of weeks everybody in the state is cold and housebound.

Winter temperatures can fall below freezing in the highlands and regularly reach lows of 20°F or below and highs in the 40s and 50s. On the deserts during this time, highs fall to the low 60s and even into the 50s, and lows regularly fall below 30°F. Only a few places in the state receive significant snowfall—Flagstaff, the Kaibab Plateau, and the White Mountains. In these places the snow can be deep enough to close roads and halt normal life.

ENVIRONMENTAL ISSUES

With its delicate and finely balanced biomes and some of the most dramatic and exotic scenery on earth, Arizona has over the generations been a haven, a laboratory, and a rallying point for environmentalists and ecologists. One of the biggest threats to the state's extremely varied ecosystems is simple growth; much of the desert has been paved over and crowded with homes, while the upland forests host droves of overbuilt homes just waiting for a wildfire to burn them to their foundations. It may seem strange that a land so naturally inhospitable to human occupation is, year after year, listed as one of the top two or three fastest-growing states in the nation. There are no signs that this trend is going to let up anytime soon. The constant influx of people has led over the years to environmental problems far beyond the mere pavement of desert and clearing of forests. Growth and the state's founding impetus to glean profit from the land have led to the overpumping of groundwater and the damming and taming of most of the state's rivers. This has altered the green riverways so completely that many species of native fish are now as good as gone, and nonnative plants line the mostly dry riverbeds, crowding out native riverine flora like cottonwoods and willows.

Climate change, scientists say, is likely to increase the state's environmental woes, and coupled with an ongoing drought that has been, more or less, eating away at the state for more than a decade, may lead to shortages on the Colorado River, water from which the vast majority of urban Arizonans depend. Some scientists have recently predicted that Lake Mead may dry up by 2025, while others believe the current human culture in Arizona may, one day in the future, suffer the same collapse as did the Anasazi, the Hohokam, and other complex societies who have tried to make a go of it here, leaving behind the ambitious ruins of their rise and fall but not much else.

There are numerous organizations fighting to save Arizona and its rare natural beauty from destruction and overuse, and over the last few decades the state, many local governments, and especially the diverse citizenry have taken a more proactive approach to conservation. Visiting Tucson's midtown neighborhoods gives the visitor the best evidence of this, where one can see an increasing number of homes with solar panels on their roofs and corrugated rainwater tanks rising from behind their fences. The federal government, which controls many of the state's most famous environmental treasures, has over the last several years set aside more and more of the remaining open and wild lands as wilderness areas and national monuments. However, in recent years the high price of copper and the rising cost of energy have led to renewed explorations and plans to dig strip mines on public lands, a reality that has again started familiar debates over resource conservation that have been raging for decades. Groups like the Nature Conservancy and the Tucson-based Sky Island Alliance and Center for Biological Diversity are using a variety of methods, including simple capitalism, science-based advocacy, and the federal courts, to make sure that large swaths of Arizona remain open and wild.

Visitors to Arizona can help keep the state beautiful and clean by adhering to a few simple, commonsense rules. First of all, as always, pack out what you pack in. Always stay on the trails, don't feed wild animals, and never, ever take any vehicle off the road or the trail, including a bike. If you're an off-highway vehicle (OHV) enthusiast, stick to the set-aside off-road areas in the national forests (which can be identified through the U.S. Forest Service's Arizona websites or at the local offices). Also, if you're visiting any of the state's many national forests during the summer, there are likely to be campfire and smoking restrictions enforced throughout the state due to high temperatures and ongoing drought. Make sure you are familiar with these restrictions and that you follow them to the letter. Nearly all of the state's huge, catastrophic wildfires in recent years have been caused by humans.

Flora and Fauna

LIFE ZONES

The state's flora is, like the land itself, extremely diverse, ranging from weird desert rarities to tall, thick evergreens.

If you pay attention to your elevation—and the "wrinkled" nature of the state assures that you are changing elevation all the time—you can generally predict what the weather will be like and which plants and animals you are likely to see; of course, it's not all strictly delineated, and the various life zones often bleed into one another. Between 4,500 and about 7,000 feet you're in the **Upper Sonoran zone,** characterized by scrub oak, piñon pine, juniper, manzanita, and sagebrush grasslands; this zone is often called the chaparral. The midlands of the state, at around 6,000 feet and higher, are marked by the **transition zone,** a scrubby land of short dry bushes stretching into the ponderosa pines. Above 8,500 feet or so, thick stands of evergreen conifers and white aspen are common. Above 9,500 feet or so, a height reached in Arizona primarily by climbing up towering mountains, the **subalpine zone** has tough Engelmann spruce and bristlecone pine, and above that it's all barren rocks and tundra.

Trees and Bushes

The official Arizona state tree is the paloverde, a green-skinned desert-dweller that can grow up to 25 feet high. The tree proliferates throughout the Lower Sonoran zone and is often a close neighbor to the saguaro, the baby buds of which use the paloverde's cover to hide and grow. Other common desert trees are the ubiquitous mesquite, which has often been used for firewood and building, and whose beans have nourished people and animals alike. Both the mesquite and the paloverde bloom yellow in the spring.

Ironwood trees, drought-resistant evergreens, grow along slopes and washes in the desert. Bushy plants crowd the desert as well: Creosote is everywhere, as is stickery, **catclaw,**

and **rabbitbrush,** all of which bloom yellow. Adding a little red to the bloom-time is the **ocotillo,** which is everywhere in the desert and resembles a sprouting group of pipe cleaners. Throughout the desert and into the chaparral of the transition zones you'll see several sword-cluster species of **agave,** an important plant to the human population in that it can be turned into mescal and tequila. The *agave parryi,* or **century plant,** blooms only once with a tall stalk of yellow flowers.

In the scrublands and chaparral and higher you'll see scrub oak, piñon pine, juniper, manzanita, and other brushy trees. In the high country, above 6,000 feet or so, you'll see ponderosa pine mainly. Higher still, in the mountain forests near the North Rim of the Grand Canyon, in the White Mountains and elsewhere, fir, spruce, and aspen forests dominate.

an agave plant

© TIM HULL

Along many waterways you'll see big cottonwoods and willows and sycamores.

Cacti

The most famous of Arizona's cacti, the **saguaro,** looks like it does because it is perfect: Every form has a function. Its green skin allows for photosynthesis, normally the job of leaves on less individualistic plants. Its spongy flesh and ribbed contours encourage water storage; the saguaro can collect and store up to 200 gallons of water from a single rainfall, which can get it through the year. Its telltale needles protect it from the incessant gnawing of hungry desert creatures. Its splashy white blossoms (seen in April, May, and June—the blossoms are Arizona's official state flower) and its juicy red fruits (eaten for eons by the desert's native inhabitants) assure the rising of another generation. The best place to commune with these perfectly adapted desert plants is Saguaro National Park near Tucson.

You'll see various species of cactus

The saguaro is the most famous of Arizona's cacti.

throughout the Lower and into the Upper Sonoran zones. Most cactus are easily recognizable if you know their names: **organ pipe, barrel, beaver tail, claret cup,** and **hedgehog** cactus generally look like their sobriquets suggest, albeit spiky and standoffish versions. The famous **prickly pear** cactus can be identified by its red fruit-blooms, which are turned into jellies and even margarita mix.

Wildflowers

In the early spring, especially after a rainy winter, the desert bajadas, the sloping flatland that stretches out from the desert mountain ranges, and valleys bloom with color as dormant wildflowers burst back to life. Various shades of photogenic whites, yellows, blues, reds, and purples contrast with the uniform rich green of the well-watered springtime desert to create a truly beautiful but ephemeral scenery. Some of the most common bloomers are the light-purple **Arizona lupine,** the deep yellow **Mexican gold poppy,** the dark pink **Parry's penstemon (or Parry's beardtongue),** and the virginal white **desert lily.** In summer the northland meadows and grasslands bloom with wild color as well. The best, most accessible places to see wildflowers in the spring are Picacho Peak State Park between Phoenix and Tucson and the Superstition Mountains east of Phoenix. You'll also see the desert in bloom in places like Saguaro National Park near Tucson and throughout the Santa Cruz Valley south of Tucson.

FAUNA
Mammals

Arizona's official state mammal is the **ringtail,** a relative of the raccoon often called a ringtailed cat or a miner's cat because of its rodent-eating proclivities. Its huge, bushy, white-and-black-ringed tail is its identifying feature, but it's not likely you'll see one unless you're nocturnal. The **mountain lion,** or cougar, is found, and hunted, throughout the state; smaller **bobcats** are often seen lounging near water features in Sonoran Desert backyards, and scrawny **coyotes** can be spotted quickly

a male Gambels quail

The **California condor** has been reintroduced into the wild around Grand Canyon country. Though not a native to the state, the jagged canyon country was deemed a perfect place to acclimate the threatened, prehistoric-looking bird into the wild.

Water birds, including the elegant **great blue heron,** hang around the state's riparian areas, and **wild turkeys** are somewhat common in oak and pine woodlands. One of the most common birds in the desert is the **Gambels quail,** which can often be seen crossing streets followed by a ragged line of tiny offspring. The **turkey vulture** is constantly soaring slowly in the ever-blue dryland sky. Various owl species are common in the woodlands and the deserts, and the **gila** and the **acorn woodpecker** are always tapping away at some tree or woodland home.

Southern Arizona is a mecca for bird enthusiasts, who stalk the region's sky island mountain ranges looking for rare subtropical birds like the **elegant trogon,** a green, red, white, and black bird related to the jungle-loving quetzal.

Fish

The **apache trout,** a gold-and-black native Arizona species, is the official state fish. Because of changes to the ecosystem and other factors, 28 of the state's 31 native fish are threatened, endangered, or as good as extinct. Still, in the mountain streams and lakes popular with anglers, you'll find rainbow and brown trout, bass, and others. In the lowland lakes there's bass, crappie, sunfish, catfish, and trout.

Reptiles

The desert is known as the home of the rattlesnake, seen more and more these days as the suburban attack on the desert continues. A few species of rattlesnake are found in Arizona. The **western diamondback,** which has lent its name to the state's world-champion professional baseball team, lives in the desert and the mountains and has deadly venom. Its skin is gray with brown diamond-shaped splotches along the back and a series of black-and-white bands just

crossing highways throughout the state. In the western deserts a few **bighorn sheep** still cling to the dry rocky cliffs.

A few different species of **jackrabbit** can be found all over, and **white-tailed deer** and **mule deer** live from the bottom of the Grand Canyon to the mountain heights and most places in between. **Pronghorn** live on the high grasslands in herds. The **collared peccary,** or **javelina** (which resembles a wild pig), is everywhere in the desert and the transition zone, so much so that they are generally considered pests. The **black bear** lives in the mountains throughout the state, and various species of **bats** come out in the Arizona night, responsible for pollinating and continuing the state's signature cactus forests.

Birds

The small, flitting **cactus wren,** which lives among the spiky plants, is the Arizona state bird, while the tall **roadrunner** may be its most recognizable. The **red-tailed hawk** proliferates in the desert sky, hunting rodents.

© JULIA NELSON/123RF.COM

a western diamondback

above its rattle. As with nearly all animals, the diamondback will leave you alone if you afford it the same courtesy. The light-brown **western rattlesnake** lives throughout the state, and the **Arizona ridge-nosed rattlesnake** lives in the woodlands of southeastern Arizona, a reddish-brown or gray hunter of rodents and lizards.

Several different species of **lizard** can be seen all over the lowlands, doing push-ups on hot rocks. The desert's most recognizable residents, these tiny leftover dinosaurs come in many shapes and sizes. One of the biggest is the fat and venomous **gila monster,** with its beady skin and languid looks. The monster can be seen sunning itself sometimes in and around Tucson. The only venomous lizard in the United States should be given a wide berth if encountered.

The slow and wise **desert tortoise** hides out from the desert sun in its burrow, and if it makes it past its soft-shell youth—when it's a favorite of predatory birds—it can live up to a hundred years or more. Frogs and toads in Arizona include the **Arizona tree frog,** a lime-green forest resident, and the **western spadefoot toad,** which lives in the desert in a burrow, a blotchy greenish brown with gray tints.

Insects and Arachnids

The **bark scorpion** is the crabby, pinching demon of the desert underworld; its venom is dangerous if it finds its way to the blood. The **grand western cicada** makes a racket in the woodlands on summer evenings. The hirsute **desert tarantula** looks much meaner than it is, cruising about in the early morning and early evening. You're bound to encounter gnats and mosquitoes and other tiny pests in desert riparian areas and around upland lakes.

History

PREHISTORIC CULTURES

Small bands of ice-age migrants were probably moving through North America as many as 20,000 years ago, but the pioneer Southwesterners are still widely considered to be the **Clovis** people (named for their spear points, first found in Clovis, New Mexico), who hunted big game in what is now Arizona about 10,000 to 16,000 years ago. Climate change and the overexploitation of the mammoths and great ground sloths of the Pleistocene ended this epoch by about 8,000 BC. From then until pottery-making cultures began to rise around the time of Jesus, the Archaic-era hunter-gatherers made a long, successful go of it here, moving between the forested highlands and the deserts seasonally to hunt and gather wild foods. By the late Archaic period these bands were living in semipermanent camps in pit houses and were growing corn likely introduced by migrants from Mesoamerica.

The first millennium AD saw the rise of several sophisticated and mostly sedentary cultures in Arizona, the most successful of which were the **Anasazi** on the Colorado Plateau, the **Sinagua** in the Verde Valley and volcanolands around Flagstaff, the **Mogollon** in eastern Arizona and New Mexico, the **Salado** in the region around the Little Colorado River, and the **Hohokam** in the river valleys of the Sonoran Desert. These cultures would rise and fall in stages, with rises generally coinciding with wet times and falls subsequent to droughts.

By AD 700 or so the Anasazi were building above-ground, rock-and-mud urbanlike villages that would become known as pueblos, from the Spanish for town or city. The Anasazi culture would briefly rise to become something of an empire in the plateau country, with New Mexico's Chaco Canyon as its ruling capital.

A separate culture, but one related in many ways to the Anasazi, flourished in the Flagstaff and Verde Valley regions from around AD 500 to 1425. Called the Sinagua, which means

"without water" in Spanish, the group mostly lived around Sunset Crater near Flagstaff until AD 700, when several bands migrated below the Mogollon Rim to live along the Verde River and among the red rocks of Sedona. The Sinagua built impressive cliff dwellings and huge sandstone apartment-style pueblos that can still be seen and visited today. The Sinagua culture survived the eruption of Sunset Crater in 1064 and thrived as part of an important regional trade route for centuries.

Known for their elegant black-and-white Mimbres pottery, the Mogollon people lived in scattered villages in the pine forests of west-central New Mexico and east-central Arizona from around AD 150 to about 1400, when they are thought to have been absorbed into the Anasazi regime. The Salado people lived in the Tonto Basin northeast of Phoenix from about AD 1150 to the 1400s. One of their cliff dwellings above the Salt River can still be seen today at Tonto National Monument. On the low deserts, the Hohokam constructed a network of irrigation canals in the river valleys around what are now Phoenix and Tucson, and lived in complex, hierarchical agricultural societies that built adobe great houses and ceremonial ball courts.

Around AD 1150 many of the dramatic cliff dwellings, built by various cultures and scattered from the desert to the pines to the rocky lands of the Colorado Plateau, began to appear throughout the Southwest. These cultures had mostly run their course by AD 1450 due to a variety of factors—ecological, climatic, and social. For generations the monuments and ruins they left behind have fascinated scientists and tourists alike.

Sometime in the 1400s or before, the Athapaskan culture migrated south to the area from the far north in Canada; these tribes would later become those known as the **Apache** and the **Navajo.** These tribes were not related to any of the cultures living in the region at

petroglyphs at the Palatki ruins, near Sedona

© JOE MORELLI/123RF.COM

the time they arrived. The Apache eventually moved to southeastern Arizona, where they would have an epochal battle for supremacy with the U.S. Army in the late 19th century, while the Navajo stayed in the Colorado Plateau area and learned about dry-land farming from their Puebloan neighbors, while also spending a good amount of time raiding those same neighbors. They would eventually be nearly killed off by the U.S. Army under the direction of Kit Carson. After a long and brutal internment outside of their harsh but beloved Four Corners lands, the Navajo signed a treaty with the United States in 1868 that allowed them to return to the plateau country, where they remain today and have grown to become North America's largest tribe. The **Hopi,** who live on a small reservation on three mesas in the middle of the Navajo Nation, are the descendants of the Anasazi who lived in the region's dramatic cliff dwellings and pueblos. They were never forced off the land that they consider to be their homeland—the same harsh and seemingly inhospitable mesas they still live

on today—but they were subject, as were the Navajo and Apache, to periodic attempts by the federal government to "Americanize" them by sending their children to government-run schools off the reservation, forcing them into a cash and labor economy very different from their subsistence lifestyle, and converting them to Christianity. A large number of Navajo today are Christians, and there are churches throughout the reservation. Many Hopi have held on to their native religious beliefs and seem to live in a separate, more ancient time.

THE EUROPEANS ARRIVE

The impenetrable northern reaches of the Spanish Empire in Mexico were essentially unexplored by Europeans when **Alvar Nuñez Cabeza de Vaca** found himself shipwrecked and lost in the grasslands and deserts of what is now the southwestern United States and northern Mexico in the 1520s. And though he and his companions—one of them, Estevan, was a Moorish slave or indentured servant—probably never made it to Arizona proper, the tales they told of their adventures when they finally returned to Mexico City inspired subsequent explorations in the great north. In 1539 Fray Marcos de Niza and Estevan trekked north to discover the Seven Cities of Cibola, rumors of which Estevan and Cabeza de Vaca had heard during their ordeal. Estevan scouted ahead and was killed by the Zuni, who lived not in golden cities but in regular old mesa-top pueblos not too different from those that still exist on the Hopi reservation in Arizona and in the Rio Grande Valley of New Mexico. Nevertheless, de Niza's report suggested that the golden cities may indeed be a reality, and that was enough to inspire an ambitious expedition in 1540 led by **Francisco Vasquez de Coronado** in search of the reported riches. Coronado found none, but his expedition moved through what is now eastern Arizona. In the 1690s **Father Eusebio Francisco Kino** began his journeys into southern Arizona and Sonora, bringing cattle to the region for the first time and establishing several long-lasting missions, including San Xavier del Bac near Tucson, to this day still celebrating mass in its dark, cool interior. By the 1750s the Spanish crown had established a presidio or fort at Tubac, which was moved to the Santa Cruz Valley near Tucson in 1775. Southern Arizona comprised the northern reaches of the Spanish New-World empire, though it was sparsely populated and was a violent, dangerous place to live. Spanish cattle ranchers and other hardy settlers fought Apaches and others for the right to live in the region, but for decades the north would remain too isolated and too dangerous to grow much. The Mexicans won their independence from Spain in 1821 and so took over administration of the vast northlands. The wilderness was exploited somewhat for its resources, used for cattle ranching and placer mining by tough Mexican explorers, but mostly it was too far from the center of power and was too dangerous to be of much worth to the new nation.

In the later 1820s trappers, hunters, and mountain men like James Ohio Pattie, Antoine Leroux, and Pauline Weaver became some of the first Anglo Americans to venture through Arizona, in search of beaver pelts. Such men would in turn guide the **Army of the West** and the Mormon Battalion through the state in 1846 and 1847 during the Mexican-American War, which was fought primarily in Mexico. After the war ended in 1848, much of what is now the Southwest became U.S. property, and in 1850 a huge area that included Arizona and New Mexico became the New Mexico Territory. In 1854 the land between the Gila River and the Mexican border—southern Arizona, basically—was added to the territory through the **Gadsden Purchase.**

In 1849 and for several years afterward, thousands of Americans passed through Arizona headed for gold and glory in California. Those hard-rock, hard-luck miners would return east to the state a few years later in search of the gold and silver most of them had failed to find on the coast. Several boundary, land, railroad, and scientific surveys of Arizona and the West during the 1850s brought this far corner of the continent greater attention and interest from the East.

TERRITORIAL YEARS

It was the increasing mining activity in the state that, among other factors, led President Lincoln to establish the Arizona Territory in 1863, disconnecting it from the huge conglomerate of land called New Mexico. The capital was established at Prescott, in the state's mineral-laden midlands, and the East's economic exploitation of the land, albeit on a much smaller scale than it would become, commenced. During the Civil War, Tucson was a confederate hotbed for a time before being occupied by the U.S. Army. After the Civil War ended, immigration and exploration of the Southwest picked up considerably. Still, when **John Wesley Powell** completed the first river run through the Grand Canyon in 1869, the population of the territory was less than 10,000 persons.

Settlers trickled in over the coming years, spurred here to find treasure, to cure their tuberculosis, and for adventure, science, and cheap land made available by the federal Homestead and Desert Land Acts. Despite this, the territory remained a wild and dangerous place for most. The Apache, Navajo, and other tribes didn't feel they should have to give up the land they had conquered to white settlers, many of whom were looking to get rich quick exploiting the land and then leave. From 1871 until **Geronimo**'s final surrender in 1886, the U.S. Army fought a brutal war with the Apache and other tribes. The Apache were eventually defeated at a high cost to both parties, and some bands were sent to Oklahoma, where they became prisoners of war for many years. They struggled to hold to their traditional ways and remain a strong culture, but privation and the machinations of a government that did not understand them took their toll. Eventually the Apaches were allowed to return to Arizona to reservations that include parts of their traditional homelands, and today they operate successful casinos and resorts.

With the end of the Apache wars the territory moved one step closer to large-scale settlement and development. In the 1880s the railroad arrived and transformed the region, bringing in more people and materials than ever before. By 1889 the Phoenix area had already begun to dominate the territory, and with the construction of Roosevelt Dam on the Salt River in 1911, the valley's agricultural boom was just on the horizon. In 1912, Arizona entered the union as the 48th state.

STATEHOOD AND BEYOND

The first half of the 20th century in Arizona was dominated by the era of reclamation. The federal government used taxpayer money to develop the state's water resources, damming rivers for irrigation, water storage, and hydroelectric power, creating a huge agricultural industry in the process. Phelps Dodge and other mining giants ripped huge holes in the land to extract low-grade copper, while Anglo owners and managers on the whole treated the Mexican and Native American miners and

Arizona entered the union in 1912.

© KAVRAM/123RF.COM

those who worked in the agricultural industry as seasonal laborers—without whom Arizona agriculture would not have been possible—poorly, even criminally on many occasions.

At the same time, more residents and visitors began to realize that there was more to the fantastic Arizona landscape than profit and loss, and this era saw the rise of national parks and monuments, national forests, and state-level protection of important lands. Beginning around the 1920s, boosters in Phoenix and Tucson and elsewhere began to see the economic benefits of attracting tourists to the sunny state, and by 1950 or so tourism had replaced the extractive industries in importance. During the two world wars the federal government set up training bases and military installations in the state that led to a growth spurt, and the advent of swamp coolers and air conditioners stimulated a population boom in Arizona that has yet to really let up.

Economy and Government

ECONOMY

Arizona's economy for much of the past was ruled by the boom-and-bust realities of the extractive and agricultural industries. Worldwide prices, the fickleness of the market, and the constant threat of a destructive act of nature made economic life here before World War II a wild ride. Booms in the cattle industry in the 1890s and cotton before and during World War I created large industries in the state virtually overnight. The overgrazing of an arid-land open range and monocultural agriculture took their individual tolls, and both of these members of the state's well-known "Five C" economy actually influenced life here on a major scale for a relatively short time. The other of the Five C's (sometimes four)—copper, cotton, cattle, citrus, and climate—have fared better than cotton and cattle, both of which are now very minor elements of the state's economy. Copper mining, the state's claim to fame in economic circles for several generations, was nearly moribund until the mid-2000s, when worldwide prices hit record levels (thanks, in large part, to a global building boom centered in China, and the ubiquity of copper in consumer electronic products and other modern necessities). Previously mothballed pits have opened again, and startup firms from outside the state are searching the desert for new pit sites. This may be just a blip on the overall economic radar screen, however. The extractive and agricultural industries are no longer the primary economic engines of Arizona and the western states and haven't been for some time. According to a recent report by the Tucson-based Sonoran Institute, fewer than 5 percent of the West's counties have more than 20 percent of employment in traditional extractive industries, and agriculture and ranching made up just 4 percent of total employment in the West as of 2000.

A boom in single-family housing and urban and suburban development has enraptured the state for several decades, though as of this writing that boom has predictably gone bust. Still, despite its boom-and-bust ways, the state has often been somewhat impervious to national economic slowdowns, primarily because of its always-steady growth. Growth fuels itself, and an economy that is growing is always perceived to be healthy. Between 2000 and 2006, Arizona's population grew by about 20 percent. The deep truth of the Arizona economy, and one that holds for the entire West, is that the service industry (much of it tourism related), with its low wages and transient workers, is the hottest-running economic engine here and has been for many years. All over the West, non-labor income like investments, disability, and retirement payments come in a close second to the service industry as a top economic driver.

The median household income in Arizona is about $44,000 with 2.6 people per household. Some 15 percent of Arizonans live below the poverty line.

GOVERNMENT

Arizona's government has had a contrary relationship with the federal establishment since before statehood. The state's entrance into the union was delayed for some time because the legislature, backed by a majority of the public, refused to give up a section of its constitution that allowed for the popular recall of judges. Today the bickering between the two continues over public land issues and border control. The truth is that the federal government made Arizona, and it still controls a good portion of the land in the state. With history as an example, it's easy to see that had the federal government not protected huge portions of the state as national forests, monuments, parks, and wilderness areas, outside (mostly eastern) economic interests would have used that land for their own profit, as they have the majority of Arizona's natural resources since long before statehood.

Tucson's Homegrown Movie Industry

It may have been the myth of what the West was supposed to be that kept Arizona from becoming the western seat of the film industry instead of just a poor relation, if one is to take for truth a story often related, with minor variations, in most histories about the western march of the movie business.

It is an apocryphal-sounding story about fate's privilege, a story that Bob Shelton, former owner of Old Tucson Studios, told me several years ago over lunch.

In 1914, he said, the legendary producer Adolph Zukor sent Cecil B. DeMille and Samuel Goldwyn to Flagstaff, in northern Arizona. Zuker had the year before bought the rights to *The Squawman*, a Broadway play with a typical Western theme. DeMille and Goldwyn, looking for alkaline flats and purple sage, stepped off the train into snow, finding themselves surrounded not by mesas and cacti but by white-capped mountains and near-alpine vistas. "I thought Arizona was a desert," one might have said to the other.

If they had traveled a day or so south to Tucson—then the principal urban area in the young state—they would have found exactly what they were looking for, and the climate and the variation might have persuaded them to set up shop, or so the speculation goes. But they didn't go south and they didn't stay in Flagstaff; instead, they headed farther west and stopped when they ran out of land. They rented a barn and made the first full-length Western. Thus Hollywood was born, and Arizona passed over as a candidate for the western seat of a fledgling industry that would irrevocably transform the world.

That's not to say that the movie industry didn't come to southern Arizona; it did, and to a certain extent it still does. There were a few films produced here in the early days, and a few studios set up offices, including those of the Al Jennings Production Company, which had an office here in 1918. Jennings was a former outlaw whose ambition was to release the Western

bandit from the romantic sentimentality that dominated much of the media coverage of that famous, and to a large extent made-up, Western lifestyle. Such exceptions aside, however, after Hollywood was established not much happened here until Columbia Pictures came in 1939 and built **Old Tucson,** a purported replica of Tucson circa 1860. Columbia came to film an outdoor epic aptly titled *Arizona,* starring William Holden and Jean Arthur. Other productions trickled in, bringing with them a host of myth-making stars to a region that was already falling back on hackneyed stories of cowboys and Indians, outlaws and gunfighters, saloon girls and freedom, in its search for a national identity.

For a while Old Tucson fell into disrepair and near obscurity; then, in 1959, Shelton bought the land and put some money into the moldering complex. He opened for business in 1960. In Shelton, Tucson found its most active impresario. Shelton is credited today by many in the industry for single-handedly making Tucson, for a time, a major film location. When Tucson's film industry was at its peak, between the 1960s and the early 1990s, the community was doing $20 million in film business per year, according to Shelton.

"It grew very substantially to the point where, at the peak of our prosperity, we could field three full film crews out of Tucson, and that was attractive to the industry," Shelton told me. "There was a time when I had John Wayne, Clint Eastwood, Lee Marvin, and Burt Lancaster all working on films at Old Tucson at the same time."

Dubbed the "Hollywood of the Desert," Tucson at its peak was third only to Hollywood and New York in film production. Though not much of what was made here will be remembered, most of it forgettable Westerns, TV episodes, and commercials, there were dozens of good, and even a few great, movies made in Tucson during the heyday, including *Hombre, Duel in the Sun, El Dorado,* and *Gunfight at the O.K. Corral.*

the Arizona capitol building in Phoenix

The state's government for most of its history has been interested, like nearly everybody else, in developing and taking from the land, and the various land-hungry interests who at one time or another were in favor—be they mining, agricultural, ranching, or military—have dictated policy. This is not as true today as it has been in the past, however.

While Arizona is known today as a staunchly "red" state, that has not always been the case and it likely won't be for much longer.

Progressive Democrats ruled the state for a few generations until **Barry Goldwater** and the conservative revolution found success here and on the national stage in the 1960s. Since then the state has been a Republican stronghold, and a conservative one at that. There are a few "blue" enclaves, notably Tucson and the Navajo Nation. However, the state's demographics seem to be changing, and the voter rolls are swelling not with Republicans and Democrats, but with Independents.

People and Culture

Most Arizona residents are émigrés to the state, and most have lived here a relatively short time. The majority of the state's 6.1 million residents live in Pima and Maricopa Counties, in and around the two large urban areas of Tucson and Phoenix. About a million persons live in Pima County and some 3.7 million live in Maricopa. About 13 percent of Arizonans are over 65, but 26 percent are under 18. The former statistic is expected to rise significantly as more and more baby boomers retire and move to the sunbelt, just as their parents did in the 1960s and 1970s. On par with nationwide averages, about 81 percent of Arizonans are high school graduates, and 24 percent have at least a bachelor's degree. A full 68 percent of Arizonans own their homes.

While the majority of Arizonans are still in most corners of the West referred to as Anglos, and the state was largely founded and developed by Anglos—much more so than was its neighbor New Mexico—people of Latino origin have a significant influence on the economy and culture here, especially in Southern Arizona and in both large urban areas. According to the U.S. Census Bureau, 29 percent of Arizonans are of Hispanic or Latino origin, compared to 15 percent nationwide. The influence of Latino culture, especially that of Mexico, can be seen throughout the state. Much of the finest art, music, and food to be found in Arizona has its origins in Mexico, to which the entire land area of the state used to belong, not too long ago.

Native Americans make up about 5 percent of the population; the largest tribe, the Navajo Nation, has some 298,000 members. Other tribes include the O'odham people, formerly called the Papago and Pima. The **Tohono O'odham** (the Desert People) live on a large reservation southwest of Tucson and operate casinos near the city. In the Phoenix area, the **Akimel O'odham** (the River People), or the Gila River Indian Community, live on a reservation and operate casinos as well. Other tribes in the state include the Hopi, the Yavapai near Prescott, the Western Apache bands, and the Colorado River tribes of western Arizona.

Unlike many of the other Native American nations on the continent, Arizona's tribes are still living today on what they consider their ancestral homelands, albeit smaller portions of that homeland set aside by the federal government under the reservation system. And while poverty is generally the rule on these reservations, Arizona's Native Americans have made important contributions to the artistic, cultural, political, and economic life of the state. The finest artists to come out of Arizona are Native American, and many are known the world over for their arts and crafts based on traditional designs and patterns but adapted and evolved to speak to a contemporary world.

Most of the state's Native American tribes have compacts allowing them to operate casinos, and those casinos are popular and profitable; still, many Arizona Native Americans live below the poverty line, even though access to education, health care, and jobs has increased somewhat over the years.

RELIGION

Religious life in Arizona is diverse and complex. **Catholicism** is popular among Latino residents and with many Anglos as well, while the **Church of Jesus Christ of Latter-day Saints,** or the Mormons, has been established in some rural areas of the state since the 19th century.

A 2008 Pew Forum survey found that 25 percent of Arizonans identified as Catholics, and 23 percent identified as Evangelical Protestants. Mainline Protestants make up about 15 percent of the religious population, and LDS adherents are about 4 percent. A surprising 22 percent see themselves as "unaffiliated." Members of historically Black Protestant churches make up 3 percent of the population,

Arizona's Native American Arts and Crafts

There are hundreds of Native American artists living in Arizona. The majority are Hopi and Navajo, and they live on reservations in the far northeastern corner of the state. Many Indian artists sell their work at markets and fairs held throughout the year in Phoenix, Tucson, Flagstaff, and elsewhere. Silverwork, carvings, pottery, rugs, and paintings of the Hopi, Navajo, and others have been highly desired since territorial days.

Because it's made by Native Americans, many people approach this art with a lot of preconceived notions; especially prevalent are notions about authenticity and tradition. Some people expect every Indian artist and artisan to be adhering to some ancient set of guidelines set down before real time began, a method that washes each squash-blossom necklace and kachina doll carving with some undeniable spiritual patina. Like most artistic movements, however, the provenance of the Southwestern Indian Arts and Crafts tradition is far more complex.

Think of these artists as working within similar confines as did painters and sculptors of the Western European tradition before and during the Renaissance. Such artists were bound more often than not to paint and sculpt imagery from the Bible or Greek and Roman mythology, and they could count on their public immediately recognizing the scenes and characters they depicted. However, within this rather narrow tradition, there existed astonishing variety.

Consider, as an example, the story of how silverwork was introduced to the Navajo. In the 1850s, Navajo ironworker Atsidi Sani (Old Smith) added silver to the old Navajo tradition of making jewelry out of shell and stone. The Hopi and Zuni later learned from the Navajo. The oral tradition says the Southwest's Indians were taught metal work in general by the Europeans; Atsidi Sani is said to have learned silversmithing from a smith called Nakai Tsosi or "Thin Mexican." More and more Navajo learned the art during the tribe's tragic imprisonment at Fort Sumner at Bosque Redondo, and the Navajo are said to have taught their Pueblo neighbors, mostly the Hopi and the Zuni, to work silver.

The silver in the early days and for a long time after mostly came from Mexican and U.S. coins. Reservation traders like John Lorenzo Hubbell, at Ganado, paid the Navajo to teach it to each other, then sold the products to tourists. Some of the best silversmiths gave up raising livestock and farming and were able to become full-time artisans, a pattern that still plays out today.

It was during the golden age of Southwestern tourism that the authenticity of Indian jewelry became an issue. The artists were, of course, encouraged to create work specifically for tourists, who flocked to the reservations and pueblos on the Fred Harvey Indian Detours. Writer and trader Mark Bahti writes that these pieces were often lightweight, with "horses, tipis, arrows, thunderbirds . . . designed to fit the tourist notion of what Indian jewelry was *supposed* to look like." But, as Bahti points out, what was Indian jewelry actually "supposed" to look like? Nobody could really say, and they still can't. By the 1920s, manufactured copies were being made outside the Southwest and then shipped in to be sold as authentic, spurring the artists to join together in co-ops and guilds, many of which are still in operation and are still training new artists.

The 1970s brought about a boom in the market for Pueblo and Navajo jewelry, and today there is a really diffuse sense of what is traditional and what is innovative. Innovation—the artist responding not only to tradition but to the world around him or her—can be seen everywhere at Indian markets throughout Arizona.

Catholicism is practiced by 25 percent of Arizona's residents. Pictured is an image of the Virgin of Guadalupe at San Xavier.

2 percent are Jewish, and 1 percent is Buddhist. Jehovah's Witnesses also make up 1 percent of the population.

LANGUAGE

The majority of Arizonans speak English, though some 26 percent of residents speak a language other than English at home (likely Spanish), according to the U.S. Census Bureau. From time to time over the years there have been calls for and votes on making English the official language of the state, usually attending some new round of anger and fear over illegal immigration, which, owing more than anything else to Arizona's proximity to Mexico, is an ever-present political issue. The reality is that Spanish is used throughout the state and especially in the urban areas. You'll see and hear it everywhere. You may also hear several Native American languages as you travel around the state, including the intricate Hopi language and the Navajo tongue, which was used by the famous code talkers of World War II—one of the only "codes" never to be broken.

THE ARTS

Most of the prominent non-Native American artists and writers associated with Arizona were émigrés. **Edward Abbey,** author of the *Monkey Wrench Gang* and many other books, continues, nearly two decades after his death, to influence writing and environmental politics in the state. A friend of Abbey's, Doug Peacock (Hayduke from Abbey's novel) has written an excellent war memoir, *Walking It Off,* and several books about grizzly bears. Another Abbey friend, Tucsonan **Charles Bowden,** has a national reputation as a nonfiction writer and has produced some of the best books ever about the disaffection and dark ironies of sunbelt culture. Tucson resident **Leslie Marmon Silko** wrote the closest thing we yet have to an Arizona epic: her *Almanac of the Dead* examines the ancient and contemporary Southwest and the confluence of the two. The prolific **Zane Grey,** one of the progenitors of the Western genre, spent a lot of time in Arizona's Rim Country and based many of his books in the state.

The German painter **Max Ernst** came to Arizona in 1946, settling in Sedona and painting the state's surrealistic landscapes in the manner it deserved. His work is on display at the **Phoenix Art Museum.** There are hundreds of painters and sculptors living and working in Arizona today. Many of them congregate in Sedona, Tucson, Tubac, Bisbee, and Jerome. Each of these towns and cities has many galleries dedicated to individual artists, styles, and groups. The famed **Cowboy Artists of America** group was founded in Sedona in 1965, and the aesthetic traditions of the group are still highly visible in the state's galleries and museums.

Arizona has produced a few pop stars, most notably **Linda Ronstadt,** whose family has deep roots in Tucson. **Alice Cooper** grew up in the Valley of the Sun and still resides there, operating a popular downtown rock-and-jock-themed restaurant and bar. The Tempe music scene had a minor worldwide reputation in the 1990s thanks to bands like the **Gin Blossoms** and the **Refreshments.** Singer **Stevie Nicks** is from the Phoenix area, as is **Wayne Newton.**

Thanks to its desert scenery and always-clear skies, Arizona has had a vibrant movie-making scene on and off since the silent era. Classic films like *Arizona, Stagecoach,* and *Oklahoma* were filmed in the state, along with *The Planet of the Apes, The Three Amigos,* and hundreds of others. The fortunes of Arizona's film industry tend to rise and fall with the popularity of the Western.

ESSENTIALS

Getting There and Around

BY AIR

If you're flying into Arizona, you'll likely find yourself at **Phoenix Sky Harbor International Airport** (3400 E. Sky Harbor Blvd., 602/273-3300, www.phoenix.gov/skyharborairport). One of the Southwest's largest airports, Sky Harbor has three terminals served by many domestic and international airlines. The airport is just three miles east of downtown Phoenix and easy to find. There's a free shuttle system that will take you between terminals.

The only other serious choice is **Tucson International Airport** (520/573-8000, www.tucsonairport.org), which hosts a few airlines and offers daily flights to both coasts and other destinations. If you book a flight to Tucson it may be slightly more expensive than flying into Sky Harbor in Phoenix, and you probably won't get a direct flight; in many cases, you'll have to fly into Sky Harbor, switch planes, and then fly south to Tucson—just a 1.5-hour drive on I-10. If you're renting a car anyway, it's probably a better idea to fly into Phoenix and then drive from there, unless you are just going to Tucson and Southern Arizona; then a direct flight into TIA makes more sense.

Flagstaff, Prescott, Tusayan near the Grand Canyon, Yuma, and other towns have airports,

© TIM HULL

though they are small and offer mostly regional routes. There are also several smaller regional airports around the Valley of the Sun, offering regional flights to Southwestern and West Coast ports. If you're coming from the West Coast or some other Southwestern city, you might look into regional flights to your Arizona destination; otherwise, Sky Harbor and then a rental car is your best bet no matter where you're headed in Arizona.

BY TRAIN

Amtrak's Southwest Chief Route, which mirrors the old Santa Fe Railway's Super Chief Route of the grand Fred Harvey days, stops twice daily (one eastbound, one westbound) at Flagstaff's classic **downtown depot** (1 E. Route 66, 800/872-7245, www.amtrak.com), the former Santa Fe headquarters and also the town's visitors center (800/842-7293). The route crosses the country from Chicago to L.A., dipping into the Southwest through northern New Mexico and northern Arizona. There are long-term plans for a high-speed railway between Phoenix and Tucson, and possibly to other parts of the state, though likely such a useful project is a generation or more away from being realized. The Southwest, while built and populated largely by the railroads, continues to hold strong to the car culture, and that isn't going to change anytime soon.

BY CAR

You need a personal vehicle to get around in Arizona. A significant part of the fun of a visit to the great Southwest is the road trip, and there's just too much scenery and too many spur-of-the-moment stops to go any other way. Ideally, for everyone involved, we'd all ride our bikes across the state. We'd see everything up close and slow, the air would be clean, and we'd all be in great shape and great friends. It's feasible to do such a thing, for there are innumerable back roads throughout the state that allow one to quit the Interstate slipstream; from time to time you'll see a weighted-down group of riders pulling trailers and looking dead-eyed along one of the two-lanes through the desert,

but one suspects the elevation challenges in this hump-backed land would be too great for most us. It's a good idea to reserve a rental car before you travel. But don't rent it at the Phoenix Sky Harbor Airport; the airport charges exorbitant taxes and fees that make a short taxi ride to an off-airport rental place well worth it.

If you'd like to carry your home along with you on the Arizona road, or you desire to relive a favorite sitcom moment or two, look into renting an RV. All over the state these days you'll see rented RVs touring the monuments and landscapes of the West, packed with families and groups of friends. In Phoenix, check out **RV Rental Outlet** (2126 W. Main St., Mesa, 480/461-0023, 480/461-0025, or 888/461-0023, www.rvrentaloutlet.com).

From Los Angeles: The major road routes into and through the state are I-10, I-40, and I-8. I-10 is the best and really the only practical way to get from Los Angeles to Phoenix and Tucson, a distance of 373 miles (5 hours) and 488 miles (7 hours), respectively. To reach Flagstaff and the Grand Canyon from Los Angeles, take I-40, a distance of 486 miles (7 hours), with another 78 miles (1.5 hours) to the Grand Canyon. I-40 also passes by Williams, another gateway to the Grand Canyon. L.A. is 431 miles (6 hours) from Williams, all of it along the interstate, and it's another 60 miles (1 hour) to the South Rim from there.

From Las Vegas: The main route from Las Vegas to Flagstaff, Williams, and the Grand Canyon runs along Highway 93 to I-40. The popular South Rim section of Grand Canyon National Park is 277 miles from Las Vegas (it's 4 hours from Las Vegas to Flagstaff, and then another 1.5 hours to the Grand Canyon).

The drive across the rocky, jagged desert from Las Vegas to Phoenix is 300 miles (about 5 hours). Most of the drive, save for a short jog on I-40 near Kingman, is on U.S. 93, a scenic desert highway that moves through some of the most ruggedly beautiful outbacks in the Southwest and crosses the Colorado River near Hoover Dam.

From Phoenix: To reach Arizona's northland (which includes Flagstaff, the Grand Canyon,

Prescott, the Mogollon Rim, and Sedona) from Phoenix, take I-17 out of the valley. I-17 goes all the way to Flagstaff where it hooks into I-40, a distance of about 150 miles (2 hours).

BY BUS

Greyhound (www.greyhound.com) provides bus service between major towns, mostly along the Interstate routes. This isn't a very efficient way to travel around Arizona, but you could do it. Check out the website for schedules and station locations.

BY BIKE

The two most bike-friendly towns in Arizona are Tucson, in the southern, desert portion of the state, and Flagstaff, in the cool mountainous pine forest. Both have more or less completed hundreds of miles of bike paths and bike lanes, making it possible to live in both places with just a bike for transportation. However, for about three months out of the year it is either too hot in Tucson or too cold in Flagstaff to ride much. Both Flagstaff and Tucson have large and active biking communities that consistently push for more trails and lanes.

Grand Canyon National Park's South Rim has become increasingly bike-friendly in recent years. You can take your own bike or rent one inside the park. Biking is actually an ideal way to see the park—much better than driving to each of the lookouts and having to park and get out of the car, and it's faster than walking. It's mostly a summertime activity, however, considering the park's relatively high elevation; come early November, you'll likely find it too cold to enjoy the ride.

TOURS

If you're looking for the knowledgeable assistance of an expert, you can hire **Open Road Tours** (602/997-6474, www.openroadtours. com) to guide and shuttle you in comfort all over the state. Such tours are only recommended for those who enjoy groups. Arizona's tourist track is well established and easy to negotiate, and a tour guide is not necessary. Most of the best sights are controlled by the federal government, specifically the National Park Service, and rangers are always on hand to answer questions and give free, informative tours.

Accommodations and Food

ACCOMMODATIONS

Arizona is known around the world for the high-luxury resort accommodations offered in Tucson, Phoenix, Scottsdale, Sedona, and elsewhere. The best of these spa resorts appear to require their own zip code and guidebook, and the rich and pampered people who frequent them can spend weeks in Arizona without venturing beyond the gates. The best of these all-inclusive, posh spa-resorts in Phoenix, Scottsdale, Tucson, and Sedona are listed in the chapters for those cities.

The state is also fortunate to have a number of historic hotels still in operation, though updated and remodeled; and there are also not a few boutique hotels and bed-and-breakfasts operating out of historic buildings that used to serve some important territorial function. In the old mining town of Jerome in North-Central Arizona, the **Jerome Grand Hotel** used to be the once-thriving boomtown's hospital. Another old mining town, Bisbee, in Southern Arizona, has a B&B operating out of a former schoolhouse. Of course, the most distinctive accommodations in both towns are widely thought to be haunted. There are several elegant hotels from the 1920s and 1930s still operating, though with new-century comforts and conveniences, including the **Hassayampa Inn** in downtown Prescott and **La Posada** in Winslow.

Bed-and-breakfast inns proliferate throughout Arizona, and nearly every region has several. Many of the best B&Bs can be contacted through the **Arizona Association of Bed and**

Clothing Optional Accommodations

There's something about the powerful Arizona sun, especially when it shines hard on the desert country, that makes one want to wear as few clothes as possible. While this usually isn't recommended, what with society's conventions and the danger of overexposure to the dastardly rays, those who enjoy the popular world of "naturism" will want to check out one of the clothing-optional resorts in the desert just north of Phoenix. **Shangri La Ranch** (44444 N. Shangri La Rd., New River, 623/465-5959, www.shangrilaranch.com, office hours 10am-5pm daily, $32 per couple daily fee, $70-105 for a room, $10 per

night camping, $15 for RV hookup) is a family-oriented nudist resort with rooms, camping, and an RV park. It offers numerous activities, a huge swimming pool, and a friendly staff. Although no bathing suits are allowed in the pool, the philosophy of Shangri La seems to be live and let live, so you can "ease into" the nudist lifestyle if you're not already a committed naturist. The setting is gorgeous, way out in the scrubby desert about 45 minutes north of Sky Harbor Airport off I-17 near New River. This is most definitely a family place, so they expect you to be respectful and adhere to the rules of conduct.

Breakfast Inns (www.arizona-bed-breakfast.com).

If you're just looking for a place to flop between adventures, there is an abundance of chain hotels in every major city and town, and in small towns near national parks and monuments and off the interstates.

FOOD

The local-food revolution has not missed Arizona; throughout the state you'll find numerous restaurants dedicated to using local and all-natural ingredients, harking back to a simpler time when we knew a bit more about our food. In the old mining towns of Bisbee in Southern Arizona and Jerome in Northern Arizona, you'll find a few high-style restaurants serving an eclectic blend of Southwestern and haute cuisine. In Scottsdale, Phoenix, and throughout the Valley of the Sun, your head will spin from all the options, most of them highly creative and dedicated to a fusion of the native and the new. On the high grassland plains in Winslow, just south of the Navajo Nation, you'll find one of the best restaurants in the Southwest, **The Turquoise Room,** inside the refurbished and beautiful **La Posada** hotel, a restaurant that reaches back to the past of the Fred Harvey Company, when elegant

accommodations and fine dining on locally grown and prepared food were the norm, even in the outback—which Winslow in many ways still is today. On the very edge of the Grand Canyon you'll find surprisingly creative and delicious cuisine at the beautiful **El Tovar** restaurant in Grand Canyon Village. Head to either the Navajo or Hopi Reservation nearby, and you can sample the native cuisine, centered mainly around mutton and corn and a kind of Mexican-Native American amalgam called the Navajo (or Hopi) taco—a delicious hunk of fry bread piled high with meat and beans.

Mexican Food

Because so many Arizona residents are from somewhere else, you'll find all the world cuisines well represented in even the most seemingly out-of-the-way places; however, one style reigns supreme: Mexican food. The cuisine of Mexico is very popular throughout the United States these days, and travelers to Arizona and the border region are likely to have at least a passing knowledge of the favorites. However, in Southern Arizona, the Valley of the Sun, and most of the other parts of the state, you'll experience a higher quality and more authentic dining experience than you can find at the big national chains. Tucson and Nogales (especially if you cross "the line" and try one of the restaurants in the tourist section of Nogales, Sonora, Mexico) are the best places in the state to eat Mexican food. In Tucson you'll find dozens of restaurants featuring a variety of regional Mexican foods, but the most prevalent is the style of northern Mexico, "El Norte"—after all, it wasn't that long ago that this region was not the extreme south of the United States, but rather the extreme north of Mexico.

A ranching frontier, northern Mexico—specifically the states of Sonora and Chihuahua—have a cuisine based on beef, beans, cheese, and chilies—the comfort food of Mexico. You are more likely to find flour tortillas in northern Mexico than in the central and southern regions, as the desert and semidesert land is harder on corn than on wheat. A popular ranchland delicacy is machaca, also called carne seca—dried, shredded beef that is available at nearly every restaurant as a filling for burritos and tacos or on its own. Many Tucson restaurants are famous for their carne asada, or grilled meat—thin strips of beef spiced and grilled and then stuffed in tacos or burritos or served on its own with rice and beans. Another popular northern dish is menudo, available at many Tucson and Phoenix-area taco stands and restaurants. It's a kind of soup made with tripe and hominy and cow's foot and is said to cure hangovers—it is often offered only on the weekends.

Throughout the southern portion of the state it's also easy to find excellent Mexican seafood. Tucson is only four or five hours from the Sea of Cortez, and many locals have vacation homes along the desert coast. Places serving fish tacos, shrimp cocktail, and other seafood delights abound. There are also a few restaurants in the state that serve a more complex, gourmet version of Mexican cuisine. At these places, listed in the Tucson and Phoenix restaurant sections, you'll be able to sample the intricate moles and chicken and pork dishes of central and southern Mexico.

Tips for Travelers

In many ways Arizona was saved by tourists. If travelers didn't love the state's scenery and history so much, the Grand Canyon may have long ago been strip-mined and the last of the desert paved over. Instead, the natural wonders have been to a large degree saved forever, and a vibrant and busy tourism industry has grown up here. Because of this, it's easy to be a tourist in Arizona; herein you'll find a few tips to make it even easier.

INTERNATIONAL TRAVELERS

The many national parks and monuments in Arizona are well equipped for international tourists. They all offer guides and other literature in a variety of major languages and are used to working with international travelers. Arizona and the Southwest in general are very popular destinations for European and Japanese travelers especially, and in the summer, no matter where you're from, you could very well meet one of your compatriots on the South Rim or at Monument Valley.

The U.S. government's **Visa Waiver Program** allows tourists from 37 countries to visit without a visa for up to 90 days. To check if your country is on the list go to http://travel.state.gov/index.html. Even with a waiver, you still need to bring your passport and present it at the port of entry.

ACCESS FOR TRAVELERS WITH DISABILITIES

Many of the best sights in Arizona are accessible to disabled travelers in one way or another. The Grand Canyon and most of the other major federal parks have accessible trails and viewpoints. For advice and links to other helpful Internet resources, go to www.disabledtravelers.com, which is based in Arizona and is full of accessible travel information, though it's not specific to the state. The **National**

Accessible Travelers Database may also be helpful. For questions specific to Arizona, you may want to contact the state Department of Administration's **Office for Americans with Disabilities** (100 N. 15th Ave., Ste. 361, Phoenix, 602/542-6276 or 800/358-3617, or TTY 602/542-6686, www.azada.gov).

TRAVELING WITH CHILDREN

A family trip around Arizona is necessarily a road trip. Is there such a thing as an entirely kid-friendly road trip? At any rate, Arizona is an ideal place for an active, outdoor vacation involving the whole family. Most of the major sights, especially the national parks and monuments, cater to families and offer a host of fun and educational programs for kids. Phoenix and Tucson both have excellent zoos, both of them kid-centric. Rangers at all the parks and monuments are usually eager to explain and illuminate the sights for kids, and the **Junior Rangers** program, offered at most of the parks, is a fun and educational way to get your kids engaged with nature—and it even includes a photo-ready swearing-in ceremony. Children under 16 are admitted free to federal parks, monuments, and recreation areas.

SENIOR TRAVELERS

The best thing those 62 years old or older can do before visiting Arizona is to purchase an **America the Beautiful–National Parks and Federal Recreational Lands Senior Pass.** This golden ticket will get you and up to three adults into every national park and monument for the rest of your life. It costs just $10, paid one time in person at any federal park. In Arizona, where most of the best attractions and sights are under federal control, this adds up to big savings and should encourage all families to bring along grandma and grandpa wherever they go.

The popular **Elderhostel** (11 Ave. de Lafayette, Boston, MA 02111, 800/454-5768, www.elderhostel.org) organization offers several programs in Arizona; go to www.elderhostel.org/programs/state.asp?whatState=AZ for an up-to-date list.

GAY AND LESBIAN TRAVELERS

Arizona is no more or no less gay friendly than most other states. The gay community is strong and diverse in both Phoenix and Tucson, the state's two major cities. There aren't really gay districts, as such, though in Phoenix the **Melrose District,** on 7th Avenue between Camelback and Indian School Roads, is sometimes considered one.

The **Greater Phoenix Gay & Lesbian Chamber of Commerce** (P.O. Box 2097, Phoenix, AZ 85001, 602/266-5055, www.gpglcc.org) has lists of the state's gay and gay-friendly accommodations. The Valley's *Echo Magazine* (602/266-0550, www.echomag.com) is an excellent source of news and culture for the gay community.

In Tucson, *The Tucson Observer* (520/622-7176, www.tucsonobserver.com) has news about the local gay community, and **Wingspan** (425 E. 7th St., 520/624-1779, www.wingspan.org) is the Old Pueblo's GLBT community center.

CONDUCT AND CUSTOMS

Be polite and friendly and you'll get along in Arizona just fine; it may not look like other places, but Arizona is very much a typical American state. Most of the rural areas are ruled by conservative values and politics, though a strong and vocal minority of more liberal wilderness lovers and runaway hippies exists in nearly every forest and desert town of any size. The college towns—Tucson, Flagstaff, and Tempe—tend to be more liberal than the rest of the state.

On the Navajo, Hopi, Western Apache, and other Native American reservations throughout the state, don't take pictures without asking first, and don't drive off road for any reason—that's somebody's land and livelihood. On the Hopi Reservation, don't enter a village without first stopping at a store or a village office to ask permission. It's a good idea to hire a guide to take you around, as there are many places that are off limits without one.

Health and Safety

THE ARIZONA SUN

Whether you're hiking deep into Grand Canyon or walking sun-splattered paths through a saguaro forest or simply strolling through the Phoenix Zoo, you must be aware that the incessant sun, the driving reason for most visits to Arizonaland, can quickly become a dangerous threat to your health. To eliminate this threat, thus allowing you to bask only in the sun's friendly attributes, practice moderation and prevention. Rather than worship, the sun requires timidity: Stay in the shadows, covered from head to toe. If you're not willing to do this, as most aren't, then at least wear a hat with a wide brim, use high-SPF sunscreen, cover your neck, and, preferably, wear long sleeves. This applies not only to backcountry desert adventurers and hikers; mere sightseekers, especially those with fresh-faced children in tow, are just as susceptible to sun- and heat-related health issues—more so, in fact: The less fit you are, the higher the danger.

The least of what the sun can do to you is not to be taken lightly. A **sunburn,** which comes on quicker than you'd think, can lead to skin cancer, and that can lead to death. If you get a sunburn, there's little you can do, save try to make yourself more comfortable. Stay out of the sun, of course, and try to keep cool and hydrated. There are dozens of over-the-counter balms available, but simple aloe works as well as anything. A popular home remedy is to gently dab the burned areas with vinegar. If the burn starts to blister, reaching the dreaded third-degree stage, skin cancer becomes a very real threat. Again, the best way to avoid sunburn is to stay out of the sun; barring that, cover up and follow common sense. Those with fair skin and children should be even more cautious.

Hikers, shoppers, sightseers, golfers, and anybody else exerting themselves under high-heat conditions should watch out for **dehydration.** When your body becomes dangerously depleted of fluids, you'll notice first that you are not urinating regularly and your saliva has dried up. You may become irritable and confused; your skin may turn gray and your pulse may race. Children especially can become dehydrated quickly. The best way to avoid dehydration is to limit your exertion during the hottest part of the day and to drink a lot of water. If you feel the symptoms of dehydration coming on, get to a cool, comfortable place, take in fluids, and rest.

Hikers should take along a few packets of electrolyte powder, similar to Gatorade and the like, and a separate water bottle to mix it in—these can be life-savers. If you exert yourself in the heat and sun and fail to replace the fluids flowing out, your body can become depleted of electrolytes and fluids. Such is the path to **heat exhaustion,** a dangerous condition that can turn fatal if not treated. You begin to feel nauseated, dizzy, and weak, and your muscles cramp. Again, if you experience any of these symptoms, get to a cool, comfortable place quickly and drink water and something with sodium and potassium in it, like an electrolyte drink.

Dehydration and heat exhaustion, while dangerous and unpleasant, pale when compared to **heat stroke,** sometimes called sun stroke or heat hyperpyrexia, a severe, dangerous health threat that is frequently fatal or, if not fatal, often changes a victim's future health significantly and irrevocably. Heat stroke occurs when the body's temperature-regulating capacity fails; this can be caused by either relatively short exposure to extremely high heat—like, say, a short, strenuous run on a 120°F July afternoon in Yuma—or prolonged exposure to relatively high temperatures, as in a 15-mile hike in 90°F heat. And that's only if you're in good shape. It would take far less to cause heat stroke in most of us. The first and most important sign of heat stroke is a lack of sweating. If you stop sweating in a situation where you *should* be sweating, take notice. Sweating is your body's way of regulating its temperature, so it stands to reason that if you stop sweating, there may be something wrong with your body. Your heart rate will speed up noticeably and your skin will become dry; you'll get a headache and become confused. At its worst, heat stroke leads to unconsciousness, convulsions, and death. Once you notice you're not sweating, you must get help immediately: Get to an emergency room as soon as possible.

ALTITUDE SICKNESS

The mountains in Arizona reach up to 12,000 feet rarely, and more frequently up to 10,000 feet. Though most visitors won't be going that high, you should be aware that a few of the state's mountain towns sit between 5,000 and 8,000 feet above sea level. Lowlanders in relatively good shape may get headaches, a little dizziness, and shortness of breath while walking around Flagstaff or other of the state's mountain towns, but very few will experience serious altitude sickness—the result of not getting enough oxygen, and therefore not enough blood flow to the brain. Still, take it easy in the higher elevations if you begin to feel tired and out of breath, dizzy, or euphoric. If you have heart or lung problems, you need to be more aware in the higher elevations; the best thing to do is to get a prescription for oxygen from your doctor and carry it with you if you plan on spending a lot of time in the mountains.

HIKING SAFETY

Most hiking safety is based on common sense: Take enough water, wear a hat and good shoes, take along something to eat, don't go alone, and make sure somebody knows where you're going and when you're planning on being back. In the desert, such common sense takes on added meaning. It's best to avoid taking long, strenuous hikes in the desert between May and September. Unless you're a masochist or a tough guy or girl without mercy, you probably won't enjoy it, and it can get very dangerous very fast. If you do go out in the summer, however, don't go out during the hottest part of the day—stick to early morning or evening, though even at these times the heat can be brutal.

Besides the usual hiking gear that every hiker should have—water, food, a hat, shoes, etc.—Arizona hikers should carry a **tourniquet** with them; if you happen to get bitten by a rattlesnake or a scorpion—not a very likely occurrence at all—you'll want to tie the tourniquet around the area to slow the blood flow, and the venom, until you can get to a hospital and the antivenin. The best way to avoid a snakebite is to avoid snakes. They are not going to bother you unless you bother them or surprise them. Keep an eye on the ground while you're hiking; if a snake, rattler or otherwise, is in your general vicinity, leave the area. Cover your ankles and keep your hands and feet out of dark holes, and don't put your hands on a rock without looking at it first.

OTHER CONCERNS

West Nile virus and the **Hanta virus** are the long-shot threats to your health in Arizona, and both can be avoided by taking precautions. Use insect repellent to ward off the former and simply stay away from rodents to avoid the latter.

Threats from humans come in all the usual forms. Lock your vehicle wherever you go, even in the most remote locations. Don't pick up hitchhikers, anywhere.

Information and Services

COMMUNICATIONS

Arizona has five **area codes.** For eastern Maricopa county, including Tempe, Mesa, and most of Scottsdale, dial 480; for Phoenix proper, dial 602; for western Maricopa county, dial 623; for all of Southern Arizona, including Tucson, dial 520; and for all of Northern Arizona, including Prescott, Flagstaff, Jerome, the Grand Canyon, and western Arizona (including Yuma and Lake Havasu City), dial 928.

Your **cell phone** will work in most parts of Arizona, though there are large swaths of the Navajo and Hopi Reservations where cell service is spotty at best, and mostly nonexistent. Cell phones don't usually work in the backcountry, but it's worth taking it along just in case.

You'll find high-speed wireless **Internet** service throughout the state at the majority of hotels and motels, and in cafés and libraries everywhere. Even the remote reservation lands are wired in.

TIME ZONES

Arizona is in the Mountain Time Zone (MST) and is one of the few places in the country that does not switch over to daylight saving time from the second Sunday in March to the first Sunday in November. The Navajo Nation in northeastern Arizona, because it spreads across three states, does switch to daylight saving time, adding even a time change to complete the foreign-country feel of that region.

MAPS AND TOURIST INFORMATION

The **Arizona Office of Tourism** (1110 W. Washington St., Ste. 155, Phoenix, 602/364-3700 or 866/275-5816, www.arizonaguide.com) will send you a free print or electronic version of the official state guide, and its website is full of information and lists of accommodations, events, and restaurants throughout the state. If you're planning to spend a lot of time in the state's national forests, you can get maps and information beforehand from the **National Forest Service, Southwestern Region** (333 Broadway SE, Albuquerque, NM, 505/842-3292, www.fs.fed.us/r3), or from the websites for the individual forests, listed in the chapters in which they appear. The **Arizona BLM State Office** (1 N. Central Ave., Ste. 800, Phoenix, 602/417-9200, www.blm.gov/az/st/en.html) also has a lot of information on the state's wildlands, and the **Arizona State Parks Department** (1300 W. Washington, Phoenix, 602/542-4174, www.azstateparks.com) has information on all the parks managed by the state. Passes and reservations for state and federal parks can be obtained and made online or at the parks themselves.

MEDIA

Arizona has just two major daily newspapers, the *Arizona Republic* in Phoenix and the *Arizona Daily Star* in Tucson. The *Republic* is more of a statewide newspaper, while the *Star* focuses on Southern Arizona. You'll find the *Republic* at newsstands and newspaper vending machines throughout the state, while the *Star* is typically available only in Southern Arizona. In North-Central Arizona, the daily *Prescott Courier* and the *Daily Sun* in Flagstaff cover the northland well, including all the happenings at the Grand Canyon and the Navajo Nation. In Western Arizona, the *Yuma Sun* is the only daily newspaper.

For alternative news, commentary, and arts and entertainment coverage, check out the free weekly *Phoenix New Times,* covering the Valley of the Sun. In Tucson, the free *Tucson Weekly* offers in-depth coverage of the news and art and entertainment scene in Southern Arizona. Both weeklies publish annual "best of" issues, which list readers' picks of the best restaurants, bars, shops, and attractions in the state's two major urban areas.

Tucson and Phoenix both have network

Tucson's Community Radio

Hidden away in an old brick house in Tucson's Armory Park Historic District is one of the best radio stations in the West.

Since the early 1980s **KXCI Community Radio** (220 S. 4th Ave., 520/622-5924 request line, 520/623-1000 office line, www.kxci.org) has been broadcasting an outrageously eclectic mixture of music, news, and cultural programming that has contributed greatly to making Tucson a place where people slightly left of center feel welcome and comfortable. This full-time job is done by a staff of mostly volunteer, non-professional DJs, many of whom learn the ropes in a DJ class offered annually by the station.

Most weekdays the majority of daytime air is taken up by the "Music Mix," a brew of new and old alternative rock, roots, country, Latino, jazz, electronica, world music, and classic pop that's so unpredictable you shouldn't be surprised to hear Willie Nelson followed by the White Stripes followed by a new tune from your favorite Afghani hip-hop artist.

Most nights there's a lineup of genre-specific shows. Mondays feature a "locals only" broadcast that showcases the best of Tucson's fertile music scene, while on Tuesdays country-western, alternative country, and Americana rule. Wednesday is Latino night, and on Saturday you'll hear bluegrass in the morning and in the afternoon Kidd Squidd's Mystery Jukebox, during which the Kidd, who has an unmatched knowledge of music in all its forms, plays a few hours' worth centered around a creative theme.

Because KXCI is supported by grants and donations from listeners, there are no commercials and nobody is beholden to an absentee corporation dictating playlists. This can make for near daily discoveries of music that you didn't know was out there. Tune in to KXCI at 91.3 on the FM dial, or at www.kxci.org.

---

television affiliates, as does Flagstaff. Outside of Southern Arizona, which looks toward Tucson for all its television news, you'll mostly see the local news out of Phoenix.

All three of the state's universities operate National Public Radio stations (Phoenix: KJZZ FM 91.5; Tucson: KUAZ FM 89.1; Flagstaff: KNAU FM 88.7), which offer public radio news programs throughout the day.

MONEY

Despite its largely rural character, Arizona is set firmly in the 21st century. Even in the most out-of-the-way areas, you'll be able to use your credit or debit card with impunity. However, it's always a good idea to carry some cash, especially if you're headed to the Navajo and Hopi Reservations, where it is not uncommon for phone lines, and therefore credit card machines, to go down, and you may find yourself in need of gas but with no way to pay for it.

Foreign travelers can exchange their money at banks throughout the state; check the website www.xe.com for up-to-date exchange rates.

If you cross the border into Mexico and remain in the tourist and shopping areas, you don't need to exchange your money. Shops and restaurants in Nogales, Arizona, and other border towns are happy to take your dollars.

BUSINESS HOURS

While the majority of businesses in Arizona keep regular hours, in many areas the business hours change with the season. In Tucson, Phoenix, Yuma, and all the other desert cities and towns, you may find some places closed during the hottest months of the summer (July and August). Call ahead and don't take anything for granted if you're planning a trip to the desert during those infernal months. In winter, some of the small towns of the White Mountains go into hibernation, and many businesses close for weeks or months at a time. Again, it's best to call ahead.

RESOURCES

Suggested Reading

HISTORY

Armstrong, William Patrick. *Fred Harvey: Creator of Western Hospitality.* Bellmont, AZ: Canyonlands Publications, 2000. A slim introduction to Harvey and his accomplishments. Available at many Grand Canyon bookstores, it puts a positive spin on the "Civilizer of the West" and the marketing of the Southwestern style.

Bandelier, Fanny, trans. *The Journey of Alvar Nuñez Cabeza de Vaca.* Chicago: Rio Grande Press, 1964. This strange first-person account marks the true beginnings of American literature. The conquistador spent years of privation with various northern-Mexico Indian tribes after being shipwrecked near Florida in the late 1520s. He became a slave, a shaman, and a trader before finally finding his way back to Mexico and inspiring the later explorations of the Southwest by the Spanish.

Corel, Edwin. *The Gila: River of the Southwest.* New York: Holt, Rinehart and Winston, 1951. Using Arizona's once-mighty east-west riverway as his hub, Corel jumps off in many directions, exploring human history and culture under the influence of the Gila, which, along with its major tributaries—the Salt, the Santa Cruz, the San Pedro, and the Verde—has been the main pumping artery of Arizona civilization for centuries.

Hall, Sharlot M. (Crampton, C. Gregory, ed.). *Sharlot Hall on the Arizona Strip: A Diary of a Journey Through Northern Arizona in 1911.* Flagstaff: Northland Press, 1975. Hall, a semifamous regional writer of the frontier and early statehood, took an arduous trip to the isolated Arizona Strip and lived to write about it. The editor's notes provide a short but thorough introduction to the human history of the region.

Jones, Billy M. *Health-Seekers in the Southwest 1817-1900.* Norman: University of Oklahoma Press, 1967. A scholarly but readable study of health migration in the 19th century. It turns out, according to Jones, that the Wild West was really a "health frontier" full of reluctant settlers who ventured west to cure TB and other ailments.

Limerick, Patricia Nelson. *The Legacy of Conquest: The Unbroken Past of the American West.* New York: W. W. Norton & Company, 1987. An unromantic reconsideration of the history of the Western frontier. Limerick finds that it was a distinctly American hunger for resources, profit, and real estate that built and ruled the West, not the six-gun and its stoic, free-shooting hero.

Luckingham, Bradford. *The Urban Southwest.* El Paso: Texas Western Press, 1982. A study of the rise of four major Southwestern cities, including Phoenix and Tucson.

Martin, Douglas D. *An Arizona Chronology: The Territorial Years, 1846-1912.* Tucson: University of Arizona Press, 1962.

Martin, Douglas D. (Patricia, Paylore, ed.). *An Arizona Chronology: Statehood 1913-1936.* Tucson: University of Arizona Press, 1966. A retired newspaperman, Douglas spent years searching through old Arizona newspapers, gathering the major headlines from 1846 to 1936. The series provides a general and surprisingly entertaining understanding of the march of Arizona history.

Powell, Lawrence Clark. *Arizona: A History.* Albuquerque: University of New Mexico Press, 1990. A more recent edition of the book first published in 1976, Powell's history is not a definitive blow-by-blow but rather a series of essays on various chapters in Arizona's history and culture. A much-admired Southwestern writer, librarian, and scholar, Powell lived in Tucson for many years. His *Southwest: Three Definitions* (Benson, AZ: Singing Winds Bookshop, 1990) is an excellent trilogy of essays on the landscape and culture of the Southwest.

Sheridan, Thomas. *Arizona: A History.* Tucson: University of Arizona Press, 1995. A very well written and informative general history.

Smith, Dean. *The Great Arizona Almanac: Facts About Arizona.* Portland, OR: WestWinds Press, 2000. Former newspaperman Smith compiled this almanac, with entries on Arizona history, travel, current events, famous residents, mileage charts, zip codes, and area codes. It's in dire need of a new edition but is still very useful and interesting.

Sonnichsen, C. L. *Tucson: The Life and Times of an American City.* Norman: University of Oklahoma Press, 1982. A thorough telling of the Old Pueblo's long history from its founding in 1776 as a presidio up to the early 1980s.

Waters, Frank. *The Colorado.* New York: Holt, Rinehart and Winston, 1951. The great Western writer known for his novel *The Man Who Killed the Deer,* Waters was also a master of nonfiction. Though he penned this book about the Colorado River and all that it influences in the 1940s, in a Southwest unrecognizable from what it is today, the greater part of his story still seems true—a classic of that "sense of place" all writers seek.

NATIVE AMERICANS, ANTHROPOLOGY, AND ARCHAEOLOGY

Dentdale, Jennifer Nez. *Reclaiming Diné History: The Legacies of Navajo Chief Manuelito and Juanita.* Tucson: University of Arizona Press, 2007. A compelling account of the Navajo Nation written by the first Navajo woman to earn a Ph.D. in history. Dentdale gives the oral history of her people just as much, if not more, credence than she does the mostly Anglo-written accounts that claim to be official and complete. This method reveals, among other things, that women played a much larger role in traditional Navajo society than "colonial" records credit.

Hall, Edward T. *West of the Thirties: Discoveries Among the Navajo and Hopi.* New York: Doubleday, 1994. The great anthropologist tells stories about his work with the Navajo and Hopi during the Great Depression, evoking a time when the remote Indian Country was practically inaccessible.

Houk, Rose. *Sinagua.* Tucson: Western National Parks Association, 1992. Pick up this short volume at any of the national parks or monuments you're sure to visit in Arizona; it's a concise introduction to the Sinagua and their land, part of a series sold throughout the state.

Kosik, Fran. *Native Roads: The Complete Motoring Guide to the Navajo and Hopi Nations.* Tucson: Rio Nuevo, 2005. Kosik knows the reservation lands well and includes a lot of fascinating historical tidbits; recommended to anyone wishing to go deeper than most into Indian Country.

Lamb, Susan. *A Guide to Navajo Rugs.* Tucson: Western National Parks Association, 1992.

Lamb, Susan. *A Guide to Pueblo Pottery.* Tucson: Southwest Parks and Monuments Association, 1996. These handy guides, available at park and monument bookshops and most of the gift shops and tourist attractions in Indian Country, explain the basics of rug and pottery identification—just enough to hook you in and whet your appetite for collecting the arts and crafts of the Navajos and Pueblos.

Waters, Frank. *Book of the Hopi.* New York: Penguin, 1963. Though this history of the Hopi and retelling of their myths and legends sometimes gets a cold shoulder from scholars, Waters's book has a narrative thrust that makes the Hopi story seem immediate and meaningful not just to the Hopi and a few anthropologists, but to all of us.

Wright, Barton. *The Complete Guide to Collecting Kachina Dolls.* Flagstaff: Northland Press, 1977. A classic guide to the kachina spirits and what they mean.

GRAND CANYON

Ghiglieri, Michael P. and Thomas M. Myers. *Over the Edge: Death in Grand Canyon.* Flagstaff: Puma Press, 2001. A popular collection of macabre stories about tumblers and jumpers, drowners, and killers in the Grand Canyon. One of the few books of its kind that is updated quite regularly.

Grattan, Virginia L. *Mary Colter: Builder upon Red Earth.* Grand Canyon: The Grand Canyon Association, 1992. A very readable account of architect Mary Colter's life and career. Colter seems to be little known outside the Southwest, though she deserves a wider reputation for her fanciful Grand Canyon creations and the rustic Arts-and-Crafts elegance of her Harvey Houses.

Hughes, Donald. *In the House of Stone and Light.* Grand Canyon Natural History Association, 1978. A relatively short, well-written account of the human history of the Grand Canyon, concentrating mainly on the Anglo development of the South Rim and the evolution of Grand Canyon National Park.

Powell, John Wesley. *The Exploration of the Colorado River and Its Canyons.* New York: Dover, 1961. A reprint of Powell's 1895 classic *Canyons of the Colorado,* this firsthand account of two journeys through the canyon on the Colorado River is essential reading (and it is surprisingly readable) for anyone interested in the continuing story of the confluence of man and Grand Canyon.

Schullery, Paul. *The Grand Canyon: Early Impressions.* Boulder: Colorado Associated University Press, 1981. Includes essays by John Muir and others, showing that writers and other visitors have struggled mightily to describe and comprehend the canyon since people have been visiting it.

THE ENVIRONMENT AND NATURAL HISTORY

Carter, Jack L. et al. *Common Southwestern Native Plants: An Identification Guide.* Silver City, NM: Mimbres Press, 2003. A thorough but easy-to-use guide to plants you're likely to see in Arizona; includes common species of the deserts, the forested mountains, and the plateau country.

Grubbs, Bruce. *Desert Sense: Camping, Hiking & Biking in Hot, Dry Climates.* Seattle: The Mountaineers Books, 2004. If you're going to be hiking or riding a bike in the desert, especially if you're doing it in the summer, consider picking up this or a similar book to familiarize yourself with desert survival beyond the basics of bringing water and wearing a hat.

Kavanagh, James, ed. *The Nature of Arizona.* Blaine, WA: Waterford Press, 1996. A useful all-in-one guide specific to the state; most guides attempt to lump everything together under "Southwest." Lists and provides illustrations of the state's flora and fauna, including mammals, snakes, fish, birds, and spiders.

Logan, Michael F. *The Lessening Stream: An Environmental History of the Santa Cruz River.* Tucson: University of Arizona Press, 2002. A professor paints an attractive and elegiac portrait of what the river used to be like and explains why it isn't like that anymore.

Olin, George. *50 Common Mammals of the Southwest.* Tucson: Western National Parks Association, 2000. An introduction to Arizona's mammals; slim with attractive illustrations, part of a series available throughout the state.

Quinn, Meg. *Wildflowers of the Southwest.* Tucson: Rio Nuevo, 2000. If you're going to be hiking in the desert in spring, pick up this guide to the many wildflowers that bloom throughout the state.

HIKING

Berkowitz, Alan. *Grand Canyon North Kaibab Trail Guide.* Grand Canyon Association, 2005.

Thybony, Scott. *Grand Canyon Bright Angel Trail Guide.* Grand Canyon Association, 2004.

Thybony, Scott. *Grand Canyon Hermit Trail Guide.* Grand Canyon Association, 2005.

Thybony, Scott. *Grand Canyon South Kaibab Trail Guide.* Grand Canyon Association, 2006. Pick up these small, inexpensive guides to the major Grand Canyon trails at most canyon-area bookstores. They contain a lot of information for being so small, and several color photos show you what's ahead. Each guide also includes an interesting history of the trail.

Tessmer, Martin. *50 Hikes in Arizona.* Woodstock, VT: The Countryman Press, 2004. An excellent guide to the best hiking trails in the state, with detailed descriptions of each trail and precise directions to the trailheads. Includes all regions of the state.

Warren, Scott, S. *100 Classic Hikes in Arizona.* Seattle, WA: The Mountaineers Press, 2000. Has 50 more hikes than *50 Hikes in Arizona.* For those looking not only for the best, most popular hikes but also the less known and little used.

LITERATURE

Abbey, Edward. *The Monkey Wrench Gang.* New York: Harper Collins, 2000. Abbey's best-known novel, first published in 1975, is a crazy comic Western with radical environmentalists as its heroic gang of outlaws.

Abbey, Edward. *One Life at a Time, Please.* New York: Henry Holt and Company, 1987. Abbey was the Southwest's resident poet-provocateur, a major influence on a few generations of western writers and environmentalists. It has yet to be decided if he was writing literature disguised as polemics or the other way around, but he is an essential voice in the long project to justify the ways of the West to the rest of the country. This volume of essays from the late 1970s and the 1980s includes his thoughts on Lake Powell.

Bowden, Charles. *Blue Desert.* Tucson: University of Arizona Press, 1986.

Bowden, Charles. *Frog Mountain Blues.* Tucson: University of Arizona, 1987. Bowden's voice is overwhelming once you get into it. His essays, reportage, and nature writing chronicle the darker side of the sunbelt.

Internet Resources

TOURISM SITES

Arizona Office of Tourism
www.arizonaguide.com
The official site for the state's Office of Tourism has basic information on the state's regions and lists various possible itineraries.

Discover Navajo
www.discovernavajo.com
The official site of the Navajo Nation's tourism group has basic information about visiting the nation—where to stay, what to do, and what not to do. It has a large number of links to tour companies.

Flagstaff Convention and Visitors Bureau
www.flagstaffarizona.org
This site has general information on visiting Flagstaff, the northland, and the Grand Canyon along with helpful listings.

Grand Canyon National Park
www.nps.gov/grca
The Grand Canyon's official website has basic information on the park; go here for information about backcountry permits. For reservations and information on the park's accommodations, go to the **Xanterra South Rim** site at www.grandcanyonlodges.com.

Greater Phoenix Convention & Visitors Bureau
www.visitphoenix.com
The official site for Phoenix and the Valley of the Sun has a pretty comprehensive list of restaurants and hotels in the valley.

Metropolitan Tucson Convention and Visitors Bureau
www.visittucson.org
This is Tucson and Southern Arizona's official tourism site.

Sedona Chamber of Commerce
www.visitsedona.com
The official site for Sedona tourism has general information on Sedona, Oak Creek Canyon, Red Rock Country, and the Verde Valley.

Yuma Visitors Bureau
www.visityuma.com
The official site for Yuma and the lower Colorado River region.

NEWS AND CULTURE

Arizona Daily Star
www.azstarnet.com
Tucson's morning daily is free on this site, with news and information on all of Southern Arizona.

Arizona Republic
www.azcentral.com
The state's largest newspaper is free online every day, and the site has a robust Arizona travel guide and a useful dining and entertainment section.

Phoenix New Times
www.phoenixnewtimes.com
This site is the best place to go for entertainment and cultural listings and alternative news and commentary about life in the Valley of the Sun.

Tucson Weekly
www.tucsonweekly.com
Southern Arizona's best source of alternative news, political blogs, and cultural and entertainment news and listings.

Index

List of Maps

Acknowledgments

This edition is dedicated, with love and thanks, to Katie Sanderson. Thanks also to all the folks at Avalon for their help, confidence, and patience, especially my editor, Kathryn Ettinger. I would also like to thank my parents, Kathleen and Roger Hull, for all of their support over the years. Also thanks to Carol Sanderson for all of her kindness and the many clippings she sent me while I was researching this new edition. Thanks to my sister, Janis Barrett, and her family for their support, and to my brother, Thomas Hull, and his wife, Candy Hull. Thanks to Gregg Turkington, a.k.a. Neil Hamburger, for his suggestions. And thanks to my great friends Ryan and Regina Lord and Jason and Jen Shaw for their support and encouragement.

MAP SYMBOLS

▭▭▭	Expressway	(	Highlight	✈	Airport	⚓	Golf Course
▭▭▭	Primary Road	○	City/Town	✗	Airfield	℗	Parking Area
▭▭▭	Secondary Road	◉	State Capital	▲	Mountain	▱	Archaeological Site
▭ ▭ ▭	Unpaved Road	✹	National Capital	✛	Unique Natural Feature	⌂	Church
- - - -	Trail	★	Point of Interest			⛽	Gas Station
··········	Ferry	•	Accommodation	⟋	Waterfall	⤼	Dive Site
▬▬▬	Railroad	▼	Restaurant/Bar	⚲	Park	▩	Mangrove
▭▭▭	Pedestrian Walkway	■	Other Location	⬮	Trailhead	▭	Reef
▥▥▥	Stairs	∧	Campground	☼	Lighthouse	▭	Swamp

CONVERSION TABLES

°C = (°F - 32) / 1.8
°F = (°C x 1.8) + 32
1 inch = 2.54 centimeters (cm)
1 foot = 0.304 meters (m)
1 yard = 0.914 meters
1 mile = 1.6093 kilometers (km)
1 km = 0.6214 miles
1 fathom = 1.8288 m
1 chain = 20.1168 m
1 furlong = 201.168 m
1 acre = 0.4047 hectares
1 sq km = 100 hectares
1 sq mile = 2.59 square km
1 ounce = 28.35 grams
1 pound = 0.4536 kilograms
1 short ton = 0.90718 metric ton
1 short ton = 2,000 pounds
1 long ton = 1.016 metric tons
1 long ton = 2,240 pounds
1 metric ton = 1,000 kilograms
1 quart = 0.94635 liters
1 US gallon = 3.7854 liters
1 Imperial gallon = 4.5459 liters
1 nautical mile = 1.852 km

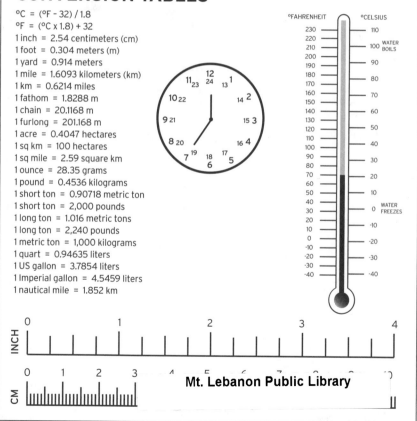

MOON ARIZONA & THE GRAND CANYON
Avalon Travel
a member of the Perseus Books Group
1700 Fourth Street
Berkeley, CA 94710, USA
www.moon.com

Editor and Series Manager: Kathryn Ettinger
Copy Editor: Mary Calvez
Graphics Coordinator: Elizabeth Jang
Production Coordinator: Elizabeth Jang
Cover Design: Faceout Studios, Charles Brock
Moon Logo: Tim McGrath
Map Editor: Albert Angulo
Cartographer: Stephanie Poulain
Indexer: Greg Jewett

ISBN-13: 978-1-61238-761-1
ISSN: 2372-1693

Printing History
1st Edition – 1986
12th Edition – July 2014
5 4 3 2 1

Text © 2014 by Tim Hull.
Maps ® 2014 by Avalon Travel.
All rights reserved.

Some photos and illustrations are used by permission and are the property of the original copyright owners.

Front cover photo: Antelope Canyon © Tim Hull

Title page photo: Pima County Courthouse in Tucson © Tim Hull

Interior photos: p. 4 running donkeys near the Navajo Nation © Tim Hull; p. 5 Arizona Capitol building in Phoenix © Kenny Tong/123rf.com; p. 6 (top left) Hotel San Carlos in downtown Phoenix © Derrick Neill/123rf.com, (top right) blooming flowers in Monument Valley © Tim Hull, (bottom) Hubbell Trading Post National Historic Site © Tim Hull; p. 7 (top) an Arizona bighorn sheep seen on a hiking trail © Eric Snyder, (bottom left) Tucson view © Tim Hull, (bottom right) lightning in the Grand Canyon

© designpics/123rf.com, p. 8 Marble Canyon in the Arizona Strip © Tim Hull; p. 9 (top) *Circle of Peace* by sculptor Gary Price at St. Mary's Basilica in Phoenix, photo © Chris Boswell/123rf.com, (bottom left) carvings in Scottsdale © Tim Hull, (bottom right) San Xavier del Bac in Tucson © Tim Hull; p. 11 © Tim Hull; p. 12 (top left) © Tim Hull, (top right) © Alexey Stiop/123rf.com; p. 14 *Intertribal Greeting* by sculptor Doug Hyde (Nez Perce/Assiniboine/Chippewa), photo © Visions Of America LLC/123rf.com; pp. 16-17 © Tim Hull; p. 18 NPS photo by Michael Quinn; p. 19 © Tim Hull; p. 20 © Eric Snyder; p. 21 NPS photo by Michael Quinn; p. 22 (left) © Jason Hindman/123rf.com, (right) © Tim Hull; p. 23 © Tim Hull; p. 24 © Tim Hull; p. 25 (top) © Chris Putnam/123rf.com, (bottom) © Richard Semik/123rf.com; p. 26 © Frederic Prochasson/123rf.com

Back cover photo: a gila woodpecker peeks out from its nest inside a saguaro cactus © Koji Hirano/123rf.com

Printed in Canada by Friesens

KEEPING CURRENT

If you have a favorite gem you'd like to see included in the next edition, or see anything that needs updating, clarification, or correction, please drop us a line. Send your comments via email to feedback@moon.com, or use the address above.